Managing the Waterway

Hampton Roads, VA to Biscayne Bay, FL

by
Mark and Diana Doyle

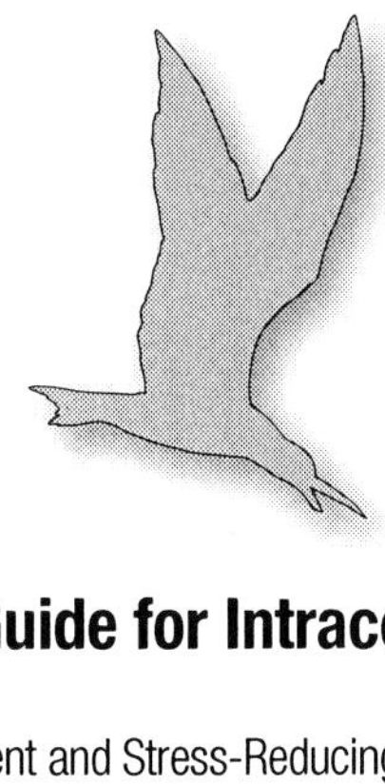

An Enriched Cruising Guide for Intracoastal Waterway Travelers

The Unique Content and Stress-Reducing Format Enable You to
Confidently Plan Your Trip and Pilot Your Vessel While Learning About and Enjoying the
Intracoastal Waterway's Wildlife, History, and Culture

Printed in the United States of America.

Published by semi-local publications LLC

Visit us at www.semi-local.com or www.managingthewaterway.com

Publisher Cataloging-in-Publication Data
Doyle, Mark Stephen, 1956—
Managing the waterway, Hampton Roads, VA to Biscayne Bay, FL : an enriched cruising guide to the Intracoastal Waterway / Mark and Diana Doyle.—1st ed.
p. cm.
ISBN-13: 978-0-9758617-0-7
ISBN-10: 0-9758617-0-0
1. Boats and boating—Atlantic Intracoastal Waterway—Guidebooks. 2. Atlantic Intracoastal Waterway—Guidebooks. 3. Atlantic Intracoastal Waterway—History. 4. Natural History—Atlantic Coast (U.S.). 5. Marinas—Atlantic Intracoastal Waterway—Guidebooks. I. Doyle, Diana Richards, 1963—II. Title.
GV776.A845D69 2005
797.1 0975—dc22 2004195460

"Thank God for Charleston," by Virginia Mixson Geraty. Used by permission.

Maps and illustrations by Mark S. Doyle.

For ordering information, including bulk discounts or custom orders, contact:

semi-local publications LLC
4706 38th Avenue South
Minneapolis, MN 55406
612-729-4411
sales@semi-local.com

Marinas or chandleries, for inclusion or updates, contact:

marinas@semi-local.com or stores@semi-local.com

Navigational conditions are subject to change at any time. The information in this book does not replace navigational charts and reference to current USCG Local Notices to Mariners. The maps, descriptions, illustrations, and reference locator waypoints in this guide are not to be used for navigation. The authors have made all efforts to ensure the accuracy of the information; however, neither the authors nor the publisher make any warranty of any kind with regard to the accuracy or completeness of the information contained herein.

Information about Waterway Marine Facilities and services are based on facility responses: no guarantee is made as to its accuracy nor do semi-local publications LLC or the authors endorse any of the facilities described herein.

The author and publisher shall not be liable in any event of incidental or consequential damages in connection with the use of this information. Use of this publication is at the reader's sole risk and discretion. Furthermore, in any event, the liability of semi-local publications LLC, if any, shall never exceed the amount paid by the original purchaser for this guide.

Produced on an iMac G5 using Adobe Creative Suite Premium. Primary typefaces include Agenda, Helvetica Neue, Myriad Pro, StonePrint, and Times New Roman PS.

Author's Note

"Beware! Here be dragons," warned the early mariners' charts about areas yet uncharted. Today the Atlantic Intracoastal Waterway is exceptionally well charted and maintained. But this does not mean the Waterway is static. Channels shift, anchorages shoal, and aids are moved, renumbered, or lost. Today, the dragons are changing navigational conditions.

Just prior to publication, in only a single month, over 75 locations along the ICW between Hampton Roads and Biscayne Bay required a listing in the Coast Guard Local Notice to Mariners, including new shoal areas, recently sunk wrecks, new security zones, and bridge changes or closures. There were eight proposals for changing existing ICW bridge schedules or for the construction of new bridges! The Coast Guard listed approximately 100 temporarily damaged, missing, or inoperable aids between Hampton Roads and Biscayne Bay!

This is why the Notices to Mariners are issued *weekly*. Do not be surprised—in fact, as a vigilant navigator you should expect—to spot several chart inaccuracies each day.

> **Caution:** There will be minor and major discrepancies between your charts and what you experience along the Waterway.

With or without the hurricane season of 2004, anchorage depths are also subject to change, particularly at entrances vulnerable to shoaling. The anchorage depths listed are based on NOAA charted depths and reported depths.

> **Caution:** Sound your way carefully into any anchorage due to possible shoaling and depth changes.

We used the latest charts at the time of writing. We made multiple contact attempts to all Waterway Marine Facilities. We verified telephone numbers and websites. We obtained the latest bridge schedules and numbers from the USCG Bridge Divisions and regional Departments of Transportation. Waypoints provided by these facilities were corroborated using digital cartography.

> **Caution:** The ICW is too winding to steer to the latitude/longitude coordinates provided! Only use the waypoints to locate or identify a marina, facility, turning buoy, or anchorage on your charts.

We believe we have amassed the latest and most correct data possible. However, conditions do change and errors slip through. To receive notice of these changes and errors by email, send your email address to:

errata@semi-local.com

And please do send us your ICW questions. We'll try to answer them in a vignette in the next edition!

mark@managingthewaterway.com
diana@managingthewaterway.com

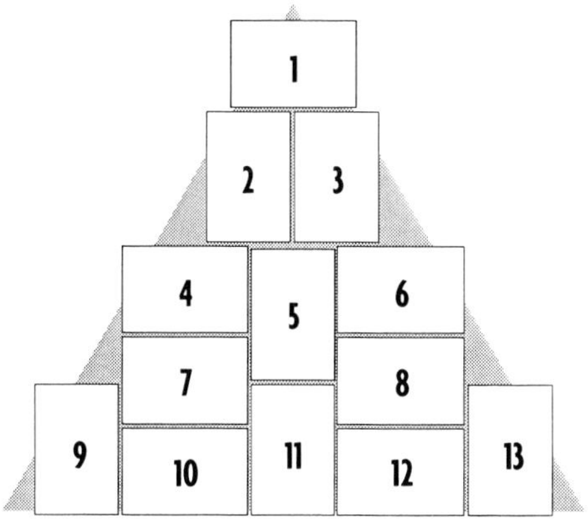

On the Cover

On the Cover

1. Great Egret. Photo courtesy of Everglades Day Safari.
2. Trawler on ICW. Photo courtesy of Flagler County Chamber of Commerce.
3. Shuttle Launch, Cape Canaveral. Photo courtesy of NASA.
4. Bottle-nosed Dolphin. Photo courtesy of NASA.
5. Osprey on Manatee Speed Zone Sign. Photo courtesy of Mary Bowman & Smithsonian Marine Station.
6. Grouper Groupies. Photo courtesy of St. Lucie County Tourist Development Council.
7. Fort Macon and Kids. Photo courtesy of Crystal Coast Tourism Development Authority.
8. St. Augustine Alligator Farm. Photo by Author.
9. Caribbean 1500 Start. Photo courtesy of West Marine Caribbean 1500.
10. Coconut Grove. Photo courtesy of Greater Miami Convention & Visitors Bureau.
11. Roseate Spoonbill. Photo courtesy of NASA.
12. Statute Mile Marker 195. Photo courtesy of RosalieAnn Figge Beasley.
13. St. Simons Island Light. Photo courtesy of Brunswick-Golden Isles Convention & Visitors Bureau.

Acknowledgments

It is said that a book is better than its authors. What an understatement! *Managing the Waterway* couldn't have been written without help from an army (or navy?) of contributors. We thank you all!

We relied heavily on the expertise of many government organizations, including the U.S. Army Corps of Engineers, the U.S. Coast Guard, NASA, NOAA, and the National Weather Service. We truly appreciate the resources and services your organizations provide for marine safety and information. Several individuals were particularly helpful, including Michael Brodhead at the USACE Office of History, Barry Dragon and Michael Lieberum of the USCG Seventh District Bridge Operations, Waverly Gregory of the USCG Fifth District Bridge Division, Robert Milici at the U.S. Geological Survey, Ralph Moses at the Virginia USACE, Jerry Rogers of the Norfolk District Army Corps of Engineers, and Wayne Stacey of the USCG Office of Boating Education. In addition, countless state and local offices, including city public affairs offices, tourism and development councils, chambers of commerce, and regional film boards, provided materials and answered questions.

Many non-profits work hard to support boaters and the Atlantic Intracoastal Waterway. Special thanks to David Roach and Brenda Sullivan of the Florida Inland Navigation District (www.aicw.org), Rosemary Lynch of the Atlantic Intracoastal Waterway Association (www.atlintracoastal.org), Lin Olsen of the Great Bridge Battlefield & Waterways History Foundation (www.gbbattlefield-waterways.com), and George Ramsey of the Virginia Canals & Navigations Society (organizations.rockbridge.net/canal). As usual, the Seven Seas Cruising Association (www.ssca.org) was a treasure trove of cruiser-relevant information.

Several individuals contributed their subject matter expertise, patiently fielding our arcane questions. Particular thanks to Susan Carson, local historian of Southport, North Carolina; Alan Jones of Carr-Jones Associates for IT advice; Will Doar, South Carolina Geological Survey; Dr. Richard Myers, Virginia Department of Conservation and Recreation; Tim Rulon at NOAA; and Susan Scott, marine science writer for the *Honolulu Star-Bulletin* and former ICW cruiser. Virginia Bach provided library science information on everything from CIP to LCCNs then patiently read an early draft. For insights into the workings of marine publishing, thanks to Patricia Bohanan at First Mate Yacht Services in St. Augustine; Vivien Godfrey of Bluewater Books & Charts in Ft. Lauderdale; Corinne Kanter, author of *The Cruising K.I.S.S. Cookbook* series; and Kathy Parsons, author of *Spanish for Cruisers* and *French for Cruisers*.

The photographs in this book were graciously contributed. Thanks to Kathy Hill of the Smithsonian Marine Station at Fort Pierce for coordinating with local photographers and a big thanks to the photographers themselves. Patricia Holm generously provided additional photos of Vero Beach. RosalieAnn Beasley (a.k.a. GrandmaR) provided images from her VirtualTour.com pages. Everglades Day Safari in Ft. Lauderdale (www.ecosafari.com) provided photographs taken on their safaris.

For copy editing, thanks to Sylvia Messner and to Becca Hillan, former copy editor and now co-owner of T&C Canvas in Ft. Myers.

We especially appreciate the time and comments provided by the seasoned cruisers who armchair sailed or ICW "test-drove" our early drafts. Thanks to David Allester & Eileen Quinn of Little Gidding, Gene Barnes, Alex & Diane Allmayer-Beck of Ariel III, RosalieAnn Figge Beasley (a.k.a. Grandma Rosalie) of RosalieAnn, Bart & Leah Bolger, Jon & Elma Brein, Paul Butterfield of Liberty, Dee Carstarphen of Muskrat, Larry & Sharon Duhaime of Lead Free Too, Frank & Joanne Finney of Fantasy Island, Larry & Bobbi Graham of Tortuga, Charles & Corinne Kanter, Rick & Pam Kilmer of The Cat's Aweigh, Mike Martin of Distant Music, Cliff & Bezy McKay of Ceilidh, Bruce McKenna & Barbara Fagan of Messin' About, Sean McKenna of Rugrats, Robert & Jo Mellis of Quiet Passage, Dawn Nye of Cruisehound, Bill Saville of Atarax, Bob Soper, Kent Utley of Mortar Offer, Cindy Wallach of Majestic, Stephen Watterson of Witch of Endor, Norm & Judy Woods of Integrity, and Mike & Amy Woolf. Fair winds and following seas to all!

We are especially indebted to our friend Paul Pregent who patiently listened to our half-baked ideas and meticulously oversaw the craftsmanship and manufacturing of this book.

And finally, thanks to our son Morgan...for all the little ways he helps by being aboard.

Expanded Table of Contents

List of Illustrations

List of Photos

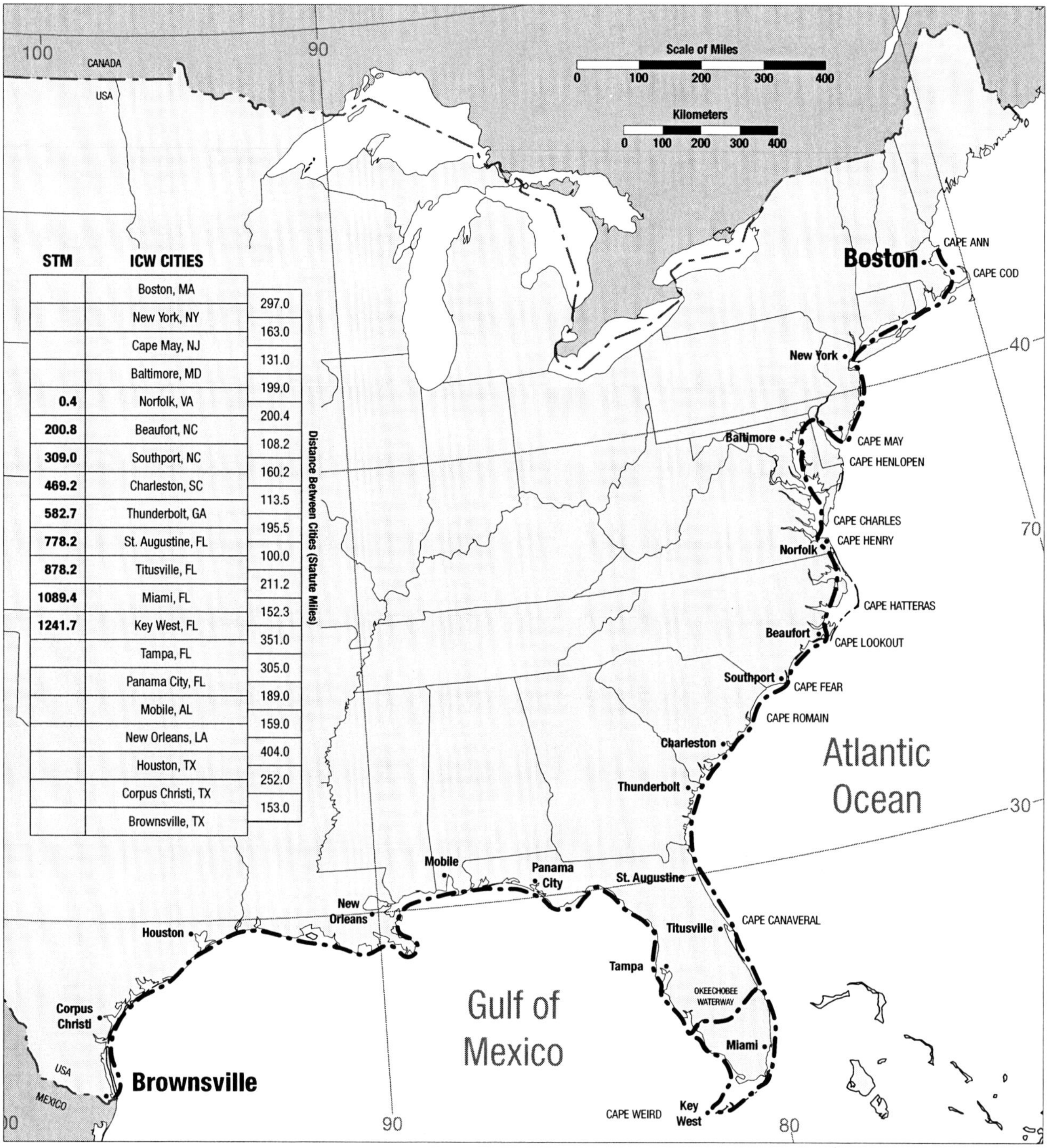

STM	ICW CITIES	Distance Between Cities (Statute Miles)
	Boston, MA	
		297.0
	New York, NY	
		163.0
	Cape May, NJ	
		131.0
	Baltimore, MD	
		199.0
0.4	Norfolk, VA	
		200.4
200.8	Beaufort, NC	
		108.2
309.0	Southport, NC	
		160.2
469.2	Charleston, SC	
		113.5
582.7	Thunderbolt, GA	
		195.5
778.2	St. Augustine, FL	
		100.0
878.2	Titusville, FL	
		211.2
1089.4	Miami, FL	
		152.3
1241.7	Key West, FL	
		351.0
	Tampa, FL	
		305.0
	Panama City, FL	
		189.0
	Mobile, AL	
		159.0
	New Orleans, LA	
		404.0
	Houston, TX	
		252.0
	Corpus Christi, TX	
		153.0
	Brownsville, TX	

The Intracoastal Waterway

From Boston to Brownsville, the Intracoastal Waterway is a nearly 4000-mile route behind natural barrier islands, connecting bays and coastal rivers along the Atlantic and Gulf coasts.

The Atlantic portion connects creeks, rivers, sounds, and bays from Massachusetts Bay to Florida Bay, and includes the Cape Cod and Chesapeake & Delaware (C&D) canals.

The Gulf portion includes the Okeechobee Waterway, Mobile Bay, Mississippi Sound, the Sabine-Neches Waterway, and Galveston Bay.

America's ICW—A Dream Fulfilled

Nearly 4000 miles long, the Intracoastal Waterway takes advantage of one of the most extensive protected coastlines in the world.

Even the Great Barrier Reef in Australia runs only 1200 miles along its coast. The Inside Passage, a naturally protected inland route from Seattle, Washington to Skagway, Alaska, is a mere 1000 miles.

First envisioned by our nation's founders over two hundred years ago, the Intracoastal Waterway is an awe-inspiring engineering feat. Delayed and postponed for generations, a World War and an economic crash provided the impetus for its completion. Only then did the country have the federal unity to complete the original dream of a nationally managed, protected inland route for commerce and defense. ▲

Managing the Waterway

...Before it manages you!

Mark's Perspective

The first time I ran the ICW my heart rate never went below 120! Between running aground, and waiting to run aground, my mouth was so dry I couldn't spit for a week. I thought if I could only reach Florida—back to civilization and wide-open water—I'd be rescued from this damn ditch!

Years later, after many statute miles, dawn finally broke over Marblehead. If I stopped fighting it, and figured out how to manage the waterway, I might actually enjoy those 1098 miles.

What if I prepared a daily summary of bridges and restrictions? What if I outlined acceptable anchorages and marinas at pre-calculated distances?

What if I stopped trying to do laundry in Norfolk, or pulling up to R.E. Mayo's shrimp dock needing an email connection?

What if I didn't arrive at Alligator River hoping for a grocery stop only to leave with Little Debbie snack cakes and Slim Jims? What if I put together a list of spares and re-stocked in Wrightsville Beach or St. Augustine?

In other words, what if I began **Managing the Waterway**?

We all can't be locals. But we certainly can learn to be semi-locals. This guide is the guide I always wished for. I hope it lowers your heart rate and skyrockets your fun quotient!

March 2005

OVER THE years, we've found it's simple—either you manage the Waterway or the Waterway manages you. If you find yourself stressed by the uncertainty of day-to-day challenges, it's easy to forget why you went cruising in the first place: to slow the pace and enjoy the local sights, sounds, and experiences. The Intracoastal Waterway is either a collection of beautiful bays, sounds, and rivers, or it becomes an alternate I-95 to Florida.

Planning ahead is the key to enjoying the incredible sights and stories behind the Intracoastal Waterway. With the right resources and a bit of foresight, your vessel becomes your magic carpet ride through this slice of waterfront America.

But it's not enough to have lots of information—all cruising guides include massive amounts of information. What matters most is how that information is organized. As captain, you need information presented concisely and consistently. You want details when you need them—or if you're overwhelmed at that moment, you need to be able to focus on the high-level essentials.

To help accomplish the goal of a relaxed and enjoyable cruise, we strive to provide the information you need, where and when you need it. Whether novice or old salt, sailor or trawler, sightseer or delivery crew, you can customize the guide's use by referring to different sections at different times in different situations. We hope this new design for a cruising guide offers you the opportunity to fully enjoy one of the world's most extensive protected inland waterways.

CRUISERS TRIANGLE

When it comes to your vessel and crew, first things first. In 1943, the psychologist Abraham Maslow conceptualized this idea in what he called a *Hierarchy of Needs*. He organized his concept into a tiered, triangular icon built up of tasks in order of priority. Each successive level builds upon the other, defining needs to be met before moving to the next level.

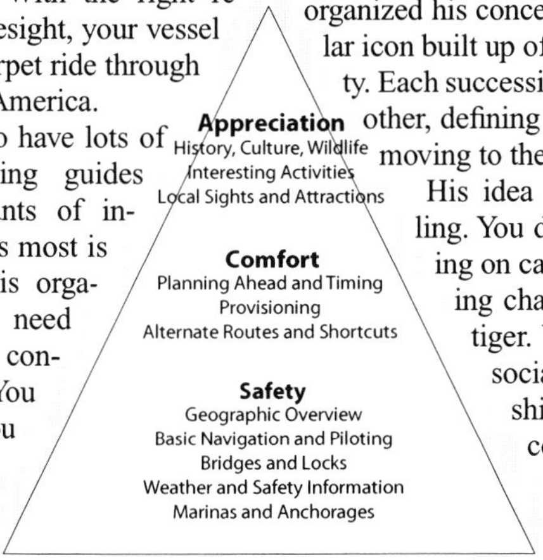

Cruisers Triangle – Managing the Waterway

His idea is simple and compelling. You don't spend time reflecting on cave painting if you're being chased by a saber-toothed tiger. You don't worry about social groups and friendships if you're hungry, cold, and sitting out in the driving rain.

Traveling the ICW is not a life-challenging expedition, but it's still governed by Maslow's triangle. When you're managing a transiting vessel, basic needs come first: safe piloting, safety for the crewmembers, and secure overnight moorage. Only when these demands are met can attention to other activities. No matter what the experience of captain and crew, moving *any* vessel over *any* 1000 miles takes planning.

Photo by Jonas N. Jordan — Courtesy of U.S. Army Corps of Engineers

Thunderbolt, GA

SAFETY

Each time we reach a new geography, we're reminded of the salience of the CRUISERS TRIANGLE™ and our hierarchy of needs. We're starting over: finding moorage in unfamiliar ports, adapting to local anchoring conditions, deciphering weather patterns, and locating groceries, laundry, and marine supplies.

Even if you're an experienced cruiser, if you're unfamiliar with the Intracoastal Waterway you must start at the bottom of the CRUISERS TRIANGLE. The first challenges are safely piloting and securing your vessel.

For new cruisers, *Managing the Waterway* helps you move off the bottom of the triangle by providing crucial safety and navigation information in a simple and accessible format. We organize basic piloting information in a concise mile-by-mile column with a Rolling Header™ of important safety information. With this information at your fingertips, you have immediate answers to safety questions:

- What are my anchoring opportunities tonight?
- Where is the next marina?
- Will I be able to find sufficient fuel stops?
- Where are the security zones and what is required?
- Which WX weather station is appropriate for my location?
- NOAA predicts severe thunderstorms for Horry County; does this affect me?
- Where is the next range so I don't run aground?
- Whom do I call locally if I run aground?
- Where is the closest Coast Guard station?

Courtesy of Yaskin Engineering

Photo by Pat Yaskin **Donald Ross Bridge** (STM 1009.4)

COMFORT

To move up the Cruisers Triangle, you must become proactive rather than reactive. You can schlep all over town to hunt for a marine part. You can eat canned food when you run out of produce. You can wait for a bridge opening by circling for 20 minutes.

Or you can have access to the information you need to plan ahead. You can minimize waiting and delays, eliminate long safaris for supplies, and know when you'll have easy access to stores and services. With the right information, you can plan ahead and do the same tasks better and in less time.

As you move up the Cruisers Triangle, you can make the trip more comfortable by precisely timing transits, provisioning when it is convenient, or selecting alternate routes to accommodate weather conditions. At this level of the Cruisers Triangle, managing a vessel is less about piloting aid-to-aid and more about coordinating a smooth transit. You need the information to answer your planning questions:

- What delays or concerns are in today's transit?
- How many bridge delays are in the next 20 miles so I can adjust my estimated arrival time?
- Should I speed up or slow down to time the next restricted bridge?
- Where are the alternate ICW routes? Why use them?
- How much tide should I allow for docklines or scope?
- How can I locate marine supplies near the ICW?
- Will there be a grocery store at the next stop?
- Where will laundry, propane, Internet, or a post office be available?

Courtesy of Everglades Day Safari

Great Egret

APPRECIATION

Cruisers are naturally curious folk. Their wanderlust fuels their curiosity for new experiences, drawing them from the security of their land homes. For most cruisers the reward of a moving vessel is the daily excitement of new places, scenery, activities, and acquaintances. Your vessel is your magic carpet!

There is so much to see and experience along the way. The challenge is to not hurriedly pass it by as you navigate from aid to aid and mile to mile. When you have safety and comfort tasks under control, you can turn to appreciation. If you're at the top of the Cruisers Triangle, you're able to watch more than your depth sounder and the next dayboard, appreciating the sights and stories along the Waterway.

Managing the Waterway is an enriched cruising guide. In addition to detailed information on navigation, our Interpretive Vignettes tell the story of the Intracoastal Waterway. These stories provide detailed and entertaining insights to the regional flora and fauna, history and folklore, and local culture and attractions. In the Interpretive Vignettes you'll find answers to appreciation questions:

- What is the story behind the Rock Pile?
- I'd like to see a ______; where should I look?
- What is the legend behind this unusual name?
- Was Forrest Gump really filmed here?
- What are those strange sounds at night at anchor?
- What was this area like 50, 100, or 1000 years ago?
- What is there to do or see in this area?
- How can I keep up-to-date on regional fishing regs?
- What books can I read to experience the local culture?

Join a support organization for advice and fellowship. Sailors seem to gravitate to the Seven Seas Cruising Association (www.ssca.org; 954/771-5660); trawler owners to the Marine Traders Owners Association (www.mtoa.net). Additionally, women cruisers may wish to check out Women Aboard (www.womenaboard.com; 877/WMN-ABRD).

NOT A LOCAL, BUT A SEMI-LOCAL

You'll never be a *local*, but MTW can help make you a *semi-local*. Why simply transit mileposts and signposts when there is so much more? It's the legends and sites between these mileposts that make the Waterway one of the richest inland passages in the world. ▲

Are you a semi-local?
Try out these north-to-south ICW pronunciations:

A. Mackay Island, NC
B. Neuse River, NC
C. Beaufort, NC
D. Bogue Sound, NC
E. Horry County, SC
F. Socastee Bridge, SC
G. Winyah Bay, SC
H. St. Helena Sound, SC
I. Beaufort, SC
J. Calibogue Sound, SC
K. Daufuskie Island, SC
L. Ossabaw, GA
M. Sapelo Sound, GA
N. Brevard County, FL
O. Eau Gallie, FL
P. Wabasso, FL
Q. Pompano Beach, FL

Answers: A. MACK-ee; B. NOOS; C. BO-fuhrt; D. rhymes with "vogue"; E. O-ree; F. SAW-kuh-stee; G. WIN-yaw; H. HE-luh-nuh; I. Byoo-fuhrt; J. kal-uh-BO-gee; K. dah-FUSS-key; L. AH-suh-baw; M. SAP-uh-lo; N. bruh-VAHRD; O. oh-GAH-lee; P. wuh-BASSO; Q. PAWM-puh-no.

Source: The Columbia Gazetteer of North America

Managing the Guide

...How to Use this Book

Diana's Perspective

For most of us, traveling the Intracoastal Waterway is a dream come true.

You've worked hard your whole life and this is one of your rewards! A thousand miles of changing scenery, incredible wildlife, and fascinating maritime communities.

But the ICW can be a hard ride. When Mark jokes about grocery safaris or points to a spot he "late-night anchored", I think "Wow, what a rough way to go!"

Cruising isn't an easy lifestyle; why make it harder? Given moving the boat, running a household, and home schooling, we have a very full schedule. But learning to **manage the waterway** has made it, well, enjoyable.

Planning allows us time to stop more, see more, do more, and learn more. But you can only do that if you have the information you need, organized in an accessible format.

Planning ahead is our key to having the time and composure to look beyond the navigation aids.

Can you imagine missing the eco-tour of a lifetime because navigation, moorage, or provisioning worries drove your agenda?

We hope our guide removes some of those worries; then we'll take you on that tour!

Diana

March 2005

WE'VE USED them all. And with more than a dozen ICW publications on the market, it's fair to ask "Why another?"

Each book had its merits, but we found we were using a handful of cruising guides, supplemented by additional reference publications. We carried a road atlas for county names. We used government publications for tides, Coast Guard, and weather resources. We purchased regional guidebooks for local tourism information. We relied on private booklets to locate towing companies or marine stores. What we really needed was an *enriched* guide, one melding all of this information in a concise, accessible format.

Managing the Waterway's simplest single improvement is "pulling it all together," providing captain and crew with information they need, when and where they need it.

How do you clean out your garage? Most people start by throwing every item onto the driveway. Then ask: What is necessary? How is it used? How often do I need it?

That's what we did with MTW. We took an overwhelming quantity of information and re-packed the garage. We asked ourselves what information was needed in a cruising guide. We pondered how information should and would be accessed, redesigning the layout away from appendices or alphabetical lists.

We extracted and highlighted information usually relegated to reference tables or government publications and included it on *each* page as it's needed.

Using newspaper design tricks, the pages are chock-full of information. This means less page-flipping in the cockpit. So wherever you are in the Cruisers Triangle—a newbie focused on piloting or a seasoned snowbird hoping to spot wildlife—the info is right in front of you!

A PILOTING GUIDE

Of course we include detailed mile-by-mile piloting information, alerting you to marinas, anchorages, cuts and canals, bridges, junctions, ranges, inlets, security zones, and alternative routes.

There are approximately 350 Waterway Marine Facilities, each with contact, approach, and services information. And nearly 300 anchorages, each described at its statute mile rather than grouped in an anchoring section. The 141 bridges are also detailed at their statute mile, rather than listed in an appendix. We integrate hundreds of GPS waypoints. Cautions and piloting concerns are described mile-by-mile and highlighted in a unique Rolling Header™ at the top of each page, letting you manage potential delays or safety concerns.

A NAUTICAL RESOURCE

We weave in important reference information from official publications. Each marina and anchorage listing includes its local spring tidal range. The Big Picture™ maps show counties and the locations of NOAA weather towers. The Rolling Header on each page highlights the nearest NOAA weather broadcast, Coast Guard station, and towing companies. We identify 192 Waterway Chandleries, with distances from the closest ICW marinas.

AN ICW TOUR

Over 260 Interpretive Vignettes delve into regional history, culture, and wildlife. Part history text, part field guide, part tour book, these story clips (and 200 photos & illustrations) take you on a colorful pre-cruise. We include over 1200 websites & telephone numbers for local resources and Featured Attractions.

A WORKBOOK

We demanded a slim and light design—small enough to toss in a bag and take ashore. MTW is a cruising guide designed to make the trip with you: it's a *workbook*, not a coffee table book. With UV-coated cover protection, lightfast inks, and a higher quality Wire-O binding, it's a book for the salt air not for the shelf.

Fold the book over on its spine, clip it against the wind, and mark it up with underlining for emphasis, time logs, destination notes, taped business cards, or highlighting. This is *your* cruising guide, these are your notes and reflections; the book only gets better with your annotations! ▲

❶ ICW Track
Get an overview of the ICW's route as it winds along rivers, runs behind barrier islands, and crosses open sounds.

❷ Transit Counties
Severe weather warning for Hyde County? Check the counties along the ICW route and know when a weather warning applies to you.

❸ Inland Counties
Look to the ghosted county names to locate inland counties mentioned in approaching weather forecasts.

❹ Cities and Mileages
Use the distance table for quick estimates of travel time between cities and towns.

❺ Seasonal Temperatures
Note the average high temperature for daytime exposure, or average seasonal low temperature for evenings at anchor. Also in Celsius for metric-minded cruisers.

❻ Sounds, Bays, and Capes
A lighthouse icon marks the major capes mentioned in NOAA broadcasts. Major sounds and bays are also labeled.

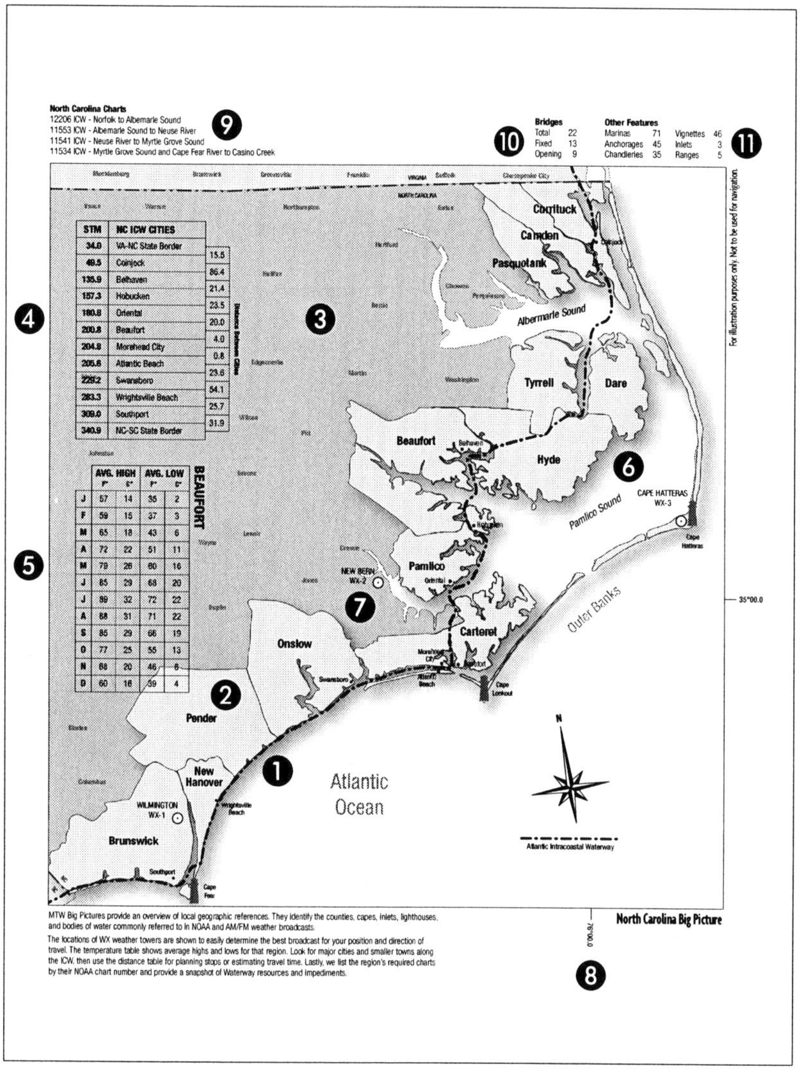

❼ NOAA Weather Towers
Locate the closest WX weather tower for the appropriate weather broadcast.

❽ Latitude and Longitude
Latitude and longitude tics provide a sense of your north or south (and east or west) progression.

❾ Required Charts
A list of required NOAA charts.

❿ Bridge Summary
Get a "feel" for the state's bridge situation and make plans accordingly. Each summary is broken out by fixed and opening bridges.

⓫ Additional Features Summary
An overview of what's ahead for that state. The number of marinas, anchorages, chandleries, vignettes, inlets, and ranges is given.

STATE BIG PICTURES

Each state begins with a boater-centric visual overview of the geography, called a Big Picture™. Use Big Pictures in lieu of a road atlas to locate counties, cities, sounds, and capes commonly referred to in local NOAA or AM/FM weather broadcasts. Specifically geared to ICW cruisers, these overview maps include the ICW route, weather tower locations, and summaries of that state's Waterway attributes.

The Big Picture for each state includes tables for ICW city distances and average seasonal temperatures. Look to the upper left for a list of required NOAA charts. In the upper right, each state's features, including bridges, marinas, anchorages, chandleries, inlets, and ranges, give an overview of what's coming.

❶ State Summary
A brief introduction to each state's maritime and ICW history, its geographic regions along the ICW, and its navigational characteristics.

❷ Waterway Boundaries
The ICW is a series of rivers, bays, and sounds. Your trip through Virginia transits Hampton Roads to North Landing River.

❸ ICW Statute Miles
Note the boundaries of the state by its ICW miles.

❹ Bridges/Locks Radio Watch
As you enter a new state, remember to hail bridges and locks on the appropriate channel. VHF 13 is common, with South Carolina and Florida the exceptions. They monitor VHF 09. Additionally, VHF 13 lets you eavesdrop on commercial traffic movement and alerts.

Virginia

❷ Hampton Roads to North Landing River

❸ ❹ The Old Dominion State
ICW Statute Mile -16.4 to 34.0
Bridges and Locks Monitor VHF 13

❶ VIRGINIA'S INTRACOASTAL Waterway is a history tour spanning two hundred years. No other 34-mile section intersects so many important events in the emergence of our nation.

In Virginia, the *entire* Intracoastal Waterway is a historical site. The Dismal Swamp Canal, envisioned by George Washington and painstakingly hand-dug by slaves, is the oldest continually operating man-made canal in the U.S. Today it is listed in the National Register of Historic Places and designated a National Civil Engineering Landmark.

The Albemarle & Chesapeake Canal, originally surveyed in 1772, was completed in 1859. Until the steam shovel was invented, cutting 14 miles through swamps and tidal marshes remained an impractical dream.

These rivers and canals were central to America's early conflicts. The Revolutionary War was fought along the banks of the Waterway, as Loyalists and Patriots battled for control of strategic routes. One of the most pivotal battles of the Revolutionary War, the Battle of Great Bridge, took place at a pinch-point bridge crossing over the Waterway. The victory allowed the establishment of an essential supply line from the Carolinas and Virginia to Washington's army in the north.

As the Civil War unfolded, Hampton Roads, not too far from the Mason-Dixon line, was at the center of this conflict. The famous "Battle of the Ironclads," the face-off between the *Monitor* and the *Merrimack*, took place in Hampton Roads. You pass near the site as you transit between Fort Wool and Fort Monroe, the fort where Confederate President Jefferson Davis was imprisoned.

This maritime history surrounds Virginia's Intracoastal Waterway. There are scores of commemorative sites and exhibits, ranging from Civil War forts to high-tech naval museums. Virginia is the "history channel" of the Intracoastal Waterway tour.

Courtesy of City of Norfolk

An Elephant Has the Right of Way

The short transit through Virginia spans scenery as well as history. This short ICW stretch, only five percent of the distance to Miami, has some of the most varied experiences of the entire Waterway. The route begins in a shipping port busy with commerce and ends in a remote wetland area of canoe trails.

The transformation begins just south of the Dismal Swamp Canal junction at STM 7.2. North of this junction, the Waterway passes through a noisy, bustling, developed industrial port. To the south, it transforms into a quiet woodland riverine passage. By the time you reach Currituck Sound in North Carolina, you have experienced the transition from battleships to water moccasins, from merry-go-rounds to nesting osprey.

HAMPTON ROADS

To a mariner, a "road" means an anchorage. Nautically speaking, a road is an anchorage that is less sheltered than a harbor. Hampton Roads, formed by the confluence of the James, Nansemond, and Elizabeth Rivers, is one of the largest sheltered bays in the area, an important road since colonial times.

Although the harbor has been called Hampton Roads since the 1600s, this name has only been used for the southeastern region of Virginia since 1983. At that time the jurisdictions bordering the harbor decided to share a regional identity as Hampton Roads. This designation now includes the Southside (independent cities of Norfolk, Portsmouth, Virginia Beach, Suffolk, and Chesapeake); the Peninsula (independent cities of Hampton and Newport News); and the counties of Isle of Wight, James City, Surry, and York.

Today Hampton Roads is one of the eastern seaboard's most strategic ports, home to the world's largest naval base.

❺

Regions ❻
Hampton Roads
On to the North Carolina Border

Inlets ❼
Chesapeake Bay Entrance

U.S. Coast Guard ❽
District Five: 757/398-6272
Group Hampton Roads: 757/483-8568
Station Portsmouth: 757/483-8527

NOAA Weather Towers ❾
WX-2 Heathsville
WX-1 Norfolk

Security Zones ❿
Norfolk Naval Shipyard
Norfolk Naval Base

Canal Information ⓫
757/201-7606

Lighthouses ⓬
Thimble Shoal Light
Old Point Comfort Light
Fort Wool Light
Portsmouth Lightship

Fishing Information ⓭
www.dgif.state.va.us/fishing

Managing the Waterway © 2005 | Hampton Roads to North Landing River | VA-25

❺ State Highlights
A column of quick reference information and contacts for that state.

❻ State Regions
Regional names, often used by locals, with different geographies and navigational concerns. The STATE SUMMARY describes each region in detail.

❼ Inlets
Recommended inlets for ICW cruising vessels.

❽ U.S. Coast Guard
Telephone numbers for the state's Coast Guard district office, groups, and stations.

❾ NOAA Weather Towers
A reminder of NOAA WX weather tower locations.

❿ Security Zones
Overview of upcoming security zones, described in detail in the NAV COLUMN.

⓫ Additional Local Contacts
Local contacts unique to that state, such as Virginia's canal information, North Carolina's Camp Lejeune firing range hotline, or Florida's recorded shuttle launch schedule.

⓬ Lighthouses
A list of each state's lighthouses visible from the ICW.

⓭ Fishing Information
Link to this site for up-to-date information on licenses, catch limits, and in many cases, online permits.

STATE INTRODUCTIONS

Before you start ticking off the miles, the STATE INTRODUCTION provides reference information and practical advice for each region.

We begin with a column of STATE HIGHLIGHTS. Glance to this column for quick reminders of regions, inlets, Coast Guard stations, weather towers, security zones, ICW telephone numbers, lighthouses, and fishing regulations.

The STATE SUMMARY describes the regional characteristics and navigational concerns in more detail. Divided into geographic regions, read these summaries to get a sense of the Waterway's different experiences. Each STATE SUMMARY ends with the state's BOOK AND FILM PICKS, a collection of regional recommendations for your cruise.

❷ Rolling Header (Enlarged)

SAFETY INFO

NOAA Weather
WX-2 Heathsville, VA
WX-1 Norfolk, VA
WX-3 Cape Hatteras, NC

USCG
Station Portsmouth, VA
VHF 16 or 09/22A
757/483-8527

❸

Sea Tow
Hampton Roads, VA
VHF 16/18
757/496-1999

TowBoatU.S.
Portsmouth, VA
VHF 16/19
757/441-9656

HEADS UP!

0.7 North Harbor Ferry Crossing
2.5 N&P Belt Line RR Bridge
2.7 Jordan Bridge
3.5 Norfolk Southern RR Bridge
5.8 Gilmerton Bridge
5.8 Norfolk Southern RR Bridge
7.2 Dismal Swamp Canal (SB)
7.7 Ship Traffic (NB)
8.8 Dominion Blvd. Bridge

❹

11.5 Great Bridge Lock
11.5 No Lunar Tides (SB)
12.1 Atlantic Intracoastal Bridge
13.8 Norfolk Southern RR Bridge
15.2 Centerville Turnpike Bridge
20.2 North Landing Bridge
34.0 VA-NC Border
41.5 Currituck Ferry Crossing
49.6 Coinjock Coast Guard Station

5.8 Gilmerton Bridge
VHF 13; 757/545-15
Double bascule; ve
Restricted year rou
0830 and 1530-173

bows; river
en deve
ntua

SAFETY INFO

NOAA Weather
WX-2 Heathsville, VA
WX-1 Norfolk, VA
WX-3 Cape Hatteras, NC

USCG
Station Portsmouth, VA
VHF 16 or 09/22A
757/483-8527

Sea Tow
Hampton Roads, VA
VHF 16/18
757/496-1999

TowBoatU.S.
Portsmouth, VA
VHF 16/19
757/441-9656

HEADS UP!

0.7 North Harbor Ferry Crossing
2.5 N&P Belt Line RR Bridge
2.7 Jordan Bridge
3.5 Norfolk Southern RR Bridge
5.8 Gilmerton Bridge
5.8 Norfolk Southern RR Bridge
7.2 Dismal Swamp Canal (SB)
7.7 Ship Traffic (NB)
8.8 Dominion Blvd. Bridge

11.5 Great Bridge Lock
11.5 No Lunar Tides (SB)
12.1 Atlantic Intracoastal Bridge
13.8 Norfolk Southern RR Bridge
15.2 Centerville Turnpike Bridge
20.2 North Landing Bridge
34.0 VA-NC Border
41.5 Currituck Ferry Crossing
49.6 Coinjock Coast Guard Station

❶

5.8 Gilmerton Bridge ✓
VHF 13; 757/545-1512
Double bascule; vertical 11 feet.
Restricted year round: M-F except holidays, 0630-0830 and 1530-1730 hrs.

5.8 Norfolk Southern RR Bridge ✓
(Gilmerton Railroad Bridge)
Single bascule; vertical 7 feet; usually open.

7.1 Interstate 64 Bridge ✓
VHF 13; 800/305-5799
Double bascule; vertical 65 feet.
Opens with 24-hour notice. Bridge currently lists eight telephone numbers. Call 800/305-5799 M-F 0700-1730 hrs or leave message after hours to arrange opening.

1134 Hrs

❺

7.2 Junction | Dismal Swamp Alternate Route ✓
to Southbound Navigation Only
78.8 74.6-mile alternate route.
Exit ICW N of R30. Proceed WNW into well-marked entrance channel. Rejoin ICW at G1 "AR" (Alligator River).
Caution: Dismal Swamp Canal closes occasionally due to water conditions. Call 757/201-7606 for information and updates.

Take North in spring?

7.7 Heads Up | Ship Traffic ❼ ✓
to Northbound Navigation Only
-12.0 This stretch of Hampton Roads has a high concentration of commercial ship traffic.

8.8 Dominion Boulevard Bridge ✓
(Steel Bridge)
VHF 13; 757/547-0521
Double bascule; vertical 12 feet.
Restricted year round: M-F except holidays, 0630-0830 and 1600-1800 hrs.
Restricted Memorial Day to Labor Day: M-F except holidays, 0830-1600 hrs, opens every hour on the half-hour.

❻

11.5 Great Bridge Lock ❽ ✓
VHF 13; 757/547-3311
Restricted year round: 0600-1900 hrs. Northbound, opens on the hour timed with the Atlantic Intracoastal Bridge. Southbound, opens at quarter after and remains open until quarter of the hour.
Caution: If you are new to locking, you may wish to review Manage the Transit, Locks.

MTW HelmClip™
www.semi-local.com
612.728.4411

11.5 Albemarle and Chesapeake Canal ❾ ✓
to Southbound Navigation Only
19.7 8.2-mile land cut.
No anchorages, two marinas, fuel available.

11.5 No Lunar Tides ❿
to Southbound Navigation Only
185.5 174-mile non-tidal zone.
From Great Bridge Lock (STM 11.5) to Adams Creek (STM 185.5), tides and currents are primarily dictated by recent wind conditions.

12.0 Free Dock
Tie up on SW wall between lock and bridge. 24-hour limit. [STR 0.0] ⓫

Passing through, you are but one of nearly 15,000 boats locking through annually.

A nice park with services and trails is on the north side of the locks. This park is popular with locals, who come to yacht-watch from the bleachers and, in their words, "imagine what the people on board do for a living."

Make sure your rudder is amidships before engaging gear! Odds are, your last move was toward the wall—and the rudder is still in that position. ⓭

GREAT BRIDGE VISITOR CENTER

Like Pearl Harbor, sometimes a single battle is credited with turning the tide of citizen support. The Battle of Great Bridge, fought in the beginning of the American Revolution in 1775, was one such battle. Considered the "Southern Bunker Hill," the victory at Great Bridge demoralized many Southern Loyalists, converting them and other cautious residents to the Patriot cause.

At the start of the Revolution, the route through the town of Great Bridge was the only land route to Norfolk from the south. But when British troops crossing this swampy area reached the pinch-point of Great Bridge, they were defeated by Patriot troops, eventually forcing the British to evacuate Norfolk.

You can learn more about the history of this area and both Waterway canals at the new Great Bridge Battlefield and Waterways Visitor Center. In conjunction with construction of the new bridge, a new visitor center is scheduled to be open and fully operational by December 2006. The center will include a large park on both sides of the canal, walking trails, an education and visitor center, and docks for boaters.

Great Bridge Battlefield & Waterways ⓯
www.gbbattlefield-waterways.com
Telephone TBA

OXBOWS

The North Landing River once was a meandering mature river. The chart still shows the old bow-shaped bends in the river. These bends, called oxbows, are created as the outer banks are scoured by years of erosion. You can identify the age of a river by the sharpness of the oxbows; rivers begin relatively straight then develop sharper switchbacks. Eventually a river can even wind back on itself, cutting off an oxbow and creating a new island. ⓬

The North Landing River's largest oxbows were bypassed by sections of straight channels, dug in the late 1800s. But the river is still beautiful, and abandoned oxbows with enough depth offer quiet and safe anchorage.

NORTH LANDING RIVER

Over 10,000 acres along the North Landing River are protected as part of a Natural Area Preserve. The area is mostly wetlands, including the only "pocosin" (elevated peat bog) area in Virginia. *Pocosin* is a Native American

Courtesy of VA Canals and Navigations Society

Photo by George Ramsey **Osprey on North Landing River** ⓮

word for "swamp-on-a-hill."

Marshes along this river are flooded with wind-driven rather than lunar tides. High tide occurs when a south wind pushes water up from Currituck Sound. A north wind sucks water back down into Currituck Sound, creating a low tide. These wind tides can change the water level along the North Landing River by as much as two feet.

The tributaries of this wild area are accessible by designated canoe trails, also open to motorized dinghies. If you stay at Pungo Ferry Marina (STM 28.4) or one of the nearby anchorages, Altons Creek canoe trail picks up just northwest of Pungo Ferry Bridge. The self-guided tour leads 2.5 miles up Altons Creek to the preserve's floating dock. Boaters are welcome to leave dinghies at this dock and walk the wide footpath and boardwalk to the main park entrance (0.4 miles). Self-guided tour brochures are available at the main park entrance.

VA-36 Hampton Roads to North Landing River Managing the Waterway © 2005

---

❶ Nav Column

Reversible for southbound or northbound travel. Landmarks spanning other entries—security zones, cuts, canals, ranges, or alternate routes—are listed at both southbound and northbound boundaries.

❷ Rolling Header™

Each header "rolls" with that page's Safety Info and Heads Up!.

❸ Safety Info

Tune to the boldface WX station for the strongest signal. Note the next south- or northbound tower. Locate and contact the closest Coast Guard and towing stations.

❹ Heads Up!™

These entries are **excerpts** from the Nav Column and **only include** opening bridges, security zones, or other hazards. The bottom entry of the left-hand column is locked to that page's center statute mile. Scan the right-hand column for southbound (or up for northbound) landmarks that impact your safety or schedule. Boldface entries are detailed on that page.

❺ Statute Mile Column

The statute mile column is convenient for notes or logging your time.

❻ MTW HelmClip™

Fold the book on its spine, clip the outer edge to hold pages against the wind, and slide up and down to mark your current location.

❼ Mark Your Progress

Check off your south- or northbound progress on the gray S or N. In an emergency, anyone on board can communicate your vessel's approximate location by noting the last check mark.

❽ Restricted Bridges & Locks

Opening bridges list primary name, alternate names, land-based identifying routes, VHF, telephone contact (if available), bridge type, vertical clearance, restricted hours, and additional cautionary notes.

NAVIGATION and APPRECIATION

The Nav Column lists mile-by-mile piloting information. It details marinas, anchorages, cuts & canals, bridges, junctions, ranges, inlets, security zones, and alternate routes. Following the ICW convention, all mileage is in statute miles. We include full-service marinas, repair yards, free docks, visitor centers, inns, dry stores, yacht clubs, and community marinas. Distance off the ICW is noted within parentheses.

The Rolling Header combines customized Safety Info and a Heads Up! to help you manage upcoming delays or safety concerns. The header "rolls," highlighting that page's *nearest access* services or information.

Interpretive Vignettes follow the miles, telling the stories behind the ICW. They highlight regional flora & fauna, history & folklore, and pop culture & local events.

❾ Cautions & Notes

Cautions such as security zones, reversing buoyage, and strong currents are noted. Additionally, services are listed for all canals and cuts.

❿ South- or Northbound Only

Landmarks relevant in only one direction are noted with Southbound Navigation Only or Northbound Navigation Only.

⓫ Tidal Ranges

Use the local spring tidal range—noted as [STR] with an optional (TS) at government tide stations—to adjust your lines at fixed docks, set your anchoring scope, or as a rough proxy for current.

⓬ Interpretive Vignettes

266 crisp, focused stories describe the sights and tales of the ICW.

⓭ Cruising Tips

Over 75 tips highlight ideas to make your trip easier and safer.

⓮ Photos & Illustrations

200 photos and illustrations give you a visual preview of the Waterway.

⓯ Featured Attractions

Websites and telephone numbers for local festivals, museums, parks, lighthouses, visitor centers, tourism offices, and ferry schedules.

Avoid missing important landmarks by highlighting the Southbound Navigation Only or Northbound Navigation Only entries before you leave. We use two different colored highlighters.

Don't wait! Flip through the guide and skim the tips. You may choose to implement some tips ahead of time, or wait until you reach a geography for its area-relevant tip.

❶ Waterway Marine Facilities

Identifies all Waterway Marine Facilities with transient dockage or fuel docks. Turn to its statute mile for navigation details. Facilities in boldface type responded to an information survey and are detailed with a Waterway Business Card.

❷ Waterway Business Cards™

Provided free for any Waterway Marine Facility completing a survey. A summary of services designed to be photocopied and cut out as wallet cards, bring a Waterway Business Card ashore for reference information.

❸ Contact Information

For reservations or inquiries, receiving forwarded mail, or arranging a delivery.

❹ Marine Facilities & Services

Check the availability of a pump-out, mail forwarding, fax machine, marine parts and service, haul-out, propane, laundry, pool, Internet land-line or wi-fi, courtesy car or bike, groceries, restaurants, post office, and library. Survey distances are "Walk" (less than two miles), "Taxi" (two to 10 miles), or "N/A" (more than 10 miles).

❷

Brunswick Landing Marina — STM 679.5

2429 Newcastle Street
Brunswick, GA 31520

912/262-9264 ✆
912/262-9327 (fax)

VHF 16/68

Depth	12	**Laundry**	On-Site
Diesel/Gas	D/G	**Pool**	No
Pumpout	Yes	**Internet/WiFi**	I
Mail/Fax	M/F	**Car/Bike**	No
Service	On-Site	**Groceries**	Walk
Parts	On-Site	**Restaurant**	Walk
Haulout	50T	**Post Office**	Walk
Propane	Taxi	**Library**	Walk

Jekyll Harbor Marina — STM 684.4
www.jekyllharbor.com

One Harbor Road
Jekyll Island, GA 31527

912/635-3137 ✆
912/635-2633 (fax)

VHF 16/72 ❸ ❹

Depth	12	**Laundry**	On-Site
Diesel/Gas	D/G	**Pool**	Yes
Pumpout	Yes	**Internet/WiFi**	I/W
Mail/Fax	M/F	**Car/Bike**	C/B
Service	On-Call	**Groceries**	Walk
Parts	On-Call	**Restaurant**	On-Site
Haulout	No	**Post Office**	Walk
Propane	Taxi	**Library**	N/A

❶ Georgia Waterway Marine Facilities

This table summarizes all known Waterway marine facilities, their location along the ICW, and their telephone number. Each is listed as either offering transient (T) dockage or not—and whether they have a fuel dock with diesel (D), gas (G), or neither.

582.3	Savannah Bend Marina	912/897-3625	T	D/G
582.4	**Hinckley Yacht Services**	912/629-2400	No	No
582.7	**Bahia Bleu Marina**	912/354-2283	T	D/G
583.2	**Thunderbolt Marine**	912/356-3875	T	D/G
585.5	**Sail Harbor Marina & Boatyard**	912/897-2896	T	No
585.5	**Hogans' Marina**	912/897-3474	T	G
585.5	The Landings	912/598-1901	No	D/G
589.9	**Isle of Hope Marina**	912/354-8187	T	D/G
600.9	Delegal Creek Marina	912/598-0023	T	D/G
613.7	Kilkenny Marina	912/727-2215	T	D/G
662.2	**Two Way Marina**	912/265-0410	T	D/G
664.2	Hampton River Club Marina	912/638-1210	T	D/G
670.7	Troupe Creek Marina	912/264-3862	No	G
677.2	**Golden Isles Marina**	912/634-1128	T	D/G
679.5	**Brunswick Landing Marina**	912/262-9264	T	D/G
683.6	Jekyll Wharf Marina	912/635-3152	T	D/G
684.4	**Jekyll Harbor Marina**	912/635-3137	T	D/G
712.3	Lang's Marina East	912/882-4452	T	D/G

In preparing this guide, each facility received multiple fax, email, and telephone contacts. Waterway Business Cards are included for those who supplied basic facility and services information. Non-bold type indicates non-response. However, an additional telephone call was made to assure the accuracy of transient, fuel, and contact information. If you are interested in non-responding facilities and their services, you should contact them directly.

❺ Georgia Waterway Chandleries

This table lists marine equipment suppliers within easy reach of the ICW, their telephone number and address, and their location relative to ICW marinas and anchorages.

Mackay Marine	912/354-4542	2911 River Drive, Thunderbolt, GA 31404	0.2 miles from Bahia Bleu Marina
Woo's Hardware	912/897-1366	205 Johnny Mercer Boulevard, Savannah, GA 31410	1.2 miles from Sail Harbor Marina
West Marine Savannah	912/352-2660	7700 Abercorn Street, Savannah, GA 31406	4.9 miles from Isle of Hope Marina
BoatU.S. Savannah	912/925-2363	11607 Abercorn Street, Savannah, GA 31419	7.0 miles from Isle of Hope Marina
Home Depot Savannah	912/921-0158	11180 Abercorn Street, Savannah, GA 31419	7.0 miles from Isle of Hope Marina
Lowe's Savannah	912/927-0000	11114 Abercorn Street, Savannah, GA 31419	7.0 miles from Isle of Hope Marina
Boater's World	912/925-0216	13015 Abercorn Street, Savannah, GA 31419	7.6 miles from Isle of Hope Marina
Bass Pro Shops Outdoor World	912/961-4200	14045 Abercorn Street, Savannah, GA 31419	7.7 miles from Isle of Hope Marina
Island Ace Hardware	912/638-3800	1701 Frederica Road, St. Simons Island, GA 31522	2.2 miles from Golden Isles Marina
The Bedford Sportsman	912/638-5493	3405 Frederica Road, St. Simons Island, GA 31522	3.7 miles from Golden Isles Marina
Central Hardware	912/265-3510	1730 Norwich Street, Brunswick, GA 31520	0.9 miles from Brunswick Landing Marina
Georgia Ace Hardware	912/265-1321	205 Monck Street, Brunswick, GA 31520	1.0 miles from Brunswick Landing Marina
West Marine Brunswick	912/264-6222	1919 Glynn Avenue, Brunswick, GA 31520	1.9 miles from Brunswick Landing Marina
Home Depot Brunswick	912/264-2025	200 Altama Connector, Brunswick, GA 31520	4.0 miles from Brunswick Landing Marina
Boater's World	912/261-9790	147 Altama Connector, Brunswick, GA 31525	4.5 miles from Brunswick Landing Marina
Maxwell True Value Family Center	912/635-2205	16 Beachview Drive, Jekyll Island, GA 31527	0.6 miles from Jekyll Harbor Marina
Kings Bay Ace Hardware	912/729-2648	1292 Osborne Road, St. Marys, GA 31558	1.3 miles from Lang's Marina East

❻

Managing the Waterway © 2005 GA-117

❺ Waterway Chandleries

North to south, 192 marine supply stores along the ICW. Telephone numbers for pre-ordering parts, confirming an item is in stock, placing an item on hold, or asking about delivery.

❻ MapQuest® Distances

Plan your access to supplies. Dock or anchor near the reference Waterway Marine Facility for access to that Waterway Chandlery.

FACILITIES AND SERVICES

Plan ahead for moorage and supplies with 349 Waterway Marine Facilities and 192 Waterway Chandleries. Marinas that completed an information survey received a Waterway Business Card, detailing their contact information and services.

Use the Waterway Marine Facilities table to quickly identify transient dockage and locate fuel docks. Every facility in the table is described in the Nav Column at its statute mile.

Find the closest marine supplies with the Waterway Chandleries table, which includes national marine stores, independent chandleries, national home centers, and local hardware stores. Home centers let you pay less for items such as tubing, duct tape, buckets, and cleansers. Local hardware stores in small maritime communities often stock an extensive inventory of marine supplies.

Photocopy the Waterway Business Card pages before you depart. Store them in a folder ready to cut out for quick wallet references for you, crew members, or guests.

❶ **Mixed Metric DST Table™**

Corrects for ICW Mixed Metrics (Knots and Statute Miles)

D = S x T

Distance = Speed x Time

Nautical miles (conve❸om statute miles) = knots x hh:mm

Distance (Statute Miles)

Speed (Knots)	1.0	1.5	2.0	2.5	3.0	3.5	4.0	4.5	5.0	5.5	6.0	6.5	7.0	7.5	8.0	8.5	9.0	9.5	10.0
4	00:13	00:20	00:26	00:33	00:39	00:46	00:52	00:59	01:05	01:12	01:18	01:25	01:31	01:38	01:44	01:51	01:57	02:04	02:10
6	00:09	00:13	00:17	00:22	00:26	00:30	00:35	00:39	00:43	00:48	00:52	00:56	01:01	01:05	01:10	01:14	01:18	01:23	01:27
8	[illegible] ❺	00:10	00:13	00:16	00:20	00:23	00:26	00:29	00:33	00:36	00:39	00:42	00:46	00:49	00:52	[illegible]	[illegible] ❹	01:02	01:05
10	00:05	00:08	00:10	00:13	00:16	00:18	00:21	00:23	00:26	00:29	00:31	00:34	00:36	00:39	00:42	00:44	00:47	00:50	00:52
12	00:04	00:07	00:09	00:11	00:13	00:15	00:17	00:20	00:22	00:24	00:26	00:28	00:30	00:33	00:35	00:37	00:39	00:41	00:43
14	00:04	00:06	00:07	00:09	00:11	00:13	00:15	00:17	00:19	00:20	00:22	00:24	00:26	00:28	00:30	00:32	00:34	00:35	00:37
16	00:03	00:05	00:07	00:08	00:10	00:11	00:13	00:15	00:16	00:18	00:20	00:21	00:23	00:24	00:26	00:28	00:29	00:31	00:33
18	00:03	00:04	00:06	00:07	00:09	00:10	00:12	00:13	00:14	00:16	00:17	00:19	00:20	00:22	00:23	00:25	00:26	00:28	00:29
20	00:03	00:04	00:05	00:07	00:08	00:09	00:10	00:12	00:13	00:14	00:16	00:17	00:18	00:20	00:21	00:22	00:23	00:25	00:26

❷ **Example One:** A restricted bridge is 8.5 STM ahead and opens in 55 minutes. You want to catch the opening but you've slowed down to enjoy the scenery and don't want to speed up needlessly only to idle in front of the bridge. Solution: adjust RPMs for 8.0 knots SOG to time the opening perfectly.

Example Two: You regularly motor at several fixed RPM. You know (and GPS confirms) that 3000 RPM averages 10 knots. The Great Bridge Lock is 7 STM ahead and closes in 30 minutes. Solution: SOG must be 12 knots or higher to make this locking. Either increase RPM or consider stopping in Great Bridge for a stroll.

Example Three: Averaging 16 knots over the day, at 1400 hrs you've decided it's time to get off this ride! A recommended marina is 14 STM ahead. With no restricted bridges, security zones, or other hindrances, how long until tie-up? Solution: doubling the time in the 16 Knot/7.0 STM cell gives you an ETA of 46 minutes.

❶ Correcting for Mixed Metrics

Use this table to determine boat speed to make a bridge opening, or estimate time to an anchorage, or ICW distances traveled at a given boat speed over a length of time.

❷ Example One

A restricted bridge is 8.5 statute miles ahead and opens in 55 minutes. Should you speed up to make the opening or slow down to avoid idling at the bridge?

❸ First Step

Choose the distance column: 8.5 statute miles.

❹ Second Step

The bridge opens in 55 minutes. Scan down the 8.5 column to find a time 55 minutes or less in order to make the opening.

❺ Final Step

Read across the row to the speed in knots. To time this bridge opening, you need an average speed over the ground (SOG) of 8 knots.

MAKING THE MATH EASY!

The old distance-speed-time problem may seem trivial, until you remember the ICW is measured in statute miles and your vessel's speed is displayed in nautical miles per hour (knots). It's like driving a car in Canada where distances are displayed in kilometers and your speedometer reads in miles per hour. In either case, you have a mixed metric problem.

Before you shrug off mixed metrics, remember the Mars Climate Orbiter was lost because engineers forgot to convert miles to kilometers! If you fail to adjust for mixed metrics, you won't lose a space ship, but you may misestimate arrival times at restricted bridges. It's no fun to arrive at the Ben Sawyer Bridge, just north of Charleston, three minutes after the start of their two-hour evening restriction.

❶

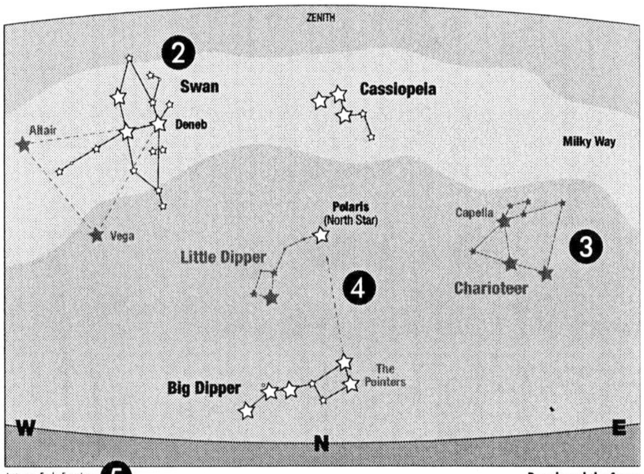

Autumn, Early Evening ❺

Deneb and the Swan

❶ Look Overhead

The sky's zenith is directly over your head. Look to the horizon labels for North and South orientation.

❷ Primary References

Look for the primary constellations and references highlighted in the vignette. The size of the star icon corresponds to its magnitude or brightness. We use three sizes: very bright, typically visible away from light pollution, and difficult to see even in dark anchorages.

❸ Secondary References

Ghosted references are not described in the vignette, but are easily visible or are mentioned in another vignette. Not all visible stars are shown!

❹ Pointers and Helpers

Dashed lines lead you from star to star to help navigate the sky.

❺ Season and Time

As an example, look for this night sky in autumn, in the early evening.

AUTUMN AND SPRING CONSTELLATIONS

Mariners love stars, even if they can't always locate Arcturus or Sirius. And stars and mariners go back a long way.

We include eight astronomy Interpretive Vignettes, introducing you to the stories behind some bright constellations and stars, such as the Dragon, Deneb and the Swan, Regulus and the Lion, Andromeda, Pegasus, Scorpio, and the Pleiades. Learn about precession and look for the Great Nebula, the farthest object visible to the naked eye.

Each Interpretive Vignette includes a Star Chart, helping you locate major spring and fall stars as you transit the ICW.

Managing the Transit

...A Little on What to Expect

THE WATERWAY was a rough ride in 1912 when Henry Plummer took his catboat on the inland route from Massachusetts to Florida.

Back then, notched boards nailed to posts marked the channels. If the top corner of the board was cut off, the deeper water was closer to the post (whatever "closer" meant). If the bottom corner was cut off, deep water was "farther off." This system was, at best, rough and the dredging was worse so Plummer's three-foot draft was constantly touching bottom. As his teenage son and faithful crewmember recounted later, running aground four to five times a day "became more than just monotonous."

Today the Waterway is maintained by a fleet of dredges and is well marked with dayboards, buoys, and range markers. Piloting the ICW is now fairly straightforward, especially if you work with the navigation system that has evolved over the years. It doesn't mean you won't touch bottom, but at least you can enjoy a more relaxing trip than Plummer.

This chapter overviews basic characteristics of the Atlantic Intracoastal Waterway, including aids, bridge protocol, boat traffic, running aground, and inlet safety.

AIDS TO NAVIGATION

There are two important facts to remember about aids along the Intracoastal Waterway: they run clockwise around the coast and they are uniquely marked.

Because the ICW runs along the shore, the conventional adage of "red, right, returning from seaward" becomes unclear. To clarify, the Coast Guard adopted the following clockwise convention: moving in a southerly direction along the Atlantic Coast, then in a northerly, then westerly direction along the Gulf Coast, is considered returning from seaward. You can remember this rule as "red, right, returning to Texas."

Occasionally, given the ICW's frequent crossing and joining of established waterways, you often experience a sudden change in lateral buoyage. For example, colored aids to navigation "swap sides" three times near the Savannah River intersection.

To prevent confusion, the aids of the Intracoastal Waterway are uniquely marked. Every dayboard or buoy—in additional to its regular numbering, shape, and color characteristics—shows a yellow reflective symbol. When traveling southbound, a yellow reflective square indicates a port-side mark. A yellow reflective triangle indicates a starboard-side mark.

Caution: Expect to see yellow squares on *triangular* (red) dayboards and yellow triangles on *square* (green) dayboards. This is common as the ICW meanders and intersects channels with buoyage having opposite cardinal significance!

Some mariners complain they have trouble spotting the yellow ICW marks. Keep a heavy, steady pair of binoculars handy

Bridges Along the Waterway

There are seven types of bridges along the Atlantic Intracoastal Waterway between Hampton Roads and Biscayne Bay, including the only pontoon bridge in operation on the East Coast. The seven bridge types are: fixed, lift, pontoon, single-bascule, double-bascule, single-pivot swing, and double-pivot swing.

Courtesy of U.S. Army Corps of Engineers

Photo by Tony Santana

Palm Valley Fixed Bridge (STM 758.8)

Photo by Rosalie Beasley

Jordan Lift Bridge (STM 2.7)

Courtesy of NCDOT

Sunset Beach Pontoon Bridge (STM 337.9)

Courtesy of U.S. Army Corps of Engineers

Atlantic Intracoastal Bascule Bridge (STM 12.1)

Courtesy of NCDOT

Alligator River Swing Bridge (STM 84.2)

Courtesy of VA Canals and Navigations Society

Photo by George Ramsey

Albermarle Sound "N"

and you'll have no trouble sighting them. Binoculars may be necessary not only in poor visibility conditions, but if the symbol is faded or if the sun shadows the aid.

Always verify each upcoming aid's yellow square or triangle, especially around inlets and river junctions. The simple habit of verifying each Waterway mark (which becomes second nature after a few days) saves a lot of grief. If you take a wrong turn, you may still be in deep water because you've wandered into a non-ICW channel. You now need to re-locate the ICW channel, which will likely put you on the wrong side of an aid, in shallow water.

Before you leave, register your dinghy at your local Department of Motor Vehicles or Department of Natural Resources (depending on your state). Florida considers a *motorized* dinghy a separate vessel requiring its own registration and legal identification.

DAYBOARDS

Dayboards are the most common navigational aid along the Waterway. Look for dayboards in three forms: mounted on a single piling, on a dolphin (a collection of strapped, teepee-like pilings), or on a larger piling structure. The type of mounting has no navigational significance.

The dayboards are conventional, with triangular red dayboards marked with even numbers, and square green dayboards marked with odd numbers. The numbers are large and very visible, unless the sun is low on the horizon and the board is silhouetted.

The numbers on the dayboards typically increment or decrement one-by-one. It's a good habit to keep track of the numbers, searching for the next number in the sequence. However, the dayboard numbers do not continue for the entire route of the Intracoastal Waterway; the numbers would be too large. Sequences stop and start over, often at an inlet junction or other geographic feature.

In addition, some aids are lit. A good rule of thumb is: if an aid is lit, it's lit for a reason. Lighted aids are much more expensive to build and maintain. Heed lit aids and think about why they are lit.

Along the Intracoastal Waterway, a lit aid calls attention to an important junction, turn, or hazard. In addition, the light's *characteristics* (color and rhythm) have significance. A colored light has lateral significance. For example, a flashing green light calls your attention to keeping the aid on the appropriate side of your vessel. A quick flashing light typically identifies a turn requiring an abrupt, rather than a gradual, course change.

DROP AIDS

Because of the shifting and shoaling nature of the Waterway, the Coast Guard often places small temporary *drop aids,* or *floaters*, to supplement larger permanent aids.

These aids are typically small nuns or cans designated with an additional letter. For example, a red drop aid between R2 and R4 would be labeled R2 "A". As with all Intracoastal Waterway aids, drop aids also show the ICW yellow square or triangle.

Since drop aids are placed in areas of shoaling they should be given a wide berth.

Plan at least a month ahead for holidays or family traditions so you're not caught short-supplied. Items such as cards, party favors, gifts, and cooking ingredients can be difficult to find.

Photo by Rosalie Beasley

STM 195

MILE MARKERS

Beginning at Norfolk, Virginia, and ending in Brownsville, Texas, the Intracoastal Waterway is measured in *statute* miles, rather than nautical miles. These are the same mile measures (1 statute mile = 5,280 feet) used on land.

However, since vessels measure their speed in knots, namely *nautical* miles per hours, statute miles wreak havoc with estimating travel time. A nautical mile is approximately 6,076 feet per mile, so the conversion is ugly. The Mixed Metric DST Table on the cover flap lets you quickly overcome these mixed metrics.

The statute mile convention is firmly entrenched, with STM markers shown on NOAA charts every five miles. Along much of the Waterway, the statute miles are marked with ICW mile marker boards. These small signs, when available, are white with black lettering. They may be attached to a dayboard, piling, tree, or even painted on a rock!

On your charts, the Waterway's route is marked with a thin light purple line. This line, used on all ICW charts as a convention, is referred to as the *magenta line*.

RANGES

Ranges are very common along some stretches of the Waterway, particularly shallow areas with cross currents. Ranges are marked on charts as black dashed lines. In reality, range boards are large rectangular dayboards (taller than wide) painted in three vertical stripes. Occasionally, locals have built a range, which may be as simple as a set of poles.

The important task is to stay on a *front range* by looking ahead and keeping the forward (lower) and rear (higher) range markers directly in line. With a *back range*, this involves occasionally glancing back over your stern. Keeping the range markers aligned will assure you stay mid-channel.

To correct your course, follow this simple rule: steer to the lower range marker.

Don't become so fixated on the range you continue past its intended departure. The channel typically ends and turns *before* the range aids are reached or out of sight. Be on the lookout for the buoy or dayboard marking the end of the range line. Every season several boaters, pleased with their precision range running, forget to depart the line before they've hit shallow water.

BRIDGES

The official overhead clearance along the Intracoastal Waterway is 65 feet above mean high water. However, the Julia Tuttle Bridge in Miami (STM 1087.2), with a fixed clearance

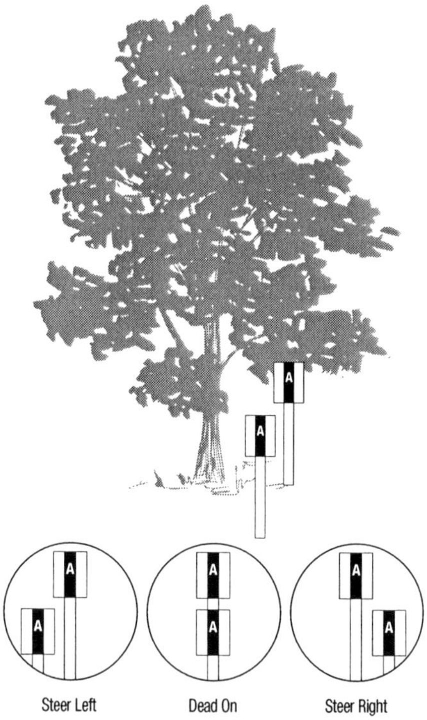

Steer to the Lower Range Marker

of 56 feet, is an exception. Southbound vessels taller than 56 feet must exit the Waterway by Port Everglades and return no sooner than Government Cut, Miami.

In addition, some of the 65-foot bridges have been reported short, so vessels with heights over 62 feet should use caution or watch the tides. For example, the Wilkerson Bridge in North Carolina (STM 125.9) has a reported fixed clearance of 64 feet.

As boating and land traffic increases, the old low-clearance opening bridges continue to be removed, replaced by fixed 65-foot spans. But there are still over eighty opening bridges between Hampton Roads and Biscayne Bay. Nearly two-thirds of these are in Florida.

The term, *restricted openings* are times a bridge does not open on request. For example, during restricted hours, a bridge may open on the hour and half-hour only. Holidays refer to federal holidays, in which case the usual rush-hour restrictions do not apply.

Caution: Bridge schedules change! For example, Broward County recently completed a three-month trial of simplified openings. Pending a final decision, bridge schedules between STM 1055.0 and STM 1074.0 may change. Temporary and permanent bridge restrictions are published in the Local Notice to Mariners.

Restricted hours may also refer to a block of time when the bridge does not open for recreational traffic, such as during the morning and evening rush hours. If you accidentally arrive at a bridge during its restricted hours, the bridge will not open for you as a pleasure craft.

Even during restricted hours, bridges open for commercial traffic. During a blackout period, you may be able to "sneak through" with a commercial vessel. Clear this with the bridge tender before proceeding.

If it is not during restricted hours, begin by hailing the bridge on the VHF, using that state's bridge channel (VHF 13 or 09). Only call the bridge tender if you are unable to hail them by VHF.

Caution: A bridge will typically not open unless you officially request an opening. Circling in front of the bridge is not considered a bridge opening request and, if you are a lone vessel, will often result in you missing the opening.

Remember, it is equally important to state a *non*-intention. As a courtesy, if you are approaching a bridge and do not intend to pass through, hail the bridge tender and advise him. For example, many boaters stop at Alligator River Marina for inexpensive diesel or an overnight stay. This marina is approached southbound by coming right up to the Alligator River Swing Bridge, turning hard to starboard, and following the bridge into the basin. You will have a very agitated bridge tender if you approach the bridge for three miles at flank speed without making radio contact!

Bridge tenders have other duties, so they may not respond to you immediately. Wait a reasonable amount of time before hailing again. Additionally, re-naming bridges seems to have become a modern-day government sporting activity. We have endeavored to list all bridge name alternatives which may be in favor this season. If one doesn't work, try another.

Courtesy of U.S. Army Corps of Engineers

ICW Bridge Construction

According to Coast Guard regulations (technically not part of the Inland Rules), you may also hail a drawbridge by sounding one prolonged blast, followed within three seconds by one short blast, "repeated until acknowledged by the bridge tender." Unfortunately, this strategy usually backfires. No one likes being honked at and you'll usually end up waiting until another boat requests an opening. Forget the horn.

The inland rules of the road dictate who has the right of way in passing situations. Vessels with a *following* current have right-of-way over vessels motoring up current. If you are heading against the current, stand off until the other vessels clear the bridge opening. With the possibility of a strong current setting them onto the bridge, the boat *with* the current needs your courtesy and room to pass through safely.

Rather than assume a "first-come, first-served" lineup for the bridge opening, hail your fellow cruisers and suggest queueing up in order of hull speed. This will make everyone's life easier, avoiding the post-opening jockeying, passing, and rock-and-roll.

TYPES OF BRIDGES

There are seven types of bridges along the Waterway between Hampton Roads and Biscayne Bay, including the only pontoon bridge in operation on the East Coast. The seven bridge types are: fixed, lift, pontoon, single-bascule, double-bascule, single-pivot swing, and double-pivot swing.

Fixed bridges are 65 feet at mean high water with two exceptions: the 56-foot height of the Julia Tuttle Causeway Bridge in Miami and the reported 64-foot height of the Wilkerson Highway Bridge in North Carolina.

Lift bridges rise horizontally and are typically railroad bridges. Most railroad bridges along the Waterway are *unmanned* and left in the open position unless a train is approaching. If the bridge is closing for an approaching train, light and sound signals will warn you as a precursor to lowering. Some bridges sound warnings well in advance (such as five minutes and one minute prior). Bridges that are more frequently raised and lowered have more aggressive signaling procedures.

The pontoon bridge, located in southern North Carolina, technically has zero clearance since it is floating. This means even the smallest boats must request an opening, which can back up small boat traffic near the bridge on busy days. On exceptionally low tides the pontoon bridge may not be able to open. Be sure to wait until the cable, which opens and closes the bridge, is slack and drops to the bottom of the channel before passing through.

Bascule bridges (from the French word for "seesaw") open on a counterbalanced device that lets the un-weighted end rise as the weighted end is allowed to fall. On a single-bascule bridge, there is a single counterbalance and the bridge lifts from one edge. On a double-bascule bridge, two bascules lift in the center. Watch your mast or flybridge on single-bascule bridges: the passage is narrower and the maximum height is not in the center of the passage.

Swing bridges pivot or rotate to open. Never crowd a swing bridge: it may need the area in front of the spans in order to rotate open. Stay further back and wait until the spans have fully opened. In the case of single-pivot swing bridges, the entire structure will rotate on the center support. Pass through on the side showing large fenders on both the bridge support and bank side.

LOCKS

If you take the Albemarle & Chesapeake Canal route, there is only one lock between Hampton Roads and Biscayne Bay. Located at STM 11.5 in Great Bridge, Virginia, the Great Bridge Lock is a very manageable and well-maintained lock. Depending on the wind-driven tides, the lift is between one and four feet. Although wind is an issue on many locks, we have never experienced significant windage in the Great Bridge Lock.

Arriving from the north, the lock opens at a quarter past each hour and remains open until a quarter before the hour. If you arrive during this window, confirm any signal lights (green means clear to enter) and pro-

Photo by Author

Great Bridge Lock: Child's Play!

ceed to the south wall for recreational craft. Arriving from the east (northbound), the lock opens timed with the opening of the new bascule bridge at Great Bridge. As with bridges, if possible, consider the hull speeds of the vessels and try to enter the lock in a logical order to minimize passing after you exit the lock.

Unlike many locks along the Erie Canal, the Great Bridge Lock is clean and has forgiving rubber walls, so you won't need extra lock equipment. If it is your first time locking, we suggest over-preparing by having lines ready at the bow and stern, fenders to starboard, gloves on, and two boat hooks ready.

In truth, in over 300 lockings, this is the easiest lock we've ever come across. The recreational wall is rubberized and the short lift is gentle and non-turbulent. Barring unusual wind conditions, you can easily fend off with your hand or boat hook. You may lock through with commercial vessels, which use the north wall by the lock office. The lock tender is usually busy with the commercial traffic on the north side so do not expect help coming alongside.

When paralleling the wall, be aware of wall effect (also called canal or bank effect). This phenomenon, which slowly points you toward the lock wall and generates thousands of dollars of gelcoat repairs a year, is created by the drag of a vessel's waves on the wall. Many boaters enter a lock too quickly and then have to back down hard, or enter too slowly and have to throttle up. Both of these abrupt maneuvers create prop-wash in the lock chamber, which can move your, or someone else's, vessel unpredictably.

To minimize wall effect, avoid closely paralleling the wall. Instead, enter the lock six feet away from the wall, gradually narrowing the gap as you approach your tie-up position. Entries should be smooth (meaning not changing RPM) and slow (about two knots) until you reach your position as lead boat in the chamber or behind the last boat that entered before you.

For the same reason, always push off laterally from the wall before you start moving forward to exit. Have the bow and stern person simultaneously push away from the wall until the boat is parallel to the wall six to eight feet away. This will put you away from the wall and prevent you from being sucked back in by wall effect.

Avoid slipping into cell-phone chat on the (very public) VHF, also known as the "coconut telegraph." Don't broadcast your boat name, evening plans, or make negative comments about other boaters, the locals, bridge tenders, or facilities.

BOAT TRAFFIC

Some lengths of the Waterway are solitary, but other stretches are busy with boat traffic. Every helmsperson should be familiar with the basic sound signals of the Rules of the Road, particularly those used along the Waterway. In addition, because of the commercial operations on the Waterway, you must be familiar with the day shapes of working vessels. Lights are not reviewed since transiting the Waterway after dusk is not recommended.

SOUND SIGNALS AND PASSING

The Atlantic Intracoastal Waterway is covered by the Inland Rules. This means power-driven vessels are required to signal proposed intentions to all visible vessels within one-half mile or to reach a passing agreement by radio. In reality, very few vessels use sound signals along the Waterway. This is probably by courtesy rather than by ignorance. Admittedly, few vessels appreciate being honked at prior to being passed.

The Inland Rules allow for radio agreement in lieu of passing signals. While underway, we always maintain a scanning radio watch on VHF 09, 13, and 16, and accept this chatter as a part of our day. The radio lets you communicate intentions to larger approaching commercial craft. We only use sound signals when someone does not respond to our VHF hail and there is doubt about intentions.

Often a commercial vessel will hail you and say "one whistle." Because of the clos-

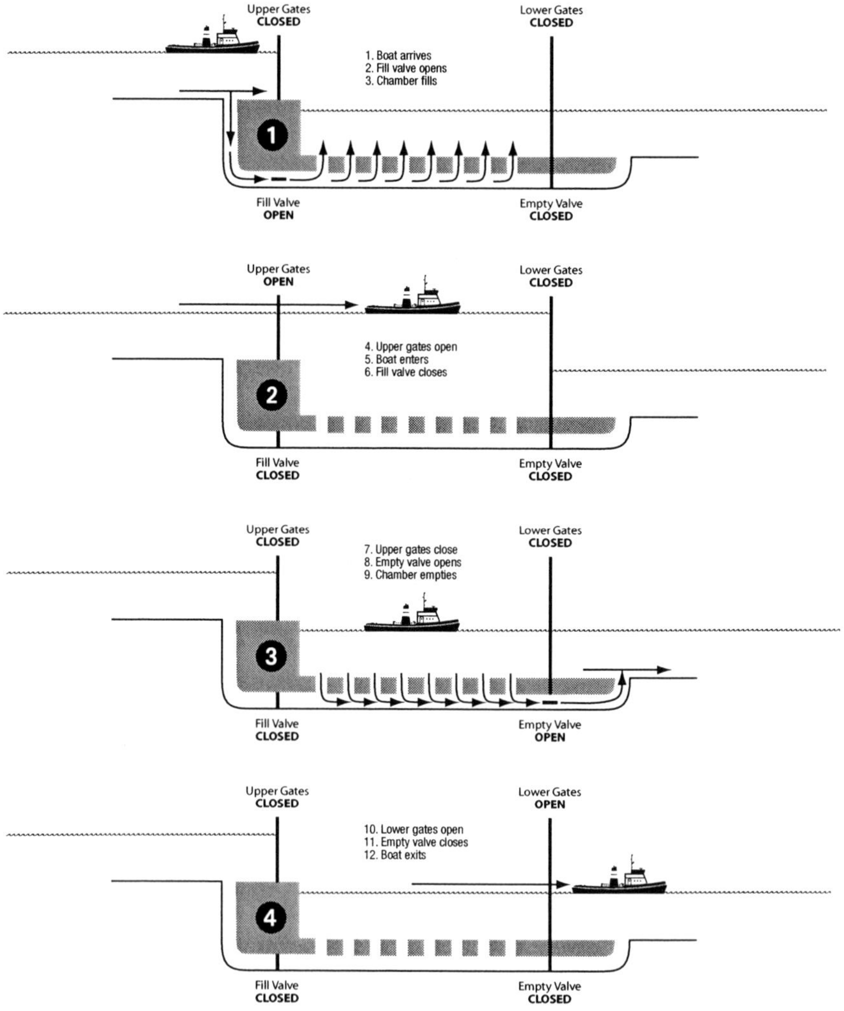

How a Lock Works: No Pumps, Only Gravity!

er quarters, Inland Rules are more of a dialogue than the International Rules: vessels signal intent and then wait for a response before the action is taken.

To review, one whistle (or one short blast on the horn) signals they intend to leave you on their port side. In an approaching situation, this means you would pass port to port. You must agree to the arrangement by responding "one whistle" or "port-to-port" on the VHF or sounding one short blast on your horn. Even better, confirm a signal in a different way to avoid miscommunication, such as "I'll hold to the reds."

Courtesy of Greater Ft. Lauderdale CVB

Tight Quarters Up New River

"Two whistles," or two short blasts, signals the intent to leave you on their starboard side (whether overtaking or approaching). Again, you should reply with two short blasts or a verbal agreement on your VHF.

The norm, like driving cars, is to pass port to port. However, not all proposed passing by commercial vessels is port-to-port. If you are already far to your port side in a channel, or a larger commercial vessel needs his port side of a turn, a starboard-to-starboard passing may make more sense.

If you are unsure or concerned, signal five short blasts, signifying danger or failure to understand the other vessel's intentions, or continue a dialogue on VHF 13.

Finally, three short blasts signals a vessel is operating astern propulsion. On a small vessel this most likely means backing up. On a large commercial vessel it may only mean *backing down* (engines operating astern) as a means to slow down.

DAY SHAPES TO KNOW

Correctly reading day shapes allows you to quickly understand a commercial vessel's activity and your appropriate actions when approaching. We review a handful of day shapes commonly seen along the Waterway.

Because the Waterway is continually shoaling and shifting, working dredges are common. You can confidently approach a dredge by remembering the saying "diamonds are a captain's best friend." A working dredge shows two diamond day shapes in a vertical line on the side on which another vessel may pass. The dredge shows two balls in a vertical line on the side on which it is working. Pass the dredge on the side marked by the diamonds; its gear and operations are on the other side.

A vessel restricted in her ability to maneuver shows three day shapes in a line: ball-diamond-ball. A dredge may show this shape in addition to the two diamonds and two balls designating the passing side. A tug engaged in a towing operation that restricts its ability to deviate from its course also shows the ball-diamond-ball sequence.

Vessels engaged in fishing, whether at anchor or underway, show one of two day shapes: two cones with their apexes together in a vertical line, one above the other, or a basket day shape (if less than 20 meters). Trawlers are fishing vessels that drag a dredge net through the water (such as shrimpers). Trawlers show the same day shapes as fishing vessels. In addition, if the fishing vessel has outlying gear extending more than 150 meters horizontally from the vessel, it shows a cone upward on the side of the gear.

If you see a tug with a tow showing a single diamond day shape (not part of the ball-diamond-ball sequence), expect the tow to be exceptionally long (over 200 meters). Similarly, any partially submerged tow is marked with single diamond day shapes, forward or forward and aft.

A vessel at anchor shows a round ball day shape. For example, a working boat such as a dredge must show this day shape if it is anchored. The only exception is a vessel less than 20 meters anchored in a special anchorage area. However, designated special anchorage areas are rare along the ICW.

Finally, larger sailing vessels are required to show a steaming cone if under power with raised sails. For sailboats over 12 meters with sails up and the engine on, a conical day shape pointing downward signals the vessel is under power and has assumed the right-of-way burden of a power vessel rather than a sailing vessel.

Vessel Engaged in Dredging

Eventually you will encounter a working dredge. Although monitoring VHF 16 and 13, they often will not respond to pleasure craft: (1) they are busy working and (2) believe they are already communicating with day shapes.

Using binoculars, remain in the marked channel and slowly approach the dredge until you can clearly make out the day shapes. The obstruction exists on the side with two balls in a vertical line.

You may safely pass the dredge on the side displaying two diamonds in a vertical line. Remember the saying, "Diamonds are a Captain's Best Friend."

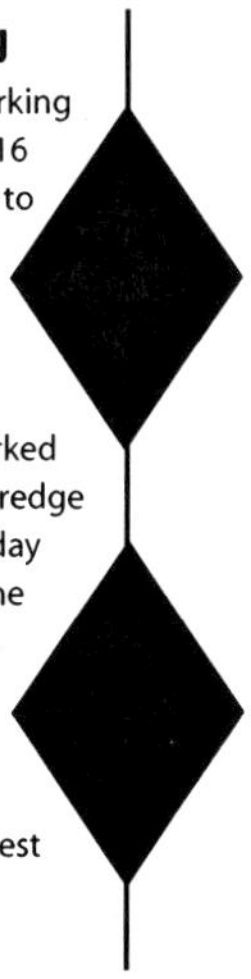

Diamonds Are a Captain's Best Friend

That's in theory. We're offering a round of free drinks to anyone with evidence of a steaming cone properly used on the Waterway.

A current Vessel Safety Check reduces boardings by the USCG. To find the examiner nearest you, call the USCG Info Line at 800/368-5647, visit www.safetyseal.net, or locate the closest U.S. Power Squadron at www.usps.org.

RUNNING AGROUND

Some people joke there are two kinds of vessels on the Intracoastal Waterway: those currently aground and those soon to be aground. If you are from Maine or the Georgian Bay in Canada, the thought of touching bottom is appalling.

Photo by Rosalie Beasley

Dredge with Dayshapes

Drawing an embarrassing less-than-three-feet, we grounded recently when we moved to the side of a narrow cut for an approaching tug and tow. Even President Warren Harding and his crew ran aground and had to be rescued twice in two days in 1923: once on a sandbar south of Hillsboro Lighthouse and then again in New River Sound. You're in good company.

The good news is it's almost always mud or soft sand, not rocks. If you accept the Waterway conditions are always in flux, then touching bottom need not imply you are a poor navigator. Because conditions change, the ICW's magenta line depicted on your chart may not be a deep and perfect trench.

Since the average cost for a "soft ungrounding" is $500, most experienced ICW cruisers recommend broader towing coverage. The basic towing plan included with a BoatU.S. membership is only $50 per incident—barely enough to get the towboat's ignition started.

An unlimited coverage plan, either from Sea Tow or TowBoatU.S., costs just over $100 per year.

Sea Tow
www.seatow.com
800/473-2869

TowBoatU.S.
www.boatus.com/towing
800/888-4869

Learn from the pros. Notice that commercial vessels are always underway with radar. Long-range keeps a weather eye and short-range assists in locating and staying (ranging) in mid-channel.

PREVENTING GROUNDINGS

Unlike the Bahamas, don't expect to be able to read the water to locate the channel. Inland waters are too dark with tannin or churned up with sand and mud. Don't be deceived by what coastal pilots call "flyers," cloud shadows on the water that look like shoals. Instead, rely on Coast Guard-maintained navigational aids and your depth sounder.

However, you can and should read the current at each dayboard or buoy. Constantly look astern to check for set. Verify you are still in the channel by looking back to the last two or three aids. Your wake will show if you are still in the channel, or if you're being set. Obviously you cannot simply drive the boat forward to the next aid or your banana path will set you far outside the buoy-to-buoy channel.

To stay in the channel, drive your vessel like a tugboat. Use the aids as they were intended: for larger, less maneuverable commercial craft. Take large *tug turns* at each aid, rounding the aid in a wide arc like a tug and barge. The aids are placed for these large vessels and their propellers continuously scour the channel. We have actually followed a large commercial vessel through a shoaled area, our depth sounder beeping wildly through the churned water, while the barge literally plowed a channel.

Finally, expect (and accept!) errors in the existence and location of aids. Aids shift and are missing. Drop aids are added on new shoals. Conditions constantly change along the Waterway, depending on weather and the funding available for dredging.

Because of this, don't rely on your chartplotter as a perfect image of the world. Remember, your chartplotter shows a precise image of a government-issued chart. It's not a precise image of the world outside your dodger.

Caution: If you're driving a chartplotter screen or driving the GPS, you are driving an outdated digital road map and expecting exact depictions of the world. Trust your eyes before you trust digital cartography.

WHEN THINGS GO WRONG

If you do touch bottom, stay calm and follow four simple steps.

First, begin by evaluating your situation. Will you get tide help or harm? Similarly, are you getting helped or harmed by the wind? Where is the deep water relative to your boat? The answers to these questions determine how quickly you need to proceed through the remaining steps or if you should call professional help immediately.

Try to back off the shoal by shifting weight on your vessel. Move crewmembers or hang on booms to list or de-trim your vessel. Then gently try to back off. Good, or inarguably better, water is almost always behind you.

If this doesn't work, turn to non-professional help. The easiest way is to ask a passing boat (preferably a power boat, which can be as small as a recreational fishing boat or dinghy) to throw you a passing wake. With your engines lightly in reverse, at the height of the wake your vessel should float and back off of the shoal.

Passing vessels can also provide a light tow. Boaters are usually more than willing to help, but reluctant to go near the area where you grounded. If you're sitting on the hard, don't expect any sane vessel to be willing to leave the channel.

Remember you can always tow yourself by loading your anchor in your dinghy, setting it as a kedge anchor, and using your windlass or winch to haul yourself off the shoal.

If none of these steps work, or if tidal help is uncertain, call the pros. Telephone or hail the closest Sea Tow or TowBoatU.S. station. Do not waste valuable time calling the Coast Guard; they do not tow boats unless "lives are in danger."

If you call a towing company, understand and communicate with them (before they touch your boat) whether the procedure is considered towing or salvage. Towing involves attaching to a grounded boat to refloat it. Salvage is the recovery of a sinking or stranded boat and typically involves equipment such as air bags, pumps, or multiple towing vessels. Obviously salvage is much more involved (legally and with your insurance company) than towing.

If the answer is salvage, then ask the company (called the salvor) to give you a fixed price or a price based on time and materials in writing before beginning. Sometimes a salvor does not want to give a price before they begin, preferring to make a salvage claim afterwards based on the cost. If so, ask them to use the BoatU.S. Open Form Yacht Salvage Contract, which assures a claim can go to binding arbitration if negotiation with your insurance company fails. A copy of this contract is available at the BoatU.S. website (www.boatus.com/salvage). Be sure your insurance covers what you think it does (up to the full value of your boat) and there is no deductible for salvage costs.

Will you need weekly or monthly oil changes? At home, many boaters only change their oil once a season. But the miles really add up along the ICW. Make sure you have enough oil, filters, impellers, and belts to perform frequent pit stops.

SECURITY ZONES

Any area, whether permanent or temporary, in which navigation is restricted for security or safety reasons, is part of a security zone.

A security zone is a prohibited area in order to safeguard harbors or vessels or waterfront facilities from sabotage, such as around the Highway Bridge in Charleston Harbor or near Cape Canaveral prior to a shuttle launch.

Courtesy of U.S. Army Corps of Engineers

Photo by Jonas N. Jordan

Savannah Freighters

These zones may be moveable. For example, the naval vessel protection zone is a moveable security zone around every naval vessel. Boaters should stay at least 500 yards away from any navy vessel. If you must enter this zone because of navigational restrictions, you must maintain a minimum safe speed. In all circumstances you must monitor VHF 16 when near government vessels. Under no circumstances may a recreational boat be within 100 yards of a navy vessel.

A safety zone is an area where access is limited for safety reasons. It may be stationary, such as the area around Camp Lejeune during firing exercises, or moveable, such as the zone around a vessel carrying hazardous cargo.

semi-local publications LLC

Photo by Author

Submarine Moving Security Zone

A regulated navigation area is an area where navigation is permitted but additional navigational rules apply. For example, you can enter the area around Kings Bay, Georgia, but must transit at minimum speed for steerageway.

In addition to the regular security, safety, and regulated navigation zones, the Coast Guard also designates temporary zones for short periods or in particular circumstances. Examples are closures during high security events such as the G-8 summit, around a vessel transporting nuclear materials, during the loading or unloading of military vessels, or in a blasting or dredging area. Listen on VHF 16 for the Coast Guard Broadcast Notice to Mariners and then switch to VHF 22A for details.

One of the simplest and cheapest ways to maintain email contact is with a PocketMail Composer (www.pocketmail.com; 877/362-4543). Using an acoustic coupler, this 3-inch by 6-inch handheld device lets you send and receive email from any phone by simply dialing a toll-free number.

Courtesy of PocketMail

PocketMail Composer

A FEW WORDS ON ANCHORING

Ask 12 cruisers the best way to anchor and you'll get 13 opinions. Part art, part science, nothing replaces a good book on anchoring—such as *The Complete Book of Anchoring and Mooring* by Earl Hinz—and a bit of experience.

Nevertheless, here are a baker's dozen of generally-accepted, high-level observations from our years of traveling and anchoring along the Intracoastal Waterway.

Although anchorages vary—from small tidal creeks to the lee of causeway bridges—remember that anchoring fundamentals (location, equipment, deployment, protection, scope) remain the same.

Anchorages look different from the "inside." Turn on your GPS before entering an anchorage. Then you can exit confidently—in faint morning light or even in fog—by retracing your electronic "bread crumb" trail.

Be on the lookout for shoaling areas as you enter an anchorage. In river or creek anchorages, this means favoring the scoured outside turn of oxbows and bends.

Always take an inventory of how other vessels are anchored. Are they on chain or nylon rode? One anchor or two? If two, are they Bermuda (two anchors at 45°), Bahamian (two anchors at 180°), or bow-and-stern moored? Based on these observations, make *compatible* decisions.

In tight anchorages, be alert for snags or shoals in your swinging circle. You may need to reduce your swing by reducing scope, using two anchors, or using chain rather than nylon rode.

To greatly reduce swing, many cruisers choose to Bahamian moor. Set your first anchor then drift down current paying out twice your intended scope. Drop the second anchor and pull in half the scope on your first anchor's rode.

Avoid bow and stern anchoring in heavy tidal areas. Current running against your transom is extremely unsettling. And, if not executed precisely, you may find yourself wound up on your two rodes like a twisted playground swing. Save this technique for anchoring in a narrow cut where you must restrict *all* swinging into the channel.

Check the local tidal range—listed in the NAV COLUMN as spring tidal range [STR]—to determine your scope. Since spring tidal range is a worst-case scenario, calculating from this number should result in sufficient scope.

Use the spring tidal range [STR] as a proxy for local current. Generally speaking, higher tidal ranges mean more current!

Finally, once you've checked your set, don't neglect the importance of proper anchor lighting.

Always use an anchor light! It's not just a courtesy; it's the law. No matter how remote the setting, whenever we're tempted to save a few amps, we think of the possibility of a large outboard skimming through its local waters after dark.

Sailboats should add a small light at deck level, visible along the horizon. A single masthead light may satisfy USCG requirements but is not where close-quarter boat traffic is looking.

The new low-voltage masthead lights are even less visible. High in the sky, their faint bluish-white light bears a striking resemblance to Sirius, a bright bluish-white star!

Like Tom Bodett, you'll want to keep a light on! Many communities enforce running lights and, yes, this includes your dinghy. We urge you to read the nav rules and comply. What light(s) you show vary by tender size, speed, and type. Even a rowing dinghy must have a clearly visible white light available.

WEATHER

The executive summary of weather along the Atlantic Intracoastal Waterway is captured in a single word: *northers*. The predominant weather pattern, particularly during the fall and winter, is a series of northerlies passing through, each cycle lasting a few days.

The cycle begins with a light southerly breeze and fair weather. Then the wind shifts to the northwest and increases in intensity, often blowing as high as 40 mph from the northwest. The wind continues to shift slowly to the northeast, and the speed decreases as it clocks around to the east then southeast. As the wind moves through the southern quadrant, the wind drops to a light breeze. The light winds and fair weather return, until the wind clocks toward the northwest and the cycle begins again.

By being aware of these cycles of wind direction and speed, you can plan your transit days accordingly. Not only sailboats need to work with the wind. Manage your transit by working with the pattern of weather cycles along the Waterway.

An excellent source for weather information is Weather Underground. This site provides up-to-date marine forecasts including satellite images, sea temperatures, storm conditions, and even astronomy sky views.

Weather Underground
www.wunderground.com/MAR/

Courtesy of St. Lucie County TDC

Ft. Pierce Inlet

LEAVING THE ICW

Leaving the ICW—often called "going outside," "jumping offshore," or simply "bumping out"—is controversial among cruisers. Many cruisers get tired of the restricted bridge openings and shallow water, opting for some offshore legs. For sailboats, there is the allure of a sail to break up the monotony of powering the Waterway. Or, because of your vessel's height or draft, you may need to bump out occasionally, such as to avoid the 56-foot Julia Tuttle bridge or the continual shoaling near Lockwoods Folly.

Before you go, take note of the length of each inlet in calculating your offshore passage. The transit out and back can add hours to a day trip, particularly for slower vessels.

And remember, there is a reason the federal government (and private companies) invested so much effort and money creating and maintaining a sheltered inland route for boat traffic. Conditions outside the Waterway are almost always a rougher ride than behind the barrier islands. You have left a protected waterway (even if it is a choppy bay or sound) for the ocean.

Check weather and sea conditions near each inlet. Inlets can be very rough when an onshore wind opposes an ebbing tidal current. It's very difficult to assess inlet conditions from seaward. You only see the smooth backs of the waves as they roll toward the inlet. Call ahead to a Coast Guard station near your destination port to get the local weather forecast—it may be very different than your port of departure. ▲

Bridges		**Other Features**			
Total	13	Marinas	21	Vignettes	17
Fixed	3	Anchorages	10	Inlets	1
Opening	10	Chandleries	12	Ranges	0

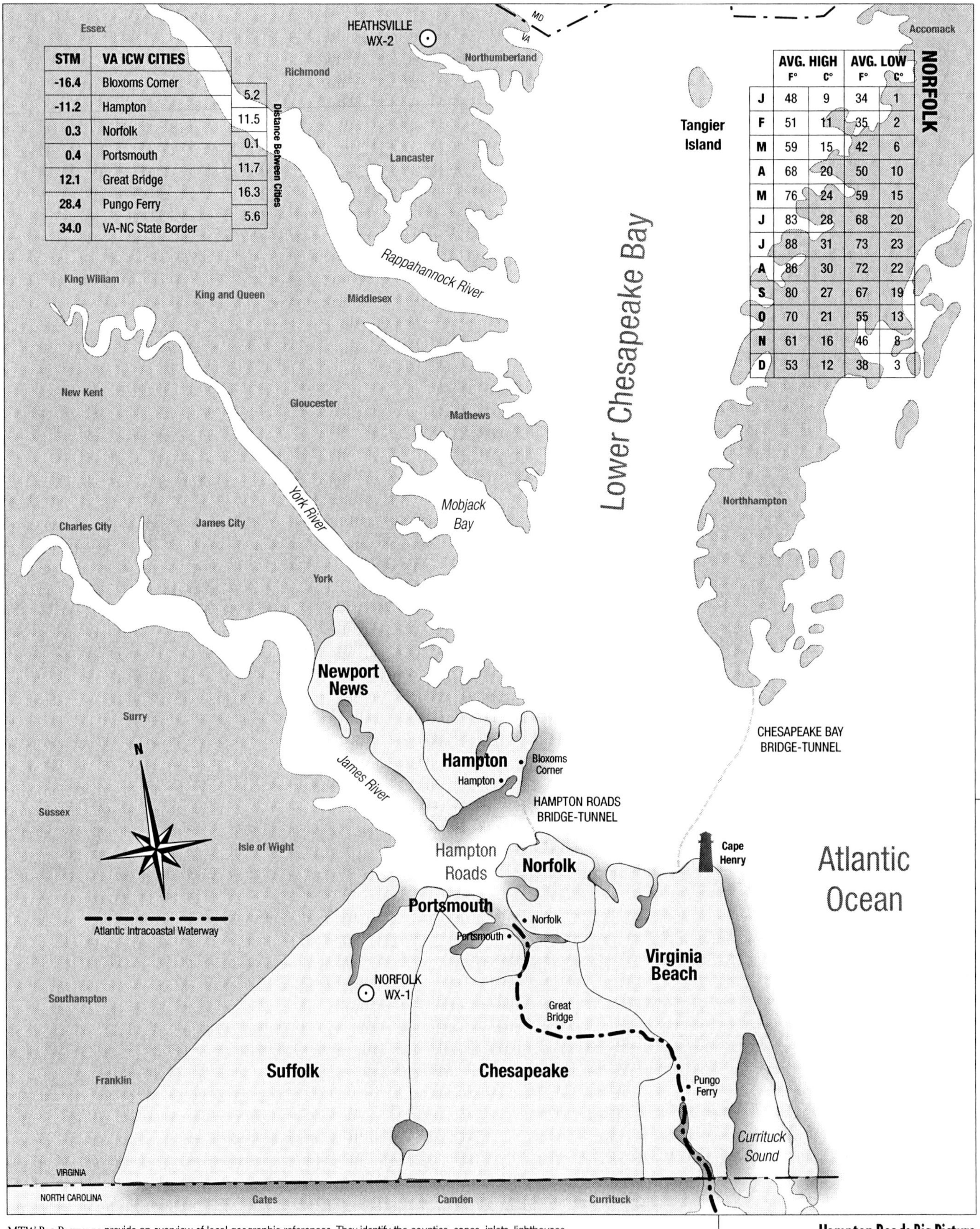

STM	VA ICW CITIES	Distance Between Cities
-16.4	Bloxoms Corner	
		5.2
-11.2	Hampton	
		11.5
0.3	Norfolk	
		0.1
0.4	Portsmouth	
		11.7
12.1	Great Bridge	
		16.3
28.4	Pungo Ferry	
		5.6
34.0	VA-NC State Border	

NORFOLK

	AVG. HIGH F°	AVG. HIGH C°	AVG. LOW F°	AVG. LOW C°
J	48	9	34	1
F	51	11	35	2
M	59	15	42	6
A	68	20	50	10
M	76	24	59	15
J	83	28	68	20
J	88	31	73	23
A	86	30	72	22
S	80	27	67	19
O	70	21	55	13
N	61	16	46	8
D	53	12	38	3

MTW Big Pictures provide an overview of local geographic references. They identify the counties, capes, inlets, lighthouses, and bodies of water commonly referred to in NOAA and AM/FM weather broadcasts.

The locations of WX weather towers are shown to easily determine the best broadcast for your position and direction of travel. The temperature table shows average highs and lows for that region. Look for major cities and smaller towns along the ICW, then use the distance table for planning stops or estimating travel time. Lastly, we list the region's required charts by their NOAA chart number and provide a snapshot of Waterway resources and impediments.

Virginia

Hampton Roads to North Landing River

The Old Dominion State
ICW Statute Mile -16.4 to 34.0
Bridges and Locks Monitor VHF 13

Regions
Hampton Roads
On to the North Carolina Border

Inlets
Chesapeake Bay Entrance

U.S. Coast Guard
District Five: 757/398-6272
Group Hampton Roads: 757/483-8568
Station Portsmouth: 757/483-8527

NOAA Weather Towers
WX-2 Heathsville
WX-1 Norfolk

Security Zones
Norfolk Naval Shipyard
Norfolk Naval Base

Canal Information
757/201-7606

Lighthouses
Thimble Shoal Light
Old Point Comfort Light
Fort Wool Light
Portsmouth Lightship

Fishing Information
www.dgif.state.va.us/fishing

VIRGINIA'S INTRACOASTAL Waterway is a history tour spanning two hundred years. No other 34-mile section intersects so many important events in the emergence of our nation.

In Virginia, the *entire* Intracoastal Waterway is a historical site. The Dismal Swamp Canal, envisioned by George Washington and painstakingly hand-dug by slaves, is the oldest continually operating man-made canal in the U.S. Today it is listed in the National Register of Historic Places and designated a National Civil Engineering Landmark.

The Albemarle & Chesapeake Canal, originally surveyed in 1772, was completed in 1859. Until the steam shovel was invented, cutting 14 miles through swamps and tidal marshes remained an impractical dream.

These rivers and canals were central to America's early conflicts. The Revolutionary War was fought along the banks of the Waterway, as Loyalists and Patriots battled for control of strategic routes. One of the most pivotal battles of the Revolutionary War, the Battle of Great Bridge, took place at a pinch-point bridge crossing over the Waterway. The victory allowed the establishment of an essential supply line from the Carolinas and Virginia to Washington's army in the north.

As the Civil War unfolded, Hampton Roads, not too far from the Mason-Dixon line, was at the center of this conflict. The famous "Battle of the Ironclads," the face-off between the *Monitor* and the *Merrimack*, took place in Hampton Roads. You pass near the site as you transit between Fort Wool and Fort Monroe, the fort where Confederate President Jefferson Davis was imprisoned.

This maritime history surrounds Virginia's Intracoastal Waterway. There are scores of commemorative sites and exhibits, ranging from Civil War forts to high-tech naval museums. Virginia is the "history channel" of the Intracoastal Waterway tour.

Courtesy of City of Norfolk

An Elephant Has the Right of Way

The short transit through Virginia spans scenery as well as history. This short ICW stretch, only five percent of the distance to Miami, has some of the most varied experiences of the entire Waterway. The route begins in a shipping port busy with commerce and ends in a remote wetland area of canoe trails.

The transformation begins just south of the Dismal Swamp Canal junction at STM 7.2. North of this junction, the Waterway passes through a noisy, bustling, developed industrial port. To the south, it transforms into a quiet woodland riverine passage. By the time you reach Currituck Sound in North Carolina, you have experienced the transition from battleships to water moccasins, from merry-go-rounds to nesting osprey.

HAMPTON ROADS

To a mariner, a "road" means an anchorage. Nautically speaking, a road is an anchorage that is less sheltered than a harbor. Hampton Roads, formed by the confluence of the James, Nansemond, and Elizabeth Rivers, is one of the largest sheltered bays in the area, an important road since colonial times.

Although the harbor has been called Hampton Roads since the 1600s, this name has only been used for the southeastern region of Virginia since 1983. At that time the jurisdictions bordering the harbor decided to share a regional identity as Hampton Roads. This designation now includes the Southside (independent cities of Norfolk, Portsmouth, Virginia Beach, Suffolk, and Chesapeake); the Peninsula (independent cities of Hampton and Newport News); and the counties of Isle of Wight, James City, Surry, and York.

Today Hampton Roads is one of the eastern seaboard's most strategic ports, home to the world's largest naval base.

The Waterway passes through the cities of Hampton, Norfolk, and Portsmouth before entering the Elizabeth River. Because most southbound boats arrive in Hampton Roads from the Chesapeake Bay, we've stepped back from the official start of the Waterway—at the mouth of the Elizabeth River between Norfolk and Portsmouth—to include navigation and marina information for the entire area.

Hampton is part of what is called "the Peninsula." The center of town is at the mouth of the Hampton River, but many boaters also stop at charted Bloxoms Corner. Called "Salt Ponds" by locals, Bloxoms Corner is a quiet residential district of Hampton. Fort Monroe, a military base technically independent of Hampton, lies along the Waterway between Bloxoms Corner and Hampton's city center. Hampton's turnoff is at STM –11.2. Downtown Hampton is a small city geared for boaters, with very accessible services and many attractions.

Mile Zero at Hospital Point

The official start of the Intracoastal Waterway is at the mouth of the Elizabeth River between Portsmouth and Norfolk. This location, called "Mile Zero," is located at Hospital Point, marked by the famous government aid R36.

The convenient Elizabeth River ferry makes Norfolk and Portsmouth a single resource for transiting boaters. Both cities are geared to maritime visitors. Large marinas and marine services abound, making either of these two towns excellent pit stops for boat maintenance. They are large cities, so there are many shopping areas and activities for visitors, ranging from maritime museums to annual festivals on the cities' marina docks.

Marinas are abundant in Hampton Roads. There are many public and private marinas and several yacht clubs offering reciprocal privileges. In addition, many of the marinas have extensive facilities with full repair and haul-out capabilities.

But despite heavy waterfront development, there are also surprisingly many anchorages. Hampton Roads is created by the influx of several rivers and creeks, many of which offer protection, such as up the Lafayette River at STM –3.5 or Willoughby Bay at STM –9.0. Most of the cities of Hampton Roads also maintain designated anchorages.

But don't expect an anchorage in Hampton Roads to be the peaceful anchorage of a Maine cove. Remember, it's Hampton Roads, one of the largest and most active commercial ports in the world. One of the most famous Hampton Roads anchorages, the Hospital Point anchorage in Portsmouth, is typical. Let's just say it puts you in the middle of things. It's easy to access everything you need from this anchorage; but be prepared for noise and wash. Some cruisers love this anchorage; others hate it. Perhaps everyone should try it once and decide for him or herself.

Large boat traffic is the main navigation concern in Hampton Roads. As one of the world's deepest natural ice-free harbors, the port of Hampton Roads is very busy with commercial vessels. Shipyards, military bases, fishing fleets, and freighters combine to create a lot of traffic. In fact, Hampton Roads is the third largest U.S. port in terms of tonnage, after New Orleans and Houston.

Despite this traffic, Hampton Roads is not the "freighter freeway" that some describe. The channels are wide and well marked. As a small vessel, you can and should take advantage of the edges of the channels. There is plenty of space for maneuverability. Keep a vigilant eye for larger commercial traffic and stay out of the way.

As a major naval port, it is important to be aware of restricted navigation areas. In brief, keep away from naval installations. The Waterway channel passes near the Norfolk Navy Yard. Don't be surprised if you are approached, identified, and possibly even escorted by a Coast Guard patrol boat along this stretch.

Remember that all Navy vessels and cruise ships are within a "moving protection zone." Boaters should stay at least 500 yards away from any Navy vessel unless this is not possible due to navigation conditions such as a narrow channel. If you must enter the 500-yard zone, you must maintain a minimum safe speed. In all circumstances you must monitor VHF 16 when near government vessels. Under no circumstances can a recreational boat be within 100 yards of a Navy vessel. In addition, depending on their cargo, freighters and loading docks at

Photo by Jeff Greenburg

Elizabeth River Ferry

shipyards may also invoke the 500-yard restricted navigation area.

If you are heading southbound from Norfolk or Portsmouth, be sure to note the three restricted bridges between STM 2.7 and STM 8.8. To accommodate rush hour traffic, these three bridges (Jordan, Gilmerton, and Dominion Boulevard Bridges) do not open during rush hour. Most importantly, the bridges are closed between 0630 and 0830 hrs and 1530 and 1800 hrs. Use the MIXED METRIC DST TABLE on the cover tab to calculate your early morning start in order to clear these bridges.

Hampton Roads
www.visithamptonroads.com

Collect toll-free numbers for businesses you use regularly: financial institutions, insurance or credit card companies, and medical offices. Today, many businesses have toll-free numbers for out-of-state callers.

ON TO THE NORTH CAROLINA BORDER

There are two routes to the Alligator River in North Carolina, both historic land cuts: the Virginia Cut (called Route 1 on the charts) or the Great Dismal Swamp Canal (Route 2).

In this first edition of *Managing the Waterway*, we focus on Virginia Cut because it remains the primary route for Waterway travelers. Virginia Cut, which roughly parallels the Dismal Swamp route, is wider and deeper and now carries most of the commercial traffic and the deeper draft recreational boats. Route 1 has a single lock, deeper water, more services, and more traffic.

However, we suggest you take the Dismal Swamp at least once. It's only three miles longer than Virginia Cut and is a lovely trip. A fantastic visitor center offers free dockage at its 150-foot face dock. However, there are fewer services and shallower water along Route 2. Occasionally the Dismal Swamp route closes due to water conditions or dredging delays. Call 757/201-7606 for information and updates before you choose this route.

The Albemarle & Chesapeake canal connects the Elizabeth River, which has lunar tides, with the North Landing River and Currituck Sound, which have wind-driven tides. The single lock at Great Bridge—the only lock on Route 1—balances the lunar- and wind-driven tides. "South" of the lock any change in the water level is wind-driven, forced upriver from Currituck Sound.

semi-local publications LLC

Photo by Author

Great Bridge Lock

The Great Bridge Lock at STM 11.5 is a very manageable and well-maintained lock. Depending on the wind-driven tides, the lift is between one and four feet. Although wind is an issue on many locks, we have never experienced significant windage in the Great Bridge Lock.

Southbound, the lock opens at a quarter past each hour and remains open until a quarter before the hour. If you arrive during this window, confirm any signal lights (green means clear to enter) and proceed to the *south* wall. Northbound, the lock opens timed with the opening of the new bascule bridge at Great Bridge.

The south, non-commercial vessel wall is rubberized and the short lift is gentle and non-turbulent. Unless it's very windy, you can easily fend off with your hand or boat hook. You may lock through with commercial vessels, which use the north wall by the lock office. The lock tender is usually busy with the commercial traffic on the north side, so don't expect help.

A visitor center for boaters is planned as part of the construction of the new bridge at Great Bridge. Opening in December 2006, the facility will include a large park along the canal, walking trails, a visitor center and museum, and docks and information for boaters.

As you pass the junction with the Dismal Swamp Canal route, the look and feel of the Waterway transforms.

The industrial activity ends and the Waterway becomes quiet natural rivers stitched together with land cuts. The Albemarle & Chesapeake Canal blends with the North Landing River, with short land cuts to bypass the oxbows of this meandering river.

As you approach North Carolina, the area becomes more and more remote. North Landing River crosses a wild area of unusual and valuable wetlands owned by the State of Virginia and the Nature Conservancy. Over 10,000 acres are set aside to preserve land that has more rare plants, animals, and natural communities than any place east of the Blue Ridge. These marshes and swamps are punctuated by Baldcypress and Loblolly Pine, and are abundant with wildlife. You'll pass through these wild wetlands until the river opens up at Currituck Sound and the North Carolina border. Marinas become smaller and scarcer along the North Landing River. The more populated areas of Virginia Beach, which spans from the North Landing River north to the Chesapeake Bay and east to the Atlantic, are miles away.

As the Waterway becomes more remote, anchorages become abundant. Many of the oxbows or wide spots in the channel offer excellent overnight protection.

Away from the noise and bustle of Hampton Roads, southern Virginia is more typical of the Waterway experience through North and South Carolina and Georgia: smaller towns, many anchorages, and meandering natural waterways.

Dismal Swamp Canal Visitor Center
www.dismalswamp.com
252/771-8333

Battlefield and Waterways Visitor Center
www.gbbattlefield-waterways.com
Telephone TBA

Save your money! Buy inexpensive and lightweight cotton towels. Expensive, plush towels will only fade and prematurely wear flagging on deck and drying in the harsh sun. Cheap towels take up less room, absorb better, and dry faster onboard or with other clothes in the laundromat dryer.

VIRGINIA BOOK AND FILM PICKS

With his teenage son and a cat as crew, Henry Plummer left Massachusetts to sail the inland passage to Florida. The year was 1912 and the Intracoastal Waterway was very different than today. There were few marinas, minimal dredging, and only primitive navigation aids.

Courtesy of U.S. Army Corps of Engineers

Photo by Jonas N. Jordan

Great Blue Heron

Plummer chronicles his travels in *The Boy, Me and the Cat: Life Aboard a Small Boat from Massachusetts to Florida and Back.*

You think you have grievances about the Waterway? This book puts today's small boating inconveniences into perspective. Without aids and dredging, they ran aground constantly. Their meals were largely what they could catch. They ate oysters, plovers, turtles—and anything else that swam, flew, or crawled. Meanwhile their landlubber cat was completely traumatized by life aboard a 24-foot boat.

Courtesy of U.S. Fish & Wildlife Service

North American Raccoon

Nearly 100 years later, this book still ranks as the best travelogue ever written about the Intracoastal Waterway.

Dee Carstarphen's book, *Narrow Waters*, subtitled "an artist's memoir of sailing through sound, swamp, city, forest, marsh, and glade," is a travelogue in words and watercolor illustrations. It covers the ICW from the Chesapeake to the Dry Tortugas with beautiful illustrations and rich handwritten annotations. ▲

SAFETY INFO

NOAA Weather	**Sea Tow**
WX-2 Heathsville, VA	Hampton Roads, VA
WX-1 Norfolk, VA	VHF 16/18
WX-3 Cape Hatteras, NC	757/496-1999
USCG	**TowBoatU.S.**
Station Portsmouth, VA	Portsmouth, VA
VHF 16 or 09/22A	VHF 16/19
757/483-8527	757/441-9656

HEADS UP!

NB	No Northbound Heads Up!
NB	No Northbound Heads Up!
NB	No Northbound Heads Up!
NB	No Northbound Heads Up!
NB	No Northbound Heads Up!
NB	No Northbound Heads Up!
NB	No Northbound Heads Up!
NB	No Northbound Heads Up!
-12.0	**Ship Traffic (SB)**
-9.0	Security Zone Enforced (SB)
-5.0	Security Zone Enforced (NB)
0.0	Hospital Point, ICW Mile "0"
0.1	Bridge Caution (SB)
0.7	North Harbor Ferry Crossing
2.5	N&P Belt Line RR Bridge
2.7	Jordan Bridge
3.5	Norfolk Southern RR Bridge
5.8	Gilmerton Bridge

-16.4 Before Mile "0"
to Hampton Roads
0.0 If you haven't already provisioned in the Chesapeake, take advantage of the excellent staging anchorages and marinas in Hampton Roads:

- Bloxoms Corner | Salt Ponds
- Old Point Comfort
- Hampton
- Willoughby Bay
- Lafayette River
- Western Branch
- Scotts Creek
- Norfolk and Portsmouth

-16.4 Bloxoms Corner | Salt Ponds
Approach G3 N37.03.271
STR 2.8 feet W076.15.536
Traveling SSW down the lower Bay, look for Approach G3 and Bloxoms Corner G1 and R2 (SW of charted Grand View Pier). Proceed NW into privately maintained channel.
Entrance channel is a well-aided break in the beach with 6 feet at low water. Turn to port aggressively at the last green dayboard to avoid being swept NNW toward the marsh.
See Salt Ponds Skimmers.

- **Southall Landings Marina** (1.4)
  VHF 16/09 N37.03.510
  757/850-9929 W076.17.148
  Marina is to starboard in gated community.
- **Bloxoms Corner Anchorage** (1.5)
  Anchor 6-9 feet N37.03.429
  STR 2.8 feet W076.17.213
  Anchorage is past marina where pond opens up. Move out of channel to WNW.
- **Salt Ponds Marina** (1.6)
  VHF 16/09 N37.03.223
  757/850-4300 W076.17.236
  Marina is to port. Transient dockage and fuel dock are beyond charted basin to port.

-12.0 Junction | Chesapeake Bay Entrance (13.0)
Well Aided N36.57.942
Well Lit W076.04.661
From Old Point Comfort Light, proceed E then ESE along charted Thimble Shoal Channel to the Chesapeake Bay Bridge-Tunnel.
Waypoint is between G5 and R6.

-12.0 Old Point Comfort Light
Lighthouse to NW.
The official entrance to Hampton Roads.
See Fort Monroe and Fort Wool.

-12.0 Heads Up | Ship Traffic
to Southbound Navigation Only
7.7 This stretch of Hampton Roads has a high concentration of commercial ship traffic.

-11.5 Old Point Comfort Marina (0.0)
VHF 16/68 N37.00.246
757/788-4308 W076.18.866
Exit main ship channel SSW of Old Point Comfort Light. Proceed NNW into charted Phoebus Channel. Marina is to starboard in charted small basin W of Fort Monroe. [STR 3.0 (TS)]

THE ATLANTIC FLYWAY

Welcome to the world of migrants. You are a small part of a huge migration along the Atlantic flyway, the major corridor between the Arctic, Caribbean, and South America. Twice a year, hundreds of species transit this corridor, moving with the seasons and weather patterns.

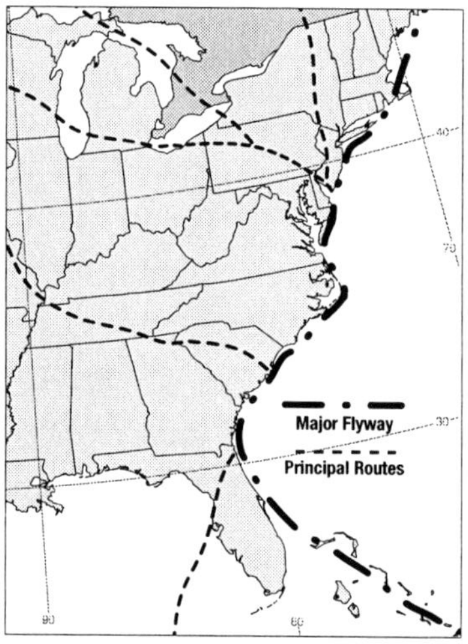

Courtesy of www.birdnature.com

The Atlantic Flyway

Think of a flyway as a migration highway with off-ramps for different species. Large waterfowl—like geese or swans—hop on this turnpike in the Arctic Circle and exit at Currituck or Albemarle Sound. Smaller birds—Robins or Palm Warblers—exit further south in Florida. Some of the colorful tropical songbirds, like the bright red Scarlet Tanagers, continue to destinations in South America or the southern Caribbean.

Like you, your avian companions transit during favorable wind conditions. No sense burning up scarce energy bucking a headwind. Smaller songbirds, in fact, need to ride the leading edge of a front. Look for flocks of small migrating birds as each front passes through. Watch for swarms of swallows flying low over the water. Look over areas of open water for geese or swans resting in huge rafts. We are all travelers with the weather on the Atlantic flyway.

SALT PONDS SKIMMERS

Sitting in your cockpit in the evening, you may be startled by what sounds like the cry of a newborn baby. This loud coarse "aaaaw" is the cry of a Black Skimmer, a unique bird that feeds on small fish by slicing the water with its elongated lower bill.

Watch for skimmers on calm evenings, slicing back and forth along the placid fairway. Skimmers are incredibly graceful in the air, able to fly just above the surface of the water and execute hairpin turns while foraging.

But their huge bills are a liability on land. Young skimmers get tired holding up their own beaks. Like school kids resting their chins on their desks, tired young skimmers sometimes sprawl comically forward, resting their heavy bills on the ground.

FORT MONROE AND FORT WOOL

Now that you're south of the Mason-Dixon line (the line separating youse from y'all), many passing sites will date back to the Civil War. Two examples are sentinels Fort Monroe and Fort Wool—guarding the entrance to Hampton Roads at STM -12.0. As you pass Old Point Comfort, Fort Monroe and the Old Point Comfort Lighthouse are on the point to the north and Fort Wool is on the island to the south.

Courtesy of NASA

Black Skimmer

Fort Monroe is an active military post and the location of Old Point Comfort Marina, open to eligible personnel (STM -11.5). If you stay at Old Point Comfort Marina, you can conveniently visit the Casement Museum chronicling Fort Monroe's somber history (Confederate President Jefferson Davis was imprisoned here) and view the Old Point Comfort Lighthouse.

Fort Wool is located on the small island known as The Rip-Raps, which

SAFETY INFO

NOAA Weather	Sea Tow
WX-2 Heathsville, VA	Hampton Roads, VA
WX-1 Norfolk, VA	VHF 16/18
WX-3 Cape Hatteras, NC	757/496-1999
USCG	**TowBoatU.S.**
Station Portsmouth, VA	Portsmouth, VA
VHF 16 or 09/22A	VHF 16/19
757/483-8527	757/441-9656

HEADS UP!

NB	No Northbound Heads Up!
NB	No Northbound Heads Up!
NB	No Northbound Heads Up!
NB	No Northbound Heads Up!
NB	No Northbound Heads Up!
NB	No Northbound Heads Up!
NB	No Northbound Heads Up!
-12.0	Ship Traffic (SB)
-9.0	Security Zone Enforced (SB)
-5.0	Security Zone Enforced (NB)
0.0	Hospital Point, ICW Mile "0"
0.1	Bridge Caution (SB)
0.7	North Harbor Ferry Crossing
2.5	N&P Belt Line RR Bridge
2.7	Jordan Bridge
3.5	Norfolk Southern RR Bridge
5.8	Gilmerton Bridge
5.8	Norfolk Southern RR Bridge

is basically a big pile of rocks built up from dumping ballast in the early 1800s on a natural shoal. Unfortunately, piling heavy rocks on a sandy wet shoal is a bad engineering strategy, so the island continued to settle over time, delaying the construction of the Fort. Fort Wool was still incomplete by the start of the Civil War, but was used anyway. Its claim to fame was an experimental cannon, called the Sawyer Gun, which could fire a cannonball all the way to where you now see the towering gray ships at the Norfolk Naval Shipyard.

THE MONITOR AND THE MERRIMACK

Today the Norfolk Naval Shipyard, with its huge battleships and dry docks, dominates Hampton Roads. It was the site of the first dry dock (which took seven years to build in the 1920s) and the birthplace of the modern steel battleship. It was here the first armored ship, the *U.S.S. Merrimack*, was built.

The original Merrimack was a wooden steam-powered warship, abandoned by the Union Navy when they lost their base at Norfolk. To open the supply of food and munitions, the Confederates had to break the blockade of Hampton Roads. They re-fitted the captured Merrimack with new decks and sides of 2-foot-thick wood covered with 4-inch-thick iron. The Merrimack left the shipyard with a new name (*C.S.S. Virginia*) and a new look: the old wooden ship was now decks awash with heavy armor, looking like a clunky riveted submarine.

In 1862, the *C.S.S. Virginia* steamed into Hampton Roads to confront the Union blockade. Union shells bounced off the armored sides and the Virginia left unharmed. But the Civil War arms race was underway. The Union Navy also had an armored ship in the works. The *U.S.S. Monitor* arrived overnight to protect the blockade fleet. The Virginia and the Monitor fought for four hours to a stalemate.

The "Battle of Ironclads" at Hampton Roads was the first time in history two iron ships met in combat at sea. At Hampton Roads, the age of wooden warships ended, and the era of modern steel battleships began.

CANNON BALLS AND BRASS MONKEYS

Cannons were the weapons of choice during these conflicts. But storing scores of round heavy cannonballs on the deck of a ship required a special device called a *brass monkey*. A monkey was a metal plate with sixteen round indentations, creating a 30-ball pyramid of one ball resting on four resting on nine resting on sixteen. The plates needed to be brass or the iron cannonballs would rust to the plate.

Courtesy of West Marine Caribbean 1500

Caribbean 1500 Start

But when brass cools, it contracts more and contracts faster than iron. So, if the temperature dropped too far and too fast, the brass indentations would shrink and the cannon balls would escape off the monkey, rolling all over the deck. When this happened, the crew would complain it was (literally), "cold enough to freeze the balls off a brass monkey."

So next time you're freezing cold, pushing those last few miles down the Waterway to that night's port...you can complain about the cold relative to the balls on a brass monkey.

HAMPTON

With multiple choices for docking or anchoring, Hampton is an accessible and convenient stop for cruisers. In addition to provisioning, Hampton has several unique attractions. The Virginia Air and Space Center is within walking distance. It includes dozens of hands-on air and space exhibits and an interactive aviation gallery. Over 30

Old Point Comfort Marina, part of a military base, is open to "authorized patrons": (1) active or retired military personnel, (2) active or retired Department of Defense employees, (3) NASA employees, and (4) possibly by 2005, all federal employees.

-11.2 Hampton

Exit main ship channel SW of Old Point Comfort Light. Use second channel, **not** charted Phoebus Channel. Proceed NNW and follow channel into Hampton River. [STR 3.1 (TS)]

Hampton is a small nautically oriented town loaded with marine services and providing mass transit to groceries and chandleries.

SEE HAMPTON.

- **Bluewater Yachting Center** (2.4)
  VHF 16/72 N37.00.959
  757/723-6774 W076.20.531
  Marina is to port.
- **Sunset Boating Center** (3.0)
  VHF 16; 757/722-3325
  Exit Hampton Channel at G17. Proceed W into charted Sunset Creek. Marina is ahead.
- **Hampton Yacht Club** (2.6)
  VHF 16 N37.01.209
  757/722-0711 W076.20.641
  Yacht club is to port.
  Accepts guests of members and offers reciprocal rights to members of accredited yacht clubs.
- **Hampton Anchorage** (2.8)
  Anchor 8-10 feet N37.01.400
  STR (TS) 3.1 feet W076.20.466
  Anchorage is to starboard opposite Downtown Hampton Public Piers.
- **Downtown Hampton Public Piers** (2.9)
  VHF 16 N37.01.455
  757/727-1276 W076.20.497
  Marina is to port before fixed bridge.

-9.2 Junction | Hampton Roads

Proceed westerly for Newport News and James River destinations.

Continue southerly into charted Norfolk Harbor Reach for Norfolk, Portsmouth, and ICW.

-9.0 Willoughby Bay

There are two charted entrances to Willoughby Bay. The southern entrance at Sewells Point is much preferred with better depth and less crosswind.

Exit main ship channel at G5. Proceed ESE along Sewells Point Channel. Depart channel S of G7. [STR 3.0]

- **Willoughby Harbor Marina** (2.4)
  VHF 16/09 N36.57.863
  757/583-4150 W076.17.705
  Proceed E across Willoughby Bay. Marina is in charted northern hook.
- **Rebel Marina** (2.4)
  VHF 16; 757/588-6022
  Proceed E across Willoughby Bay. Marina is W of Willoughby Harbor Marina.

SAFETY INFO

NOAA Weather
WX-2 Heathsville, VA
WX-1 Norfolk, VA
WX-3 Cape Hatteras, NC

USCG
Station Portsmouth, VA
VHF 16 or 09/22A
757/483-8527

Sea Tow
Hampton Roads, VA
VHF 16/18
757/496-1999

TowBoatU.S.
Portsmouth, VA
VHF 16/19
757/441-9656

HEADS UP!

NB	No Northbound Heads Up!
NB	No Northbound Heads Up!
NB	No Northbound Heads Up!
NB	No Northbound Heads Up!
NB	No Northbound Heads Up!
-12.0	Ship Traffic (SB)
-9.0	**Security Zone Enforced (SB)**
-5.0	**Security Zone Enforced (NB)**
0.0	**Hospital Point, ICW Mile "0"**
0.1	**Bridge Caution (SB)**
0.7	North Harbor Ferry Crossing
2.5	N&P Belt Line RR Bridge
2.7	Jordan Bridge
3.5	Norfolk Southern RR Bridge
5.8	Gilmerton Bridge
5.8	Norfolk Southern RR Bridge
7.2	Dismal Swamp Canal (SB)
7.7	Ship Traffic (NB)

• **Willoughby Bay Anchorage** (3.3)
Anchor 8-10 feet N36.57.571
STR 3.0 feet W076.16.597
Proceed easterly across Willoughby Bay. Anchor in NE corner.

-9.0 Heads Up | Norfolk Naval Base S N
to Southbound/Northbound Navigation
-5.0 Security Zone enforced.
Caution: Stay to the red side of channel and expect contact from a patrol boat.

-3.5 Lafayette River Anchorage (2.4) S N
Anchor 6-8 feet N36.54.334
STR (TS) 3.2 feet W076.18.385
Exit main ship channel between G21 and G23. Proceed NE into channel. Anchorage is before fixed bridge (vertical 24 feet), ESE of R14, opposite Norfolk Yacht & Country Club.

-2.2 Western Branch S N
Exit main ship channel NNW of R30. Proceed SSW, then westerly along channel. [STR 3.1 (TS)]

• **Western Branch Diesel** (1.3)
VHF 16; 757/673-7000
Facility is to N.
Engine service and repairs. No transient dockage. Uses Virginia Boat & Yacht facilities.

• **Virginia Boat & Yacht** (1.4)
VHF 16; 757/673-7167
Marina is to N.

• **Western Branch Bridge** (1.5)
Fixed; vertical 45 feet.

• **Nautical Boats & Marina** (1.6)
VHF 16; 757/483-6148
Marina is to N.
Hard hit by Hurricane Isabel but re-building.

-0.5 Scott Creek S N
Exit main ship channel at R34. Proceed W into channel. [STR 3.4]

• **Portsmouth Boating Center** (0.7)
VHF 16/68 N36.50.766
757/397-2092 W076.18.893
Marina is at G5.

• **Scott's Creek Marina** (0.8)
VHF 16/68 N36.50.791
757/399-2628 W076.19.008
Marina is to starboard.

0.0 ICW Mile "0" S N
This portion of the Atlantic Intracoastal Waterway, which most people think of as *the* ICW, begins here off Hospital Point at R36.
See Norfolk and Portsmouth.

0.1 Heads Up | Bridge Caution S N
Southbound Navigation Only
Southbound travelers must time their passage with the rush-hour blackouts of the Jordan, Gilmerton, and Dominion Boulevard Bridges.
Use the Mixed Metric DST Table on the cover tab to calculate *your* early start.
For example, our relatively slow-moving vessel (6.5 knots or 7.5 stm/hr) requires us to be un-

historic aircraft are displayed, including the Apollo 12 Command Module, a DC-9 passenger jet, and a replica 1903 Wright Flyer.

The Hampton Carousel, a restored turn-of-the-century merry-go-round, is adjacent to the Air and Space Center. This carousel attracts thousands of visitors a year and is one of only 200 antique carousels remaining in the United States. It is a rare and beautiful example of American folk art, painstakingly carved and painted by German, Italian, and Russian immigrant artisans. The work is so detailed the veins in the horses' necks and legs are visible.

Hampton is also the port of departure for the West Marine Caribbean 1500. Each November, a flotilla of about 70 boats departs Hampton on a 7- to 12-day cruising rally to Tortola, British Virgin Islands.

The Mariners' Museum is located nearby in the city of Newport News. This 550-acre park includes several spectacular galleries with more than 50 full-size vessels. Their hand-carved boat models are so detailed they require a magnifying glass.

Virginia Air & Space Center
www.vasc.org
757/727-0900

Hampton Carousel
757/727-6381

West Marine Caribbean 1500
www.carib1500.com
757/223-5070

Mariners' Museum
www.mariner.org
800/581-7245

WHY THE ARMY CORPS?

Government floating aid R36, known to boaters as *Mile Zero*, welcomes you to the unofficial start of the ICW. All mileage, from here to Key West, is measured from this location.

Today the Army Corps of Engineers is in charge of the ICW, but it wasn't always this way. In the 1800s the Waterway was owned by an assortment of for-profit private companies. The federal government would deed rights to a company to dig a land cut between two natural bodies of water and the company would attempt to recoup its investment through tolls. Many of the early portions of the Waterway were hand-dug by slave labor.

Courtesy of City of Norfolk

Norfolk Waterside

But this system didn't fare well. The private companies discovered that profits were poor. Over time, they failed to honor their maintenance obligations. So in the early 1900s the U.S. government began to nationalize the Waterway, re-claiming rights from private holdings. With slave labor no longer an option, the federal government turned this huge project over to the Army Corps, the only government agency with the engineering skills and shovel-power for the job.

During that isolationist era of American history, national security was not much of a concern. Entire sections of the Waterway remained incomplete and there was a backlog of maintenance work on existing sections.

Of course, national security became paramount within a couple of decades. With U-boats prowling the Atlantic seaboard, a reliable inland passage became a priority. Emergency Public Works funds during the 1930s pushed the completion of the remaining sections of a federal waterway.

Save big bucks! Collect preferred customer cards for each grocery chain. The first time you visit a Food Lion or Winn-Dixie, visit the customer service counter. They will issue a free card, valid in all stores, yielding preferred sales prices. Carry your supermarket "playing card" set when you go ashore and pay discount prices no matter what store is in that town.

NORFOLK AND PORTSMOUTH

If you are tired of anchors, as in ground tackle, and are ready for anchors, as in malls, Waterside Marina is purported to be the only marina on the Intracoastal Waterway within two blocks of a Nordstrom-caliber mall.

And thanks to the Elizabeth River ferry, events and services on both sides of the river are accessible from all

SAFETY INFO

NOAA Weather
WX-2 Heathsville, VA
WX-1 Norfolk, VA
WX-3 Cape Hatteras, NC

USCG
Station Portsmouth, VA
VHF 16 or 09/22A
757/483-8527

Sea Tow
Hampton Roads, VA
VHF 16/18
757/496-1999

TowBoatU.S.
Portsmouth, VA
VHF 16/19
757/441-9656

HEADS UP!

NB	No Northbound Heads Up!
NB	No Northbound Heads Up!
NB	No Northbound Heads Up!
-12.0	Ship Traffic (SB)
-9.0	Security Zone Enforced (SB)
-5.0	Security Zone Enforced (NB)
0.0	Hospital Point, ICW Mile "0"
0.1	Bridge Caution (SB)
0.7	**North Harbor Ferry Crossing**
2.5	**N&P Belt Line RR Bridge**
2.7	**Jordan Bridge**
3.5	**Norfolk Southern RR Bridge**
5.8	Gilmerton Bridge
5.8	Norfolk Southern RR Bridge
7.2	Dismal Swamp Canal (SB)
7.7	Ship Traffic (NB)
8.8	Dominion Blvd. Bridge
11.5	Great Bridge Lock

Norfolk and Portsmouth marinas and anchorages. The ferry operates seven days a week, crosses twice an hour, takes bicycles, and is only $1 (50¢ for seniors). The ferry stops at three locations: Waterside Marina in Norfolk, and North Landing and High Street Landing in Portsmouth. In Norfolk, the Norfolk Electric Transit (NET) runs a free circuit of the downtown area every few minutes.

semi-local publications LLC

Photo by Author

"Mile Zero" R36

Additionally, there is a public dinghy dock at Waterside Marina.

Norfolk and Portsmouth have many restaurants, but few grocery stores. A local supermarket, G.W. Marketplace, provides van transportation for cruisers from the Waterside dinghy dock. For a small fee, they will also accept email orders for delivery when you arrive.

Festivals are a near-monthly occurrence in Portsmouth and Norfolk. Southbound in the fall you can attend the Caribbean Festival (late-August), the Seafood Sampler (mid-September), the Mile Marker Zero Rendezvous (September), or the Virginia Wine Fest (mid-October).

Northbound in the spring don't miss the Virginia Beer Festival (mid-May), Harborfest (mid-June), the Cajun Food Fest (late-June), and the Cock Island Race (late-June).

The Portside/Old Harbor Market which previously had open-air restaurants is closed. The bandstand remains and hosts summer concerts. The new nTelos Pavilion in Harbor Center also has large open-air concerts. You can also visit Norfolk Naval Base and Air Station, responsible for doubling the population of Norfolk during World War II. For fascinating insights into naval architecture and the science of battleships, tour the Battleship *U.S.S. Wisconsin* or visit Nauticus, the National Maritime Center.

Portsmouth celebrated its 250th birthday in 2002 and its Olde Towne district is still rich with historical architecture. The city provides a narrated horse-drawn carriage tour or you can take a self-guided walking tour. At least three other museums are nearby: the Portsmouth Naval Shipyard Museum, the Portsmouth Lightship Museum, and the Children's Museum.

For answers to your questions, the Visit Hampton Roads website lists hours, fees, and other information for all museums and events in this area.

Elizabeth River Ferry
www.hrtransit.org
757/222-6100

Norfolk Electric Transit
www.norfolk.gov/visitors
757/222-6100

G.W. Marketplace
email: gwmarketplace@cox.net
757/625-1507

Norfolk Naval Base & Air Station
www.navstanorva.navy.mil
757/444-7955

Nauticus, the National Maritime Center
www.nauticus.org
800/664-1080

Portsmouth Naval Shipyard Museum
www.portsnavalmuseums.com
757/393-8591

Portsmouth Lightship Museum
www.portsnavalmuseums.com
757/393-8741

Children's Museum
www.childrensmuseumva.com
757/393-5258

Hampton Roads Info
www.visithamptonroads.com

GREAT BRIDGE LOCK

If you've already come through the Erie Canal's 30-plus locks, including the 170-foot drop of Waterford's Flight of Five, the Great Bridge Lock is miniscule. If not, the Great Bridge Lock is a great first! It is the only lock along the Virginia Cut route and has between one and four feet of rise (depending on the wind-driven tides). It has relatively little turbulence, easy-to-use cleats, and forgiving rubber walls on the south or recreational boater side.

derway by 0500 hrs to beat the 0630 hrs bridge blackouts.

0.1 Hospital Point Anchorage (0.1)
Anchor 10-14 feet N36.50.723
STR 3.4 feet W076.17.970
Exit ICW SSE of R36. Proceed SW to anchor among the fleet.

0.3 Tidewater Yacht Agency (0.2)
VHF 16; 757/393-2525
Exit ICW opposite Town Point. Proceed WSW to marina entrance. Marina is charted bulkheaded facility. [STR 3.4]

0.4 Waterside Marina (0.2)
VHF 16/68 N36.50.581
757/625-3625 W076.17.494
Exit ICW SSW of Town Point. Proceed ENE to marina. [STR 3.4]
Marina is easily identified as a signature Rouse Company waterfront development (Boston's Faneuil Hall, Baltimore's Harborplace, Jacksonville's Jax Landing, and Miami's Bayside).

0.5 Colonna Yachts (1.1)
No VHF Watch N36.50.347
757/627-0738 W076.16.579
Exit ICW at Waterside Marina. Proceed ESE into charted Eastern Branch. Facility is to S. [STR 3.4]
Mega-yacht refit and repair only. No transient dockage.
Caution: It is easy to stray ESE into charted Eastern Branch. Proceed southerly to continue along ICW.

0.7 North Harbor Landing (0.1)
First charted basin S of Tidewater Yacht Agency. [STR 3.4]

- **Ferry Crossing**
  Ferry crosses in a triangle, stopping at two locations in Portsmouth (North Harbor and High Street) and at Waterside Marina in Norfolk.
  See Norfolk and Portsmouth.
- **Free Dock**
  2-hour tie-up allowed to sightsee, stretch, or walk the dog. Also handy if you ran foul current down Hampton Roads and will hit the bridge blackouts ahead.

1.0 Ocean Marine Yacht Center (0.1)
VHF 16/09; 757/399-2920
Marina is to W. [STR 3.3]

2.5 Norfolk & Portsmouth Belt Line RR Bridge
(N&P Railroad Bridge)
Lift; vertical 6 feet; usually open.

2.7 Jordan Bridge
VHF 13; 757/545-4695
Lift; vertical 15 feet.
Restricted year round: M-F except holidays, 0630-0830 and 1530-1730 hrs.

3.5 Norfolk Southern RR Bridge
Lift; vertical 10 feet; usually open.

SAFETY INFO

NOAA Weather
WX-2 Heathsville, VA
WX-1 Norfolk, VA
WX-3 Cape Hatteras, NC

USCG
Station Portsmouth, VA
VHF 16 or 09/22A
757/483-8527

Sea Tow
Hampton Roads, VA
VHF 16/18
757/496-1999

TowBoatU.S.
Portsmouth, VA
VHF 16/19
757/441-9656

HEADS UP!

0.7 North Harbor Ferry Crossing
2.5 N&P Belt Line RR Bridge
2.7 Jordan Bridge
3.5 Norfolk Southern RR Bridge
5.8 Gilmerton Bridge
5.8 Norfolk Southern RR Bridge
7.2 Dismal Swamp Canal (SB)
7.7 Ship Traffic (NB)
8.8 Dominion Blvd. Bridge
11.5 Great Bridge Lock
11.5 No Lunar Tides (SB)
12.1 Atlantic Intracoastal Bridge
13.8 Norfolk Southern RR Bridge
15.2 Centerville Turnpike Bridge
20.2 North Landing Bridge
34.0 VA-NC Border
41.5 Knotts Island Ferry Crossing
65.0 Albermarle Sound Crossing (SB)

5.8 Gilmerton Bridge
VHF 13; 757/545-1512
Double bascule; vertical 11 feet.
Restricted year round: M-F except holidays, 0630-0830 and 1530-1730 hrs.

5.8 Norfolk Southern RR Bridge
(Gilmerton Railroad Bridge)
Single bascule; vertical 7 feet; usually open.

7.1 Interstate 64 Bridge
VHF 13; 800/305-5799
Double bascule; vertical 65 feet.
Opens with 24-hour notice. Bridge currently lists eight telephone numbers. Call 800/305-5799 M-F 0700-1730 hrs or leave message after hours to arrange opening.

7.2 Junction | Dismal Swamp Alternate Route
to Southbound Navigation Only
78.8 74.6-mile alternate route.
Exit ICW N of R30. Proceed WNW into well-marked entrance channel. Rejoin ICW at G1 "AR" (Alligator River).
Caution: Dismal Swamp Canal closes occasionally due to water conditions. Call 757/201-7606 for information and updates.

7.7 Heads Up | Ship Traffic
to Northbound Navigation Only
-12.0 This stretch of Hampton Roads has a high concentration of commercial ship traffic.

8.8 Dominion Boulevard Bridge
(Steel Bridge)
VHF 13; 757/547-0521
Double bascule; vertical 12 feet.
Restricted year round: M-F except holidays, 0630-0830 and 1600-1800 hrs.
Restricted Memorial Day to Labor Day: M-F except holidays, 0830-1600 hrs, opens every hour on the half-hour.

11.5 Great Bridge Lock
VHF 13; 757/547-3311
Restricted year round: 0600-1900 hrs. Northbound, opens on the hour timed with the Atlantic Intracoastal Bridge. Southbound, opens at quarter after and remains open until quarter of the hour.
Caution: If you are new to locking, you may wish to review MANAGE THE TRANSIT, LOCKS.

11.5 Albemarle and Chesapeake Canal
to Southbound Navigation Only
19.7 8.2-mile land cut.
No anchorages, two marinas, fuel available.

11.5 No Lunar Tides
to Southbound Navigation Only
185.5 174-mile non-tidal zone.
From Great Bridge Lock (STM 11.5) to Adams Creek (STM 185.5), tides and currents are primarily dictated by recent wind conditions.

12.0 Free Dock
Tie up on SW wall between lock and bridge. 24-hour limit. [STR 0.0]

Passing through, you are but one of 15,000 boats locking through annually.

A nice park with services and trails is on the north side of the locks. This park is popular with locals, who come to yacht-watch from the bleachers and, in their words, "imagine what the people on board do for a living."

Make sure your rudder is amidships before engaging gear! Odds are, your last move was toward the wall—and the rudder is still in that position.

GREAT BRIDGE VISITOR CENTER

Like Pearl Harbor, sometimes a single battle is credited with turning the tide of citizen support. The Battle of Great Bridge, fought on December 9, 1775, was one such battle. Considered the "Southern Bunker Hill," the victory at Great Bridge demoralized many Southern Loyalists, converting them and other cautious residents to the Patriot cause.

At the start of the Revolution, the route through the town of Great Bridge was the only land route to Norfolk from the south. But when British troops crossing this swampy area reached the pinch-point of Great Bridge, they were defeated by Patriot troops, eventually forcing the British to evacuate Norfolk.

You can learn more about the history of this area and both Waterway canals at the new Great Bridge Battlefield and Waterways Visitor Center. In conjunction with construction of the new bridge, a new visitor center is scheduled to be open and fully operational by December 2006. The center will include a large park on both sides of the canal, walking trails, visitor center and museum, and docks for boaters.

Great Bridge Battlefield & Waterways
www.gbbattlefield-waterways.com
Telephone TBA

OXBOWS

The North Landing River once was a meandering mature river. The chart still shows the old bow-shaped bends in the river. These bends, called oxbows, are created as the outer banks are scoured by years of erosion. You can identify the age of a river by the sharpness of the oxbows; rivers begin relatively straight then develop sharper switchbacks. Eventually a river can even wind back on itself, cutting off an oxbow and creating a new island.

The North Landing River's largest oxbows were bypassed by sections of straight channels, dug in the late 1800s. But the river is still beautiful, and abandoned oxbows with enough depth offer quiet and safe anchorage.

NORTH LANDING RIVER

Over 10,000 acres along the North Landing River are protected as part of a Natural Area Preserve. The area is mostly wetlands, including the only "pocosin" (elevated peat bog) area in Virginia. *Pocosin* is a Native American word for "swamp-on-a-hill."

Courtesy of VA Canals and Navigations Society

Photo by George Ramsey **Osprey on North Landing River**

Marshes along this river are flooded with wind-driven rather than lunar tides. High tide occurs when a south wind pushes water up from Currituck Sound. A north wind sucks water back down into Currituck Sound, creating a low tide. These wind tides can change the water level along the North Landing River by as much as two feet.

The tributaries of this wild area are accessible by designated canoe trails, also open to motorized dinghies. If you stay at Pungo Ferry Marina (STM 28.4) or one of the nearby anchorages, Altons Creek canoe trail picks up just northwest of Pungo Ferry Bridge. The self-guided tour leads 2.5 miles up Altons Creek to the preserve's floating dock. Boaters are welcome to leave dinghies at this dock and walk the wide footpath and boardwalk to the main park entrance (0.4 miles). Self-guided tour brochures are available at the main park entrance.

The Nature Conservancy
www.tnc.org/virginia

SAFETY INFO

NOAA Weather
WX-2 Heathsville, VA
WX-1 Norfolk, VA
WX-3 Cape Hatteras, NC

USCG
Portsmouth, VA
VHF 16 or 09/22A
757/483-8527

Sea Tow
Hampton Roads, VA
VHF 16/18
757/496-1999

TowBoatU.S.
Portsmouth, VA
VHF 16/19
757/441-9656

HEADS UP!

5.8	Norfolk Southern RR Bridge
7.2	Dismal Swamp Canal (SB)
7.7	Ship Traffic (NB)
8.8	Dominion Blvd. Bridge
11.5	Great Bridge Lock
11.5	No Lunar Tides (SB)
12.1	**Atlantic Intracoastal Bridge**
13.8	**Norfolk Southern RR Bridge**
15.2	**Centerville Turnpike Bridge**
20.2	**North Landing Bridge**
34.0	VA-NC Border
41.5	Knotts Island Ferry Crossing
65.0	Albermarle Sound Crossing (SB)
78.8	Dismal Swamp Canal (NB)
80.0	Albermarle Sound Crossing (NB)
84.2	Alligator River Bridge
157.0	Hobucken Coast Guard Station
185.5	No Lunar Tides (NB)

THIS EON'S POLE STAR

At night, all stars appear to rotate around the North Star, the landmark designating the North Celestial Pole of our night sky. American slaves looked to the North Star to lead them to freedom. The song "Follow the Drinking Gourd" refers to the Big Dipper as a drinking gourd, as this constellation was known in Africa. The front edge of the Dipper points straight at (about five lengths) the North Star, or Polaris.

Over the night and the seasons, the constellations rotate around Polaris. Some constellations, like Cassiopeia and Cepheus, are always visible in the Northern Hemisphere so are called *circumpolar* constellations. Cassiopeia (pronounced Cass-ee-o-PEE-ah) is nearly overhead with its distinctive "M" or "W" pattern of bright stars always facing open to the North Star. Cassiopeia's husband, King Cepheus (pronounced SEFF-ee-us) faces her with bright stars forming a face and triangular hat.

But Polaris hasn't always been the pole star. The earth's poles are slowly shifting in a process called *precession*. When Columbus sailed, mariners had to make allowances for Polaris's distance from the true pole. The North Star at the time of the construction of the Great Pyramid, about 2600 BC, was Thuban, a faint star in the constellation Draco. In "only" 100 years, Polaris will begin to drift away from the true pole and there won't be another pole star until about 4000 AD (the star Er Rai). Polaris is and has been our closest pole star: it's less than one degree from the true North Celestial Pole … at least until the next century.

OSPREY

Ospreys are constant companions along the Waterway, guarding large stick nests on top of dayboards, diving feet first to catch fish with their sharp talons, and waking you in the morning with their loud, shrill whistles.

These raptors, sometimes called fish hawks, are a symbol of the recovery of many species along the Waterway. Two decades ago they were nearly wiped out by the pesticide DDT, which entered the food chain and caused their eggshells to be so thin the eggs were crushed by the roosting parents.

Ospreys are now common along the Waterway. Identify the Osprey by its white breast, brown wings and back, and dark eye stripe. Watch them as they fly off with a fish in their feet: their talons are long and sharp, their toes are rough to grip a slippery fish, and they hold the fish head forward as they fly off to dine in a nearby tree.

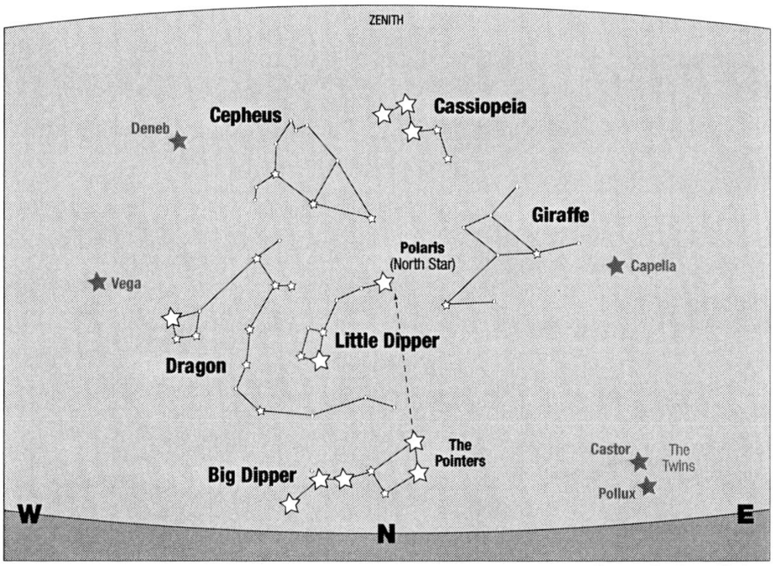

Autumn, Early Evening

Circumpolar Constellations

12.1 Atlantic Intracoastal Bridge
(Great Bridge Bridge)
VHF 13; 757/482-8250
Double bascule; vertical 7 feet.
Restricted year round: 0600-1900 hrs, opens on the hour.
New five-lane bascule replaced old two-lane swing bridge.
See Great Bridge Visitor Center.

12.2 Free Dock
Exit ICW SE of bridge. Dock is to N. [STR 0.0]

12.6 Atlantic Yacht Basin (0.1)
VHF 16/68 N36.43.180
757/482-2141 W076.13.938
Exit ICW W of Highway Bypass Bridge. Marina is to S in charted basin. [STR 0.0]

12.9 Highway Bypass Bridge
(Route 168)
Fixed; vertical 65 feet.

13.8 Norfolk Southern RR Bridge
Single bascule; vertical 7 feet; usually open.

15.1 Centerville Waterway Marina (0.1)
VHF 16; 757/547-4498
Marina is to N. [STR 0.0]

15.2 Centerville Turnpike Bridge
(Route 170)
VHF 13; 757/547-3631
Single-pivot swing; vertical 4 feet.
Restricted year round: M-F except holidays, 0630-0830 and 1600-1800 hrs.
Restricted year round: M-F except holidays, 0830-1600 hrs, opens on the hour and half-hour.

19.7 to 11.5 Albemarle and Chesapeake Canal
Northbound Navigation Only
8.2-mile land cut.
No anchorages, two marinas, fuel available.

20.2 North Landing Bridge
(Route 165)
VHF 13; 757/482-3081
Double-pivot swing; vertical 6 feet.
Restricted year round: 0600-1900 hrs, opens on the hour and half-hour.

24.6 North Landing River Anchorage (North)(0.1)
Anchor 5-7 feet N36.40.206
STR 0.0 feet W076.03.831
Exit ICW S of G23. Proceed SW above small island into oxbow.

26.4 North Landing River Anchorage (South)(0.1)
Anchor 8-10 feet N36.38.665
STR 0.0 feet W076.03.629
Exit ICW N of R32. Proceed SW into charted deep water NNW of R32.

28.4 Pungo Ferry Marina (0.1)
VHF 16; 757/721-3299
Exit ICW SSW of G41. Marina is to E. [STR 0.0]
Often difficult to hail. Approach the main dock, running parallel to the ICW, to contact marina

SAFETY INFO

NOAA Weather
WX-2 Heathsville, VA
WX-1 Norfolk, VA
WX-3 Cape Hatteras, NC

USCG
Station Portsmouth, VA
VHF 16 or 09/22A
757/483-8527

Sea Tow
Albemarle Sound, NC
VHF 16/09 or 11
252/312-9612

TowBoatU.S.
Coinjock, NC
VHF 16
757/286-1591

HEADS UP!

7.7	Ship Traffic (NB)
8.8	Dominion Blvd. Bridge
11.5	Great Bridge Lock
11.5	No Lunar Tides (SB)
12.1	Atlantic Intracoastal Bridge
13.8	Norfolk Southern RR Bridge
15.2	Centerville Turnpike Bridge
20.2	North Landing Bridge
34.0	**VA-NC Border**
41.5	Knotts Island Ferry Crossing
65.0	Albermarle Sound Crossing (SB)
78.8	Dismal Swamp Canal (NB)
80.0	Albermarle Sound Crossing (NB)
84.2	Alligator River Bridge
157.0	Hobucken Coast Guard Station
185.5	No Lunar Tides (NB)
200.8	Beaufort Channel Bridge (2.7)
203.8	Morehead City RR Bridge

staff. They will direct you to a tie-up based on your draft. Proceed carefully; water shallows quickly along bulkhead.

28.4 Pungo Ferry Anchorage (North)(0.1) S N
Anchor 6-8 feet N36.37.092
STR 0.0 feet W076.03.004
Exit ICW SSW of G41. Proceed W into southern oxbow entrance.
See North Landing River.

28.7 Pungo Ferry Bridge S N
(Route 726)
Fixed; vertical 65 feet.
Caution: This is one of many bridges with disputed heights. Once charted at 60 feet, now charted at 65 feet, but reported as less. Check the boards before proceeding.

29.0 Pungo Ferry Anchorage (South)(0.1) S N
Anchor 6-8 feet N36.36.760
STR 0.0 feet W076.03.149
Exit ICW SW of R42. Slowly proceed NNW out of channel.

30.3 Blackwater Creek Anchorage (0.2) S N
Anchor 6-8 feet N36.35.783
STR 0.0 feet W076.03.768
Exit ICW at R46. Proceed NW into Blackwater Creek.

34.0 VA-NC Border S N
North Landing River (Sandy Point G63)

A KINGFISHER NAMED HALCYON

You will see many yachts named *Halcyon* between here and Miami, and you'll also see a bird named halcyon.

In Roman mythology, a beautiful goddess named Alcyone, grieving the loss of her shipwrecked husband, threw herself off a cliff into the sea and became a kingfisher. So the Romans called their kingfisher Halcyon and associated the bird's nesting time with good seafaring weather.

Today the name lives on among contemporary mariners as a boat name, meaning happy or peaceful.

The word is also part of the Belted Kingfisher's scientific name, *Ceryle alcyon*. The Belted Kingfisher is common along the North Landing River. Recognize it as a stocky bright blue bird with a white preacher's collar, a crest, and an oversized bill. Before you spot it, listen for its warning call of a raucous rattle. Kingfishers perch on branches overhanging the water, diving to grab a small fish, crayfish, or frog.

GREAT BLUE HERON

The Great Blue Heron is one of the most common wading birds along the Waterway. These tall thin birds in blue-gray, white, and beige are usually seen wading slowly at the edge of quiet waters, standing still as a statue until they snatch a fish or frog.

Many people incorrectly call these birds "cranes." Cranes have larger bodies and are found inland. Some Southerners call the Great Blue Heron by the name "po' Joe," because they are so tall and scrawny. Imagine being four feet tall and weighing only six pounds!

Most of the time these waders are solitary. Great Blue Herons only congregate during breeding season to form large, loud rookeries. One of Virginia's largest heron rookeries is here in the North Landing River area.

Keep a road atlas on board. It's a great reference source for locating airports, major roads, hometowns of old and new friends, and as a map for rental car outings.

WATER SNAKES: FRIEND OR FOE?

Cottonmouths, or Water Moccasins, do live in the North Landing River area. But the vast majority of swimming snakes between here and Florida are harmless water snakes. Water snakes, such as the Brown Water Snake or the Banded Water Snake, can also be large and look mean, but are non-venomous. Every year hundreds of harmless water snakes die because people with good intentions think they are killing a poisonous Water Moccasin.

Courtesy of U.S. Fish and Wildlife Service

Northern Water Snake

Next time you see a snake near the water, take time to observe it. Unlike water snakes, Cottonmouths often do not retreat when approached, so you may have a chance of seeing one along the riverbanks. In the water, Cottonmouths can rest on the surface and typically swim with most of their body above water. Water snakes usually swim with only the front third of their body above water, and then sink when they stop wiggling.

In either case, if you don't bother them, they won't bother you. Snakes may not be popular, but they are as important to the environment as a Carolina Wren or a Bottle-nosed Dolphin. ▲

Virginia Waterway Business Cards

Southall Landings Marina
STM -16.4

www.southallmarina.com

333 Mainsail Drive
Hampton, VA 23664

757/850-9929 (phone)
757/850-7622 (fax)

VHF 16/09

Depth	7	**Laundry**	Walk
Diesel/Gas	No	**Pool**	On-Site
Pumpout	Yes	**Internet/WiFi**	I
Mail/Fax	M/F	**Car/Bike**	C
Service	On-Call	**Groceries**	Walk
Parts	On-Call	**Restaurant**	Walk
Haulout	No	**Post Office**	Walk
Propane	Taxi/Taxi	**Library**	Taxi

Salt Ponds Marina
STM -16.4

www.saltpondsmarinaresort.com

11 Ivory Gull Crescent
Hampton, VA 23664

757/850-4300 (phone)
757/851-4893 (fax)

VHF 16/09

Depth	8-12	**Laundry**	On-Site
Diesel/Gas	D/G	**Pool**	2
Pumpout	Yes	**Internet/WiFi**	I
Mail/Fax	M/F	**Car/Bike**	B
Service	On-Site	**Groceries**	Taxi
Parts	On-Site	**Restaurant**	On-Site
Haulout	No	**Post Office**	Walk
Propane	Taxi	**Library**	Taxi

Old Point Comfort Marina
STM -11.5

www.monroemwr.com

P.O. Box 51106
Fort Monroe, VA 23651

757/788-4308 (phone)
757/788-4354 (fax)

VHF 16/68

Depth	12	**Laundry**	On-Site
Diesel/Gas	D/G	**Pool**	2
Pumpout	Yes	**Internet/WiFi**	I
Mail/Fax	M/F	**Car/Bike**	No
Service	On-Call	**Groceries**	Walk
Parts	On-Call	**Restaurant**	On-Site
Haulout	6T	**Post Office**	Walk
Propane	Taxi	**Library**	Walk

Bluewater Yachting Center
STM -11.2

www.bluewateryachtsales.com

One Marina Road
Hampton, VA 23669

757/723-6774 (phone)
757/722-7668 (fax)

VHF 16/72

Depth	8	**Laundry**	On-Site
Diesel/Gas	D/G	**Pool**	Yes
Pumpout	Yes	**Internet/WiFi**	I
Mail/Fax	M/F	**Car/Bike**	No
Service	On-Site	**Groceries**	Walk
Parts	On-Site	**Restaurant**	On-Site
Haulout	37T/100T	**Post Office**	Walk
Propane	Taxi	**Library**	Walk

Hampton Yacht Club
STM -11.2

www.hamptonyc.com

4707 Victoria Boulevard
Hampton, VA 23669

757/722-0711 (phone)
757/722-4700 (fax)

VHF 16

Depth	8	**Laundry**	Walk
Diesel/Gas	No	**Pool**	No
Pumpout	Yes	**Internet/WiFi**	I/W
Mail/Fax	F	**Car/Bike**	B
Service	On-Call	**Groceries**	Walk
Parts	On-Call	**Restaurant**	Walk
Haulout	1T/5T	**Post Office**	Walk
Propane	Taxi	**Library**	Walk

Downtown Hampton Public Piers
STM -11.2

www.downtownhampton.com

756 Settlers Landing Road
Hampton, VA 23669

757/727-1276 (phone)
757/727-1255 (fax)

VHF 16/09

Depth	10	**Laundry**	Taxi
Diesel/Gas	No	**Pool**	Yes
Pumpout	Yes	**Internet/WiFi**	I
Mail/Fax	M/F	**Car/Bike**	B
Service	On-Call	**Groceries**	Taxi
Parts	On-Call	**Restaurant**	Walk
Haulout	No	**Post Office**	Walk
Propane	Taxi	**Library**	Walk

Willoughby Harbor Marina
STM -9.0

www.willoughbyontheweb.com

1525 Bayville Street
Norfolk, VA 23503

757/583-4150 (phone)
757/583-1846 (fax)

VHF 16/09

Depth	10	**Laundry**	On-Site
Diesel/Gas	No	**Pool**	Plan '05
Pumpout	Yes	**Internet/WiFi**	I/W
Mail/Fax	M/F	**Car/Bike**	No
Service	On-Call	**Groceries**	Taxi
Parts	On-Call	**Restaurant**	On-Site
Haulout	No	**Post Office**	Taxi
Propane	Taxi	**Library**	Taxi

Portsmouth Boating Center
STM -0.5

www.portsmouthboating.com

1244 Bay Street
Portsmouth, VA 23704

757/397-2092 (phone)
757/297-6923 (fax)

VHF 16/68

Depth	8-10	**Laundry**	On-Site
Diesel/Gas	D/G	**Pool**	No
Pumpout	Yes	**Internet/WiFi**	I
Mail/Fax	M/F	**Car/Bike**	B
Service	On-Site	**Groceries**	Walk
Parts	On-Site	**Restaurant**	Walk
Haulout	70T	**Post Office**	Walk
Propane	Walk	**Library**	Walk

Photocopy the "business card" of any Waterway facility. Then cut out the copy and take it ashore for easy reference!

Scott's Creek Marina

STM -0.5

Six Harper Avenue
Portsmouth, VA 23707

757/399-2628 (phone)
757/399-8260 (fax)

VHF 16/68

Depth	12	**Laundry**	On-Site
Diesel/Gas	No	**Pool**	Yes
Pumpout	Yes	**Internet/WiFi**	No
Mail/Fax	M/F	**Car/Bike**	No
Service	On-Call	**Groceries**	Walk
Parts	On-Call	**Restaurant**	Walk
Haulout	No	**Post Office**	Walk
Propane	Taxi	**Library**	Taxi

Waterside Marina

STM 0.4

www.watersidemarina.com

333 Waterside Drive
Norfolk, VA 23510

757/625-3625 (phone)
757/625-3626 (fax)

VHF 16/68

Depth	20	**Laundry**	On-Site
Diesel/Gas	No	**Pool**	No
Pumpout	No	**Internet/WiFi**	I/W
Mail/Fax	M/F	**Car/Bike**	No
Service	On-Call	**Groceries**	Walk
Parts	On-Call	**Restaurant**	45
Haulout	No	**Post Office**	Walk
Propane	NA	**Library**	Walk

Colonna Yachts (Repair)

STM 0.5

www.colonnayachts.com

2401 Kimball Terrace
Norfolk, VA 23504

757/627-0738 (phone)
757/627-5562 (fax)

No VHF Watch

Depth	13	**Laundry**	Taxi
Diesel/Gas	Truck	**Pool**	No
Pumpout	Truck	**Internet/WiFi**	I
Mail/Fax	M/F	**Car/Bike**	C
Service	On-Site	**Groceries**	Taxi
Parts	On-Site	**Restaurant**	Taxi
Haulout	1000T	**Post Office**	Taxi
Propane	Walk	**Library**	Taxi

Atlantic Yacht Basin

STM 12.6

www.atlanticyachtbasin.com

2615 Basin Road
Chesapeake, VA 23322

757/482-2141 (phone)
757/482-1682 (fax)

VHF 16/68

Depth	12	**Laundry**	On-Site
Diesel/Gas	D/G	**Pool**	No
Pumpout	Yes	**Internet/WiFi**	I
Mail/Fax	M/F	**Car/Bike**	C
Service	On-Site	**Groceries**	Walk
Parts	On-Site	**Restaurant**	Walk
Haulout	60T/300T	**Post Office**	Taxi
Propane	Walk	**Library**	Walk

Virginia Waterway Marine Facilities

This table summarizes all known Waterway Marine Facilities, their location along the ICW, and their telephone number. Each is listed as either offering transient (T) dockage or not—and whether they have a fuel dock with diesel (D), gas (G), or neither.

-16.4	**Southall Landings Marina**	757/850-9929	T	No
-16.4	**Salt Ponds Marina**	757/850-4300	T	D/G
-11.5	**Old Point Comfort Marina**	757/788-4308	T	D/G
-11.2	**Bluewater Yachting Center**	757/723-6774	T	D/G
-11.2	Sunset Boating Center	757/722-3325	No	D/G
-11.2	**Hampton Yacht Club**	757/722-0711	No	No
-11.2	**Downtown Hampton Public Piers**	757/727-1276	T	No
-9.0	**Willoughby Harbor Marina**	757/583-4150	T	No
-9.0	Rebel Marina	757/588-6022	T	No
-2.2	Western Branch Diesel	757/673-7000	No	No
-2.2	Virginia Boat & Yacht	757/673-7167	T	No
-2.2	Nautical Boats & Marina	757/483-6148	T	No
-0.5	**Portsmouth Boating Center**	757/397-2092	T	D/G
-0.5	**Scott's Creek Marina**	757/399-2628	T	No
0.3	Tidewater Yacht Agency	757/393-2525	T	D/G
0.4	**Waterside Marina**	757/625-3625	T	No
0.5	**Colonna Yachts**	757/627-0738	No	No
1.1	Ocean Marine Yacht Center	757/399-2920	T	D/G
12.6	**Atlantic Yacht Basin**	757/482-2141	T	D/G
15.1	Centerville Waterway Marina	757/547-4498	No	No
28.4	Pungo Ferry Marina	757/721-3299	T	D/G

Boldface type indicates the facility completed a survey and is highlighted in a Waterway Business Card. Each facility received multiple fax, email, and telephone requests. A final telephone call was made to verify the accuracy of transient, fuel, and contact information.

Virginia Waterway Chandleries

This table lists marine equipment suppliers within easy reach of the ICW, their telephone number and address, and their location relative to ICW marinas and anchorages.

The Batten Pocket	Recently Closed	529 Bridge Street, Hampton, VA 23669	0.4 miles from Downtown Hampton Public Piers
Home Depot Hampton	757/827-5121	1413 Armistead Avenue, Hampton, VA 23666	1.7 miles from Downtown Hampton Public Piers
Lowe's Hampton	757/896-4930	2002 Powhatan Parkway, Hampton, VA 23666	2.8 miles from Downtown Hampton Public Piers
Boater's World Hampton	757/827-1613	2145 Coliseum Drive, Hampton, VA 23666	3.8 miles from Downtown Hampton; near Coliseum Mall
West Marine Hampton	757/825-4900	2121 W. Mercury Blvd., Hampton, VA 23666	3.9 miles from Downtown Hampton; near Coliseum Mall
Lowe's Portsmouth	757/405-9980	4040 Victory Blvd., Portsmouth, VA 23701	4.3 miles from Portsmouth Boating Center; near Tower Mall
W.T. Brownley Company	888/622-2540	226 E. Main Street, Norfolk, VA 23510	0.1 miles from Waterside Marina
West Marine Norfolk	757/466-1826	5616 E. Virginia Beach Blvd., Norfolk, VA 23502	5.7 miles from Waterside Marina; near Military Circle Mall
Boater's World Norfolk	757/461-0151	5950 E. Virginia Beach Blvd., Norfolk, VA 23502	6.0 miles from Waterside Marina; near Military Circle Mall
The Marine Store	757/482-2680	2615 Basin Road, Chesapeake, VA 23322	On-site Atlantic Yacht Basin
Lowe's Chesapeake	757/436-0707	1308 N. Battlefield Blvd., Chesapeake, VA 23320	3.2 miles from Atlantic Yacht Basin
Home Depot Battlefield	757/548-8478	1400 Tintern Lane, Chesapeake, VA 23320	3.4 miles from Atlantic Yacht Basin

North Carolina Charts
12206 ICW - Norfolk to Albemarle Sound
11553 ICW - Albemarle Sound to Neuse River
11541 ICW - Neuse River to Myrtle Grove Sound
11534 ICW - Myrtle Grove Sound and Cape Fear River to Casino Creek

Bridges	
Total	22
Fixed	13
Opening	9

Other Features			
Marinas	71	Vignettes	46
Anchorages	45	Inlets	3
Chandleries	35	Ranges	5

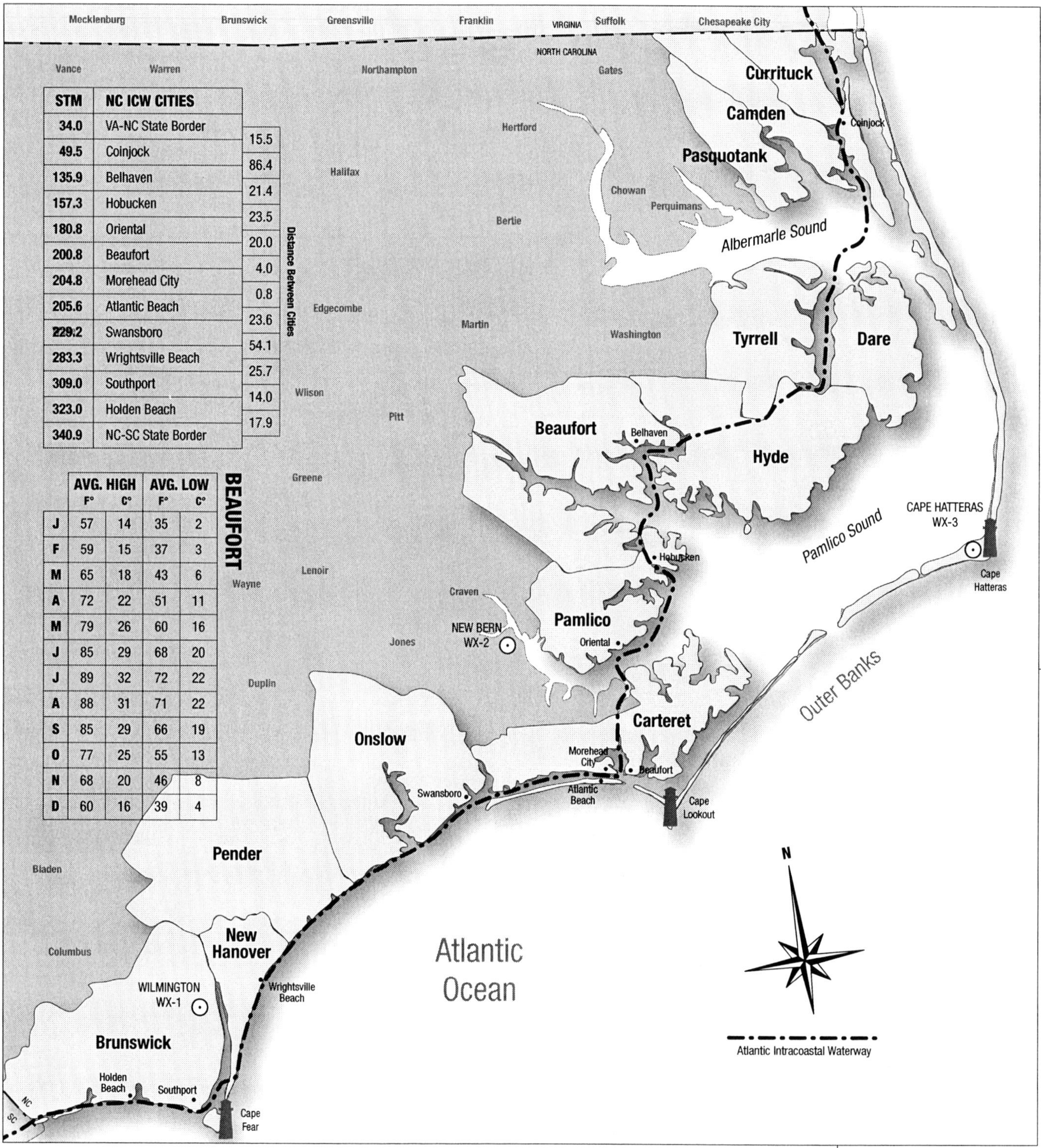

STM	NC ICW CITIES	Distance Between Cities
34.0	VA-NC State Border	15.5
49.5	Coinjock	86.4
135.9	Belhaven	21.4
157.3	Hobucken	23.5
180.8	Oriental	20.0
200.8	Beaufort	4.0
204.8	Morehead City	0.8
205.6	Atlantic Beach	23.6
229.2	Swansboro	54.1
283.3	Wrightsville Beach	25.7
309.0	Southport	14.0
323.0	Holden Beach	17.9
340.9	NC-SC State Border	

BEAUFORT

	AVG. HIGH F°	AVG. HIGH C°	AVG. LOW F°	AVG. LOW C°
J	57	14	35	2
F	59	15	37	3
M	65	18	43	6
A	72	22	51	11
M	79	26	60	16
J	85	29	68	20
J	89	32	72	22
A	88	31	71	22
S	85	29	66	19
O	77	25	55	13
N	68	20	46	8
D	60	16	39	4

For illustration purposes only. Not to be used for navigation.

MTW Big Pictures provide an overview of local geographic references. They identify the counties, capes, inlets, lighthouses, and bodies of water commonly referred to in NOAA and AM/FM weather broadcasts.

The locations of WX weather towers are shown to easily determine the best broadcast for your position and direction of travel. The temperature table shows average highs and lows for that region. Look for major cities and smaller towns along the ICW, then use the distance table for planning stops or estimating travel time. Lastly, we list the region's required charts by their NOAA chart number and provide a snapshot of Waterway resources and impediments.

North Carolina

North Landing River to Little River Inlet

The Tar Heel State
ICW Statute Mile 34.0 to 340.9
Bridges Monitor VHF 13

Regions
Albemarle
Pamlico-Neuse
Crystal Coast
Cape Fear Coastal

Inlets
Beaufort Inlet
Masonboro Inlet
Cape Fear River Entrance

U.S. Coast Guard
District Five: 757/398-6486
Station Hobucken: 252/745-3131
Group Fort Macon: 252/247-4570
Station Fort Macon: 252/247-4583
Station Emerald Isle: 910/354-2719
Station Wrightsville Beach: 910/256-2615
Station Oak Island: 910/278-1133

NOAA Weather Towers
WX-3 Cape Hatteras
WX-2 New Bern
WX-1 Wilmington

Security Zones
Camp Lejeune Firing Range

Camp Lejeune ICW Closure Information
910/451-3064

Lighthouses
Bald Head Island Light
Oak Island Light

Fishing Information
www.ncfisheries.net/recreational.htm

NORTH CAROLINA boaters are grateful for an inland waterway. With a coastline known as the "Graveyard of the Atlantic," it would be ungrateful to slight the ICW. Without this 300-mile inland route, transiting the North Carolina coast would mean a long and dangerous passage around Cape Hatteras, Cape Lookout, and Cape Fear. If you haven't appreciated the Waterway yet, North Carolina is the place.

With dangerous inlets, shoals, and capes, North Carolina developed very differently than its neighboring coastal states. Virginia and South Carolina, with their large protected harbors and easy ocean access, dominated maritime commerce. And where there's commerce, there's money. Bustling ports, merchant wealth, and cosmopolitan cities developed on South Carolina's and Virginia's harbors.

But North Carolina largely missed out on the boom. You won't find large commercial and naval ports like Norfolk, nor cosmopolitan cities like Charleston. In North Carolina, the towns along the Waterway are smaller maritime communities, such as Belhaven, Oriental, Morehead City, Beaufort, and Southport.

So as you enter North Carolina, in some ways you leave civilization behind. For example, if there's a place along the Waterway you're going to lose cell coverage, it will likely be in North Carolina.

Yet several boater-friendly villages and towns punctuating the quiet rural stretches make this one of our favorite cruising areas. For many of the small communities, visiting boaters are an important part of the local economy. Some towns—such as Elizabeth City, Oriental, and Beaufort—are havens for retired cruisers. Their culture welcomes transiting boaters, offering dinghy access, courtesy cars, and well-maintained town dock facilities. Be sure to patronize the local stores and restaurants in these friendly communities.

Courtesy of Crystal Coast TDA

Fort Macon Ranger and Kids

Navigational concerns come with the territory. Rather than traffic and bridge openings, wind and shoaling take top billing.

Everyone has heard about the wind and waves of North Carolina's sounds. Large shallow bays behind extensive barrier islands create unique boating conditions. High winds have a lengthy fetch over Albemarle and Pamlico Sound. Combined with incredibly shallow depths, and an opposing current, the waves can become quite nasty.

Plan intelligently when you cross these sounds. Remember that sea conditions are created by *past and present* wind conditions. If a strong wind has shifted, expect an unsettling cross-sea. Note the wind direction from the previous 24 to 48 hours and wait out unfavorable conditions.

If you are entering a river mouth from a sound, be aware of the combination of wind and river current. If the wind opposes the current, conditions can be treacherous. Time your travel near the mouths of large rivers, especially the Neuse, for light or following winds.

South of Beaufort, the Waterway becomes a narrow lagoon behind barrier islands. In this region, between Beaufort and Southport, fetch is less of a concern. Instead, shoaling and reversing currents take top navigation priority.

The broken barrier islands and the narrow passage of Bogue Sound create strong currents near the inlets. These currents not only set your vessel off course, they create notoriously shifting sandbars. In this area, expect to see "drop aids" (small, often uncharted aids marking the *latest* shoal edge).

The sandy bottom shoals quickly to the edges of the Waterway. It's easy to panic when you see wading birds standing in the water a few beam widths from your vessel. It's very disconcerting; but don't worry, there is a channel through these flats.

A final tip for North Carolina, useful for all shoal areas of the Waterway: learn to drive like a tug.

Why should you care how the tugs run the Waterway? Because it's shallow along this stretch and tugs define the channel. The Waterway is maintained with federal dollars for *commercial* vessels, not for pleasure boaters. So the channels are placed to accommodate the wide turns of tugs with tows. And the constant scouring of the large powerful tug props reinforce the channel. So if you want to minimize your chance of grounding—drive like a tug.

To paraphrase Carl the greenskeeper: to drive like a tug, you must think like a tug. Think slow turning, slow-to-stop, minimal maneuverability, and pushing a long barge. No sober tug captain is going to bang a sharp turn around a Waterway aid. Instead, they will approach the aid, leaving a wide berth and carve a very wide turn, actually called a "tug turn." Then they will run a straight range line from the end of that turn to a point port or starboard of their next aid, again in preparation for a wide arcing turn.

Most recreational boaters do not naturally tug-turn navigation aids. The most common error is to cling to the aids, believing that they mark the deep water. But if you drive the aids like a connect-the-dots game, you'll miss the channel.

Even as a small boat, if you have any significant draft, do not turn close to an aid. The aid does not mark the deep water! Aids mark the *pivot point* used by large vessels to arc their turn. Swing wide like a tug, safely away from the aid, and you are more likely to stay in the deepest water.

Wilmington District Shoaling Updates
www.saw.usace.army.mil/nav/map.htm

ALBEMARLE

Through northern North Carolina, the Waterway jumps from sound to sound, connected by narrow sheltered rivers. From the woods of the North Landing River, you open into the 15-mile stretch of Currituck Sound. Then the Waterway weaves through pine forests again before opening to the expanse of Albemarle Sound.

The Albemarle region is one of the most unpopulated areas of the Intracoastal Waterway. Transiting the North Landing River or the Alligator River, Norfolk or Miami seem light-years away. The open water, the winding rivers, the wildlife, and the solitude make fire sirens and navy ships a distant memory.

There are no large towns here. And small towns, such as Coinjock, are often only places where a rural road meets the Waterway. But the waterfront is busy in other ways: commercial shrimpers head back and forth and local residents fish from their bass boats.

Don't expect luxury resorts here. There are plenty of fine marinas, but they are modest. Many are fishing camps, gas stations with dockage, or working docks that welcome transient boaters. There are also plenty of safe anchorages without the tide and current hassles you'll find further south.

A helpful internet resource—spanning all coastal regions of North Carolina—is the ICW-Net. This cooperative website, supported by advertising, was created as a forum for small coastal communities to present their attractions, events, and history. For information on the Albemarle region:

ICW-Net Albemarle
www.albemarle-nc.com

Carry two 11-lb aluminum propane tanks instead of one 20-lb steel tank. Although you won't be able to take advantage of "exchanges," two smaller aluminum tanks are lighter, won't rust, and have a 10% higher combined capacity. Additionally, you'll always have a spare tank to use until you have an opportunity to refill the other. And you'll especially thank us for this advice next time you're carrying a full tank back to your boat along a hot, dusty county road.

PAMLICO-NEUSE

The pattern of large open sounds, connected by rivers or cuts, continues. Wide rivers, such as the Neuse, open onto Pamlico Sound. In fact, the Neuse River, measuring six miles across its mouth, is the widest river in the United States.

Many of the same conditions apply to Pamlico Sound as Albemarle Sound. Shallow, with miles of fetch, it can kick up with ugly wave conditions, particularly if the wind has cycled. The wind and wave *combination* is of paramount concern.

In addition, as you approach the Neuse River, any wind from the northeast collides with the river current, creating unpleasant and potentially dangerous conditions. Heed the wind direction on your transit day—and the day prior—and avoid transiting this area with heavy northerly winds.

The Pamlico-Neuse region is a bit more populated than the northern sounds, but it is still a rural and small-town geography. Several of these towns, such as Belhaven and Oriental, have developed viable town centers along the Waterway. These towns are exceptionally welcoming to boaters. Some, such as Oriental, seem to center their existence on the cruising community. These towns depend on marine tourism, so they offer comfortable marinas and many shops geared specifically to boaters.

This region marks a change in the marine climate. Warmer water lies just to the south of the Neuse River. The weather may not be noticeably warmer, but statistically the climate and water temperature shifts as you approach Beaufort and Morehead City. This change in marine climate is one of the reasons many southbound boaters sight their first Bottle-nosed Dolphins in the lower Neuse, at the Adams Creek junction.

ICW-Net Pamlico
www.pamlico.com

CRYSTAL COAST

The Crystal Coast differs in both climate and culture from the northern sound regions. The Crystal Coast is a popular tourist destination, drawing visitors from all over the country to its beaches, history, and dive wrecks.

The "Crystal Coast" is the designator for Carteret and Onslow counties, and includes part of the Outer Banks, Cape Lookout, part of Bogue Sound, and the communities of Beaufort, Morehead City, Atlantic Beach, Emerald Isle, and Swansboro. The coast is "crystal" for its clear water and sandy beaches. Divers love the region for the shipwrecks, a by-product of North Carolina's notorious capes and inlets. Expect to see this slogan of regional pride on everything, from Crystal Coast Yellow Cab to Crystal Coast Wireless.

Courtesy of NOAA

Photo by Marge Beaver

Fort Macon and Beaufort Inlet

Tourists flock to the barrier beach towns for the sand and surf. The towns, although still small, provide many services for boaters, including marinas along the island and mainland sides of Bogue Sound (pronounced like "vogue"). But with locals and tourists flocking to the water, the downside is the marine traffic. On weekends, the Waterway near Beaufort and Morehead City can be an aquatic freeway as weekend warriors spar for speed and space.

Beaufort and Morehead City, two cities on opposite sides of the Newport River, are as different as most "twin" cities across a river. In fact, they offer boaters complementary amenities.

The cruisers' stereotype is sailboats turn east for Beaufort and powerboats turn west into Morehead City. This stereotype isn't precisely true, but it underscores cultural differences between the two towns. Morehead City offers more marine industry, fishing, and shopping services. Beaufort offers historical sites and small-town shops.

South of Beaufort, the Waterway takes advantage of Bogue Sound, a 30-mile stretch sheltered from the Atlantic Ocean by small barrier islands. Bogue Sound is a long narrow lagoon, only two miles wide.

The Waterway continues behind the barrier islands for another 50 miles, through a narrow, shoaling stretch broken by many small inlets. Don't even think about using these inlets: they require local knowledge to navigate their constantly shifting channels.

But transiting boaters must pay attention to the inlets for their currents and shoals. Lunar tides influence the Waterway from Oriental southward, with tidal ranges of three to four feet near Beaufort, increasing to five feet as you approach South Carolina.

Courtesy of Crystal Coast TDA

WWII German U-352

The greater tides create reversing currents at river or inlet mouths. Because of the effect of narrow ocean inlets, river mouths, and the lagoon, the current constantly changes direction along the Waterway.

If you are one of those diligent navigators who checks current tables to calculate the most efficient travel time, you'll just have to let it go. You can calculate all you want for southern North Carolina; it won't make any difference.

There are so many small inlets that a moving vessel may experience a different current every hour or so. It's nearly impossible to favorably time currents over an eight-hour period. Accept the fact that these contrary currents typically cancel each other out during the course of a transit day.

ICW-Net Crystal Coast
www.crystalcoast.com

CAPE FEAR COASTAL

This region, centered at the city of Wilmington, includes Pender, New Hanover, and Brunswick counties. Although the ICW does not pass directly through Wilmington, it does transit many of its surrounding towns including: Wrightsville Beach, Carolina Beach, Southport, Bald Head Island, Long Beach, Holden Beach, Ocean Isle, and Sunset Beach.

The Cape Fear River dictates the navigation in this region. Both the inlet and the river can be extremely ornery, but the Waterway offers protection and an easy passage with only a little planning.

Although Cape Fear Inlet is a large ocean inlet, it is not recommended for northbound departures or southbound arrivals. Its exposure, strong currents, and 30-mile Frying Pan Shoals make it a poor alternative to the more sedate Masonboro Inlet only 23 miles to the north.

Most of North Carolina's inlets are not recommended for cruising boaters. They typically span two extremes: small inlets with shifting channels or large inlets with open exposure and currents. But Beaufort Inlet and Masonboro Inlet are exceptions. Many boaters choose to go outside for this 64 nm run. This manageable day sail avoids the shoal passages along the Waterway through Pender, Onslow, and southern Carteret counties.

As you approach the Cape Fear River, you must consider the current. Unlike Bogue Sound to the north, you should not attempt to oppose the currents of this large and powerful river.

With a current that can run to six knots, expect white caps if the river current is opposing the wind direction. The prudent tactic is to time your passage with favorable wind conditions and a *slight* carrying tide.

Don't get overzealous and attempt to time the maximum ebb or flood. There are times when there can be too much help. In a large cruising vessel, a six-knot current on the transom feels like white-water rafting a bathtub. The tiny savings in time is not worth diminished vessel maneuverability.

If you accidentally find yourself bucking the current, move out of the main ship channel. Move into shallower water to minimize the effect of the river's current.

Lastly, there is little reason for a small recreational boater to religiously follow the ship channel ranges like a 200-foot freighter. Move to the edge of the channel and leave the main channel to the big boys.

ICW-Net Cape Fear
www.azaleacoast.com

NORTH CAROLINA BOOK AND FILM PICKS

With video rental stores few and far between, the North Carolina Waterway is a great place for reading. North Carolina has been overshadowed in the movie business by South Carolina, who has wooed Hollywood with its photogenic southern locales and large financial incentives. Most films set in the Carolinas are shot in South Carolina.

But North Carolina has several excellent bookstores catering to boaters. The quiet rivers and creeks are perfect for anchoring out and reading about two subjects near and dear to North Carolina's historical heart: pirates and wind.

Our image of pirates is driven largely by stereotypes from Disney movies, usually involving prosthetic hooks and plank walking. But it turns out this is fiction. To see pirate life from the inside, read the non-fiction book *Mistress of the Seas*, by John Carlova.

Carlova tells the story of Anne Bonny, a sexy rebellious young woman from a middle-class family who became a legend among pirates. She was the lover of several famous pirates, ran her own crew, and skirted the law by hiding in the Bahamas. In telling her story, the intricacies of piracy as an early-American business and lifestyle come to life. And it's nothing like Disney!

And what better place to read about the wind than North Carolina? With its broad sounds known for their nasty fetch, the magnitude of the wind becomes a daily part of life aboard a cruising vessel.

It was Admiral Francis Beaufort who promoted the idea of measuring the wind using an observable scale. The town of Beaufort, North Carolina was not named after this Beaufort, but no matter. In fact, Beaufort of the wind scale fame removed his name whenever it showed up on a map. In his old age he finally acquiesced, allowing his name to be used for a sea discovered in the search for the Northwest Passage.

A new book, *Defining the Wind* by Scott Huler, is a fascinating story of Beaufort and the development of the wind scale that bears his name. Like Dava Sobel's book, *Longitude*, Huler weaves a tale of scientific discovery, "borrowed" inventions, and the fight to promote unconventional thinking.

Children can understand the Beaufort scale with the beautiful children's book, *The Rising of the Wind: Adventures Along the Beaufort Scale*, by Jacques Yvart and Claire Forgeot. The book's illustrations were originally part of a dare: an artist claimed he could communicate anything with art. So his challenger, who happened to be a sailor, responded, "Okay, then paint the Beaufort scale." The result is astounding: illustrations that convey the visual sense of each of the twelve winds using land, near shore, and open ocean scales.

North Carolina has two popular bookstores catering to transiting boaters. Hodge Podge, near the docks in Oriental, specializes in used books but is able to special order. Scuttlebutt Nautical Books is located in Beaufort near the town docks. By calling ahead, you can have your book picks ready when you arrive in port. ▲

Hodge Podge Gently Used Books
Oriental, NC
252/249-3670

Scuttlebutt Nautical Books
Beaufort, NC
252/728-7765

SAFETY INFO

NOAA Weather
WX-2 Heathsville, VA
WX-1 Norfolk, VA
WX-2 New Bern, NC

USCG
Station Portsmouth, VA
VHF 16 or 09/22A
757/483-8527

Sea Tow
Albemarle Sound, NC
VHF 16/09 or 11
252/312-9612

TowBoatU.S.
Coinjock, NC
VHF 16
757/286-159

HEADS UP!

8.8	Dominion Blvd. Bridge
11.5	Great Bridge Lock
11.5	No Lunar Tides (SB)
12.1	Atlantic Intracoastal Bridge
13.8	Norfolk Southern RR Bridge
15.2	Centerville Turnpike Bridge
20.2	North Landing Bridge
34.0	**VA-NC Border**
41.5	**Knotts Island Ferry Crossing**
65.0	**Albermarle Sound Crossing (SB)**
78.8	Dismal Swamp Canal (NB)
80.0	Albermarle Sound Crossing (NB)
84.2	Alligator River Bridge
157.0	Hobucken Coast Guard Station
185.5	No Lunar Tides (NB)
200.8	Beaufort Channel Bridge (2.7)
203.8	Morehead City RR Bridge
235.2	Camp Lejeune Firing Range (SB)

34.0 VA-NC Border
North Landing River (Sandy Point G63)

41.5 Knotts Island | Currituck Ferry Crossing
Be on the lookout for occasional ferry traffic. No signals visible from ICW.

48.8 North Carolina Cut
to Southbound Navigation Only
51.5 2.7-mile land cut.
US Coast Guard (closed), no anchorages, two marinas, fuel available.

49.3 Midway Marina & Motel
VHF 16/09 N36.21.001
252/453-3625 W075.56.913
Marina is to NW. [STR 0.0]

49.4 Coinjock Marina
VHF 16; 252/453-3271
Marina is to SE. [STR 0.0]

49.5 Harrison's Marina
VHF 16; 252/453-2631
Marina is to NW.
Closed due to Isabel damage; no current plans to re-open. [STR 0.0]

49.6 USCG Station Coinjock (Closed)
Typically listed in cruising guides, this charted station has been closed for some time. Your next southbound station is Hobucken at STM 157.0.

50.1 Coinjock Bridge
(US 158)
Fixed; vertical 65 feet.

51.5 North Carolina Cut
to Northbound Navigation Only
48.8 2.7-mile land cut.
US Coast Guard (closed), no anchorages, two marinas, fuel available.

56.5 Buck Island Anchorage (North)(0.1)
Anchor 6-8 feet N36.16.043
STR 0.0 feet W075.57.488
Exit ICW N of G153. Proceed E to charted deep water N of Buck Island.

58.2 Buck Island Anchorage (South)(0.7)
Anchor 6-8 feet N36.15.365
STR 0.0 feet W075.57.299
Exit ICW SSE of G157. Follow charted deeper water to E then NNW beyond charted 7-foot tongue.

61.2 Broad Creek Anchorage (1.7)
Anchor 6-8 feet N36.11.922
STR 0.0 feet W075.57.185
Exit ICW at G163. Proceed westerly to mouth of Broad Creek.

65.0 Albemarle Sound Crossing
to Southbound Navigation Only
80.0 15-mile open water crossing.
Wait for settled weather and time the crossing for early morning or early evening.
See Albemarle Waves.

MACKAY ISLAND NATIONAL WILDLIFE REFUGE

Every year, millions of migratory waterfowl arrive to spend the winter at Currituck Sound. Flocks of thousands of birds have been spotted rafting around Mackay Island (pronounced MACK-ee), including white Snow Geese and Tundra Swans. No wonder the name Currituck Sound comes from the Indian word *Coratank*, meaning wild geese.

To accommodate all these visitors, the Mackay Island National Wildlife Refuge protects over 8,000 acres of wetlands. You can see the refuge to your east as you cross the Virginia-North Carolina border (STM 38.5).

Scan the horizon for rafts of geese, ducks, or swans. You are probably familiar with the Canada Goose. You may also spot Snow Geese: white with black-tipped wings. Tundra Swans are all white and easily separated from alien Mute Swans by their black rather than orange bills. Tundra Swans (formerly called Whistling Swans for their noise when flying) are our native "American" swans. These beautiful birds mate for life and travel each year between their breeding grounds at the Arctic Circle and the mild protected bays of North Carolina.

DENEB AND THE SWAN (AUTUMN)

As Tundra Swans migrate along the shoreline, the swan constellation Cygnus follows the Milky Way across the fall sky.

To find the Swan, look west and slightly below zenith for the bright first-magnitude star Deneb. Deneb is part of the summer triangle, visible high in the west, made up of a trio of bright stars: Deneb, Vega, and Altair.

Deneb traces its name back to Arabic nomads, who navigated the desert using stars long before ocean navigators. Deneb means tail in Arabic and it forms the tail of the Swan. Look for the clear cross pattern—also called the Northern Cross—a constellation looking like a swan flying with its long neck to the west.

Attach a whistle and personal strobe to each PFD. Most man overboard incidents actually occur inland, in squalls or rough weather. If someone goes overboard, even in inland waters such as Albemarle Sound, it's much easier to locate them in the wave clutter and poor visibility with the help of sound and light safety devices.

SEDGES HAVE EDGES

It's probably apparent why this area is known as the Great Marsh. If you're traveling south, you haven't seen anything yet. Wait until you get to Georgia, where you will see *a lot* of marsh grass. If you've already experienced Georgia, it's still worth appreciating the marsh grass here.

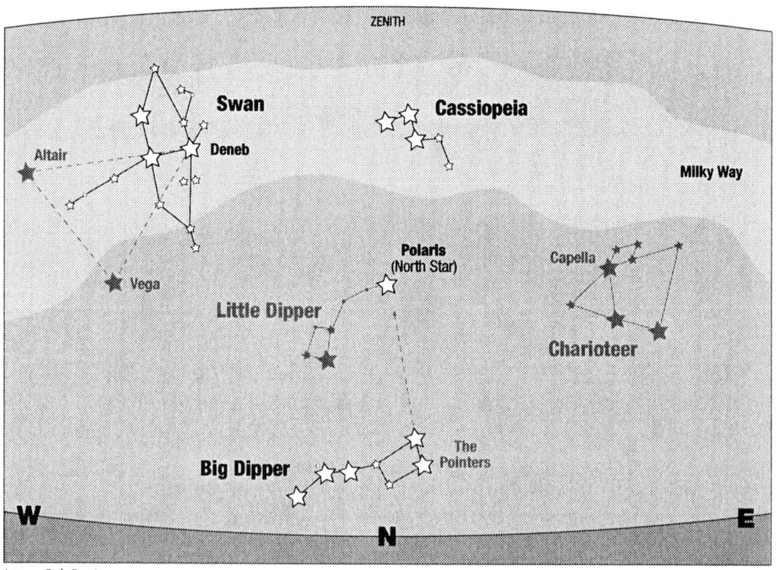

Autumn, Early Evening

Deneb and the Swan

SAFETY INFO

NOAA Weather
WX-2 Heathsville, VA
WX-1 Norfolk, VA
WX-3 Cape Hatteras, NC

USCG
Station Hobucken, NC
VHF 16 or 09/22A
252/745-3131

Sea Tow
Albemarle Sound, NC
VHF 16/09 or 11
252/312-9612

TowBoatU.S.
Coinjock, NC
VHF 16
757/286-1591

HEADS UP!

11.5	No Lunar Tides (SB)
12.1	Atlantic Intracoastal Bridge
13.8	Norfolk Southern RR Bridge
15.2	Centerville Turnpike Bridge
20.2	North Landing Bridge
34.0	VA-NC Border
41.5	Knotts Island Ferry Crossing
65.0	Albermarle Sound Crossing (SB)
78.8	**Dismal Swamp Canal (NB)**
80.0	**Albermarle Sound Crossing (NB)**
84.2	**Alligator River Bridge**
157.0	Hobucken Coast Guard Station
185.5	No Lunar Tides (NB)
200.8	Beaufort Channel Bridge (2.7)
203.8	Morehead City RR Bridge
235.2	Camp Lejeune Firing Range (SB)
240.5	Camp Lejeune Firing Range (NB)
240.7	Onslow Beach Bridge

Although these grass-like plants can all look alike, marshes are home to a great variety of plants, including sedges, rushes, and marsh grass. Bet you didn't know the marsh grass jingle to remember the differences:

Sedges have edges,
Rushes are round,
Grasses have leaves that go to the ground.

So, in general, sedges have edged stems in cross-section, including saw grass, which is common in Florida. Rushes have round seemingly leafless stems. Black Needle Rush is the very thin spiky plant that looks like a knitting needle sticking out of the ground, sometimes with a flower-like tuft blossoming out the side. True grasses, like the mats of greenish-yellow cordgrass along the shallow shores, have leaves that form an overlapping sheath around the stem.

Courtesy of U.S. Fish & Wildlife Service

Tundra Swans

Before the days of Purina duck chow, marsh grass was a valuable commodity. The marshes near STM 45.0 were once a source of wild celery and sago grass, sold around the world as duck food.

PROUD TO BE A TAR HEEL

Ever wonder why North Carolinians are proud to be called tar heels?

During the Civil War, North Carolina soldiers had a reputation for never retreating, even after they were abandoned by supporting troops from other states. So it was said that North Carolinians fought as if they had tar on their heels, meaning they would never run from a fight.

ALBEMARLE WAVES

Just ask any cruiser, and they'll tell you about the waves on Albemarle Sound—that there is something frighteningly different about a four-foot Albemarle wave versus a four-foot ocean swell.

And it's not just cruiser folklore, it's scientifically true. Both Albemarle and Pamlico Sounds produce these unique waves. Albemarle Sound may be 50 miles long, but it's only 20 feet deep. And shallow depths do strange things to the waves.

Waves are energy formed by the wind over the water. Remember, waves move *energy*, not water (the water molecules circle from crest to trough in each wave). As the energy force increases, say by greater winds, the wavelength also increases.

Unless of course, the water is shallow, in which case the length between waves is suppressed. But the energy still has to go somewhere, so it forces the waves to be taller and closer together. The same force wind in the ocean would produce shorter smoother waves with longer wavelengths.

So it's not just your stomach's imagination: waves on Albemarle and Pamlico Sounds are a much rougher ride!

TANNIN

In North Carolina, the water changes to a dark rich brown color. Many boaters describe the color like strong tea, or coffee without milk. The tea or coffee analogy is a good one: the substance coloring the water, called tannin, is the same substance that makes tea and coffee brown. Tannin is naturally released from the roots and decaying leaves of cypress and juniper trees that line the North Carolina cuts.

But tannin doesn't make the water "dirty." In fact, sailing ships sought out water with tannin because it wouldn't spoil as quickly. Each ship had to store months of drinking water in dark, dank wooden barrels called *scuttlebutts.*

After months percolating in a scuttlebutt, freshwater becomes pond-like. The water, teeming with algae and bugs, was called "lively water." So tannin, which increases the acidity of the water, kept the water a little less lively a little bit longer.

But just like coffee or tea, tannin's colored molecules create stubborn stains. For modern white fiberglass

67.2 Junction | Chowan River or Outer Banks
Southbound Navigation Only
Exit ICW SSW of G173.
Proceed westerly for charted Chowan River, town of Edenton, and other western Albemarle Sound destinations.
Proceed SSE to charted Outer Banks and Pamlico Sound destinations.

69.4 Albemarle Sound "N" (0.1)
Large tower to NW.

72.4 Albemarle Sound "AS" (0.2)
Large tower to NW.

75.7 Albemarle Sound "S" (0.3)
Large tower to NW.

78.8 Junction | Chowan River or Outer Banks
Northbound Navigation Only
Exit ICW NNE of G1 "AR".
Proceed westerly for charted Chowan River, town of Edenton, and other western Albemarle Sound destinations.
Proceed easterly to pick up charted Outer Banks and Pamlico Sound routes.

78.8 Junction | Dismal Swamp Alternate Route
to 7.2
Northbound Navigation Only
74.6-mile alternate route.
Exit ICW at G1 "AR". Proceed NNE to Pasquotank River.
Rejoin ICW below I-64 bridge at R30 (Southern Branch Elizabeth River).
Caution: Dismal Swamp Canal closes occasionally due to water conditions. Call 757/201-7606 for information and updates.

80.0 Albemarle Sound Crossing
to 65.0
Northbound Navigation Only
15-mile open water crossing.
Wait for reasonable weather and time the crossing for early morning or early evening.
SEE ALBERMARLE WAVES.

81.5 Little Alligator River Anchorage (2.0)
Anchor 6-8 feet N35.55.910
STR 0.0 feet W076.01.523
Exit ICW NNW of G9. Proceed W around Sandy Point.
SEE ALLIGATOR RIVER AND ITS CARNIVORES.

84.1 Alligator River Marina (1.3)
VHF 16; 252/796-0333
Exit ICW NNE of bridge. Proceed WNW along bridge to marina breakwater. [STR 0.0]

84.2 Alligator River Bridge
(US 64)
VHF 13; 252/796-7261
Single-pivot swing; vertical 14 feet; on request.
Caution: Bridge does not open if winds exceed 34 knots.

88.0 Milltail Creek Anchorage (3.2)
Anchor 6-9 feet N35.50.481
STR 0.0 feet W075.58.391

SAFETY INFO

NOAA Weather	Sea Tow
WX-1 Norfolk, VA	Albemarle Sound, NC
WX-3 Cape Hatteras, NC	VHF 16/09 or 11
WX-2 New Bern, NC	252/312-9612
USCG	**TowBoatU.S.**
Station Hobucken, NC	Belhaven, NC
VHF 16 or 09/22A	VHF 16
252/745-3131	252/943-2151

HEADS UP!

13.8	Norfolk Southern RR Bridge	157.0	Hobucken Coast Guard Station
15.2	Centerville Turnpike Bridge	185.5	No Lunar Tides (NB)
20.2	North Landing Bridge	200.8	Beaufort Channel Bridge (2.7)
34.0	VA-NC Border	203.8	Morehead City RR Bridge
41.5	Knotts Island Ferry Crossing	235.2	Camp Lejeune Firing Range (SB)
65.0	Albermarle Sound Crossing (SB)	240.5	Camp Lejeune Firing Range (NB)
78.8	Dismal Swamp Canal (NB)	240.7	Onslow Beach Bridge
80.0	Albermarle Sound Crossing (NB)	260.8	Surf City Bridge
84.2	Alligator River Bridge	278.1	Figure Eight Island Bridge

Exit ICW SE of R18. Proceed ESE to charted Milltail Creek.

A narrow and winding creek providing excellent protection for small boats who like a "snug" anchorage. Not recommended for sailboats.

88.1 Second Creek Anchorage (1.5)
Anchor 6-8 feet N35.50.611
STR 0.0 feet W076.03.217
Exit ICW SSE of R18. Proceed W to a spot slightly S of Second Creek entrance.

101.2 Logging Camp Anchorage (0.5)
Anchor 6-8 feet N35.39.771
STR 0.0 feet W076.02.178
Exit ICW NW of G39. Proceed S to charted old logging camp channel. Anchor E of channel.

102.2 Deep Point Anchorage (0.1)
Anchor 6-9 feet N35.40.448
STR 0.0 feet W076.03.495
Exit ICW E of G43. Proceed N.

103.2 Bear Point Anchorage (0.1)
Anchor 6-8 feet N35.40.581
STR 0.0 feet W076.04.381
Exit ICW at R46. Proceed NNE.

104.2 Tuckahoe Point Anchorage (0.2)
Anchor 7-9 feet N35.40.354
STR 0.0 feet W076.05.617
Exit ICW between G49 and R52. Proceed NNW to charted deep water.

104.9 Alligator River-Pungo River Canal
to Southbound Navigation Only
126.1 21.2-mile land cut.
No anchorages, no marinas, no fuel.

113.9 Fairfield Bridge
Fixed; vertical 65 feet.

125.9 Wilkerson Bridge
(Walter B. Jones Bridge)(US 264)
Fixed; vertical 64 feet.
Caution: The clearance is listed as 64 feet. Check boards before proceeding.

126.1 Alligator River-Pungo River Canal
to Northbound Navigation Only
104.9 21.2-mile land cut.
No anchorages, no marinas, no fuel.

126.4 Pungo River
to Southbound Navigation Only
145.9 Buoyage reverses at G27 "PR".
Look for yellow reflective ICW triangles and squares on aids.

127.4 Pungo River Anchorage (0.6)
Anchor 8-10 feet N35.33.516
STR 0.0 feet W076.28.097
Exit ICW at R24. Proceed NNW.

129.5 Scranton Creek Anchorage (1.9)
Anchor 8-10 feet N35.30.538
STR 0.0 feet W076.28.086
Exit ICW at Satterthwaite Point. Proceed SSE into

vessels, this means your boat will develop an ICW-moustache after a few weeks. Boats completing the ICW earn this distinctive bow stain.

Tannin is a stubborn stain. But it wipes off easily with household toilet bowl cleanser or Marykate On & Off Hull and Bottom Cleaner. A tiny amount is sufficient to remove the stain. And if the hull is freshly waxed, it will stain less!

Courtesy of U.S. Fish & Wildlife Service

Sliders Basking

BALDCYPRESS

Baldcypress trees are one of the main sources of tannin in the water. Baldcypress (technically not "bald" cypress) is not a true cypress tree but a deciduous redwood, losing its needles every winter. Northerners may know another deciduous conifer: the Tamarack, or what Mainers call a "hackamatack."

Baldcypress are easy to identify with their knobby knees rising above water level. These knees, or pneumatophores, are extensions of the root system protruding from the ground. The knees develop only when the tree grows in water, presumably to provide oxygen to the roots in the rising brackish water.

The gnarly look of Baldcypress makes them look old—and they often are. Baldcypress can live for 600 years. An old-growth cypress could have sprouted before Columbus discovered the New World. Nicknamed "wood eternal" because they have rot-resistant heartwood, they were liberally harvested in the 1930s and 1940s to make items resistant to rot. Since it's slow to rot, Baldcypress was used for barrels, fences, hulls of PT boats, and of course, coffins.

Now these trees are seldom harvested. The wetlands are too fragile and the trees grow much too slowly to sustain a reasonable timber supply.

FLYPAPER FOR DEMONS

See the bright green beach-ball-sized clumps growing on nearly dead trees? Long ago, the Anglo-Saxons believed life was generated spontaneously from animal droppings. The growth of a living plant on a dead branch must come from the droppings of birds. So the Anglo-Saxons named this plant "dung-on-a-twig," using the word for dung ("mistel") and twig ("tan"). We call it mistletoe.

Mistletoe was sacred to the Celtic Druids, whose nature-based religion believed anything growing without its roots in the soil was mystical. So the spontaneity of mistletoe on oak branches embodied life and fertility. It was gathered at the summer and winter solstices as part of the Druid's religious ceremonies.

Versions of these beliefs about mistletoe continued around the world. When enemies met under mistletoe in the forest they were to lay down their arms and observe a truce until the next day. In the Middle Ages, branches of mistletoe were hung from ceilings to ward off evil spirits, described sarcastically in modern times as "flypaper for demons."

Today, we decorate homes with mistletoe at Christmas, just after the winter solstice, in a tradition surviving from Druid and other pre-Christian traditions. Kissing under the mistletoe brings fertility, good will, and peace.

Courtesy of U.S. Army Corps of Engineers

Photo by Jonas N. Jordan

Cypress Swamp

SAFETY INFO

NOAA Weather
WX-1 Norfolk, VA
WX-3 Cape Hatteras, NC
WX-2 New Bern, NC

USCG
Station Hobucken, NC
VHF 16 or 09/22A
252/745-3131

Sea Tow
Albemarle Sound, NC
VHF 16/09 or 11
252/312-9612

TowBoatU.S.
Belhaven, NC
VHF 16
252/943-2151

HEADS UP!

15.2	Centerville Turnpike Bridge
20.2	North Landing Bridge
34.0	VA-NC Border
41.5	Knotts Island Ferry Crossing
65.0	Albermarle Sound Crossing (SB)
78.8	Dismal Swamp Canal (NB)
80.0	Albermarle Sound Crossing (NB)
84.2	Alligator River Bridge
157.0	Hobucken Coast Guard Station
185.5	No Lunar Tides (NB)
200.8	Beaufort Channel Bridge (2.7)
203.8	Morehead City RR Bridge
235.2	Camp Lejeune Firing Range (SB)
240.5	Camp Lejeune Firing Range (NB)
240.7	Onslow Beach Bridge
260.8	Surf City Bridge
278.1	Figure Eight Island Bridge
283.2	Wrightsville Beach Bridge

THE OTHER CHRISTMAS PLANT

The coastal plains of the Southeast are home to two native plants associated with Christmas. American Holly—with spiny, dark green glossy leaves, red berries, and small waxy white flowers—grows wild in dense green patches along the Waterway.

Courtesy of NASA

Belted Kingfisher

To the Druids, holly was revered because it stayed green when other trees, such as the sacred oaks, lost their leaves. Its bright red berries symbolized the sacred menstrual blood of their Goddess.

Every winter, the Celts cut holly branches and placed them around their homes to provide winter shelter for the tiny forest fairies. The first holly branches brought into the house portended who would rule the home for the coming year: husband or wife.

Unlike most plants, a holly tree is either a male or a female, noticeable in the flowers. Bring a male sprig in first and the male runs the show. On our boat, the domestic power struggle over yard plants ended long ago. Flowers!

With the rise of Christianity in the British Isles, the symbolism of holly, but not its sacredness, changed. As late as the 18th century, felling a holly tree was associated with bad luck. The berries now symbolize the drops of Christ's blood, the prickly leaves, Jesus's crown of thorns.

Don't lose 'em overboard! Use twice as many clothespins as you would at home on the laundry line. Doubling up foils a strong breeze which can easily flag a towel and pop a single clothespin. Additionally, clip two clothespins on each edge below the lifeline.

SALINITY GAUGES

When the Alligator-Pungo canal opened, salt water mixed with the surrounding low-lying marshes. Today you can see the vestiges of this ocean-river cocktail: the bare silver skeletons of dead cypress trees rising up from the marsh. Baldcypress can tolerate brackish water, but die if the water becomes too saline.

You can use Baldcypress, and other plants you see, as clues to the water's salinity. If it's mildly brackish, Baldcypress thrives. If the water is very salty, cypress swamps are replaced by salt-tolerant cordgrasses.

Salt water causes dehydration in plants, so any plant growing in saline soil or water has ways to lock in the limited freshwater. Wax Myrtle locks in moisture with its small waxy leaves. Some plants in extreme salt environments have no leaves at all. Instead of leaves, glasswort, which grows on the islands around Beaufort, has strange-looking little green branching tubes. These tubes make it look like an alien life form, but are very effective at storing salt and absorbing and retaining freshwater.

Every year the level of salt water rises, perhaps due to global warming. Because of the rising water, the coastal southern states lose several thousand acres of wetland forests a year—killed by salt water and forced to evolve to salt-tolerant grass marshes.

THE CARNIVORES OF ALLIGATOR RIVER

Yes, the Alligator River was named after the American Alligator. As recently as the 1930s, 15-foot alligators

Courtesy of NASA

Namesake of Alligator River

charted Scranton Creek.

131.7 Dowry Creek S N
Exit ICW at G15. Proceed N into charted Upper Dowry Creek. [STR 0.0]

- **Dowry Creek Marina** (1.1)
  VHF 16/71 N35.31.974
  800/824-7035 W076.32.098
  Marina is to port.
- **Dowry Creek Anchorage** (1.2)
  Anchor 6-7 feet N35.32.116
  STR 0.0 feet W076.32.058
  Anchorage is beyond marina as water shoals.

135.9 Belhaven S N
Exit ICW at G1 "BC". Proceed NW into Pantego Creek to Belhaven. [STR 0.0]
SEE BELHAVEN.

- **River Forest Marina** (1.3)
  VHF 16; 252/943-2151
  Marina is behind breakwater to starboard.
- **Belhaven Anchorage** (Southeast)(1.6)
  Anchor 8-10 feet N35.31.854
  STR 0.0 feet W076.37.333
  Anchorage is WSW of R8. Beware of charted 3-foot shoal.
- **Captain Robbs' Yard & Marina** (1.9)
  VHF 16; 252/943-2110
  Facility is closed with no plans to re-open.
- **Belhaven Waterway Marina** (2.0)
  VHF 16/09 N35.32.187
  252/944-0066 W076.37.447
  Marina is to starboard, opposite G9.
- **Belhaven Anchorage** (Northwest)(2.5)
  Anchor 7-9 feet N35.32.390
  STR 0.0 feet W076.37.971
  Anchorage is between R12 and fixed bridge.

136.3 Pungo Creek Anchorage (2.8) S N
Anchor 7-9 feet N35.30.716
STR 0.0 feet W076.38.629
Exit ICW WNW of Durants Point. Proceed westerly into Pungo Creek. Round Windmill Point.

140.3 Jordan Creek Anchorage (1.2) S N
Anchor 8-10 feet N35.27.280
STR 0.0 feet W076.36.024
Exit ICW abeam Tyson Point. Proceed W to Jordan Creek. Anchor in charted 9-foot tongue.

140.4 Slade Creek Anchorage (1.7) S N
Anchor 8-10 feet N35.27.529
STR 0.0 feet W076.33.085
Exit ICW NW of Sandy Point. Proceed easterly to Slade Creek. Round July Point.

145.9 Pungo River S N
to Northbound Navigation Only
126.4 Buoyage reverses.
Look for yellow reflective ICW triangles and squares on aids.
SEE PUNGOTEAGUE AND MACHAPUNGO.

146.5 Junction | Pamlico River or Outer Banks S N
Southbound/Northbound Navigation

SAFETY INFO

NOAA Weather
WX-3 Cape Hatteras, NC
WX-2 New Bern, NC
WX-1 Wilmington, NC

USCG
Station Hobucken, NC
VHF 16 or 09/22A
252/745-3131

Sea Tow
Beaufort, NC
VHF 16/7 or 9 or 79
252/728-6551

TowBoatU.S.
Belhaven, NC
VHF 16
252/943-2151

HEADS UP!

15.2	Centerville Turnpike Bridge
20.2	North Landing Bridge
34.0	VA-NC Border
41.5	Knotts Island Ferry Crossing
65.0	Albermarle Sound Crossing (SB)
78.8	Dismal Swamp Canal (NB)
80.0	Albermarle Sound Crossing (NB)
84.2	Alligator River Bridge
157.0	**Hobucken Coast Guard Station**
185.5	No Lunar Tides (NB)
200.8	Beaufort Channel Bridge (2.7)
203.8	Morehead City RR Bridge
235.2	Camp Lejeune Firing Range (SB)
240.5	Camp Lejeune Firing Range (NB)
240.7	Onslow Beach Bridge
260.8	Surf City Bridge
278.1	Figure Eight Island Bridge
283.2	Wrightsville Beach Bridge

Exit ICW SSE of "PR".
Proceed westerly for Bath, Washington, and western Pamlico River destinations.
Proceed southeasterly to Ocracoke, Outer Banks, and Pamlico Sound destinations.
SEE MASON-DIXON LINE OF THE MARINE WORLD.

153.0 Snode Creek Anchorage (0.5)
Anchor 4-6 feet N35.18.144
STR 0.0 feet W076.37.609
Exit ICW NNW of G11. Proceed W into Snode Creek.

153.7 Eastham Creek Anchorage (0.6)
Anchor 5-7 feet N35.17.747
STR 0.0 feet W076.36.364
Exit ICW at G13. Proceed ENE into Eastham Creek. Anchor NE of G3.

154.1 Campbell Creek Anchorage (0.4)
Anchor 5-7 feet N35.17.072
STR 0.0 feet W076.37.222
Exit ICW N of Long Neck Point. Proceed WSW into charted 7-foot tongue.

155.4 Upper Spring Creek Anchorage (0.1)
Anchor 5-6 feet N35.16.328
STR 0.0 feet W076.35.955
Exit ICW at G19. Ease NE just off ICW.

157.0 USCG Station Hobucken
Charted USCG station is to W.

157.1 Hobucken Bridge
(Routes 33/304)
Fixed; vertical 65 feet.

157.3 R.E. Mayo Company
No VHF Watch; 252/745-5331
Facility is to W. [STR 0.0]
Working shrimp dock provides limited transient dockage as space allows. Pull up along straight wharf south of the facility. The wharf is unstaffed.
If you need help docking, circle in the canal and ask a fellow cruiser to take your lines.
SEE HOBUCKEN.

157.5 Jones Bay Anchorage (0.3)
Anchor 5-6 feet N35.14.356
STR 0.0 feet W076.35.091
Exit ICW S of G21. Proceed ESE into Jones Bay.
Caution: Wind dramatically changes the depth in Jones Bay. There is typically more water than charted. Proceed slowly.

159.7 Gale Creek Anchorage (0.1)
Anchor 6-8 feet N35.12.622
STR 0.0 feet W076.35.462
Exit ICW at G23. Proceed W to charted deep pocket.
Caution: Avoid cable area shown on chart.

161.2 Bear Creek Anchorage (1.9)
Anchor 6-8 feet N35.11.777
STR 0.0 feet W076.36.458
Exit ICW SE of G27. Carefully proceed SW around charted shoal then northwesterly into Bear Creek.

inhabited the river. Now you'll have to travel further south to see alligators. But there are plenty of other interesting carnivores in this wild area.

Alligator River National Wildlife Refuge (STM 90.0) adjoins the Waterway to the east, one of the last eastern strongholds of the Black Bear. It's also protected habitat for the endangered Red Wolf. Red Wolves were recently reintroduced to this refuge, chosen because of its remoteness, natural water moat, and small coyote population.

If you anchor along Alligator River, such as at Milltail Creek (STM 88.0), you may hear the call of a Red Wolf. Listen at night for an eerie musical series of howls, very distinct from the high-pitched more dog-like howl of coyotes. You can listen (and perhaps howl along) to a Red Wolf call online at the North Carolina Zoological Society's website.

North Carolina Zoological Society
www.fieldtripearth.org/article.xml?id=683

LOBLOLLY PINES

Many important species of trees line the ICW and it can make the trip more enjoyable to identify them.

The "pine" is one of the South's most important trees—honored as the state tree of North Carolina and a cornerstone of the South's early economy.

The Loblolly Pine is the most common pine along the Alligator and Pungo Rivers. It was a common plantation tree and one of many important timber trees to the Southern economy. Look for its long clear stems (and if you can get close enough, its 6- to 7-inch needles in clusters of threes). As you move toward southern North Carolina, start to look for the grander Longleaf Pine, and in Florida, the Slash Pine.

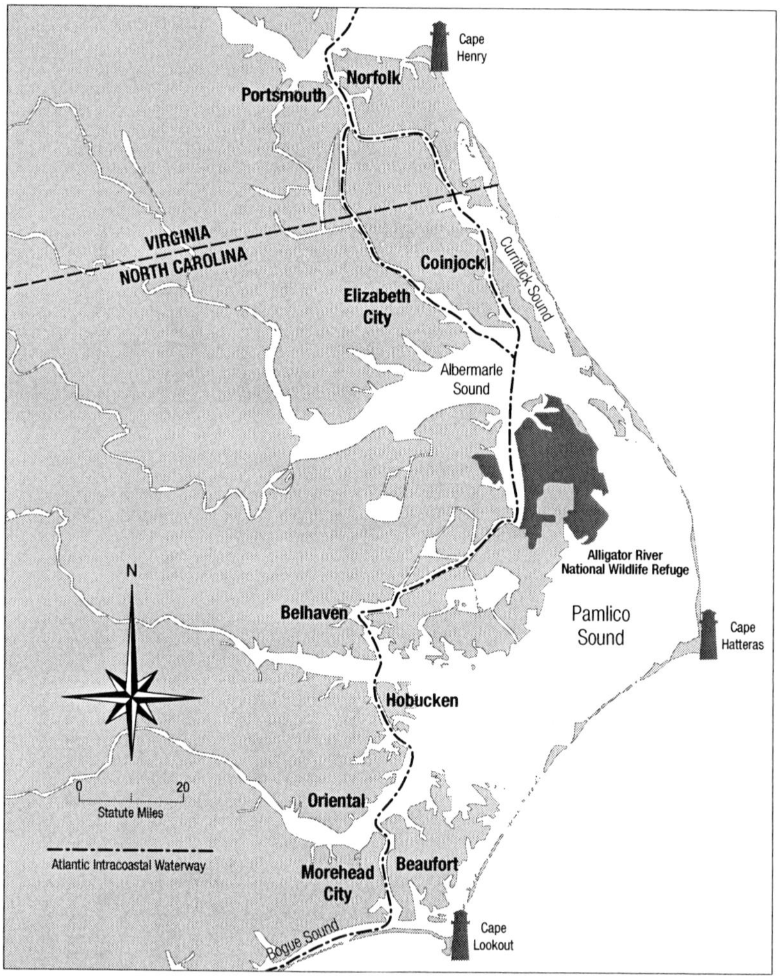

North Carolina Sounds

SAFETY INFO

NOAA Weather
WX-3 Cape Hatteras, NC
WX-2 New Bern, NC
WX-1 Wilmington, NC

USCG
Station Hobucken, NC
VHF 16 or 09/22A
252/745-3131

Sea Tow
Beaufort, NC
VHF 16/7 or 9 or 79
252/728-6551

TowBoatU.S.
Oriental, NC
VHF 16/10
252/249-1180

HEADS UP!

15.2	Centerville Turnpike Bridge
20.2	North Landing Bridge
34.0	VA-NC Border
41.5	Knotts Island Ferry Crossing
65.0	Albermarle Sound Crossing (SB)
78.8	Dismal Swamp Canal (NB)
80.0	Albermarle Sound Crossing (NB)
84.2	Alligator River Bridge
157.0	Hobucken Coast Guard Station
185.5	No Lunar Tides (NB)
200.8	Beaufort Channel Bridge (2.7)
203.8	Morehead City RR Bridge
235.2	Camp Lejeune Firing Range (SB)
240.5	Camp Lejeune Firing Range (NB)
240.7	Onslow Beach Bridge
260.8	Surf City Bridge
278.1	Figure Eight Island Bridge
283.2	Wrightsville Beach Bridge

TURNING THE SWEETGUM SCARLET

In the fall, the Sweetgum tree is unmistakable with its brilliant scarlet leaves. During other seasons, look for its five-pointed star-shaped leaves and its spiky dangling seedpod balls.

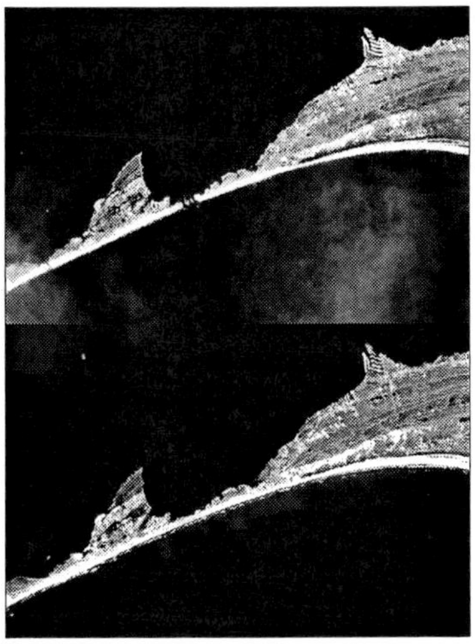

Courtesy of EROS Data Center, NASA

Isabel Alters Hatteras (Top)

As fall arrives, Sweetgum trees turn red and the constellation Great Bear drops in the sky toward the treetops. In Native American legends, these two seasonal changes are connected. Ancient hunters kill Great Bear and the great animal collapses behind the autumn trees. Its blood turns the trees crimson as it disappears below the horizon.

Look for Great Bear, or Ursa Major, as part of the Big Dipper, with the ladle like a saddle and the tip of the handle forming the bear's nose.

Store extra bedding, towels, or heavy clothes such as sweatshirts in your cabin settee pillows. Buy pillows you like and remove the foam or batting. Replace with your storage items zipped into a cotton pillow protector, which keeps them clean and dry. This trick saves space and you have easy access to your extra warm clothing from the cockpit!

BALD EAGLE

Don't be surprised if you look up into a dead tree and see a majestic Bald Eagle nonchalantly watching your vessel pass. Bald Eagles are fairly common along the Waterway, but often keep a regal-like low profile.

The trick to spotting a bald eagle is to look for clues. Since Bald Eagles are the alpha bird among raptors, other birds don't like eagles in their territory. Agitated Ospreys or crows are often the first clue to look for a Bald Eagle. If the Ospreys are shrieking and circling, check the trees. You'll often see a large Bald Eagle trying to ignore the machinations of the Ospreys. Sometimes an Osprey will even dive-bomb an eagle, pestering it until it moves further down the river.

BELHAVEN

Belhaven, with a population of about 2,000, is a small waterfront town. Like many small American towns, the center of town is Water Street and Main Street. You can find several services in town, including a regional hospital with a quality emergency room, library, post office, hardware store, drug store, and bank.

Just up Water Street to Main, you pass a stately Victorian mansion. This is River Forest Manor, now an inn and restaurant and part of the River Forest Marina.

Back in 1899, the big money in this region was in lumber and rails. John Wilkinson, the President of Roper Lumber and Vice-President of Norfolk & Southern Railroad, built the River Forest Manor.

He hired craftsmen for the interior detailing, which included carved ceilings and oak mantels for the eleven fireplaces, leaded cut-glass windows, crystal chandeliers, tapestries, mahogany wainscoting, and a mosaic. Wilkinson

Courtesy of VA Canals and Navigations Society

Photo by George Ramsey

How to Spot a Bald Eagle

161.3 Hurricane Harbour Marina (5.0)
VHF 16; 252/745-3369
Exit ICW SE of G27. Proceed WSW to charted R4, then westerly beyond Petty and Wise Points to G5. Marina is ahead, SW of Windmill Point.
Although your chartkit may not cover the Bay River extension, this route is wide, six-plus feet deep, and well-aided. [STR 0.0]

161.4 Bonner Bay Anchorages
Exit ICW SE of G27. Proceed southwesterly to Bonner Bay.

- **Long Creek Anchorage** (3.4)
  Anchor 8-12 feet N35.09.123
  STR 0.0 feet W076.34.975
  Ease E into Long Creek.
- **Spring Creek Anchorage** (3.9)
  Anchor 6-10 feet N35.08.475
  STR 0.0 feet W076.35.801
  Ease SW into Spring Creek.

164.6 Junction | Neuse River Shortcut
to 175.0
Southbound Navigation Only
8.9-mile shortcut.
Exit ICW 0.25 STM abeam G1. Proceed SSE to leave R2 0.25 STM to starboard. Abeam R2, turn SW to leave R4 0.25 STM to starboard. Abeam R4, turn WSW to leave R6 0.1 STM to starboard. Rejoin the magenta line southbound at STM 175.0, just beyond Gum Thicket Shoal.
We take very few shortcuts on the ICW. The magenta line is well traveled and better maintained, which spares us the more exciting stories of prop snags or hitting uncharted, submerged piles.
However, boat traffic seems to have worn a groove in the magenta line in several places. You can save 1.5 miles and get a better look at the scenery by running the aids off Maw Point Shoal, Piney Point Shoal, and Gum Thicket Shoal.
Caution: We only recommend this or any other shortcut with excellent wind, sea, and visual conditions.

167.1 Junction | Neuse River to Outer Banks
Southbound/Northbound Navigation
Exit ICW E of Neuse River Junction light. Proceed southeasterly for Ocracoke, Outer Banks, and Pamlico Sound destinations.

173.6 Dowdy Point Anchorage (3.0)
Anchor 6-8 feet N35.05.781
STR 0.0 feet W076.35.671
Exit ICW between R4 and R6. Proceed NNW to Broad Creek entrance. Follow channel and anchor N of G3.

175.0 Junction | Neuse River Shortcut
to 164.6
Northbound Navigation Only
8.9-mile shortcut.
Depart ICW at STM 175.0. Proceed ENE to leave R6 0.1 STM to port. Abeam R6, continue ENE to leave R4 0.25 STM to port. Abeam R4, turn NE to leave R2 0.25 STM to port. Abeam R2, turn NNW to leave G1 0.25 STM to port. Rejoin the magenta line northbound at Bay River G1, between Maw and Bay Points.

SAFETY INFO

NOAA Weather	**Sea Tow**
WX-3 Cape Hatteras, NC	Beaufort, NC
WX-2 New Bern, NC	VHF 16/7 or 9 or 79
WX-1 Wilmington, NC	252/728-6551
USCG	**TowBoatU.S.**
Station Fort Macon, NC	Oriental, NC
VHF 16 or 09/22A	VHF 16/10
252/247-4583	252/249-1180

HEADS UP!

20.2	North Landing Bridge	200.8	Beaufort Channel Bridge (2.7)
34.0	VA-NC Border	203.8	Morehead City RR Bridge
41.5	Knotts Island Ferry Crossing	235.2	Camp Lejeune Firing Range (SB)
65.0	Albermarle Sound Crossing (SB)	240.5	Camp Lejeune Firing Range (NB)
78.8	Dismal Swamp Canal (NB)	240.7	Onslow Beach Bridge
80.0	Albermarle Sound Crossing (NB)	260.8	Surf City Bridge
84.2	Alligator River Bridge	278.1	Figure Eight Island Bridge
157.0	Hobucken Coast Guard Station	283.2	Wrightsville Beach Bridge
185.5	No Lunar Tides (NB)	319.5	Lockwoods Folly Inlet Area (SB)

Caution: We only recommend this or any other shortcut with excellent wind, sea, and visual conditions.

178.5 South River Anchorage (5.5)
Anchor 8-12 feet N34.58.043
STR 0.0 feet W076.34.771
Exit ICW S of Cockle Point. Proceed SSE to South River entrance. Follow channel to charted remains of Lukens.

180.8 Junction | Neuse River
Southbound/Northbound Navigation
Exit ICW NW of G7 Garbacon Shoal Light.
Proceed WSW for Whittaker Creek, Oriental, and western Neuse River destinations.
Proceed SW, then southerly to continue ICW southbound (Adams Creek).
Proceed northerly to continue ICW northbound.
Caution: Southbound, many first-time ICW travelers mistakenly continue along the Neuse River. To continue ICW southbound, enter Adams Creek at STM 185.0.

Whittaker Creek (0.5)
At Neuse River Junction, continue 0.5 STM WSW. Exit Neuse River and proceed northerly to charted Whittaker Creek channel. [STR 0.0]

- **Whittaker Creek Yacht Harbor** (1.9)
  VHF 16; 252/249-0666
  Marina is on Whittaker Point where channel splits.
- **Sailcraft Service** (2.0)
  No VHF Watch; 252/249-0522
  Bear left at split. Facility is to port. Repair yard with no transient dockage.
- **Deaton Yacht Service** (2.2)
  VHF 16/10 N35.01.880
  252/249-1180 W076.41.177
  Bear left at split. Proceed westerly into first charted creek to facility. Repair yard with no transient dockage.

Oriental (1.1)
At Neuse River Junction, continue 1.1 STM WSW. Exit Neuse River and proceed northerly to charted Oriental channel. Proceed in channel to harbor breakwater R8. [STR 0.0]
SEE ORIENTAL.

- **Oriental Marina & Inn** (1.9)
  VHF 16/71 N35.01.484
  252/249-1818 W076.41.720
  Proceed easterly to main harbor (Raccoon Creek). Marina is to starboard.
- **Oriental Public Docks** (1.9)
  No VHF Watch; No Tel.
  Proceed easterly to main harbor (Raccoon Creek). Town docks are dead ahead at The Bean, a favorite coffee and ice cream shop.
  Room for 2 boats, enforced 48-hour limit, no facilities.
- **Oriental Harbor Marina** (1.8)
  VHF 16/78 N35.01.447
  252/249-3783 W076.41.857

also included a most un-Victorian architectural detail—but something the rich and famous now expect in their home design—a spa-style bathtub large enough for two people.

The Manor has been an inn since 1941, with a guest registry which has included James Cagney, Tallulah Bankhead, Robert Ripley, Harvey Firestone, Burl Ives, Twiggy, Roy Clark, Neal Sedaka, and Walter Cronkite.

PUNGOTEAGUE AND MACHAPUNGO

Over 400 years ago, the Pungo River was an Indian settlement, "discovered" by English explorers in 1585.

Most of the names in this region are from Native American history. Both the Machapungo and Pungoteague tribes lived here, naming their tribes from the word "pungo" meaning dust. The Machapungo's name, not to be outdone, means "much dust."

Pungo, or dust, may seem like an odd identifier for a tribe—until you notice the sandy soil characteristic of the Pungo River basin.

MASON-DIXON LINE OF THE MARINE WORLD

You may be well south of the Mason-Dixon line, but you just crossed the imaginary line called "the Mason-Dixon line of the marine world" by environmentalist and science writer Rachel Carson (See The Edge of the Sea).

Across Pamlico Sound, Cape Hatteras juts into the Atlantic. The Labrador Current flows from the north; the Gulf Stream flows from the south. The two currents converge at Hatteras, dividing the marine species into "northerners" and "southerners": cold-water species like cod, mackerel, and pollock to the north and warm-water species like Spanish mackerel, mullet, and grouper to the south.

HOBUCKEN

Hobucken is a great place to stop and experience firsthand a working shrimp dock. The commercial facilities at R.E. Mayo welcome transient boaters and offer great protection. The area is wooded and quiet. It has all the character you'd expect from a site where the facilities are a wooden outhouse with a crescent moon on the door.

You may be unfamiliar with moon cutouts on outhouses, but they're there for a reason. In the days before electricity, the occupant needed a bit of light and ventilation. Obviously a big square cutout window won't work for privacy on an outhouse. Supposedly there were originally two cutout symbols: a star for the men's privy and a crescent moon for the women's.

semi-local publications LLC

Photo by Author
R.E. Mayo Restrooms

But even back then men didn't clean their bathrooms. The men's facilities quickly became dirty and in disrepair and soon everyone preferred the cleaner women's privies. By the 1800s everyone was using the outhouses ventilated with the moon and the symbols had lost their gender meaning. And so today's arrangement evolved: co-ed bathrooms cleaned by women.

MOSQUITOES: WHY ME?

Mainers joke that Tenant's Harbor is where fog is made. On some nights it feels as if mosquitoes are made in the marshes of Pamlico County.

But don't be paranoid and think you're the only victim. Mosquitoes also bite turtles' necks and legs, alligators' tender skin around their eyes, between snakes' scales, and wading birds' long naked legs. Mosquitoes are equal opportunity bloodsuckers.

There are countless dietary folk remedies, including a diet rich in ginseng, bananas, garlic, brewer's yeast, or Mrs. Paul's Fish Sticks. Too bad ice cream or chips aren't on the list. Once again, forget the fad diet and reach for the DEET.

If the insects are particularly bad, using a red navigation light for reading at night attracts fewer insects to your screens than bright white lights.

SAFETY INFO

NOAA Weather
WX-3 Cape Hatteras, NC
WX-2 New Bern, NC
WX-1 Wilmington, NC

USCG
Station Fort Macon, NC
VHF 16 or 09/22A
252/247-4583

Sea Tow
Beaufort, NC
VHF 16/7 or 9 or 79
252/728-6551

TowBoatU.S.
Oriental, NC
VHF 16/10
252/249-1180

HEADS UP!

20.2	North Landing Bridge
34.0	VA-NC Border
41.5	Knotts Island Ferry Crossing
65.0	Albermarle Sound Crossing (SB)
78.8	Dismal Swamp Canal (NB)
80.0	Albermarle Sound Crossing (NB)
84.2	Alligator River Bridge
157.0	Hobucken Coast Guard Station
185.5	**No Lunar Tides (NB)**
200.8	Beaufort Channel Bridge (2.7)
203.8	Morehead City RR Bridge
235.2	Camp Lejeune Firing Range (SB)
240.5	Camp Lejeune Firing Range (NB)
240.7	Onslow Beach Bridge
260.8	Surf City Bridge
278.1	Figure Eight Island Bridge
283.2	Wrightsville Beach Bridge
319.5	Lockwoods Folly Inlet Area (SB)

ORIENTAL

Oriental once was a fishing, farming, and lumber community with a sawmill and a train stop. But in the 1950s both the train and the sawmill closed, devastating the small town's economy.

Ten years later, sailors discovered Oriental. In 1960 only four sailboats listed Oriental as their hailing port. Today over 2,000 boats call Oriental home. With over 3,000 boats total, Oriental has three times more boats than people. Many of its residents are former cruisers who have swallowed the anchor, choosing to retire to Oriental for its great sailing on the Neuse River and Pamlico Sound.

Courtesy of NASA

Dolphin at Play

In fact, Oriental bills itself as "the sailing capital of North Carolina." The town has a vibrant downtown area along the waterfront and an active art community. Many boaters enjoy the nautical collection at Hodge Podge Used Books or the marine items at Inland Waterway Treasure Company. Beginning in 2004, the town hosts a regional boat show in September at the Oriental Harbor Marina.

Hodge Podge Used Books
252/249-3670

Inland Waterway Treasure Company
252/249-1797

Oriental Boat Show Info
www.pamlico-nc.com/ocr
www.orientalharbor.com

DOLPHIN OR PORPOISE?

Just as alligators are not crocodiles, dolphins are not porpoises. Many boaters mistake dolphins for porpoises. But here in the warmer waters just north of Adams Creek, and inland south to Florida, the most likely Cetacean is the Atlantic Bottle-nosed Dolphin.

And like alligators and crocodiles, one obvious difference between dolphins and porpoises is their snouts. Dolphins have a pointed nose, called a beak. Porpoises have a flat nose with no beak, more like the front of a small whale. Look for the flatter-nosed Harbor Porpoise in colder, northern New England harbors.

semi-local publications LLC

Photo by Author

Dolphin Escort

NORTHERN HARRIER

As you transit through the marshes, look for the flap-and-glide pattern of the marsh hawk, coursing back and forth across the flats.

The marsh hawk, officially called the Northern Harrier, is a streamlined hawk with thin wings and a long tail. It may be brown or gray, but the distinctive white rump is always a clincher. Harriers show up along the entire length of the Waterway, but their numbers are declining, most likely due to loss of habitat.

If you watch a marsh hawk course back and forth over the marshes, you may see one with a small bird or snake in its claws. They feed by gliding low along creeks and over the marsh grass, dropping like a stone onto a small mammal, snake, frog, or bird. In residential areas a harrier will swoop over an open area of lawn, plucking an inattentive robin or squirrel right off the manicured grass.

THE FIRST LINK

Secretary of the Treasury Albert Gallatin first envisioned an Atlantic Intracoastal Waterway in 1808, arguing for a comprehensive federally managed inland route from Boston, Massachusetts to St. Marys, Georgia. Gallatin optimistically expected his pet project to cost $3 million and take ten years. But no one was interested.

For the rest of the 1800s, private companies or local governments dug canals, hoping to make a profit from

Marina is before fixed bridge, to starboard.

- **Oriental Anchorage** (1.7)
  Anchor 6-10 feet N35.01.321
  STR 0.0 feet W076.42.024
  Anchorage is between breakwater and fixed bridge.
- **Oriental Bridge** (1.8)
  Fixed; vertical 45 feet.
- **Greens Creek Anchorage** (2.3)
  Anchor 5-6 feet N35.01.460
  STR 0.0 feet W076.42.596
  Proceed beyond fixed bridge into charted Greens Creek. Anchor beyond G3.

185.5 No Lunar Tides
to Northbound Navigation Only
11.5 174-mile non-tidal zone.
From Adams Creek (STM 185.5) to Great Bridge Lock (STM 11.5), tides and currents are primarily dictated by recent wind conditions.
SEE DOLPHIN OR PORPOISE?

185.5 Range "A"
to Southbound/Northbound Navigation
186.9 Adams Creek
1.5-mile range.

187.7 Cedar Creek Anchorage (0.2)
Anchor 6-8 feet N34.55.995
STR 0.5 feet W076.38.892
Exit ICW at G9. Proceed E into charted tongue.

187.7 Range "B"
to Southbound/Northbound Navigation
189.7 Adams Creek
2.0-mile range.

191.5 Adams Creek Canal
to Southbound Navigation Only
197.2 5.7-mile land cut.
No anchorages, one marina, fuel available.

194.2 Sea Gate Marina (0.2)
VHF 16/09 N34.51.000
252/728-4126 W076.41.500
Exit ICW at charted basin. Proceed W. Marina is to port. [STR 2.1]

195.9 Core Creek Bridge
(Route 101)
Fixed; vertical 65 feet.

196.0 Bock Marine (0.1)
No VHF Watch; 252/728-6855
Facility is to E. Repair yard with no transient dockage.

197.2 Adams Creek Canal
to Northbound Navigation Only
191.5 5.7-mile land cut.
No anchorages, one marina, fuel available.

197.3 Jarrett Bay Boatworks (0.1)
No VHF Watch; 252/728-2690
Facility is to E. Boat builder and repair yard with no transient dockage.

SAFETY INFO

NOAA Weather
WX-3 Cape Hatteras, NC
WX-2 New Bern, NC
WX-1 Wilmington, NC

USCG
Station Fort Macon, NC
VHF 16 or 09/22A
252/247-4583

Sea Tow
Beaufort, NC
VHF 16/7 or 9 or 79
252/728-6551

TowBoatU.S.
Beaufort, NC
VHF 16
252/728-5088

HEADS UP!

34.0	VA-NC Border
41.5	Knotts Island Ferry Crossing
65.0	Albermarle Sound Crossing (SB)
78.8	Dismal Swamp Canal (NB)
80.0	Albermarle Sound Crossing (NB)
84.2	Alligator River Bridge
157.0	Hobucken Coast Guard Station
185.5	No Lunar Tides (NB)
200.8	**Beaufort Channel Bridge (2.7)**
203.8	Morehead City RR Bridge
235.2	Camp Lejeune Firing Range (SB)
240.5	Camp Lejeune Firing Range (NB)
240.7	Onslow Beach Bridge
260.8	Surf City Bridge
278.1	Figure Eight Island Bridge
283.2	Wrightsville Beach Bridge
319.5	Lockwoods Folly Inlet Area (SB)
322.5	Lockwoods Folly Inlet Area (NB)

197.7 Core Creek Range S N
to Southbound/Northbound Navigation
199.5 Core Creek
1.8-mile range.

200.8 Junction | Beaufort Alternate Route S N
to Southbound Navigation Only
204.2 5.3-mile alternate route.

Exit ICW at G "RS". Proceed S along charted channel, locally known as Russell Slough, to a point NW of Gallants Point. Proceed SE into Gallants Channel.

Proceed southerly to G15 and Town Creek. [STR 3.5 (TS)]

Continue southerly for Beaufort bridges and Beaufort. [STR 3.6]

Rejoin ICW southbound at Morehead City Turning Basin.

Caution: Transiting the Beaufort area may be confusing. See accompanying chartlet, "Beaufort and Approaches."

SEE BEAUFORT AND MOREHEAD CITY.

- **Town Creek Marina** (2.7)
  VHF 16/08 N34.43.514
  252/728-6111 W076.39.839
  Exit at G15. Proceed E. Marina is to port.
- **Discovery Diving** (2.8)
  VHF 10 N34.43.367
  252/728-2265 W076.39.860
  Exit at G15. Proceed E. Facility is on S side of basin, opposite marina.
  Dive shop with no transient dockage. Air and dinghy dock available.
- **Town Creek Anchorage** (2.8)
  Anchor 8-10 feet N34.43.464
  STR 3.5 feet W076.39.779
  Exit at G15. Proceed E. Anchorage is beyond marina.
- **Beaufort Channel Bridge** (2.7)
  (US 70)
  VHF 13; 252/728-3279
  Double bascule; vertical 13 feet.
  Restricted year round: 0600-2200 hrs, opens on the hour and half-hour, except no openings M-F 0630-0800 and 1630-1800 hrs.
- **Beaufort RR Bridge** (2.7)
  Charted but has been removed.
- **Beaufort Inn** (2.8)
  No VHF Watch; 252/728-2600
  Inn is to E. Cannot sleep on boat; must be a guest at the Inn.
- **Spouter Inn** (3.1)
  No VHF Watch; 252/728-5190
  Restaurant is to NE. Dock and dine.
- **Beaufort Gulf Docks** (3.2)
  VHF 16; 252/728-6000
  Fuel dock is to NE.
- **Beaufort Town Docks** (3.3)
  VHF 16; 252/728-2503
  Proceed ESE along waterfront. Town Docks are to NE.

the tolls or improve trade for their local economy. Any national attention to canals went to the northern states, especially New York and the Great Lakes.

It wasn't until 1906, nearly 100 years after Gallatin's proposal, that the Atlantic Deeper Waterways Association formed to lobby again for the construction of an inland waterway. Congress agreed to authorize a survey of the proposed project. Based on this survey, the Army Corps recommended a 12-foot deep canal between Norfolk, Virginia and Beaufort, North Carolina. Approval for several other large projects—including Beaufort, South Carolina to the Florida border and Beaufort, North Carolina to Sneads Ferry, North Carolina—followed within the next few years.

So the Waterway transformed from pieces of cuts and canals into a vision for a nationally managed inland waterway. By some accounts, the first major project of the contemporary government-controlled Atlantic Intracoastal Waterway between Norfolk and Miami began here in 1911, connecting the Neuse River to the Newport River at Beaufort, through a swamp once called the Open Grounds.

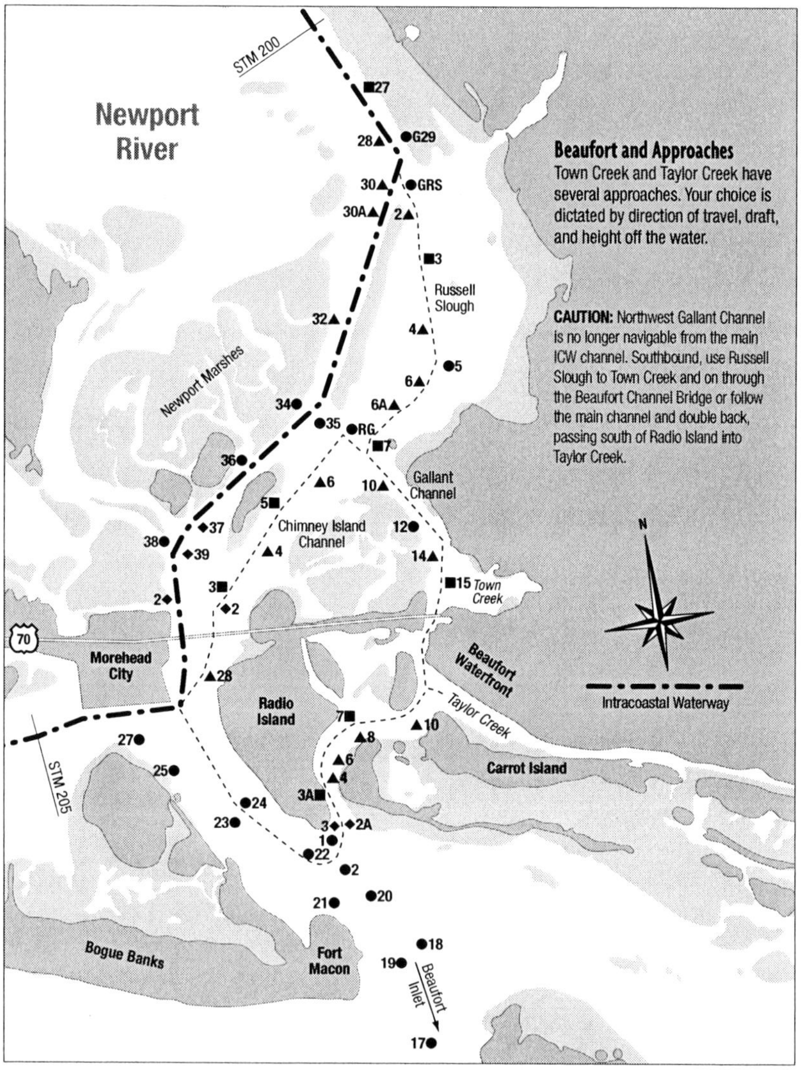

For illustration purposes only. Not to be used for navigation.

Beaufort and Approaches

SAFETY INFO

NOAA Weather
WX-3 Cape Hatteras, NC
WX-2 New Bern, NC
WX-1 Wilmington, NC

USCG
Station Fort Macon, NC
VHF 16 or 09/22A
252/247-4583

Sea Tow
Beaufort, NC
VHF 16/7 or 9 or 79
252/728-6551

TowBoatU.S.
Beaufort, NC
VHF 16
252/728-5088

HEADS UP!

65.0	Albermarle Sound Crossing (SB)
78.8	Dismal Swamp Canal (NB)
80.0	Albermarle Sound Crossing (NB)
84.2	Alligator River Bridge
157.0	Hobucken Coast Guard Station
185.5	No Lunar Tides (NB)
200.8	Beaufort Channel Bridge (2.7)
203.8	**Morehead City RR Bridge**
235.2	Camp Lejeune Firing Range (SB)
240.5	Camp Lejeune Firing Range (NB)
240.7	Onslow Beach Bridge
260.8	Surf City Bridge
278.1	Figure Eight Island Bridge
283.2	Wrightsville Beach Bridge
319.5	Lockwoods Folly Inlet Area (SB)
322.5	Lockwoods Folly Inlet Area (NB)
337.9	Sunset Beach Bridge
340.9	NC-SC Border

Don't fight it; when cruising, you become your boat. Most people will remember your boat's name, design, and hailing port...but not your name. It becomes, "Remember that couple from Minnesota with the kid on a PDQ catamaran we met in Marathon?" Print boat cards for your vessel. Laid out similar to business cards, include your boat name, design, and hail port; crew names; email; cell phone; and mailing address.

SEINING FOR MENHADEN

You don't need an alarm clock in Beaufort or Morehead City. The early morning purse-seiners, heading out to round up schools of menhaden, wake the lazy slumbering cruisers.

Beaufort is home to the only North Carolina menhaden fish factory still in operation. If you visit in June, Beaufort Fisheries opens to the public as part of the Beaufort Old Homes Tour.

Atlantic Menhaden (pronounced MEN-hay-den) is a 15-inch herring-like fish. It's abundant along the Atlantic and Gulf coasts, its catch exceeding the tonnage of all other species combined.

Large schools of menhaden are encircled with a net, drawn in like a purse to capture thousands of fish. The fish are pumped into large refrigerated holds for transfer to the processing plant, where they are ground to meal and the oil rendered.

Courtesy of NOAA

Photo by Bob Williams

Menhaden Boat

Although early colonists were hungry enough to eat menhaden, these small, oily, bony fish are now considered inedible to humans. Native Americans used menhaden for fertilizer—the Indian word for menhaden, "munnawhatteaug," means fertilizer—and it is believed the Native Americans showed early colonists how to improve their corn crops with menhaden.

Today menhaden are processed for the protein and oil. Each year Beaufort Fisheries produces 7,500 tons of menhaden meal and 400,000 gallons of menhaden oil. But all this fish processing comes at a cost: as Beaufort gentrifies, many residents complain about the stench of fish oil and offal.

Courtesy of Crystal Coast TDA

NC Maritime Museum

You probably don't realize it, but you almost certainly have menhaden products aboard your vessel. Do you have margarine, salad dressing, or sports drinks on board? What about pet food, lipstick, or vitamin supplements with Omega 3? Did you know menhaden oil is used in marine lubricants, paints, and caulking compound?

Beaufort Old Homes Tour
www.historicbeaufort.com
800/575-7483

BEAUFORT AND MOREHEAD CITY

Two cities on opposite sides of the Newport River, Beaufort and Morehead City have all the amenities for boaters.

Morehead City, along Route 70, has the larger grocery stores and shopping centers. But if you stay in Beaufort you can borrow a courtesy car—from the Beaufort Docks or the North Carolina Maritime Museum—for your Morehead City provisioning.

Beaufort (pronounced BO-fort) is known for its museums, history, and waterfront shops. The North Carolina Maritime Museum has displays of boat building and thousands of shells (with free admission). For charts or guides, visit Scuttlebutt Nautical Books and Bounty along the waterfront on Front Street.

Beaufort and Morehead City host several annual festivals. The Wooden Boat Show is held in Beaufort every May. Morehead City hosts the North Carolina Blackbeard Fest, also held in May. For fall transits, Morehead City's Seafood Festival is every October.

- **Taylor Creek Anchorages** (3.4)
  Anchor 8-14 feet N34.42.843
  STR 3.6 feet W076.39.845
  Anchorages are opposite and beyond Town Docks.
  SEE SHACKLEFORD HORSES.
- **Olde Towne Yacht Club** (4.1)
  VHF 16; 252/726-3066
  Yacht club is on eastern tip of Radio Island as you head seaward toward inlet.

To rejoin the ICW, proceed southerly beyond Pivers and Radio Islands and intercept the charted Morehead City Channel S of Radio Island. Proceed NW into turning basin to rejoin magenta line southbound.

202.2 Heads Up | Gallants Channel (Closed) S N
Southbound/Northbound Navigation
ICW R34 and G35 Pair
Caution: The charted northwest extension of Gallants Channel is closed due to shoaling. For Town Creek and Beaufort destinations, use Russell Slough, Chimney Island Channel, or the Beaufort main channel.

203.6 Morehead City Yacht Basin (0.6) S N
VHF 16/71 N34.43.368
252/726-6862 W076.42.273
Exit ICW N of twin bridges. Proceed W along channel. Marina is to port. [STR 3.7]

203.7 Junction | Chimney Island Channel S N
Northbound Navigation Only
Exit ICW N of twin bridges. Proceed NE in Chimney Island Channel to pick up Gallants Channel SE to Town Creek destinations.

203.8 Morehead City Bridge S N
(US 70)
Fixed; vertical 65 feet.

203.8 Morehead City RR Bridge S N
(Beaufort and Morehead Railroad Bridge)
Single-bascule; vertical 4 feet; usually open.

204.2 Junction | Beaufort or Beaufort Inlet S N
Southbound/Northbound Navigation
Exit ICW in charted turning basin. Proceed SSE along charted Morehead City Channel.
Caution: Transiting the Beaufort area may be confusing. See accompanying chartlet, "Beaufort and Approaches."

- **Beaufort** (2.5)
  Exit channel between R22 and R20. Pick up Beaufort Channel at R2 and proceed northerly.
  See description of Beaufort marinas and anchorages at STM 200.8.
- **Beaufort Inlet** (4.2)
  Well Aided N34.39.759
  Well Lit W076.40.371
  Continue southerly to inlet. Waypoint is between G9 and R10.
  Given the preponderance of Carolina capes, their attendant shoals, and subsequent long inlets, you usually save considerable distance by staying inside.

SAFETY INFO

NOAA Weather
WX-3 Cape Hatteras, NC
WX-2 New Bern, NC
WX-1 Wilmington, NC

Sea Tow
Beaufort, NC
VHF 16/7 or 9 or 79
252/728-6551

USCG
Station Fort Macon, NC
VHF 16 or 09/22A
252/247-4583

TowBoatU.S.
Beaufort, NC
VHF 16
252/728-5088

HEADS UP!

65.0	Albermarle Sound Crossing (SB)	240.5	Camp Lejeune Firing Range (NB)
78.8	Dismal Swamp Canal (NB)	240.7	Onslow Beach Bridge
80.0	Albermarle Sound Crossing (NB)	260.8	Surf City Bridge
84.2	Alligator River Bridge	278.1	Figure Eight Island Bridge
157.0	Hobucken Coast Guard Station	283.2	Wrightsville Beach Bridge
185.5	No Lunar Tides (NB)	319.5	Lockwoods Folly Inlet Area (SB)
200.8	Beaufort Channel Bridge (2.7)	322.5	Lockwoods Folly Inlet Area (NB)
203.8	Morehead City RR Bridge	337.9	Sunset Beach Bridge
235.2	Camp Lejeune Firing Range (SB)	340.9	NC-SC Border

Typically, "bumping out" is better left until Georgia and Florida. However, a common one-day jump is from Beaufort Inlet to Masonboro Inlet at Wrightsville Beach. This 72 STM (63 NM) leg is a straight run and for sailboaters, under the right wind conditions, a fine sail.

At Beaufort Inlet G9 and R10 pair, proceed WSW to Masonboro Inlet (sea buoy RW "A").

204.8 Morehead City
Exit ICW along seawall W of State Port Terminal. Proceed N to Morehead City channel. [STR 3.7 (TS)]
When approaching or leaving Morehead City, you may alternately join Morehead City channel at ICW R4 at STM 206.0.
SEE BEAUFORT AND MOREHEAD CITY.

- **Portside Marina** (0.4)
  VHF 16/10 N34.43.126
  252/726-7678 W076.42.312
  Marina is to N.
- **Dockside Yacht Club** (0.5)
  VHF 16; 252/247-4890
  Yacht club is to N.
- **Sanitary Fish Market & Restaurant** (0.6)
  VHF 16 N34.43.175
  252/247-3111 W076.42.707
  Facility is to N.
- **Morehead Gulf Docks** (0.7)
  VHF 16; 252/726-5461
  Fuel dock is to N.
- **Capt. Bill's Waterfront Restaurant** (0.8)
  No VHF Watch; 252/726-2166
  Restaurant is to N. May be able to stay overnight after dining. No power; no water. Gate is locked when restaurant closes.
- **Russell Yachts** (0.9)
  No VHF Watch; 252/240-2826
  Facility is to N. Repair yard with no transient dockage.

205.6 Atlantic Beach Marinas
Exit ICW at G3. Proceed SW to Fl (2+1) R bifurcated channel marker. [STR 4.3 (TS)]

- **Anchorage Marina** (1.1)
  VHF 16; 252/726-4423
  Proceed SW in charted Money Island Bay channel. Marina is at end of channel.
- **Fort Macon Marina** (1.1)
  VHF 16/09,68 N34.42.051
  252/726-2055 W076.43.815
  Marina is W of Anchorage Marina.
- **Atlantic Beach Causeway Marina** (1.5)
  VHF 16; 252/726-6977
  At bifurcated channel marker, bear westerly, then southerly, along bridge. Marina is at end of channel. Limited draft; call ahead.

206.7 Atlantic Beach Bridge
(Route 1182)
Fixed; vertical 65 feet.

209.2 Peletier Creek
Exit ICW at G7. Proceed N into Peletier Creek. ENE spur leads to first three facilities.

Because of treacherous and shifting waters, Beaufort and Morehead City are popular destinations for diving sunken wrecks. If you are dive certified, several local dive shops offer outings. If breathing compressed air is not your thing, you can visit the Fort Macon State Park, on the barrier island across from Beaufort and Morehead City, to walk, swim, or join a tour of the fort.

North Carolina Maritime Museum
www.ah.dcr.state.nc.us
252/728-7317

Scuttlebutt Nautical Books and Bounty
252/728-7765

Wooden Boat Show
http://ncmm-friends.org/
252/728-7317

North Carolina Blackbeard Fest
252/808-0440

Morehead City Seafood Festival
252/726-6273

Fort Macon State Park
www.ils.unc.edu/parkproject
252/726-3775

Save your back! Buy a Pack-N-Roll, available at Boaters' World and other stores, which folds open to carry a milk-crate full of heavy items. Use the Pack-N-Roll for cans and liquids and save the boat bag for light items such as paper goods, produce, and bread.

THE EDGE OF THE SEA

Rachel Carson wrote her first book, *The Edge of the Sea*, about the estuaries surrounding Beaufort. Portions of the islands across from Beaufort along Taylor Creek are named in her honor. You can dinghy along Taylor Creek and stop at the Rachel Carson Reserve to walk or swim or join a guided tour.

Rachel Carson was a nature writer, aiming her pen at pesticides in the late 1950s. During a time when post-war sentiment cheered "better living through chemistry," Carson nailed DDT like a contemporary investigative reporter. She fought her own illnesses—including arthritis, ulcers, and breast cancer—but finished her landmark book *Silent Spring* in 1962.

The book was controversial, to say the least. When the editors at Reader's Digest saw the book they cancelled her contract to run a condensed version.

But forty years later, Carson is remembered as "the mother of the environmental movement." DDT was linked to the near-extinction of several species, including the symbol of America, the Bald Eagle.

So when you see a Bald Eagle along the Waterway, remember Rachel Carson's last efforts. And thanks to her, you should see one of these majestic birds. No longer an endangered species, our national symbol is now a symbol of the recovery of a species.

Rachel Carson Reserve
252/728-2170

SHACKLEFORD HORSES

Across from the Beaufort waterfront, feral horses graze on saltmarsh cordgrass. You can see the horses from the anchorage, as you dinghy along Taylor Creek, or from a walk on the Rachel Carson Reserve. Although they are technically wild, you can often get very close in your dinghy. But watch or photograph them from a distance. You're too close if you interrupt their feeding and they stop grazing.

Some people call them wild ponies, but these Shackleford horses are neither ponies nor a toy breed. Stories about their origins are mixed. They may be descendants of diminutive horses brought by early explorers, possibly as early as the conquistadors. But whether their descendants were left behind from an abandoned colony or survivors of a shipwreck is unknown.

semi-local publications LLC

Photo by Author **Shackleford Horses**

Small horses travelled as cargo on early sailing ships and were used to explore marshy coastal areas. At one time these "marsh tackies" were abundant along the coastal islands, as far south as Florida's Tolomato River. But as development encroached in the 1940s, North Carolina's remaining wild horses were placed on Shackleford Banks to roam wild and graze on marsh grass.

SAFETY INFO

NOAA Weather	Sea Tow
WX-3 Cape Hatteras, NC	Beaufort, NC
WX-2 New Bern, NC	VHF 16/7 or 9 or 79
WX-1 Wilmington, NC	252/728-6551
USCG	**TowBoatU.S.**
Station Fort Macon, NC	Beaufort, NC
VHF 16 or 09/22A	VHF 16
252/247-45837	252/728-5088

HEADS UP!

65.0	Albermarle Sound Crossing (SB)	240.5	Camp Lejeune Firing Range (NB)
78.8	Dismal Swamp Canal (NB)	240.7	Onslow Beach Bridge
80.0	Albermarle Sound Crossing (NB)	260.8	Surf City Bridge
84.2	Alligator River Bridge	278.1	Figure Eight Island Bridge
157.0	Hobucken Coast Guard Station	283.2	Wrightsville Beach Bridge
185.5	No Lunar Tides (NB)	319.5	Lockwoods Folly Inlet Area (SB)
200.8	Beaufort Channel Bridge (2.7)	322.5	Lockwoods Folly Inlet Area (NB)
203.8	Morehead City RR Bridge	337.9	Sunset Beach Bridge
235.2	Camp Lejeune Firing Range (SB)	340.9	NC-SC Border

QUEEN ANNE'S REVENGE

In 1718, Blackbeard, one of the world's most notorious pirates, lost his flagship, *Queen Anne's Revenge*, in Beaufort Inlet. Soon afterward, his luck worsened. He was captured a few months later and decapitated, his head hung from the victorious ship. But Queen Anne's Revenge was never found.

Until a few years ago. Nearly 300 years after the wreck, a private shipwreck exploration firm based in Beaufort discovered a wreck presumed to be Blackbeard's flagship. The company's insight was using historical accounts to recreate the likely location of the inlet's *early-eighteenth century* entrance channel and bars. After nearly a decade of searching, they located the wreck partially submerged on a sandy bottom in only 20 feet of water.

For several months, the exploration team and the North Carolina Department of Cultural Resources secretly worked to verify the vessel's identity. All evidence points to this truly being Blackbeard's ship. As the divers continue to excavate and clean the items, the definitive evidence will be an article with the insignia "La Concorde," the original name of the captured ship.

Courtesy of National Park Service

Cape Lookout Light

Archaeological work began in 1997, but it will take 15 years to excavate, clean, and catalog the items. Until then, the entire area is a security zone, monitored by an underwater electronic surveillance system to ward off looters.

Queen Anne's Revenge
www.qaronline.org

WILL YOU SWALLOW ANYTHING?

Gulls are everywhere along the Waterway. They have learned boats mean food, whether it's offal from fishing or chicken from a stern grill.

We've found out firsthand that a gull cannot be intimidated when it comes to food. In a tug-of-war battle over a chicken breast, Mark had the spatula advantage but the gull had the advantage of flight. Mark gripped the chicken breast with tongs while the gull pulled on the chicken with its beak, flapping backward with its strong wings. Mark took advantage of a defensive opening, swatting the bird with the spatula, but the bird was persistent. In the end it was a draw. The grilled meat dropped into the water, Neptune's treat.

Courtesy of NOAA

Laughing Gull

Gulls may be the aggressive pigeons of the sea, but they have a rich etymological history. In ancient Breton along the French coast, the word for gull, *goelaff*, means to weep. We interpret the gull's plaintiff cry differently today, calling our most common gull along the Waterway, "Laughing Gull."

The English word for gull comes from the medieval Cornish word *gullan*, meaning throat. Our words gullet and gullible evolved from the root word gull. So today, a person is gullible if he'll swallow anything—just like the omnivorous gull.

Mark your anchor rode using plastic wire ties. They are easily seen, easily felt at night in the dark, and tough enough to run through a windlass. Loop the tie through a chain link or line ply then snip the tail short. Develop a color/number scheme to signal how much you have payed out, such as one green is 20 feet, two greens are 40 feet...one yellow is 120 feet, two yellows are 140 feet...one red is 220 feet, etc.

CORMORANT

Cormorants give many people the creeps. For centuries, these dark oily birds lurking under the water have symbolized evil and the underworld.

Anchorage and Coral Bay Marina are beyond this turnoff. [STR 1.6]

Caution: Creek entrance may have only 4 feet during low tide. Creek has 6-8 feet inside.

- **Taylor Boat Works** (0.4)
  VHF 16; 252/726-6374
  Marina is to starboard. Repair yard with no transient dockage.
- **Harbor Master** (0.5)
  VHF 16; 252/726-2541
  Facility is to starboard.
- **70 West Marina** (0.6)
  VHF 16; 252/726-5171
  Marina is closed. Transient wet slips are closed due to condo and dockominium development. Dry store only.
- **Peletier Creek Anchorage** (0.4)
  Anchor 6-8 feet N34.43.687
  STR 1.6 feet W076.46.876
  Anchorage is at fork.
- **Coral Bay Marina** (0.7)
  VHF 16; 252/247-4231
  Marina is to port. Dry store with no transient dockage.

210.5 Spooners Creek S N
Exit ICW at G9. Proceed N into Spooners Creek. [STR 1.4 (TS)]

Caution: Creek entrance may have only 4 feet during low tide. Creek has 6-8 feet inside.

- **Spooners Creek Yacht Harbor** (0.4)
  VHF 16; 252/726-2060
  Marina is to port.
- **Spooners Creek Anchorage** (0.5)
  Anchor 5-7 feet N34.43.811
  STR (TS) 1.4 feet W076.48.436
  Anchorage is beyond marina.

224.9 Island Harbor Marina (0.4) S N
VHF 16; 252/354-3106
Exit ICW at R42. Proceed S between spoil islands to marina. [STR 2.5]
Limited draft; call ahead.

225.9 Emerald Isle Bridge S N
Fixed; vertical 65 feet.

226.0 Heads Up | Camp Lejeune S N
Southbound Navigation Only
Because the Camp Lejeune firing range starts at STM 235.2, this is a good place to check on the base's schedule.
Listen on VHF 16, AM 530, or hail Swansboro Coast Guard. Control boats monitor VHF 16/82.

227.8 Flying Bridge Restaurant (0.1) S N
VHF 16; 252/393-2416
Exit ICW W of G45 "A". Proceed N into charted basin. [STR 2.6]
Dock and dine with some transient space. Limited draft; call ahead.

228.5 Dudley's Marina (0.1) S N
VHF 16; 252/393-2204

SAFETY INFO		
	NOAA Weather	**Sea Tow**
	WX-3 Cape Hatteras, NC	Beaufort, NC
	WX-2 New Bern, NC	VHF 16/7 or 9 or 79
	WX-1 Wilmington, NC	252/728-6551
	USCG	**TowBoatU.S.**
	Station Emerald Isle, NC	Swansboro, NC
	VHF 16 or 09/22A	VHF 16
	910/354-2719	910/326-1861

HEADS UP!

80.0	Albermarle Sound Crossing (NB)	260.8	Surf City Bridge
84.2	Alligator River Bridge	278.1	Figure Eight Island Bridge
157.0	Hobucken Coast Guard Station	283.2	Wrightsville Beach Bridge
185.5	No Lunar Tides (NB)	319.5	Lockwoods Folly Inlet Area (SB)
200.8	Beaufort Channel Bridge (2.7)	322.5	Lockwoods Folly Inlet Area (NB)
203.8	Morehead City RR Bridge	337.9	Sunset Beach Bridge
235.2	**Camp Lejeune Firing Range (SB)**	340.9	NC-SC Border
240.5	**Camp Lejeune Firing Range (NB)**	347.0	Numerous Rock Ledges (SB)
240.7	**Onslow Beach Bridge**	347.3	Little River Bridge

Exit ICW at R46 "A". Proceed ENE to marina. [STR 2.5]

229.1 Swansboro Anchorage (0.3) S N
Anchor 6-10 feet N34.41.156
STR 2.5 feet W077.07.060
Exit ICW NW of G47. Proceed ENE into White Oak River. Anchor between R4 and fixed bridge.

229.2 Casper's Marina (0.1) S N
VHF 16/09 N34.41.117
910/326-4462 W077.07.300
Exit ICW at R46 "C". Marina is ahead. [STR 2.5]
SEE SWANSBORO.

233.4 Tiara Basin Anchorage (0.2) S N
Anchor 7-9 feet N34.38.797
STR 2.1 feet W077.10.804
Exit ICW ENE of G55. Proceed NNW into charted channel and basin.
Basin houses Tiara Boats, who discourages anchoring. Best to arrive late and leave early.

235.2 Camp Lejeune Firing Range Safety Zone S N
to Southbound/Northbound Navigation
240.5 ICW may be closed.
If training exercises are underway, patrol boats block the ICW.
Listen on VHF 16, AM 530, or hail Swansboro Coast Guard. Control boats monitor VHF 16/82.
SEE CAMP LEJEUNE.

240.7 Onslow Beach Bridge S N
VHF 13; 910/450-7376
Single-pivot swing; vertical 12 feet.
Restricted year round: 0700-1900 hrs, opens on the hour and half-hour.

244.5 Mile Hammock Bay Anchorage (0.3) S N
Anchor 8-12 feet N34.33.083
STR 3.5 feet W077.19.494
Exit ICW between R66 and G67. Proceed NE into Mile Hammock Bay.
SEE CAMP LEJEUNE.

246.6 Swan Point Marina (0.1) S N
VHF 16; 910/327-1081
Exit ICW between R2 and R4. Marina is to W. [STR 3.5]

246.7 New River Marina (0.1) S N
VHF 16; 910/327-2106
Exit ICW between R2 and R4. Marina is to W. [STR 3.5]

252.2 Heads Up | Camp Lejeune S N
Northbound Navigation Only
Because the Camp Lejeune firing range starts at STM 240.5, this is a good place to check on the base's schedule.
Listen on VHF 16, AM 530, or hail Swansboro Coast Guard. Control boats monitor VHF 16/82.

252.3 North Topsail Beach Bridge S N
(Route 210)
Fixed; vertical 65 feet.

In China, cormorants are valuable to fishermen. With a ring around each bird's neck and a long thin line for a leash, fishermen release cormorants into the water to capture fish. The cormorants catch the fish in their mouths but the collar ring prevents them from swallowing the fish. The birds are pulled in with the string, unloaded of their catch, and released back to the sea for another mouthful of fish. A very effective fishing lure, but probably not sanctioned by animal rights groups.

Courtesy of Smithsonian Marine Station
Photo by Marcia Geyer
Cormorant Drying Out

In the U.S., the Double-crested Cormorant, which is common along the Waterway, is protected under the 1972 Migratory Bird Treaty Act. Its population plummeted during the use of the pesticide DDT but has since rebounded to historic highs. Now cormorants have the opposite problem: they are so common the U.S. Fish and Wildlife Service recently proposed allowing states to "control cormorants by lethal means." As the cormorant population rises, there is concern about the impact on populations of freshwater game fish, one of the food sources of this skilled underwater hunter.

Although they look oily, cormorants do not have oil on their feathers. Unlike ducks, which any hunter knows are extremely oily, cormorants' feathers become drenched with water. So cormorants are commonly seen perched in the sun, wings in a spread-eagle pose, drip-drying their feathers.

LAUGHING GULLS

In the winter, the Laughing Gull is one more drab, grayish gull, distinguished only by a gray splotch behind its eye. But as spring approaches, it transforms to clean white plumage with a jet-black hood and bright red bill. During breeding season, they perch on pilings and advertise their status by displaying their blood red mouth lining and belting out their nasal high-pitched laugh: ha-ha-ha-haah-haah-haah-haah.

We call them Laughing Gulls from their call, but the Spaniards noticed another gull habit. In Spanish, they are called *guanaguanare*, from the Incan word *huana* for dung.

SWANSBORO

Since the days of an Algonquin Indian settlement, the location where White Oak River meets Bogue Inlet has been coveted. It eventually became the town of Swannsborough—named after the former speaker of the North Carolina House of Commons, Samuel Swann—and developed a thriving shipbuilding and commercial fishing industry.

But this narrow stretch of Waterway, behind the barrier islands between Beaufort and Wrightsville Beach, was one of North Carolina's last completed sections of the Waterway. Completed in 1932 at a cost of $13 million, or $175 million in today's dollars, this important segment allowed boats to avoid the numerous shifting shoals of local inlets.

Courtesy of USCG
Photo by Zachary A. Crawford
Training at Camp Lejeune

Today Swansboro is a quaint waterfront town, a fishing village supported in part by the nearby Marine Corps base. The town has several small shops and popular local restaurants. To find anything you want or need, visit the town's website which has a very organized pull-down menu listing all business information by category.

Swansboro Info
www.tourswansboro.com

SAFETY INFO

NOAA Weather
WX-2 New Bern, NC
WX-1 Wilmington, NC
WX-2 Myrtle Beach, SC

USCG
Station Wrightsville Beach
VHF 16 or 09/22A
910/256-2615

Sea Tow
Wrightsville Beach, NC
VHF 16/71 or 79
910/452-3798

TowBoatU.S.
Wrightsville Beach, NC
VHF 16/11
910/367-0868

HEADS UP!

185.5 No Lunar Tides (NB)
200.8 Beaufort Channel Bridge (2.7)
203.8 Morehead City RR Bridge
235.2 Camp Lejeune Firing Range (SB)
240.5 Camp Lejeune Firing Range (NB)
240.7 Onslow Beach Bridge
260.8 Surf City Bridge
278.1 Figure Eight Island Bridge
283.2 Wrightsville Beach Bridge
319.5 Lockwoods Folly Inlet Area (SB)
322.5 Lockwoods Folly Inlet Area (NB)
337.9 Sunset Beach Bridge
340.9 NC-SC Border
347.0 Numerous Rock Ledges (SB)
347.3 Little River Bridge
349.0 The Rock Pile (SB)
352.2 The Rock Pile (NB)
353.4 Barefoot Landing Bridge

CAMP LEJEUNE

Officially known as Marine Corps Base Camp Lejeune, this 246-square-mile base is home to 50,000 marines and navy personnel. An additional 100,000 military family members and retirees live in the surrounding area.

The Waterway transits through a ten-mile stretch of the base, including a four-mile firing range. You can see the watchtower at the northern entrance to the firing range. Further inland are man-made hills, such as Poggemeyer's Peak, where instructors watch as marine units practice with automatic weapons, grenade launchers, and .50-caliber machine guns. The base has 54 live-fire ranges, 89 maneuver areas, and 25 tactical landing zones.

Courtesy of MCB Camp Lejeune

Mile Hammock Bay (circa 1940)

Mile Hammock Bay is located at STM 244.5. Today you can anchor in this small man-made harbor, but cannot go ashore. During World War II marines practiced amphibious landings in this protected bay. Because of the offshore threat of German U-boats, marines could not practice their operations off Onslow Beach. So a full-scale mock-up of a troop transport ship was built on the inland side of the Waterway—a $175,000 military set for trainees to practice climbing up and down the netting with a full pack and rifle.

Camp Lejeune is still an active training base, training about 40,000 marines per year. It's hard to fathom the scope of Camp Lejeune and its program, but just think about how much those hungry trainees eat at the end of a day running through the North Carolina woods. Each day, Camp Lejeune's mess hall serves up a staggering 858 gallons of milk and 1,577 dozen eggs.

TOPSAILS

Topsail Beach, Topsail Island, Topsail Creek, Topsail Inlet. The area south of Bogue Inlet is riddled with small tricky inlets between barrier islands—very popular with pirates in the days when ships flew topsails.

Locals may have watched the seaward horizon for pirates' sails approaching over the low barrier islands. One account describes ships approaching the inlets, looking over the barrier islands for the topsails of hidden pirate ships. If pirates' topsails were spotted they would quickly move along the coast to a safer inlet.

Either way, topsails clearly served as early warning systems in the days of sailing ships.

VERRAZZANO'S ARRIVAL

Searching for a new shorter route to Cathay, Giovanni de Verrazzano's course was interrupted by an unknown body of land. When Verrazzano and his crew landed along these narrow barrier islands in 1524, they documented the earliest known descriptions of the shores of the New World and its native inhabitants. Verrazzano's journals describe a people who

> *"go altogether naked except only that they cover their privy parts with certain skins of beasts like unto martens, which they fasten onto a narrow girdle made of grass, very artfully wrought, hanged about with tails of divers and other beasts, which round about their bodies hang dangling down to their knees. Some of them wear garlands of birds' feathers."*

Verrazzano continued north along the coast, mistakenly believing he had reached the Pacific Ocean when he arrived at Pamlico Sound. This misinterpretation implied that North America was a long and very narrow isthmus. It would take more than a century for this skewed depiction to disappear from many maps.

Fortunately for Verrazzano, he made a better call when he discovered New York Bay. He was the first European to arrive at the narrow bay entrance between what is now Staten Island and Brooklyn. Today a bridge at that bay is named in his honor: the Verrazzano-Narrows Bridge.

260.7 Beach House Marina (0.3)
VHF 16; 910/328-2628
Exit ICW NE of bridge. Proceed S to Surf City channel. Marina is charted behind small island. [STR 3.2]

260.8 Surf City Bridge
(Routes 50/120)
VHF 13; 910/328-4291
Single-pivot swing; vertical 12 feet.
Restricted year round: 0700-1900 hrs, opens on the hour.

263.7 Topsail Sound Anchorage (0.1)
Anchor 7-9 feet N34.24.539
STR 3.2 feet W077.35.699
Exit ICW at R86. Proceed S just off ICW and under small spoil island.
SEE TOPSAILS.

264.2 Anchors Away Boatyard (0.1)
VHF 16; 910/270-4741
Exit ICW ENE of R90. Marina is to NNW. Repair yard with no transient dockage. [STR 3.3]
Formerly Marker 90 Boatyard.

266.5 Harbour Village Marina (0.1)
VHF 16; 910/270-4017
Exit ICW at R94. Marina is to NW. [STR 3.3]

278.1 Figure Eight Island Bridge
VHF 13; 910/686-2018
Single-pivot swing; vertical 20 feet.
Restricted year round: opens on the hour and half-hour.

279.0 Waterway Marine Service (0.3)
No VHF Watch; 910/686-0284
Exit ICW at charted Pages Creek. Proceed N into shallow creek. Facility is to port. Repair yard with no transient dockage. [STR 4.1]

279.8 Coastal Carolina Yacht Yard (0.3)
No VHF Watch N34.15.493
910/686-0004 W077.46.763
Exit ICW NE of R122 where chart indicates Piles PA. Proceed NW into charted basin. Facility is to NW. [STR 4.2]

279.8 Oak Winds Marina (0.3)
VHF 16/09 N34.15.417
910/509-1942 W077.46.633
Exit ICW NE of R122 where chart indicates Piles PA. Proceed NW into charted basin. Marina is to N. [STR 4.2]

283.2 Wrightsville Beach Bridge
(Route 74)
VHF 13; 910/256-2886
Double bascule; vertical 20 feet.
Restricted year round: 0700-1900 hrs, opens on the hour.
SEE WRIGHTSVILLE BEACH.

283.3 Wrightsville Beach Marina (0.1)
VHF 16; 910/256-6666
Marina is to SE. [STR 4.5]

SAFETY INFO

NOAA Weather
WX-2 New Bern, NC
WX-1 Wilmington, NC
WX-2 Myrtle Beach, SC

USCG
Station Wrightsville Beach
VHF 16 or 09/22A
910/256-2615

Sea Tow
Wrightsville Beach, NC
VHF 16/71 or 79
910/452-3798

TowBoatU.S.
Wrightsville Beach, NC
VHF 16/11
910/367-0868

HEADS UP!

200.8	Beaufort Channel Bridge (2.7)
203.8	Morehead City RR Bridge
235.2	Camp Lejeune Firing Range (SB)
240.5	Camp Lejeune Firing Range (NB)
240.7	Onslow Beach Bridge
260.8	Surf City Bridge
278.1	Figure Eight Island Bridge
283.2	Wrightsville Beach Bridge
319.5	Lockwoods Folly Inlet Area (SB)
322.5	Lockwoods Folly Inlet Area (NB)
337.9	Sunset Beach Bridge
340.9	NC-SC Border
347.0	Numerous Rock Ledges (SB)
347.3	Little River Bridge
349.0	The Rock Pile (SB)
352.2	The Rock Pile (NB)
353.4	Barefoot Landing Bridge
365.4	Seaboard Coast Line RR Bridge

283.3 Bridge Tender Marina (0.1)
VHF 16; 910/256-6550
Marina is to NW. [STR 4.5]

283.4 Dockside Marina (0.1)
VHF 16/09,10 N34.12.923
910/256-3579 W077.48.941
Marina is to NW. [STR 4.5]

283.4 Motts Channel
Exit ICW at G25. Proceed SE into marked channel leading to Wrightsville Beach and Masonboro Inlet. [STR 4.5]

- **Atlantic Marine** (0.3)
  VHF 16; 910/256-9911
  Facility is to NE. Dry store with no transient dockage.
- **Seapath Yacht Club** (0.5)
  VHF 16; 910/256-3747
  Marina is to NE.
- **Motts Channel Anchorage** (1.6)
  Anchor 8-12 feet N34.12.453
  STR 4.5 feet W077.47.913
  Leave Motts Channel SE of R14. Proceed NE toward fixed bridge.
  Public dinghy dock at SE corner of bridge. Dinghies cannot be left overnight.
- **Masonboro Inlet** (4.2)
  Follow charted Banks Channel along Wrightsville Beach shore.
  See inlet comments at STM 285.1.

285.1 Junction | Masonboro Inlet (2.2)
Moderately Aided N34.10.296
Poorly Lit W077.47.872
Exit ICW at G129. Proceed SE through Shinn Creek to Masonboro Inlet.
Waypoint is at RW "A" sea buoy. The inlet is short but well breakwatered. [STR 4.5 (TS)]
Given the preponderance of Carolina capes, their attendant shoals, and subsequent long inlets, you usually save considerable distance by staying inside.
Typically, "bumping out" is better left until Georgia and Florida. However, a common one-day jump is from Beaufort Inlet to Masonboro Inlet at Wrightsville Beach. This 72 STM (63 NM) leg is a straight run and for sailboaters, under the right wind conditions, a fine sail.
At Masonboro Inlet sea buoy RW "A", proceed ENE to Beaufort Inlet (G9 and R10 pair).

286.9 Masonboro Sound Anchorage (0.3)
Anchor 6-10 feet N34.10.300
STR 4.5 feet W077.50.303
Exit ICW SW of R130. Proceed E into charted tongue.

288.1 Masonboro Boat Yard & Marina (0.2)
VHF 16/09 N34.09.471
910/791-1893 W077.51.391
Exit ICW SW of G135. Proceed NW into Whiskey Creek in privately maintained channel. Marina is to port. [STR 4.5]

Courtesy of NOAA

Photo by Bob Williams

Purse Seining

WRIGHTSVILLE BEACH

Until World War I, Wrightsville Beach was a summer retreat, accessible only by boat or train. Today, Wrightsville Beach is a small island community linked to the mainland by the Wrightsville Beach Bridge. There are plenty of services at this stop: restaurants, marine supplies, bookstores, groceries, and a shopping mall with a West Marine about a half-mile west of the bridge.

Besides the sand and sun, Wrightsville Beach draws visitors to the Airlie Gardens, located at STM 283.3 just south of the bridge on the mainland side before Bradley Creek. These gardens were once part of a 155-acre estate (with a 2,200 acre hunting preserve) owned by a New York and Newport society family who lived it up Gatsby-style. The gardens were reputed to have had a half-million azalea bushes and exotic plants from all over the world. Today the Gardens are open to the public. You can take a self-guided tour through the grounds, featuring the 450-year-old Airlie Oak, or visit for an outdoor folk or jazz concert.

Airlie Gardens
www.airliegardens.org
910/793-7531

Stop trying to lasso that piling! To place and retrieve lines on pilings—without entertaining the whole marina—buy a Shurhold 3-in-1 Boat Hook, available at West Marine and other stores. To make it really easy, mount the 3-in-1 on a telescoping pole.

MONEY ISLAND AND BURIED TREASURE

Money Island and Money Point, reputedly Captain Kidd's hidey-holes in the late 1600s, are located just south of Bradley Creek. These small inlets, isolated islands, and winding creeks were perfect hiding places for pirates. Legend has it pirates hid their loot on these islands until the early 1700s.

But Money Island has never lived up to its name. Many people remain convinced treasure is buried on the island, but still no chests of gold have been found. Instead, other treasures were uncovered as the Waterway was excavated. A dredge found a large cask of wine, buried for decades in the sandy muck. And local archaeologists struck another type of gold when a dredge, operating just south of Wrightsville Beach, unearthed a complete set of mastodon bones.

After grocery shopping, discard cardboard egg cartons at the dock and place the eggs in plastic egg suitcases, those reusable egg containers sold in camping stores. You can also re-use a foam egg carton. They protect your eggs and let you keep paperboard waste off the boat, which becomes even more important as you approach the humid south.

THE CARNIVORES OF CAROLINA BEACH

Snows Cut, at STM 297, passes through the Carolina Beach State Park. The park, with riverbank fishing and six miles of easy walking trails, is accessible to boaters both by marina or boat ramp.

You may notice the Flytrap Trail, a half-mile loop beginning near the marina. Carolina Beach is famous for its unusual plants—plants that eat meat!

Venus Flytraps, Sundews, Bladderwort, Pitcher Plants, and Butterwort all thrive in this boggy, acidic, mineral-poor soil.

Carnivorous plants can survive in this poor soil because they've evolved a different way to obtain nutrients. In fact, you won't find carnivorous plants in nutrient-rich soil. If the soil has plenty of nutrients, catching insects is terribly inefficient and a waste of precious resources. Non-carnivorous plants quickly overgrow and out-compete carnivorous plants, forcing them out of that habitat.

The Venus Flytrap grows abundantly here, native to an area within 75 miles of Wilmington. Look for the Venus Flytrap producing traps anytime be-

SAFETY INFO

NOAA Weather
WX-2 New Bern, NC
WX-1 Wilmington, NC
WX-2 Myrtle Beach, SC

USCG
Station Oak Island, SC
VHF 16 or 09/22A
910/278-1133

Sea Tow
Wrightsville Beach, NC
VHF 16/71 or 79
910/452-3798

TowBoatU.S.
Southport, NC
VHF 16/11
910/457-7141

HEADS UP!

200.8	Beaufort Channel Bridge (2.7)
203.8	Morehead City RR Bridge
235.2	Camp Lejeune Firing Range (SB)
240.5	Camp Lejeune Firing Range (NB)
240.7	Onslow Beach Bridge
260.8	Surf City Bridge
278.1	Figure Eight Island Bridge
283.2	Wrightsville Beach Bridge
319.5	Lockwoods Folly Inlet Area (SB)
322.5	Lockwoods Folly Inlet Area (NB)
337.9	Sunset Beach Bridge
340.9	NC-SC Border
347.0	Numerous Rock Ledges (SB)
347.3	Little River Bridge
349.0	The Rock Pile (SB)
352.2	The Rock Pile (NB)
353.4	Barefoot Landing Bridge
365.4	Seaboard Coast Line RR Bridge

Courtesy of Crystal Coast TDA

Kayaking Cape Lookout

tween spring and the first frost. The traps are modified leaves, shaped like a clamshell with livid colors inside that lure small insects. When an insect touches the fine trigger hairs on the trap, the trap slowly closes and entraps the prey. The plant then secretes digestive fluids to break down the insect and absorb its nutrients. About three to five days later the trap re-opens. But catching insects is hard work for a plant: each trap can only open and close three times before dying.

Carolina Beach State Park
www.ils.unc.edu/parkproject
910/458-8206

LONGLEAF PINE

The Longleaf Pine, named for its 10- to 16-inch graceful arching needles, is the granddaddy of southern pines. At the time of Spain's arrival, the Southeast was one of the largest pure-type forests in the world: a 1500-mile belt of Longleaf Pine forest covering the coastal plains from Virginia to Texas.

The Longleaf Pine is the state tree of North Carolina and the pride of the South. Although the broad expanses of grand trees are gone, the Longleaf Pine forest remains a crucial habitat throughout the Southeast. Like the Spotted Owl in the Pacific Northwest, the endangered Red-cockaded Woodpecker needs mature stands of Longleaf Pine in order to nest.

In a marriage of wildlife conservation and military training, Camp Lejeune has set aside its large stand of mature Longleaf Pine forest for wildlife. Firing practices and training exercises are scheduled around the animals' breeding areas.

The animals, at least the woodpeckers, don't seem to mind the distant sound of gunfire. Camp Lejeune's Longleaf Pine forest now supports one of the most robust populations of the endangered Red-cockaded Woodpecker. Both trainees and woodpeckers share the woods, staking out their turf with their own rat-a-tat-tat noises.

Who hails the medic *for you*? You may be confident operating the VHF but a guest may not. Purchase and post clear direction placards, available pre-printed at marine stores, by your radio for emergencies.

FORT FISHER

With remote and treacherous shores, Cape Fear Inlet was the perfect setting for blockade running. During the Civil War, ships quietly steamed into the mouth of the river, hoping to reach the protection of Forts Fisher or Caswell. But if a ship was cornered, the crew was instructed to ground and set fire to the boat.

During the last days of the Civil War, Fort Fisher guarded the only remaining port open to the Confederates. But the fort was eventually captured, with hundreds of additional casualties when munitions accidentally exploded. For decades afterward, skeletons of Confederate and Federal troops were exposed as the ocean washed away the earthworks under the fort.

Today Fort Fisher, Fort Anderson, and Fort Caswell are in ruins, but the visitor center at Fort Fisher documents their history. A visit to the fort is free and a quarter-mile trail surrounds its remains. The NC Underwater Archaeology Center, with exhibits on artifacts uncovered in underwater explorations, and the NC Aquarium, are also located at Fort Fisher. A ferry departs from Southport for $2 roundtrip.

Fort Fisher
www.ils.unc.edu/parkproject
910/458-5798

293.8 Inlet Watch Yacht Club (0.1)
VHF 16/09 — N34.04.702
910/799-5756 — W077.53.196
Exit ICW between G155 and G155 "A". Proceed WNW into privately maintained channel. Marina is to port. [STR 4.7]

295.1 Oceana Marina (0.1)
VHF 16; 910/458-5053
Exit ICW at G161. Marina is to SE. [STR 4.7]

295.2 Carolina Beach Anchorage (0.5)
Anchor 12-14 feet — N34.03.102
STR 4.7 feet — W077.53.358
Exit ICW at G161 for Carolina Beach channel. Proceed southerly to G5. Anchor between G5 and charted island.

295.2 Snows Cut
to Southbound Navigation Only
296.8 1.6-mile land cut.
No anchorages, no marinas, no fuel.
Caution: Both ends of Snows Cut can be confusing. Southbound, be sure to pick out the range early and head southerly, down Cape Fear River, rather than northerly toward Wilmington.

295.7 Carolina Beach Bridge
(Snows Cut Bridge)(US 421)
Fixed; vertical 65 feet.

296.8 Snows Cut
to Northbound Navigation Only
295.2 1.6-mile land cut.
No anchorages, no marinas, no fuel.
Caution: Both ends of Snows Cut can be confusing. Northbound, be sure to turn northerly, rather than turn S into Carolina Beach channel.

296.9 Range "A"
to Southbound/Northbound Navigation
297.3 Snows Cut Entrance
0.4-mile range.
Southbound, pick up this range immediately upon exiting Snows Cut.

297.0 Carolina Beach State Park Marina
VHF 16/09 — N34.03.005
910/458-7770 — W077.55.157
Exit ICW in Range "A", near G165. Proceed E into charted basin. [STR 4.4]
SEE THE CARNIVORES OF CAROLINA BEACH.

297.3 Range "B"
to Southbound/Northbound Navigation
298.7 Snows Cut Entrance
1.4-mile range.
Northbound, exit Cape Fear River at G33, heading northeasterly to leave G177 to starboard.
Caution: When the current is running, it is extremely easy to be swept off course before you pick up the range.

299.0 Cape Fear River Advisory
to Southbound Navigation Only
308.5 Buoyage reverses.
Look for yellow reflective ICW triangles and

SAFETY INFO

NOAA Weather
WX-2 New Bern, NC
WX-1 Wilmington, NC
WX-2 Myrtle Beach, SC

USCG
Station Oak Island, SC
VHF 16 or 09/22A
910/278-1133

Sea Tow
Ocean Isle, NC
VHF 16/79
910/575-7839

TowBoatU.S.
Southport, NC
VHF 16/11
910/457-7141

HEADS UP!

203.8	Morehead City RR Bridge
235.2	Camp Lejeune Firing Range (SB)
240.5	Camp Lejeune Firing Range (NB)
240.7	Onslow Beach Bridge
260.8	Surf City Bridge
278.1	Figure Eight Island Bridge
283.2	Wrightsville Beach Bridge
319.5	Lockwoods Folly Inlet Area (SB)
322.5	Lockwoods Folly Inlet Area (NB)
337.9	Sunset Beach Bridge
340.9	NC-SC Border
347.0	Numerous Rock Ledges (SB)
347.3	Little River Bridge
349.0	The Rock Pile (SB)
352.2	The Rock Pile (NB)
353.4	Barefoot Landing Bridge
365.4	Seaboard Coast Line RR Bridge
366.0	Numerous Rock Ledges (NB)

squares on aids.

Cape Fear River is appropriately named: winds always seem to be blowing at the mouth, the current runs to 6 knots, and there is ship traffic day and night.

We typically time our transit to take advantage of the current but have learned not to be greedy. If you maximize the current's lift, you will also be getting on and off the river with maximum cross current.

And if the wind opposes the current, river conditions here can be treacherous.

Lastly, if you find yourself bucking the current, move out of the main ship channel into shallower water to minimize the adverse effect.

See The Fear in Cape Fear.

308.5 Junction | Cape Fear River Entrance

Exit ICW abeam Battery Island. Proceed southerly along main ship channel for Bald Head Island and Cape Fear River Entrance. [STR 4.7]

- **Bald Head Island Marina** (2.8)
  VHF 16/11 or 09 N33.52.617
  910/457-7380 W078.00.017
  Exit main ship channel at G13 "A". Proceed SE to charted keyhole basin.
  See Bald Head Lighthouse.
- **Cape Fear River Entrance** (5.8)
  Well Aided N33.50.379
  Well Lit W078.01.764
  Continue southerly along main ship channel. Waypoint is at R8.
  We only use this inlet when departing for or arriving from southern destinations. Frying Pan Shoals, which extends over 30 miles seaward, makes northbound departures or southbound arrivals impractical.

308.5 Cape Fear River Advisory
to Northbound Navigation Only
299.0 Buoyage reverses.

Look for yellow reflective ICW triangles and squares on aids.

See comments at STM 299.0.

309.0 Southport Harbor

Exit ICW between G1 and R2 "A", to easternmost charted basin. Proceed N into Southport Harbor. [STR 4.6 (TS)]

See Stuart House & Southport.

- **Town Marina Free Docks** (0.1)
  Designated T-head is to port.
  24-hour limit; 4-5 feet at low tide; room for 1 boat.
- **Provision Company Free Docks** (0.1)
  Restaurant is to NE.
  Free overnight stay with meal purchase. Room for 2-3 boats.
- **Southport Anchorage** (0.2)
  Anchor 7-8 feet N33.55.037
  STR (TS) 4.6 feet W078.01.472
  Proceed to center of basin. Room for 1 or 2 boats only.

NC Underwater Archaeology Center
910/452-9042

North Carolina Aquarium
www.ncaquariums.com
910/458-8257

STUART HOUSE

Stuart House, once located on the waterfront next to the Quarantine Station on Bay Street, was the center of the Southport community. In the late 1800s this inn and popular gathering place served up 50¢ meals of fresh fish, clams, crab, shrimp, and oysters. All the lawyers and judges coming down the river to the county seat stopped at Stuart House on their way through.

New Hanover County Public Library

Stuart House

Stuart House was also famous for its proprietor, Kate Stuart, known to locals as "Miss Kate." In 1879, the captain of a Clyde Lines steamer left his young daughter at Stuart House while he made one of his voyages. When the Captain's ship returned, the girl was so excited she ran right off the end of the dock into the strong tidal current of the Cape Fear River. Kate Stuart, dressed in long skirts and petticoats, jumped into the water and saved the child.

Thereafter, for as long as Miss Kate lived, the Clyde Lines steamers blew their whistles three times in salute as they passed her home. She responded by waving a white handkerchief, or at night, lighting a lantern. When she was too old to acknowledge the whistles, her servants came out to wave.

Miss Kate passed away in 1929 at the age of 84. Hurricane Hazel irreparably damaged Stuart House in the 1950s and it had to be torn down. Over the years the story passed on incorrectly in most Waterway histories, stemming from a mistake in an out-of-town newspaper report about ships lowering flags in her honor. But locals, such as Southport historian and long-time resident Susan Carson, still remember hearing the sound of the three toots as the ships passed by, knowing the salute was in gratitude to Miss Kate.

SOUTHPORT

You can learn more about the history of Southport at the North Carolina Maritime Museum's Southport Branch. Or visit Orton Plantation Gardens, just north of Southport on Orton Point. If you have a sense of déjà vu at Orton Gardens, don't worry. You probably have seen the plantation house before: over forty movies have been shot on location here, including *The Divine Secrets of the Ya-Ya Sisterhood* (2002).

Southport is also the ferry hub to Fort Fisher and Bald Head Island. The state ferry crosses to Fort Fisher for a $2 round-trip fare. The Bald Head Island Ferry is pricier ($15 round-trip), but provides access to the Bald Head Lighthouse, the beaches, and the Bald Head Island Club golf course.

NC Maritime Museum, Southport Branch
www.ah.dcr.state.nc.us/sections/maritime
910/457-0003

Orton Plantation Gardens
www.ortongardens.com
910/371-6851

Fort Fisher State Ferry
800/368-8969

Bald Head Island Ferry
910/457-5003

Bald Head Island Club
910/457-7310

WHITE IBIS

As you transit the Cape Fear area, look for striking White Ibises with their black-tipped wings and downward curving scarlet red bills. Over 9,000 pairs nest on tiny Battery Island, a 100-acre island off Bald Head Island. Five to ten percent of the entire North American population of White Ibis crowd onto this island, safe from raccoons that cannot cross the strong currents of the Cape Fear River.

Cape Fear also provides the ibis parents with a kids menu. Young ibis are like children: picky eaters who need bland food. The adults prefer a salty menu of local crabs, but the little tykes can't take the sodium. Fortunately, young ibis love crayfish, which are abundant in the area's swamps. The bland and easy crayfish are the ibis

SAFETY INFO

NOAA Weather	**Sea Tow**
WX-2 New Bern, NC	Ocean Isle, NC
WX-1 Wilmington, NC	VHF 16/79
WX-2 Myrtle Beach, SC	910/575-7839
USCG	**TowBoatU.S.**
Station Oak Island, SC	Southport, NC
VHF 16 or 09/22A	VHF 16/11
910/278-1133	910/457-7141

HEADS UP!

203.8	Morehead City RR Bridge	337.9	Sunset Beach Bridge
235.2	Camp Lejeune Firing Range (SB)	340.9	NC-SC Border
240.5	Camp Lejeune Firing Range (NB)	347.0	Numerous Rock Ledges (SB)
240.7	Onslow Beach Bridge	347.3	Little River Bridge
260.8	Surf City Bridge	349.0	The Rock Pile (SB)
278.1	Figure Eight Island Bridge	352.2	The Rock Pile (NB)
283.2	Wrightsville Beach Bridge	353.4	Barefoot Landing Bridge
319.5	**Lockwoods Folly Inlet Area (SB)**	365.4	Seaboard Coast Line RR Bridge
322.5	**Lockwoods Folly Inlet Area (NB)**	366.0	Numerous Rock Ledges (NB)

equivalent of serving up a quick kids dinner of mac 'n' cheese.

One of the easiest ways to live off the land is crabbing. All you need is a piece of string, chicken necks, and a net. Tie the chicken neck onto the string and lower the bait to the seabed. When you feel a crab nibbling, slowly pull up the string. About a foot from the surface, the dining crab will realize what is happening and drop off. Be ready with your net underwater and catch it as it lets go.

THE FEAR IN CAPE FEAR

Cape Fear doesn't have a very inviting name. And it shouldn't. This region has seen a lot of fear over the centuries, from the terror of pirates to the scuttles of blockade running. And some of the most treacherous shoals along the Atlantic are located at Frying Pan Shoals, extending thirty miles out to sea. The Atlantic Ocean rolls in to Cape Fear with full force, earning the North Carolina coast the nickname "Graveyard of the Atlantic."

BALD HEAD LIGHTHOUSE

Bald Head Light is abandoned now, but it was once an important lighthouse for this treacherous region. The station, established in 1796, became North Carolina's first lighthouse. But the light was extinguished during the blockade running of the Civil War and not re-lit until 1880.

Seamen nicknamed the lighthouse "Old Baldy" after the lighthouse survived hurricane after hurricane. In the 1980s the Old Baldy Foundation restored the structure and it is now listed on the National Register of Historic Places.

Although you won't directly pass the lighthouse on the Intracoastal Waterway, a two-mile detour off the magenta line will put you there. Bypass the Waterway's cut into Southport and continue a short distance out Cape Fear River Entrance. You can see the lighthouse on the south end of Smith Island. The octagonal brick lighthouse rises 90 feet overlooking Cape Fear River and the Atlantic.

LOCKWOODS FOLLY

Lockwoods Folly is a small inlet, not recommended for non-local boats and, in fact, not recommended for Mr. Lockwood himself.

Lockwood unintentionally put himself on the map when he erringly built a wooden boat, intending to launch it through the local inlet. But the boat's draft was too deep, forcing Lockwood to abandon his brand-new vessel, high and dry, in the too-shallow inlet.

The inlet recently shoaled again, a victim of dredging budget cuts. This highly visible incident received enough attention to garner special government assistance. Without similar funding, the Waterway will once again become inaccessible to deep draft vessels.

semi-local publications LLC

Photo by Paul Pregent

Living Off the Land

To support the Waterway, join the Atlantic Intracoastal Waterway Association for a $35 fee. This advocacy group provides online and email ICW updates and lobbies to maintain the inlets and channels of the Waterway.

AIWA
www.atlintracoastal.org

CALABASH COOKING

Calabash-style seafood is a popular menu item in southern North Carolina. Exit Little River at STM 341.8, and wander up the Calabash River to the town of Calabash, a small town famous for its seafood.

In the 1800s the area was called Pea Landing, since peanuts were grown around Calabash and shipped by way

309.3 Southport Marina (0.1)
VHF 16/09 N33.55.034
910/457-5261 W078.01.701
Exit ICW E of R2 "A". Proceed N into marina basin. [STR 4.6]

310.1 Indigo Plantation & Marina (0.1)
VHF 16; 910/457-7380
Exit ICW between G3 and G5. Marina is to N. [STR 4.6]

310.2 Dutchman Creek Anchorage (0.2)
Anchor 4-7 feet N33.55.252
STR 4.6 feet W078.02.691
Exit ICW at G5. Proceed N into creek.

311.1 South Harbour Village Marina (0.1)
VHF 16 N33.55.279
910/454-7486 W078.03.718
Exit ICW E of G9. Marina is to N. [STR 4.6]

311.8 Yaupon Beach Bridge
(Route 133)
Fixed; vertical 65 feet.

314.8 St. James Plantation (0.1)
VHF 16; 910/253-0463
Exit ICW W of R16. Marina is to N. [STR 4.6]

319.5 Heads Up | Lockwoods Folly Inlet Area
to Southbound Navigation Only
322.5 This area is consistently a problem for transiting cruisers due to frequent dredging and new marker placement. Be extremely vigilant.
Caution: Expect uncharted "drop aids" and/or aid renumbering.
SEE LOCKWOODS FOLLY.

320.2 Blue Water Point Marina (0.5)
VHF 16; 910/278-1230
Exit ICW at R36. Proceed S to marina. [STR 4.8]

322.5 Heads Up | Lockwoods Folly Inlet Area
to Northbound Navigation Only
319.5 See Lockwoods Folly Inlet comments at STM 319.5.

323.0 Holden Beach Marina (0.1)
VHF 16; 910/842-5447
Marina is to N. [STR 4.8]

323.5 Holden Beach Bridge
(Route 130)
Fixed; vertical 65 feet.

329.7 Hughes Marina (0.2)
No VHF Watch; No Telephone
Exit ICW E of G77. Proceed N into Shallotte River. Marina is to port. [STR 5.4 (TS)]
Tie up and walk to house to pay for dockage.

333.7 Ocean Isle Bridge
(Route 904)
Fixed; vertical 65 feet.

335.6 Pelican Pointe Marina (0.1)
VHF 16/10 N33.53.416
910/579-6440 W078.28.322
Exit ICW between R98 and G99. Marina is to N. [STR 5.1]

SAFETY INFO

NOAA Weather	Sea Tow
WX-1 Wilmington, NC	Ocean Isle, NC
WX-2 Myrtle Beach, SC	VHF 16/79
WX-1 Charleston, SC	910/575-7839
USCG	**TowBoatU.S.**
Station Oak Island, SC	Little River, SC
VHF 16 or 09/22A	VHF 16/14 or 11
910/278-1133	843/249-0244

HEADS UP!

240.5	Camp Lejeune Firing Range (NB)	347.0	Numerous Rock Ledges (SB)
240.7	Onslow Beach Bridge	347.3	Little River Bridge
260.8	Surf City Bridge	349.0	The Rock Pile (SB)
278.1	Figure Eight Island Bridge	352.2	The Rock Pile (NB)
283.2	Wrightsville Beach Bridge	353.4	Barefoot Landing Bridge
319.5	Lockwoods Folly Inlet Area (SB)	365.4	Seaboard Coast Line RR Bridge
322.5	Lockwoods Folly Inlet Area (NB)	366.0	Numerous Rock Ledges (NB)
337.9	**Sunset Beach Bridge**	371.0	Socastee Bridge
340.9	**NC-SC Border**	406.0	Winyah Bay Entrance (SB)

337.9 Sunset Beach Bridge S N

VHF 13; 910/579-6473

Pontoon; vertical 0 feet.

Restricted April 1-November 30: 0700-1900 hrs, opens on the hour.

Restricted June 1- September 30: SA-SU and holidays, 0700-2100 hrs, opens on the hour.

Caution: Do not proceed until cable is completely lowered underwater. Bridge may not open in extremely low tide.

340.9 NC-SC Border S N

Little River Inlet (ENE of R116)

of Little River to Wilmington. Calabash became its own village in 1883, but only incorporated as a town in 1973.

By the 1930s Calabash was a busy fishing village. As the story goes, locals gathered at the docks as the workboats returned. They cooked up big pots of seafood for the hungry crew, serving the meal under the trees at the waterfront. Over time, this small-town tradition of frying up large portions of batter-dipped fish and shrimp transformed into open-air dockside restaurants. By the 1940s, Calabash became known for its lightly battered, deep-fried fresh seafood.

You can't fix it if you can't see it! Every boat tool kit should include a 12-volt trouble light for working in dark engine or bilge areas. Available at home centers or auto supply stores, it's simply a bulb in a protective plastic cage, with a hook to hang in whatever cramped area you need light.

THE LION (SPRING)

If your birthday is between July 23 and August 22, you can see your zodiac sign in the night sky. Look southwest of the sky's zenith, just below the Big Dipper, for the constellation Leo, or the Lion.

Find the Lion by spotting Regulus, the bluish-white, first-magnitude star southwest of the Big Dipper. You can pinpoint Regulus precisely by using the two stars of the Dipper's bowl next to the handle and drawing a straight line past the paw of Great Bear. This imaginary line will first pass through a bright star of the Lion's shoulder, then to the bright star Regulus at the Lion's rearward front foot. Look for the bright star Denebola forming the Lion's tail.

The Lion is part of the Zodiac, a belt of twelve constellations circling the sky. The word Zodiac in Greek means "animal circle," referring to a time more than 4000 years ago when all constellations of the Zodiac were animals.

Some Zodiac constellations, such as the Virgin or Water Carrier, are no longer interpreted as animals. But the twelve constellations and their symbols are still associated with twelve divisions of the year. ▲

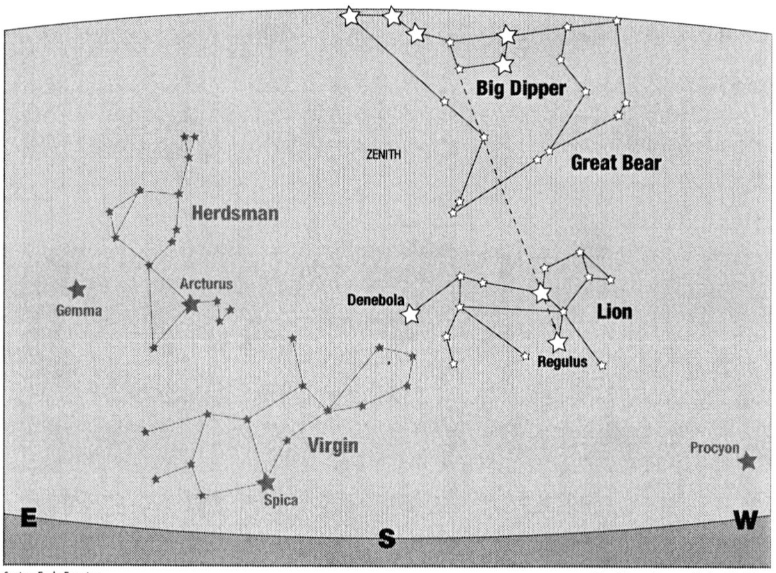

Spring, Early Evening

The Lion, Part of the Zodiac

North Carolina Waterway Business Cards

Midway Marina & Motel
STM 49.3

www.midwaymarina.com

157 Coinjock Dev. Road
Coinjock, NC 27923

252/453-3625
252/453-4842

VHF 16/09

Depth	12	**Laundry**	On-Site
Diesel/Gas	D/G	**Pool**	Yes
Pumpout	Yes	**Internet/WiFi**	I/W
Mail/Fax	M/F	**Car/Bike**	No
Service	On-Call	**Groceries**	On-Site
Parts	On-Call	**Restaurant**	On-Site
Haulout	No	**Post Office**	Walk
Propane	Taxi	**Library**	Taxi

Dowry Creek Marina
STM 131.7

www.dowrycreekmarina.com

110 Spinnaker Run Road
Belhaven, NC 27813

800/824-7035
252/943-2898

VHF 16/71

Depth	8	**Laundry**	On-Site
Diesel/Gas	D/G	**Pool**	Yes
Pumpout	Yes	**Internet/WiFi**	I
Mail/Fax	M/F	**Car/Bike**	C
Service	On-Call	**Groceries**	Taxi
Parts	On-Call	**Restaurant**	Taxi
Haulout	No	**Post Office**	Taxi
Propane	Taxi	**Library**	Taxi

Belhaven Waterway Marina
STM 135.9

www.belhavenmarina.com

332 East Water Street
Belhaven, NC 27810

252/944-0066
252/944-0069

VHF 16/09

Depth	7	**Laundry**	On-Site
Diesel/Gas	No	**Pool**	Spa
Pumpout	Yes	**Internet/WiFi**	I
Mail/Fax	M/F	**Car/Bike**	B
Service	On-Site	**Groceries**	Taxi
Parts	On-Site	**Restaurant**	Walk
Haulout	35T/75T	**Post Office**	Walk
Propane	Walk	**Library**	Walk

Deaton Yacht Service (Repair)
STM 180.8

www.deatonyacht.com

1306 Neuse Drive
Oriental, NC 28571

252/249-1180
252/249-0664

VHF 16/10

Depth	6	**Laundry**	Taxi
Diesel/Gas	No	**Pool**	No
Pumpout	Yes	**Internet/WiFi**	No
Mail/Fax	F	**Car/Bike**	No
Service	On-Site	**Groceries**	Walk
Parts	On-Site	**Restaurant**	Walk
Haulout	25T	**Post Office**	Walk
Propane	Taxi	**Library**	Taxi

Oriental Harbor Marina
STM 180.8

www.orientalharbor.com

P.O. Box 217
Oriental, NC 28571

252/249-3783
252/249-3770

VHF 16/78

Depth	8	**Laundry**	On-Site
Diesel/Gas	No	**Pool**	Yes
Pumpout	Yes	**Internet/WiFi**	I/W
Mail/Fax	M/F	**Car/Bike**	C/B
Service	On-Call	**Groceries**	Walk
Parts	On-Call	**Restaurant**	Walk
Haulout	No	**Post Office**	Walk
Propane	Walk	**Library**	N/A

Oriental Marina & Inn
STM 180.8

www.orientalmarina.com

103 Wall Street
Oriental, NC 28571

252/249-1818
252/249-0529

VHF 16/71

Depth	6	**Laundry**	On-Site
Diesel/Gas	D/G	**Pool**	Yes
Pumpout	No	**Internet/WiFi**	I/W
Mail/Fax	M/F	**Car/Bike**	B
Service	On-Call	**Groceries**	Walk
Parts	On-Call	**Restaurant**	Walk
Haulout	No	**Post Office**	Walk
Propane	Taxi	**Library**	N/A

Sea Gate Marina
STM 194.2

729 Sea Gate Drive
Newport, NC 28570

252/728-4126
252/728-6694

VHF 16/09

Depth	6	**Laundry**	On-Site
Diesel/Gas	D/G	**Pool**	No
Pumpout	No	**Internet/WiFi**	No
Mail/Fax	F	**Car/Bike**	No
Service	On-Call	**Groceries**	Taxi
Parts	On-Call	**Restaurant**	Taxi
Haulout	No	**Post Office**	Taxi
Propane	Taxi	**Library**	Taxi

Town Creek Marina
STM 200.8

www.towncreekmarina.com

232 West Beaufort Road
Beaufort, NC 28516

252/728-6111
252/728-4053

VHF 16/08

Depth	12	**Laundry**	On-Site
Diesel/Gas	D/G	**Pool**	No
Pumpout	Yes	**Internet/WiFi**	I/W
Mail/Fax	M/F	**Car/Bike**	C
Service	On-Site	**Groceries**	Walk
Parts	On-Site	**Restaurant**	On-Site
Haulout	50T	**Post Office**	Walk
Propane	Taxi	**Library**	Walk

Photocopy the "business card" of any Waterway facility. Then cut out the copy and take it ashore for easy reference!

Discovery Diving (Diving)

STM 200.8

www.discoverydiving.com

414 Orange Street
Beaufort, NC 28516

252/728-2265
252/728-2581

VHF 10/10

Depth	5	**Laundry**	Walk
Diesel/Gas	No	**Pool**	No
Pumpout	No	**Internet/WiFi**	No
Mail/Fax	M/F	**Car/Bike**	No
Service	On-Call	**Groceries**	Taxi
Parts	On-Call	**Restaurant**	Walk
Haulout	No	**Post Office**	Walk
Propane	Taxi	**Library**	Walk

Morehead City Yacht Basin

STM 203.6

www.moreheadcityyachtbasin.com

208 Arendell Street
Morehead City, NC 28557

252/726-6862
252/726-1939

VHF 16/71

Depth	10	**Laundry**	On-Site
Diesel/Gas	D/G	**Pool**	No
Pumpout	Yes	**Internet/WiFi**	I/W
Mail/Fax	M/F	**Car/Bike**	C
Service	On-Call	**Groceries**	Walk
Parts	On-Call	**Restaurant**	Walk
Haulout	No	**Post Office**	Walk
Propane	Taxi	**Library**	Walk

Portside Marina

STM 204.8

www.portsidemarina.com

209 Arendell Street
Morehead City, NC 28557

252/726-7678
252/726-6923

VHF 16/10

Depth	12	**Laundry**	On-Site
Diesel/Gas	D/G	**Pool**	No
Pumpout	No	**Internet/WiFi**	No
Mail/Fax	M/F	**Car/Bike**	No
Service	On-Site	**Groceries**	Walk
Parts	On-Site	**Restaurant**	Walk
Haulout	No	**Post Office**	Walk
Propane	Taxi	**Library**	Walk

Sanitary Fish Market (Restaurant)

STM 204.8

www.sanitaryfishmarket.com

501 Evans Street
Morehead City, NC 28557

252/247-3111
252/247-5110

VHF 16/68

Depth	15	**Laundry**	Taxi
Diesel/Gas	No	**Pool**	No
Pumpout	No	**Internet/WiFi**	No
Mail/Fax	No	**Car/Bike**	No
Service	No	**Groceries**	Walk
Parts	No	**Restaurant**	On-Site
Haulout	No	**Post Office**	Walk
Propane	Taxi/Taxi	**Library**	Walk

Fort Macon Marina

STM 205.6

www.visitnc.com

417 E. Fort Macon Road
Atlantic Beach, NC 28512

252/726-2055
252/726-5299

VHF 16/09 or 68

Depth	4	**Laundry**	No
Diesel/Gas	G	**Pool**	No
Pumpout	No	**Internet/WiFi**	No
Mail/Fax	F	**Car/Bike**	No
Service	On-Site	**Groceries**	Taxi
Parts	On-Site	**Restaurant**	Walk
Haulout	No	**Post Office**	Taxi
Propane	N/A	**Library**	Taxi

Casper's Marina

STM 229.2

www.caspersmarina.com

301 Water Street
Swansboro, NC 28584

910/326-4462
910/326-4628

VHF 16/09

Depth	10	**Laundry**	Walk
Diesel/Gas	D/G	**Pool**	No
Pumpout	Yes	**Internet/WiFi**	I
Mail/Fax	M/F	**Car/Bike**	B
Service	On-Call	**Groceries**	Walk
Parts	On-Call	**Restaurant**	Walk
Haulout	No	**Post Office**	Walk
Propane	Walk	**Library**	Taxi

Coastal Carolina Yacht Yard (Repair)

STM 279.8

www.coastalcarolinayachtyard.com

2107 Middle Sd. Loop Rd.
Wilmington, NC 28411

910/686-0004
910/686-0008

No VHF Watch

Depth	4	**Laundry**	No
Diesel/Gas	No	**Pool**	No
Pumpout	No	**Internet/WiFi**	No
Mail/Fax	M/F	**Car/Bike**	No
Service	On-Site	**Groceries**	Taxi
Parts	On-Site	**Restaurant**	Taxi
Haulout	25T	**Post Office**	Taxi
Propane	N/A	**Library**	Taxi

Oak Winds Marina

STM 279.8

2127 Middle Sd. Loop Rd.
Wilmington, NC 28411

910/509-1942
910/686-6006

VHF 16/09

Depth	5	**Laundry**	On-Site
Diesel/Gas	No	**Pool**	No
Pumpout	Yes	**Internet/WiFi**	No
Mail/Fax	M/F	**Car/Bike**	No
Service	On-Call	**Groceries**	Walk
Parts	On-Call	**Restaurant**	Walk
Haulout	No	**Post Office**	Taxi
Propane	Taxi	**Library**	Taxi

Dockside Marina

STM 283.4

www.docksidewb.com

1306 Airlie Road
Wilmington, NC 28403

910/256-3579 (phone)
910/256-0012 (fax)

VHF 16/09 or 10

Depth	15	**Laundry**	Walk
Diesel/Gas	D/G	**Pool**	No
Pumpout	No	**Internet/WiFi**	I
Mail/Fax	M	**Car/Bike**	No
Service	On-Call	**Groceries**	Walk
Parts	On-Call	**Restaurant**	On-Site
Haulout	No	**Post Office**	Walk
Propane	Walk	**Library**	Walk

Masonboro Boat Yard

STM 288.1

www.masonboro.com

609 Trails End Road
Wilmington, NC 28409

910/791-1893 (phone)
910/791-9777 (fax)

VHF 16/09

Depth	7	**Laundry**	On-Site
Diesel/Gas	No	**Pool**	No
Pumpout	No	**Internet/WiFi**	I
Mail/Fax	M/F	**Car/Bike**	C
Service	On-Site	**Groceries**	Taxi
Parts	On-Site	**Restaurant**	Walk
Haulout	19T	**Post Office**	Taxi
Propane	Taxi	**Library**	Taxi

Inlet Watch Yacht Club

STM 293.8

www.inletwatch.com

801 Paoli Court
Wilmington, NC 28409

910/392-7106 (phone)
910/392-7564 (fax)

VHF 16/09

Depth	6	**Laundry**	Taxi
Diesel/Gas	D/G	**Pool**	Yes
Pumpout	No	**Internet/WiFi**	No
Mail/Fax	F	**Car/Bike**	No
Service	On-Site	**Groceries**	Walk
Parts	On-Site	**Restaurant**	Taxi
Haulout	30T	**Post Office**	Walk
Propane	Taxi	**Library**	Taxi

Carolina Beach State Park

STM 297.0

www.ncsparks.net

P.O. Box 475
Carolina Beach, NC 28428

910/458-7770 (phone)
910/458-6350 (fax)

VHF 16/09

Depth	4	**Laundry**	On-Site
Diesel/Gas	D/G	**Pool**	No
Pumpout	Yes	**Internet/WiFi**	No
Mail/Fax	No	**Car/Bike**	No
Service	On-Call	**Groceries**	Walk
Parts	On-Call	**Restaurant**	Walk
Haulout	No	**Post Office**	Walk
Propane	Taxi	**Library**	Taxi

Bald Head Island Marina

STM 308.5

www.baldheadisland.com

5411 Overbrook Road
Bald Head Island, NC 28461

910/457-7380 (phone)
910/457-7403 (fax)

VHF 16/11 or 09

Depth	8	**Laundry**	On-Site
Diesel/Gas	D/G	**Pool**	No
Pumpout	Yes	**Internet/WiFi**	I/W
Mail/Fax	M/F	**Car/Bike**	No
Service	On-Call	**Groceries**	Walk
Parts	On-Call	**Restaurant**	On-Site
Haulout	No	**Post Office**	Walk
Propane	N/A	**Library**	Taxi

Southport Marina

STM 309.3

www.visitnc.com

606 W. West Street
Southport, NC 28461

910/457-5261 (phone)
910/457-0050 (fax)

VHF 16/09

Depth	5	**Laundry**	On-Site
Diesel/Gas	D/G	**Pool**	No
Pumpout	Yes	**Internet/WiFi**	I
Mail/Fax	M/F	**Car/Bike**	No
Service	On-Site	**Groceries**	Taxi
Parts	On-Site	**Restaurant**	On-Site
Haulout	70T	**Post Office**	Walk
Propane	Taxi	**Library**	Walk

South Harbour Village Marina

STM 311.1

www.southharbourvillage.com

4909 Fish Factory Road
Southport, NC 28461

910/454-7486 (phone)
910/457-6930 (fax)

VHF 16/68

Depth	10	**Laundry**	On-Site
Diesel/Gas	D/G	**Pool**	No
Pumpout	Yes	**Internet/WiFi**	I
Mail/Fax	M/F	**Car/Bike**	No
Service	On-Call	**Groceries**	Walk
Parts	On-Call	**Restaurant**	On-Site
Haulout	No	**Post Office**	Taxi
Propane	Taxi	**Library**	Taxi

Pelican Pointe Marina

STM 335.6

2000 Sommersett Road
Ocean Isle Beach, NC 28469

910/579-6440 (phone)
910/579-8535 (fax)

VHF 16/10

Depth	6	**Laundry**	Taxi
Diesel/Gas	D/G	**Pool**	No
Pumpout	No	**Internet/WiFi**	I
Mail/Fax	M/F	**Car/Bike**	C
Service	On-Site	**Groceries**	Walk
Parts	On-Site	**Restaurant**	Walk
Haulout	10T	**Post Office**	Walk
Propane	Walk	**Library**	Taxi

North Carolina Waterway Marine Facilities

This table summarizes all known Waterway Marine Facilities, their location along the ICW, and their telephone number. Each is listed as either offering transient (T) dockage or not—and whether they have a fuel dock with diesel (D), gas (G), or neither.

49.3	**Midway Marina & Motel**	252/453-3625	T	D/G
49.4	Coinjock Marina	252/453-3271	T	D/G
49.5	Harrison's Marina	Closed	No	No
84.1	Alligator River Marina	252/796-0333	T	D/G
131.7	**Dowry Creek Marina**	800/824-7035	T	D/G
135.9	River Forest Marina	252/943-2151	T	D/G
135.9	Captain Robbs' Yard & Marina	Closed	No	No
135.9	**Belhaven Waterway Marina**	252/944-0066	T	No
157.3	R.E. Mayo Company	252/745-5331	T	No
161.3	Hurricane Harbour Marina	252/745-3369	T	No
180.8	Whittaker Creek Yacht Harbor	252/249-0666	T	D/G
180.8	Sailcraft Service	252/249-0522	No	No
180.8	**Deaton Yacht Service**	252/249-1180	No	No
180.8	**Oriental Harbor Marina**	252/249-3783	T	No
180.8	**Oriental Marina & Inn**	252/249-1818	T	D/G
194.2	**Sea Gate Marina**	252/728-4126	T	D/G
196.0	Bock Marine	252/728-6855	No	No
197.3	Jarrett Bay Boatworks	252/728-2690	No	No
200.8	**Town Creek Marina**	252/728-6111	T	D/G
200.8	**Discovery Diving**	252/728-2265	No	No
200.8	Beaufort Inn	252/728-2600	No	No
200.8	Spouter Inn	252/728-5190	No	No
200.8	Beaufort Gulf Docks	252/728-6000	No	D/G
200.8	Beaufort Town Docks	252/728-2503	T	D/G
200.8	Olde Towne Yacht Club	252/726-3066	T	D/G
203.6	**Morehead City Yacht Basin**	252/726-6862	T	D/G
204.8	**Portside Marina**	252/726-7678	T	D/G
204.8	Dockside Yacht Club	252/247-4890	T	No
204.8	**Sanitary Fish Market**	252/247-3111	T	No
204.8	Morehead Gulf Docks	252/726-5461	T	D/G
204.8	Capt. Bill's Waterfront Restaurant	252/726-2166	No	No
204.8	Russell Yachts	252/240-2826	T	No
205.6	Anchorage Marina	252/726-4423	T	D/G
205.6	**Fort Macon Marina**	252/726-2055	T	G
205.6	Atlantic Beach Causeway Marina	252/726-6977	T	D/G
209.2	Taylor Boat Works	252/726-6374	No	No
209.2	Harbor Master	252/726-2541	T	No
209.2	70 West Marina	252/726-5171	No	No
209.2	Coral Bay Marina	252/247-4231	No	D/G
210.5	Spooner's Creek Yacht Harbor	252/726-2060	T	D/G
224.9	Island Harbor Marina	252/354-3106	T	D/G
227.8	Flying Bridge	252/393-2416	T	No
228.5	Dudley's Marina	252/393-2204	T	D/G
229.2	**Casper's Marina**	910/326-4462	T	D/G
246.6	Swan Point Marina	910/327-1081	T	D/G
246.7	New River Marina	910/327-2106	T	D/G
260.7	Beach House Marina	910/328-2628	T	D/G
264.2	Anchors Away Boatyard	910/270-4741	No	No
266.5	Harbour Village Marina	910/270-4017	T	D/G
279.0	Waterway Marine Service	910/686-0284	No	No
279.8	**Coastal Carolina Yacht Yard**	910/686-0004	No	No
279.8	**Oak Winds Marina**	910/509-1942	T	No
283.3	Wrightsville Beach Marina	910/256-6666	T	D/G
283.3	Bridge Tender Marina	910/256-6550	T	D/G
283.4	**Dockside Marina**	910/256-3579	T	D/G
283.4	Atlantic Marine	910/256-9911	No	G
283.4	Seapath Yacht Club	910/256-3747	T	D/G
288.1	**Masonboro Boat Yard & Marina**	910/791-1893	T	No
293.8	**Inlet Watch Yacht Club**	910/392-7106	T	D/G
295.1	Oceana Marina	910/458-5053	T	D/G
297.0	**Carolina Beach State Park Marina**	910/458-7770	T	D/G
308.5	**Bald Head Island Marina**	910/457-7380	T	D/G
309.3	**Southport Marina**	910/457-5261	T	D/G
310.1	Indigo Plantation & Marina	910/457-7380	T	No
311.1	**South Harbour Village Marina**	910/454-7486	T	D/G
314.9	St. James Plantation	910/253-0463	T	D/G
320.2	Blue Water Point Marina	910/278-1230	T	D/G
323.0	Holden Beach Marina	910/842-5447	T	D/G
329.7	Hughes Marina	No Telephone	T	No
335.6	**Pelican Pointe Marina**	910/579-6440	T	D/G
341.8	Marsh Harbour Marina	Closed	No	No

Boldface type indicates the facility completed a survey and is highlighted in a Waterway Business Card. Each facility received multiple fax, email, and telephone requests. A final telephone call was made to verify the accuracy of transient, fuel, and contact information.

North Carolina Waterway Chandleries

This table lists marine equipment suppliers within easy reach of the ICW, their telephone number and address, and their location relative to ICW marinas and anchorages.

Riddick & Windley Hardware	252/943-2205	235 Pamlico Street, Belhaven, NC 27810	0.4 miles from Belhaven Waterway Marina
Inland Waterway Treasure Co.	252/249-1797	305 Hodges Street, Oriental, NC 28571	0.1 miles from Oriental Marina & Inn
West Marine Express	252/249-3200	1104 Broad Street Exit, Oriental, NC 28571	1.0 miles from Oriental Harbor Marina
Beaufort Ace Home Center	252/728-3111	1511 Live Oak Street, Beaufort, NC 28516	1.1 miles from Town Creek Marina
Scuttlebutt Nautical Books	252/728-7765	433 Front Street, Beaufort, NC 28516	0.1 miles from Beaufort Town Docks
Barbour's Marine Supply	800/682-2643	410 Hedrick Street, Beaufort, NC 28516	0.7 miles from Beaufort Town Docks
Ace Hardware & Marine	252/726-6620	600 Arendell Street, Morehead City, NC 28557	0.5 miles from Morehead City Yacht Basin
Williams True Value Hardware	252/726-7158	3011 Bridges Street, Morehead City, NC 28557	2.2 miles from 70 West Marina
Jones Brothers Marine	252/726-8404	5136 Highway 70, Morehead City, NC 28557	2.5 miles from 70 West Marina
West Marine Morehead City	252/240-2909	4950 Arendell Street, Morehead City, NC 28557	0.7 miles from Coral Bay Marina
Lowe's Morehead City	252/727-5011	5219 Highway 70, Morehead City, NC 28557	1.7 miles from Coral Bay Marina
Beach True Value Hardware	252/726-9647	407 Atlantic Beach Cswy., Atlantic Beach, NC 28512	0.6 miles from Fort Macon Marina
West Marine Express	252/247-3356	407 Atlantic Beach Cswy., Atlantic Beach, NC 28512	0.6 miles from Fort Macon Marina
Boater's World Atlantic Beach	252/240-0055	1010 W. Fort Macon Road, Atlantic Beach, NC 28512	1.1 miles from Fort Macon Marina
Sound Ace Hardware	252/354-4640	300 Emerald Plantation Road, Emerald Isle, NC 28594	0.6 miles from Island Harbor Marina
Waters Ace Hardware	910/326-1538	778 West Corbett Avenue, Swansboro, NC 28584	1.3 miles from Casper's Marina
East Coast Sports	910/328-1887	409 Roland Avenue, Surf City, NC 28445	On-site Beach House Marina
Surf City Hardware	910/328-3251	14021 NC Highway 50, Surf City, NC 28445	1.2 miles from Beach House Marina
Coastal Carolina Marine	910/798-6200	6332 Oleander Drive, Wilmington, NC 28403	1.7 miles from Bridge Tender Marina
Craft American Hardware	910/256-4782	7002 Wrightsville Avenue, Wilmington, NC 28403	0.7 miles from Dockside Marina
West Marine Wilmington	910/256-7878	1994 Eastwood Road, Wilmington, NC 28403	0.7 miles from Dockside Marina
Home Depot Wilmington	910/790-3770	210 Eastwood Road, Wilmington, NC 28403	3.4 miles from Dockside Marina
Boater's World Wilmington	910/452-3000	317 South College Road, Wilmington, NC 28403	4.7 miles from Dockside Marina
Lighthouse Marine Supply	910/392-5005	291 N. Green Meadows Drive, Wilmington, NC 28405	5.3 miles from Atlantic Marine
Lowe's South Wilmington	910/397-0137	5110 South College Road, Wilmington, NC 28412	4.0 miles from Masonboro Boat Yard
Bame Ace Hardware	910/395-1904	3516 South College Road, Wilmington, NC 28412	4.1 miles from Masonboro Boat Yard
Boat Parts R Us	910/392-0589	521 Soundside Drive, Wilmington, NC 28412	2.0 miles from Inlet Watch Yacht Club
Cape Fear Marine & Tackle	910/397-0068	6132 Carolina Beach Road, Wilmington, NC 28412	3.4 miles from Inlet Watch Yacht Club
Bame Ace Hardware	910/458-8266	1021 N. Lake Park Blvd., Carolina Beach, NC 28428	1.6 miles from Carolina Beach State Park Marina
Island Tackle & Hardware	910/458-3049	801 N. Lake Park Blvd., Carolina Beach, NC 28428	1.8 miles from Carolina Beach State Park Marina
West Marine Express	910/458-5712	1401 N. Lake Park Blvd., Carolina Beach, NC 28428	2.1 miles from Carolina Beach State Park Marina
Lowe's Southport	910/454-8761	5084 Southport Supply Road SE, Southport, NC 28461	3.2 miles from Southport Marina
GPS Store	910/575-9544	6899 Beach Drive SW, Ocean Isle Beach, NC 28469	0.9 miles from Pelican Pointe Marina
Ocean Isle True Value	910/579-0575	6685 Beach Drive SW, Ocean Isle Beach, NC 28469	1.6 miles from Pelican Pointe Marina
Calabash True Value Hardware	910/579-3513	10050 Beach Drive SW, Calabash, NC 28467	Dinghy from Calabash River anchorage

South Carolina Charts

11534 ICW - Myrtle Grove Sound and Cape Fear River to Casino Creek
11518 ICW - Casino Creek to Beaufort River
11507 ICW - Beaufort River to St. Simons Sound

Bridges	
Total	20
Fixed	13
Opening	7

Other Features			
Marinas	56	Vignettes	54
Anchorages	68	Inlets	5
Chandleries	35	Ranges	13

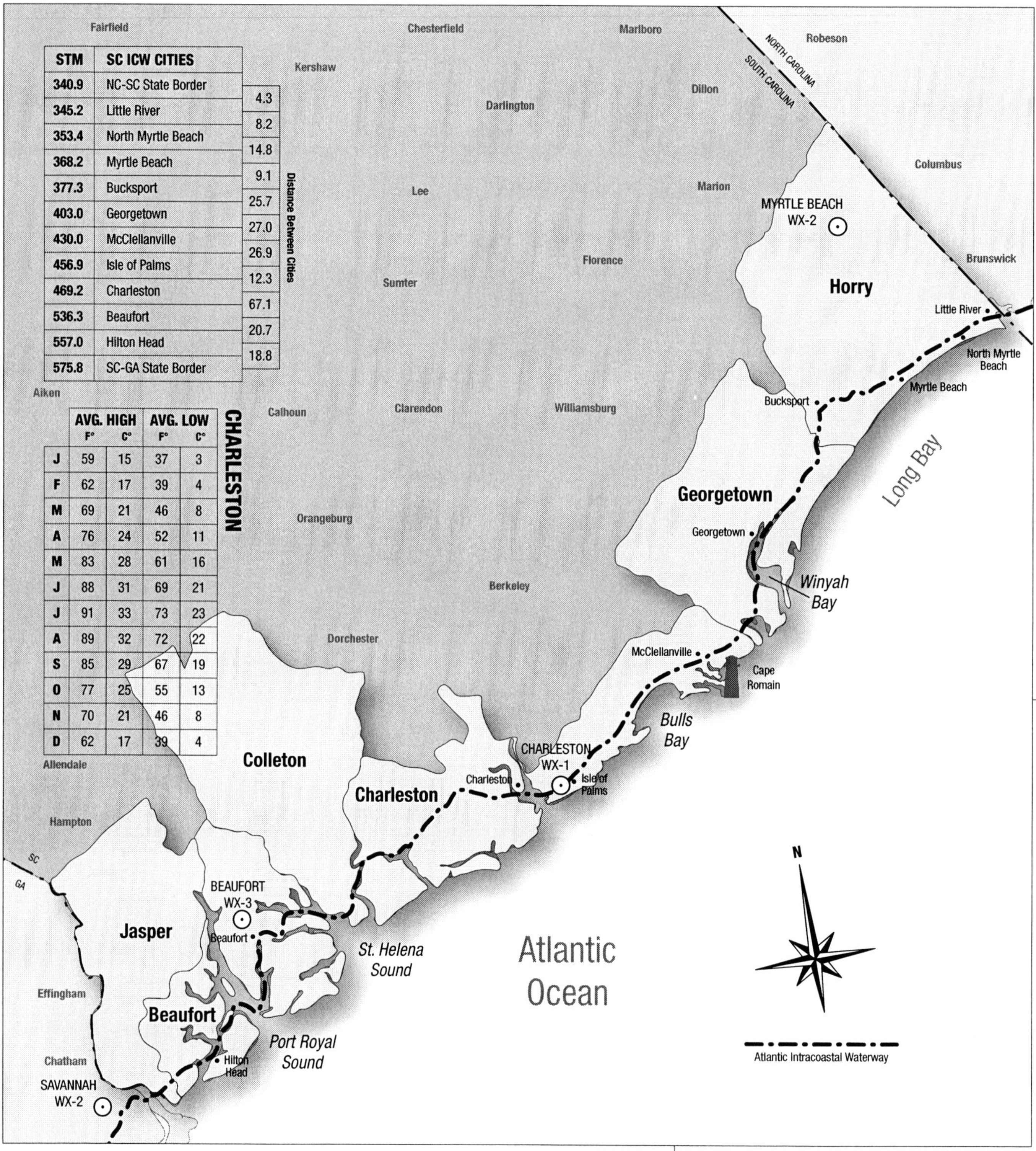

STM	SC ICW CITIES	Distance Between Cities
340.9	NC-SC State Border	
		4.3
345.2	Little River	
		8.2
353.4	North Myrtle Beach	
		14.8
368.2	Myrtle Beach	
		9.1
377.3	Bucksport	
		25.7
403.0	Georgetown	
		27.0
430.0	McClellanville	
		26.9
456.9	Isle of Palms	
		12.3
469.2	Charleston	
		67.1
536.3	Beaufort	
		20.7
557.0	Hilton Head	
		18.8
575.8	SC-GA State Border	

CHARLESTON

	AVG. HIGH		AVG. LOW	
	F°	C°	F°	C°
J	59	15	37	3
F	62	17	39	4
M	69	21	46	8
A	76	24	52	11
M	83	28	61	16
J	88	31	69	21
J	91	33	73	23
A	89	32	72	22
S	85	29	67	19
O	77	25	55	13
N	70	21	46	8
D	62	17	39	4

For illustration purposes only. Not to be used for navigation.

33°00.0

79°30.0

MTW Big Pictures provide an overview of local geographic references. They identify the counties, capes, inlets, lighthouses, and bodies of water commonly referred to in NOAA and AM/FM weather broadcasts.

The locations of WX weather towers are shown to easily determine the best broadcast for your position and direction of travel. The temperature table shows average highs and lows for that region. Look for major cities and smaller towns along the ICW, then use the distance table for planning stops or estimating travel time. Lastly, we list the region's required charts by their NOAA chart number and provide a snapshot of Waterway resources and impediments.

South Carolina

Little River Inlet to Savannah River

The Palmetto State
ICW Statute Mile 340.9 to 575.8
Bridges Monitor VHF 09

Regions
The Grand Strand
Northern Lowcountry
Southern Lowcountry

Inlets
Winyah Bay Entrance
Charleston Roads
North Edisto River Entrance
St. Helena Sound
Port Royal Sound

U.S. Coast Guard
District Seven: 305/415-6800
Station Georgetown: 843/546-2742
Group Charleston: 843/724-7632
Station Charleston: 843/724-7616

NOAA Weather Towers
WX-2 Myrtle Beach
WX-1 Charleston
WX-3 Beaufort

Security Zones
Hwy. 17 Bridge, Charleston Harbor
I-526 Bridge, Charleston Harbor

Lighthouses
Cape Romain Light
Sullivans Island Light
Harbour Town Light

Fishing Information
www.dnr.state.sc.us

SOUTH CAROLINA and North Carolina really are different. And, although they're often collectively referred to as "the Carolinas," a boater visiting each state's oldest waterfront settlements can't help but notice these differences.

It's not just that South Carolina is warmer than North Carolina; the culture is different. South Carolina is the Deep South: palm trees, southern cooking, and plantation architecture. South Carolina's harbors, much more hospitable than North Carolina's, led to the development of a wealthy plantation society with booming aristocratic cities like Charleston, Beaufort, and Georgetown.

This economic head start and cosmopolitan culture still influence South Carolina's coast. As you transit South Carolina, you'll notice more luxury marinas and more world-class resort destinations, such as Myrtle Beach or Hilton Head.

South Carolina's Lowcountry draws visitors from around the world. Charleston's Spoleto USA, a 17-day art festival in May and June, is an internationally recognized cultural event.

Filmmakers have also discovered the Lowcountry. Every year several major films are shot in communities along South Carolina's Waterway. South Carolina is so photogenic the *state* has been called a movie star.

Mel Gibson's *The Patriot* (2000) was filmed in Georgetown. And *Cold Mountain* (2003) with Jude Law, Nicole Kidman, and Renée Zellweger, was filmed in Charleston. Beaufort was a location for the filming of *G.I. Jane* (1997) with Demi Moore, and *Something to Talk About* (1995) with Julia Roberts and Dennis Quaid.

Several contemporary classics, including *The Big Chill* (1983), *Prince of Tides* (1991), and *Forrest Gump* (1994), were all filmed in Beaufort. *The Legend of Bagger Vance* (2000) with Matt Damon and Will Smith, was filmed near Beaufort and Charleston. South Carolina's film credits roll on and on.

Paramount Promotional Image

Forrest Gump at St. Helena Sound

The Waterway is a magic carpet ride through the history and culture of South Carolina's coast. You'll literally pass through the world-famous golf courses of Myrtle Beach—an aerial tram ferries golfers overhead—and weave through abandoned plantations around the once-booming port town of Georgetown.

You'll pass the upscale residential communities around Charleston and may choose to anchor or dock in the center of this historic town. The legendary resort communities of the Lowcountry, including Hilton Head Island, all lie along the ICW.

And don't forget the food! Lowcountry "cuisine"—not the place, but its *food*—was listed in the 2004 bestselling book *1,000 Places to See Before You Die*.

Lowcountry cooking is unique. Based on the African traditions of the Gullah communities, it starts with local seafood such as shrimp, oysters, crab, and fish. Then it adds African and plantation vegetables: okra, peanuts, benne (African for sesame seeds), rice, tomatoes, field peas, greens, tomatoes, corn, hot peppers, or watermelon. Many of the dishes are one-pot creations, with names like Hoppin' John, Frogmore stew, or she-crab soup.

Log your time toward a USCG captain's license. After 360 days of operating a small vessel, you qualify to sit for your OUPV (Operator of an Uninspected Passenger Vessel) exam. Convenient testing centers are located in Charleston, 843/720-3250 and Miami, 305/536-6548.

THE GRAND STRAND

The northern South Carolina coast, stretching 60 miles along the Atlantic Ocean, is known as the Grand Strand. Although most of coastal South Carolina is flat low country, you wouldn't realize it as you transit the Grand Strand region of the Waterway. The 28-mile Pine Island Cut, one of the last sections to be completed along the Norfolk-Miami route, is deep and narrow.

Rather than following a meandering inland river route through the lowlands, engineers drew a straight line through the high country. The Waterway becomes a path unlike anything nature could ever create, a straight, narrow, high-banked land cut.

The cut parallels the coast, passing through the resort communities of North Myrtle Beach and Myrtle Beach. Because the Waterway is a deep cut, it's difficult to see the resorts and golf courses beyond its banks. Sometimes the only clue to the development around you is the frequency of a new 65-foot bridge. Don't be surprised to see new uncharted bridges under construction. Development has not slowed.

Pine Island Cut has its own unique navigational concerns. Overall, piloting is easy along this stretch: simply stay in the middle of the easy-to-follow engineered cut. However, be alert for floating logs and branches that fall from the eroding banks.

Because it's a narrow 28-mile run, there are no recommended anchorages along its length. There are many popular marinas, but if you prefer to anchor you must plan ahead. This is not the place to plunk it at twilight when you feel like stopping for the day. Plan ahead to anchor before or after Pine Island Cut.

Within Pine Island Cut, there is an extremely narrow and rocky stretch called the "Rock Pile." The channel narrows considerably and is lined on both sides with rock ledges. Depending on the tide, the ledges may not be visible!

Boaters disagree on the best time to transit the Rock Pile. Some experienced boaters prefer a high tide, for the obvious reason that there is more water depth. The other camp (ourselves included) prefers a low tide so the rock ledges are visible along the sides of the channel. At low tide the channel is obvious. At high tide you can be lulled into believing the entire cut is part of the navigable channel.

Courtesy of Charleston CVB

Shem Creek, Mt. Pleasant

Regardless of where you fall on the high-tide-versus-low-tide debate, you should always attempt to transit on a *rising* tide. Then if you do lose the channel, nature will correct for your mistake with time.

You also must consider traffic when entering the Rock Pile. First, listen on the radio to determine if any large commercial vessels are transiting the Rock Pile. They will issue a securité on VHF 16 and 13. Second, depending on the size and maneuverability of your vessel and visibility conditions, issue a securité yourself as you approach.

If you hear a securité, answer with your position and negotiate passage. Wait at the entrance. Do not attempt to pass a tug and barge in this narrow area!

The rolling HEADS UP! reminds you when the Rock Pile, or any other important land cut, is on your planning horizon.

Courtesy of NOAA

Photo by Susan D. McKay

Meeting Reach, Isle of Palms

NORTHERN LOWCOUNTRY

The northern Lowcountry's winding rivers, lined with moss-laden trees, are a welcome respite from the narrow straight runs, concrete high-rise bridges, and eroding banks of the Grand Strand. Here the Waterway blends with the natural landscape, following a series of historical rivers.

Because the Waterway connects from river to river with short land cuts, it's important to keep a heads up for junctions. The ICW route is clearly marked by the magenta line on your charts, but doesn't always follow what appears to be the largest channel or river.

In some cases, the junctions are sharp turns from a wide body of water into a narrow channel. For example, the tiny Estherville Minim Creek Canal entrance is a sharp turn off large Winyah Bay. It's very easy to miss the canal entrance and continue out the wide and well-marked Winyah Channel.

Caution: As reminders to scout for a cut's turnoff, the mile-by-mile NAV COLUMN and the rolling HEADS UP! note these tricky junctions at the appropriate statute mile.

There are very few towns along this stretch. Much of the land in the northern Lowcountry has been preserved in large tracts, including the Francis Marion National Forest and the Cape Romain National Wildlife Refuge.

Anchorages are abundant throughout this preserved marshland, with a good anchorage about every four miles. Then again, as with any small tributary creek anchoring, expect shallow depths and plan ahead for swing. Although the current is generally less than the marshlands of Georgia, avoid outer curves where deeper depths indicate a daily scouring by the current. There are also several opportunities to anchor within Cape Romain National Wildlife Refuge—one of the eastern seaboard's largest and most remote wildlife areas—much of it accessible only to boaters.

With about 10,000 residents, Georgetown is the largest Waterway town in the northern Lowcountry. Boaters give Georgetown mixed reviews. Some cruisers love Georgetown's working shrimp docks, historic architecture, and quaint walking streets. It's a comfortable stop with several marinas, an anchorage, shops for supplies, and fresh shrimp sold right off the boats. Other cruisers remember Georgetown as a noisy harbor with a cabbage-like sour smell coming from the west. The harbor is quieter now that Georgetown Steel is closed. Whether the paper mill dominates your impression of Georgetown depends on which way the wind is blowing when you visit.

As you leave Cape Romain National Wildlife Refuge and approach Charleston Harbor, the Waterway enters the suburban residential developments north of Charleston. These planned communities also offer several marina opportunities.

SOUTHERN LOWCOUNTRY

The southern Lowcountry, extending from Charleston to Savannah, is the stereotype of the genteel South. The cities are slow-paced and welcoming, with beautiful historical architecture and tasteful attractions for visitors.

Courtesy of Charleston CVB

Lighthouse Steeple

If you choose to stay in Charleston, many of the local marinas put you within walking distance of the heart of this historic city. If you are provisioning, the city has a good public transportation system. In addition, most marinas provide courtesy vans.

Although Charleston also provides two anchorages, this is a great opportunity to spring for the dockage fee. The marinas are very reasonably priced considering Charleston is an expensive tourist destination. Charleston is also a great place to use any bikes lashed to your lifelines, or rent some to go exploring.

Courtesy of Charleston CVB

Charleston Carriage Tours

Between Charleston and Savannah, the Waterway transits a low country of winding rivers through marshland, punctuated by pine-and-palmetto high ground. These stunning natural surroundings continue to attract new residents. Many resorts and residential communities now dot the coastal islands, including legendary Hilton Head Island.

Beaufort is a favorite stop for cruisers, a small version of Charleston with a historic district and town center adjacent to the town docks. With its upscale shops, restaurants, and stately antebellum architecture, this town is sophisticated beyond its small 10,000-person population. The town welcomes boaters, with a popular anchorage and a first-rate downtown marina.

These are tidal rivers, with five- to six-foot tides and corresponding tidal currents. Be sure to consider changes in the current when anchoring, and adjust your scope for the tidal range.

At marinas, ask ahead about the current and rely on dock help. The currents at Beaufort and Charleston marinas can be unsettling, even to an experienced captain.

If you arrive during a strong current, ask for advice and request dockhands to stand by and take your lines. You can even borrow our favorite warcry, "Foam the runways, we're coming in!"

Bring a bit of home along! Screw multi-photo frames (upside down) to your bulkheads. By securely anchoring the frame, you can safely take family photos along for the trip. And you can easily slip the glass *up*, and swap out older photos to occasionally change your decor.

SOUTH CAROLINA BOOK AND FILM PICKS

South Carolina's rich cultural history is reflected in the scores of books and films about its people and history.

As you transit the Waccamaw and Pee Dee Rivers, or pass through the Francis Marion National Forest, you can read about General Francis Marion, known locally as "The Swamp Fox." His hideout was near the Waterway along the Pee Dee River. Robert D. Bass's book, *Swamp Fox*, is extremely popular among history buffs and is a great read for a rainy day at anchor.

If history reading makes you sleepy, the emotionally moving film *The Patriot* (2000) will keep you awake. Mel Gibson's character, Benjamin Martin, is based on the Swamp Fox's role in the Revolutionary War. But the film is not an accurate biography of Marion's life. To tell the best dramatic story, the writers and producers combined elements from the lives of Francis Marion, Elijah Clarke, Brigadier General Daniel Morgan, Andrew Pickens, and Thomas Sumter.

Author Julia Peterkin recounts a different history along the Waccamaw River. She grew up on the Brookgreen Plantation, a white child raised by Gullah-speaking African Americans who worked the plantation. Her novels, particularly *Black April* which was written in 1927, are fascinating depictions of African American life on a plantation in Gullah-speaking coastal South Carolina. Her literary skill earned her a Pulitzer Prize in 1929.

Columbia/Tristar Promotional Image

Pat Conroy's Prince of Tides

As you reach Charleston, *Wind from the Carolinas*, by Robert Wilder, tells the story of a family's history over the generations. His settings migrate between Charleston and the Bahamas. This light read is wildly popular in the Bahamas, where it's sold in many small shops. Even if you are not continuing on to the Bahamas, the story is the engrossing account of the Loyalists in Charleston and their struggles to start a new life in the Bahamas after the Revolution.

While anchored or docked in Beaufort, you can view the local sites on the silver screen. The classic film *Forrest Gump* (1984) with Tom Hanks, was filmed all around Beaufort, including the local shrimp docks. The baby-boomer classic *Big Chill* (1983) was filmed at the Fripps House, a short distance from the Beaufort town docks. You'll recognize many scenes from downtown Beaufort watching this film.

Daufuskie Island, just north of the Georgia Border, was the setting for Beaufort-bred author Pat Conroy's first book. His story, *The Water is Wide* (later made into the mediocre John Voight film *Conrack*), describes his year as an idealistic young teacher on this isolated Gullah-speaking island. Conroy went on to write the bestselling book and then the screenplay, *Prince of Tides*, made into a movie with Nick Nolte and Barbra Streisand in 1991.

Wherever you are in South Carolina, or even neighboring North Carolina or Georgia, you may want to try Lowcountry cooking in your own galley. John Martin Taylor's book is a classic. Martin, who grew up casting shrimp nets off Hilton Head Island, launched the culinary revival of Lowcountry cooking with his book *Hoppin' John's Lowcountry Cooking: Recipes and Ruminations from Charleston and the Carolina Coastal Plain.* ▲

SAFETY INFO	**NOAA Weather** WX-1 Wilmington, NC **WX-2 Myrtle Beach, SC** WX-1 Charleston, SC **USCG** Station Oak Island, SC VHF 16 or 09/22A 910/278-1133	**Sea Tow** Ocean Isle, NC VHF 16/79 910/575-7839 **TowBoatU.S.** Little River, SC VHF 16/14 or 11 843/249-0244

HEADS UP!			
240.7	Onslow Beach Bridge	347.3	Little River Bridge
260.8	Surf City Bridge	349.0	The Rock Pile (SB)
278.1	Figure Eight Island Bridge	352.2	The Rock Pile (NB)
283.2	Wrightsville Beach Bridge	353.4	Barefoot Landing Bridge
319.5	Lockwoods Folly Inlet Area (SB)	365.4	Seaboard Coast Line RR Bridge
322.5	Lockwoods Folly Inlet Area (NB)	366.0	Numerous Rock Ledges (NB)
337.9	Sunset Beach Bridge	371.0	Socastee Bridge
340.9	**NC-SC Border**	406.0	Winyah Bay Entrance (SB)
347.0	**Numerous Rock Ledges (SB)**	410.5	Estherville Minim Canal (SB)

340.9 NC-SC Border S N
Little River Inlet (ENE of R116)

341.8 Junction | Calabash, NC or Little River Inlet S N
Exit ICW at ICW R2. [STR 5.4]

- **Calabash River Anchorage** (0.2)
  Anchor 5-7 feet N33.52.354
  STR 5.4 feet W078.34.182
  Proceed NNE to Calabash River R2. Ease out off channel to a point between R2 and G3.
- **Marsh Harbour Marina** (0.9)
  No VHF Watch; No Telephone
  Proceed northeasterly up the Calabash River to Calabash.
  Marina closed with no plans to re-open.
- **Little River Inlet** (3.9)
  Proceed southerly along channel to charted Little River Inlet. [STR 5.5 (TS)]
  Used by local commercial and sport fishing boats.

344.2 B&W's Marina (0.1) S N
VHF 16; 843/280-8954
Exit ICW at G9. Marina is to NNW. [STR 5.1 (TS)]
Locals report the marina has closed.

345.2 Crickett Cove Marina (0.1) S N
VHF 16/12 N33.51.826
843/249-7169 W078.37.349
Exit ICW at G11. Marina is to N. [STR 5.1]

346.0 Coquina Harbor S N
Exit ICW at G13. Proceed N into charted basin. [STR 4.9]

- **Lightkeeper's Marina** (0.3)
  VHF 16; 843/249-8660
  Marina is to port.
- **Myrtle Beach Yacht Club** (0.4)
  VHF 16; 843/249-5376
  Marina is to port.
- **Coquina Yacht Club** (0.4)
  VHF 16/09 N33.51.816
  866/249-9333 W078.38.300
  Marina is to starboard.

346.4 Silver Coast Marina (0.1) S N
VHF 16/14 N33.51.550
843/249-1000 W078.38.522
Exit ICW between G13 and R14. Marina is to N. [STR 4.9]

346.8 Pine Island Cut S N
to Southbound Navigation Only
374.8 28-mile land cut.
No anchorages, eight marinas, fuel available.
SEE THE LAST LINK.

347.0 Anchor Marina (0.1) S N
VHF 16; 843/249-7899
Exit ICW ENE of bridge. Marina is to SSE. [STR 4.6]

347.0 Numerous Rock Ledges S N
to Southbound Navigation Only
366.0 NOAA Chart No. 11534, Cautionary Note E states: "Numerous rock ledges have been reported abut-

CABBAGE PALMETTO

A cabbage palmetto and a crescent moon: these joined symbols represent South Carolina. Even the renowned logo designer Paul Rand—of UPS®, IBM®, and ABC® advertising fame—would be envious of this logo.

But no one got paid for this one: the palm-and-moon logo was designed over 200 years ago during the Revolutionary War. It's still wildly popular, printed on everything including T-shirts, coffee mugs, and fishing caps.

Courtesy of National Park Service

Fort Sumter Palmetto Logs

The original flag of South Carolina, designed by Colonel Moultrie in 1775, included only the crescent moon on a dark blue background. The cabbage palmetto was added later to commemorate Moultrie's heroic defense of Fort Sullivan, now Fort Moultrie.

The fort, located on Sullivans Island near Charleston (STM 464), was built with local palmetto logs. Conveniently, palmetto wood is soft and spongy thus enabling the fort's unique walls to absorb the impact of British cannonballs. The Patriots held their position, and the cabbage palmetto became a symbol of South Carolina's independence.

The Cabbage Palmetto, also called Sabal Palmetto, is a native palm in the Southeast and grows abundantly along the Waterway. It's distinctive in the wild with its thick lattice trunk and overlapping brown broken fronds underneath the live growth.

THE LAST LINK

Pine Island Cut (STM 347 to STM 375) was the last section of the Waterway to be completed. It opened in 1936 with an appropriately raucous local celebration. And it's no wonder it was last: unlike most of the Waterway, this section required dynamite.

Horry County (pronounced O-ree) residents had discussed the possibility of a canal since the 1800s. So in the 1930s, when the federal government proposed funding a canal from Little River to Winyah Bay, local officials assumed the canal would follow a seven-mile route connecting the Little River to the Waccamaw River. This was great news for the county: a new canal would revitalize the Conway county seat by putting it back on a commercial waterway.

But things don't always work out your way. Instead, the Army Corps chose a straight 28-mile cut along Myrtle Beach, bypassing Conway altogether. Perhaps it was the engineering challenge. The proposed route resulted in the longest man-made cut along the entire length of the Intracoastal Waterway.

IF YOU'RE ON THE ROCKS, IT'S THE SCHIST

The infamous "Rock Pile," at STM 347 to STM 366 along Pine Island Cut, is actually fossiliferous limestone, not schist. But if you scrape your hull you won't care what kind of rock it is. Instead, curse the engineers who chose this deep, rocky route for the cut.

When the Army Corps began work on Pine Island Cut in the early 1930s, they quickly discovered a problem. They had no trouble with the Pleistocene marine sands and clays, but then they hit Cretaceous limestone with marl pits. Needless to say, progress slowed.

Cretaceous limestone, found at the lowest point of the Rock Pile, is 65 million to 144 million years old, formed at the end of the dinosaur age when modern mammals and flowering plants evolved. The good news about Cretaceous limestone is it's loaded with interesting fossils. The bad news is it's quite a challenge if you're trying to dig a canal.

Private contractors were needed to blast the area before dredges could re-

SAFETY INFO

NOAA Weather
WX-1 Wilmington, NC
WX-2 Myrtle Beach, SC
WX-1 Charleston, SC

USCG
Station Oak Island, SC
VHF 16 or 09/22A
910/278-1133

Sea Tow
Myrtle Beach, SC
VHF 16/10
843/385-0217

TowBoatU.S.
Myrtle Beach, SC
VHF 16/14 or 11
843/249-0244

HEADS UP!

319.5 Lockwoods Folly Inlet Area (SB)
322.5 Lockwoods Folly Inlet Area (NB)
337.9 Sunset Beach Bridge
340.9 NC-SC Border
347.0 Numerous Rock Ledges (SB)
347.3 Little River Bridge
349.0 The Rock Pile (SB)
352.2 The Rock Pile (NB)
353.4 Barefoot Landing Bridge
365.4 Seaboard Coast Line RR Bridge
366.0 Numerous Rock Ledges (NB)
371.0 Socastee Bridge
406.0 Winyah Bay Entrance (SB)
410.5 Estherville Minim Canal (SB)
411.0 South Island Ferry Crossing
462.3 Ben Sawyer Bridge
469.0 Charleston Coast Guard Station
470.8 Wappoo Creek Bridge

move the spoils. As the rock became more and more of a challenge, the engineers continued to commensurately narrow the channel.

It took about two years to blast and drill through the area, but the project was ultimately successful. Literally millions of tons of material were removed, at a bargain cost of 19¢ per cubic yard. In the end, the $4.8 million project from Cape Fear River to Winyah Bay, boosted by public works funds, was completed under budget.

Photo by Rosalie Beasley

Rafting at Barefoot Landing

NORTH MYRTLE BEACH

Beyond the banks of the Waterway, the seaside resort of North Myrtle Beach bustles with activity. New construction is everywhere and several large bridges have been built to accommodate the growing local and tourist traffic.

This is the land of golf courses: over 80 courses dot the greater Myrtle Beach area. Many of these courses line the Waterway, but are hard to see because of their elevation. The aerial tramway, at STM 356.3, ferries golfers across the Waterway on the 27-hole public Waterway Hills Golf Club.

Many boaters look forward to a stop at Barefoot Landing (STM 353.7) to access its 100 specialty shops, 13 factory outlets, and 13 restaurants. This village resort and shopping complex maintains a dock along the Waterway where boaters are welcome to tie up overnight for free. However, the 500-foot dock is typically crowded so expect to raft.

Myrtle Beach Golf Courses
http://golfmb.com
Barefoot Landing
www.bflanding.com
843/272-8349

THE CAROLINA SHAG

No, it's not Austin Power's shag—although it may lead to that! In the Carolinas, to "shag" is to dance a popular beachside swing dance. The Carolina shag is the official state dance of South Carolina.

The dance presumably originated in Myrtle Beach in the 1930s and was popular through the wartime 1940s. Dancing the shag is making a big comeback, so expect to see this dance when you have dinner ashore. The shag is usually danced to rhythm and blues, oldies, or Motown in the sand on the beach, so it's also called "beach dancing" or the "beach swing."

To prevent your hanging lockers and clothing from getting a musty smell, place a fabric softener sheet or two inside like a sachet.

BUCKSPORT, MAINE OR SOUTH CAROLINA?

Yes, they are related. Bucksport, South Carolina was named after Mr. Buck, who came from Maine and whose family of shipbuilders founded Bucksport, Maine. Young Mr. Buck came to South Carolina in search of cheap lumber.

semi-local publications LLC

Photo by Author

Golf Tram Over Waterway

He found it in Bucksport, South Carolina, which became a major lumber-shipping center. Logs were harvested and hauled from the local swamps and floated down the Waccamaw River to the ships.

Today Bucksport is a small quiet town with 340 families.

SPANISH MOSS

The Waccamaw River is a wild peaceful river, banked by abandoned rice fields and live oaks abundantly draped with Spanish Moss.

ting the deep portion of the Intracoastal Waterway channel from Nixon Crossroads to Latitude 33.42.51 N. Mariners should use extreme caution to avoid grounding in this area."

The narrowest and rockiest stretch is "The Rock Pile" (STM 349.0 TO STM 352.2).

347.1 Nixon Crossroads Bridge
Fixed; vertical 65 feet. [STR 4.6 (TS)]

347.2 Harbourgate Marina (0.1)
VHF 16/12 N33.51.126
843/249-8888 W078.39.349
Exit ICW between bridges. Marina is to S. [STR 4.6]

347.3 Little River Bridge
VHF 09; 843/280-5919
Single-pivot swing; vertical 7 feet; on request.

348.3 Dock Holidays Marina (0.1)
VHF 16/10 N33.50.569
843/280-6354 W078.40.134
Exit ICW between R14 "A" and G15. Marina is to SSE in charted basin. [STR 3.9]

349.0 Heads Up | The Rock Pile
to Southbound/Northbound Navigation
352.2 Begins near G15 and ends near charted VORTAC tower.
Issue a securité on VHF 16 and 13 to warn commercial traffic you will be transiting the narrows: "Securité, securité, securité; this is the motor [or sailing] vessel [your-boat-name] approaching the Rock Pile southbound [or northbound]."
SEE IF YOU'RE ON THE ROCKS.

353.4 Barefoot Landing Bridge
VHF 09; (Would Not Provide)
Single-pivot swing; vertical 31 feet; on request.
SEE NORTH MYRTLE BEACH.

353.7 Barefoot Landing (0.1)
No VHF Watch N33.48.060
843/272-8349 W078.44.796
Docks are to SSE. [STR 3.3]
Free dock with access to factory outlet complex. 72-hour limit. No services. Expect to raft.

353.7 Barefoot Resort Yacht Club
VHF 16/10 N33.48.077
843/390-7900 W078.44.848
Marina is to NNW. New facility opening in 2005. [STR 3.3]

355.6 Conway Bypass Twin Bridges
Fixed; vertical 65 feet.

356.3 Overhead Cable Car
Vertical 67 feet.
This gondola whisks golfers from the parking lot to the pro shop of Waterway Hills Golf Club.

358.1 Grande Dunes Bridge
Fixed; vertical 65 feet.
Caution: Older charts may not show several new 65-foot fixed bridges along this stretch. This is a dead-reckoning caution only.

SAFETY INFO

NOAA Weather
WX-1 Wilmington, NC
WX-2 Myrtle Beach, SC
WX-1 Charleston, SC

USCG
Station Georgetown, SC
VHF 16 or 09/22A
843/546-2742

Sea Tow
Myrtle Beach, SC
VHF 16/10
843/385-0217

TowBoatU.S.
Myrtle Beach, SC
VHF 16/14 or 11
843/249-0244

HEADS UP!

340.9 NC-SC Border
347.0 Numerous Rock Ledges (SB)
347.3 Little River Bridge
349.0 The Rock Pile (SB)
352.2 The Rock Pile (NB)
353.4 Barefoot Landing Bridge
365.4 Seaboard Coast Line RR Bridge
366.0 Numerous Rock Ledges (NB)
371.0 Socastee Bridge
406.0 Winyah Bay Entrance (SB)
410.5 Estherville Minim Canal (SB)
411.0 South Island Ferry Crossing
462.3 Ben Sawyer Bridge
469.0 Charleston Coast Guard Station
470.8 Wappoo Creek Bridge
472.2 Elliott Cut (SB)
472.5 Elliott Cut (NB)
536.0 Ladies Island Bridge

358.2 Marina at Grande Dunes S N
VHF 16/10 N33.46.081
843/315-7777 W078.48.823
Exit ICW WSW of bridge. Marina is to SSE. New facility opening soon. [STR 2.2]

360.6 Grissom Parkway Bridge S N
Fixed; vertical 65 feet.

365.4 Highway 501 Bridge S N
Fixed; vertical 65 feet.

365.4 Seaboard Coast Line RR Bridge S N
Single bascule; vertical 16 feet; usually open.

366.0 Numerous Rock Ledges S N
to Northbound Navigation Only
347.0 See Cautionary Note and Comment at STM 347.0.

368.2 Hague Marina (0.1) S N
VHF 16/68 N33.41.735
843/293-2141 W078.57.655
Exit ICW at charted oxbow. Proceed SW, into oxbow, to marina. [STR 2.2]

371.0 Socastee Bridge S N
VHF 09; 843/347-3525
Single-pivot swing; vertical 11 feet; on request.
This bridge (pronounced SAW-cuss-tee) was scheduled for removal upon completion of the 65-foot fixed bridge. Local residents apparently have equal passion for convenience and historic preservation. The bridge is now on the historic register, blocking its demolition forever.

371.2 Route 544 Bridge S N
Fixed; vertical 65 feet.

373.3 Osprey Marina (0.1) S N
VHF 16; 843/215-5353
Exit ICW W of R26. Marina is to S. [STR 2.3]

374.8 Pine Island Cut S N
to Northbound Navigation Only
346.8 28-mile land cut.
No anchorages, eight marinas, fuel available.

374.8 Enterprise Creek Anchorage (0.2) S N
Anchor 6-10 feet N33.40.331
STR (TS) 2.4 feet W079.03.774
Exit ICW at G27. Proceed NNW to Enterprise Creek.

375.6 Waccamaw River Anchorage (0.1) S N
Anchor 10-14 feet N33.39.930
STR 2.5 feet W079.04.247
Exit ICW at G29. Proceed N into charted oxbow.

377.0 Bucksport Anchorage (North)(0.1) S N
Anchor 10-12 feet N33.39.262
STR 2.6 feet W079.05.634
Exit ICW at G35. Proceed NW.

377.2 Bucksport Anchorage (South)(0.1) S N
Anchor 12-17 feet N33.39.175
STR 2.6 feet W079.05.748
Exit ICW at R36. Proceed NW into charted oxbow. Bucksport Plantation renovations and dock expansion have encroached into this anchorage.

Spanish Moss is neither Spanish nor moss. It's an air plant in the pineapple family. The great botanist Carl Linnaeus named these plants as the genus *Tillandsia*, after one of his Swedish students. This student, Elias Tillands, would get so seasick he once chose to walk more than a thousand miles around the Gulf of Bothnia rather than cross it in a boat. Since these air plants grew in trees, Linnaeus assumed they hated water and named them after his student who would do anything to stay away from water.

semi-local publications LLC

Photo by Author **Horse Riders Along the Waterway**

Actually, Spanish Moss likes water, but only in the form of high humidity. Those long strands hanging from tree branches are living plants, gleaning moisture from the air and rainwater. Spanish Moss has a fuzzy velvety feel and if you look closely you can see the greenish living center. Sometimes, tiny yellowish flowers show at the base of the threadlike leaves. Spanish Moss doesn't kill or harm its host tree: the roots are lightly attached and don't penetrate the wood.

Over the years, Spanish Moss has been harvested for many uses. Native Americans made rope with Spanish Moss. During the Revolutionary War it was used as gun wadding. Mattresses were stuffed with Spanish Moss during the Plantation Era. As late as the 1900s it was used for upholstery filling and filters for air conditioners.

Today we simply enjoy the dramatic effect of Spanish Moss, hanging from the dark gnarled branches of mature live oaks, a symbol of the South.

RICE FIELDS

Before the Civil War, rice fields covered mile after mile of the marshes along the Waterway. Using slave labor, the land was cleared, partitioned by dikes, and the water level managed by a system of wooden floodgates. These fields fueled the prosperity of the large coastal plantations, with over half of the nation's rice crop produced in South Carolina.

Every May to November, when the rice fields were flooded with river water, the white families left their large plantation houses for their coastal homes, often only a few miles across the river. The hot and humid summer months created malodorous fields—conditions believed to be unhealthy and malarial for the young plantation children. The slaves remained to tend and harvest the crop.

The rice and indigo fields are long gone, part of a local economy that collapsed after the Civil War. If you scan the horizon, you may see a remaining upright chimney of a rice mill or clusters of chimneys from old slave quarters. The floodgates have rotted away; the tide rolls over these marshes as it did centuries before.

BELGIAN ROCKS

It's hard to imagine the Waccamaw River as a major center of commerce. Yet it was once an important shipping center for the area's huge plantations, such as Laurel Hill, Springfield, The Oaks, Fairfield, and Arcadia.

Large boats docked at wooden wharves along these shores to pick up plantation produce. The stone ballast of the empty ships was exchanged for the weight of rice at the plantation wharves. By the 1800s the banks of the Waccamaw were lined at low tide with small round stones, called "Belgian rocks," supposedly brought from Europe and discarded as ships' ballast.

You may still spot a collection of Belgian rocks at low tide along the Waterway in South Carolina or Georgia. Over time most of the Belgian rocks have been collected and put to other uses. Rocks along the Waccamaw were gathered to pave the cobblestone streets of Charleston.

GULLAH

Gullah is still spoken in some communities in the rural Lowcountry. It's a Creole dialect, combining English with

SAFETY INFO		
	NOAA Weather	**Sea Tow**
	WX-1 Wilmington, NC	Georgetown, SC
	WX-2 Myrtle Beach, SC	VHF 16/9
	WX-1 Charleston, SC	843/527-4136
	USCG	**TowBoatU.S.**
	Station Georgetown, SC	Georgetown, SC
	VHF 16 or 09/22A	VHF 16/11
	843/546-2742	843/833-1951

HEADS UP!

340.9	NC-SC Border	406.0	Winyah Bay Entrance (SB)
347.0	Numerous Rock Ledges (SB)	410.5	Estherville Minim Canal (SB)
347.3	Little River Bridge	411.0	South Island Ferry Crossing
349.0	The Rock Pile (SB)	462.3	Ben Sawyer Bridge
352.2	The Rock Pile (NB)	469.0	Charleston Coast Guard Station
353.4	Barefoot Landing Bridge	470.8	Wappoo Creek Bridge
365.4	Seaboard Coast Line RR Bridge	472.2	Elliott Cut (SB)
366.0	Numerous Rock Ledges (NB)	472.5	Elliott Cut (NB)
371.0	Socastee Bridge	536.0	Ladies Island Bridge

West African languages. The words evolved as African slaves journeyed from Africa through the West Indies to the Southern plantations.

Try to understand this phrase from Virginia Mixson Geraty's Gullah poem, "Thank God for Charleston":

De moon done rise
en' de win' fetch de smell ob de maa'sh
F'um de haa'buh ob de lan' wuh uh lub'.

The Gullah community also has their own unique African-derived beliefs and customs, related to the natural world around them. For example, as recreational boaters we're scared of an ebb tide. Ebb water means if you ground your vessel it's only going to get worse over the next several hours. To the Gullah community, the ebb tide was believed to have the pull of death. So birthing needed to be completed before the tide turned, or life could be pulled away with it.

THE TRANSLATION

In American English, the Gullah poem describes the Lowcountry:

The moon has risen now
and the wind brings the smell of the marsh
From the harbor of the land that I love.

BROOKGREEN PLANTATION

Julia Peterkin, who grew up as a child on the Brookgreen Plantation near STM 384, wrote about Gullah life on the rice plantations. Her novels tell the story of the plantation-based Gullah community, accurately capturing the dialect and beliefs of this African culture.

But Peterkin was white, not black. So when her novel *Black April* was published in 1927, she was criticized both by whites and blacks for writing with an African American perspective.

It wasn't long, though, until the African American community praised her novels as insightful and accurate portrayals of Lowcountry life. Peterkin continued to document the life of African Americans, winning the Pulitzer Prize for her novel *Scarlet Sister Mary* in 1929.

Her childhood home, the Brookgreen Plantation, is located on the eastern banks of the Waterway at STM 384. Sandy Island, the setting of *Black April*, is to the west. Today the Brookgreen Garden is open to the public, with fountains, a sculpture garden, and over 4,000 acres of native gardens.

Brookgreen Garden
www.brookgreen.org
843/235-6000

WAY DOWN UPON THE PEE DEE RIVER

How about: "Way down upon the Pee Dee River, far, far away..."? Hmm, doesn't quite have the right ring to it. That's what Stephen Foster thought as he wrote the American classic "The Swannee River (Old Folks at Home)."

As the story goes, the Pee Dee River, which joins the Waccamaw River just north of Georgetown, appeared in Foster's early drafts of the song. But Foster wasn't happy with the cadence. So he went to his brother's printing shop in Pittsburgh, asking for an atlas. From it he chose the Suwannee, crossing out "Pee Dee" and replacing it with the abbreviated two-syllable "Swannee."

Instead of singing about the Pee Dee River, American children sing about the Suwannee, located in the Florida Panhandle. The song is now Florida's state song, but ironically, Foster never set foot in Florida. His song captures the Southern plantation life of this area—but come to think of it, he never set foot in South Carolina either!

Columbia Tristar Promotional Image

Mel Gibson as The Patriot

Add easy lighting to dark hanging lockers and lazarettes with Moonlights. These small round battery-powered lights turn on and off when you tap them. A two-pack costs $3.97 at Home Depot stores.

377.3 Bucksport Plantation Marina (0.1) S N
VHF 16; 843/397-5566
Exit ICW between R36 and R38. Marina is to W. [STR 2.6 (TS)]
SEE BUCKSPORT.

380.6 Prince Creek Anchorage (North)(0.3) S N
Anchor 14-20 feet N33.36.283
STR 2.7 feet W079.05.127
Exit ICW at R44. Proceed ESE into Prince Creek.

381.2 Bull Creek Anchorage (1.2) S N
Anchor 16-20 feet N33.36.510
STR 2.7 feet W079.06.358
Exit ICW SW of R48. Give the shoal at R48 a wide berth as you proceed northerly into Bull Creek. Continue around first bend.

382.4 Prince Creek Anchorage (South)(0.4) S N
Anchor 12-14 feet N33.34.885
STR 2.7 feet W079.05.769
Exit ICW at G53. Proceed NE into Prince Creek.

383.6 Cow House Creek Anchorage (North)(0.2) S N
Anchor 6-10 feet N33.33.651
STR 3.2 feet W079.05.441
Exit ICW at G57. Proceed WSW into Cow House Creek.

383.7 Wacca Wache Marina (0.1) S N
VHF 16/10 N33.33.712
843/651-2994 W079.05.172
Exit ICW between G57 and R58. Marina is to E at charted basin. [STR 3.2 (TS)]
SEE BROOKGREEN PLANTATION.

384.4 Cow House Creek Anchorage (South)(0.2) S N
Anchor 6-8 feet N33.33.106
STR 3.2 feet W079.05.446
Exit ICW at G61. Proceed NW into Cow House Creek.

386.5 Sandhole Creek Anchorage (0.2) S N
Anchor 6-8 feet N33.31.635
STR 3.4 feet W079.06.853
Exit ICW at R66. Proceed NW into Sandhole Creek.

388.2 Reserve Harbor Marina (0.1) S N
VHF 16; 843/235-8262
Exit ICW at G71. Marina is to SE. [STR 3.8]

388.8 Thoroughfare Creek Anchorage (1.0) S N
Anchor 12-16 feet N33.30.832
STR (TS) 3.9 feet W079.08.700
Exit ICW at G73. Proceed W into Thoroughfare Creek. Anchor at charted Belin.

394.2 Heritage Plantation Marina (0.1) S N
VHF 16/10 N33.26.418
843/237-3650 W079.10.768
Exit ICW at charted flashing pair of private aids. Marina is to SE. [STR 4.1 (TS)]

395.4 Butler Island Anchorage (0.4) S N
Anchor 10-16 feet N33.25.650
STR 4.1 feet W079.11.932
Exit ICW between G83 and R84. Pass well N of

SAFETY INFO

NOAA Weather
WX-2 Myrtle Beach, SC
WX-1 Charleston, SC
WX-3 Beaufort, SC

USCG
Station Georgetown, SC
VHF 16 or 09/22A
843/546-2742

Sea Tow
Georgetown, SC
VHF 16/9
843/527-4136

TowBoatU.S.
Georgetown, SC
VHF 16/11
843/833-1951

HEADS UP!

347.0	Numerous Rock Ledges (SB)
347.3	Little River Bridge
349.0	The Rock Pile (SB)
352.2	The Rock Pile (NB)
353.4	Barefoot Landing Bridge
365.4	Seaboard Coast Line RR Bridge
366.0	Numerous Rock Ledges (NB)
371.0	Socastee Bridge
406.0	**Winyah Bay Entrance (SB)**
410.5	Estherville Minim Canal (SB)
411.0	South Island Ferry Crossing
462.3	Ben Sawyer Bridge
469.0	Charleston Coast Guard Station
470.8	Wappoo Creek Bridge
472.2	Elliott Cut (SB)
472.5	Elliott Cut (NB)
536.0	Ladies Island Bridge
575.8	SC-GA Border

Butler Island shoal and proceed southwesterly to anchor behind island.

401.1 Lafayette Bridge S N
(US 17)
Fixed; vertical 65 feet. [STR 4.2 (TS)]

402.8 Georgetown Landing Marina (1.2) S N
VHF 16/10 or 68 N33.21.868
843/546-1776 W079.15.968
Exit ICW SW of river junction "W". Proceed NNE toward Great Pee Dee River fixed bridge. Marina is before bridge to NW. [STR 4.2]
See Way Down upon the Pee Dee River.

403.0 Georgetown S N
Exit ICW at R40. Proceed N into Sampit River. At junction "S" bear right into charted town harbor for three marinas and the anchorage; bear left for Johnson's Marina. [STR 4.3 (TS)]
See Indigo & Georgetown.

- **Hazzard Marine** (0.8)
  VHF 16/68 N33.21.578
  843/527-3625 W079.16.783
  Marina is to starboard.
- **The Boat Shed Marina** (1.0)
  VHF 16/68 N33.21.677
  843/546-4415 W079.16.805
  Marina is to starboard.
- **Georgetown Anchorage** (1.2)
  Anchor 8-10 feet N33.21.849
  STR (TS) 4.3 feet W079.16.990
  Anchorage is to port, anywhere along charted island, opposite charted clock tower.
- **Harborwalk Marina** (1.3)
  VHF 16/68 N33.21.812
  843/546-4250 W079.16.911
  Marina is to starboard, in center of town, by the clock tower.
- **Johnson's Marina** (2.5)
  VHF 16/10 N33.21.389
  843/545-8633 W079.18.688
  Proceed westerly up Sampit River beyond charted fixed bridge (vertical 65 feet). Marina is to port approximately one mile beyond bridge.

403.0 Winyah Bay Ship Channel S N
to 406.0 Southbound/Northbound Navigation Buoyage reverses.
Look for yellow reflective ICW triangles and squares on aids.

406.0 Junction | Winyah Bay Entrance (13.2) S N
Well Aided N33.11.570
Well Lit W079.07.161
Exit ICW at R30. Proceed southeasterly in main ship channel. Waypoint is at R4.
Caution: Southbound ICW travelers must bear off S in charted Western Channel to pick up the Estherville Minim Creek Canal to Charleston.
See North Island.

406.1 Belle Isle Marina (0.3) S N
VHF 16; 843/546-8491
Exit ICW S of R30. Proceed WNW in privately

THE SWAMP FOX

The Pee Dee River may have missed the boat for musical fame, but it scored historical fame as the hideout of "The Swamp Fox."

The 250,000-acre Francis Marion National Forest, running for about 20 miles along the west side of the Waterway south of McClellanville, is named after the Swamp Fox, a.k.a. General Francis Marion. The release of the film *The Patriot* (2000) with Mel Gibson's character loosely based on Francis Marion, renewed interest in the story of the Swamp Fox.

Francis Marion was a diminutive Revolutionary War General who earned his nickname by lurking in the swamps, ambushing the British with a small guerilla band, and then disappearing back into the swamps before the British knew what hit them. Marion would raid British supply depots and rescue captured American prisoners of war. Since he grew up in this area, he knew these swamps intimately. The Swamp Fox's hideout was Snow's Island in the Pee Dee River.

The British never caught Marion, nor found his hideout. To this day, South Carolina children boast about Marion's elusiveness in a schoolyard jingle:

Swamp Fox, Swamp Fox, tail on his hat.
Nobody know where the Swamp Fox at.
Swamp Fox, Swamp Fox, hiding in the glen.
He run away to fight again.

PARLEZ-VOUS FRANCAIS?

Have you noticed that many of the names in this area are French? Some of the names, such as Horry County, (pronounced O-ree) and named after another local Revolutionary War hero, Peter Horry, are still pronounced in the French style.

Both Marion and Horry were Huguenots, descended from French settlers who left France in the 1500s during the Protestant Reformation. These French dissidents were dissatisfied with the domination of the Catholic Church in France and sought to develop a more democratic religion.

In defiance of Catholicism and the monarchy, the Protestants who met in secret were called Huis Genooten, or "house fellows," derived from Flemish or German. Eventually the name evolved to "Huguenot."

In 1535, an edict was issued ordering the extermination of Protestant heretics. For decades afterward, Huguenots were persecuted. Thousands fled France, many seeking the safety of the religiously tolerant American Colonies. Many settled in South Carolina, becoming successful planters growing rice, indigo, cotton, and silk.

Use milk crates in large lockers to create instant removable partitions. They drain naturally and keep snorkel gear, shore power cords, and other miscellaneous gear organized. Because they are plastic they're light, wash easily, and dry quickly.

INDIGO

Despite our blue-jeans culture, most Americans are unfamiliar with indigo. At one time, indigo was the foundation for this region's economy, creating fortunes rivaling the European aristocracy. It was the cash crop of choice before the plantations switched to rice in the early 1800s. But just as the rice industry collapsed during the Civil War, the indigo trade ended with the Revolutionary War. Prices crashed as cheap indigo from India and the East Indies glutted the market.

Indigo Field Marks

In the 1700s there was a tremendous demand for blue dye, the most difficult color to produce in a natural dye. Indigo is a plant in the pea family with bluish-tinged leaves. Ferment the leaves and you get a rich dark-blue dye. Before a synthetic substitute was developed in 1870, indigo was the only way to create a blue color.

Georgetown indigo was coveted for

SAFETY INFO		
	NOAA Weather	**Sea Tow**
	WX-2 Myrtle Beach, SC	Georgetown, SC
	WX-1 Charleston, SC	VHF 16/9
	WX-3 Beaufort, SC	843/527-4136
	USCG	**TowBoatU.S.**
	Station Georgetown, SC	Georgetown, SC
	VHF 16 or 09/22A	VHF 16/11
	843/546-2742	843/833-1951

HEADS UP!		
	349.0 The Rock Pile (SB)	462.3 Ben Sawyer Bridge
	352.2 The Rock Pile (NB)	469.0 Charleston Coast Guard Station
	353.4 Barefoot Landing Bridge	470.8 Wappoo Creek Bridge
	365.4 Seaboard Coast Line RR Bridge	472.2 Elliott Cut (SB)
	366.0 Numerous Rock Ledges (NB)	472.5 Elliott Cut (NB)
	371.0 Socastee Bridge	536.0 Ladies Island Bridge
	406.0 Winyah Bay Entrance (SB)	575.8 SC-GA Border
	410.5 Estherville Minim Canal (SB)	578.4 Wilmington River Cut-off (NB)
	411.0 South Island Ferry Crossing	579.9 Causton Bluff Bridge

its colors, ranging from coppers to purples. Winyah Bay (pronounced WIN-yaw) was the center of the international indigo trade, overseen by an aristocratic society of plantation owners, called the Winyah Indigo Society. The group still operates today as a philanthropic society in Georgetown, located at Cannon and Prince Streets.

Indigo now grows wild throughout the area, self-seeded volunteers from an industry abandoned over 200 years ago. Look for clusters of pea-like yellow flowers and small clover-like round leaves with a noticeable blue-green tinge and you've found indigo.

GEORGETOWN

Georgetown is the third oldest city in South Carolina, once rivaling Charleston as South Carolina's major port. During the boom years of indigo and rice, Georgetown developed into a town with beautiful colonial architecture, much of which still stands today.

If you'd like to walk and see the historic architecture, pick up the Historic Seaport Georgetown brochure, available at most marinas or at shops in the business district. This small map lists 63 historic buildings dating back to 1737, all within a few blocks of the waterfront. If you don't want to walk, a similar tram tour departs from the center of town under the clock tower.

Today Georgetown is a town of about 10,000 people, supported by a mix of modern industries. The small revitalized downtown has many shops, including restaurants, banks, gift shops, and marine stores. In the center of town, the old market and meeting building with the clock tower, is the Rice Museum.

Shrimping and a paper mill are now the main industries in Georgetown, especially since the bankruptcy of Georgetown Steel. Commercial fishing boats bring their catch to the docks southeast of the downtown waterfront. You can buy fresh seafood off the boats at Independent Seafood, located at the bottom of Cannon Street by the docks.

Depending on the wind, you may also notice the paper mill. Some cruisers complain about the sour smell from the mill, located at the west end of the harbor. But one has to admire Georgetown's resiliency to economic conditions that have continually forced this small town to adapt.

Rice Museum
843/546-7423

NORTH ISLAND

Crossing Winyah Bay, before turning into the Estherville Minim Creek Canal at STM 410.5, look seaward and you might spot the long peninsula of North Island.

North Island is believed to be one of the first attempted settlements by the Spanish. They arrived in 1526 to build a new community, but dissension among the colonists—including the death of their leader, slave insurrections, and Native American raids—decimated the group. The remaining 150 members quickly gave up on the settlement idea and returned to Spain. The next group of European settlers didn't arrive until the early 1700s, finding a sheltered haven at the head of Winyah Bay in what is now Georgetown.

The anchorage at North Island also hosted two most-welcome visitors during the Revolutionary War. French Generals Lafayette and DeKalb anchored there in 1777, secretly meeting with Patriot leaders at the Huger Plantation. It was at North Island they offered France's aid to colonial America in her fight against the British.

Find, or buy and drink (our choice), a *box* of wine. The empty bag-in-a-box packaging is perfect for safely transporting used motor oil from your boat to an oil recycling drop-off. Hmmm...let's see: that's one box of wine every 100 engine hours, right?

TOM YAWKEY'S FIELD OF DREAMS

Along the eastern banks of the Estherville Minim Creek Canal, the land is preserved as the Tom Yawkey Wildlife Center Heritage Preserve. The late Tom Yawkey, former owner of the Boston Red Sox, willed the land to the state of South Carolina as a waterfowl management area. The preserve is only accessible by the South Island Ferry at STM 411.

At one time, farmers placed migrating waterfowl in the same category as rats, locusts, and weevils. Every spring,

maintained channel to marina. [STR 4.1]
Marina is undergoing dredging and major reconstruction. Scheduled for completion fall 2005.

410.5 Estherville Minim Creek Canal S N
to Southbound Navigation Only
415.4 4.9-mile land cut.
No anchorages, no marinas, no fuel.
Caution: Southbound, be alert for the right-angle turn at R2 to follow the ICW magenta line SW to Charleston.

411.0 South Island Ferry Crossing S N
Lights signal a ferry crossing. Speed limit strictly enforced near ferry and boat ramps. [STR 4.3 (TS)]
See Tom Yawkey Wildlife Center.

415.4 Estherville Minim Creek Canal S N
to Northbound Navigation Only
410.5 4.9-mile land cut.
No anchorages, no marinas, no fuel.

415.6 Minim Creek Anchorage (Northwest)(0.4) S N
Anchor 8-10 feet N33.11.580
STR 4.6 feet W079.16.676
Exit ICW between R4 and G5. Proceed northwesterly into Minim Creek around first bend.

415.6 Minim Creek Anchorage (Southeast)(0.3) S N
Anchor 8-10 feet N33.11.337
STR 4.6 feet W079.16.366
Exit ICW between R4 and G5. Proceed southeasterly into Minim Creek.

416.6 Range "A" S N
to Southbound/Northbound Navigation
417.0 Little Crow Island
0.4-mile range.

417.0 Range "B" S N
to Southbound/Northbound Navigation
417.4 Crow Island
0.4-mile range.

418.0 North Santee River Anchorage (0.7) S N
Anchor 8-10 feet N33.10.693
STR 4.7 feet W079.18.587
Exit ICW E of R18. Proceed NW. Anchor in charted 8- to 10-foot shallows.

418.3 45.5-mile Land Cut S N
to Southbound Navigation Only
463.8 45.5-mile land cut.
14 anchorages, two marinas, fuel available.

420.1 South Santee River Anchorage (Northwest)(0.3) S N
Anchor 9-12 feet N33.09.077
STR 4.8 feet W079.19.417
Exit ICW between R22 and R24. Proceed NW.

420.1 South Santee River Anchorage (Southeast)(0.4) S N
Anchor 10-12 feet N33.08.701
STR 4.8 feet W079.18.766
Exit ICW between R22 and R24. Proceed SE.

430.0 Leland Oil Company (0.5) S N
VHF 16; 843/887-3641
Exit ICW at G35. Proceed N into charted Jeremy

SAFETY INFO

NOAA Weather WX-2 Myrtle Beach, SC **WX-1 Charleston, SC** WX-3 Beaufort, SC	**Sea Tow** Charleston, SC VHF 16/10 843/881-8949
USCG Station Charleston, SC VHF 16 or 09/22A 843/724-7616	**TowBoatU.S.** Charleston, SC VHF 16/12 843/795-4699

HEADS UP!

352.2	The Rock Pile (NB)	469.0	Charleston Coast Guard Station
353.4	Barefoot Landing Bridge	470.8	Wappoo Creek Bridge
365.4	Seaboard Coast Line RR Bridge	472.2	Elliott Cut (SB)
366.0	Numerous Rock Ledges (NB)	472.5	Elliott Cut (NB)
371.0	Socastee Bridge	536.0	Ladies Island Bridge
406.0	Winyah Bay Entrance (SB)	575.8	SC-GA Border
410.5	Estherville Minim Canal (SB)	578.4	Wilmington River Cut-off (NB)
411.0	South Island Ferry Crossing	579.9	Causton Bluff Bridge
462.3	Ben Sawyer Bridge	592.4	Skidaway Narrows Bridge

Creek to town of McClellanville. Facility is to starboard. [STR 5.8 (TS)]
Previously known as Leland Marine.
See McClellanville & Oyster Recycling.

430.0 Five Fathom Creek Anchorages S N
Exit ICW at Town Creek G25. Proceed southwesterly in charted Town Creek to Five Fathom Creek.

- **Five Fathom Creek Anchorage** (Northeast)(0.9)
  Anchor 8-12 feet N33.03.950
  STR 5.8 feet W079.27.881
  Upon entering Five Fathom Creek, hook NE and anchor by R20.
- **Five Fathom Creek Anchorage** (Southwest)(2.4)
  Anchor 10-14 feet N33.02.915
  STR 5.8 feet W079.28.772
  Below G17, hook NE to charted 10-foot tongue.

435.7 Awendaw Creek Anchorage (0.8) S N
Anchor 8-10 feet N33.02.096
STR 5.8 feet W079.32.265
Exit ICW at R48. Proceed SSW, then easterly, to charted deepwater tongue.

439.0 Graham Creek Anchorage (0.3) S N
Anchor 6-8 feet N33.00.545
STR 5.7 feet W079.35.338
Exit ICW at R64. Proceed S into Graham Creek.
See Cape Romain.

448.3 Price Creek Anchorage (1.2) S N
Anchor 14-20 feet N32.53.406
STR 5.7 feet W079.39.858
Exit ICW at R86. Proceed NE then southeasterly into Price Creek.

450.8 Capers Creek Anchorage (0.2) S N
Anchor 8-10 feet N32.52.447
STR 5.8 feet W079.42.204
Exit ICW at R94. Proceed S to charted 10-foot pocket.

451.4 Whiteside Creek Anchorage (North)(0.2) S N
Anchor 10-14 feet N32.52.273
STR 5.8 feet W079.42.796
Exit ICW NE of R96. Proceed NW into Whiteside Creek.

451.5 Whiteside Creek Anchorage (South)(0.2) S N
Anchor 6-8 feet N32.51.943
STR 5.8 feet W079.42.708
Exit ICW at R96. Proceed S down Whiteside Creek. Anchor E of G97.

454.7 Dewees Creek Anchorage (Northwest)(0.9) S N
Anchor 18-20 feet N32.50.453
STR 5.8 feet W079.44.870
Exit ICW between G109 and R110. Proceed NW to first unnamed creek to starboard. Proceed NE into creek. Anchor around first bend.
See Sewee Bay Middens.

454.7 Dewees Creek Anchorage (Southeast)(1.1) S N
Anchor 12-16 feet N32.49.902
STR 5.8 feet W079.43.662
Exit ICW between G109 and R110. Proceed easterly then N behind Big Hill Marsh Island.

thousands of game birds descended on their crops. Plantation owners employed seasonal "bird minders" to sit on embankments in the fields and shoo the birds with muskets, rawhide whips with crackers, and tin noisemakers. Frustrated farmers even resorted to baiting the fields with carrion, intentionally attracting turkey vultures to frighten away other birds.

Today, of course, migratory birds are protected under the Migratory Bird Treaty Act. The Yawkey Preserve, covering North Island, South Island, and most of Cat Island, provides valuable habitat for their annual migrations.

Tom Yawkey Wildlife Center
843/546-6814

ANDROMEDA (AUTUMN)

It's not a constellation, but the Great Square is an important celestial landmark. Look for a very large square of four bright stars, visible in early fall just south of the sky's zenith.

The Great Square is the jumping off point for two constellations: Andromeda and Pegasus. Andromeda is the chained lady, her head at the northeast corner of the Great Square as she lies back, chained by her right arm. According to the myth, Andromeda is the daughter of Queen Cassiopeia and King Cepheus, both visible around the North Star (See This Eon's Pole Star).

But Queen Cassiopeia boasted of her daughter's beauty one too many times. The jealous sea nymphs convinced Poseidon to send a sea monster, the Whale, to ravage Ethiopia's coast.

In order to save his land, the King appeased the monster by chaining Andromeda to a rock in the sea. Fortunately, brave Perseus spotted Andromeda, killed the monster, and carried her off on his winged horse, Pegasus.

In late fall, the constellations of this myth are visible: Andromeda, Cassiopeia, Cepheus, Perseus, Pegasus, and the Whale.

THE FARTHEST YOU CAN SEE

On a moonless night in a dark anchorage, look carefully near Andromeda's bent knee. You may see a hazy smudge of light. This is the spiral galaxy Great Nebula, a galaxy other than our own Milky Way galaxy, and the most distant object visible with the naked eye.

MCCLELLANVILLE

Once busy with shucking houses and oyster canneries, McClellanville was the center of the local oyster industry. But honestly, when was the last time you saw (or ate) a canned oyster? These days, people want fresh oysters on the half shell, not slimy morsels in a jar. As tastes changed, the shucking and canning businesses closed.

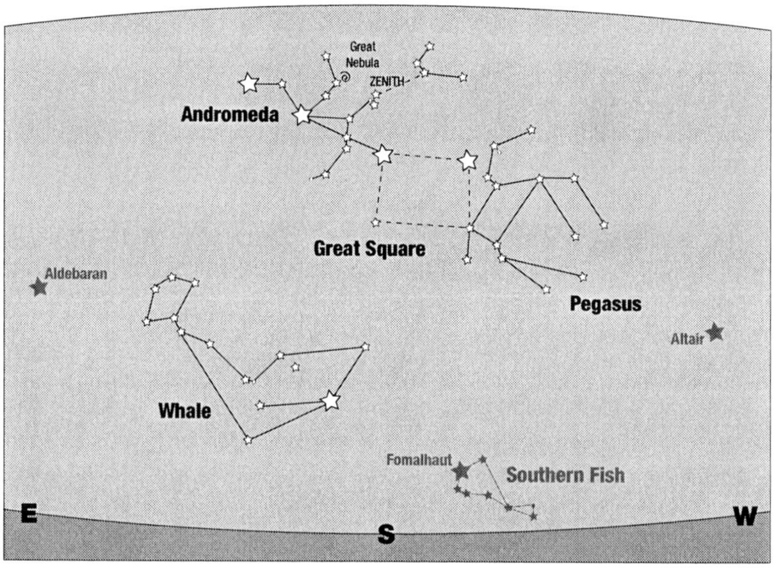

Autumn, Late Evening

Andromeda and the Great Square

SAFETY INFO

NOAA Weather	Sea Tow
WX-2 Myrtle Beach, SC	Charleston, SC
WX-1 Charleston, SC	VHF 16/10
WX-3 Beaufort, SC	843/881-8949
USCG	**TowBoatU.S.**
Station Charleston, SC	Charleston, SC
VHF 16 or 09/22A	VHF 16/12
843/724-7616	843/795-4699

HEADS UP!

352.2	The Rock Pile (NB)	469.0	Charleston Coast Guard Station
353.4	Barefoot Landing Bridge	470.8	Wappoo Creek Bridge
365.4	Seaboard Coast Line RR Bridge	472.2	Elliott Cut (SB)
366.0	Numerous Rock Ledges (NB)	472.5	Elliott Cut (NB)
371.0	Socastee Bridge	536.0	Ladies Island Bridge
406.0	Winyah Bay Entrance (SB)	575.8	SC-GA Border
410.5	Estherville Minim Canal (SB)	578.4	Wilmington River Cut-off (NB)
411.0	South Island Ferry Crossing	579.9	Causton Bluff Bridge
462.3	**Ben Sawyer Bridge**	592.4	Skidaway Narrows Bridge

Fortunately, local restaurants and grocery stores still consume massive quantities of shrimp. McClellanville, with only about 180 families, is home to a large shrimping fleet and the South Carolina Shrimpers Association. If you pass by in early May, stop in for the Blessing of the Fleet and enjoy the town's Lowcountry shrimp festival.

Lowcountry Shrimp Festival
843/887-3712

semi-local publications LLC

Photo by Author **Shrimpers at McClellanville**

OYSTER RECYCLING

Now that oysters are sold by the bushel in their shells, what happens to all those shells? Back when oysters were cleaned at a shucking house, the shells could be returned to the estuary. Now, with oysters distributed all over the state and shucked in small quantities at restaurants or backyard oyster roasts, most shells never make it back to the bay. They end up in landfills or dumped in driveways as a cheap do-it-yourself paving surface.

But oyster beds need oyster shells to repopulate. During the summer, oysters spawn and release free-swimming larvae, called spat, into the water. About two weeks later, the spat attach to a suitable surface, called *cultch*, and begin building their own shells. The best source of cultch? Old oyster shells.

Unless oyster shells are returned for cultch, the next generation of oysters suffer. So if you walk the dock at McClellanville, you may see an unusual recycling receptacle: the oyster shell drop-off site. Instead of aluminum or glass, oyster shells are the local recyclable, re-used to maintain the area's shellfish beds.

SEWEE BAY MIDDENS

Disposing of oyster shells is not a new problem. The Native Americans ate massive quantities of shellfish, leaving behind centuries of accumulated shells. These mounds of pre-history kitchen waste are called middens.

Large middens have been found all along the Waterway, left from the many Native American communities that used these inland waters for settlements or transportation.

Although most middens were lost to development, occasionally you can still spot a midden along the Atlantic or Gulf Intracoastal Waterway.

Several middens are located along the shores of Sewee Bay at about STM 445. Piles of oyster shells and pottery shards were also found further south at Porcher Bluff, charted as the high ground beyond the marshes west of G105 at about STM 454. Look for unusual mounds of land, now covered with vegetation.

OYSTERCATCHERS

Ever try to open an oyster shell? It's not easy. An oyster shell can break a thin stainless-steel knife blade; that's why you have to use a specially designed oyster knife. But there is a wading bird that can open oysters with its bill: the oystercatcher.

Look for the American Oystercatcher flying by your boat or feeding along the banks. This large chunky wader is distinctive with its heavy bright red bill, black back, and white underparts. Or listen for an oystercatcher approaching with its alarmingly loud and clear "whee-whee-whee-whee" whistle.

CAPE ROMAIN

The Cape Romain National Wildlife Refuge is described as the greatest natural wildlife area on the Atlantic coast. It protects 64,000 acres of wilderness, much of it inaccessible because of dense undergrowth and wetlands.

But your magic carpet takes you in comfort through 24 miles of the refuge. There are several anchorages between STM 430 and STM 452 where you can explore the wilds by dinghy.

Look for wood storks, ibis, plovers, sandpipers, oystercatchers, terns, mergansers, and several species of herons. Unfortunately, the Sewee Visitor Center, serving the Cape Romain National Wildlife Refuge and the

456.0 Seven Reaches Creek Anchorage (0.2)
Anchor 6-8 feet N32.48.912
STR 5.9 feet W079.45.163
Exit ICW at G115. Proceed W to charted 7-foot sounding.
SEE RESORTS OLD AND NEW.

456.9 Isle of Palms Marina (0.1)
VHF 16/71 N32.48.318
843/886-0209 W079.45.541
Exit ICW WSW of R116. Marina is to SE. [STR 5.9]

458.8 Isle of Palms Bridge
Fixed; vertical 65 feet.
Caution: Clearance reported at less than 65 feet. Check boards before proceeding.

461.1 Inlet Creek Anchorage (0.3)
Anchor 10-14 feet N32.47.054
STR 5.9 feet W079.49.499
Exit ICW WSW of G119. Proceed N to Inlet Creek.

462.3 Ben Sawyer Bridge
VHF 09; 843/883-3581
Single-pivot swing; vertical 31 feet. [STR 5.9 (TS)]
Restricted year round: M-F except holidays, 0700-0900 and 1600-1800 hrs.
Restricted year round: SA-SU and holidays, 0900-1900 hrs, opens on the hour.

462.4 Toler's Cove Marina (0.2)
VHF 16; 843/881-0325
Exit ICW WSW of bridge. Proceed NW in privately maintained channel. Marina is to starboard. No transient dockage. [STR 5.9]

463.8 45.5-mile Land Cut
to 418.3
Northbound Navigation Only
45.5-mile land cut.
14 anchorages, two marinas, fuel available.
SEE FORT MOULTRIE.

463.8 Range "C"
to 464.1
Southbound/Northbound Navigation
Sullivans Island
0.3-mile range.

464.5 Junction | Charleston Roads (7.7)
Well Aided N32.42.028
Well Lit W079.45.805
Exit ICW SW of R130. Proceed southeasterly out channel.
Waypoint is between G13 and R14.
SEE FORT SUMTER & THE HUNLEY SUBMARINE.

464.5 Junction | Cooper River
Exit ICW SW of R130. Proceed northwesterly up Cooper River. [STR 5.0 (TS)]
The Cooper River winds northerly to Patriots Point, the town of Mount Pleasant, and Charleston (east) destinations.
SEE CHARLESTON: CITY OF ARRIVALS.

- **Charleston Harbor Marina** (2.7)
  VHF 16/72 N32.47.158
  888/856-0028 W079.54.654
  Exit Cooper River ship channel between R34

SAFETY INFO

NOAA Weather
WX-2 Myrtle Beach, SC
WX-1 Charleston, SC
WX-3 Beaufort, SC

USCG
Station Charleston, SC
VHF 16 or 09/22A
843/724-7616

Sea Tow
Charleston, SC
VHF 16/10
843/881-8949

TowBoatU.S.
Charleston, SC
VHF 16/12
843/795-4699

HEADS UP!

353.4	Barefoot Landing Bridge
365.4	Seaboard Coast Line RR Bridge
366.0	Numerous Rock Ledges (NB)
371.0	Socastee Bridge
406.0	Winyah Bay Entrance (SB)
410.5	Estherville Minim Canal (SB)
411.0	South Island Ferry Crossing
462.3	Ben Sawyer Bridge
469.0	**Charleston Coast Guard Station**
470.8	Wappoo Creek Bridge
472.2	Elliott Cut (SB)
472.5	Elliott Cut (NB)
536.0	Ladies Island Bridge
575.8	SC-GA Border
578.4	Wilmington River Cut-off (NB)
579.9	Causton Bluff Bridge
592.4	Skidaway Narrows Bridge
706.0	Kings Bay Security Zone (SB)

and R36. Proceed NE to charted marina breakwater at Patriots Point.

- **Charleston Maritime Center** (2.8)
  VHF 16/69 N32.47.275
  843/853-3625 W079.55.417
  Exit Cooper River ship channel between R34 and R36. Proceed SW, north of Shutes Folly Island, to marina in charted basin.
- **Cooper River Marina** (7.6)
  VHF 16/11 N32.49.820
  843/554-0790 W079.56.250
  Continue northwesterly up Cooper River. Proceed on either side of Drum Island (under either fixed bridge, vertical 135 feet) to charted Shipyard Creek. Proceed WNW into creek. Marina is to starboard.

469.0 USCG Station Charleston S N
Charted USCG station is to NE.
Caution: Security zone marked by buoys.

469.2 Junction | Ashley River and Charleston S N
Exit ICW NW of Coast Guard base at R4. Proceed northwesterly up Ashley River.
The Ashley River leads to the city of Charleston (west) destinations. [STR 6.2]
SEE CHARLESTON ARCHITECTURE.

- **Charleston "Old" Anchorage** (0.2)
  Anchor 12-20 feet N32.46.563
  STR 6.2 feet W079.56.992
  The old anchorage NW of R4 is now home to the City Marina's MegaDock facilities.
- **Charleston City Marina** (0.3)
  VHF 16/68 N32.46.653
  843/723-5098 W079.57.163
  Marina is to starboard before high-rise bridge.
  The marina no longer offers overnight mooring balls for transients.
- **Charleston "New" Anchorage** (0.4)
  Anchor 16-20 feet N32.46.591
  STR 6.2 feet W079.57.230
  Anchorage is opposite City Marina in charted designated anchorage at G5.
- **Ashley River Fixed Bridge** (0.6)
  Fixed; vertical 56 feet. [STR 6.2 (TS)]
  Caution: This is NOT an ICW 65-foot bridge!
- **Ashley Marina** (0.7)
  VHF 16/71 N32.46.884
  843/722-1996 W079.57.447
  Marina is to starboard.
  Recently sold. Converting to dockominiums.
- **Ripley Light Marina** (0.7)
  VHF 16; 843/766-2100
  Marina/Yacht Club is closed. Transient wet slips are closed due to condo and dockominium development.
  Fuel dock is active, in charted 10-foot canal.
- **Ashley River Bridges** (0.9)
  (US 17)
  VHF 09; 843-577-7605
  Twin bascule; vertical 18 and 14 feet.
  Restricted year round: M-F 0700-0900 and 1600-1900 hrs, 12-hour notice required.

Francis Marion State Forest, is located about eight miles from charted Garris Landing on Highway 17.

Cape Romain National Wildlife Refuge
http://caperomain.fws.gov
843/928-3264

RESORTS OLD AND NEW

There once were two resorts near STM 456. Isle of Palms, on the east side of the Waterway, was a refuge from the summer heat of Charleston. In the early 1900s Charlestonians could take a ferry across to Mt. Pleasant, then ride the trolley along Sullivans Island to the cooler barrier island beaches of Isle of Palms.

Goat Island, on the west side of the Waterway across Meeting Reach, attracted a different clientele. During Prohibition, bootleggers used this island as their hangout.

Today Isle of Palms is a residential community, developed after World War II to provide housing for returning veterans, and, later in the 1970s, by the same company that developed Hilton Head Island. Isle of Palms' 900-acre resort, Wild Dunes, includes a marina, golf courses, beaches—and, of course, plenty of legal alcohol.

THE GOLD BUG

Edgar Allen Poe's short mystery, *The Gold Bug*, takes place along the shores of Sullivans Island, near STM 464. Poe was stationed nearby in Charleston and wrote this cryptographic story shortly after he left the army.

The story tells the tale of an eccentric who has retreated to Sullivans Island to live in peaceful poverty. He finds a gold bug and a partially buried piece of parchment with a cryptograph. When the note is solved, it contains directions to a site on the island. In its coding scheme, the note leads to: K6††') ;(85)?(8

The code is relatively simple, so this short story was used in grammar schools in the early 1900s to teach the logic of codes. Like a Wheel of Fortune game of the 1840s, it can be solved using common letter frequencies. To get you started:) is a s, K is a K, and ; is a t. Vanna has offered one vowel for free: the number 8 is an e.

FORT MOULTRIE

When South Carolina seceded from the Union, Fort Moultrie was one of a quartet of forts guarding Charleston Harbor. Fort Moultrie stood on Sullivans Island, Fort Sumter in the mid-

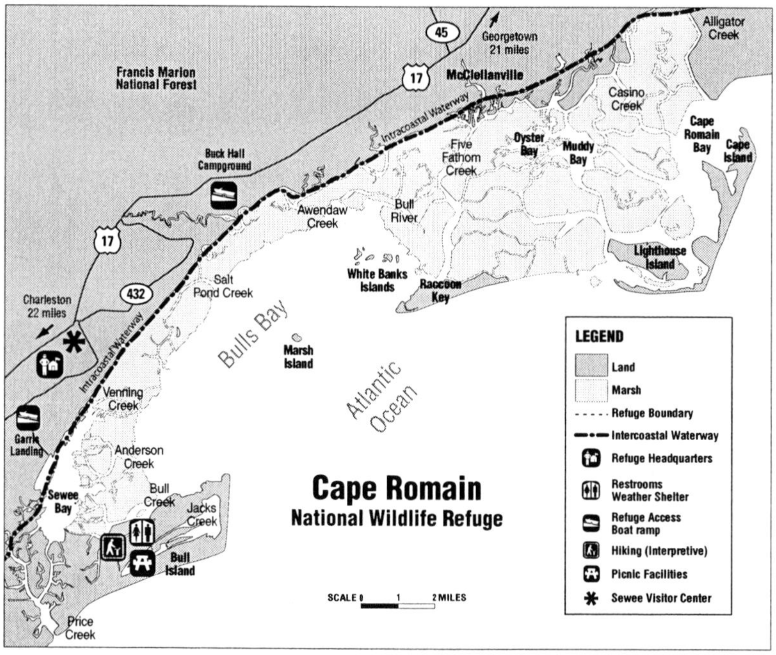

Courtesy of Cape Romain National Wildlife Refuge

Cape Romain National Wildlife Refuge

SAFETY INFO

NOAA Weather	**Sea Tow**
WX-2 Myrtle Beach, SC	Charleston, SC
WX-1 Charleston, SC	VHF 16/10
WX-3 Beaufort, SC	843/881-8949
USCG	**TowBoatU.S.**
Station Charleston, SC	Charleston, SC
VHF 16 or 09/22A	VHF 16/12
843/724-7616	843/795-4699

HEADS UP!

366.0	Numerous Rock Ledges (NB)	**472.5**	**Elliott Cut (NB)**
371.0	Socastee Bridge	536.0	Ladies Island Bridge
406.0	Winyah Bay Entrance (SB)	575.8	SC-GA Border
410.5	Estherville Minim Canal (SB)	578.4	Wilmington River Cut-off (NB)
411.0	South Island Ferry Crossing	579.9	Causton Bluff Bridge
462.3	Ben Sawyer Bridge	592.4	Skidaway Narrows Bridge
469.0	Charleston Coast Guard Station	706.0	Kings Bay Security Zone (SB)
470.8	**Wappoo Creek Bridge**	713.0	Kings Bay Security Zone (NB)
472.2	**Elliott Cut (SB)**	713.7	Cumberland Sound Channel (NB)

dle of Charleston Harbor, Fort Johnson on James Island, and Castle Pinckney on Shutes Folly Island. These four forts combined their strengths well: Charleston was never conquered from the sea.

The fort at Fort Moultrie is actually "Fort Moultrie III." Originally called Fort Sullivan, the initial structure was a little fort made of palmetto logs. Under the leadership of Colonel Moultrie, Fort Sullivan successfully defended Charleston against the British in 1776 (See Cabbage Palmetto). A larger, more substantial structure—named in the Colonel's honor—was built, destroyed in a 1804 hurricane, and rebuilt in 1809.

Fort Moultrie's real strength was its strategic position, not its structure. Ships entering the harbor were sitting ducks for Fort Moultrie's guns. Shoals at the entrance to Charleston Harbor forced ships to enter the harbor from the south, on a range heading directly toward the fort. If a ship didn't maintain the heading, she ran aground. But maintaining the heading put her right in the line of fire, unable to fire until she cleared the range and turned broadside into the harbor.

Fort Moultrie National Monument
www.nps.gov/fomo
843/883-3123

FORT SUMTER

No fort is as famous in American history as Fort Sumter. On April 12, 1861, Confederate Commander Beauregard received orders to "proceed to reduce it." The rebels began an artillery barrage from the batteries ringing Charleston Harbor. The Union garrison inside Fort Sumter fired back, but the fort's wooden barracks caught fire and the men were forced to surrender. A Confederate horse was the only fatality during the 34-hour artillery exchange.

But when Beauregard granted permission to the surrendering troops to fire a 100-gun salute before lowering the Stars and Stripes, one of the shots misfired and killed two Union soldiers. So in an ironic twist, the first two official deaths of the Civil War were friendly fire—the first of 620,000 men who would die in the 4-year civil strife.

Fort Sumter is now a National Monument, accessible by private boat or ferry. A concession ferry provides transportation for $12, departing from Patriots Point in Mt. Pleasant and the Fort Sumter Visitor Education Center, located in downtown Charleston next to the aquarium.

Columbia/Tristar Promotional Image

Robert Gould Shaw and Broderick

The sandy spit of land, on the mainland across from Fort Sumter, is important in African American history. Black Union troops launched a suicidal attack from this spit, challenging a Confederate redoubt called Battery Wagner. The battle on this spit transformed the attitudes of both Northern and Southern whites about the fighting ability of black soldiers. The story of these troops is told in the film *Glory* (1989), starring Matthew Broderick, Morgan Freeman, and Denzel Washington.

Fort Sumter National Monument
www.nps.gov/fosu
843/883-3123

Fort Sumter Tours/Ferry
800/789-3678

South Carolina Aquarium
www.scaquarium.org
843/720-1990

THE HUNLEY SUBMARINE

The first submarine to sink an enemy vessel, the *H.L. Hunley*, made several tragic test voyages here in Charleston Harbor. Like any "first," the Hunley had its share of problems. But this clunky hand-cranked vessel, currently being conserved by archaeologists at the Warren Lasch Conservation Center, is more sophisticated than historians first believed.

The Hunley is mostly remembered for its tragic failures. Since the only oxygen supply was the submarine's volume, any unexpected delay meant the oxygen would be dangerously depleted. The first crew drowned in 1863 when a wake from a passing steamer

- **Dolphin Cove Marina** (3.0)
  VHF 16; 843/744-2562
  Continue northerly up Ashley River. Marina is to starboard.

469.9 Mark Clark Expressway Bridge S N
(James Island Expressway Bridge)
Fixed; vertical 67 feet.

470.8 Wappoo Creek Bridge S N
VHF 09; 843/852-4157
Double bascule; vertical 33 feet. [STR 6.0 (TS)]
Restricted June 1-September 30 and December 1-March 30: M-F except holidays, 0630-0900 and 1600-1830 hrs.
Restricted April 1-May 31 and October 1-November 30: M-F except holidays, 0600-0900 and 1600-1830 hrs.
Restricted April 1-November 30: M-F, 0900-1600 hrs; and SA-SU and holidays, 0900-1900 hrs; opens on the hour and half-hour.

471.1 Wappoo Creek Anchorage (0.2) S N
Anchor 10-14 feet N32.45.897
STR 6.0 feet W079.58.828
Exit ICW W of bridge. Proceed SW into oxbow. Anchor behind small island.

472.2 Elliott Cut S N
to 472.5 Southbound/Northbound Navigation
0.3-mile land cut.
Caution: Elliott Cut can run 6.5 knots at max ebb.

472.6 Junction | Stono River S N
Exit ICW NW of R18. Proceed southerly down Stono River. [STR 6.0]
Caution: Buoyage reverses in Stono River.

- **Buzzards Roost Point Anchorage** (0.8)
  Anchor 8-12 feet N32.45.560
  STR 6.0 feet W080.00.531
  Anchorage is opposite R16 "A" in charted 7- to 10-foot tongue.
- **Buzzard's Roost Marina** (1.0)
  VHF 16; 843/559-5516
  Marina is to starboard before bridge.
- **Stono River Bridge** (1.1)
  Fixed; vertical 65 feet.
  New fixed bridge replaces charted 8-foot swing bridge.
- **Stono Marina** (1.2)
  VHF 16; 843/559-2307
  Marina is to starboard after bridge.

473.7 Range "A" S N
to 475.2 Southbound/Northbound Navigation
Stono River
1.5-mile range.
We typically pick up (southbound) or leave (northbound) Range "A" at G21.

475.5 Stono River Anchorage (North)(0.2) S N
Anchor 6-10 feet N32.46.775
STR 6.1 feet W080.03.214
Exit ICW at G23. Proceed northerly to charted

SAFETY INFO

NOAA Weather
WX-2 Myrtle Beach, SC
WX-1 Charleston, SC
WX-3 Beaufort, SC

USCG
Station Charleston, SC
VHF 16 or 09/22A
843/724-7616

Sea Tow
Charleston, SC
VHF 16/10
843/881-8949

TowBoatU.S.
Charleston, SC
VHF 16/12
843/795-4699

HEADS UP!

371.0	Socastee Bridge
406.0	Winyah Bay Entrance (SB)
410.5	Estherville Minim Canal (SB)
411.0	South Island Ferry Crossing
462.3	Ben Sawyer Bridge
469.0	Charleston Coast Guard Station
470.8	Wappoo Creek Bridge
472.2	Elliott Cut (SB)
472.5	Elliott Cut (NB)
536.0	Ladies Island Bridge
575.8	SC-GA Border
578.4	Wilmington River Cut-off (NB)
579.9	Causton Bluff Bridge
592.4	Skidaway Narrows Bridge
706.0	Kings Bay Security Zone (SB)
713.0	Kings Bay Security Zone (NB)
713.7	Cumberland Sound Channel (NB)
714.0	GA-FL Border

7- to 8-foot tongue.
Caution: When leaving anchorage, be careful to exit tongue easterly to avoid charted shoal.

475.8 Range "B" S N
to Southbound Navigation Only
476.5 Stono River
0.7-mile range.

476.3 Ross Marine (0.1) S N
VHF 16/79 N32.46.316
843/559-0379 W080.03.849
Exit ICW in Range "B". Facility is to SSE. [STR 6.2]

476.5 Range "B" S N
to Northbound Navigation Only
475.8 Stono River
0.7-mile range.

477.1 Range "C" S N
to Southbound/Northbound Navigation
477.9 Stono River
0.8-mile range.

478.1 Range "D" S N
to Southbound/Northbound Navigation
478.8 Stono River
0.7-mile range.

479.3 John F. Limehouse Bridge S N
Fixed; vertical 65 feet. [STR 6.5 (TS)]

479.8 Stono River Anchorage (South)(0.1) S N
Anchor 5-7 feet N32.46.988
STR 6.5 feet W080.06.891
Exit ICW ENE of G39. Proceed NW into oxbow. Less water than charted; do not enter very far.

487.7 Church Creek Anchorage (0.5) S N
Anchor 8-12 feet N32.42.560
STR 7.5 feet W080.11.080
Exit ICW at G77. Proceed ESE into charted Church Creek.
See Church Flats and Cook's Kitchen.

487.8 Range "A" S N
to Southbound/Northbound Navigation
488.7 Wadmalaw (pronounced WAHD-muh-law) Sound
0.9-mile range.

492.8 Wadmalaw Island Anchorage (0.2) S N
Anchor 15-18 feet N32.40.142
STR 7.6 feet W080.14.206
Exit ICW between G95 and G97. Proceed northerly into charted tongue.

494.0 Wadmalaw River Anchorage (0.2) S N
Anchor 12-15 feet N32.39.385
STR 7.6 feet W080.14.763
Exit ICW between R100 and G101. Proceed northeasterly into charted tongue.

495.5 Toogoodoo Creek Anchorage (1.9) S N
Anchor 8-12 feet N32.39.678
STR (TS) 7.3 feet W080.16.599
Exit ICW midway between Toogoodoo Creek and Tom Point Creek. Proceed northerly into creek. Anchor around bend as water shallows.

flooded the sub at its mooring. A few weeks later, half of the second crew, including the designer H.L. Hunley, died during a test dive.

In 1864 the Hunley went back out into Charleston Harbor. This time it rammed a spar with a black powder charge into a Federal blockade ship, becoming the first submarine to sink an enemy warship. Sadly, the submarine failed to return, sinking as a tomb on the seabed.

The Hunley was discovered in 1995 and raised in 2000. Only last year were the remains of the third crew placed with the other Hunley crew members, at the Magnolia Cemetery in Charleston, where many of the city's Confederate casualties are buried.

You can see the Hunley, on weekend afternoons when archaeologists are not at work, at the Warren Lasch Conservation Center.

Hunley Submarine
Warren Lasch Conservation Center
www.hunley.org
866/866-9938

CHARLESTON: CITY OF ARRIVALS

When we think of the arrival of immigrants to America, Ellis Island comes to mind. But much earlier in American history, Charleston was the port of entry for many—from the first American Jews to countless African slaves.

If a Charlestonian traces his or her ancestry to "the three ships," it means they are descended from the first settlers of Charleston. In 1669, three ships of colonists sailed from England to the New World. But on the voyage, hurricanes wrecked two of the ships, forcing the passengers to crowd aboard the single remaining vessel. This ship, called the Carolina, arrived months later in Charleston, starting a new community in this protected harbor.

The first American Jews also arrived through the port of Charleston. Jews began arriving from Spain in 1695, fleeing the persecution of the Inquisition. Until the early 19th century, Charleston had the largest Jewish population in the country, with a quarter of all American Jews living in South Carolina. The temple Kahal Kadosh Beth Elohim, on Hasell Street, was built in 1840 and is considered by many to be the birthplace of Reform Judaism in America. You can enter the sanctuary on weekday mornings. The oldest remaining Jewish burial ground in the South is nearby at the cemetery on Coming Street.

Charleston was also busy with slave traffic. A third of all Africans brought to this country as slaves first touched American soil here in Charleston. Slave auctions were held in the hall at Six Chalmers Street, now the Slave Mart Museum.

Charles Towne Landing State Historic Site
843/852-4200

Kahal Kadosh Beth Elohim
www.kkbe.org
843/723-1090

Slave Mart Museum
843/724-7395

The Charleston Museum
www.charlestonmuseum.org
843/722-2996

Courtesy of Charleston CVB

Charleston Architecture

CHARLESTON ARCHITECTURE

Charleston is a sophisticated modern city with very un-modern architecture. It is a city of church spires instead of skyscrapers, cobblestone streets and antebellum architecture instead of postwar housing.

Ironically, it was poverty following wealth that saved Charleston's beautiful architecture. Before the Civil War, Charleston was living it up as the center of plantation wealth. Hundreds of plantation owners and merchants built elaborate townhouses in Charleston as city residences, complete with lav-

SAFETY INFO

NOAA Weather
WX-1 Charleston, SC
WX-3 Beaufort, SC
WX-2 Savannah, GA

USCG
Station Charleston, SC
VHF 16 or 09/22A
843/724-7616

Sea Tow
Charleston, SC
VHF 16/10
843/881-8949

TowBoatU.S.
Charleston, SC
VHF 16/12
843/795-4699

HEADS UP!

371.0	Socastee Bridge
406.0	Winyah Bay Entrance (SB)
410.5	Estherville Minim Canal (SB)
411.0	South Island Ferry Crossing
462.3	Ben Sawyer Bridge
469.0	Charleston Coast Guard Station
470.8	Wappoo Creek Bridge
472.2	Elliott Cut (SB)
472.5	Elliott Cut (NB)
536.0	Ladies Island Bridge
575.8	SC-GA Border
578.4	Wilmington River Cut-off (NB)
579.9	Causton Bluff Bridge
592.4	Skidaway Narrows Bridge
706.0	Kings Bay Security Zone (SB)
713.0	Kings Bay Security Zone (NB)
713.7	Cumberland Sound Channel (NB)
714.0	GA-FL Border

ish formal gardens and ornate interior designs. They lived in high style with balls and banquets, a lively arts culture, and European educations.

Courtesy of Charleston CVB

Sweetgrass Baskets

That lifestyle came to a crash after the Civil War, when Charleston slid into an economic depression triggered by the collapse of the rice market. Unlike many other cities emerging from the ruins of the Civil War, Charleston was too poor to rebuild. The pre-Civil War buildings had to suffice. Thankfully, old buildings were repaired and maintained rather than torn down and rebuilt.

Today these historic structures are incredibly valuable, both historically and economically. They are no longer maintained out of frugal economic necessity. Today's real estate values are staggering. A "moderate" Charleston single-family historic townhouse now sells for between $1 million and $3 million; a mansion in the historic district can push $7 million.

To learn about the architectural history of Charleston, take a narrated walking or carriage tour leaving from the City Market. The tours highlight the history of the buildings and the design principles that made these houses comfortable in the southern heat before air conditioning.

If you arrive in the spring, between late March and mid-April, scores of private homes are open to the public through the Annual Festival of Houses and Gardens. Tickets are $45 and the properties vary daily. Or, for $15, you can join a walking tour leaving from 108 Meeting Street.

In the fall, between late September and mid-October, the city also opens its doors for self-guided candlelight walking tours of private homes and gardens. The walks depart every Thursday, Friday, and Saturday evenings and are sponsored by the Preservation Society of Charleston.

Annual Festival of Houses & Gardens
www.historiccharleston.org
843/722-3405

Preservation Society of Charleston
843/722-4630

Find out what's good to eat and interesting to see! Check out the local visitor center for restaurant guides, free brochures and maps, calendars of events, and local bus routes and schedules. They can usually answer any question: from where to get supplies to what's happening for free that evening.

OLD CITY MARKET

Old City Market, a collection of sheds on Market Street between Meeting and East Bay Streets, was once an outdoor produce and fish market. Today it is a collection of restaurants, shops, and local produce and craft stands.

Fanner baskets, also called sweetgrass baskets, are sold in the Old City Market, locally made by descendants of the slaves who cultivated the rice. Made of grass, pine, or palmetto fronds, these baskets were used to winnow rice on the plantations. The grains were tossed into the air and the wind "fanned" the chaff from the rice.

Large flat baskets similar to these are still used in Sierra Leone, on the west coast of Africa. Most of the slaves brought to the Carolina plantations were captured from the Rice Coast of Africa, where rice had been grown for centuries. The slaves brought their language—now evolved into Gullah—their music, and their craft of coiled, decorative baskets.

495.7 Tom Point Creek Anchorage (0.8)
Anchor 8-12 feet N32.38.700
STR 7.3 feet W080.16.779
Exit ICW at charted Tom Point Creek. Proceed NNW into creek.

496.6 Junction | North Edisto River Entrance
Exit ICW ESE of R110 (White Point). Proceed southeasterly down North Edisto River. [STR 7.1]
Caution: Buoyage reverses in North Edisto River and companion creeks.

- **Steamboat Creek Anchorage** (2.1)
  Anchor 12-15 feet N32.36.633
  STR 7.1 feet W080.16.769
  Exit river at R2. Proceed westerly into Steamboat Creek.
- **Rockville Marine** (7.2)
  VHF 16; 843/559-1124
  Exit river SE of charted Front Range (Q 16ft). Proceed N into Bohicket Creek. Continue N into Adams Creek. Facility is to starboard. [STR 6.7]
  Repair yard with no transient dockage.
- **Bohicket Marina** (9.3)
  VHF 16; 843/768-3461
  Exit river SE of charted Front Range (Q 16ft). Proceed N into charted Bohicket Creek. Continue northeasterly up Bohicket Creek beyond Cherry Point. Marina is to starboard at charted docks near Haulover Creek. [STR 6.7]
- **North Edisto River Entrance** (12.0)
  Moderately Aided N32.31.318
  Moderately Lit W080.06.759
  Continue SE out inlet. Waypoint is at R2 "NE".

501.3 McKinley Washington Jr. Bridge
Fixed; vertical 65 feet. [STR 7.2 (TS)]

501.6 Fishing Creek Anchorage (0.9)
Anchor 8-12 feet N32.38.706
STR 7.2 feet W080.20.704
Exit ICW at R132. Proceed northerly into Fishing Creek.
See Whooping Island.

502.7 Watts Cut
to Southbound/Northbound Navigation
504.3 1.6-mile land cut.
No anchorages, no marinas, no fuel.

504.4 South Edisto River Anchorage (North)(1.2)
Anchor 6-10 feet N32.36.833
STR 7.1 feet W080.24.274
Exit ICW W of G143. Proceed northwesterly up South Edisto River.

505.1 Range "A"
to Southbound/Northbound Navigation
506.0 South Edisto River
0.9-mile range.

507.5 South Edisto River Anchorage (Mid)(0.3)
Anchor 8-10 feet N32.34.569
STR 7.1 feet W080.23.262
Exit ICW at R152. Proceed NE to pocket in front of charted house.
See Prospect Hill Plantation.

SAFETY INFO		
	NOAA Weather	**Sea Tow**
	WX-1 Charleston, SC	Charleston, SC
	WX-3 Beaufort, SC	VHF 16/10
	WX-2 Savannah, GA	843/881-8949
	USCG	**TowBoatU.S.**
	Station Charleston, SC	Beaufort, SC
	VHF 16 or 09/22A	VHF 16
	843/724-7616	912/898-9659

HEADS UP!

406.0	Winyah Bay Entrance (SB)	575.8	SC-GA Border
410.5	Estherville Minim Canal (SB)	578.4	Wilmington River Cut-off (NB)
411.0	South Island Ferry Crossing	579.9	Causton Bluff Bridge
462.3	Ben Sawyer Bridge	592.4	Skidaway Narrows Bridge
469.0	Charleston Coast Guard Station	706.0	Kings Bay Security Zone (SB)
470.8	Wappoo Creek Bridge	713.0	Kings Bay Security Zone (NB)
472.2	Elliott Cut (SB)	713.7	Cumberland Sound Channel (NB)
472.5	Elliott Cut (NB)	714.0	GA-FL Border
536.0	Ladies Island Bridge	720.7	Kingsley Creek RR Bridge

507.6 Old Range "B" S N
to Southbound/Northbound Navigation
507.9 South Edisto River
0.3-mile range.
This range is still charted, but no longer used.

509.2 South Edisto River Anchorage (South)(0.4) S N
Anchor 8-12 feet N32.33.697
STR 7.1 feet W080.24.636
Exit ICW between R156 and G157. Proceed NNW toward Alligator Creek.
Caution: When leaving anchorage, rejoin ICW at top, rather than middle, of charted Range "C".

509.2 Range "C" S N
to Southbound/Northbound Navigation
509.9 South Edisto River
0.7-mile range.

511.1 St. Pierre Creek Anchorage (4.3) S N
Anchor 15-18 feet N32.31.926
STR 7.1 feet W080.21.438
Exit ICW E of R162. Proceed southeasterly down South Edisto River. Turn NNE, into St. Pierre Creek.

511.2 Fenwick Cut S N
to Southbound/Northbound Navigation
511.5 0.3-mile land cut.
No anchorages, no marinas, no fuel.

511.6 Fenwick Island Anchorage (South)(0.8) S N
Anchor 12-15 feet N32.31.365
STR 7.1 feet W080.24.550
Exit ICW SW of R164. Proceed southerly to Fenwick Island. Anchor off charted Seabrook.

512.0 Fenwick Island Anchorage (North)(0.1) S N
Anchor 12-15 feet N32.32.132
STR (TS) 7.1 feet W080.25.044
Exit ICW W of R164. Proceed NE.

513.5 Mosquito Creek S N
Exit ICW at R166. Proceed northwesterly up Ashepoo River. Turn N into Mosquito Creek at Bennetts Point. [STR 7.3]

- **B&B Seafood** (1.8)
  No VHF Watch; 843/844-2322
  Facility is to port.
- **Mosquito Creek Anchorage** (2.0)
  Anchor 10-12 feet N32.33.512
  STR 7.3 feet W080.27.162
  Anchor beyond B&B Seafood.

513.6 Ashepoo Coosaw Cutoff (East) S N
to Southbound/Northbound Navigation
515.0 1.4-mile land cut.
No anchorages, no marinas, no fuel.

515.1 Rock Creek Anchorage (Southeast)(0.5) S N
Anchor 12-16 feet N32.30.644
STR 7.2 feet W080.27.741
Exit ICW at R172. Proceed SE down Rock Creek.

515.6 Unnamed Range S N
to Southbound/Northbound Navigation
516.2 Rock Creek
0.6-mile range.

This will be the only time we'll suggest adding weight! When a bank is available, stock up on rolls of quarters. Since you can easily burn through $10 at one laundry session, buy $20 or $30 of quarters. It's amazing how often the change machines are out of order!

CHURCH FLATS AND COOK'S KITCHEN

Back when the only mode of transportation was boat, the meandering creeks south of Charleston were the local roads. These creeks took residents to and from church and to and from Charleston where goods were bought and sold.

"Church Flats" is located just south of G63 at about STM 485. Supposedly parishioners traveled to this spot for the local church, timing their arrival with the rising tide and returning home on the ebb tide.

Just a bit further south, near STM 487, is a wide marshy area once called "Cook's Kitchen." The marsh was called a kitchen, not for its bountiful harvests, but because it was a popular rest stop for hot food. Families traveling northbound to provision and sell their goods in Charleston would stop at the marsh at Cook's Kitchen to prepare a big meal before arriving at the bustling city.

WHOOPING ISLAND

The River Styx had a ferryman, named Charon, who allowed travelers to cross into Hades by paying him an obolus, an ancient Greek coin.

Charon may have demanded a price, but at least he stayed awake. To cross the North Creek, just south of G133, travelers needed to rouse the laid-back ferryman. As the story's told, locals had to "whoop" at the top of their lungs to wake the ferryman and get his attention. So the island at this old ferry crossing is now called Whooping Island.

PROSPECT HILL PLANTATION

Just south of G151, at STM 507, the charts show a single structure inauspiciously marked "House."

This large white house overlooking the Waterway is the Prospect Hill Plantation, built in 1790. The design is attributed to James Hoban, the architect of the other White House, the one at 1600 Pennsylvania Avenue.

LOWCOUNTRY MUD

Lowcountry mud isn't "mud." The sticky malodorous mud of these sulfurous tidal marshes has its own name: plough (pronounced pluff).

The name plough was coined back in the early 1800s, when planters discovered the local marsh mud was rich with nutrients. The mud was harvested and spread over fields of Sea Island cotton as a soil treatment. Since it was plowed into the fields, it was called plough mud, or eventually, simply "plough."

Courtesy of Beaufort Online

Set for Big Chill and Great Santini

COOSAW ISLAND

When the Union won the Civil War, it faced a quandary: what to do with the African American slaves freed from the Southern plantations.

In another one of the federal government's ambitious relocation plans, Federal troops were instructed to confiscate several of the outer islands, including Coosaw and Hilton Head Islands. The island properties were sold for taxes to emancipated African Americans, who settled on these remote islands to make a subsistence living fishing and farming. The islands were islands of poverty: as late as 1937 Coosaw Island had no automobiles, telephones, or bathtubs.

Today, Coosaw, Ladys, St. Helena, and Hilton Head Islands are linked to the mainland by bridges. Island living is now fashionable, and the islands have been transformed into modern, expensive—and largely white—residential developments.

"I can't hear you!" Spray your VHF deck connections with Corrosion Block every few months. It dramatically improves your VHF radio's transmission and reception.

SAFETY INFO

NOAA Weather
WX-1 Charleston, SC
WX-3 Beaufort, SC
WX-2 Savannah, GA

USCG
Station Tybee, GA
VHF 16 or 09/22A
912/786-5440

Sea Tow
Charleston, SC
VHF 16/10
843/881-8949

TowBoatU.S.
Beaufort, SC
VHF 16
912/898-9659

HEADS UP!

406.0	Winyah Bay Entrance (SB)	575.8	SC-GA Border
410.5	Estherville Minim Canal (SB)	578.4	Wilmington River Cut-off (NB)
411.0	South Island Ferry Crossing	579.9	Causton Bluff Bridge
462.3	Ben Sawyer Bridge	592.4	Skidaway Narrows Bridge
469.0	Charleston Coast Guard Station	706.0	Kings Bay Security Zone (SB)
470.8	Wappoo Creek Bridge	713.0	Kings Bay Security Zone (NB)
472.2	Elliott Cut (SB)	713.7	Cumberland Sound Channel (NB)
472.5	Elliott Cut (NB)	714.0	GA-FL Border
536.0	**Ladies Island Bridge**	720.7	Kingsley Creek RR Bridge

BEAUFORT

The first thing a boater needs to know about Beaufort is how to pronounce the city's name. It's Bew-furt, not Bo-fort.

Bo-fort is the town with the same name further north. Bo-fort was originally called Fishtowne, an apt name given the menhaden industry, but not a good marketing choice. So Bo-fort was renamed in 1709 for Henry Somerset, the second Duke of Beaufort.

Bew-furt was also named after the Duke of Beaufort, but for some reason unknown to local historians in either town, the two towns pronounce the name differently. As Bo-fort points out, they pronounce the name with the "correct" French pronunciation. Bew-furt pronounces the name as they please, thank you very much!

Today Beaufort is a vibrant waterfront town, with beautiful architecture dating to the 1700s and all the amenities a transiting boater needs. It's the second oldest city in South Carolina and, like Charleston, was largely saved from the physical destruction of the Civil War.

Paramount Pictures Promotional Image

Pop Culture Abounds on the Waterway

The best way to appreciate the town is to take the walking tour, following the free map available in town. The walk highlights many unusual homes, including "The Castle," a medieval-style antebellum mansion overlooking the Waterway. The Beaufort National Cemetery, created in 1862 by President Lincoln, is also a beautiful walk. It has 12,000 graves of Confederate soldiers set among live oak trees.

Beaufort's historical architecture also attracts filmmakers. The Fripp House on Short Street, called Tidalholm and built in 1853, is the house in the films *The Big Chill* (1983) and *The Great Santini* (1979). *Forrest Gump* (1994) was also filmed in Beaufort, with the shrimp dock scenes shot at shrimp shacks across the river on St. Helena Island. After filming those movies, William Hurt, Tom Berringer, and Tom Hanks were all so impressed with the Beaufort area they each bought local properties.

If you're a baby-boomer, can you name the (then) unknown actor who portrayed Alex's corpse in *The Big Chill*? Lawrence Kasdan, the director, felt so badly about cutting scenes of a live Alex he promised the actor a role in his next picture, *Silverado*. The movie proved enough of a success to launch this unknown actor's film career.

If your dogs are barking after walking all the local sites, stop at a restaurant and enjoy the unofficial seafood dish of South Carolina: frogmore stew.

By the way, the answer to the question above is Kevin Costner.

Beaufort Visitor Center
www.beaufortsc.org
800/638-3525

FROGMORE STEW

No, frogmore stew is not made with frog legs—or, thankfully, any other frog parts. Frogmore is a community on St. Helena Island, identified by the post office with a giant metal frog in front. The stew, also called Lowcountry stew, is a seafood boil with shrimp, crab, sausage, and corn-on-the-cob chunks.

The stew's origin is relatively recent: historians point out the sausage used in the stew only came to the Lowcountry with immigrants in the 1940s. The owner of Gay Seafood in Beaufort claims to have invented the recipe when he prepared a cookout of leftovers for fellow National Guardsmen. Since then its popularity has grown and several area restaurants now serve variants of this Lowcountry dish.

RUDDY TURNSTONE

Look for this tame little sandpiper skittering along the docks in South Carolina in late fall or early spring. A migrant, they spend the breeding season in the Arctic, decked out in striking rufous, brown, and black plumage.

In the winter months they hang out

516.3 Rock Creek Anchorage (Northwest)(0.4)
Anchor 8-12 feet N32.31.768
STR 7.2 feet W080.29.018
Exit ICW ENE of G177. Proceed NW up Rock Creek.

516.4 Ashepoo Coosaw Cutoff (West)
to Southbound/Northbound Navigation
517.7 1.3-mile land cut.
No anchorages, no marinas, no fuel.

518.2 Junction | St. Helena Sound (16.0)
Well Aided N32.21.551
Poorly Lit W080.18.434
Exit ICW ESE of R186. Proceed southeasterly down Coosaw River. Waypoint is at G1.

521.5 Dataw Island Marina (4.7)
VHF 16/68 N32.27.148
843/838-8410 W080.34.659
Exit ICW at charted Parrot Creek. Proceed southerly into Parrot Creek marked channel. [STR 7.9]
Honor all aids (red, right, returning). At R6, turn westerly into Morgan River. Charted marina is to port on Datha Island.
See Coosaw Island.

527.7 Range "A"
to Southbound/Northbound Navigation
528.7 Coosaw River
1.0-mile range.

530.1 Brickyard Creek Anchorage (0.2)
Anchor 8-10 feet N32.29.332
STR 8.6 feet W080.41.214
Exit ICW at R214. Proceed southeasterly into oxbow.
Caution: Previously, this anchorage was entered from the southern oxbow. Recent shoaling now makes it preferable to enter from the north.

534.5 Marsh Harbor Boatyard (0.3)
VHF 16; 843/521-1500
Exit ICW between R232 and G233. Proceed NE to privately maintained channel. Facility is to starboard. [STR 8.4]
Repair yard with no transient dockage.

535.9 Factory Creek
Exit ICW E of bridge. Proceed southeasterly into Factory Creek channel. [STR 8.3]

- **Lady's Island Marina** (0.8)
  VHF 16; 843/522-0430
  Marina is to starboard.
- **Factory Creek Anchorage** (1.2)
  Anchor 10-12 feet N32.25.257
  STR 8.3 feet W080.39.109
  Anchorage is beyond marina.

536.0 Ladies Island Bridge
VHF 09; 843/521-2111
Single-pivot swing; vertical 30 feet.
Restricted year round: M-F except holidays, 0700-0900 and 1600-1800 hrs.
Restricted year round: M-F except holidays, 0900-1600 hrs, opens on the hour and half-hour.

SAFETY INFO

NOAA Weather
WX-1 Charleston, SC
WX-3 Beaufort, SC
WX-2 Savannah, GA

USCG
Station Tybee, GA
VHF 16 or 09/22A
912/786-5440

Sea Tow
Savannah, GA
VHF 16/11
912/897-4304

TowBoatU.S.
Beaufort, SC
VHF 16
912/898-9659

HEADS UP!

406.0	Winyah Bay Entrance (SB)
410.5	Estherville Minim Canal (SB)
411.0	South Island Ferry Crossing
462.3	Ben Sawyer Bridge
469.0	Charleston Coast Guard Station
470.8	Wappoo Creek Bridge
472.2	Elliott Cut (SB)
472.5	Elliott Cut (NB)
536.0	Ladies Island Bridge
575.8	SC-GA Border
578.4	Wilmington River Cut-off (NB)
579.9	Causton Bluff Bridge
592.4	Skidaway Narrows Bridge
706.0	Kings Bay Security Zone (SB)
713.0	Kings Bay Security Zone (NB)
713.7	Cumberland Sound Channel (NB)
714.0	GA-FL Border
720.7	Kingsley Creek RR Bridge

536.3 Downtown Marina of Beaufort (0.2)
VHF 16/68 N32.25.765
843/524-4422 W080.40.447
Exit ICW W of bridge. Marina is to N. [STR 8.2 (TS)]
Caution: There is considerable current at these docks. Contact marina for docking assistance.
SEE BEAUFORT & RUDDY TURNSTONE.

536.4 Free Docks (0.2)
Exit ICW W of bridge. Dock is to N. [STR 8.2]
Free daytime tie-up. No overnight dockage.
Caution: Free docks are W of marina. Do not use the concrete bulkhead E of marina, which is used by small cruise ships and large tour boats. Wind and wash conditions are dangerous.

536.5 Beaufort Anchorage (0.1)
Anchor 14-22 feet N32.25.762
STR 8.2 feet W080.40.685
Exit ICW between G239 and R240. Proceed N.

538.4 Beaufort River Anchorage (0.4)
Anchor 8-14 feet N32.24.935
STR 8.2 feet W080.40.517
Exit ICW NNE of R242 (Spanish Point). Proceed NNE into charted tongue.

539.5 Port Royal Landing Marina (0.2)
VHF 16 N32.23.745
800/326-7678 W080.40.759
Exit ICW N of bridge. Proceed W. [STR 8.2]

539.6 Beaufort River Bridge
Fixed; vertical 65 feet.

541.7 Port Royal Anchorage (1.5)
Anchor 8-14 feet N32.22.511
STR 8.4 feet W080.41.829
Exit ICW at G41. Proceed NW up Battery Creek. Anchorage is beyond G47 off municipal pier.

541.7 Beaufort River Main Ship Channel
to Southbound Navigation Only
547.8 Buoyage reverses.
Look for yellow reflective ICW triangles and squares on aids.

544.0 Cowen Creek Anchorage (2.3)
Anchor 7-10 feet N32.21.767
STR 8.5 feet W080.38.884
Exit ICW between R36 and G33. Proceed E, leaving Range "C" lower light to port. Turn northerly up Cowen Creek. Anchor off Cat Island.
SEE SAIL NAKED.

547.8 Junction | Port Royal Sound (14.5)
Well Aided N32.05.055
Well Lit W080.35.028
Exit ICW at G27. Proceed southerly to inlet.
Waypoint is at RW "P" sea buoy.
Although this inlet is long, it leads southward so is a great jumping-out spot for Florida.
SEE PARRIS ISLAND.

547.8 Beaufort River Main Ship Channel
to Northbound Navigation Only
541.7 Buoyage reverses.

in drab non-breeding plumage, eating small crustaceans and dodging boaters along the docks. But these friendly, tame dock mascots are still pretty in their winter coats of mottled brown and white feathers.

Normally turnstones do just that: turn stones. When they're not dock walking, they eat by chasing after a retreating wave, turning over small stones using their bill like a farmer with a crowbar. If a stone is too big for one sandpiper they'll even work together, digging out the supporting sand and prying together like kids moving a giant snowball.

SAIL NAKED

Cat Island, just south of Beaufort at STM 544, was a local attention-getter in the early 1930s. Back in the days when swimsuits looked like today's winter long underwear, Cat Island was famous (or infamous) as the headquarters of a nudist colony.

PARRIS ISLAND

Parris Island, at STM 546, is the home of the Parris Island Marine Corps Recruit Depot, an intimidating name where more marines experience boot camp than any other location. Since 1949, when it established a women's battalion, it has been the only training program for female marines. Today about 19,000 male and female recruits train on Parris Island each year.

A staggering number of recruits have passed through Parris Island since it opened in 1891. During the single month of December 1941, following Pearl Harbor, 5,000 trainees arrived here, with another 9,000 the following month. During the war years of 1941 to 1945, over 200,000 marines trained at Parris Island.

One can only wish each year's recruits better luck through this tough 12-week program than the French Protestants had in 1562. After a miserable experience with insects, illness, and humidity, the settlers gave up on Parris Island, opting to return to religious persecution and prison cells back in France.

ST. HELENA ISLAND AND MARSH TACKIES

There was little food for the livestock of the African Americans who lived on these sandy islands. But the small horses, or marsh tackies, that plowed their fields and pulled their carts needed to be fed.

So the local island residents relied on wild provender. As late as the 1930s, islanders gathered at the large marsh at the southern end of St. Helena Island, near STM 547. They paddled the marsh in small boats, harvesting the abundant marsh grass like hay to feed their horses over the winter.

Courtesy of NOAA

American Avocet

STILTS, AVOCETS, AND PLOVERS

Lowcountry marshes are thick with shorebirds. There are so many sizes and shapes it sometimes seems as if there's a marsh bird for every leg length and beak style. Legs vary from the ridiculously long, seemingly double-jointed legs of the Black-necked Stilts to the stubby legs of the plovers. Some waders have tiny short bills, like the Sanderlings on the sandy shores, while others like the American Avocet have long thin elegant up-curved bills.

What's with all the different beaks and legs?

Even though marshes are incredibly rich ecosystems, shorebirds can't all eat the same thing. So, like complementary friends where one likes cake and the other likes frosting, shorebird species have evolved legs and bills to divvy up the mud. Every species has its own bill type and leg length—each feeding on food at different water, sand, or mud depths.

With 23 different species of shorebirds along the ICW, sharing makes a lot more sense than competing.

SKULL CREEK

No, skulls were not unearthed here. Skull Creek, from STM 553 to STM 558,

SAFETY INFO

NOAA Weather
WX-1 Charleston, SC
WX-3 Beaufort, SC
WX-2 Savannah, GA

USCG
Station Tybee, GA
VHF 16 or 09/22A
912/786-5440

Sea Tow
Savannah, GA
VHF 16/11
912/897-4304

TowBoatU.S.
Beaufort, SC
VHF 16
912/898-9659

HEADS UP!

410.5	Esterville Minim Canal (SB)
411.0	South Island Ferry Crossing
462.3	Ben Sawyer Bridge
469.0	Charleston Coast Guard Station
470.8	Wappoo Creek Bridge
472.2	Elliott Cut (SB)
472.5	Elliott Cut (NB)
536.0	Ladies Island Bridge
575.8	SC-GA Border
578.4	Wilmington River Cut-off (NB)
579.9	Causton Bluff Bridge
592.4	Skidaway Narrows Bridge
706.0	Kings Bay Security Zone (SB)
713.0	Kings Bay Security Zone (NB)
713.7	Cumberland Sound Channel (NB)
714.0	GA-FL Border
720.7	Kingsley Creek RR Bridge
739.1	Sisters Creek Bridge

was supposedly once called "Skulk Creek," but the "k" got lost as the two words were pronounced together quickly. Local legend says Native Americans used this area to stage attacks on Europeans settlers, "skulking" along the creek to sneak up on the island settlements.

PINCKNEY ISLAND

Pinckney Island, at STM 555, is named after General Pinckney, who lived on this island in his later years.

The Pinckneys are legendary in the Lowcountry. Charles Pinckney was a commander during the Revolutionary War, a signer of the U.S. Constitution, and an 1804 and 1808 presidential candidate. Mrs. Pinckney is credited with the early agricultural experiments with indigo that led to its local commercial cultivation (See Indigo).

Pinckney didn't live on the island until 1804, when he returned to clear the maritime forest and create a plantation growing the coveted long-staple Sea Island cotton. By the 1840s, several hundred slaves worked the plantation.

Like many other farmers, the Civil War ended the Pinckney's plantation prosperity. In the 1930s, the island was virtually abandoned. It was eventually sold, after 200 years of Pinckney ownership, to the wife of a New York banker.

Ellen Bruce, the new owner, replanted hardwoods and pines, cleared ponds to attract waterfowl and put about 70 percent of the fields back into cultivation. After several more owners through the 1950s and 1960s, the land was granted to the government in 1975, becoming the 4,000-acre Pinckney Island National Wildlife Refuge.

Garbage is a real inconvenience aboard a boat. To minimize your galley refuse, unpack everything you can at the dock after you shop. Dispose of excess packaging and transfer food and non-food items to zip lock bags or reusable plastic containers.

HILTON HEAD ISLAND

Mention Hilton Head and most people think of stunning golf courses. In fact, the Colleton River Plantation Golf Course was where Bagger Vance (Will Smith) helped Rannulph Junuh (Matt Damon) get his swing and his girl back in *The Legend of Bagger Vance* (2000).

This island also has an interesting history as a former stronghold of the Gullah community. If you arrive in February, you can participate in the Native Islander Gullah Celebration, which highlights the local music, history, and food of the Sea Islands' Gullah residents.

DreamWorks SKG Promotional Image

Bagger Vance (Will Smith)

Hilton Head Island had a rough start as a European settlement. First the Spanish tried in 1521, then the French in 1562, then the Spanish again, all abandoning the island. The first English ship arrived from Barbados in 1663, captained by (you guessed it!) William Hilton.

At that time, the Yemassee—Spanish-speaking Indians pushed north from Florida by the Spaniards—inhabited the island. You can still see the remnants of the Yemassee's mysterious giant shell rings in Pines Forest Preserve and on the north end of the island off Squire Pope Road.

During the Civil War, Hilton Head and the surrounding islands were taken early. Attention was focused on the bigger port of Charleston, so the two forts protecting Port Royal Sound, Fort Walker on Hilton Head Island and Fort Beauregard at Bay Point, were equipped with only 19 functioning guns. More than 12,000 Union troops invaded the area in one of the earliest amphibious assaults of our history—and the largest naval assault until the D-Day invasion of Normandy. The Union troops used captured Fort Walker as the base for a strangling naval blockade, described as a major factor in the South's defeat.

Today Hilton Head is a wealthy resort island with 250 restaurants, 25 golf courses, 378 tennis courts, and 10

Look for yellow reflective ICW triangles and squares on aids. [STR 7.7 (TS)]

Caution: Many cruisers continue NW along the main ship channel toward Port Royal, missing the northerly ICW turnoff to Beaufort.

SEE ST. HELENA ISLAND AND MARSH TACKIES.

553.5 Skull Creek Anchorage (0.7) S N
Anchor 8-10 feet N32.15.100
STR 8.0 feet W080.44.738
Exit ICW at R6. Proceed southwesterly beyond Seabrook Landing heading toward marina.
SEE SKULL CREEK.

554.8 Skull Creek Marina (0.2) S N
VHF 16/10, 09, 68 N32.14.800
843/681-8436 W080.44.900
Exit ICW between G9 "A" and R10. Proceed E to marina. [STR 8.0]

555.4 Hilton Head Boathouse (0.2) S N
VHF 16; 843/681-2628
Exit ICW at G13. Proceed SE to facility. [STR 8.0]
Dry store with no transient dockage.
SEE PINCKNEY ISLAND.

557.0 Hilton Head Harbor Marina (0.1) S N
VHF 16/12 N32.13.446
843/681-3256 W080.46.227
Exit ICW at R20. Proceed SW to marina. [STR 8.0]
Formerly Outdoor Resorts, also known as Hilton Head Harbor RV Resort & Marina.

557.5 J. Wilton Graves Twin Bridges S N
Fixed; vertical 65 feet.
SEE HILTON HEAD ISLAND.

558.0 Range "A" S N
to Southbound/Northbound Navigation
558.4 Skull Creek
0.4-mile range.

558.4 Windmill Harbour Marina (0.3) S N
VHF 16/14 N32.12.909
843/681-9235 W080.46.977
Exit ICW abeam Ferry Point. Proceed NE to marina in charted keyhole basin.
Enter marina through a small lock easily operated by crew or marina staff. [STR 0.0]

563.4 Bryan Creek Anchorage (1.4) S N
Anchor 8-10 feet N32.10.464
STR 8.2 feet W080.49.404
Exit ICW between R30 and R32. Proceed northerly into charted Bryan Creek, avoiding Middle Marsh Island shoal.

563.9 Junction | Broad Creek S N
Exit ICW ESE of R32. Proceed SSE, leaving G1 to port, up Broad Creek. [STR 8.4]

- **Opossum Point Anchorage** (3.8)
  Anchor 12-16 feet N32.10.810
  STR 8.4 feet W080.46.767
  Anchorage is at bend in creek, opposite Opossum Point.

SAFETY INFO

NOAA Weather
WX-1 Charleston, SC
WX-3 Beaufort, SC
WX-2 Savannah, GA

USCG
Station Tybee, GA
VHF 16 or 09/22A
912/786-5440

Sea Tow
Savannah, GA
VHF 16/11
912/897-4304

TowBoatU.S.
Tybee, GA
VHF 16/11
912/786-5283

HEADS UP!

410.5	Estherville Minim Canal (SB)
411.0	South Island Ferry Crossing
462.3	Ben Sawyer Bridge
469.0	Charleston Coast Guard Station
470.8	Wappoo Creek Bridge
472.2	Elliott Cut (SB)
472.5	Elliott Cut (NB)
536.0	Ladies Island Bridge
575.8	SC-GA Border
578.4	Wilmington River Cut-off (NB)
579.9	Causton Bluff Bridge
592.4	Skidaway Narrows Bridge
706.0	Kings Bay Security Zone (SB)
713.0	Kings Bay Security Zone (NB)
713.7	Cumberland Sound Channel (NB)
714.0	GA-FL Border
720.7	Kingsley Creek RR Bridge
739.1	Sisters Creek Bridge

- **Palmetto Bay Marina** (4.2)
  VHF 16; 843/785-3910
  Marina is to starboard.
- **Palmetto Bay Yacht Center** (4.3)
  VHF 16; 843/686-5989
  Facility is to starboard.
  Repair yard with no transient dockage.
- **Broad Creek Bridge** (4.4)
  Fixed; vertical 65 feet.
- **Wexford Plantation Yacht Harbor** (4.9)
  VHF 14/14 N32.10.736
  843/686-8813 W080.45.609
  Exit creek at G7. Proceed S to marina.
- **Broad Creek Marina** (5.4)
  VHF 16/14 N32.11.032
  843/681-3625 W080.45.355
  At R8, marina is to port.
- **Shelter Cove Marina** (6.8)
  VHF 16; 843/842-7001
  Exit creek between R18 and G19. Marina channel is to starboard.

564.0 Harbour Town Yacht Basin (0.9)
VHF 16/68 N32.08.318
843/671-2704 W080.48.918
Exit ICW SE of R32. Proceed SSE to marina in charted basin. [STR 8.3 (TS)]
Marina is easily recognized by red-and-white striped lighthouse.
SEE HARBOUR TOWN LIGHT.

565.6 Bull Island Anchorage (1.3)
Anchor 8-12 feet N32.09.865
STR 8.4 feet W080.51.484
Exit ICW E of R34. Proceed N into Bull Creek.
SEE BLOODY POINT.

567.7 Daufuskie Marina (0.1)
VHF 16/71 N32.07.873
843/341-4898 W080.52.466
Marina is to SE. [STR 8.3]
Also known as Melrose Landing or Daufuskie Island Resort & Spa.
SEE WATCH YOUR WAKE.

568.5 Cooper River Anchorage (1.0)
Anchor 12-16 feet N32.08.583
STR 8.3 feet W080.53.226
Exit ICW NE of G37. Proceed northerly.
Caution: Beyond the bend lie power cables with vertical clearance of 55 feet.

570.4 New River Anchorage (North)(0.6)
Anchor 8-10 feet N32.06.767
STR (TS) 8.1 feet W080.54.193
Exit ICW NE of R40. Proceed northwesterly into New River.

572.3 New River Anchorage (South)(1.5)
Anchor 14-18 feet N32.04.893
STR 8.1 feet W080.53.460
Exit ICW SE of R42. Proceed southeasterly into New River.

marinas. A staggering 2.5 million people visit the island each year.

Hilton Head Island
www.hiltonheadisland.org
800/523-3373

Native Islander Gullah Celebrations
www.gullahcelebration.com
877/650-0676

HARBOUR TOWN LIGHT

The 90-foot red-and-white striped lighthouse, at STM 564, marks the Waterway's southern junction with Calibogue Sound (pronounced Kal-uh-BO-gee). It's a new lighthouse, built in 1970, but is notable as the first privately built lighthouse since the early 1800s. It's located at the Harbour Town Yacht Basin on Hilton Head Island and is open to the public.

THE SCORPION (LATE SPRING-EARLY AUTUMN)

For over 6,000 years, the constellation around the star Antares has been visualized as a scorpion. Antares is the Scorpion's heart, a first-magnitude red star called the "rival of Mars" for its color. Mariners may remember using Antares for sights in celestial navigation. Look for Antares and the Scorpion low in the sky to the south when you are in the southern U.S. latitudes.

According to myth, the Scorpion killed Orion when the Goddess Juno sent it to sting Orion's heel. So Scorpion and Orion were placed in opposite

Courtesy of Hilton Head Island CVB

Harbour Town Light

parts of the sky. The Scorpion is visible in the summer, Orion in the winter. When one rises, the other sets...locked in eternal battle.

SNAP, CRACKLE, POP

As you reach warmer water, you may be startled by loud crackling noises coming from your hull at night. The sound has been described as "Rice Krispies popping," "bacon frying in a skillet," or "the crackling of dry twigs burning."

Contrary to cruiser legend, the noise is not caused by krill eating the growth on your hull. According to several marine biologists, it's the sound of snapping shrimp.

Scientists have only recently discovered how these tiny shrimp make so much noise. At first they thought it was the snapping of the shrimps' enlarged claws. And it is...sort of.

The noise is not the claw snapping,

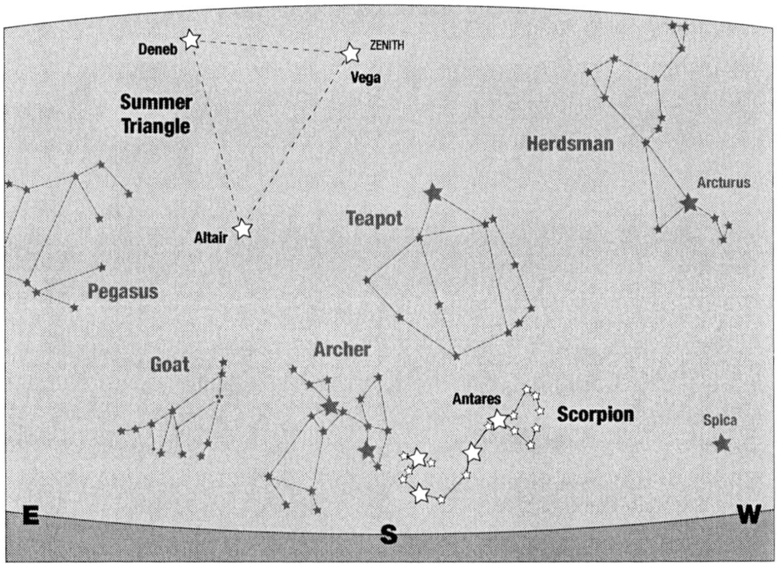

Late Spring, Late Evening to Early Autumn, Early Evening

Summer Triangle and Scorpion Rising

SAFETY INFO		
	NOAA Weather WX-3 Beaufort, SC **WX-2 Savannah, GA** WX-1 Jacksonville, FL	**Sea Tow** Savannah, GA VHF 16/11 912/897-4304
	USCG Station Tybee, GA VHF 16 or 09/22A 912/786-5440	**TowBoatU.S.** Tybee, GA VHF 16/11 912/786-5283

HEADS UP!

410.5	Estherville Minim Canal (SB)	578.4	Wilmington River Cut-off (NB)
411.0	South Island Ferry Crossing	579.9	Causton Bluff Bridge
462.3	Ben Sawyer Bridge	592.4	Skidaway Narrows Bridge
469.0	Charleston Coast Guard Station	706.0	Kings Bay Security Zone (SB)
470.8	Wappoo Creek Bridge	713.0	Kings Bay Security Zone (NB)
472.2	Elliott Cut (SB)	713.7	Cumberland Sound Channel (NB)
472.5	Elliott Cut (NB)	714.0	GA-FL Border
536.0	Ladies Island Bridge	720.7	Kingsley Creek RR Bridge
575.8	**SC-GA Border**	739.1	Sisters Creek Bridge

it's the cavitation from the water jet made by its high-speed closure. Just like the cavitation from your propeller, the water jet from the claw snapping shut (at 62 mph!) changes the water pressure and forms tiny cavitation bubbles. When the low-pressure bubbles pop, the telltale crack is produced.

In warm waters, these small one-inch shrimp are abundant and noisy—so noisy they can conceal submarines from sonar. Snapping shrimp snap at 200 decibels, well above the 120-decibel human hearing pain threshold. So next time you're trying to sleep, think of the thousands of snappers in the water around your hull, busily conducting their own coconut telegraph at a frequency of 300 kHz, stunning prey, defending territory, and communicating with other shrimp.

BLOODY POINT

Traveling down Calibogue Sound, or rounding the corner northbound into Calibogue Sound, you can spot the Haig Point Light on the northern end of Daufuskie Island (pronounced Dah-FUSS-key). Bloody Point is nearby.

There are two accounts of what happened at Bloody Point. One version describes Native Americans chased to the end of Daufuskie Island by the British, where men, women, and children were slaughtered at the edge of the sea.

Another version tells it as the breaking point in a series of Native American raids on Europeans living on the island. During one of these raids, the Indians found the whiskey stash. As they camped at the northeast end of Daufuskie, hooting it up on the whiskey, other residents spotted the campfires. Frustrated with the raids, they encircled the camp and separated the Indians from their canoes. All the Indians were murdered, except one, who supposedly swam the ten miles back to Tybee Island. As the story goes, there never was another Indian raid on Daufuskie Island.

Oral histories evolve over three hundred years, but everyone agrees the blood on Bloody Point is Indian blood.

Calibrate an *empty* water tank by filling it in five-gallon jerry jug increments. Mark the levels with a permanent marker and/or verify your tank gauge.

WATCH YOUR WAKE

In 1969, Patrick Conroy, the author of the books and screenplays *Prince of Tides* and *The Great Santini*, spent a year as an idealistic young teacher on Daufuskie Island. He struggled with Gullah-speaking students who couldn't read, didn't know what country they lived in, and had never seen a telephone or car. He later recounted his experiences in *The Water is Wide*.

One of Conroy's goals for the school year was to teach the children to swim. With alligators on the freshwater side, and currents on the saltwater side, few had ever learned to swim. But the islanders feared "snowbirds" more than alligators or currents. They recounted stories of islanders who fell into the water, sinking like a rock only to resurface drowned several days later.

Yes, the snowbirds are us—cruising boaters. Conroy describes the unfortunate scenario: a great white yacht, heading southbound on the first breath of winter, doesn't bother to cut its engine speed when passing a fisherman or crabber working in a small home-built bateau. In the rush to locate the next channel marker to Florida, the captain often never notices the small, capsized boat he leaves behind.

In the end, Conroy taught only three children to dog paddle. Their fear of the water was so ingrained most of the children refused to even step into the water. ▲

572.3 Walls Cut S N
to Southbound/Northbound Navigation
572.6 0.3-mile land cut.
No anchorages, no marinas, no fuel.

572.6 Wright River Anchorage (Southeast)(0.6) S N
Anchor 11-15 feet N32.04.385
STR 8.1 feet W080.55.059
Exit ICW WNW of G43. Proceed S down Wright River.

573.5 Wright River Anchorage (Northwest)(0.5) S N
Anchor 8-12 feet N32.05.335
STR 8.1 feet W080.56.336
Exit ICW at R48. Proceed NW up Wright River.

573.5 Fields Cut S N
to Southbound/Northbound Navigation
575.5 2.0-mile land cut.
No anchorages, no marinas, no fuel.

575.8 SC-GA Border S N
Savannah River (G35)
Caution: The ICW crosses the Savannah River. Large commercial ship traffic can suddenly appear, steaming on the fast-moving current.

South Carolina Waterway Business Cards

Crickett Cove Marina

STM 345.2

www.crickettcove.com

4495 Baker Street
Little River, SC 29566

843/249-7169
843/280-3426

VHF 16/12

Depth	5	**Laundry**	On-Site
Diesel/Gas	D/G	**Pool**	No
Pumpout	Yes	**Internet/WiFi**	No
Mail/Fax	M/F	**Car/Bike**	No
Service	On-Call	**Groceries**	Walk
Parts	On-Call	**Restaurant**	On-Site
Haulout	No	**Post Office**	Walk
Propane	Taxi	**Library**	Taxi

Coquina Yacht Club

STM 346.0

www.coquinayachtclub.com

4208 Coquina Harbor Drive
Little River, SC 29566

866/249-9333
843/249-8643

VHF 16/09

Depth	6	**Laundry**	On-Site
Diesel/Gas	No	**Pool**	No
Pumpout	No	**Internet/WiFi**	I
Mail/Fax	M/F	**Car/Bike**	No
Service	On-Call	**Groceries**	Walk
Parts	On-Call	**Restaurant**	On-Site
Haulout	No	**Post Office**	Walk
Propane	Walk	**Library**	Taxi

Silver Coast Marina

STM 346.4

www.silvercoastmarina.com

4430 Kingsport Road
Little River, SC 29566

843/249-1000
843/249-8468

VHF 16/14

Depth	12	**Laundry**	Walk
Diesel/Gas	G	**Pool**	No
Pumpout	No	**Internet/WiFi**	No
Mail/Fax	F	**Car/Bike**	No
Service	On-Site	**Groceries**	Walk
Parts	On-Site	**Restaurant**	Walk
Haulout	60T	**Post Office**	Walk
Propane	Walk	**Library**	Walk

Harbourgate Marina

STM 347.2

www.harbourgatemarina.com

2120 Sea Mountain Highway
N. Myrtle Beach, SC 29582

843/249-8888
843/249-1144

VHF 16/12

Depth	10	**Laundry**	On-Site
Diesel/Gas	D/G	**Pool**	No
Pumpout	No	**Internet/WiFi**	No
Mail/Fax	M/F	**Car/Bike**	No
Service	On-Call	**Groceries**	Walk
Parts	On-Call	**Restaurant**	On-Site
Haulout	No	**Post Office**	Taxi
Propane	Walk	**Library**	Taxi

Dock Holidays Marina

STM 348.3

www.thegrandstrand.com

1525 13th Ave. North
N. Myrtle Beach, SC 29582

843/280-6354
843/280-9002

VHF 16/10

Depth	7	**Laundry**	On-Site
Diesel/Gas	D/G	**Pool**	No
Pumpout	Yes	**Internet/WiFi**	I
Mail/Fax	M/F	**Car/Bike**	No
Service	On-Call	**Groceries**	Walk
Parts	On-Call	**Restaurant**	On-Site
Haulout	No	**Post Office**	Taxi
Propane	Taxi	**Library**	Taxi

Barefoot Landing

STM 353.7

www.bflanding.com

4898 Hwy. 17 South
N. Myrtle Beach, SC 29582

843/272-8349
843/272-1052

No VHF Watch

Depth	14	**Laundry**	Taxi
Diesel/Gas	No	**Pool**	No
Pumpout	No	**Internet/WiFi**	No
Mail/Fax	No	**Car/Bike**	No
Service	No	**Groceries**	Walk
Parts	No	**Restaurant**	On-Site
Haulout	No	**Post Office**	Taxi
Propane	N/A	**Library**	Taxi

Barefoot Resort Yacht Club

STM 353.7

www.barefootresortclub.com

4980 Barefoot Resort Bridge
N. Myrtle Beach, SC 29582

843/390-7900
843/390-7070

VHF 16/10

Depth	8	**Laundry**	On-Site
Diesel/Gas	D/G	**Pool**	Yes
Pumpout	Yes	**Internet/WiFi**	I/W
Mail/Fax	F	**Car/Bike**	B
Service	On-Call	**Groceries**	Walk
Parts	On-Call	**Restaurant**	On-Site
Haulout	No	**Post Office**	Walk
Propane	N/A	**Library**	Taxi

Marina at Grand Dunes

STM 358.2

www.granddunes.com/marina

8201 Marina Parkway
Myrtle Beach, SC 29572

843/315-7777
843/315-7778

VHF 16/10

Depth	8	**Laundry**	On-Site
Diesel/Gas	D/G	**Pool**	Yes
Pumpout	Yes	**Internet/WiFi**	I/W
Mail/Fax	M/F	**Car/Bike**	C
Service	On-Call	**Groceries**	Taxi
Parts	On-Call	**Restaurant**	Walk
Haulout	No	**Post Office**	Walk
Propane	Taxi	**Library**	N/A

Photocopy the “business card” of any Waterway facility. Then cut out the copy and take it ashore for easy reference!

Hague Marina

STM 368.2

One Hague Drive
Myrtle Beach, SC 29577

843/293-2141 (phone)
843/293-2140 (fax)

VHF 16/68

Depth	9	**Laundry**	On-Site
Diesel/Gas	D/G	**Pool**	No
Pumpout	No	**Internet/WiFi**	I
Mail/Fax	M/F	**Car/Bike**	C
Service	On-Site	**Groceries**	Taxi
Parts	On-Site	**Restaurant**	Walk
Haulout	35T	**Post Office**	Taxi
Propane	Walk	**Library**	Taxi

Wacca Wache Marina

STM 383.7

www.wwmarina.com

1950 Wachesaw Road
Murrells Inlet, SC 29576

843/651-2994 (phone)
843/651-1056 (fax)

VHF 16/10

Depth	8	**Laundry**	On-Site
Diesel/Gas	D/G	**Pool**	No
Pumpout	Yes	**Internet/WiFi**	I/W
Mail/Fax	M/F	**Car/Bike**	No
Service	On-Call	**Groceries**	Taxi
Parts	On-Call	**Restaurant**	Taxi
Haulout	No	**Post Office**	Taxi
Propane	Taxi	**Library**	Taxi

Heritage Plantation Marina

STM 394.2

1823 Heritage Drive
Pawleys Island, SC 29585

843/237-3650 (phone)
843/235-0854 (fax)

VHF 16/10

Depth	32	**Laundry**	On-Site
Diesel/Gas	No	**Pool**	No
Pumpout	Yes	**Internet/WiFi**	Walk
Mail/Fax	M	**Car/Bike**	No
Service	On-Call	**Groceries**	Taxi
Parts	On-Call	**Restaurant**	On-Site
Haulout	No	**Post Office**	Taxi
Propane	N/A	**Library**	Taxi

Georgetown Landing Marina

STM 402.8

www.georgetownlandingmarina.com

432 Marina Drive
Georgetown, SC 29440

843/546-1776 (phone)
843/546-7832 (fax)

VHF 16/10 or 68

Depth	6	**Laundry**	On-Site
Diesel/Gas	D/G	**Pool**	Yes
Pumpout	Yes	**Internet/WiFi**	I
Mail/Fax	M/F	**Car/Bike**	No
Service	On-Call	**Groceries**	Taxi
Parts	On-Call	**Restaurant**	On-Site
Haulout	No	**Post Office**	Taxi
Propane	Taxi	**Library**	Walk

Hazzard Marine

STM 403.0

200 South Meeting Road
Georgetown, SC 29440

843/527-3625 (phone)
No Fax (fax)

VHF 16/68

Depth	10	**Laundry**	On-Site
Diesel/Gas	D/G	**Pool**	No
Pumpout	Yes	**Internet/WiFi**	I/W
Mail/Fax	M/F	**Car/Bike**	B
Service	On-Site	**Groceries**	Walk
Parts	On-Site	**Restaurant**	Walk
Haulout	60T	**Post Office**	Taxi
Propane	Walk	**Library**	Walk

The Boat Shed Marina

STM 403.0

www.theboatshedmarina.com

18 South St. James Street
Georgetown, SC 29440

843/546-4415 (phone)
843/546-5142 (fax)

VHF 16/68

Depth	9	**Laundry**	Walk
Diesel/Gas	D/G	**Pool**	No
Pumpout	Yes	**Internet/WiFi**	I/W
Mail/Fax	M/F	**Car/Bike**	No
Service	On-Call	**Groceries**	Walk
Parts	On-Call	**Restaurant**	Walk
Haulout	No	**Post Office**	Taxi
Propane	Walk	**Library**	Walk

Harborwalk Marina

STM 403.0

www.harborwalkmarina.com

525 Front Street
Georgetown, SC 29440

843/546-4250 (phone)
843/546-2395 (fax)

VHF 16/68

Depth	12	**Laundry**	Walk
Diesel/Gas	D/G	**Pool**	No
Pumpout	No	**Internet/WiFi**	No
Mail/Fax	M	**Car/Bike**	No
Service	On-Call	**Groceries**	Walk
Parts	On-Call	**Restaurant**	Walk
Haulout	No	**Post Office**	Taxi
Propane	Walk	**Library**	Walk

Johnson's Marina

STM 403.0

894 Trout Road
Georgetown, SC 29440

843/545-8633 (phone)
843/545-8633 (fax)

VHF 16/10

Depth	16	**Laundry**	On-Site
Diesel/Gas	D/G	**Pool**	No
Pumpout	No	**Internet/WiFi**	No
Mail/Fax	M/F	**Car/Bike**	No
Service	On-Site	**Groceries**	Taxi
Parts	On-Site	**Restaurant**	Walk
Haulout	No	**Post Office**	Taxi
Propane	Taxi	**Library**	Taxi

Isle of Palms Marina

STM 459.6

www.iopmarina.com

50 41st Avenue
Isle of Palms, SC 29451

843/886-0209 (phone)
843/886-0058 (fax)

VHF 16/71

Depth	9	**Laundry**	On-Site
Diesel/Gas	D/G	**Pool**	No
Pumpout	Yes	**Internet/WiFi**	I/W
Mail/Fax	M/F	**Car/Bike**	No
Service	On-Call	**Groceries**	Taxi
Parts	On-Call	**Restaurant**	On-Site
Haulout	No	**Post Office**	Taxi
Propane	On-Site	**Library**	N/A

Charleston Harbor Marina

STM 464.5

www.charlestonharbormarina.com

24 Patriots Point Road
Mt. Pleasant, SC 29464

888/856-0028 (phone)
843/856-8540 (fax)

VHF 16/72

Depth	15	**Laundry**	On-Site
Diesel/Gas	D/G	**Pool**	On-Site
Pumpout	Yes	**Internet/WiFi**	I/W
Mail/Fax	M/F	**Car/Bike**	C
Service	On-Call	**Groceries**	Walk
Parts	On-Call	**Restaurant**	On-Site
Haulout	No	**Post Office**	Taxi
Propane	Taxi	**Library**	Taxi

Charleston Maritime Center

STM 464.5

http://ci.charleston.sc.us/

10 Wharfside Street
Charleston, SC 29401

843/853-3625 (phone)
843/577-6673 (fax)

VHF 16/69

Depth	6	**Laundry**	Walk
Diesel/Gas	D/G	**Pool**	No
Pumpout	Yes	**Internet/WiFi**	I
Mail/Fax	M/F	**Car/Bike**	No
Service	On-Call	**Groceries**	Walk
Parts	On-Call	**Restaurant**	Walk
Haulout	No	**Post Office**	Walk
Propane	Walk	**Library**	Walk

Cooper River Marina

STM 464.5

www.ccprc.com

1010 Juneau Avenue
N. Charleston, SC 29405

843/554-0790 (phone)
843/744-4140 (fax)

VHF 16/11

Depth	5	**Laundry**	On-Site
Diesel/Gas	No	**Pool**	No
Pumpout	Yes	**Internet/WiFi**	I
Mail/Fax	M/F	**Car/Bike**	No
Service	On-Call	**Groceries**	Taxi
Parts	On-Call	**Restaurant**	Taxi
Haulout	No	**Post Office**	Taxi
Propane	Taxi	**Library**	Taxi

Charleston City Marina

STM 469.2

www.charlestoncitymarina.com

17 Lockwood Drive
Charleston, SC 29401

843/723-5098 (phone)
843/853-1840 (fax)

VHF 16/68

Depth	20	**Laundry**	On-Site
Diesel/Gas	D/G	**Pool**	No
Pumpout	Yes	**Internet/WiFi**	I/W
Mail/Fax	M/F	**Car/Bike**	Shuttle
Service	On-Call	**Groceries**	Walk
Parts	On-Call	**Restaurant**	Walk
Haulout	No	**Post Office**	Walk
Propane	Walk	**Library**	Walk

Ashley Marina

STM 469.2

www.ashleymarina.com

33 Lockwood Drive
Charleston, SC 29401

843/722-1996 (phone)
843/720-3623 (fax)

VHF 16/71

Depth	22	**Laundry**	On-Site
Diesel/Gas	D/G	**Pool**	No
Pumpout	Yes	**Internet/WiFi**	I/W
Mail/Fax	M/F	**Car/Bike**	Shuttle
Service	On-Site	**Groceries**	Walk
Parts	On-Site	**Restaurant**	Walk
Haulout	No	**Post Office**	Walk
Propane	Walk	**Library**	Walk

Ross Marine

STM 476.3

www.rossmarine.com

2676 Swygert Boulevard
Johns Island, SC 29455

843/559-0379 (phone)
843/559-3172 (fax)

VHF 16/79

Depth	12	**Laundry**	Taxi
Diesel/Gas	D/G	**Pool**	No
Pumpout	No	**Internet/WiFi**	No
Mail/Fax	M/F	**Car/Bike**	B
Service	On-Site	**Groceries**	Taxi
Parts	On-Site	**Restaurant**	Taxi
Haulout	30T/70T	**Post Office**	Taxi
Propane	Taxi	**Library**	Taxi

Dataw Island Marina

STM 521.5

www.datawmarina.com

100 Marina Drive
Dataw Island, SC 29920

843/838-8410 (phone)
843/838-8412 (fax)

VHF 16/68

Depth	20	**Laundry**	On-Site
Diesel/Gas	D/G	**Pool**	No
Pumpout	Yes	**Internet/WiFi**	I
Mail/Fax	M/F	**Car/Bike**	B
Service	On-Site	**Groceries**	Taxi
Parts	On-Site	**Restaurant**	Taxi
Haulout	35T	**Post Office**	Taxi
Propane	N/A	**Library**	Taxi

Downtown Marina of Beaufort

STM 536.3

1006 Bay Street
Beaufort, SC 29902

843/524-4422 (phone)
843/524-8437 (fax)

VHF 16/68

Depth	18	**Laundry**	On-Site
Diesel/Gas	D/G	**Pool**	No
Pumpout	Yes	**Internet/WiFi**	I/W
Mail/Fax	M/F	**Car/Bike**	C
Service	On-Call	**Groceries**	Taxi
Parts	On-Call	**Restaurant**	Walk
Haulout	No	**Post Office**	Walk
Propane	Taxi	**Library**	Walk

Port Royal Landing Marina

STM 539.5

www.portroyallandingmarina.com

One Landing Drive
Port Royal, SC 29935

800/326-7678 (phone)
843/525-9166 (fax)

VHF 16/12

Depth	8	**Laundry**	On-Site
Diesel/Gas	D/G	**Pool**	No
Pumpout	Yes	**Internet/WiFi**	I/W
Mail/Fax	M/F	**Car/Bike**	C/B
Service	On-Call	**Groceries**	Walk
Parts	On-Call	**Restaurant**	On-Site
Haulout	No	**Post Office**	Taxi
Propane	Taxi	**Library**	Taxi

Skull Creek Marina

STM 554.8

www.theskullcreekmarina.com

One Waterway Lane
Hilton Head, SC 29926

843/681-8436 (phone)
843/681-3946 (fax)

VHF 16/10

Depth	7	**Laundry**	On-Site
Diesel/Gas	D/G	**Pool**	No
Pumpout	Yes	**Internet/WiFi**	No
Mail/Fax	M/F	**Car/Bike**	C/B
Service	On-Call	**Groceries**	Taxi
Parts	On-Call	**Restaurant**	Walk
Haulout	35T	**Post Office**	Taxi
Propane	Taxi	**Library**	Taxi

Hilton Head Harbor Marina

STM 557.0

www.hiltonheadharbor.com

43 Jenkins Road
Hilton Head, SC 29925

843/681-3256 (phone)
843/689-2197 (fax)

VHF 16/12

Depth	18	**Laundry**	On-Site
Diesel/Gas	D/G	**Pool**	Yes
Pumpout	No	**Internet/WiFi**	I
Mail/Fax	No	**Car/Bike**	No
Service	On-Call	**Groceries**	Taxi
Parts	On-Call	**Restaurant**	On-Site
Haulout	No	**Post Office**	Taxi
Propane	Delivered	**Library**	Taxi

Windmill Harbour Marina

STM 558.4

161 Harbour Passage
Hilton Head, SC 28512

843/681-9235 (phone)
843/681-9394 (fax)

VHF 16/14

Depth	8	**Laundry**	On-Site
Diesel/Gas	D/G	**Pool**	Yes
Pumpout	Yes	**Internet/WiFi**	I
Mail/Fax	M/F	**Car/Bike**	No
Service	On-Call	**Groceries**	Taxi
Parts	On-Call	**Restaurant**	Walk
Haulout	No	**Post Office**	Taxi
Propane	Taxi	**Library**	Taxi

Wexford Plantation Yacht Harbor

STM 563.9

www.wexfordplantation.com

113 Wexford Club Drive
Hilton Head, SC 29928

843/686-8813 (phone)
843/686-4345 (fax)

VHF 16/14

Depth	8	**Laundry**	Walk
Diesel/Gas	No	**Pool**	Yes
Pumpout	Yes	**Internet/WiFi**	No
Mail/Fax	M/F	**Car/Bike**	No
Service	On-Call	**Groceries**	Walk
Parts	On-Call	**Restaurant**	On-Site
Haulout	No	**Post Office**	Walk
Propane	Taxi	**Library**	Walk

Broad Creek Marina

STM 563.9

18 Simmons Road
Hilton Head, SC 29926

843/681-3625 (phone)
843/689-9451 (fax)

VHF 16/14

Depth	12	**Laundry**	On-Site
Diesel/Gas	D/G	**Pool**	No
Pumpout	Yes	**Internet/WiFi**	I
Mail/Fax	F	**Car/Bike**	No
Service	On-Call	**Groceries**	Taxi
Parts	On-Call	**Restaurant**	Taxi
Haulout	No	**Post Office**	Taxi
Propane	Taxi	**Library**	Taxi

Harbour Town Yacht Basin

STM 564.0

www.harbourtown.com

149 Lighthouse Road
Hilton Head, SC 29928

843/671-2704 (phone)
843/671-0433 (fax)

VHF 16/68

Depth	8	**Laundry**	On-Site
Diesel/Gas	D/G	**Pool**	Yes
Pumpout	Yes	**Internet/WiFi**	I/W
Mail/Fax	M/F	**Car/Bike**	B
Service	On-Call	**Groceries**	Taxi
Parts	On-Call	**Restaurant**	Walk
Haulout	No	**Post Office**	Walk
Propane	Taxi	**Library**	Taxi

Daufuskie Marina STM 567.7

P.O. Box 23285
Hilton Head, SC 29925

843/341-4898
843/341-4848

VHF 16/71

Depth	18	**Laundry**	Walk
Diesel/Gas	D/G	**Pool**	Yes
Pumpout	No	**Internet/WiFi**	No
Mail/Fax	M/F	**Car/Bike**	No
Service	On-Call	**Groceries**	Taxi
Parts	On-Call	**Restaurant**	On-Site
Haulout	No	**Post Office**	On-Site
Propane	N/A	**Library**	N/A

South Carolina Waterway Marine Facilities

This table summarizes all known Waterway Marine Facilities, their location along the ICW, and their telephone number. Each is listed as either offering transient (T) dockage or not—and whether they have a fuel dock with diesel (D), gas (G), or neither.

344.2	B&W's Marina	Closed	No	No
345.2	**Crickett Cove Marina**	843/249-7169	T	D/G
346.0	Lightkeeper's Marina	843/249-8660	T	No
346.0	Myrtle Beach Yacht Club	843/249-5376	T	D/G
346.0	**Coquina Yacht Club**	866/249-9333	T	No
346.4	**Silver Coast Marina**	843/249-1000	T	G
347.0	Anchor Marina	843/249-7899	T	D/G
347.2	**Harbourgate Marina**	843/249-8888	T	D/G
348.3	**Dock Holidays Marina**	843/280-6354	T	D/G
353.7	**Barefoot Landing**	843/272-8349	T	No
353.7	**Barefoot Resort Yacht Club**	843/390-7900	T	D/G
358.2	**Marina at Grande Dunes**	843/315-7777	T	D/G
368.2	**Hague Marina**	843/293-2141	T	D/G
373.3	Osprey Marina	843/215-5353	T	D/G
377.3	Bucksport Plantation Marina	843/397-5566	T	D/G
383.7	**Wacca Wache Marina**	843/651-2994	T	D/G
388.2	Reserve Harbor Marina	843/235-8262	T	D/G
394.2	**Heritage Plantation Marina**	843/237-3650	T	No
402.8	**Georgetown Landing Marina**	843/546-1776	T	D/G
403.0	**Hazzard Marine**	843/527-3625	T	D/G
403.0	**The Boat Shed Marina**	843/546-4415	T	D/G
403.0	**Harborwalk Marina**	843/546-4250	T	D/G
403.0	**Johnson's Marina**	843/545-8633	T	D/G
406.1	Belle Isle Marina	843/546-8491	T	D/G
430.0	Leland Oil Company	843/887-3641	T	D/G
456.9	**Isle of Palms Marina**	843/886-0209	T	D/G
462.4	Toler's Cove Marina	843/881-0325	No	D/G
464.5	**Charleston Harbor Marina**	888/856-0028	T	D/G
464.5	**Charleston Maritime Center**	843/853-3625	T	D/G
464.5	**Cooper River Marina**	843/554-0790	T	No
469.2	**Charleston City Marina**	843/723-5098	T	D/G
469.2	**Ashley Marina**	843/722-1996	T	D/G
469.2	Ripley Light Marina	Closed	No	D/G
469.2	Dolphin Cove Marina	843/744-2562	T	G
472.6	Buzzard's Roost Marina	843/559-5516	T	D/G
472.6	Stono Marina	843/559-2307	T	No
476.3	**Ross Marine**	843/559-0379	T	D/G
496.6	Rockville Marine	843/559-1124	No	No
496.6	Bohicket Marina	843/768-3461	T	D/G
513.5	B&B Seafood	843/844-2322	T	D/G
521.5	**Dataw Island Marina**	843/838-8410	T	D/G
534.5	Marsh Harbor Boatyard	843/521-1500	No	No
535.9	Lady's Island Marina	843/522-0430	T	No
536.3	**Downtown Marina of Beaufort**	843/524-4422	T	D/G
539.5	**Port Royal Landing Marina**	800/326-7678	T	D/G
554.8	**Skull Creek Marina**	843/681-8436	T	D/G
555.4	Hilton Head Boathouse	843/681-2628	No	G
557.0	**Hilton Head Harbor Marina**	843/681-3256	T	D/G
558.4	**Windmill Harbour Marina**	843/681-9235	T	D/G
563.9	Palmetto Bay Marina	843/785-3910	T	D/G
563.9	Palmetto Bay Yacht Center	843/686-5989	No	No
563.9	**Wexford Plantation Yacht Harbor**	843/686-8813	T	No
563.9	**Broad Creek Marina**	843/681-3625	T	D/G
563.9	Shelter Cove Marina	843/842-7001	T	D/G
564.0	**Harbour Town Yacht Basin**	843/671-2704	T	D/G
567.7	**Daufuskie Marina**	843/341-4898	T	D/G

Boldface type indicates the facility completed a survey and is highlighted in a Waterway Business Card. Each facility received multiple fax, email, and telephone requests. A final telephone call was made to verify the accuracy of transient, fuel, and contact information.

South Carolina Waterway Chandleries

This table lists marine equipment suppliers within easy reach of the ICW, their telephone number and address, and their location relative to ICW marinas and anchorages.

Ship Store Anchor Marina	843/249-7899	2200 Little River Neck Road, N. Myrtle Beach, SC 29582	On-site Anchor Marina
Boulineaus True Value	843/249-3556	212 Sea Mountain Highway, N. Myrtle Beach, SC 29582	2.0 miles from Anchor Marina
Carolina Boat & Yacht Sales	843/280-4920	2120 Sea Mountain Highway, N. Myrtle Beach, SC 29582	On-site Harbourgate Marina
West Marine N. Myrtle Beach	843/280-1327	900 Highway 17 North, N. Myrtle Beach, SC 29582	0.7 miles from Dock Holidays
Home Depot N. Myrtle Beach	843/280-9908	620 Highway 17 North, N. Myrtle Beach, SC 29582	0.8 miles from Dock Holidays
Dew Ace Hardware	843/249-2331	411 Main Street, N. Myrtle Beach, SC 29582	2.0 miles from Dock Holidays
Lowe's Myrtle Beach	843/626-1700	1160 Seaboard Street, Myrtle Beach, SC 29577	6.3 miles from Grande Dunes
Boater's World Myrtle Beach	843/444-9098	1110 Seaboard Street, Myrtle Beach, SC 29577	6.4 miles from Grande Dunes
Myrtle Beach Yacht Basin	843/293-2141	3675 Hague Drive, Myrtle Beach, SC 29578	0.3 miles from Hague Marina
Lowe's S. Myrtle Beach	843/650-1400	8672 Highway 17 Bypass, Surfside, SC 29575	4.3 miles from Hague Marina
Home Depot Myrtle Beach	843/916-2229	951 Oak Forest Lane, Myrtle Beach, SC 29577	4.6 miles from Hague Marina
Booty's Hardware & Marine	843/651-2593	3908 Highway 17 Business, Murrells Inlet, SC 29576	2.0 miles from Wacca Wache Marina
Home Depot Murrells Inlet	843/357-3777	12262 Highway 17 Bypass, Murrells Inlet, SC 29576	2.5 miles from Wacca Wache Marina
West Marine Murrells Inlet	843/357-6208	12078 Highway 17 Bypass, Murrells Inlet, SC 29576	3.1 miles from Wacca Wache Marina
Pawley's Island Supplies Hardware	843/237-2912	10460 Ocean Highway, Pawleys Island, SC 29585	3.1 miles from Heritage Plantation Marina
Schofield Hardware	843/546-0012	215 Church Street, Georgetown, SC 29440	0.3 miles from Georgetown Landing Marina
Bulls Bay True Value Supply	843/887-3251	10086 North Highway 17, McClellanville, SC 29458	1.8 miles from Leland Oil Company
Isle of Palms True Value Hardware	843/886-6340	1509 Palm Boulevard, Isle of Palms, SC 29451	2.3 miles from Isle of Palms Marina
Royall Ace Hardware	843/884-2551	883 Ben Sawyer Boulevard, Mt Pleasant, SC 29464	1.8 miles from Toler's Cove Marina
Boater's World Mt. Pleasant	843/971-9555	616 Coleman Boulevard, Mt. Pleasant, SC 29464	2.5 miles from Charleston Harbor Marina
East Bay True Value Hardware	843/577-9196	18 Society Street, Charleston, SC 29401	0.4 miles from Charleston Maritime Center
Luden's Outfitters	843/723-7829	78 Alexander Street, Charleston, SC 29403	0.4 miles from Charleston Maritime Center
Charleston's Rigging & Marine	843/723-7145	1304 Meeting Street Road, Charleston, SC 29405	3.0 miles from Charleston City Marina
BoatU.S. Charleston	843/763-6360	2049 Savannah Highway, Charleston, SC 29407	5.0 miles from Charleston City Marina
West Marine Charleston	843/573-0123	975 Savannah Highway, Charleston, SC 29407	2.3 miles from Ashley Marina
Boater's World Charleston	843/763-8905	1863 Sam Rittenberg Boulevard, Charleston, SC 29407	5.9 miles from Ashley Marina
Lowe's James Island	843/795-9774	770 Daniel Ellis Drive, Charleston, SC 29412	3.6 miles from Stono Marina
Bohicket Marina Ship Store	843/768-3467	1880 Andell Bluff Boulevard, Johns Island, SC 29455	On-site Bohicket Marina
Grayco Hardware	843/521-8060	180 Sea Island Parkway, Beaufort, SC 29907	0.9 miles from Lady's Island Marina
Butler Marine	843/522-9461	124 Ladys Island Drive, Beaufort, SC 29907	1.0 miles from Lady's Island Marina
Lowe's Beaufort	843/522-3144	207 Robert Smalls Parkway, Beaufort, SC 29906	3.5 miles from Downtown Marina of Beaufort
Coligny True Value Hardware	843/785-2429	1 North Forest Beach Drive, Hilton Head, SC 29928	3.0 miles from Wexford Plantation Yacht Harbor
West Marine Hilton Head	843/686-5351	890 William Hilton Parkway, Hilton Head, SC 29928	2.1 miles from Shelter Cove Marina
Boater's World Bluffton	843/836-2292	1476 Fording Island Road, Bluffton, SC 29910	5.5 miles from Daufuskie Marina
Lowe's Bluffton	843/837-8887	35 Malphrus Road, Bluffton, SC 29910	6.6 miles from Daufuskie Marina

Georgia Charts
11507 ICW - Beaufort River to St. Simons Sound
11489 ICW - St. Simons Sound to Tolomato River

Bridges	
Total	5
Fixed	3
Opening	2

Other Features			
Marinas	18	Vignettes	31
Anchorages	55	Inlets	8
Chandleries	17	Ranges	24

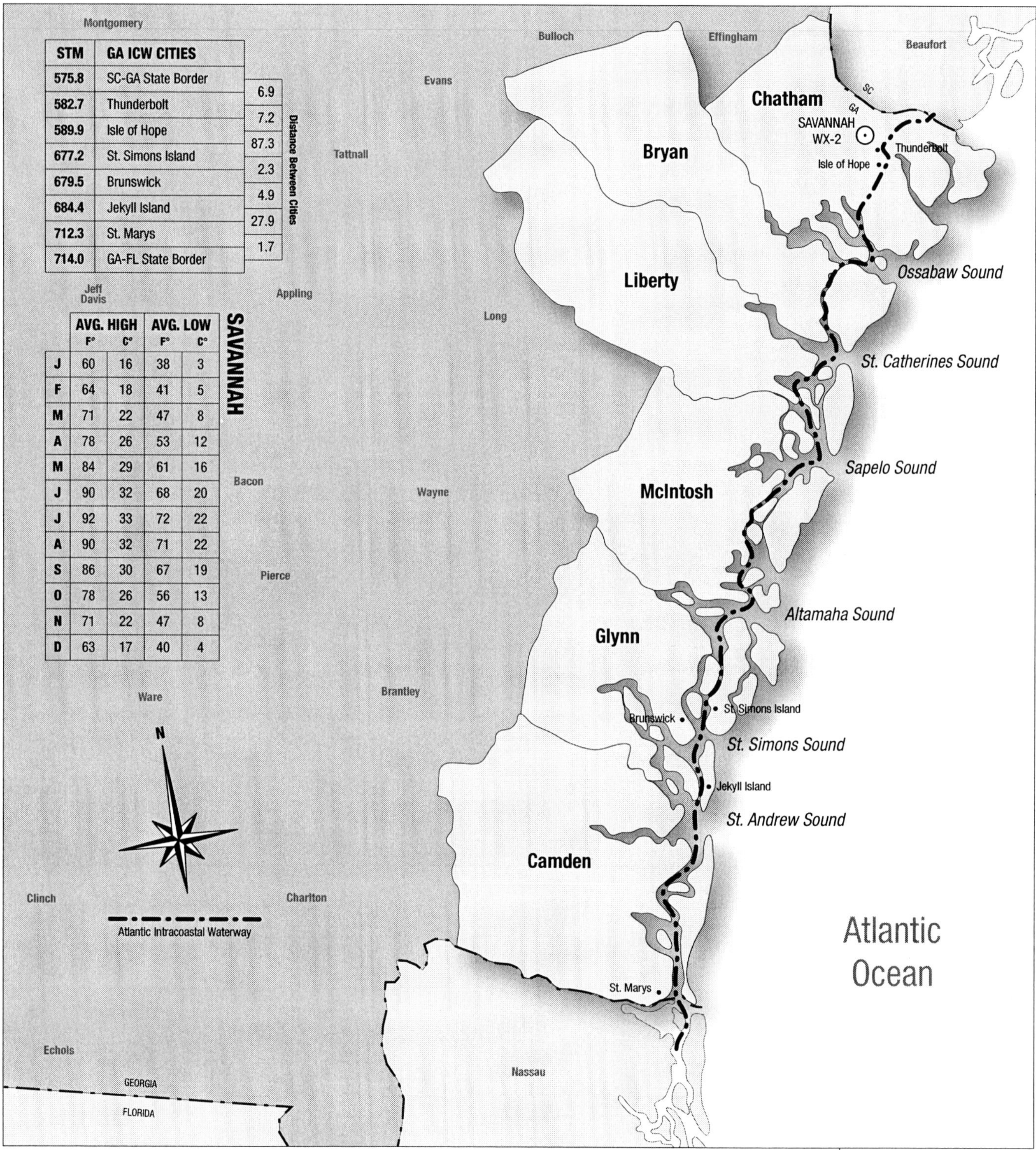

STM	GA ICW CITIES	Distance Between Cities
575.8	SC-GA State Border	
		6.9
582.7	Thunderbolt	
		7.2
589.9	Isle of Hope	
		87.3
677.2	St. Simons Island	
		2.3
679.5	Brunswick	
		4.9
684.4	Jekyll Island	
		27.9
712.3	St. Marys	
		1.7
714.0	GA-FL State Border	

SAVANNAH

	AVG. HIGH F°	AVG. HIGH C°	AVG. LOW F°	AVG. LOW C°
J	60	16	38	3
F	64	18	41	5
M	71	22	47	8
A	78	26	53	12
M	84	29	61	16
J	90	32	68	20
J	92	33	72	22
A	90	32	71	22
S	86	30	67	19
O	78	26	56	13
N	71	22	47	8
D	63	17	40	4

MTW Big Pictures provide an overview of local geographic references. They identify the counties, capes, inlets, lighthouses, and bodies of water commonly referred to in NOAA and AM/FM weather broadcasts.

The locations of WX weather towers are shown to easily determine the best broadcast for your position and direction of travel. The temperature table shows average highs and lows for that region. Look for major cities and smaller towns along the ICW, then use the distance table for planning stops or estimating travel time. Lastly, we list the region's required charts by their NOAA chart number and provide a snapshot of Waterway resources and impediments.

Georgia

Savannah River to Cumberland Sound

The Peach State
ICW Statute Mile 575.8 to 714.0
Bridges Monitor VHF 13

Regions
Savannah River to Sapelo Sound
Sapelo Sound to St. Marys River

Inlets
Savannah River Entrance
Wassaw Sound
Ossabaw Sound
St. Catherines Sound
Sapelo Sound
Doboy Sound
St. Simons Sound
St. Marys Entrance

U.S. Coast Guard
District Seven: 305/415-6800
Station Tybee: 912/786-5440
Station Brunswick: 912/267-9010

NOAA Weather Towers
WX-2 Savannah

Security Zones
Kings Bay, St. Marys River

Lighthouses
Sapelo Island Light
St. Simons Island Light
Little Cumberland Island Light

Fishing Information
www.georgiawildlife.com

GEORGIA WAS the "debatable land," caught between South Carolina and Florida in a centuries-old conflict among three imperial powers. Britain controlled the Carolinas, Spain controlled Florida, and France controlled Louisiana. Georgia was trapped in the middle.

Britain, Spain, and France all fought for this leftover territory. Although coastal Georgia was only a collection of remote sea islands with no major port, each imperial power tried to claim it as her own. The name of the game was colonial expansion, and the colonial powers were playing hardball for every piece of land.

Spain took first dibs, claiming all the sea islands from Florida north to Ossabaw Island. They named them the Golden Isles, although gold was never found. Spain protected her claim by establishing scattered plantations and forts, thinly disguised as missions. In the 1500s Spain's charts labeled the Georgia coast as Spanish territory, hoping to formalize the arrangement.

But charts are only paper, and in 1562 a French expedition set out for the Georgia coast. France challenged Spain's territorial claim and proceeded to incense the Spaniards by re-charting the rivers with French names.

Spain held on to the territory for nearly two hundred years. But these were tense times in Georgia. Each imperial power feared—and was accused of—having designs on the other's turf. In fact, Oglethorpe's Fort Frederica, near STM 670, was built in 1736 to protect the southern boundary of the British claim.

Meanwhile, Native American and pirate raids eroded the resolve of the settlers, regardless of their nationality. Pirates, including Blackbeard and Abraham, raided supply ships and plundered the missions, even stripping the missions of their bells. The Native Americans waged modern-day psychological warfare, wearing settlers down with the constant uncertainty of violence.

In the end, Georgia was nearly abandoned. Between the harassment, disease, and looming international tension, Georgia became the land in between. Spain and Britain reached a mutual agreement that neither would establish a settlement in Georgia for 50 years. It became a colonial-era DMZ: the military buffer between Spanish Florida and the British Carolinas.

Unfortunately, to many boaters, Georgia remains the forgotten region of the ICW. The state still suffers from its image as a buffer between South Carolina and Florida.

The Waterway through Georgia does meander, creating the impression you'll never get where you're going. Many cruisers complain about the switchback system of rivers that form the Waterway. Masts pass each other over the marsh-grass horizon in constantly changing directions like targets in an arcade game.

All of this twisting and turning adds up. The serpentine path of the Waterway adds more than a third—turning Georgia's 100-mile coastline into a 138-mile ride through marsh grass. It's no wonder many boaters choose to bump out at Charleston, Beaufort, St. Marys, or St. Johns and skip the Georgia Waterway altogether.

Before you bypass Georgia, we'd like you to know what you're missing.

Patricia Schultz, who wrote *1,000 Places to See Before You Die*, includes Georgia's Golden Isles in this exclusive international list. The Golden Isles are one of the most pristine and beautiful coastal areas along the Atlantic. Many of the islands have been preserved, with some of the most peaceful anchorages along the Waterway.

Georgia also offers exceptional cultural and historical experiences, without the development of the Carolinas or Florida. The Waterway puts you near areas with beautiful plantation architecture, waterfront mansions, exclusive clubs and restaurants, and cities that still reflect the culture of the Deep South.

There are not many large cities along the Georgia coast, only Savannah and Brunswick, which both lie upriver from the Waterway. Instead, the stops are small towns, like Thunderbolt or St. Simons Island.

Most visitors travel to the Georgia coast for the natural beauty and quiet of the Sea Islands. Many of these islands are carefully owned and managed, with limited access.

Boaters can experience these coveted islands in a way most landlubbers cannot.

Savannah Convention & Visitors Bureau
www.savannah-visit.com
877/728-5444

Brunswick & the Golden Isles
www.bgivb.com
800/809-1790

Coastal Georgia Website
www.coastalgeorgiaexperience.com

Georgia's coast is defined by its sea islands: a collection of relatively large unspoiled islands protecting the low-lying marshlands. Your progress through Georgia is measured by the passage of these major islands: Tybee, Wassaw, Ossabaw, St. Catherines, Blackbeard, Sapelo, Wolf, St. Simons, Jekyll, and Cumberland. Behind each island, the Waterway follows a maze of coastal rivers, with endless tributaries providing anchorages and alternate routes.

In Georgia, rivers wind back and forth so "southbound" often means an assortment of compass headings. You may actually head northwest on a southbound passage.

Although the Sea Islands offer great protection, between the islands is another story. The down side of traveling behind a chain of barrier islands is the exposure between islands. If the weather is fair and wind conditions are right, these jumps are no problem. However, they can be very choppy if the wind and current are opposed.

Fortunately, because Georgia's coast is a myriad of large rivers, there are several alternate routes for different wind conditions. The four charted alternate routes: Walburg Creek, Frederica River, St. Andrews Sound, and Brickhill River, are described in detail in the Nav Columns at their appropriate statute mile location.

Because Georgia's inlets are created by rivers flowing into large open sounds, they are not the freighter runways of the Florida coast. There are plenty of inlets: a staggering eight inlets in only 138 miles. Only Florida, with nine, has more inlets, but these are spread out over 384 miles!

Within Georgia's Intracoastal Waterway, the main navigation concerns are the tides and currents. Georgia is the land of big tides and strong currents.

To accommodate the currents, Georgia's Waterway is peppered with navigational ranges. There are 24 ranges along this short route. Most are less than a mile and simply preempt any set from the current.

Along some stretches, you hand off directly from one range to another in a "Georgia Range Square Dance." We've warned of staying on a range too long; in Georgia you might not stay on long enough. Don't cut the corners on these range pairs.

Although there are fewer marinas in Georgia, they are available. However, slower cruising boats will most likely anchor at least one night in Georgia. For those who exclusively prefer marinas, plan ahead for fueling or overnight accommodations.

Because of the currents, don't skimp on dock help. Most marinas prefer their dockhands to help rather than risk a solo, foam-the-runway, style of landing. At times, the currents can be so strong you may actually have difficulty slowly motoring into them for a landing.

Experience is an expensive teacher. We've learned to radio well in advance, ask about current conditions at the assigned slip, have fenders down, and absolutely let the dockhands do their jobs!

Courtesy of Brunswick-Golden Isles of Georgia CVB

St. Simons Island Light

The presence of currents must also be considered at Georgia's bridges. Be vigilant as you approach each bridge. Be aware of the set of the current and save some engine power in case you need to make a course correction or execute a U-turn to circle for a bridge opening.

Fortunately, Georgia has very few bridges. There are only five bridges along the Waterway in Georgia, only two requiring openings for clearance over 21 feet. Since the Georgia coast was never developed with small towns, there are not many low-clearance W.P.A.-era bridges. Most of the bridges are relatively new, built with long concrete spans over the flat marshlands to clear the 65-foot height.

Anchoring possibilities are abundant along the Georgia Waterway. Georgia has an incredible 55 anchorages along only 138 miles of the Waterway—an anchorage average of 2.5 miles. This is a great opportunity to anchor out, since many of the sites along the Sea Islands are accessible only by boat. Expect to use your dinghy often. Many of the local sites, such as Fort Frederica or Cumberland Island National Park, provide dinghy dockage to access their facilities.

Anchoring in Georgia must be done with forethought. Georgia has the highest tides between Norfolk and Miami, with about eight feet of tidal range. Note the tidal range—listed in the Nav Column as [STR] for each anchorage—and use the appropriate scope.

Avoid anchoring in a deeply scoured area of a small creek, a warning that the current may flow fast and hard. Shallow water with sediment suggests less daily current scouring. Stay more toward the inner bend of rivers where the current is generally less. Some boaters prefer to set two anchors to prevent swing. But be very careful with this arrangement; you could find your vessel wound up on your two rodes like a twisted playground swing.

Finally, you will bear witness that budgets and politics affect navigation along the ICW. The Waterway through Georgia is not used much by commercial traffic. This may be pleasant for boat traffic, but bad for funding. Commercial traffic, not pleasure boating, drives dredging budgets.

In 2005, the Savannah District lost its funding to maintain the Waterway between Port Royal Sound (STM 552) and Cumberland Sound (STM 713)—in other words, nearly all of Georgia's Waterway. This means the channel will not be maintained to authorized depths and shoaling may occur in some areas. In lieu of dredging, the Savannah District will monitor the conditions of the Waterway and publish quarterly condition reports.

If you have a deep draft vessel you may need to check with the Coast Guard or sign up for the AIWA's email updates on Waterway navigation conditions.

Savannah District Navigation
www.sas.usace.army.mil/op.htm
912/652-5061

AIWA Bulletins/Email Alerts
www.atlintracoastal.org
703/719-7273

SAVANNAH RIVER TO SAPELO SOUND

In Georgia, progress along the Waterway is measured by islands, not miles. So it helps to be familiar with the names of the Sea Islands. From the South Carolina border to Sapelo Sound (pronounced SAP-uh-lo), the islands are: Tybee, Little Tybee, Williamson, Wassaw, Ossabaw, and St. Catherines.

Tybee is Georgia's most densely developed barrier island. It's a seaside resort with restaurants, hotels, condominiums, and a residential community. But the Waterway doesn't pass near these areas, winding well inland in the lee of Tybee Island.

Little Tybee and Williamson Islands are two small islands spawned from Tybee. Both Little Tybee and Williamson were formed when sand, swept from Tybee, was deposited as a new island. Little Tybee was created over 4,000 years ago; Williamson formed only 30 years ago.

Tybee Island also marks the Savannah River inlet. The Waterway crosses the Savannah River, leaving the port of Savannah to the west and following a route through smaller towns such as Thunderbolt and Isle of Hope.

Savannah is the major city for this region of coastal Georgia, only a few miles off the Waterway. But the Savannah River is not particularly welcoming for recreational boats. It's a large commercial port with nasty currents, tides, and traffic.

Most boaters visit Savannah by stopping at the very boater-friendly communities of Thunderbolt or Isle of Hope. The historic district of Savannah is only a short bus or taxi ride away.

Wassaw Island is one of Georgia's most pristine islands. It is federally protected as a National Wildlife Refuge. The nearest town is tiny Skidaway Island, population 4,500. You're close to this town when you clear the Skidaway Narrows Bridge at STM 592.4.

Ossabaw Island was once cleared for cotton fields, but has now returned to its natural state. Jimmy Carter set aside Ossabaw Island as Georgia's first Heritage Preserve, making it the only island in Georgia reserved exclusively for educational and scientific purposes. The island is accessible only by boat.

St. Catherines is also protected from development, managed by the St. Catherines Island Foundation as part of the New York Zoological Society. Instead of a preserve for the sea island ecology, the island is home to the Wildlife Survival Center, breeding hundreds of animals from around the world for wildlife protection.

SAPELO SOUND TO ST. MARYS RIVER

South of Sapelo Sound, nationally recognized resort communities and pristine national refuge islands are (north to south): Blackbeard, Sapelo, Wolf, Egg, Little Egg, Little St. Simons, St. Simons, Jekyll, Little Cumberland, and Cumberland.

Blackbeard Island, once the hideout of the famous pirate, has been a refuge since the 1940s. The island is open to the public, both for fishing and hiking.

Sapelo, Wolf, Egg, and Little Egg Islands are also refuges. Sapelo Island is administered by NOAA as a National Estuarine Research Reserve. The island has a small community, Hog Hammock, the last intact African American Geechee community on the Georgia Coast. Wolf, Egg, and Little Egg Islands are all protected, as the Wolf Island National Wildlife Refuge, with no public use.

Little St. Simons Island is the last family-owned island along Georgia's coast, with only three owners over the last 250 years.

St. Simons Island has many property owners. It's a large island with a vibrant community, connected to the mainland by a causeway bridge. Marinas become more common near the towns of St. Simons Island and Brunswick. But there are still many anchoring opportunities.

Jekyll Island is a resort island attracting thousands of visitors each year. It's owned by the state of Georgia, and is more of a resort island than a residential community.

Little Cumberland is owned by an association of homeowners, who privately maintain the historic lighthouse and protect the island as part of the extensive Cumberland Island National Seashore.

Courtesy of U.S. Fish & Wildlife Service

Black Skimmer Flock

The southernmost of the Georgia Sea Islands, Cumberland Island, lies just north of the Georgia-Florida border. Preserved by the National Park Service, Cumberland Island is open to the public and accessible by boat or ferry.

At the Florida border, prepare to adjust to the bustle of a commercial and military port. Compared to the quiet and solitude of Lanier's marshes, St. Marys River is a shock. It's a large inlet busy with commercial and navy traffic out of Kings Bay or the port of St. Marys.

Note that the entire Kings Bay area—including large portions of Cumberland Sound and St. Marys River—is a restricted navigation area.

Caution: After 9/11, expect a more expansive security zone than shown on the chart. And don't be surprised if you are hailed and/or approached by a patrol boat.

If a ship or submarine is nearby you may be directed to a shallow area and asked to come to a complete stop, with your bow toward shore, until the vessel clears the area.

Obviously, you should maintain an *attentive* radio watch on VHF 16 as you approach and transit this area.

GEORGIA BOOK AND FILM PICKS

Ironically, one of coastal Georgia's most famous contemporary writers is from Chicago. Eugenia Price visited St. Simons Island from Illinois as a middle-aged adult, and she never left. Her series of novels about the local people and history set in romantic historical fiction novels have been steady sellers. Her St. Simons Island Trilogy, written in reverse-chronological order, consisting of *Lighthouse*, *New Moon Rising*, and *Beloved Invader*, tell the true story of the lives, tragedies, and triumphs of the people of the St. Simons Island Lighthouse and the Christ Church.

If historical romantic fiction is not your genre, Price's autobiography, *St. Simons Memoir*, is still interesting. She tells the story of her first impressions of St. Simons Island in the 1960s, describing her attempts as a mainlander (and northerner) to break through the wariness of the local island residents. She delves into the history of the local families in her research to create a historically accurate novel. Eventually she was welcomed as an adopted resident, built a house on a historic farm, and was honored by the island with Eugenia Price Day.

Georgia, with its unique southern plantation scenery, boasts an impressive slate of films. Before arriving at Georgia's anchorages, stock up on used copies of *Roots* (1977) by Alex Haley, or *Glory* (1989) with Matthew Broderick, Denzel Washington, and Morgan Freeman. Both films were shot in coastal Georgia.

The city of Savannah has become identified with a single book and movie: *Midnight in the Garden of Good and Evil*, by John Berendt. It's the true story of Savannah's inner culture—including a society patron, a transvestite, and a Santería priestess—experienced by a wide-eyed Yankee. A perfect book or film for Thunderbolt, you can walk to the Bonaventure Cemetery and experience the graveyard where the Santería rites were performed and the mystery unfolded.

Young children can learn about the wetland wading birds with the book, *Wings Along the Waterway*, by Mary Barrett Brown. Each page is a stunning two-page illustration with text introducing a shore or water bird in its habitat. ▲

SAFETY INFO		
	NOAA Weather WX-3 Beaufort, SC **WX-2 Savannah, GA** WX-1 Jacksonville, FL	**Sea Tow** Savannah, GA VHF 16/11 912/897-4304
	USCG Station Tybee, GA VHF 16 or 09/22A 912/786-5440	**TowBoatU.S.** Tybee, GA VHF 16/11 912/786-5283

HEADS UP!

411.0	South Island Ferry Crossing	**579.9**	**Causton Bluff Bridge**
462.3	Ben Sawyer Bridge	592.4	Skidaway Narrows Bridge
469.0	Charleston Coast Guard Station	706.0	Kings Bay Security Zone (SB)
470.8	Wappoo Creek Bridge	713.0	Kings Bay Security Zone (NB)
472.2	Elliott Cut (SB)	713.7	Cumberland Sound Channel (NB)
472.5	Elliott Cut (NB)	714.0	GA-FL Border
536.0	Ladies Island Bridge	720.7	Kingsley Creek RR Bridge
575.8	SC-GA Border	739.1	Sisters Creek Bridge
578.4	**Wilmington River Cut-off (NB)**	747.4	B.B. McCormick Twin Bridges

575.8 SC-GA Border S N
Savannah River (G35)
Caution: The ICW crosses the Savannah River. Large commercial ship traffic can suddenly appear, steaming on the fast-moving current.

575.8 Junction | Savannah River Entrance S N
Southbound/Northbound Navigation
Proceed northerly up Savannah River to the city of Savannah or southerly to the Savannah River entrance and Tybee Roads.

The city of Savannah has ship congestion and an industrial waterfront with few facilities for transiting ICW boaters. We recommend cruisers stay in Thunderbolt or Isle of Hope to visit this charming southern capital.

- **Savannah River Entrance** (15.1)
  Well Aided N31.58.780
  Well Lit W080.45.108
  Exit ICW at G35. Proceed southerly out Savannah River Entrance to Tybee Roads. Waypoint is between G3 and R4.
  SEE TYBEE ISLAND.

576.2 Elba Island Cut S N
to 577.4 Southbound/Northbound Navigation
1.2-mile land cut.
No anchorages, no marinas, no fuel.
SEE HOME OF THE WAVING GIRL.

577.4 St. Augustine Creek Anchorage (0.5) S N
Anchor 22-24 feet N32.03.675
STR 8.9 feet W080.59.076
Exit ICW at R8. Proceed southeasterly into St. Augustine Creek.

578.4 Wilmington River Cut-off S N
Northbound Navigation Only
Caution: It is easy to continue along Wilmington River at R "A18" or R14. If you plan to moor in Savannah, and can clear the fixed 35-foot vertical clearance bridge, you can take this shortcut. However, northbound ICW travelers should continue through Elba Island Cut.

578.7 Range "A" S N
to 579.0 Southbound/Northbound Navigation
Wilmington River
0.3-mile range.

579.0 Range "B" S N
to 579.3 Southbound/Northbound Navigation
Wilmington River
0.3-mile range.

579.9 Causton Bluff Bridge S N
(Sam Varnedoe Bascule Bridge)
VHF 13; 912/897-2511
Double bascule, vertical 21 feet.
Restricted year round: M-F except holidays, 0630-0900 and 1630-1830 hrs, opens at 0700, 0800 and 1730 hrs.
SEE BONAVENTURE CEMETERY.

582.3 Savannah Bend Marina (0.1) S N
VHF 16; 912/897-3625
Exit ICW at R34. Marina is to ESE. [STR 9.2]

TYBEE ISLAND

In the days of slaving, ships carrying human cargo were required to anchor at Tybee Island, where the slaves were quarantined before arriving in Savannah. The community on Tybee Island is still called "Lazaretto," from the word "hospital" in Spanish. Lazaretto Creek is labeled on charts, northeast of Bull River or southwest of the Savannah River inlet entrance.

The journey from Africa often took several months, with miserable conditions for the homesick captured Africans. Many slave ships locked the tribesmen and women in the dark hold with little light or air. There would be so little room the slaves had to lay in the spoon position, only to be let onto the deck once a day for a saltwater washdown, some fresh air, and some food and water. Many died from disease or committed suicide.

A slave ship typically stopped at several American ports, off-loading slaves as the labor market demanded. Weaker slaves were always chosen first. The assumption was the strong could survive a bit longer as the ship visited more ports, and as the northern weather grew harsher.

Tybee Island was one of these stops. Incoming ships anchored in the shelter of the Lazaretto River, unloading their human cargo for inspection at the hospital before proceeding to Savannah.

Don't bring paper bags, boxes, or egg cartons onto your boat! In warm moist climates, they harbor cockroach eggs. And if you do end up with palmetto bugs (a.k.a. roaches) on board, fight back with a lumpy paste of boric acid and sugar spread onto small pieces of paper. Several of these pu-pu platters should do the trick!

HOME OF THE WAVING GIRL

Elba Island, to the north of Elba Island Cut at STM 576, is the home of the waving girl. Stories from the 1880s describe a girl named Florence Martus, who lived in a little house on Elba Island overlooking the Savannah River. Every day Florence waited for her lover to return, waving to passing ships in the hope one day it would be his ship.

Sailors grew accustomed to seeing the girl waving a cloth or lantern from Elba Island as they arrived at the port of Savannah. They grew fond of her and she was known among mariners as the "Waving Girl." Some even brought her small gifts from their voyages.

Her intended never returned, but Florence—some say because she was lonely—continued to wave to each passing ship. She greeted the ships from 1887 until 1931; from age 19 until she was 63 years old.

BONAVENTURE CEMETERY

One of Savannah's biggest attractions is a cemetery: Bonaventure Cemetery, located along the Waterway just south of R30 at STM 581.3. Before you use this fact to judge Savannah tourism, you have to understand Bonaventure's connection to pop culture.

Warner Studios Promotional Image

Bonaventure Cemetery

Although the cemetery has been famous for decades (John Muir included it in his book *Thousand Mile Walk to the Gulf* in the 1860s), it was a pop culture book and film about Savannah that really put Bonaventure on the map. John Berendt's bestselling mystery book, *Midnight in the Garden of Good and Evil*, and its movie version (1997) with John Cusack and Kevin Spacey, made Bonaventure a pop culture Mecca.

The plot weaves through the Bonaventure Cemetery, described as one of America's most beautiful burial grounds with its Victorian statues, gar-

SAFETY INFO	**NOAA Weather**	**Sea Tow**
	WX-3 Beaufort, SC	Savannah, GA
	WX-2 Savannah, GA	VHF 16/11
	WX-1 Jacksonville, FL	912/897-4304
	USCG	**TowBoatU.S.**
	Station Tybee, GA	Thunderbolt, GA
	VHF 16 or 09/22A	VHF 16
	912/786-5440	912/898-9659

HEADS UP!

462.3	Ben Sawyer Bridge	592.4	Skidaway Narrows Bridge
469.0	Charleston Coast Guard Station	706.0	Kings Bay Security Zone (SB)
470.8	Wappoo Creek Bridge	713.0	Kings Bay Security Zone (NB)
472.2	Elliott Cut (SB)	713.7	Cumberland Sound Channel (NB)
472.5	Elliott Cut (NB)	714.0	GA-FL Border
536.0	Ladies Island Bridge	720.7	Kingsley Creek RR Bridge
575.8	SC-GA Border	739.1	Sisters Creek Bridge
578.4	Wilmington River Cut-off (NB)	747.4	B.B. McCormick Twin Bridges
579.9	Causton Bluff Bridge	775.0	St. Augustine Inlet Area (SB)

dens of azaleas and camellias, and live oaks hung with Spanish moss.

Old Bonaventure Cemetery is the location of the famous Bird Girl statue featured on the cover of the book and the film poster. To see this sculpture now you must visit the Telfair Museum of Art in Savannah, where it is on permanent display. Apparently the last straw for the cemetery staff was seeing tourists having a picnic on the Bird Girl tomb!

Old Bonaventure is also the burial ground for Savannah society. Civil War buffs can find the graves of Claudius Charles Wilson, involved in the battle of Chickamauga, or Josiah Tattnall, captain of the Confederate navy. Several early patriots are buried here, including Noble Wimberly Jones—a radical patriot in the American Revolution, who arrived as a 10-year-old and lived at the Wormsloe Plantation—and Edward Telfair, who went on to be the Governor of Georgia.

The New Bonaventure Cemetery is famous as the place where Minerva, the Santería priestess in Berendt's story, practices her craft in climactic scenes from the movie. Both Danny Hansford (the Billy Hanson character in the story who is killed by Jim Williams) and Jim Williams are buried here.

If you never saw the movie, you might care to look for the grave of songwriter Johnny Mercer, who wrote the lyrics or scores to over 1,000 songs, including "Charade," "Come Rain or Come Shine," "Moon River," and "Autumn Leaves."

Bonaventure Cemetery
912/651-6843

Telfair Museum of Art
www.telfair.org
912/232-1177

Wondering if your charts are current? NOAA's official list of charts and their latest edition is found at: www.chartmaker.ncd.noaa.gov/mcd/dole.htm.

THUNDERBOLT

Thunderbolt is a small town with a big name. As the only U.S. town named Thunderbolt, its name is as rare as the event that marked the town.

According to Native American legend, lightning struck the village, miraculously producing a spring of clear water where the bolt hit. "Magically," the site gave off a burnt smell long afterward...later identified as sulfur and iron from the spring water.

Today Thunderbolt is a town of about 3,000 residents, with declining shrimping and rising development. In 1996, a memorial to the shrimping industry, containing names of local families and fishermen, was erected on River Drive at Thunderbolt Bluff. Since Thunderbolt is only five miles southeast of Savannah, riverfront condominiums are in demand now.

Thunderbolt has many marinas and local services for boaters along its riverfront, including restaurants and marine businesses. Most boaters stop at Thunderbolt to visit Savannah or access its airport, avoiding the commercial traffic, two-knot current, and nine-foot tides of the port of Savannah. Savannah's public bus system, Chatham Area Transit (called the CAT), runs the #24 Bus regularly between Thunderbolt and downtown Savannah.

The CAT (Chatham Area Transit)
www.catchacat.org
912/233-5767

RIVER OTTER

In the early morning or late evening, you may spot a sleek River Otter along the banks of the Waterway. River Otters can live in fresh or salt water, but need a riparian habitat of cattails, sedges, or marsh grass for shelter.

River Otters are incredibly adapted to the marine environment. They have webbed feet, nictitating membranes to cover their eyes for swimming, nostrils and ears that close underwater, and eyes near the top of their skull to view above the water's surface while they swim. They can stay submerged for up to eight minutes.

At the heyday of fur trading, otters were nearly extirpated from Georgia. They are still trapped seasonally for their dense black to red-brown pelts, but with a single pelt selling for about $50, trapping is carefully regulated. Today the biggest threat to the river otter population is loss of habitat from coastal development.

You may see other mammals swimming in the marshes. The Marsh Rice

582.4 Hinckley Yacht Services (0.1) S N
VHF 16/68 N32.02.076
912/629-2400 W081.02.802
Exit ICW N of bridge. Facility is to W. [STR 9.2]
Formerly Tidewater Boatworks.
See Thunderbolt.

582.5 Thunderbolt Bridge S N
Fixed; vertical 65 feet. [STR 9.2 (TS)]

582.7 Bahia Bleu Marina (0.1) S N
VHF 16/68 N32.01.868
912/354-2283 W081.02.902
Exit ICW SW of bridge. Marina is to NW. [STR 9.2]

583.2 Thunderbolt Marine (0.1) S N
VHF 16/11 N32.01.458
912/356-3875 W081.02.812
Exit ICW WNW of R36. Marina is SW in charted basin. [STR 9.2]
Formerly Palmer Johnson.

584.2 Herb River Anchorage (0.4) S N
Anchor 12-14 feet N32.00.958
STR 9.2 feet W081.01.903
Exit ICW at G37. Proceed SSW into Herb River.

585.5 Turner Creek S N
Exit ICW NE of R40. Proceed ESE to charted Turners Creek. Turn NE, favoring Turners Rock, to enter creek. [STR 9.2]
Shallow 4-foot charted area is usually negated by large tidal range.

- **Sail Harbor Marina & Boatyard** (1.2)
  VHF 16/71 N32.00.510
  912/897-2896 W080.59.857
  Marina is to starboard.
  Formerly Yacht Works.
- **Hogans' Marina** (1.5)
  VHF 16/09 N32.00.584
  912/897-3474 W080.59.413
  Marina is to starboard. Easily identified by dry storage racks and two hoists.
- **Turner Creek Anchorage** (1.6)
  Anchor 8-12 feet N32.00.503
  STR 9.2 feet W080.59.462
  Continue beyond marina around bend.

585.5 Junction | Wassaw Sound S N
Exit ICW NE of R40. Proceed southerly down Wilmington River.
Buoyage reverses. Look for yellow reflective ICW triangles and squares on aids.

- **The Landings** (3.7)
  VHF 16; 912/598-1901
  Exit Wilmington River S of G23. Marina is to W at charted Priest Landing. [STR 8.5]
  Dry store and 28 wet slips for community members. Transient dockage at sister marina, Delegal Creek (STM 600.9).
- **Wassaw Sound** (14.8)
  Well Aided N31.51.438
  Moderately Lit W080.52.939
  Continue out Wilmington River to Wassaw Sound. Waypoint is at R "2W".

SAFETY INFO

NOAA Weather	Sea Tow
WX-3 Beaufort, SC	Savannah, GA
WX-2 Savannah, GA	VHF 16/11
WX-1 Jacksonville, FL	912/897-4304
USCG	**TowBoatU.S.**
Station Tybee, GA	Thunderbolt, GA
VHF 16 or 09/22A	VHF 16
912/786-5440	912/898-9659

HEADS UP!

469.0	Charleston Coast Guard Station	706.0	Kings Bay Security Zone (SB)
470.8	Wappoo Creek Bridge	713.0	Kings Bay Security Zone (NB)
472.2	Elliott Cut (SB)	713.7	Cumberland Sound Channel (NB)
472.5	Elliott Cut (NB)	714.0	GA-FL Border
536.0	Ladies Island Bridge	720.7	Kingsley Creek RR Bridge
575.8	SC-GA Border	739.1	Sisters Creek Bridge
578.4	Wilmington River Cut-off (NB)	747.4	B.B. McCormick Twin Bridges
579.9	Causton Bluff Bridge	775.0	St. Augustine Inlet Area (SB)
592.4	**Skidaway Narrows Bridge**	778.1	Bridge of Lions

589.9 Isle of Hope Marina (0.1)
VHF 16/68 N31.58.780
912/354-8187 W081.03.350
Exit ICW at R46 "A". Marina is to WNW. [STR 9.1 (TS)]
See Terrapin Farming.

590.1 Isle of Hope Anchorage (0.1)
Anchor 4-6 feet N31.58.675
STR (TS) 9.1 feet W081.03.255
Exit ICW between R46 "A" and R48. Proceed SW to charted anchorage area.
See Wormsloe Plantation.

592.4 Skidaway Narrows Bridge
(R. C. Roebling Bridge)
VHF 13; 912/352-2733
Double bascule; vertical 22 feet; on request.

594.7 Moon River Anchorage (0.4)
Anchor 6-9 feet N31.55.688
STR 8.8 feet W081.04.585
Exit ICW S of R74. Proceed NW into Moon River. Some shoaling at entrance. Anchor off Marsh Island.

597.3 Beaulieu Anchorage (1.4)
Anchor 12-14 feet N31.55.895
STR 8.8 feet W081.06.895
Exit ICW S of G79. Proceed NW to Beaulieu, avoiding shoal at Possum Point.

600.9 Delegal Creek Marina (1.6)
VHF 16; 912/598-0023
Exit ICW at R86. Proceed NE into charted Steamboat Cut and privately maintained channel. Continue northerly up Delegal Creek. Marina is beyond G11, to starboard. [STR 8.8]

601.8 Hell Gate Range
to Southbound/Northbound Navigation
602.2 Hell Gate
0.4-mile range.

602.4 Junction | Ossabaw Sound (9.9)
Moderately Aided N31.47.724
Poorly Lit W080.56.204
Exit ICW S of R92. Proceed southeasterly out South Channel. Waypoint is at RW "OS" sea buoy.
Ossabaw Sound has two charted inlets: North Channel and South Channel. South Channel is preferred because it is shorter and straighter.

606.5 Queen Bess Creek Anchorage (0.4)
Anchor 8-12 feet N31.50.376
STR 8.5 feet W081.08.618
Exit ICW between R98 and G99. Proceed SE into Queen Bess Creek. Anchor off Bear Island.

606.9 Redbird Creek Anchorage (0.9)
Anchor 8-14 feet N31.51.039
STR 8.5 feet W081.09.630
Exit ICW NE of G99. Proceed NNW into Redbird Creek.

607.3 Florida Passage Range
to Southbound/Northbound Navigation
608.4 Florida Passage
1.1-mile range.

Rat is smaller (about seven inches), with grayish-brown fur and a long thin tail. Marsh Rice Rats also swim easily, both on the surface and underwater, and nest in the marsh grasses. They are very common along the Sea Islands, and are a native species, not a pest.

If you have a manual pump marine toilet, remember to lubricate the handle to prevent damage. Every couple of weeks, pull up on the handle and lubricate the shaft with anhydrous lanolin or Superlube Teflon.

TERRAPIN FARMING

The community of Isle of Hope, at STM 590, lies in the bend along Skidaway River. The Barbee Pavilion—built by Alexander Barbee, conductor of the electric railway between Savannah and Isle of Hope—was the center of the community until the early 1900s.

Barbee settled on Isle of Hope and started "Barbee's Diamondback Terrapin Farm," described as one of the oldest turtle farms of its kind in the world. Through the 1800s, diamondback terrapin meat was considered a delicacy. The former Bannon Lodge in Thunderbolt was so famous for its terrapin stew its clientele included several presidents. Turtles were also in demand for ships' stores: they could be stored alive for weeks as a source of fresh meat simply by placing them on their backs. Unfortunately, the popularity of turtle meat nearly wiped out the wild population of terrapins.

Diamondback terrapins occur all along the Waterway and are thought to be the only turtle in the world that can live in brackish water. They are relatively small turtles, only about five to seven inches long. Look for a brown upper shell covered with plates or scales with deep diamond-shaped growth rings.

WORMSLOE PLANTATION

The Wormsloe Plantation is located just south of the Skidaway Narrows Bridge, across the marshes on the southern end of Isle of Hope. It was originally the "Wormslow" plantation, named after its large population of silkworms. Plantation owner Noble Jones, one of the first British colonists in the area, built Wormsloe in 1737 as a country estate for horticultural experiments. In addition to cotton and indigo, he raised silkworms on their required diet of mulberry trees, producing silk from the fibers of their cocoons.

Courtesy of Smithsonian Marine Station
Photo by Patricia Holm
Great Blue Heron Fishing

Despite its aristocratic formal gardens and boulevards lined with live oaks and azaleas, one has to remember that it was a jungle out there in the 1700s. The property was protected by fort-like structures. The surviving ruins of the original house, once a five-room fortified tabby house with four bastions, is one of the last remaining examples of fortified houses once common through coastal Georgia.

Today the 750-acre plantation is owned by the state and open to the public. A museum describes the history of the area. The earthworks, known during the Civil War as Fort Wymberly, are still visible. A one-mile interpretive hiking trail leads down to the tabby ruins of Wormsloe, on a bluff overlooking the marshes and waterways.

Wormsloe Historic Site
www.wormsloe.org
912/353-3023

TABBY—JUST ADD WATER

Think of tabby as the first form-poured cement technology. Since tabby has African and Arabic origins, the technology probably passed from the Moors of Africa to the Spaniards, who brought the technique to the New World in the 1500s.

All along the Georgia and South Carolina coast, foundations were built from tabby. Florida had coquina rock, which it could quarry for foundations, but Georgia and South Carolina had to rely on creating a form of concrete from abundant sand and shells.

SAFETY INFO

NOAA Weather
WX-3 Beaufort, SC
WX-2 Savannah, GA
WX-1 Jacksonville, FL

USCG
Station Tybee, GA
VHF 16 or 09/22A
912/786-5440

Sea Tow
Saint Catherines, GA
VHF 16/11
912/884-3435

TowBoatU.S.
Thunderbolt, GA
VHF 16
912/898-9659

HEADS UP!

469.0	Charleston Coast Guard Station
470.8	Wappoo Creek Bridge
472.2	Elliott Cut (SB)
472.5	Elliott Cut (NB)
536.0	Ladies Island Bridge
575.8	SC-GA Border
578.4	Wilmington River Cut-off (NB)
579.9	Causton Bluff Bridge
592.4	Skidaway Narrows Bridge
706.0	Kings Bay Security Zone (SB)
713.0	Kings Bay Security Zone (NB)
713.7	Cumberland Sound Channel (NB)
714.0	GA-FL Border
720.7	Kingsley Creek RR Bridge
739.1	Sisters Creek Bridge
747.4	B.B. McCormick Twin Bridges
775.0	St. Augustine Inlet Area (SB)
778.1	Bridge of Lions

Creating durable foundations from oyster shells and tidal sand is not easy. Preservationists at Fort Frederica recently attempted to reproduce a tabby foundation, but it was not a stunning success. They had to resort to adding cement to their shell and sand concoction. In contrast, many of the area's original tabby foundations still stand solidly 200 years later.

It is known that settlers burned huge piles of oyster shells to create lime, which was then mixed with sand, oyster shells, and water into a mortar and poured into forms. When the forms were removed, the surface was very porous, so a final coat of stucco-like lime and sand was applied.

You can see oyster shell tabby foundations all along the Waterway. Look at the base of forts; on plantation houses, such as the Reynolds home on Sapelo Island or the Wormsloe house; or on homes in historic districts, such as in Savannah or Beaufort.

Get moving! Much like commercial fishermen have a "get home" emergency system, you can mount an outboard-motor bracket on your transom. Then you can use your dinghy's outboard for emergency auxiliary power. If you lose your main engine, remove your outboard from your dinghy and hang it on your transom bracket. You won't go fast, but you'll get there!

THE HERDSMAN (AUTUMN)

The Herdsman, also called Boötes or the Bear Watcher, is one of the oldest recorded constellations, dating back over 3,000 years to the Egyptians and Greeks.

The Egyptians believed circumpolar constellations—ones that never set—were evil. Great Bear was suspected to be one of the most evil of these constellations, so Boötes, or the Bear Watcher, was believed to guard the Great Bear against fomenting evil.

The contemporary interpretation of this constellation is a herdsman, sitting down and smoking a pipe. You can locate the Herdsman from the Big Dipper. The Herdsman's main star is Arcturus, visible high in the west in September. To locate the bright star Arcturus, "follow the arc to Arcturus" by extending the sweep of the Big Dipper's handle. Once you spot Arcturus, the Herdsman constellation takes form around it with smaller fainter stars. Arcturus forms the Herdsman's lap, with a triangular body, a pentagon head with cap, and a pipe (in a triangle of lighter stars) near the end of the Big Dipper's handle.

TURKEY VULTURE

The Turkey Vulture is the raptor with a serious image problem. Word association with "vulture"? Most people think of dirty, ugly, smelly, and greedy.

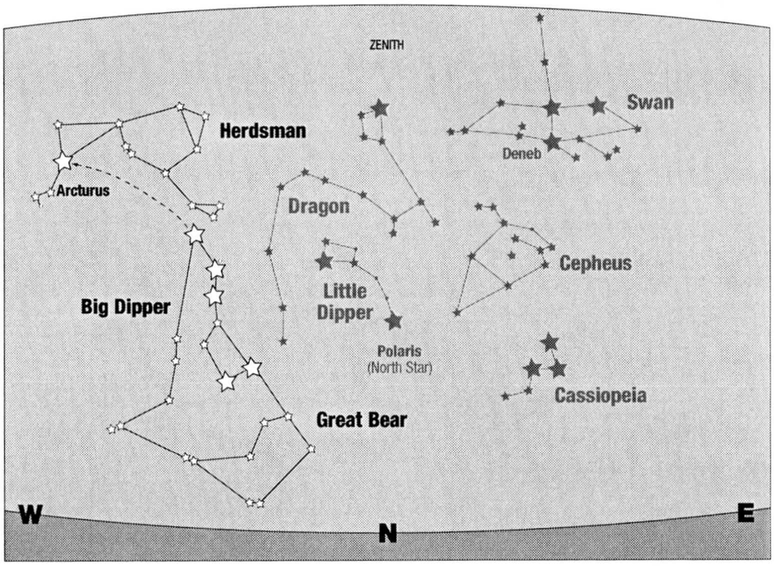

Autumn, Early Evening

Follow the Arc to Arcturus

608.5 Ossabaw Island Anchorages
Exit ICW SE of R102. Proceed easterly to anchorages.

- **Buckhead Creek Anchorage** (2.7)
  Anchor 10-12 feet N31.48.528
  STR 8.6 feet W081.07.995
  Bear S into Buckhead Creek. Take first left and proceed NNE into oxbow. Anchor off Pine Island.
- **Cane Patch Creek Anchorage** (2.5)
  Anchor 12-16 feet N31.49.324
  STR 8.6 feet W081.07.409
  Continue easterly in Cane Patch Creek. Anchor off Queen Mary Island.
- **Rush Creek Anchorage** (3.0)
  Anchor 16-20 feet N31.50.137
  STR 8.6 feet W081.06.590
  Continue northeasterly in Cane Patch Creek to charted Rush Creek basin. Anchor off unnamed islet.

610.2 Range "A"
to Southbound/Northbound Navigation
611.0 Bear River
0.8-mile range.

611.7 Range "B"
to Southbound/Northbound Navigation
612.2 Bear River
0.5-mile range.

612.3 Unnamed Anchorage (0.2)
Anchor 9-12 feet N31.47.553
STR 8.8 feet W081.09.840
Exit ICW between R104 "C" and Range "B" forward light. Proceed N into unnamed creek.

612.9 Big Tom Creek Anchorage (0.4)
Anchor 10-12 feet N31.46.612
STR 8.8 feet W081.09.236
Exit ICW at G105. Proceed ESE into Big Tom Creek.

613.7 Kilkenny Creek
Exit ICW at G107. Proceed NW into Kilkenny Creek. [STR 8.8]

- **Kilkenny Creek Anchorage** (Southeast)(0.7)
  Anchor 15-18 feet N31.46.686
  STR 8.8 feet W081.10.957
  Anchorage is before fork, in charted 12-foot shallows, where chart is labeled Kilkenny Creek.
- **Kilkenny Marina** (2.0)
  VHF 16; 912/727-2215
  Continue northwesterly in Kilkenny Creek. At fork with Lincoln Creek, favor N shore and bear to starboard. Marina is to port.
- **Kilkenny Creek Anchorage** (Northwest)(2.2)
  Anchor 8-12 feet N31.47.517
  STR 8.8 feet W081.12.028
  Anchor beyond Kilkenny Marina.

618.4 Junction | St. Catherines Sound (9.4)
Well Aided N31.40.089
Moderately Lit W081.00.142
Exit ICW ESE of R114. Proceed southeasterly to St.

SAFETY INFO

NOAA Weather	Sea Tow
WX-3 Beaufort, SC	St. Catherines, GA
WX-2 Savannah, GA	VHF 16/11
WX-1 Jacksonville, FL	912/884-3435
USCG	**TowBoatU.S.**
Station Brunswick, GA	St. Simons Island, GA
VHF 16 or 09/22A	VHF 16/10
912/267-9010	912/638-7751

HEADS UP!

469.0	Charleston Coast Guard Station	706.0	Kings Bay Security Zone (SB)
470.8	Wappoo Creek Bridge	713.0	Kings Bay Security Zone (NB)
472.2	Elliott Cut (SB)	713.7	Cumberland Sound Channel (NB)
472.5	Elliott Cut (NB)	714.0	GA-FL Border
536.0	Ladies Island Bridge	720.7	Kingsley Creek RR Bridge
575.8	SC-GA Border	739.1	Sisters Creek Bridge
578.4	Wilmington River Cut-off (NB)	747.4	B.B. McCormick Twin Bridges
579.9	Causton Bluff Bridge	775.0	St. Augustine Inlet Area (SB)
592.4	Skidaway Narrows Bridge	778.1	Bridge of Lions

Catherines Sound. Waypoint is at RW "STC" sea buoy.

618.6 Junction | Walburg Creek Alternate Route S N
to Southbound/Northbound Navigation
623.0 5.8-mile alternate route.

Southbound, exit ICW SSE of R114. Proceed SE, avoiding charted 3-foot shoal in Middle Ground. Follow St. Catherines Island to charted Walburg Creek entrance. Play the tide to rejoin ICW at R124 (North Newport River). [STR 8.3 (TS)]

Northbound, exit ICW at R124. Proceed easterly into Walburg Creek. Rejoin ICW near R114 (St. Catherines Sound).

- **Walburg Creek Anchorage**
  Anchor 16-20 feet N31.40.642
  STR 8.3 feet W081.09.533
  You may anchor anywhere in lee of St. Catherines Island.
  SEE WILDLIFE SURVIVAL CENTER.

625.4 Cattle Pen Creek Anchorage (0.5) S N
Anchor 10-14 feet N31.38.659
STR 8.3 feet W081.10.990
Exit ICW between G127 and R128. Proceed NE into Cattle Pen Creek.

630.0 Wahoo River Anchorage (1.6) S N
Anchor 12-14 feet N31.35.751
STR 8.3 feet W081.12.437
Exit ICW at G135. Proceed northwesterly, avoiding large charted shoal area, into Wahoo River.

632.4 Junction | Sapelo Sound (8.0) S N
Moderately Aided N31.31.134
Poorly Lit W081.03.882
Exit ICW S of R138. Proceed easterly to Sapelo Sound. Waypoint is at RW "S" sea buoy.
SEE BLACKBEARD ISLAND & SAPELO ISLAND LIGHT.

639.7 Front River Anchorage (0.1) S N
Anchor 8-10 feet N31.30.860
STR 8.4 feet W081.17.958
Exit ICW between R152 and G153. Proceed NW into charted Ridge River Mouth tongue.

642.3 Creighton Narrows S N
to Southbound/Northbound Navigation
642.8 0.5-mile land cut.
No anchorages, no marinas, no fuel.

643.0 Crescent River Anchorage (0.9) S N
Anchor 12-14 feet N31.29.767
STR (TS) 8.6 feet W081.20.136
Exit ICW S of G157. Proceed northwesterly up Crescent River beyond Cedar Creek fork.

643.1 Range "A" S N
to Southbound/Northbound Navigation
643.3 Crescent River
0.2-mile range.

644.1 Shellbluff Creek Anchorage (0.2) S N
Anchor 8-10 feet N31.28.554
STR 8.6 feet W081.19.987
Exit ICW S of R162. Proceed W into Shellbluff Creek.

Any sunny midday, Turkey Vultures commonly soar high on the thermals above the Waterway. With a five-foot wingspan, they soar effortlessly. Even in silhouette, high in the sky, a Turkey Vulture is easy to identify. Look for a large black bird soaring with its wings held at a pronounced dihedral; most other raptors, including Bald Eagles and Red-tailed Hawks, soar with their wings nearly flat.

Yes, vultures are funny looking and they do smell. But they are ugly and smelly for a reason. They need their heads bare instead of feathered so they can feed deep into carrion, their main food source. They also may stink for a reason. Scientists think they use their vile smell, created when they vomit when startled, to scare off threats.

Just like garbage men with their bad image, someone has to clear out the refuse! Without Turkey Vultures the place would be a mess. They are a crucial part of the food chain, removing animal carcasses before they have a chance to rot, smell, and breed disease in this warm climate. They are beautiful to watch...from a distance.

WILDLIFE SURVIVAL CENTER

St. Catherines Island is home to a low-profile retreat for internationally endangered species. Affiliated with the New York Zoological Society, the island is a modern-day Noah's Ark, breeding colonies of endangered species to be returned to zoos or the wild. The island has hosted some unusual guests, including Grevy's Zebras, Ring-tailed Lemurs, Dama Gazelles, St. Vincent Parrots, Rhinoceros Hornbills, Aldabra Tortoises, Florida Sandhill Cranes, and Jackson's Harte-beests.

The island, along Walburg Creek Alternate Route between STM 619 and STM 623, is closed to the public. However, by state law, Georgia's barrier island beaches to the high tide line are open to the public, including St. Catherines. During daylight hours, the public is allowed to use its shores up to the *high-tide line* for hiking, picnicking, or shelling. The facility and the interior of the island are absolutely off limits.

BALD EAGLES

Not too long ago, Bald Eagles were rare along the eastern seaboard. Thanks to the regulation of pesticides, the population is steadily increasing. Bald Eagles are now commonly seen along the Waterway.

Courtesy of NOAA

Black-Necked Stilt

Bald Eagles are much more abundant than most boaters realize. Since they perch quietly high in a tree, many boaters unknowingly motor past them. If you watch the other wildlife, you can locate an eagle before you even see its silhouette. Ducks or geese, which Bald Eagles consider fair prey, make themselves scarce. Other birds, like Ospreys or crows, become very agitated, screeching and sometimes mobbing the eagle. Bald Eagles chase Osprey and steal their fish, so Osprey and Bald Eagles don't get along.

So, if you see an agitated Osprey, screeching and swooping near a tree, look up. A majestic Bald Eagle is probably perched nearby, nonchalantly overlooking the Waterway, feigning indifference to the annoying lesser raptor.

It's true that anchorages provide protection, but don't settle in for the night too close to shore. Anchor 100-200 yards out. Even if the wind shifts, you'll only get the breeze not the waves. Experienced cruisers know that anchoring further out yields better ventilation, fewer insects, a lot less noise, and puts you further off a potential lee shore.

SAFETY INFO

NOAA Weather
WX-3 Beaufort, SC
WX-2 Savannah, GA
WX-1 Jacksonville, FL

USCG
Station Brunswick, GA
VHF 16 or 09/22A
912/267-9010

Sea Tow
St. Catherines, GA
VHF 16/11
912/884-3435

TowBoatU.S.
St. Simons Island, GA
VHF 16/10
912/638-7751

HEADS UP!

470.8	Wappoo Creek Bridge
472.2	Elliott Cut (SB)
472.5	Elliott Cut (NB)
536.0	Ladies Island Bridge
575.8	SC-GA Border
578.4	Wilmington River Cut-off (NB)
579.9	Causton Bluff Bridge
592.4	Skidaway Narrows Bridge
706.0	Kings Bay Security Zone (SB)
713.0	Kings Bay Security Zone (NB)
713.7	Cumberland Sound Channel (NB)
714.0	GA-FL Border
720.7	Kingsley Creek RR Bridge
739.1	Sisters Creek Bridge
747.4	B.B. McCormick Twin Bridges
775.0	St. Augustine Inlet Area (SB)
778.1	Bridge of Lions
779.0	St. Augustine Inlet Area (NB)

BLACKBEARD ISLAND

At one time, pirates and privateers were viewed as "businessmen on the margin," not unlike bootleggers during Prohibition or Mafia bosses today. In the days of maritime conflict, seizing others' ships was considered fair game. Pirates and privateers were a necessary part of the revolutionary economy, bringing home much-needed gold and munitions.

Some pirates and privateers earned near-celebrity status, joining the soirées of politicians and wealthy merchants—not too different than our politicians today when they seek out shock celebrities like Dennis Rodman or "Puff Daddy" Combs for their parties or get-out-the-vote campaigns. It used to be eye patches and a hook, now it's pink hair and body art.

But even among the pirate set, Blackbeard went for the shock factor. He braided his long black beard, smeared lampblack under his eyes, carried several pistols and knives, and boasted he never bathed. He carried long matchsticks in his hat, which he lit Halloween-style under his face at night to spook the victim ship's crew before a raid.

One of his favorite antics was to pour gunpowder into a mug of rum, set it afire, and swallow the fiery mixture. But his sense of humor was also described as "about as funny as a shipwreck." Once, he shot his pistol under a tavern table "as a joke" and took out a couple of kneecaps.

Blackbeard Island, just south of STM 633, is named after this most notorious of all pirates. Blackbeard had one of his many "branch offices" on this then-heavily-wooded island. It's rumored he buried his treasure here, but many islands are rumored to hold his treasure. Either Blackbeard had a lot of loot or it's wishful thinking on the part of treasure hunters.

In the end Blackbeard died off the coast of North Carolina without revealing his stashes. Even the beautiful Anne Bonny, the famous "mistress of the sea," couldn't seduce or tease it out of him. Maybe it was because she refused to sleep with him, complaining he stank so badly.

Blackbeard reputedly said only two people knew where his gold was buried: himself and the devil.

FRONT OR BACK DIVE?

Ever notice how pelicans and terns dive for fish all around your boat? One theory is they feed around slow-moving yachts because the fish are disoriented or brought to the surface by the agitation of the keel or propeller.

Terns are champions of the front dive. They hover for a few seconds, eyeing the water, then dive in a streamlined front entry. They rise out of the water with a single fish daintily draped in their bill, often flying off with their prize to a mate or their young.

Courtesy of NOAA

Photo by William B. Folsom

Tern Hovering

Brown Pelicans are masters of the "twisting plunge-dive." They don't hover and dive; they suddenly tilt over, collapsing their wings and plummeting in a twisting backward crash like a bucket hitting the water. Then they drag their bill full of catch to the surface, draining and swallowing their catch before flying off.

But the plunge dive has its price. To cushion the impact of eight pounds of bird hitting the water surface, Brown Pelicans have developed a chest full of air sacks, which they inflate just before striking the water. But their eyes still take a beating: the trauma eventually damages their vision. As they age, Brown Pelicans become blind, and unable to fish, ultimately die of starvation in their old age.

SAPELO ISLAND LIGHT

Remote Sapelo Island (pronounced SAP-uh-lo) has hosted a slew of lighthouses over the centuries.

The first lighthouse was built in 1820, later upgraded in the 1850s by adding a fourth-order Fresnel lens. Early in the 1900s, a new steel skeleton tower

645.0 Range "B" S N
to Southbound/Northbound Navigation
645.5 Old Teakettle Creek
0.5-mile range.

646.8 New Teakettle Creek Anchorage (1.2) S N
Anchor 8-24 feet N31.27.604
STR 7.8 feet W081.18.114
Exit ICW between R172 and G173. Proceed N into New Teakettle Creek. Continue around first bend, beyond Mary Creek.

649.3 Duplin River Anchorage (1.5) S N
Anchor 12-14 feet N31.25.563
STR 7.8 feet W081.17.705
Exit ICW NE of R178. Proceed easterly, leaving charted shoal to port, into Duplin River. Continue beyond charted ferry dock.

649.4 Junction | Doboy Sound (8.5) S N
Well Aided N31.21.181
Poorly Lit W081.11.333
Exit ICW E of R178. Proceed southeasterly to Doboy Sound. Waypoint is at RW "D" sea buoy.

649.5 Range "A" S N
to Southbound/Northbound Navigation
650.0 North River
0.5-mile range.

651.1 Back River Anchorage (0.5) S N
Anchor 8-12 feet N31.23.716
STR 7.8 feet W081.19.392
Exit ICW N of G181. Proceed E along Doboy Island into Back River.

651.2 North River Anchorage (1.9) S N
Anchor 8-12 feet N31.24.170
STR 7.8 feet W081.21.339
Exit ICW at G181. Proceed westerly into North River. Anchor around second bend.

651.8 Darien River Anchorage (0.9) S N
Anchor 12-16 feet N31.23.201
STR 7.8 feet W081.20.878
Exit ICW at G183. Proceed W into Darien River.

652.6 Range "A" S N
to Southbound/Northbound Navigation
653.0 Rockdedundy River
0.4-mile range.

653.0 Queens Island Anchorage (0.7) S N
Anchor 9-12 feet N31.22.125
STR 8.0 feet W081.19.492
Exit ICW at R190. Proceed SE into South River.
SEE WOLF ISLAND.

653.0 Range "A" S N
to Southbound/Northbound Navigation
653.3 Little Mud River
0.3-mile range.

655.5 Range "B" S N
to Southbound/Northbound Navigation
656.3 Little Mud River
0.8-mile range.

SAFETY INFO

NOAA Weather
WX-3 Beaufort, SC
WX-2 Savannah, GA
WX-1 Jacksonville, FL

USCG
Station Brunswick, GA
VHF 16 or 09/22A
912/267-9010

Sea Tow
Brunswick, GA
VHF 16/12
912/280-9428

TowBoatU.S.
St. Simons Island, GA
VHF 16/10
912/638-7751

HEADS UP!

470.8	Wappoo Creek Bridge
472.2	Elliott Cut (SB)
472.5	Elliott Cut (NB)
536.0	Ladies Island Bridge
575.8	SC-GA Border
578.4	Wilmington River Cut-off (NB)
579.9	Causton Bluff Bridge
592.4	Skidaway Narrows Bridge
706.0	Kings Bay Security Zone (SB)
713.0	Kings Bay Security Zone (NB)
713.7	Cumberland Sound Channel (NB)
714.0	GA-FL Border
720.7	Kingsley Creek RR Bridge
739.1	Sisters Creek Bridge
747.4	B.B. McCormick Twin Bridges
775.0	St. Augustine Inlet Area (SB)
778.1	Bridge of Lions
779.0	St. Augustine Inlet Area (NB)

656.6 Junction | Altamaha Sound
Southbound/Northbound Navigation

Although this appears to be a convenient point to jump out, we much prefer Doboy Sound. Altamaha Sound is shallower and has a 4-foot bar at its entrance.

Additionally, Doboy Sound is only 3 nautical miles north when entering from seaward.

An exception would be a mistimed evening approach, as Altamaha Sound is better lit.

656.6 Range "A"
to Southbound/Northbound Navigation
657.4 Altamaha Sound

0.8-mile range.

We typically pick up (southbound) or leave (northbound) Range "A" SE of R198.

657.4 Old Range "B"
to Southbound/Northbound Navigation
658.4 Altamaha Sound

1.0-mile range.

This range is partially charted but no longer used. It is now aided by R202, R204, R206, and R208.

659.1 Range "C"
to Southbound/Northbound Navigation
659.9 Altamaha Sound

0.8-mile range.

661.6 Range "A"
to Southbound Navigation Only
662.4 Buttermilk Sound

0.8-mile range.

662.2 South Altamaha River

Exit ICW Range "A" SSW of R216 "A". Proceed northwesterly into South Altamaha River channel. [STR 8.0]

Buoyage reverses. Look for yellow reflective ICW triangles and squares on aids.

- **South Altamaha River Anchorage** (0.8)
  Anchor 8-12 feet N31.18.684
  STR 8.0 feet W081.24.516
  Proceed around first bend. Anchor NE of R2.
- **Two Way Marina** (4.4)
  VHF 16/68 or 19 N31.19.684
  912/265-0410 W081.26.796
  Continue northwesterly in winding river. The river is well-aided and deep. Marina is to port before fixed bridge. [STR 6.4]
  Caution: There is considerable river current at face docks. Wait for docking assistance.

662.4 Range "A"
to Northbound Navigation Only
661.6 Buttermilk Sound

0.8-mile range.

662.4 Range "B"
to Southbound Navigation Only
662.9 Buttermilk Sound

0.5-mile range.

662.6 Buttermilk Sound Anchorage (North)(0.2)
Anchor 6-10 feet N31.17.853

replaced the brick-and-stone structure, which was left abandoned. The steel structure withstood the hurricanes, but was only in service about 30 years before it was packed up and shipped to Lake Superior's Apostle Islands. Today the brick-and-stone tower remains, abandoned for decades until it was restored in 1998.

Ferries to the island depart from Meridian and the state provides tours of the island. Most of the island is a remote state-owned nature preserve with the exception of Hog Hammock, a Gullah community of about 70 people, many descended from slaves who worked the Sapelo plantations.

By boat, the lighthouse is a two-mile detour from the magenta line. Depart the Waterway to the southeast at STM 649.5. The red-and-white striped lighthouse is visible on the southwest end of Sapelo Island.

Sapelo Island Ferry/Visitor Center
912/437-3224

McIntosh County Chamber of Commerce
www.mcintoshcounty.com
912/437-4192

FRESNEL LENSES

Think French, as in "Freh-NEL," the name of the French physicist who designed a way to use prisms to concentrate light into a powerful beam. Fresnel lenses are composed of hundreds or thousands of individual prisms, looking like a big glass beehive. Fresnel lenses were a great discovery for lighthouse technology, since even a weak light source, such as from oil lamps, could be magnified and focused to be visible dozens of miles away.

But Fresnel lenses were very expensive. Thousands of precision glass pieces had to be hand ground and polished. The work was usually done by the poorest French laborers, including children, who were paid pennies for a day of work. So most U.S. lighthouses were built with the cheaper local design of parabolic reflectors.

In the 1850s, a group of engineers, military officers, and seamen initiated a national campaign to overhaul the nation's lighthouses. This "Lighthouse Board" successfully lobbied to refit most American lighthouses with the Fresnel technology.

You can see a Fresnel lens at many of the lighthouses along the Waterway. The order of a Fresnel lens refers to the size of the lens. A first-order lens is about six feet wide and 12 feet tall; a sixth-order lens has an efficient one-foot diameter. Most ocean lighthouses use the more powerful first- or second-order lenses. Lighthouses for harbors or rivers, such as along the Waterway, are usually the smaller fourth-order lenses. The St. Simons Light has a third-order Fresnel.

Most Fresnel lenses are now replaced with modern light beacons, not because they are more effective, but because the delicate Fresnel structures are nearly impossible to repair. At today's labor rates, it would cost millions of dollars to manufacture a new Fresnel lens.

A long-stemmed lighter, sold for lighting fireplaces or barbecues, is handy on board. It's a safer way to light your galley stove and oven, oil lamps, or barbecue and can also be used to burn the cut ends of nylon or polypropylene line to prevent unraveling.

A WONDERFUL BIRD IS THE PELICAN...

...his beak can hold more than his belly can. This old ditty from 1910 is true: a Brown Pelican can hold a staggering three gallons of water in its pouch. But it can't swallow that much. Instead, it sieves its catch from the water before tipping its head back and swallowing.

The Brown Pelican is now so common along the Waterway many boaters don't realize that, until recently, it was an endangered species. Nearly extinct when it was placed on the Endangered Species List in 1978, it rebounded within a few years of protection. In 1985, the Brown Pelican was upgraded from an endangered to a threatened species in Florida, Georgia, and the Carolinas.

Brown Pelicans are masters of efficient aerodynamics. Like Canada Geese, they use a staggered follow-the-leader formation that takes advantage of the air currents created by the bird ahead. Even at a distance their flight pattern is characteristic: several flaps and then a long glide so close to the water surface it seems as if their wings will snag a wave ripple. By flying low

SAFETY INFO

NOAA Weather
WX-3 Beaufort, SC
WX-2 Savannah, GA
WX-1 Jacksonville, FL

USCG
Station Brunswick, GA
VHF 16 or 09/22A
912/267-9010

Sea Tow
Brunswick, GA
VHF 16/12
912/280-9428

TowBoatU.S.
St. Simons Island, GA
VHF 16/10
912/638-7751

HEADS UP!

470.8	Wappoo Creek Bridge
472.2	Elliott Cut (SB)
472.5	Elliott Cut (NB)
536.0	Ladies Island Bridge
575.8	SC-GA Border
578.4	Wilmington River Cut-off (NB)
579.9	Causton Bluff Bridge
592.4	Skidaway Narrows Bridge
706.0	Kings Bay Security Zone (SB)
713.0	Kings Bay Security Zone (NB)
713.7	Cumberland Sound Channel (NB)
714.0	GA-FL Border
720.7	Kingsley Creek RR Bridge
739.1	Sisters Creek Bridge
747.4	B.B. McCormick Twin Bridges
775.0	St. Augustine Inlet Area (SB)
778.1	Bridge of Lions
779.0	St. Augustine Inlet Area (NB)

over the water, they compress the air beneath their large bodies, creating an air pillow that sustains their gravity-defying glides.

Courtesy of U.S. Fish & Wildlife Service

Brown Pelican Sentinel

WOLF ISLAND

Wolf Island is one of seven islands in the Savannah Coastal Refuge, a 56,000-acre chain of islands spanning 100 miles of coastline. The chain begins at Pinckney Island National Wildlife Refuge, near Hilton Head Island in South Carolina, and ends at the Wolf Island National Wildlife Refuge between STM 653 and STM 657.

Wolf Island has been a refuge for decades, upgraded in 1975 to a National Wilderness Area with no public use facilities. All beach, marsh, and upland areas are closed to the public; wildlife observation is by boat only.

CORDGRASS

It's a *marsh*, not a swamp. Marshes are made up of grasses; swamps have trees. Officially the acres and acres of wetlands surrounding your boat in this area are called tidal marshes or spartina marshes.

Spartina is actually the genus, or group name, of a wide assortment of cordgrasses. Saltmarsh Cordgrass, Saltmeadow Cordgrass, Smooth Cordgrass, Oyster Cordgrass...there are so many different varieties of these salt-tolerant grasses they are often simply called by the group name Spartina. They all have in common an ability to tolerate saltwater flooding by excreting extra salt on their leaf edges.

Cordgrass is so abundant along the Waterway it deserves at least a few column-inches. Actually, cordgrass is crucial to the Waterway: it's the foundation of what Rafiki in *The Lion King* calls "a circle of life kind of thing."

Cordgrass holds the mud against erosion, keeps the water clean, and provides shelter to species from invertebrate mussels to Great Egrets. Cordgrass is the basis of the entire food chain. When the cordgrass dies back in late fall, the plant detritus feeds scavengers, like fish and crabs, who in turn provide food for the birds and small mammals. Large mammals, such as wild horses and deer, feed on the cordgrass like hay.

So think of the miles of cordgrass not as a swamp, but as a vast wheat field for animals. Wheat fields may be the most productive *land*, but according to biologists, these salt marshes are three times more productive than the best wheat fields.

A HEN TIDE

In the evening when your engine is off and all is quiet, listen for the loud rapid kek-kek-kek-kek of salt-water marsh hens in the marsh grass.

These brown chicken-like birds, officially called Clapper Rails, are secretive and camouflaged. They are so thin laterally—as in the expression "thin as a rail"—they nearly disappear among the marsh grass. They skulk through the grass, moving with the tide, searching for small crabs, snails, and insects along the receding water's edge.

Since high tides flood the sea of grass and flush the rails out to the edges, the locals call it a "hen tide" when the spring tide is over nine feet.

Then it's hunting time. (Bag limit is 15 per day—they're thin.) We've never eaten them, but (er, pardon the worn out phrase) we hear they taste like chicken.

STR 8.0 feet W081.24.071
Exit ICW Range "B" between R218 and R220. Proceed W to charted 9-foot pocket.

662.9 Range "B" S N
to Northbound Navigation Only
662.4 Buttermilk Sound
0.5-mile range.

663.1 Range "A" S N
to Southbound/Northbound Navigation
663.9 Mackay River
0.8-mile range.

664.0 Buttermilk Sound Anchorage (South)(0.2) S N
Anchor 8-10 feet N31.17.015
STR 8.0 feet W081.23.216
Exit ICW SSE of R222. Proceed W.

664.2 Hampton River Club Marina (3.9) S N
VHF 16; 912/638-1210
Exit ICW between R222 and G223. Proceed northeasterly in Hampton River channel. Marina is beyond G21 to starboard. [STR 8.5 (TS)]

664.9 Range "C" S N
to Southbound/Northbound Navigation
665.4 Buttermilk Sound
0.5-mile range.

665.4 Range "D" S N
to Southbound/Northbound Navigation
665.7 Buttermilk Sound
0.3-mile range.

665.9 Junction | Frederica River Alternate Routes S N
Southbound Navigation Only
7.7-mile or 12.4-mile alternate routes.
Exit ICW at G229. Proceed SE to charted alternate route. [STR 8.4]
Rejoin ICW at one of two junctions:

to For vessels that cannot clear the 9-foot fixed
673.3 bridge at Lanier Island, rejoin the ICW at STM 673.3, NW of G241 (Mackay River).

or For vessels that can clear the Lanier Island
677.5 bridge, rejoin the ICW at STM 677.5, NNW of R20 (St. Simons Sound).

- **Fort Frederica Anchorage** (3.9)
  Anchor 10-14 feet N31.13.167
  STR 8.4 feet W081.23.695
  Anchor at fort.
  Dinghy to Fort Frederica's dinghy dock and access the park for a $2 fee. A new dinghy dock is planned.
  SEE FORT FREDERICA & EBO LANDING.
- **Hawkins Creek Anchorage** (8.3)
  Anchor 8-12 feet N31.10.845
  STR 8.4 feet W081.24.845
  Beyond first junction with ICW. Anchor near Hawkins Creek entrance.
- **Frederica River Bridge** (9.3)
  Fixed; vertical 9 feet. [STR 8.0 (TS)]
  Marina and anchorage information S of Frederica River Bridge is listed at STM 677.2.

SAFETY INFO

NOAA Weather
WX-3 Beaufort, SC
WX-2 Savannah, GA
WX-1 Jacksonville, FL

USCG
Station Brunswick, GA
VHF 16 or 09/22A
912/267-9010

Sea Tow
Brunswick, GA
VHF 16/12
912/280-9428

TowBoatU.S.
St. Simons Island, GA
VHF 16/10
912/638-7751

HEADS UP!

470.8	Wappoo Creek Bridge
472.2	Elliott Cut (SB)
472.5	Elliott Cut (NB)
536.0	Ladies Island Bridge
575.8	SC-GA Border
578.4	Wilmington River Cut-off (NB)
579.9	Causton Bluff Bridge
592.4	Skidaway Narrows Bridge
706.0	Kings Bay Security Zone (SB)
713.0	Kings Bay Security Zone (NB)
713.7	Cumberland Sound Channel (NB)
714.0	GA-FL Border
720.7	Kingsley Creek RR Bridge
739.1	Sisters Creek Bridge
747.4	B.B. McCormick Twin Bridges
775.0	St. Augustine Inlet Area (SB)
778.1	Bridge of Lions
779.0	St. Augustine Inlet Area (NB)

666.2 Wallys Leg Anchorage (0.3)
Anchor 12-15 feet N31.15.449
STR 8.1 feet W081.23.997
Exit ICW at G231. Proceed WNW into Wallys Leg. Anchor off small island.

667.7 Range "A"
to Southbound/Northbound Navigation
668.1 Mackay River
0.4-mile range.

668.1 Grant Creek Anchorage (0.1)
Anchor 8-12 feet N31.14.893
STR 8.1 feet W081.25.070
Exit ICW before range lower light R "A". Proceed NE toward Grant Creek entrance.

670.7 Troupe Creek Marina (1.5)
VHF 16; 912/264-3862
Exit ICW at R238. Proceed northwesterly into charted Troup Creek. Marina is to port. [STR 8.3]
Limited transient dockage. Home to small local boats to 28 feet.

671.0 Jove Creek Anchorage (0.9)
Anchor 10-14 feet N31.13.286
STR 8.3 feet W081.25.192
Exit ICW SE of R238. Proceed northeasterly into Jove Creek. Anchor around first bend.

673.3 Hawkins Creek Anchorage (0.7)
Anchor 8-12 feet N31.10.845
STR 8.4 feet W081.24.845
Exit ICW NW of G241. Proceed southeasterly into lower Frederica River. Anchor near Hawkins Creek entrance.

673.3 Junction | Frederica River Alternate Routes
Exit ICW NW of G241. Proceed E for either northbound or southbound legs of charted Frederica River alternate routes.
See STM 665.9 or STM 677.5.

674.3 Lanier Island Bridge
Fixed; vertical 65 feet.

677.2 Lanier Island
Exit ICW W of G249. Proceed northerly, leaving Frederica River G3 to port. Continue northerly toward fixed bridge. [STR 8.0]
Caution: Older charts show G1 marking end of Lanier Island shoal. Newer charts show G3. In either scenario, approach G249 before proceeding northerly into Frederica River.

- **Lanier Island Anchorage** (2.3)
  Anchor 12-16 feet N31.09.858
  STR 8.0 feet W081.25.042
  Anchor NW in charted Special Anchorage.
- **Golden Isles Marina** (2.4)
  VHF 16/68 N31.09.950
  912/634-1128 W081.24.977
  Marina is to port before bridge.
- **Frederica River Bridge** (2.6)
  Fixed; vertical 9 feet. [STR 8.0 (TS)]

SEE MARSHES OF GLYNN.

Don't forget a dinghy anchor! Not only used to fish or snorkel but a blessing in the event of an outboard engine failure. We also often toss it out as a stern anchor to keep the dinghy off a crowded dock. Or out from under a fixed dock on a rising tide! Rig a small Danforth with 50 feet of nylon and a couple feet of chain. Prevent damage (dinghy *and* toes!) by the flukes by storing the setup in a small, self-draining plastic tub.

SEVEN SISTERS (SPRING)

These days most people associate the Seven Sisters with sailing, perhaps because of Jimmy Buffet and Desdemona, his eccentric ballad character who's building a rocket ship. But the Seven Sisters are named after a Native American story that takes place far from the tropical oceans.

Out on the northern plains, in eastern Wyoming, looms Devils Tower, not long ago made famous as the alien landing site in the film *Close Encounters of a Third Kind* (1977). The Seven Sisters are named from the creation myth of Devils Tower.

According to the legend, seven small girls, chased by a bear, climbed onto a large boulder. As they prayed for their safety, the rock lifted upward out of reach of the bear. The giant bear continued to claw at the rock, leaving deep striations along the face of rising Devils Tower. The rock pushed the girls up into the sky, where they safely remain for eternity as the Seven Sisters.

You can see the Seven Sisters, technically the Pleiades (pronounced Plee-AD-ees), in the very early spring. Find Orion, and the Pleiades are just above Orion's bow past the bright star Aldebaran. The sisters are clustered together, looking like a small silver cloud of tiny stars.

FORT FREDERICA

When James Oglethorpe founded the fort town of Frederica in 1736, he imagined a grand social experiment, a place where England's poor and unemployed could make a fresh start in the New World.

Although dreams of utopian communities were common during the Enlightenment, most never worked out as planned. Oglethorpe's vision of the poor and unemployed making a fresh start was no different. Only eleven debtor families actually came to Frederica. Instead, as with most fort-based settlements, the majority of residents were skilled laborers and soldiers.

Still, Oglethorpe successfully created and maintained an English presence in the area, which Spain considered part of her Florida territory. The Battle of Bloody Marsh on St. Simons, where the marshes ran red with Spanish blood, gave Oglethorpe a decisive victory over the Spanish.

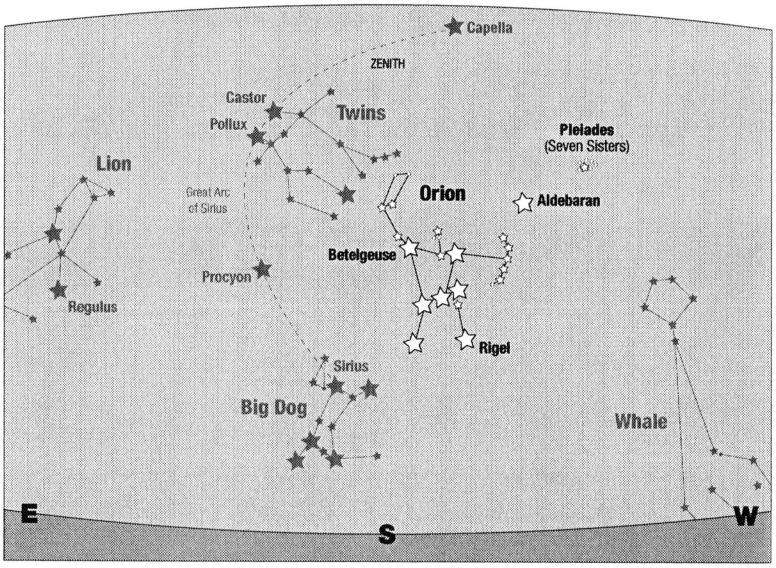

Early Spring, Early Evening

Pleiades, The Seven Sisters

SAFETY INFO

NOAA Weather
WX-2 Savannah, GA
WX-1 Jacksonville, FL
WX-2 Daytona Beach, FL

USCG
Station Brunswick, GA
VHF 16 or 09/22A
912/267-9010

Sea Tow
Brunswick, GA
VHF 16/12
912/280-9428

TowBoatU.S.
St. Simons Island, GA
VHF 16/10
912/638-7751

HEADS UP!

470.8	Wappoo Creek Bridge
472.2	Elliott Cut (SB)
472.5	Elliott Cut (NB)
536.0	Ladies Island Bridge
575.8	SC-GA Border
578.4	Wilmington River Cut-off (NB)
579.9	Causton Bluff Bridge
592.4	Skidaway Narrows Bridge
706.0	Kings Bay Security Zone (SB)
713.0	Kings Bay Security Zone (NB)
713.7	Cumberland Sound Channel (NB)
714.0	GA-FL Border
720.7	Kingsley Creek RR Bridge
739.1	Sisters Creek Bridge
747.4	B.B. McCormick Twin Bridges
775.0	St. Augustine Inlet Area (SB)
778.1	Bridge of Lions
779.0	St. Augustine Inlet Area (NB)

Courtesy of National Park Service

Seven Sisters' Devils Tower

Fort Frederica is now a national monument and its archaeological remains are open to the public. For a $2 fee, boaters can access the facility from the Fort Frederica Anchorage on the Frederica River Alternate Route.

Fort Frederica
www.nps.gov/fofr
912/638-3639

OGLETHORPE'S HUMBLE HOME

Oglethorpe built his own home, a 16 by 32 foot tabby house, just beyond the wall that enclosed the town of Frederica. This humble structure, about the size of a contemporary three-car garage, was the only home Oglethorpe ever owned in America.

Oglethorpe may not have been much of a home builder, but he was a skilled and prodigious fort builder. Within the span of a few years, he erected Fort Frederica and Fort St. Simon on St. Simons Island, and Fort Andrews and Fort William on Cumberland Island.

TALES OF A CHURCH

The Christ Church, a small wooden church set among live oak trees, is a short walk down Frederica Road from the fort. Both Charles Wesley and John Wesley, who established Methodism in this country, preached to the colonists under these live oak trees.

This simple church became famous again when a non-fiction Christian writer, Eugenia Price, visited from Chicago. She became enamored with the island's history and the story behind the church. Her first novel, *Beloved Invader*, tells the story of Anson Dodge Jr., who rebuilt the church in the 1880s in memory of his bride who died on their honeymoon.

Dodge's story captured Price's attention because he turned his tragedy into creative redemption, rebuilding the church and devoting himself to the people of St. Simons Island. Price continued the story, backward in time, in a collection of wildly successful historical novels, now called the St. Simons Trilogy.

The residents of St. Simons ultimately welcomed this Midwest transplant, dedicating a day in October as "Eugenia Price Day." She completed her last novel, *The Waiting Time*, just a few weeks before her death in 1996 at the age of 80. She is buried at the Christ Church cemetery, the church that inspired her literary career.

THE LIVE OAK

Live Oaks, with their massive trunks and broad branches hung with Spanish Moss, are revered in Georgia and honored as the state tree. Since Live Oaks can live for hundreds of years, they become personified as having experienced history, much like the Ents and their leader Treebeard in Tolkien's *Return of the King*.

Visitors often stop to see a particular Live Oak—the Live Oak where Wesley preached or the Live Oak that experienced a civil war battle.

Live Oaks, named because they stay green all year, were also an important local timber tree. Huge timbers of Live Oak, harvested from the nearby Sea Islands, were brought to Gascoigne Bluff, on the western shore of the Waterway near STM 674, to be shipped north. Some of these timbers were slated for Boston, to construct a new ship named the *USS Constitution*.

The ship's unique American materials were a success. During the War of 1812, England didn't have access to this unique Southern hardwood, and American shipwrights used it to their naval advantage. Built in part with Live Oak from the Georgia Sea Islands, the

677.5 Junction | St. Simons Sound (12.2)
Well Aided N31.03.233
Well Lit W081.15.046
Exit ICW NNW of R20. Proceed southeasterly to St. Simons Sound and Brunswick Harbor-Bar Channel. Waypoint is at RW "STS" sea buoy.
SEE ST. SIMONS ISLAND LIGHT.

677.5 Junction | Frederica River Alternate Routes
to Northbound Navigation Only
673.3 4.7-mile or 12.4-mile alternate routes.
or Exit ICW NNW of R20. Proceed northerly, leaving
665.9 Frederica River green aids to port. Continue northerly toward fixed bridge.
Caution: If your vessel cannot clear the 9-foot Frederica Bridge, you must continue northbound on the ICW or stay at Lanier Island anchorage or Golden Isles Marina (STM 677.2).
If you can clear the bridge, rejoin ICW at one of two junctions: STM 673.3 at G241 (Mackay River); or STM 665.9 at G229 (Mackay River).
Marina and anchorage information is listed at STM 665.9 and STM 677.2.

679.6 Junction | Brunswick
Exit ICW at R22. Proceed northwesterly up Brunswick River. [STR 8.4 (TS)]
- **Sidney Lanier Bridge** (3.5)
  Fixed; vertical 185 feet.
- **Brunswick Landing Marina** (5.6)
  VHF 16/68 N31.08.586
  912/262-9264 W081.29.826
  After bridge, bear N into charted East River. Marina is to starboard.

680.7 Jetty Range
to Southbound/Northbound Navigation
681.0 Jekyll Creek
0.3-mile range.
Caution: Submerged jetty at high water.

682.4 Unnamed Range
to Southbound/Northbound Navigation
682.9 Jekyll Creek
0.5-mile range.

683.6 Jekyll Wharf Marina (0.1)
VHF 16; 912/635-3152
Exit ICW at R20. Marina is to E. [STR 8.0]
Transients accommodated on 450 feet of face dock. Power and water only; showers in 2005.

684.2 Jekyll Island Anchorage (North)(0.1)
Anchor 5-8 feet N31.02.903
STR 8.0 feet W081.25.332
Exit ICW N of bridge. Proceed E.

684.3 Jekyll Creek Bridge
(SR 520)
Fixed; vertical 65 feet.
SEE JEKYLL ISLAND.

684.4 Jekyll Harbor Marina (0.1)
VHF 16/72 N31.02.758
912/635-3137 W081.25.379
Exit ICW S of bridge. Marina is to E. [STR 8.0]

SAFETY INFO

NOAA Weather	Sea Tow
WX-2 Savannah, GA	Brunswick, GA
WX-1 Jacksonville, FL	VHF 16/12
WX-2 Daytona Beach, FL	912/280-9428
USCG	**TowBoatU.S.**
Station Brunswick, GA	Jekyll Island, GA
VHF 16 or 09/22A	VHF 16/10
912/267-9010	912/638-7751

HEADS UP!

470.8	Wappoo Creek Bridge	713.0	Kings Bay Security Zone (NB)
472.2	Elliott Cut (SB)	713.7	Cumberland Sound Channel (NB)
472.5	Elliott Cut (NB)	714.0	GA-FL Border
536.0	Ladies Island Bridge	720.7	Kingsley Creek RR Bridge
575.8	SC-GA Border	739.1	Sisters Creek Bridge
578.4	Wilmington River Cut-off (NB)	747.4	B.B. McCormick Twin Bridges
579.9	Causton Bluff Bridge	775.0	St. Augustine Inlet Area (SB)
592.4	Skidaway Narrows Bridge	778.1	Bridge of Lions
706.0	Kings Bay Security Zone (SB)	779.0	St. Augustine Inlet Area (NB)

684.8 Jekyll Island Anchorage (South)(0.1) S N

Anchor 4-6 feet N31.02.500
STR 8.0 feet W081.25.430

Exit ICW between G23 and R24. Proceed E.

686.0 Junction | St. Andrews Alternate Route S N
to Southbound Navigation Only
695.8 14.6-mile alternate route.

Exit ICW between G25 and G27. Proceed westerly into Little Satilla River and charted alternate route. [STR 8.0]

This alternate route is scenic, but more importantly, a useful bypass when St. Andrews Sound is kicking up.

We recommend a maximum 4-foot draft and/or playing the tides to take advantage of this alternate route.

Rejoin ICW at R40 (Cumberland River).

- **Umbrella Creek Anchorage** (3.3)
  Anchor 6-9 feet N31.01.375
  STR 8.0 feet W081.29.355
  Exit alternate route at R "A8". Proceed WNW up Umbrella Creek.
- **Dover Creek Anchorage** (6.5)
  Anchor 10-14 feet N30.59.946
  STR 8.0 feet W081.30.936
  Exit alternate route at R "A16". Proceed NW up Dover Creek.
- **Floyd Creek Anchorage** (Northwest)(10.3)
  Anchor 9-12 feet N30.56.607
  STR 8.2 feet W081.29.849
  Exit alternate route at R "A28". Proceed NE into charted pocket.
- **Floyd Creek Anchorage** (Southeast)(13.8)
  Anchor 14-20 feet N30.55.600
  STR 8.1 feet W081.28.359
  Anchor inside Floyd Creek mouth before entering Cumberland River and rejoining ICW.

689.6 Junction | St. Andrews Sound S N

Southbound/Northbound Navigation

Although this appears to be a convenient point to bump out, St. Andrews Sound is serpentine, only moderately aided, and poorly lit. It is not recommended.

St. Simons Sound is only 7 nautical miles north when entering from seaward.

See Little Cumberland Island Light.

693.0 Little Cumberland Island Anchorage (0.3) S N

Anchor 6-10 feet N30.56.602
STR 8.0 feet W081.25.884

Exit ICW between G35 and G37. Proceed S to charted tongue.

See Marsh Tackies.

695.8 Junction | St. Andrews Alternate Route S N
to Northbound Navigation Only
686.0 14.6-mile alternate route.

Exit ICW at R40. Proceed northwesterly into Floyd Creek and charted alternate route.

Rejoin ICW between G25 and G27 (Jekyll Sound).

See STM 686.0 for comments and anchorage information.

cannonballs were reputed to bounce off the sides of the USS Constitution, earning her the nickname "Old Ironsides."

EBO LANDING

If you take the Frederica River Alternate Route, between STM 665.9 and STM 673.3, you pass Dunbar Creek just south of Fort Frederica. Up Dunbar Creek is charted Ebo Landing, where the Ebo tribe decided to return to Africa at any and all cost.

Warner Studios Promotional Image

Levar Burton as Kunta Kinte in Roots

They were seized in Nigeria and brought to a slave auction 6,000 miles away in Savannah, then purchased as a group by two families from St. Simons Island. But when the Africans were brought to their plantation along Dunbar Creek, the slaves refused to accept their fate. The Ebo chief began chanting, "The sea brought me and the sea will bring me home." Still chained to one another, they committed suicide by following their chief into the water.

For generations afterward, locals refused to fish at Ebo Landing, believing ghosts of slaves still haunted the river.

MARSHES OF GLYNN

Lanier Island, east of the Waterway at STM 674, is named for Sidney Lanier, a Georgia poet.

Lanier wrote about the Glynn County marshes in his celebrated poem, "The Marshes of Glynn," written in 1879, two years before his death:

And what if behind me to westward
The wall of the woods stands high?
The world lies east: how ample,
The marsh and the sea and the sky!
A league and a league of marsh-grass
Waist-high, broad in the blade,
Green, and all of a height,
And unflecked with a light or a shade,
Stretch leisurely off, in a pleasant plain,
To the terminal blue of the main....

Lanier found spiritual solace in the natural beauty of Georgia and often expressed these emotions in his rhythmic musical poems. But his life was not as idyllic. He volunteered for the Confederate army and was captured and imprisoned for several months. While imprisoned, he contracted tuberculosis, which plagued him for the rest of his life. He and his family often lived in poverty as he moved from job to job, attempting to support his four children. He ultimately became a lecturer at Johns Hopkins University, but died early at the age of 39.

Try to time your transits through Georgia's winding marsh channels at low tide. With seven-foot tides, water floods the marsh grasses making it difficult to see the deepwater channel. During a low but rising tide, you can easily spot the serpentine path through the "Marshes of Glynn."

ST. SIMONS ISLAND LIGHT

The lighthouse at the southern end of St. Simons Island is a replacement, built in 1872 after Confederate troops destroyed the original tabby structure as they retreated from the island. This "new" light, with its third-order Fresnel lens, is visible twenty miles out to sea.

The lighthouse is open to the public for a fee, including a Museum of Coastal History in the former lighthouse keeper's home. You can walk to the top of the 105-foot structure, which is rumored to be haunted.

Supposedly the Svendsen family, who tended the remote lighthouse at the turn of the 19th century, claimed they often heard phantom footsteps coming down the lighthouse stairs. The sound of the steps sent their dog, ironically named Jinx, into a frenzy. Perhaps the haunting is linked to the death of the original lighthouse keeper,

SAFETY INFO

NOAA Weather
WX-2 Savannah, GA
WX-1 Jacksonville, FL
WX-2 Daytona Beach, FL

USCG
Station Brunswick, GA
VHF 16 or 09/22A
912/267-9010

Sea Tow
Brunswick, GA
VHF 16/12
912/280-9428

TowBoatU.S.
Jekyll Island, GA
VHF 16/10
912/638-7751

HEADS UP!

470.8	Wappoo Creek Bridge
472.2	Elliott Cut (SB)
472.5	Elliott Cut (NB)
536.0	Ladies Island Bridge
575.8	SC-GA Border
578.4	Wilmington River Cut-off (NB)
579.9	Causton Bluff Bridge
592.4	Skidaway Narrows Bridge
706.0	**Kings Bay Security Zone (SB)**
713.0	Kings Bay Security Zone (NB)
713.7	Cumberland Sound Channel (NB)
714.0	GA-FL Border
720.7	Kingsley Creek RR Bridge
739.1	Sisters Creek Bridge
747.4	B.B. McCormick Twin Bridges
775.0	St. Augustine Inlet Area (SB)
778.1	Bridge of Lions
779.0	St. Augustine Inlet Area (NB)

who was shot by his assistant during an argument.

If you'd like to view the lighthouse from the deck of your boat, look to the south end of St. Simons Island from R20 at STM 678. For a closer look, detour about one mile east of the magenta line as you cross St. Simons Sound.

St. Simons Island Lighthouse
www.saintsimonslighthouse.org
912/638-4666

Courtesy of NOAA

Photo by Marge Beaver **Overlooking St. Simons Sound**

EGRETS

In late nineteenth century, cosmopolitan women in Europe and America demanded feathers for their hats. The flowing white feathers during breeding season, called nuptial plumes or aigrettes, were especially popular. Aigrettes sold for $32 an ounce, nearly twice the price of gold!

For every ounce of feathers shipped to the milliners, at least four adult birds were killed. In one incident, a single plume hunter shipped out four pounds of plumes. That's about $2000 worth—and a rotting heap of 250 Great Egret carcasses. By 1910 the Audubon Society counted only 1400 Great Egrets and 250 Snowy Egrets left in the four southern states.

The public was becoming offended by this needless slaughter. Congress passed the Lacey Act banning interstate shipment of birds killed in violation of state laws. But demand was still high and money led to murder. Within three years, two Audubon wardens were murdered trying to enforce the egret protection laws.

Fortunately, fashions come and go. Like all trends that trickle down the social strata, the feather-hat-look became popular among prostitutes. Some prostitutes were even paid for their services with plumes rather than cash. In a close call for the egrets, over time no respectable lady would be caught dead, so to speak, wearing an aigrette-plumed hat.

JEKYLL ISLAND

A subtropical climate with complete seclusion: Jekyll Island was the perfect site for a winter club of the ultra-rich and famous. In the 1880s this group, including the Rockefellers, Goulds, Astors, Goodyears, Morgans, Pulitzers, and Vanderbilts, built what they called "cottages" (to us commoners: "mansions") where they could ride out the northern winter with their social equals.

Each estate was huge, but to promote social interaction none included kitchens. Members were expected to dine together at the club, where a staff from Delmonico's in New York prepared the meals. To put Delmonico's into perspective, the restaurant's 100-page menu listed 370 dishes in both French and English.

By World War II, the membership of the Jekyll Island Club controlled one-sixth of the world's wealth. But in 1942, when a German U-boat torpedoed a tanker in St. Simons Sound just north of Jekyll Island, the government feared the island was too tempting a target. The Coast Guard took over and evacuated the island. In 1947 the state of Georgia purchased the island for a paltry $675,000.

Today the island is open to the masses as a popular vacation destination.

Courtesy of U.S. Fish & Wildlife Service

Birds for Feathers (circa 1930)

695.8 Floyd Creek Anchorage (Southeast)(0.8)
Anchor 14-20 feet N30.55.600
STR 8.1 feet W081.28.359
Exit ICW at R40. Proceed northwesterly into Floyd Creek. Favor NE bank.

696.3 Junction | Brickhill River Alternate Route
to Southbound Navigation Only
703.7 9.3-mile alternate route.
Exit ICW between R40 and G41. Proceed southeasterly to Brickhill River alternate route.
Rejoin ICW at R60 "A" (Crooked River).

- **Mud Creek Anchorage** (1.2)
  Anchor 12-16 feet N30.53.927
  STR 8.0 feet W081.28.076
  Bear SW into charted Mud Creek.
- **Brickhill River Anchorage** (1.0)
  Anchor 10-14 feet N30.54.184
  STR 8.0 feet W081.27.460
  Bear SE and continue in Brickhill River. Ease NE to charted 10-foot shallows to find shallower water and less current.

697.8 Shellbine Creek Anchorage (0.5)
Anchor 8-10 feet N30.54.710
STR 8.0 feet W081.29.776
Exit ICW at G43. Proceed northwesterly into Shellbine Creek. Bear left at fork.

699.3 Cabin Bluff Anchorage (0.2)
Anchor 10-12 feet N30.53.449
STR 8.0 feet W081.30.364
Exit ICW at R46. Bear S into charted tongue.

702.0 Delaroche Creek Anchorage (0.7)
Anchor 10-14 feet N30.51.660
STR 8.1 feet W081.30.309
Exit ICW at G57. Proceed SW into Delaroche Creek. Bear right at fork.

703.7 Junction | Brickhill River Alternate Route
to Northbound Navigation Only
696.3 9.3-mile alternate route.
Exit ICW at R60 "A". Proceed northeasterly to Brickhill River alternate route.
Rejoin ICW SSW of R40 (Cumberland River).
See STM 696.3 for anchorage information.

703.9 Crooked River Anchorage (0.8)
Anchor 8-12 feet N30.50.630
STR 7.9 feet W081.29.600
Exit ICW between R62 and G63 "A". Proceed W into Crooked River.

705.3 Cumberland Sound Range
to Southbound/Northbound Navigation
706.0 Cumberland Sound
0.7-mile range.

706.0 Kings Bay Security Zone
to Southbound Navigation Only
713.0 Kings Bay is an active nuclear submarine base.
Caution: Since 9/11, we have found this Security Zone has expanded. The Coast Guard has also stated, "Vessels must travel no faster than needed for steerageway."

SAFETY INFO

NOAA Weather
WX-2 Savannah, GA
WX-1 Jacksonville, FL
WX-2 Daytona Beach, FL

USCG
Station Mayport, FL
VHF 16 or 09/22A
904/564-7592

Sea Tow
Brunswick, GA
VHF 16/12
912/280-9428

TowBoatU.S.
Fernandina, FL
VHF 16/10
904/277-8511

HEADS UP!

472.2	Elliott Cut (SB)
472.5	Elliott Cut (NB)
536.0	Ladies Island Bridge
575.8	SC-GA Border
578.4	Wilmington River Cut-off (NB)
579.9	Causton Bluff Bridge
592.4	Skidaway Narrows Bridge
706.0	Kings Bay Security Zone (SB)
713.0	**Kings Bay Security Zone (NB)**
713.7	Cumberland Sound Channel (NB)
714.0	GA-FL Border
720.7	Kingsley Creek RR Bridge
739.1	Sisters Creek Bridge
747.4	B.B. McCormick Twin Bridges
775.0	St. Augustine Inlet Area (SB)
778.1	Bridge of Lions
779.0	St. Augustine Inlet Area (NB)
788.8	Crescent Beach Bridge

Expect to be contacted on VHF 16 by a patrol boat or helicopter as early as R70 (southbound) or R26 (northbound).

You may also be intercepted by a patrol boat. If so, you will be directed well off the ICW and asked to come to a complete stop, bow facing the shore, until a naval vessel clears the area.

707.9 Cumberland Sound Ship Channel S N
to Southbound Navigation Only
713.7 Buoyage reverses.

Look for yellow reflective ICW triangles and squares on aids.

711.0 Cumberland Island S N
Exit ICW at R34. Proceed NNE along Cumberland Island shore. [STR 7.3]

SEE POCKET GOPHERS.

- **Cumberland Island Anchorage** (0.9)
  Anchor 8-10 feet N30.45.164
  STR 7.3 feet W081.28.672
  Anchor opposite charted dock at Dungeness.
- **Sea Camp Anchorage** (1.7)
  Anchor 8-14 feet N30.45.886
  STR 7.3 feet W081.28.350
  Continue NNE to second charted dock.
  Dinghies may be tied up on inside of Sea Camp dock between sunrise and sunset.
- **Sea Camp Dock** (1.7)
  Day use only; no overnight dockage. Southern end of T-head is reserved for ferry. [STR 7.3 (TS)]
  Previously limited to boats less than 24 feet, but policy is being reconsidered. According to the park superintendent, boats up to 40 feet may now be allowed if space is available.
- **Greyfield Inn** (2.8)
  No VHF Watch; 904/261-6408
  Continue NNE to charted Greyfield. Dockside depth is 9 feet.
  Inn provides free dockage with room or dinner reservation on a first-come, first-served basis. May also accept transients if space available.

712.3 Junction | St. Marys S N
Exit ICW at G29. Proceed westerly up St. Marys River. [STR 6.8 (TS)]

SEE ST. MARYS THANKSGIVING.

- **Lang's Marina East** (5.3)
  VHF 16; 912/882-4452
  Marina is to starboard at E end of town. Marina is divided in east and west sections at city park.
- **Free Dock** (5.4)
  City provides free floating dock between Lang's east and west facilities. 6-hour limit. No overnight dockage.
- **St. Marys Anchorage** (5.5)
  Anchor 10-12 feet N30.43.119
  STR 6.8 feet W081.32.898
  Anchorage is past marina.

713.0 Kings Bay Security Zone S N
to Northbound Navigation Only
706.0 Kings Bay is an active nuclear submarine base.

See comments at STM 706.0.

The mansions and the Jekyll Island Club still stand, with daily tram tours provided by the Jekyll Island Museum Visitor Center.

Brunswick-Golden Isles Visitors Bureau
www.bgivb.com
800/809-1790

Jekyll Island Tours
www.jekyllisland.com
912/635-2762

LITTLE CUMBERLAND ISLAND LIGHT

When rounding R32 at STM 690, look south to the northern end of Little Cumberland Island. This is the Little Cumberland Light, a sixty-foot tower restored in 1967 by the local island association.

The original lighthouse lasted only one year at this location. The fifty-foot whitewashed tower of brick, built by the famous American lighthouse builder Winslow Lewis, was disassembled brick by brick, shipped to Amelia Island, and rebuilt. With today's construction techniques of tear-down-and-build-new, it's staggering to imagine moving a lighthouse.

Yet in the 1800s, lighthouses were disassembled and moved around like giant chess pieces. A lighthouse at Sapelo Island, also built by Lewis, was moved to the Apostle Islands in Lake Superior. Both of the relocated lighthouses survived the transplant and are still in service.

Remember, no brakes! Your dinghy can be a tug if your main engine fails. Lash it amidships with spring lines to bow and stern. Use the dinghy for power, the mother ship to steer. Go slowly; reverse on your dinghy will only spin you, not reverse your progress!

MARSH TACKIES

Georgia's coastal marshes were once home to hundreds of wild horses, called marsh tackies because they roamed and grazed the acres of salt marsh. The tackies were small working horses, let loose on the marshes in the winter to feed, then rounded up in the spring and fall for tilling and harvesting.

Descendants of these marsh tackies still roam the Cumberland Islands, now mixed with a trainload of wild mustangs relocated from Arizona in the 1920s. Look for these small wild horses along the western shore of Little Cumberland Island as you pass between STM 690 and STM 693.

Courtesy of Smithsonian Marine Station

Photo by Charles Corbeil

Snowy Egret

Scientists believe these diminutive horses are descended from horses brought centuries ago by Spanish explorers. Smaller breeds of horses were favored on those early sailing ships where space was a premium. The marsh tackies were small enough to make the transatlantic passage, but big enough to work the fields and transport people and goods through the swampy lowlands.

Recent blood typing supports this theory: the marsh tackies of the New World have been linked to a group of Spanish horses from 400 years ago.

THE HORSE LATITUDES

It's hard to imagine making a transatlantic crossing on a heavy wooden sailing ship with enough provisions for crew and farm animals. At best, the ships traveled at four to eight knots. But when they hit the mid-latitudes, between 30° to 35° N and 30° to 35° S, headway was even slower.

The mid-latitudes are notorious for their weak winds. It could take weeks for a sailing ship to pass through these areas, hence named "horse latitudes" because the horses were often the first casualties.

There are different accounts of what happened to the horses as ships were

SAFETY INFO

NOAA Weather
WX-2 Savannah, GA
WX-1 Jacksonville, FL
WX-2 Daytona Beach, FL

USCG
Station Mayport, FL
VHF 16 or 09/22A
904/564-7592

Sea Tow
Brunswick, GA
VHF 16/12
912/280-9428

TowBoatU.S.
Fernandina, FL
VHF 16/10
904/277-8511

HEADS UP!

536.0	Ladies Island Bridge
575.8	SC-GA Border
578.4	Wilmington River Cut-off (NB)
579.9	Causton Bluff Bridge
592.4	Skidaway Narrows Bridge
706.0	Kings Bay Security Zone (SB)
713.0	Kings Bay Security Zone (NB)
713.7	**Cumberland Sound Channel (NB)**
714.0	**GA-FL Border**
720.7	Kingsley Creek RR Bridge
739.1	Sisters Creek Bridge
747.4	B.B. McCormick Twin Bridges
775.0	St. Augustine Inlet Area (SB)
778.1	Bridge of Lions
779.0	St. Augustine Inlet Area (NB)
788.8	Crescent Beach Bridge
816.0	L.B. Knox Bridge
829.7	Daytona Beach Main St. Bridge

becalmed and provisions grew scarce. Many accounts describe horses being thrown overboard as the crew became unable to feed them.

This sanitized account is a bit tough to (excuse the pun) swallow—especially since the crew's other meat choice was months-old salt tack, re-hydrated by trailing it over the transom.

Tired of items being "lost aboard"? List and diagram each locker and its contents. It may sound the act of an obsessive-compulsive, but on a small boat with many crevices to cache little items, it becomes an indispensable map to your buried treasure!

POCKET "GOLFERS"

"Golfers?" a puzzled Carl (Bill Murray) asks his Scottish boss in the movie *Caddy Shack*. "Check me if I'm wrong, Sandy, but if I kill all the golfers, they're going to lock me up and throw away the key." "No, *gophers*, you great git! Not *golfers*! The little brown furry rodents."

Cumberland Island is free of golfers, but has plenty of gophers. Unlike Georgia's other Sea Islands, Cumberland has no man-made or tidal bridges linking it the mainland. So many of its inhabitants are a bit different. In addition to a unique subspecies of pocket gopher, wild horses and armadillos also roam the island.

Courtesy of National Park Service

Greyfield Inn

Pocket gophers are native to coastal Georgia and are considered pests around agriculture, golf courses, and cemeteries. But Cumberland Island is a primitive undeveloped island, preserved by the National Park Service as the Cumberland Island National Seashore. The gophers are free to dig as many large unsightly mounds as they desire.

The only public access to Cumberland Island is by boat. You can arrive by dinghy at the Sea Camp docks at STM 711 and access the island for $4 per person. The National Park Service also runs a ferry from St. Marys for $12 roundtrip. The ranger station offers tours, but the island is completely undeveloped with the exception of the Greyfield Inn, where the late John F. Kennedy Jr. and Carolyn Bessette secretly married and honeymooned.

Cumberland Island National Seashore
www.nps.gov/cuis
912/882-4335

ST. MARYS' THANKSGIVING

How could a town be more welcoming to traveling boaters than to invite them to Thanksgiving dinner? For the past three years, the town of St. Marys at STM 712.3 has shared Thanksgiving with visiting mariners. They provide the turkey, ham, and oysters; cruisers bring side dishes and desserts.

Guests and townspeople gather in the mid-afternoon in a local hotel for a buffet meal. Donations are welcome to help defray the costs and advance notice helps them plan ahead. Cruisers can listen for local details on the VHF or the SSB Cruiseheimers' Net at 0830 hrs daily on 8152 KHz. ▲

St. Marys, Georgia
www.stmaryswelcome.com
866/868-2199

713.7 Cumberland Sound Ship Channel S N
to 707.9 Northbound Navigation Only
Buoyage reverses.

Look for yellow reflective ICW triangles and squares on aids.

Caution: Northbound, it is very easy to follow the channel northwesterly into Kings Bay. Be alert for the ICW turnoff at G79.

714.0 Junction | St. Marys Entrance (7.0) S N
Well Aided N30.42.717
Well Lit W081.20.772

Exit ICW at G25. Proceed easterly to St. Marys Entrance. Waypoint is between R8 and G9.

St. Marys River is one of the best inlets along the East Coast. Submarines have very little maneuverability on the surface, so this naval inlet is wide, well aided, and well lit for ten miles.

Caution: Many electronic systems, charts, and chartkits still show the longer, dogleg channel and numbering (R14A and G15A) of 2001 charts. In either case, the above waypoint translates to the fifth pair of nav aids east of the breakwater.

714.0 GA-FL Border S N
St. Marys River (G25)

Hinckley Yacht Services (Repair)
STM 582.4

www.hinckleyyachts.com

2400 Mechanics Avenue
Savannah, GA 31404

912/629-2400
912/629-2404

VHF 16/68

Depth	12	**Laundry**	Taxi
Diesel/Gas	No	**Pool**	No
Pumpout	No	**Internet/WiFi**	I/W
Mail/Fax	M/F	**Car/Bike**	No
Service	On-Site	**Groceries**	Walk
Parts	On-Site	**Restaurant**	Walk
Haulout	35T	**Post Office**	Walk
Propane	Taxi	**Library**	Walk

Bahia Bleu Marina
STM 582.7

www.bahiableumarina.com

2812 River Drive
Thunderbolt, GA 31404

912/354-2283
912/352-4629

VHF 16/68

Depth	18	**Laundry**	On-Site
Diesel/Gas	D/G	**Pool**	No
Pumpout	No	**Internet/WiFi**	I
Mail/Fax	M/F	**Car/Bike**	No
Service	On-Call	**Groceries**	Walk
Parts	On-Call	**Restaurant**	Walk
Haulout	No	**Post Office**	Taxi
Propane	Taxi	**Library**	Walk

Thunderbolt Marine
STM 583.2

www.thunderboltmarininc.com

3124 River Drive
Savannah, GA 31404

912/356-3875
912/352-4958

VHF 16/11

Depth	15	**Laundry**	On-Site
Diesel/Gas	D/G	**Pool**	No
Pumpout	No	**Internet/WiFi**	I/W
Mail/Fax	M/F	**Car/Bike**	No
Service	On-Site	**Groceries**	Taxi
Parts	On-Site	**Restaurant**	Walk
Haulout	160T/1200T	**Post Office**	Taxi
Propane	Taxi	**Library**	Taxi

Sail Harbor Marina & Boatyard
STM 585.5

www.sailharbormarina.com

606 Wilmington Island Rd.
Savannah, GA 31410

912/897-2896
912/897-7252

VHF 16/71

Depth	9	**Laundry**	On-Site
Diesel/Gas	No	**Pool**	No
Pumpout	Yes	**Internet/WiFi**	I
Mail/Fax	M/F	**Car/Bike**	C
Service	On-Site	**Groceries**	Walk
Parts	On-Site	**Restaurant**	Walk
Haulout	30T	**Post Office**	Walk
Propane	Taxi	**Library**	Walk

Hogans' Marina
STM 585.5

www.hogansmarina.com

36 Wilmington Island Rd.
Savannah, GA 31410

912/897-3474
912/898-8929

VHF 16/09

Depth	21	**Laundry**	Walk
Diesel/Gas	G	**Pool**	No
Pumpout	Yes	**Internet/WiFi**	No
Mail/Fax	M/F	**Car/Bike**	No
Service	On-Call	**Groceries**	Walk
Parts	On-Call	**Restaurant**	Walk
Haulout	No	**Post Office**	Walk
Propane	Walk	**Library**	Walk

Isle of Hope Marina
STM 589.9

www.isleofhopemarina.com

50 Bluff Drive
Savannah, GA 31406

912/354-8187
912/354-2684

VHF 16/68

Depth	12	**Laundry**	On-Site
Diesel/Gas	D/G	**Pool**	Walk
Pumpout	Yes	**Internet/WiFi**	I/W
Mail/Fax	M/F	**Car/Bike**	C/B
Service	On-Site	**Groceries**	Walk
Parts	On-Site	**Restaurant**	Walk
Haulout	No	**Post Office**	Taxi
Propane	Taxi	**Library**	Taxi

Two Way Marina
STM 662.2

250 Ricefield Way
Brunswick, GA 31525

912/265-0410
912/261-1585

VHF 16/68 or 19

Depth	15	**Laundry**	On-Site
Diesel/Gas	D/G	**Pool**	No
Pumpout	No	**Internet/WiFi**	I
Mail/Fax	M/F	**Car/Bike**	No
Service	On-Site	**Groceries**	Taxi
Parts	On-Site	**Restaurant**	On-Site
Haulout	30T	**Post Office**	Taxi
Propane	On-Site	**Library**	Taxi

Golden Isles Marina
STM 677.2

www.gimarina.com

206 Marina Drive
St. Simons, GA 31522

912/634-1128
912/634-1786

VHF 16/68

Depth	28	**Laundry**	On-Site
Diesel/Gas	D/G	**Pool**	2005
Pumpout	Yes	**Internet/WiFi**	I/W
Mail/Fax	M/F	**Car/Bike**	C/B
Service	On-Call	**Groceries**	Walk
Parts	On-Call	**Restaurant**	On-Site
Haulout	No	**Post Office**	Walk
Propane	Taxi	**Library**	Taxi

Photocopy the "business card" of any Waterway facility. Then cut out the copy and take it ashore for easy reference!

Brunswick Landing Marina
STM 679.5

2429 Newcastle Street
Brunswick, GA 31520

912/262-9264 (phone)
912/262-9327 (fax)

VHF 16/68

Depth	12	**Laundry**	On-Site
Diesel/Gas	D/G	**Pool**	No
Pumpout	Yes	**Internet/WiFi**	I/W
Mail/Fax	M/F	**Car/Bike**	No
Service	On-Site	**Groceries**	Walk
Parts	On-Site	**Restaurant**	Walk
Haulout	50T	**Post Office**	Walk
Propane	Taxi	**Library**	Walk

Jekyll Harbor Marina
STM 684.4

www.jekyllharbor.com

One Harbor Road
Jekyll Island, GA 31527

912/635-3137 (phone)
912/635-2633 (fax)

VHF 16/72

Depth	12	**Laundry**	On-Site
Diesel/Gas	D/G	**Pool**	Yes
Pumpout	Yes	**Internet/WiFi**	I/W
Mail/Fax	M/F	**Car/Bike**	C/B
Service	On-Call	**Groceries**	Walk
Parts	On-Call	**Restaurant**	On-Site
Haulout	No	**Post Office**	Walk
Propane	Taxi	**Library**	N/A

Georgia Waterway Marine Facilities

This table summarizes all known Waterway Marine Facilities, their location along the ICW, and their telephone number. Each is listed as either offering transient (T) dockage or not—and whether they have a fuel dock with diesel (D), gas (G), or neither.

582.3	Savannah Bend Marina	912/897-3625	T	D/G
582.4	**Hinckley Yacht Services**	912/629-2400	No	No
582.7	**Bahia Bleu Marina**	912/354-2283	T	D/G
583.2	**Thunderbolt Marine**	912/356-3875	T	D/G
585.5	**Sail Harbor Marina & Boatyard**	912/897-2896	T	No
585.5	**Hogans' Marina**	912/897-3474	T	G
585.5	The Landings	912/598-1901	No	D/G
589.9	**Isle of Hope Marina**	912/354-8187	T	D/G
600.9	Delegal Creek Marina	912/598-0023	T	D/G
613.7	Kilkenny Marina	912/727-2215	T	D/G
662.2	**Two Way Marina**	912/265-0410	T	D/G
664.2	Hampton River Club Marina	912/638-1210	T	D/G
670.7	Troupe Creek Marina	912/264-3862	No	G
677.2	**Golden Isles Marina**	912/634-1128	T	D/G
679.5	**Brunswick Landing Marina**	912/262-9264	T	D/G
683.6	Jekyll Wharf Marina	912/635-3152	T	D/G
684.4	**Jekyll Harbor Marina**	912/635-3137	T	D/G
712.3	Lang's Marina East	912/882-4452	T	D/G

Boldface type indicates the facility completed a survey and is highlighted in a Waterway Business Card. Each facility received multiple fax, email, and telephone requests. A final telephone call was made to verify the accuracy of transient, fuel, and contact information.

Georgia Waterway Chandleries

This table lists marine equipment suppliers within easy reach of the ICW, their telephone number and address, and their location relative to ICW marinas and anchorages.

Mackay Marine	912/354-4542	2911 River Drive, Thunderbolt, GA 31404	0.2 miles from Bahia Bleu Marina
Woo's Hardware	912/897-1366	205 Johnny Mercer Boulevard, Savannah, GA 31410	1.2 miles from Sail Harbor Marina
West Marine Savannah	912/352-2660	7700 Abercorn Street, Savannah, GA 31406	4.9 miles from Isle of Hope Marina
BoatU.S. Savannah	912/925-2363	11607 Abercorn Street, Savannah, GA 31419	7.0 miles from Isle of Hope Marina
Home Depot Savannah	912/921-0158	11180 Abercorn Street, Savannah, GA 31419	7.0 miles from Isle of Hope Marina
Lowe's Savannah	912/927-0000	11114 Abercorn Street, Savannah, GA 31419	7.0 miles from Isle of Hope Marina
Boater's World	912/925-0216	13015 Abercorn Street, Savannah, GA 31419	7.6 miles from Isle of Hope Marina
Bass Pro Shops Outdoor World	912/961-4200	14045 Abercorn Street, Savannah, GA 31419	7.7 miles from Isle of Hope Marina
Island Ace Hardware	912/638-3800	1701 Frederica Road, St. Simons Island, GA 31522	2.2 miles from Golden Isles Marina
The Bedford Sportsman	912/638-5493	3405 Frederica Road, St. Simons Island, GA 31522	3.7 miles from Golden Isles Marina
Central Hardware	912/265-3510	1730 Norwich Street, Brunswick, GA 31520	0.9 miles from Brunswick Landing Marina
Georgia Ace Hardware	912/265-1321	205 Monck Street, Brunswick, GA 31520	1.0 miles from Brunswick Landing Marina
West Marine Brunswick	912/264-6222	1919 Glynn Avenue, Brunswick, GA 31520	1.9 miles from Brunswick Landing Marina
Home Depot Brunswick	912/264-2025	200 Altama Connector, Brunswick, GA 31520	4.0 miles from Brunswick Landing Marina
Boater's World	912/261-9790	147 Altama Connector, Brunswick, GA 31525	4.5 miles from Brunswick Landing Marina
Maxwell True Value Family Center	912/635-2205	16 Beachview Drive, Jekyll Island, GA 31527	0.6 miles from Jekyll Harbor Marina
Kings Bay Ace Hardware	912/729-2648	1292 Osborne Road, St. Marys, GA 31558	1.3 miles from Lang's Marina East

Florida Charts

11485 ICW - Tolomato River to Palm Shores
11472 ICW - Palm Shores to West Palm Beach
11467 ICW - West Palm Beach to Miami
11451 Miami to Marathon and Florida Bay

Bridges

Total	81
Fixed	28
Opening	53

Other Features

Marinas	183	Vignettes	118
Anchorages	105	Inlets	9
Chandleries	93	Ranges	1

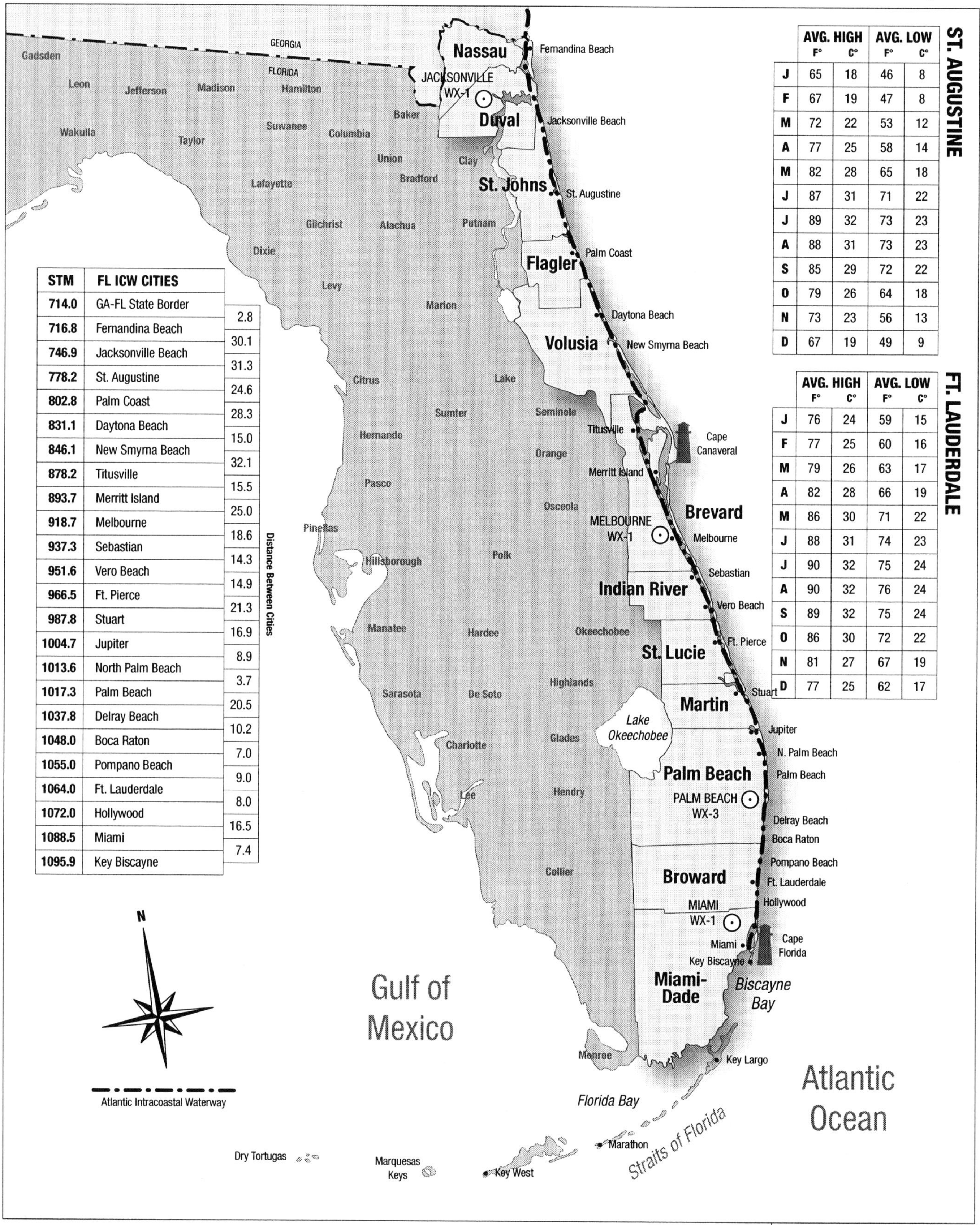

ST. AUGUSTINE

	AVG. HIGH F°	AVG. HIGH C°	AVG. LOW F°	AVG. LOW C°
J	65	18	46	8
F	67	19	47	8
M	72	22	53	12
A	77	25	58	14
M	82	28	65	18
J	87	31	71	22
J	89	32	73	23
A	88	31	73	23
S	85	29	72	22
O	79	26	64	18
N	73	23	56	13
D	67	19	49	9

FT. LAUDERDALE

	AVG. HIGH F°	AVG. HIGH C°	AVG. LOW F°	AVG. LOW C°
J	76	24	59	15
F	77	25	60	16
M	79	26	63	17
A	82	28	66	19
M	86	30	71	22
J	88	31	74	23
J	90	32	75	24
A	90	32	76	24
S	89	32	75	24
O	86	30	72	22
N	81	27	67	19
D	77	25	62	17

STM	FL ICW CITIES	Distance Between Cities
714.0	GA-FL State Border	
716.8	Fernandina Beach	2.8
746.9	Jacksonville Beach	30.1
778.2	St. Augustine	31.3
802.8	Palm Coast	24.6
831.1	Daytona Beach	28.3
846.1	New Smyrna Beach	15.0
878.2	Titusville	32.1
893.7	Merritt Island	15.5
918.7	Melbourne	25.0
937.3	Sebastian	18.6
951.6	Vero Beach	14.3
966.5	Ft. Pierce	14.9
987.8	Stuart	21.3
1004.7	Jupiter	16.9
1013.6	North Palm Beach	8.9
1017.3	Palm Beach	3.7
1037.8	Delray Beach	20.5
1048.0	Boca Raton	10.2
1055.0	Pompano Beach	7.0
1064.0	Ft. Lauderdale	9.0
1072.0	Hollywood	8.0
1088.5	Miami	16.5
1095.9	Key Biscayne	7.4

MTW Big Pictures provide an overview of local geographic references. They identify the counties, capes, inlets, lighthouses, and bodies of water commonly referred to in NOAA and AM/FM weather broadcasts.

The locations of WX weather towers are shown to easily determine the best broadcast for your position and direction of travel. The temperature table shows average highs and lows for that region. Look for major cities and smaller towns along the ICW, then use the distance table for planning stops or estimating travel time. Lastly, we list the region's required charts by their NOAA chart number and provide a snapshot of Waterway resources and impediments.

Florida

Cumberland Sound to Biscayne Bay

The Sunshine State
ICW Statute Mile 714.0 to 1097.9
Bridges Monitor VHF 09

Regions
First Coast
Space Coast
Treasure Coast
Gold Coast

Inlets
St. Marys Entrance
St. Johns Entrance
St. Augustine Inlet
Port Canaveral
Ft. Pierce Inlet
Lake Worth Inlet
Port Everglades (Ft. Lauderdale)
Port of Miami (Government Cut)
Biscayne Channel

U.S. Coast Guard
District Seven: 305/415-6800
Group Mayport: 904/247-7311
Station Mayport: 904/564-7592
Station New Smyrna: 386/428-9085
Station Port Canaveral: 321/868-4200
Station Ft. Pierce: 772/464-6100
Station Lake Worth Inlet: 561/844-4470
Station Fort Lauderdale: 954/927-1611
Group Miami: 305/535-4111
Station Miami Beach: 305/535-4368

NOAA Weather Towers
WX-1 Jacksonville
WX-2 Daytona Beach
WX-1 Melbourne
WX-3 West Palm Beach
WX-1 Miami
WX-2 Sugarloaf Key

Security Zones
Kennedy Space Center
Port of Miami (Government Cut)

Recorded Shuttle Launch Information
321/867-4636

Okeechobee Waterway Information
863/983-8101

Lighthouses
Amelia Island Light
St. Augustine Light
Ponce de Leon Inlet Light
Jupiter Inlet Light
Hillsboro Inlet Light
Cape Florida Light

Fishing Information
www.floridaconservation.org

FLORIDA WAS almost shut out of the Atlantic Intracoastal Waterway. In 1913, when the Army Corps of Engineers requested a continuation of the inland route from Beaufort, North Carolina to Key West, their request was denied.

Congress saw no reason to provide a national canal for sparsely populated Florida. The haphazard system of private canals seemed sufficient. The proposal from Beaufort southward was approved—but only to the Florida border at St. Johns River.

Well, the rest is history. Florida's population exploded during the 1900s. It's now the fourth most populous state, and still growing at an alarming rate. Nearly one thousand people move into Florida each day.

The Atlantic Intracoastal Waterway, nationalized and approved in 1927, reflects this population growth. Some sections are lined wall-to-wall (literally, with a concrete sea wall) with canal-front housing developments or high-rise condominiums. With about one in 20 residents owning a boat, South Florida's canals are choked with traffic on weekends. Large yachts line the canal edges. Between personal watercraft and luxury yachts, more money is spent on boating in Florida than any other state.

Because of its heavy use, Florida's Intracoastal Waterway is well maintained. A special state agency, the Florida Inland Navigation District (FIND), is responsible for managing the waterway system. In fact, the Brooks Memorial Bridge in Ft. Lauderdale (STM 1066) honors Commodore Brooks, a former FIND board member who was the original advocate of a national waterway from Jacksonville to Miami.

To most cruisers, Florida is the gold at the end of a rainbow: the land of warm winter months, snorkeling, sandy beaches, tiki huts, and sport fishing. As cruisers cast off from Michigan, New York, or Ontario, they dream of reaching sunny Florida.

Courtesy of St. Lucie County TDC

Up Close and Personal

But Florida and boaters have a love-hate relationship. Cruisers arrive in Florida with lingering dread from tales of Florida hassles: expensive crowded marinas, limited anchoring, dinghy fines, scores of restricted bridges, and waterways crowded with cigarette boats and personal watercraft.

All these stories are true; but some of the details are fact and some are fiction. It's the flip side of Florida being a thoroughly maritime jurisdiction. Yes, Florida has its own unique boating regulations, including rules about anchoring, licensing, taxation, and manatee zones. And its marine patrol has the manpower to enforce the laws.

Florida Inland Navigation District
www.aicw.org
561/627-3386

South Florida Marine Info Hotline
www.miasf.org
800/boat-001

Florida's Atlantic Intracoastal Waterway may cover one-third of the miles between Norfolk and Miami, but it claims nearly two-thirds of the bridges. There are 81 bridges along Florida's ICW—many with restricted opening schedules. In densely populated Palm Beach and Broward counties, it's not unusual to have a restricted bridge every few miles. With vertical clearances of only 9-, 12-, or 21-feet, these delays affect both sailboats and trawlers.

Courtesy of gssites.com/miami

Florida is Tough!

Bridge delays are a part of life in coastal Florida, both for boaters and for residents commuting to work. Fortunately, most Florida bridges open at least every half hour to accommodate the boat traffic. Many communities are working to improve this balance between boaters and commuters. Palm Beach County recently re-vamped its bridge schedules after a several-month trial. Broward County is conducting a similar study as this book goes to press.

The bridge schedules listed in the NAV COLUMN are the most up-to-date schedules at the time of press, provided by the Coast Guard's bridge division. But bridge schedules do change, both as part of a study or for construction or maintenance. If a bridge opening is critical to your passage, such as for an early departure out an inlet, you should call the bridge tender telephone number and confirm its hours.

Some cruisers avoid bridge delays by bumping out for daily ocean passages. Depending on your vessel's cruising speed and height above water, this can save considerable time. If you have a sailboat with a mast height greater than 56 feet you *must* depart the Waterway to avoid the fixed Tuttle Bridge at STM 1087.2. Southbound, exit the Waterway in Palm Beach County at Lake Worth Inlet (STM 1018.4) or at Ft. Lauderdale's Port Everglades Inlet (STM 1066.5). Northbound, exit the Waterway at Biscayne Channel (STM 1097.9) or at Miami's Government Cut (STM 1089.0).

The good news is Florida's inlets offer exceptional ocean access. There are nine well-marked and well-lit inlets along the Florida ICW, listed in the Florida STATE HIGHLIGHTS.

Florida's major inlets are designed for large ships, so they are wide and straight. Many are well lit for miles into the Atlantic, making them suitable for night arrivals or departures. However, remember that the Waterway itself is less suitable for night travel. If you intend to use an inlet at night, choose an appropriate marina or anchorage along the inlet channel.

Large vessels, such as freighters, navy ships, and cruise ships, are common near Florida's inlets. In 2001, 12 million cruise ship passengers passed through Florida ports. The Port of Canaveral—not Port of Miami (which ranks as number two)—is the busiest cruise port in the world.

Generally these large ships are not a concern. Keep an eye on your six and, as a small recreational vessel, stay to the edges of a ship channel. More important, remember that most ships—including cruise ships—are included within a 500-yard moving security zone. Stay well clear of all vessels, including ships at their berths. Don't be surprised if the Coast Guard contacts you by radio and asks you to move or change course. Be sure to actively monitor VHF 16 whenever you are near an inlet with commercial traffic.

U.S. Customs Clearance
Upon arrival from a foreign port
800/432-1216 or 800/451-0393

Salt is the enemy! If salt creeps into your cabin, from clothes or feet, everything will become damp and crunchy. Leave all salt-water-sprayed clothing in your cockpit. Keep a freshwater rinse bucket in the boarding area to dip your bare feet or shoe bottoms before you track this invisible enemy into your cabin.

Many cruisers have heard about Florida's notorious sales and use tax on recently purchased boats. Florida has a six percent sales tax and, under some conditions, extends this tax to *non-residents* who bring a boat into the state. Since many cruisers purchase a boat prior to their transit, this tax is a real concern.

First, if you're a Florida resident, you obviously owe sales tax to your home state. Florida's tax twist is the non-resident who arrives in Florida with a recently purchased vessel, but paid less than six percent sales tax in their home state. Under certain conditions, Florida can charge a use tax, equal to the difference in sales tax paid.

For example, if a boat is purchased in a state with a sales tax of four percent, the owner is required to pay an additional two percent when the boat is brought into Florida.

Use tax is not due on boats brought into Florida if all the following conditions are met: (1) The owner has owned the boat six months or longer; (2) The purchaser showed no intent to use the boat in Florida at or before the time of purchase; and (3) The boat has been used six months or longer within the taxing jurisdiction of another state. *Time spent in foreign waters, such as the Bahamas, does not count as part of the six-month period.*

Use tax becomes due when the boat is required to be titled and/or registered in Florida. Florida registration is required within 90 days after a boat enters Florida, even if the boat is currently titled and/or registered in another state. A boat that remains in Florida for more than 90 consecutive days or more than 183 days in a one-year period is required to be Florida titled and/or registered and therefore presumed to be taxable.

Obviously these rules can change at any time. And they are complicated by specific situations, such as if the boat is undergoing repairs, which invokes Florida's Safe Harbor Act and extends the use tax exemption.

If you have any questions about Florida's sales or use tax on nonresident boats, contact the Boating Section of the Department of Revenue. Two informative brochures, *Boats: Information for Owners and Purchasers* and *Florida's Boat Repair Facilities: A Safe Harbor for Taxpayers* outline the revenue laws in detail.

Florida Department of Revenue
Boat Enforcement Section
www.myflorida.com/dor
305/499-4034

In Florida, all motorized dinghies must be individually registered—either in your home state or in Florida. *Contrary to popular belief, registering your main vessel does not include umbrella registration of your dinghy.* Although you may consider your dinghy as equipment for your mother ship, it's a separate vessel according to Florida state law.

If you're skeptical your dinghy must be registered, look at all the vessels hailing from New Jersey, Ohio, Massachusetts, or Maryland with dinghy registration num-

Courtesy of MODIS Rapid Response Team, NASA

Imagery by Jacques Descloitres

Florida and Bahama Banks

bers starting with "FL." These cruisers were busted!

If you arrive in Florida with an unregistered dinghy, you need to go to a local Motor Vehicle Services office. The locations of these offices are listed on the DMV website, or call their customer service number, both listed below. Bring proof of the value of your dinghy, such as a sales receipt or insurance record. Without this proof, they will *assign* a value to your dinghy, and they don't err on the cheap side.

Florida Department of Motor Vehicles
www.dmv.org/fl-florida/boat-registration.php
850/922-9000

Because of heavy boat traffic, many Florida communities enforce anchoring laws. Fortunately, there are many anchorages along the Florida Waterway. They tend to be wide-spot anchorages, rather than oxbows, but they still offer protection. Many are simply in the lee of a large causeway bridge, which breaks the anchor-wrenching waves while providing a cooling cabin breeze.

Many Waterway towns maintain public anchorages or municipal mooring fields. Dinghy docks are often available, sometimes even at local businesses such as marinas or restaurants. This generous service allows you to access shore facilities without paying marina dock fees.

Courtesy of USCG

Photo by Harry Greene **Florida is Diving Country**

To help defray the cost of these public services, many communities charge a nominal anchoring fee or limit the number of days at their anchorage. Key West's Cow Key Channel taught local Florida governments a lesson. Today, local laws prevent squatter settlements of floating homeless from forming. The fees are usually modest and often flexible, letting you use an anchorage for a certain number of days a month. We note many of these fees and use limits in the mile-by-mile anchorage notes.

Although you may be accustomed to anchoring for free, anchoring has costs for the local community. All these visitors strain the local services. In the past ten years, the Florida Department of Environmental Protection has increased the number of pump-out stations from 135 to over 600 to provide for the increased use of the Waterway. The communities must deal with dinghy docks, water quality, public transportation, and other services open to non-residents. Many towns even allow cruisers to check out books from their libraries!

Florida also has hundreds of marinas. But it's always wise to call ahead for a marina reservation. Marinas become more crowded during the peak season. The rates also increase, particularly as you move south toward the Gold Coast.

Courtesy of USCG, 7th District

Pompano Beach Bridge

On the flip side, we once wintered too long in the Abacos and, upon returning, found ourself in Florida during the summer off-season. We stayed a month at a premium resort marina, Pier 66 in Ft. Lauderdale, for less than $1/foot/day!

It's particularly important to call ahead to marinas in Indian River, Martin, St. Lucie, and Palm Beach counties. The terrible hurricane season of 2004 damaged docks and affected the availability of transient dockage and fuel. Many marinas, such as the Ft. Pierce city docks, were decimated. Although repairs have been prompt, some marinas have quite a bit of work before they are back to full capacity.

Many cruisers joke they can tell the day of the week by the Waterway traffic. Friday through Sunday brings out all the local recreational boaters, from flat-bottomed boats fishing in the middle of the channel to PWCs ignoring the rules of the road. To avoid the weekend recreational boating madness, try to time your transits for weekdays. Sit tight at an anchorage or dock over Saturday and Sunday.

Finally, Florida's unique wildlife requires unique boating attention. The Florida Manatee—an endangered sub-species of the West Indian Manatee—is on a literal collision course with boaters. Nearly 100 manatees die every year from collisions with boats. And the total population is only about 3,000 animals. Every manatee you see, with the exception of the very young, shows prop scars on its back.

To protect the manatee, Florida has created manatee protection zones. These zones are very common near anchorages and marinas. Look for Coast Guard restricted operation symbols: a white sign with a red circle in a red square. The letters, shown in black, describe the nature of the restriction, beginning with "Manatee Zone."

Many boaters complain these signs, which require "Idle Speed/No Wake" or "Slow Speed/Minimum Wake," are vague. To clear up the confusion, *idle speed* is defined as proceeding at the minimum speed that maintains steerageway of the vessel. *Slow speed* requires the vessel to be completely off plane, settled into the water and proceeding without wake. Note the ICW channel is not exempt unless *specifically* listed on the sign, such as "Entering Manatee Zone/ICW Exempt/Slow Speed Out of ICW."

Florida, from Jacksonville to Miami, is more than one third of the journey from the start of the Atlantic Intracoastal Waterway in Norfolk. Nearly 400 of the 1098 miles between Norfolk and Miami are along Florida's extensive coastline. And Florida's several-hundred-mile coastline is varied, ranging from natural hammocks and marshes in north Florida to the skyline of Miami.

Florida divides its coast into four regions, each with unique scenery, cultures, and histories. From north to south, they are the First Coast, the Space Coast, the Treasure Coast, and the Gold Coast.

THE FIRST COAST

The First Coast includes the four northernmost Atlantic counties: Nassau, Duval, St. Johns, and Flagler. The First Coast is not only first for arriving northerners; it was the location of Florida's first settlements. Historic towns and forts, such as Fernandina, St. Augustine, and Fort Matanzas, many dating back hundreds of years to Spanish rule, are abundant in this region.

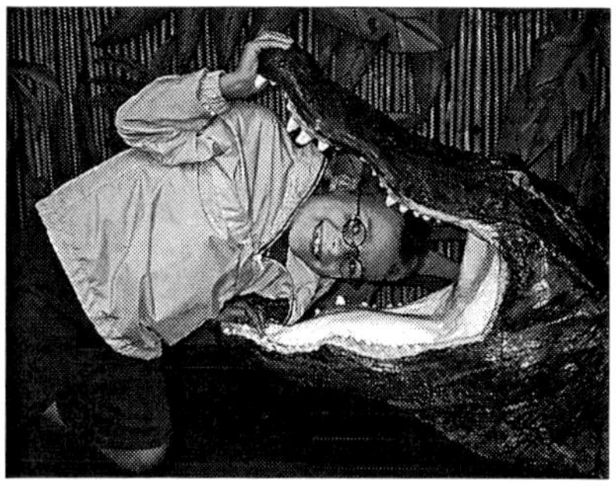

semi-local publications LLC

Photo by Author **St. Augustine Alligator Farm**

The First Coast is less hectic and less developed than its southern cousins. Northern Florida is low-key, the Old Florida or genteel South. Along the Waterway, large areas of quiet winding rivers and open marshes are protected against development. The waterfront towns, with historic buildings and lively town centers, are smaller than in mid- or South Florida. Like everywhere in Florida, tourism is still the big industry here, but it's less glitzy.

Navigationally, the First Coast presents few problems. There are many anchorages and many marinas. Anchorages do not have the crowding, restrictions, or fees of South Florida. Towns are easily accessible from the Waterway's marinas or anchorages.

Do pay attention to the tides and currents

on the First Coast. Spring tides range over five feet, so adjust your scope or docklines accordingly. For quick reference, each anchorage's spring tidal range, denoted as STR, is listed in the NAV COLUMN. Many of the anchorages are in tidal rivers, so also plan for current. Avoid deep areas that show signs of scouring; instead choose shallower pockets with accumulated sediment.

They're pricey but worth it! Hella Turbo fans are small but move lots of air to cool your cabin. They're rated at 5,000 hours and draw only 200MA@12V DC. Even on the hook in sultry South Florida, you can have a cooling breeze down below.

THE SPACE COAST

The Space Coast includes Volusia and Brevard counties (pronounced bre-VAHRD), with the larger communities of Cape Canaveral, Cocoa, Melbourne, Rockledge, and Titusville. Named for NASA's presence at Cape Canaveral, the Kennedy Space Center dominates this region. Its 140,000-acre facility has thousands of employees and spawns an extensive local technology industry.

Since the Waterway passes right by the Kennedy Space Center, many cruisers take this opportunity to watch a shuttle launch from their cockpits. A 24-hour recorded hotline provides information on scheduled launch dates. Several marinas and anchorages along the Indian River, centered above and below the Titusville Bridge at STM 878.7, provide prime viewing.

Courtesy of NASA

Shuttle Launch

If you would like to see a launch, be aware they are frequently delayed due to weather. If you have your heart set on watching a launch, you may need to wait until NASA re-approves a weather window.

The Space Coast may be the technology center of Florida's Atlantic coast, but it's also famous for its wildlife. NASA's extensive holdings create acres of land set aside against development. Miles and miles along the Waterway are protected as part of large nationally known refuges, including the Canaveral National Seashore and Merritt Island National Wildlife Refuge.

Navigationally, the Space Coast is relatively easy. The Waterway follows the Mosquito and Indian River Lagoons, wide bodies of water that are very shallow outside the channel. But the channel is well marked, with clearly visible and frequently placed dayboards.

There are a number of bridges along the Space Coast, many with restricted schedules. The NAV COLUMN provides specific restrictions on these bridges and the rolling HEADS UP! lists upcoming bridges for easier planning. The most important bridge planning occurs near Titusville. The Max Brewer Bridge (STM 878.7) and the NASA Causeway Bridge (STM 885.0) close for several hours each day for NASA's commuter traffic.

THE TREASURE COAST

The Treasure Coast, which spans Indian River, St. Lucie, and Martin counties, is named for its history of shipwrecks and buried treasure. As you transit this stretch, the INTERPRETIVE VIGNETTES highlight the shipwrecking history of this coastline.

Ft. Pierce is the hub of the Treasure Coast. Because of its inlet, Ft. Pierce is a haven for recreational boaters and marine research centers. Harbor Branch Oceanographic Institution and the Smithsonian Marine Institute are both located along the Waterway at Ft. Pierce. Ft. Pierce is also the junction to the Okeechobee Waterway, where the St. Lucie River meets the Intracoastal Waterway.

The currents near Ft. Pierce inlet and St. Lucie River are the most important navigational concern along the Treasure Coast. The current can be swift as you pass the inlet area or if you are turning up St. Lucie River to the Okeechobee Waterway. Watch your set carefully.

The Treasure Coast has many marinas and many of its communities provide anchorages or mooring fields. Some towns, such as Vero Beach and Stuart, are exceptionally welcoming, providing extensive city services to transiting boaters. For many cruisers, the Treasure Coast becomes home away from home. The region is so boater-friendly many transiting vessels choose the Treasure Coast for extended boat-repair stops, or to rest for a month from the daily boat-moving treadmill, or even to purchase a land-based home. In fact, Vero Beach has been nicknamed *Velcro* Beach for the boaters who arrive and then have trouble leaving.

THE GOLD COAST

Palm Beach, Broward, and Miami-Dade counties are aptly named the Gold Coast. This is the wealthy, opulent, decadent—and yes, crowded and expensive—region of Florida. This is the Florida of mega-yachts, complete with oil paintings and flat-screen TVs, captained by full-time professionals.

But boaters can enjoy Palm Beach, Ft. Lauderdale, and Miami on a reasonable budget. The towns provide municipal marinas or city moorings, described in the NAV COLUMN. For example, Ft. Lauderdale maintains four municipal marinas and a mooring field. Miami is becoming increasingly hospitable to boaters. Some of the Miami communities, such as Key Biscayne or Coconut Grove, break the stereotype of an ugly commercial port lined with skyscrapers.

Courtesy of Greater Miami CVB

Cape Florida Light

Surprisingly, it's also still possible to anchor along the Gold Coast. Many of the man-made lakes and canals are open for overnight stops. Some of the anchorages put you in the middle of incredibly exclusive neighborhoods. You can spend the evening at anchor with a 360-degree view of some of the most expensive real estate on the East Coast.

Unfortunately, this is South Florida, so crime needs to be on your radar. Particularly near Miami, be aware of your surroundings before you go exploring on foot. Vessels should be locked at docks, and valuables such as electronics or binoculars should be stowed or covered. Your dinghy should be locked at *all* dinghy docks in South Florida, even if the area seems safe and there is a lot of dinghy dock use.

Tides and currents become less of a concern along the Gold Coast. Instead, your piloting attention needs to focus on boat traffic and South Florida's infamous restricted bridges.

The boat traffic along the Gold Coast is noticeable and a major nuisance to slow-moving cruising vessels. Particularly on weekends, the canal is crowded with small boats, including PWCs, cigarette boats, and small fishing boats. Along some stretches, the Waterway narrows to a canal lined with

Courtesy of Greater Miami CVB

Miamarina at Bayside

sea walls. The wakes from all this haphazard traffic bounce off the sea walls, creating a choppy and unpleasant ride.

The Gold Coast's notorious restricted bridges are fact, not fiction. The last 78 miles in Florida, only 7% of the Norfolk-Miami route, has 34% of the ICW bridges. And many of these bridges have restricted hours. There are 27 restricted bridges in the three Gold Coast counties, most of them near Palm Beach and Ft. Lauderdale.

If your vessel height requires bridge openings, your travel time will suffer. In fact, don't be surprised if it takes you twice as long to make your daily average of miles.

Don't put your vessel name on your dinghy. The t/t (tender to) ruse won't circumvent Florida's dinghy registration laws and it only advertises your empty mother ship when you are ashore.

FLORIDA BOOK AND FILM PICKS

Since so few people are native Floridians, Florida is a melting pot of cultures. It may be the southern-most state, but the southern drawl of neighboring Alabama and Georgia disappears as you cross St. Marys River. Instead, the dialects come from a mix of northerners, spiced up with immigrant communities from Cuba, Haiti, Jamaica, and the Dominican Republic. Only rarely along the water will you hear a true Florida Cracker dialect.

But Florida absolutely has its own culture, captured by many nationally known local writers. Names like Carl Hiaasen, John D. MacDonald, or Randy Wayne White represent this Florida genre.

Carl Hiaasen's creative and hilarious books are required reading in Florida. Imagine characters like an ex-Governor who calls himself "Skink," lives in a swamp, and confounds wildlife wardens by wearing a transmitting panther collar. If you've never read one of Hiaasen's novels, *Tourist Season* (1986) is his first solo work. His latest novel, *Skinny Dip*, came out in 2004.

Kids can now enjoy Carl Hiaasen's naturally childish wit with his novel for young readers: *HOOT*, which won a Newbery Honor. This is true Hiaasen: a mystery involving owls, Florida developers, and precocious kids. Another Hiaasen novel for young readers, *Flush*, will debut in late 2005.

Several other excellent authors have captured Florida's culture and history for young readers. Acclaimed children's author Jean Craighead George wrote *The Missing 'Gator of Gumbo Limbo*. A local writer, Peggy Nolan, describes the Florida coast during World War II in *The Spy Who Came In From the Sea* (1999), set in Fernandina. Kate DiCamillo's first novel, *Because of Winn-Dixie*, was a 2001 Newbery Honor Book.

For a Hiaasen-style romp through the swamps of Florida—that turns out to be true—read *The Orchid Thief* (1994) by Susan Orlean. It's the story of a New York reporter (the author) who tags along with a collection of eccentric Florida Crackers and Seminole Indians. They come up with a scheme to poach rare orchids from the Everglades, violating state laws but claiming exception as Native Americans. If you have any interest in horticulture, or the contemporary Seminole tribe, Orlean's non-fiction tale is an amusing read.

But don't let the movie scare you off the book. The film *Adaptation* (2002) with Nicholas Cage and Meryl Streep, doesn't capture the book's great story, instead dwelling on a screenwriter's self-wallowing angst trying to create its screenplay. As the cliché says, the book is better than the movie.

For decades, the mystery writer John D. MacDonald represented the Florida genre of "single hero with a boat." Many contemporary Florida mystery writers, such as Randy Wayne White, are seen as continuing MacDonald's genre.

Courtesy of National Park Service

Wood Stork

If you've never read a John D. MacDonald mystery, you're missing out on a cruiser's classic. Nearly every book swap in Florida has at least one of his 21 paperbacks. Each title includes a color, beginning with *The Deep Blue Good-By* in 1964 and ending with *The Lonely Silver Rain* in 1985. The books may be decades old, but they are still wildly popular, especially among the cruising community. MacDonald's fictional character, Travis McGee, is immortal in Florida, still honored with a plaque at Bahia Mar Yachting Center.

Florida's strong tradition of mystery writing extends to female writers. Carolina Garcia-Aguilera's first novels were set in Miami's exile Cuban-American community. Her series of light chick mysteries, beginning with *Bloody Waters* (1996), are set in Little Havana, Coconut Grove, and Cuba. *Havana Heat* (2000) is one of her best.

For film picks in Florida, we choose one classic and one contemporary flick. *Body Heat* (1981) with William Hurt and Kathleen Turner, is a great way to wait out a cold rainy norther. The film was shot along the central Florida coast, including shots of the Waterway and the George Bush Boulevard Bridge (STM 1037.7).

A recent release on video, *Monster* (2003) with Charlize Theron, is a true story set in Daytona Beach. The disturbing story of a prostitute who becomes Florida's first woman executed under the death penalty, it may seem like a morbid subject for a recreational evening. But this film, which won Theron an Academy Award for best actress, is insightful and excellently produced. ▲

SAFETY INFO

NOAA Weather
WX-2 Savannah, GA
WX-1 Jacksonville, FL
WX-2 Daytona Beach, FL

USCG
Station Mayport, FL
VHF 16 or 09/22A
904/564-7592

Sea Tow
Brunswick, GA
VHF 16/12
912/280-9428

TowBoatU.S.
Fernandina, FL
VHF 16/10
904/277-8511

HEADS UP!

536.0	Ladies Island Bridge
575.8	SC-GA Border
578.4	Wilmington River Cut-off (NB)
579.9	Causton Bluff Bridge
592.4	Skidaway Narrows Bridge
706.0	Kings Bay Security Zone (SB)
713.0	Kings Bay Security Zone (NB)
713.7	Cumberland Sound Channel (NB)
714.0	**GA-FL Border**
720.7	**Kingsley Creek RR Bridge**
739.1	Sisters Creek Bridge
747.4	B.B. McCormick Twin Bridges
775.0	St. Augustine Inlet Area (SB)
778.1	Bridge of Lions
779.0	St. Augustine Inlet Area (NB)
788.8	Crescent Beach Bridge
816.0	L.B. Knox Bridge
829.7	Daytona Beach Main St. Bridge

714.0 GA-FL Border S N
St. Marys River (G25)
See Fort Clinch.

714.0 Junction | St. Marys Entrance (7.0) S N
Well Aided N30.42.717
Well Lit W081.20.772

Exit ICW at G25. Proceed easterly to St. Marys Entrance. Waypoint is between R8 and G9.

St. Marys River is one of the best inlets along the East Coast. Submarines have very little maneuverability on the surface, so this naval inlet is wide, well aided, and well lit for ten miles.

Caution: Many electronic systems, charts, and chartkits still show the longer, dogleg channel and numbering (R14A and G15A) of 2001 charts. In either case, the above waypoint translates to the fifth pair of nav aids east of the breakwater.

715.4 Tiger Point Marina & Boat Works (0.3) S N
VHF 16; 904/277-2720

Exit ICW N of G7. Proceed E to Egans Creek. Marina is to starboard at charted Old Fernandina. [STR 7.1]

716.4 Bells River Anchorage (1.1) S N
Anchor 8-14 feet N30.40.809
STR 7.1 feet W081.28.802

Exit ICW at R10. Proceed SW then NNW up Bells River. Anchor before charted 6-foot shoal.

716.5 Florida Petroleum Corporation (0.1) S N
No VHF Watch; 904/261-3200

Fuel dock is on wooden pier opposite R10. Accepts transients if you are comfortable on a fixed pier with 7-foot tide. [STR 7.1]

716.7 Fernandina Beach Anchorage (0.1) S N
Anchor 8-12 feet N30.40.316
STR 7.1 feet W081.28.123

Exit ICW NNE of R12. Anchor opposite Fernandina Harbor Marina.

716.8 Fernandina Harbor Marina (0.1) S N
VHF 16; 904/491-2090

Exit ICW NNE of R12. Marina is to ESE. [STR 7.1]
See Amelia Island Light.

719.5 Jackson Creek Anchorage (0.1) S N
Anchor 8-10 feet N30.38.667
STR 7.1 feet W081.29.005

Exit ICW N of G5. Proceed E to Jackson Creek. Entrance has shoaled to 5 feet.

719.8 Amelia River Anchorage (0.5) S N
Anchor 10-14 feet N30.38.358
STR 7.1 feet W081.29.757

Exit ICW NNW of G9. Proceed W to Amelia River.

720.6 Amelia Island Yacht Basin (0.5) S N
VHF 16; 904/277-4615

Exit ICW NNW of railroad bridge. Proceed E to charted keyhole basin. Marina is to port. [STR 7.0]

720.7 Kingsley Creek RR Bridge S N
Single-pivot swing; vertical 5 feet; usually open.

BORDER CROSSING

An imaginary line of language separates Georgia and Florida. North of the border are English names like Kings Bay, Dungeness, Stafford, and Cumberland. South of this border, the Spanish names begin: Fernandina, Vilano, Ponte Vedra, Anastasia, and Matanzas.

In the early 1800s, Fernandina was a border town, and so became one of the most coveted pieces of land in North America. Her harbor was crowded with ships from all over the world, dropping off their goods at the closest port outside U.S. import regulations.

Courtesy of Florida Inland Navigation District

Looking Over Nassau Sound

But like any border town, Fernandina attracted the darker side of commerce. Maritime hijackers hid in the marshes around Amelia Island, seizing cargo before the ships reached port. Illegal trafficking and prostitution were rampant. British spies lurked everywhere, reporting on U.S. weaknesses for the imminent conflict between America and England.

The area was in a state of anarchy—so unruly that a pirate, Louis Aury, took control of Amelia Island and claimed it for Mexico. Against U.S. laws, his outlaw government used the island as a base for wholesale slave trading.

The U.S. government finally had enough of this lawlessness in its backyard. The feds sent a man-of-war to force their surrender. Within a few years the U.S. purchased Florida from Spain, ending Fernandina's reign as the southern border town.

But the U.S. flag wasn't the last flag to fly over Fernandina. Fernandina's rule changed one more time during the Civil War when Florida joined the Confederacy. In the end, eight flags flew over this border town: the Conquistadors, the French Huguenots, Spain, England, Mexico, the Republic of Florida, the Confederate States of America, and finally, the United States of America.

FORT CLINCH

As you cross Cumberland Sound to enter Amelia River, Fort Clinch is located at the northern tip of Amelia Island, just east of R2 at STM 714.4.

Fort Clinch is one of the most complete brick forts in the country and is still open to the public. A fort was originally built on this point during the War of 1812 to prevent any more British invasions. The old fort, held by American soldiers led by General Clinch, was eventually replaced with the current brick structure. This new fort, completed in 1861 for about $750,000, was named after General Clinch.

Today you can visit the fort, part of a 1,086 acre park encompassing most of northern Amelia Island. The park includes biking and nature trails, fishing piers, and tours of the fort's restored buildings, including furnished barracks, jail cells, and the fort hospital.

Fort Clinch
www.floridastateparks.org/fortclinch
904/277-7274

AMELIA ISLAND: PERIODS AND STYLES

When Henry Flagler chose the route for his new Florida East Coast Railway, he bypassed Amelia Island and the town of Fernandina Beach.

But thanks to this rebuff, Fernandina Beach's historic architecture was spared from post-railway development. Today the town has more than 450 historic buildings. It's a small town, but 50 of its city blocks are listed on the National Register of Historic Places.

Most of the buildings are from the Victorian period, spanning from about 1840 to 1900. Contrary to common usage, *Victorian* refers to a period of time, not an architectural style. There were many architectural styles during the Victorian period. Two of these styles, Queen Anne and Italianate, have some of their most beautiful examples in Fernandina's historic district.

You can pick up a self-guided walking tour map at the local chamber of commerce. Look for the Queen Anne style,

SAFETY INFO

NOAA Weather
WX-2 Savannah, GA
WX-1 Jacksonville, FL
WX-2 Daytona Beach, FL

USCG
Station Mayport, FL
VHF 16 or 09/22A
904/564-7592

Sea Tow
Brunswick, GA
VHF 16/12
912/280-9428

TowBoatU.S.
Fernandina, FL
VHF 16/10
904/277-8511

HEADS UP!

575.8	SC-GA Border
578.4	Wilmington River Cut-off (NB)
579.9	Causton Bluff Bridge
592.4	Skidaway Narrows Bridge
706.0	Kings Bay Security Zone (SB)
713.0	Kings Bay Security Zone (NB)
713.7	Cumberland Sound Channel (NB)
714.0	GA-FL Border
720.7	Kingsley Creek RR Bridge
739.1	**Sisters Creek Bridge**
747.4	B.B. McCormick Twin Bridges
775.0	St. Augustine Inlet Area (SB)
778.1	Bridge of Lions
779.0	St. Augustine Inlet Area (NB)
788.8	Crescent Beach Bridge
816.0	L.B. Knox Bridge
829.7	Daytona Beach Main St. Bridge
830.6	Daytona Beach Memorial Bridge

the most elaborate and ornate style of the Victorian period, with towers, turrets, wrap-around porches, and fanciful details. In contrast, the Italianate style favored low roofs, wide eaves, and ornamental brackets.

You may recognize the Steamboat House, at Ash and 10th Streets, from *The Manchurian Candidate* (2004) starring Denzel Washington, Meryl Streep, and Jon Voight.

Amelia Island/Fernandina Beach
www.ameliaisland.org
800/226-3542

SHRIMPERS

Fernandina is considered the birthplace of the shrimping industry. In 1913 local fisherman began modern shrimping when they replaced rowboats and cast nets with power-driven seines and trawls. Burbank Trawl Makers, also called the Net House, is still one of the world's biggest producers of hand-sewn shrimp nets.

Courtesy of NOAA

Shrimp Trawler

Today shrimping is a capital-intensive business costing close to $1 million in capital and operating expenses.

Shrimpers must keep up with modern technology and public opinion, such as equipping their nets with turtle excluder devices. One of these devices, called a "Georgia Jumper," separates the net into a compartment where only smaller animals can enter, forcing larger animals like sea turtles out an opening in the bottom.

Each shrimp boat trawls these waters from dawn to dusk, dragging their nets along the bottom and hoping to catch 250 to 500 pounds of shrimp a day.

Amelia Island is a shrimping powerhouse. About 80% of Florida's Atlantic White Shrimp are harvested in the waters around Amelia Island, with two million pounds of shrimp delivered to Fernandina docks annually.

To join this industry in a small way, visit Amelia Island during the Annual Isle of Eight Flags Shrimp Festival on the first weekend in May. And, of course, don't forget to eat shrimp. As Bubba says, you can barbecue it, boil it, broil it, bake it, sauté it...and there's pineapple shrimp, lemon shrimp, coconut shrimp, pepper shrimp, shrimp soup, shrimp stew, shrimp salad, shrimp and potatoes, shrimp burger, shrimp sandwiches...

AMELIA ISLAND LIGHT

If you're arriving from the north, you have already passed the new lighthouse at Little Cumberland Island. The original lighthouse at Little Cumberland was moved in 1839 and still stands on the north end of Amelia Island.

Winslow Lewis, America's famous lighthouse builder, built the lighthouse (a 50-foot brick tower) and a small keeper's house for $17,000. He equipped it with the lamp-and-reflector lighting system of his own design, commonly used in early American lighthouses. The light needed winding every four hours, the task of the keeper who walked up and down the 68 granite steps (shipped from New England).

By the early 1900s the lighthouse was upgraded to a Fresnel lens and raised to 107 feet above sea level. Today the light is automated, visible along the Waterway and 19 miles out to sea. You can walk near the lighthouse, about a mile from the Fernandina waterfront, but the lighthouse is located in a private residential community and closed to the public.

AMERICAN BEACH

In the 1930s, the Afro-American Life Insurance Company, guided by its CEO A.L. Lewis, bought 200 acres at the southern end of Amelia Island.

Lewis was Florida's first black millionaire and he envisioned a place where employees and their families could enjoy the ocean. The Jim Crow era of segregation meant Florida beaches were off limits to African Americans. So Lewis created American Beach, where black Americans traveled to enjoy the ocean from the 1930s to 1950s. Famous African American performers, including Ray Charles and James Brown,

720.8 Twin Bridges
(Twin Span A1A)
Fixed; vertical 65 feet.
Caution: Bridge height reported at less than 65 feet. Check boards before proceeding.

721.0 Unnamed Range
to Southbound/Northbound Navigation
722.6 Crane Island western shore.
1.6-mile range.

724.4 Amelia City Anchorage (0.3)
Anchor 8-12 feet N30.34.887
STR (TS) 6.3 feet W081.27.978
Exit ICW between R28 and G29. Proceed SW.

725.8 Anchorages
Exit ICW at R36. [STR 6.3]

- **South Amelia River Anchorage** (0.3)
  Anchor 8-10 feet N30.34.358
  STR 6.3 feet W081.28.359
  Proceed NNE.
- **Alligator Creek Anchorage** (1.1)
  Anchor 8-10 feet N30.34.771
  STR 6.3 feet W081.28.695
  Continue beyond first anchorage then bear northwesterly to Alligator Creek.

726.7 Harrison Creek Anchorage (0.3)
Anchor 8-10 feet N30.33.871
STR 6.3 feet W081.28.239
Exit ICW between G39 and G41. Proceed N beyond Harrison Creek entrance to charted 9-foot tongue.

734.6 Talbot Island Anchorage (0.2)
Anchor 6-8 feet N30.27.328
STR 5.6 feet W081.26.992
Exit ICW at G71. Proceed WNW into oxbow.
See Isle de Sarabay.

735.0 Ft. George Island Anchorage (1.0)
Anchor 8-12 feet N30.26.419
STR 5.6 (TS) feet W081.26.076
Exit ICW at R72. Proceed SE to Ft. George River.
Dinghy to Kingsley Plantation near G5.
See Ft. George Island.

739.0 Pine Island Free Dock (0.1)
Exit ICW NE of bridge. Proceed NW to park dock. [STR 4.7]
Room for several boats. No overnight dockage. Useful to stretch your legs, walk the dog, or wait for favorable current if transiting St. Johns River to Jacksonville.

739.1 Sisters Creek Bridge
(Route 105)
VHF 09; 904/360-5300
Double bascule; vertical 24 feet; on request.

740.0 Junction | Jacksonville or St. Johns Entrance
Southbound/Northbound Navigation
Exit ICW in St. Johns River near R24.
Proceed westerly for city of Jacksonville; proceed easterly for city of Mayport and St. Johns Entrance. [STR 5.3]

SEE HUGUENOT BEACH.

- **Jacksonville Marina** (2.8)
  VHF 16; 904/246-8929
  Proceed easterly. Marina is to starboard. Formerly Mayport Marine.
- **St. Johns Entrance** (7.0)
  Well Aided N30.23.799
  Well Lit W081.21.375
  Proceed easterly out breakwater. Well lit range makes this an exceptionally easy inlet to enter at night. Waypoint is seaward of G3 and R4.

742.6 Wonderwood Bridge S N
Fixed; vertical 65 feet.
Estimated completion in October 2006.

744.1 Three Island Anchorage (0.3) S N
Anchor 16-20 feet N30.19.735
STR 4.2 feet W081.26.212
Exit ICW SSW of G17. Proceed SSE behind charted three small islands.

744.7 Atlantic Boulevard Bridge S N
Fixed; vertical 65 feet. [STR 4.2 (TS)]

744.8 Pablo Creek Marina (0.2) S N
No VHF Watch; No telephone
This once-popular marina, in the protected basin W of the ICW, is closed. Like much of the ICW's waterfront real estate it has fallen to condominiums. [STR 4.2]

746.9 Palm Cove Marina (0.6) S N
VHF 16/69 N30.17.400
904/223-4757 W081.25.880
Exit ICW N of R32. Proceed WSW in privately maintained channel. Marina is in basin. [STR 4.3]

747.3 Beach Marine (0.2) S N
VHF 16/68 N30.17.333
904/249-8200 W081.25.187
Exit ICW N of bridge. Proceed E into basin. Marina is to starboard. [STR 4.4]

747.4 B.B. McCormick Twin Bridges S N
(Beach Boulevard Bridge)(US 90)
VHF 09; 904/360-5300
Double bascule; vertical 37 feet.
Restricted April 1-May 31 and October 1-November 30: M-F, 0700-0900 and 1630-1830 hrs; and SA-SU and holidays, 1200-1800 hrs; opens on the hour and half-hour.

749.3 Pablo Creek Bridge S N
(Oak Landing Bridge)
Fixed; vertical 65 feet.

750.1 Cabbage Swamp Canal S N
to Southbound Navigation Only
760.1 10-mile land cut.
No anchorages, no marinas, no fuel.
SEE CABBAGE SWAMP.

758.8 Palm Valley Bridge S N
(Route 210)
Fixed; vertical 65 feet. [STR 5.6 (TS)]
New fixed bridge replaces old bascule bridge.

came to American Beach's restaurants and nightclubs.

Ultimately segregation ended and, combined with several bad hits by hurricanes, the allure of American Beach faded. Only 100 houses remain today, but the site is still honored as the first stop on Florida's Black Heritage Trail.

Florida's Heritage Trails
www.flheritage.com/services
800/847-7278

DRUMFISH

As Rosanna Rosannadanna says, "It's always somethin'." You're anchored out for a quiet night…and then you notice a deep booming or low-pitched grunting sound resonating through your hull. It sounds like you're bumping and sticking on your fenders—except you're at anchor, so you don't have any fenders out.

Don't worry. It's most likely a group of red or black drums, drumming with their modified swim bladders. The bladder works like a resonating chamber, making a deep underwater noise. Between February and April, drumfish swim up Florida's rivers to spawn. Scientists think drumming is related to spawning, possibly to keep the schools together. Either way, go to sleep.

If you're on a sailboat, use a deck-level light in addition to a masthead anchor light. A tiny white anchor light at the top of a mast is barely noticeable to small watercraft, whose drivers are looking for lights in their forward field of vision. Powerboats, with lower anchor lights, reduce this collision risk.

ISLANDS OF TREES

As you enter Sawpit Creek, Black Hammock Island lies to the west. In Florida, hammocks are not places to sleep in the shade, but a type of island. Like the many Inuit words for snow, in Florida there are many words for island. And the island lingo depends on the trees.

If an island is covered with hardwoods, such as live oaks or pinelands in sawgrass, it's called a *hammock*, or more precisely, a *hummock*. If the island is mangrove or pine, then it's a *key*. If the island is covered with willow or bay trees, it's a *head*. An island of cypress is a *dome*.

Florida is so flat that every few inches of elevation makes a huge difference. Raise the soil a tiny bit above the waterline and the island becomes a buttonwood hammock instead of a mangrove key.

Note: When scouting potential anchorage on the charts, note the name of the islands along Florida's Waterway. The name often provides clues about the area's elevation (protection) and original ecology (holding).

And try not to be too dejected by a new type of island common throughout South Florida: an island created by canals and covered with houses is called a *development*.

ISLE DE SARABAY

Traveling from Nassau Sound to St. Johns River, the Waterway weaves through the marshes along Sawpit and Sisters Creeks. Big Talbot Island lies to the east of the Waterway, at about STM 730 to STM 735, and Little Talbot is behind Big Talbot. Ft. George Island is south of Big Talbot.

These three islands, all state parks, are some of the last remaining undeveloped islands along the Florida coast. You can access Big Talbot State Park at one of its six boat ramps. The Ft. George River ramp is closest to the facility's visitor center.

Big Talbot was once called Isle de Sarabay, after the Timucuan leader whose people inhabited Big Talbot. Timucua villages were common in this area, dating back to 3000 BC. When the French and Spanish arrived, the Timucua tribe numbered nearly 30,000. But, like many Native American communities, they had no natural immunity to the unfamiliar diseases brought by Europeans. By the early 1800s the Timucua tribe was essentially extinct.

Big Talbot Island State Park
www.floridastateparks.org
904/251-2320

EL LAGARTO

You may come across some unusual signs posted near Big Talbot and Ft. George Islands stating: "Caution! Alligators No Swimming."

In an ironic twist, the signs protect humans and are placed by the Department of *Environmental Protection*!

SAFETY INFO

NOAA Weather
WX-2 Savannah, GA
WX-1 Jacksonville, FL
WX-2 Daytona Beach, FL

USCG
Station Mayport, FL
VHF 16 or 09/22A
904/564-7592

Sea Tow
St. Augustine, FL
VHF 16/10
904/824-9969

TowBoatU.S.
St. Augustine, FL
VHF 16/18
386/322-5582

HEADS UP!

592.4	Skidaway Narrows Bridge
706.0	Kings Bay Security Zone (SB)
713.0	Kings Bay Security Zone (NB)
713.7	Cumberland Sound Channel (NB)
714.0	GA-FL Border
720.7	Kingsley Creek RR Bridge
739.1	Sisters Creek Bridge
747.4	B.B. McCormick Twin Bridges
775.0	**St. Augustine Inlet Area (SB)**
778.1	Bridge of Lions
779.0	St. Augustine Inlet Area (NB)
788.8	Crescent Beach Bridge
816.0	L.B. Knox Bridge
829.7	Daytona Beach Main St. Bridge
830.6	Daytona Beach Memorial Bridge
838.0	Ponce de Leon Inlet Area (SB)
845.0	George Munson Bridge
847.0	Ponce de Leon Inlet Area (NB)

Alligators are present—but not abundant—in the marshes behind Big Talbot and Ft. George Islands. Although you still shouldn't consider swimming, the American Alligator is much less aggressive than its cousin, the American Crocodile, found further south in Florida. In addition to differences in temperament, alligators are found in fresh water and crocodiles in salt water. Like dolphin and porpoise, you can quickly separate the species by their noses: alligators have a broad flat snout; crocodiles have a long skinny snout. This observation is best made at a distance.

The Spanish explorers called these creatures "el lagarto," meaning "the lizard." The name eventually evolved to alligator. To spot a lagarto, look along the sunny banks for muddy slide areas. Or at night, shine a flashlight along the shore. Your light will reflect their sinister bright ruby red eyes.

Courtesy of www.jaxshells.org

Photo by William Frank

No Kidding!

FT. GEORGE ISLAND

An island is a microcosm of history. Take Ft. George Island, a two-mile long island with multiple personalities over its several-hundred-year history.

The island began as a sub-tropical jungle, the perfect location for a Spanish missionary. Or at least the island was relatively safe and there were plenty of heathens to convert. In 1600, Father Pareja, recognized as one of the great scholars of the early church, created the Mission of San Juan Del Puerto on Ft. George Island. Over 500 Native Americans joined his parish.

By 1736 the English took over. The island changed to an English outpost when Oglethorpe built Fort St. George at the north end of the island and claimed St. Johns River as the southern boundary of Georgia.

Courtesy of U.S. Fish & Wildlife Service

Surveying Alligators (circa 1950)

In the 1800s, Ft. George Island followed the times and became a plantation. The Kingsley Plantation is the oldest plantation house in Florida, built in 1813. The plantation is still standing, including the main house, kitchen house, barn, and ruins of 25 of the original slave cabins. It can be visited by dinghy from the Talbot Island or Ft. George Island anchorages at STM 734.6 or STM 735.

Zephaniah Kingsley was an odd man who had an unusual relationship with African Americans. He argued blacks were the mental equals of whites, but felt they were destined for bondage.

He created an island fiefdom where he trained thousands of slaves as artisans, allowing them to keep some proceeds of their work, but then sold his skilled slaves at premium prices. He fought for civil rights for freed men, but profited ruthlessly from the buying and selling of slaves. To top off the irony, particularly in the context of the early 1800s, he married the daughter of an African chief. Ultimately he and his wife Anna moved to Hispaniola, where their descendants still live today.

By the 1900s Ft. George Island was an island resort, purchased by the state of Florida for a state park. The island still shows the scars of its history, but four hundred years later it has returned to jungle.

Ft. George Island State Park
www.floridastateparks.org
904/251-2320

760.1 Cabbage Swamp Canal S N
to Northbound Navigation Only
750.1 10-mile land cut.
No anchorages, no marinas, no fuel.

763.6 Spanish Landing Anchorage (0.1) S N
Anchor 6-8 feet N30.04.171
STR 5.5 feet W081.22.170
Exit ICW at G19. Proceed NNW.

765.0 Pine Island Anchorage (0.3) S N
Anchor 10-12 feet N30.03.126
STR 5.4 feet W081.21.835
Exit ICW S of G25. Proceed NE to Pine Island.

766.5 Capo Creek Anchorage (0.1) S N
Anchor 8-10 feet N30.01.763
STR 5.4 feet W081.21.839
Exit ICW between R30 and R32. Proceed WSW.

767.5 Shell Bluff Landing Anchorage (0.2) S N
Anchor 8-10 feet N30.01.328
STR 5.3 feet W081.20.981
Exit ICW at G35. Proceed N to charted tongue.

769.5 Tolomato River Anchorage (0.2) S N
Anchor 12-14 feet N30.00.027
STR 5.3 feet W081.20.184
Exit ICW at R42. Proceed N then NW to anchor behind G41.

775.0 Heads Up | St. Augustine Inlet Area S N
to Southbound Navigation Only
779.0 Transiting the St. Augustine Inlet area is confusing for many cruisers. Favor the Vilano Beach shore, being sure to round R60 at the charted shoals, then head SW across Davis Shores.

Caution: This area is a minefield of aids. Many small red nuns have been placed to keep you eastward of the large shoal area at the inlet's junction. Be sure to safely round R60 as you transit this area. When in doubt, favor Cape Francis or the Vilano Beach shorelines.

775.6 Camachee Cove Yacht Harbor (0.4) S N
VHF 16/68 N29.55.036
904/829-5676 W081.18.460
Exit ICW N of bridge. Proceed W to privately maintained channel. Marina is in basin. [STR 5.2]

775.8 Usina Bridge S N
(Vilano Beach Bridge)
Fixed; vertical 65 feet.
The charted lift bridge has been removed.

776.7 Junction | St. Augustine Inlet (2.5) S N
Moderately Aided N29.54.820
Poorly Lit W081.15.200
Exit ICW at R60. Proceed easterly to St. Augustine Inlet. Waypoint is at RW "STA".

776.8 Salt Run S N
Exit ICW NE of ICW G1. Proceed SSE, leaving Salt Run G1 to port. [STR 5.2]
SEE ST. AUGUSTINE LIGHT.

- **Conch House Marina Resort** (0.8)
  VHF 16/69 N29.53.716
  904/824-4347 W081.17.710

SAFETY INFO

NOAA Weather
WX-2 Savannah, GA
WX-1 Jacksonville, FL
WX-2 Daytona Beach, FL

USCG
Station Mayport, FL
VHF 16 or 09/22A
904/564-7592

Sea Tow
St. Augustine, FL
VHF 16/10
904/824-9969

TowBoatU.S.
St. Augustine, FL
VHF 16/18
386/322-5582

HEADS UP!

706.0 Kings Bay Security Zone (SB)
713.0 Kings Bay Security Zone (NB)
713.7 Cumberland Sound Channel (NB)
714.0 GA-FL Border
720.7 Kingsley Creek RR Bridge
739.1 Sisters Creek Bridge
747.4 B.B. McCormick Twin Bridges
775.0 St. Augustine Inlet Area (SB)
778.1 Bridge of Lions
779.0 St. Augustine Inlet Area (NB)
788.8 Crescent Beach Bridge
816.0 L.B. Knox Bridge
829.7 Daytona Beach Main St. Bridge
830.6 Daytona Beach Memorial Bridge
838.0 Ponce de Leon Inlet Area (SB)
845.0 George Munson Bridge
847.0 Ponce de Leon Inlet Area (NB)
869.1 Allenhurst Bridge

Exit Salt Run channel. Proceed WSW in privately maintained channel to marina.

- **Salt Run Anchorage** (1.5)
Anchor 8-10 feet N29.53.306
STR 5.2 feet W081.17.113
Depart Salt Run channel at R16. Proceed NE slightly out of channel.

778.0 St. Augustine Anchorage (North)(0.1)
Anchor 8-12 feet N29.53.625
STR 5.3 feet W081.18.560
Exit ICW N of bridge. Proceed W.
This anchorage is the less crowded of St. Augustine's anchorages, with less current. Water is deep close to shore.

778.1 Bridge of Lions
VHF 09; 904/360-5300
Double bascule; vertical 25 feet.
Restricted year round: M-F except holidays, 0700-1800 hrs, opens on the hour and half-hour except 0800, 1200 and 1700 hrs; SA-SU and holidays, 0700-1800 hrs, opens on the hour and half-hour.
See Bridge of Lions.
Note: The Bridge of Lions will be under construction from 2005-2009. During this time, a temporary bridge will be built north of the existing bridge.

778.2 St. Augustine Municipal Marina (0.1)
VHF 16/71 N29.53.505
904/825-1026 W081.18.487
Exit ICW S of bridge. Proceed W to marina. [STR 5.3 (TS)]
The City plans to add mooring balls in the future.
See St. Augustine.

778.3 St. Augustine Anchorage (South)(0.1)
Anchor 12-18 feet N29.53.425
STR 5.3 feet W081.18.424
Exit ICW S of bridge. Proceed W.
Caution: For deep-keeled vessels, note 6-foot charted shoal.

779.0 Heads Up | St. Augustine Inlet Area
to Northbound Navigation Only
775.0 Transiting the St. Augustine Inlet area is confusing for many cruisers. Head NE across Davis Shores, being sure to round R60 at the charted shoals, then head northerly to bridge.
Caution: This area is a minefield of aids. Many small red nuns have been placed to keep you eastward of the large shoal area at the inlet's junction. Be sure to safely round R60 as you transit this area. When in doubt, favor Cape Francis or the Vilano Beach shorelines.

779.8 Fish Island Marina (0.1)
VHF 16; 904/471-1955
Exit ICW NNE of bridges. Proceed ESE to marina. [STR 5.3]

780.0 San Sebastian River
Exit ICW NNE of bridges. Proceed up charted San Sebastian River. [STR 5.3]

HUGUENOT BEACH

If Los Angeles filmmakers need to shoot a Persian Gulf scene, don't expect them to travel to the Middle East. Fortunately, they have Huguenot Beach, a much safer location just east of the Waterway along the north shore of St. Johns River.

If you depart the Waterway at St. Johns River, either to dock at Mayport or use St. Johns Entrance, look for the large elbow spit off Ft. George Island. This is Huguenot Beach. Aim your camera lens just right and it's the Persian Gulf. At least this is how cinematographers visualize these dunes.

Given the number of recent movies about the Persian Gulf, this similarity saves moviemakers a lot of expense. *G.I. Jane* with Demi Moore was filmed here in 1996. Most recently, the Persian Gulf scenes in *The Manchurian Candidate* (2004) starring Denzel Washington and Meryl Streep, were also shot at Huguenot Beach on Ft. George Island.

Even after the cleanup, the smell of diesel fuel seems to linger forever. To eliminate the odor, wipe down the spill surface with vinegar. To remove the lingering smell of vinegar...

THE CANAL THAT WASN'T

To the west of the ICW, St. Johns River leads to Jacksonville, then continues south another 40 miles to the town of Palatka. Had things turned out differently, you would have been able to shortcut to the central Gulf coast from Palatka via the 110-mile Cross Florida Barge Canal. Instead, the Gulf-to-Atlantic inland shortcut is 250 miles south at the Okeechobee Waterway.

The Cross Florida Barge Canal, intended as a major deep water ship canal, was one of the biggest public works projects ever planned for Florida. Work began in the 1930s but funding, and progress, was sporadic for decades. By the late 1960s, the idea of running freighters through the agricultural and wild lands of northern Florida didn't seem like such a great idea. Worried about its environmental impact, public opinion on the canal turned strongly negative. In 1971, with the canal only one-third complete, President Nixon signed an executive order suspending further work.

In 1998, the neglected and overgrown corridor was designated as a natural greenway. Hiking and equestrian trails were built through the old barge canal and along the natural rivers. It was named the Marjorie Harris Carr Cross Florida Greenway, in honor of the woman who led the fight to stop the canal project.

CABBAGE SWAMP

Between STM 750.1 and STM 760.1, you pass through Cabbage Swamp, named after the Cabbage Palmetto. Native Americans came to Cabbage Swamp to collect Cabbage Palmetto, a coveted food source.

Courtesy of St. Lucie County TDC

Photo by Tom Baumker

Florida Red-Bellied Cooter

They harvested the palmettos as young shoots, about the size of a head of cabbage. They probably ate them raw, like celery, cutting off the green buds and peeling off the outside fibers. Later on, perhaps after they introduced this locally grown vegetable to early settlers, Cabbage Palmetto was cooked with smoked meat. Supposedly it tastes like cauliflower, which is in the cabbage family. But despite its name, Cabbage Palmetto is a palm not a cabbage.

Lots of amps but still sour milk? A small battery-operated fan placed on the upper shelf of your refrigerator will distribute the cold air more evenly. Your food will stay fresher and your compressor will work less.

SAFETY INFO

NOAA Weather	Sea Tow
WX-2 Savannah, GA	St. Augustine, FL
WX-1 Jacksonville, FL	VHF 16/10
WX-2 Daytona Beach, FL	904/824-9969
USCG	**TowBoatU.S.**
Station Mayport, FL	St. Augustine, FL
VHF 16 or 09/22A	VHF 16/18
904/564-7592	386/322-5582

HEADS UP!

713.7	Cumberland Sound Channel (NB)	816.0	L.B. Knox Bridge
714.0	GA-FL Border	829.7	Daytona Beach Main St. Bridge
720.7	Kingsley Creek RR Bridge	830.6	Daytona Beach Memorial Bridge
739.1	Sisters Creek Bridge	838.0	Ponce de Leon Inlet Area (SB)
747.4	B.B. McCormick Twin Bridges	845.0	George Munson Bridge
775.0	St. Augustine Inlet Area (SB)	847.0	Ponce de Leon Inlet Area (NB)
778.1	Bridge of Lions	869.1	Allenhurst Bridge
779.0	St. Augustine Inlet Area (NB)	875.0	Bridge Caution (SB)
788.8	**Crescent Beach Bridge**	876.6	NASA RR Bridge

ST. AUGUSTINE

St. Augustine has many claims to old, olde, and oldest. The city, called "America's Oldest City," is officially the oldest continuously occupied European settlement in the continental United States. If you walk the tourist district you may spot the "oldest house," "oldest wooden schoolhouse," or "oldest stone fort." St. Augustine, dating back to 1565, is indeed old: it was founded 55 years before the Pilgrims landed at Plymouth Rock.

Courtesy of St. Augustine VCB

Castillo de San Marcos

If you don't let the tourist business get to you, the city has stunning architecture and many local events. During the winter months, the city is decorated with over a million tiny white lights during its Nights of Lights Festival. Art galleries open their doors with refreshments and art from 5:00 to 9:00 pm, with free transportation provided by the St. Augustine Sightseeing Train.

Flagler College, located a few blocks from the municipal marina and anchorage, offers tours of its stunning campus, formerly the Flagler Hotel built by Henry Flagler in 1887. The campus has spent more than $23 million restoring the Spanish Renaissance buildings, which include 79 Tiffany stained glass windows and an electrical and water system designed by Thomas Edison.

Castillo de San Marcos, a Spanish fort dating back to 1672, and the Mission of Nombre de Dios, where the first Easter Mass in the New World was held, are also both within easy walking distance of the marinas and anchorages.

A bit further away, across the Bridge of Lions, the Alligator Farm is worth the trip. Locals rave about this amphibian and reptile zoo, which has more in common with a small natural zoo than a farm. It's the only facility in the world with every species of crocodilian.

If you visit in March, the boardwalk takes you right through the center of a Snowy Egret rookery, so close to the boardwalk you can see the chicks. These beautiful birds, and many other waders including the endangered Wood Stork, have discovered alligators make perfect bodyguards. The alligators don't threaten the egrets' nests and their presence is a big deterrent to the Snowy Egrets' primary nest predator: the raccoon.

St. Augustine VCB
www.visitoldcity.com
800/653-2489

Flagler College Legacy Tours
www.flagler.edu
904/823-3378

Castillo de San Marcos
www.nps.gov/casa
904/829-6506

Mission of Nombre de Dios
www.missionandshrine.org
904/824-2809

Alligator Farm
www.alligatorfarm.com
904/824-3337

BRIDGE OF LIONS

For many cruisers, the Bridge of Lions is the most beautiful bridge along the Waterway. It's a classic 1920s design, with clean lines and red-roofed bridge towers, affectionately decorated with the city's banners during the day and hundreds of lights during the winter nights. Stately marble lions, balancing their paws on spheres, guard each end of the bridge.

St. Augustine VCB

Bridge of Lions

But the Department of Transportation recently declared the bridge, which is on the National Register of Historic Places, "structurally deficient and functionally obsolete." Residents rallied behind their historic bridge, securing a $45 million rehabilitation project to preserve the functionality and life of the bridge. They also insisted the lions remain on the new bridge, so they will be temporarily stored and treated until the bridge renovation is complete.

- **St. Augustine Marine** (1.0)
  VHF 16 N29.52.697
  904/824-4394 W081.18.877
  Facility is to starboard.
- **Oasis Boat Yard & Marina** (1.3)
  VHF 16; 904/824-2520
  Facility is to starboard. Repair yard with no transient dockage.
- **Oyster Creek Marina** (2.1)
  VHF 16; 904/827-0520
  Marina is to port.
  Also known as Oyster Harbor Marina.

780.4 Mickler O'Connel Bridge
(Route 312)
Fixed; vertical 65 feet.

781.1 Matanzas River Anchorage (North)(0.4)
Anchor 8-12 feet N29.50.903
STR 5.2 feet W081.18.207
Exit ICW NW of R18. Proceed SSE into charted tongue to anchor behind R20.

784.1 Matanzas River Anchorage (Mid)(0.2)
Anchor 10-12 feet N29.48.964
STR 5.1 feet W081.17.530
Exit ICW N of G31. Proceed SSE into charted tongue.

785.2 Matanzas River Anchorage (South)(0.1)
Anchor 8-10 feet N29.48.454
STR 5.1 feet W081.16.993
Exit ICW W of R38. Proceed S to charted pocket.

786.5 Butler Beach Anchorage (0.5)
Anchor 6-8 feet N29.47.302
STR 5.0 feet W081.16.160
Exit ICW at G43. Proceed SSE to Butler Beach tongue.

788.8 Crescent Beach Bridge
(Cerle Allyn Pope Bridge)(Route 206)
VHF 09; 904/360-5300
Double bascule; vertical 25 feet; on request.

792.4 Fort Matanzas Anchorage (0.4)
Anchor 8-10 feet N29.43.059
STR 5.0 feet W081.14.512
Exit ICW at G81. Proceed southeasterly in Matanzas River to anchor off Fort Matanzas.
Caution: Entrance shoaled to less than 5 feet.
Dinghy to park dock at Fort Matanzas.
SEE SPANISH BAYONETS.

796.5 Marineland Marina (0.2)
No VHF Watch; 888/279-9194
Exit ICW between G87 and G89. Proceed E in privately maintained channel to marina. [STR 4.0]
The marina is currently closed but, according to officials, should re-open by late 2006.
SEE MARINELAND.

796.7 Marineland Anchorage (0.1)
Anchor 6-8 feet N29.39.864
STR 4.0 feet W081.13.089
Exit ICW at R90. Proceed W out of ICW channel.

SAFETY INFO

NOAA Weather
WX-1 Jacksonville, FL
WX-2 Daytona Beach, FL
WX-1 Melbourne, FL

USCG
Station New Smyrna, FL
VHF 16 or 09/22A
386/428-9085

Sea Tow
Daytona/Ponce, FL
VHF 16/11 or 68 or 09
386/767-1508

TowBoatU.S.
Daytona Beach, FL
VHF 16/18
386/322-5582

HEADS UP!

714.0 GA-FL Border
720.7 Kingsley Creek RR Bridge
739.1 Sisters Creek Bridge
747.4 B.B. McCormick Twin Bridges
775.0 St. Augustine Inlet Area (SB)
778.1 Bridge of Lions
779.0 St. Augustine Inlet Area (NB)
788.8 Crescent Beach Bridge
816.0 L.B. Knox Bridge
829.7 Daytona Beach Main St. Bridge
830.6 Daytona Beach Memorial Bridge
838.0 Ponce de Leon Inlet Area (SB)
845.0 George Munson Bridge
847.0 Ponce de Leon Inlet Area (NB)
869.1 Allenhurst Bridge
875.0 Bridge Caution (SB)
876.6 NASA RR Bridge
878.7 Max Brewer Bridge

Marineland is open but boat docks are under construction.
Dinghy to Pellicer Creek | Princess Place Reserve.
SEE A FLORIDA FIRST.

799.8 Palm Coast Land Cut
to Southbound Navigation Only
808.0 8.2-mile land cut.
No anchorages, multiple marinas, fuel available.
Fox Cut is between G1 and G3.
SEE HERNANDEZ'S PLANTATION.

802.8 Palm Coast Marina (0.2)
VHF 16/69 N29.34.625
386/446-6370 W081.11.640
Exit ICW N of bridge. Proceed W into southernmost charted canal. Fuel dock and transient reception are to port, before short bridge. [STR 2.0]

803.1 Palm Coast Parkway Bridge
Fixed; vertical 65 feet.

808.0 Palm Coast Land Cut
to Northbound Navigation Only
799.8 8.2-mile land cut.
No anchorages, multiple marinas, fuel available.
Fox Cut is between G1 and G3.
SEE STRAIGHTEN THIS CURVE.

809.2 Cement Plant Anchorage (0.3)
Anchor 16-20 feet N29.29.827
STR 1.0 feet W081.08.900
Exit ICW between G11 and G13. Proceed W into charted canal to anchor beyond Sea Ray plant.

810.7 Flagler Beach Bridge
Fixed; vertical 65 feet. [STR 1.0 (TS)]

816.0 L.B. Knox Bridge
(Bulow Bridge)(High Bridge)
VHF 09; 386/441-0777
Double bascule; vertical 15 feet; on request.

817.7 Halifax Creek Anchorage (0.1)
Anchor 5-8 feet N29.23.109
STR 1.0 feet W081.05.387
Exit ICW N of R30. Proceed W.
Dinghy about 2 miles S into Tomoka Basin to see shell middens.
SEE A FREE WATERWAY & ANCIENT TRASH HEAPS.

824.9 Ormond Beach Bridge
(Route 40)
Fixed; vertical 65 feet. [STR 0.7 (TS)]
SEE ROCKEFELLER'S RETIREMENT HOME.

829.1 Seabreeze Bridge Anchorage (North)(0.1)
Anchor 8-12 feet N29.13.954
STR 1.0 feet W081.01.336
Exit ICW NNW of (old) bridge. Proceed ENE.

829.2 Seabreeze Bridge
Fixed; vertical 65 feet.

829.3 Seabreeze Bridge Anchorage (South)(0.1)
Anchor 8-12 feet N29.13.787
STR 1.0 feet W081.01.232
Exit ICW SSE of (new) bridge. Proceed ENE.

ST. AUGUSTINE LIGHT

St. Augustine Light is believed to be located near the site of the first lighthouse in Florida. In 1821, when Americans claimed this territory, they discovered an old tower, presumed to be an abandoned lighthouse built by the Spaniards.

Courtesy of St. Augustine VCB

Flagler College

Without thinking first about erosion, a replacement lighthouse was built in 1824. Within decades, storm-driven erosion undermined the land and was lapping within ten feet of the foundation. Workers tried to keep the old lighthouse working by creating jetties of brush and coquina, stalling for time until a new lighthouse could be built.

The new (1874) lighthouse on Anastasia Island was located about a half mile away. Almost identical to the lighthouses at Currituck Beach and Cape Hatteras, the 161-foot brick tower was painted barber-style in black-and-white spirals. The light is no longer in operation, but the lighthouse is open to the public. You can dinghy in from Salt Run and walk up the 219 steps for a phenomenal view of St. Augustine.

St. Augustine Lighthouse
www.staugustinelighthouse.com
904/829-0745

SPANISH BAYONETS

In 1565, when a group of French Huguenots left their settlement near Jacksonville to attack the Spaniards at St. Augustine, battle plans went badly awry. They were blown off course, unable to locate St. Augustine Inlet, and shipwrecked south of St. Augustine near Matanzas Inlet.

The Spanish discovered the Huguenots on the beach and after forcing their surrender, demanded they convert from Protestantism to Catholicism. The Frenchmen surrendered, but refused to renounce their faith. Don Pedro Menéndez de Avilés, the founder of St. Augustine, ordered the 300 Frenchmen's hands tied and led them behind the sand dunes, where they were stabbed to death. The word *matanza*, Spanish for "massacre," is the name of the river and the inlet.

Nearly two hundred years after the bloodshed, Spanish settlers built a fort on Rattlesnake Island to guard St. Augustine from backdoor enemies approaching through Matanzas Inlet. Fort Matanzas, at STM 792.4, is named after this massacre. The masonry fort still stands and is open to the public with guided tours and walking paths.

Fort Matanzas National Park
www.nps.gov/foma
904/471-0116

LA MATANZA DE LAS TORTUGAS

It's truly amazing that some animals survived the early settlers of Florida. Actually, many didn't make it. Carolina Parakeets once flew in huge green flocks over the Southeast. They were killed by hunters and wiped out by the 1920s. The Ivory-billed Woodpecker also disappeared from the Southeast, a victim of the loss of the great Longleaf Pine forests. Sea turtles barely escaped the brink of extinction, saved only by recent protection of their nests and nesting sites.

Courtesy of National Park Service

Spanish Bayonets at Fort Matanzas

For hundreds of years, hunting for sea turtles was easy pickin' along these shores. Fisherman would wait along the beaches on moonlit nights, as hundreds of turtles came out of the water to rest on the warm beach sand. A fisherman would give the signal and the men would run among the turtles, flipping

SAFETY INFO

NOAA Weather
WX-1 Jacksonville, FL
WX-2 Daytona Beach, FL
WX-1 Melbourne, FL

USCG
Station New Smyrna, FL
VHF 16 or 09/22A
386/428-9085

Sea Tow
Daytona/Ponce, FL
VHF 16/11 or 68 or 09
386/767-1508

TowBoatU.S.
Daytona Beach, FL
VHF 16/18
386/322-5582

HEADS UP!

739.1	Sisters Creek Bridge
747.4	B.B. McCormick Twin Bridges
775.0	St. Augustine Inlet Area (SB)
778.1	Bridge of Lions
779.0	St. Augustine Inlet Area (NB)
788.8	Crescent Beach Bridge
816.0	L.B. Knox Bridge
829.7	**Daytona Beach Main St. Bridge**
830.6	**Daytona Beach Memorial Bridge**
838.0	Ponce de Leon Inlet Area (SB)
845.0	George Munson Bridge
847.0	Ponce de Leon Inlet Area (NB)
869.1	Allenhurst Bridge
875.0	Bridge Caution (SB)
876.6	NASA RR Bridge
878.7	Max Brewer Bridge
885.0	NASA Causeway Bridge
890.0	Bridge Caution (NB)

them on their backs so they couldn't escape. It was a simple matter of picking up the helpless turtles.

Courtesy of NASA

Releasing a Tagged Turtle

It hasn't been long since sea turtles and their eggs were on the menu. Moonlight turtle egg hunting was popular into the 1930s. Accounts of turtle egg hunts here at STM 794 describe collecting 300 to 400 eggs in a single outing. A guide to the Waterway from 1937 described the sea turtle nests not in terms of conservation, but how to cook the eggs. "Unlike hen eggs, turtle eggs have a soft but tough shell, dented at one end. They can be boiled for hours, yet the contents will remain… soft-boiled."

Today, sea turtle nesting areas are protected and carefully monitored. Despite raccoons and beach development, they now have a fighting chance.

Add nonskid material throughout your boat. We use two kinds: (1) 3M Safety Walk Nonskid Tape on companionway steps and gelcoat areas the designer or builder "missed" and (2) Scoot-Gard or generic rubber nonskid rolls to line galley cabinets and drawers so dishes and other items won't rattle or slide. We carry a roll of butcher's paper to make templates, then easily cut replacement nonskid when soiled or to brighten up an area with a color change.

MARINELAND: YES, IT'S OPEN

We often hear, "Is Marineland open or isn't it"? Although most cruisers notice the historic oceanarium at STM 796.7, just south of G87, few people know what has happened to Marineland since its bankruptcy in 1998.

The good news is, despite setbacks from the 2004 hurricanes, Marineland is once again open to visitors. The multimillion dollar renovations are scheduled for completion by spring of 2005.

This Florida icon has survived tougher times. Marineland was built in 1938 as the world's first underwater motion picture studio. But World War II forced the closure of the facility. The marine animals had to be moved to other sites or released into the ocean. The facility quickly shifted to military research, searching for a concoction to repel sharks and save seamen.

Julia Child, then a young woman working for the OSS and not yet a famous chef, helped cook up these distasteful shark recipes.

After the war, tanks were re-stocked and tourists and filmmakers returned. Through the 1950s, films like *Creature of the Black Lagoon* and *Tarzan* were shot in Marineland's simulated ocean floor tank. Today Marineland is still used for TV film shoots, conducts research on marine mammals, and has programs for visitors.

Marineland
www.marineland.net
888/279-9194

A FLORIDA FIRST

Flagler County is committed to its parks. Already over 20 miles of land along the Waterway has been set aside as part of a National Estuarine Research Reserve, including parts of Guana, Tolmato, and Matanzas Rivers. The entire Pellicer Creek, at STM 797, is part of a 505-acre aquatic preserve, meaning the state owns and protects the creek bottom and its tidal lands and islands. Flagler County recently acquired a spectacular 1500-acre property on the south side of Pellicer Creek to add to its collection, named Princess Place Reserve.

If you stay at the Marineland anchorage (STM 796.7), you can dinghy into shallow Pellicer Creek to visit this new park. There is a small boat launch and the park is now open to the public. The property is named after the wife of an exiled Russian prince who lived at the property for over 50 years. She built a hunting lodge in 1887, the oldest standing structure in Flagler County.

Princess Sherbatoff was a home design trendsetter. Like many contemporary architects, she incorporated local materials. The design of the lodge is from New York's Adirondack Camp

829.4 Caribbean Jack's Marina (0.1)
VHF 16; 386/523-3000
Exit ICW SSE of R32. Marina is to W. [STR 1.0]

829.7 Daytona Beach Main Street Bridge
VHF 09; 386/239-6477
Double bascule; vertical 22 feet; on request.
SEE BIRTHPLACE OF SPEED.

830.2 Carlton Black Bridge
(International Speedway Boulevard)
Fixed; vertical 65 feet.

830.6 Daytona Beach Memorial Bridge
(Orange Avenue Bridge)
VHF 09; 386/239-6540
Double bascule; vertical 21 feet.
Restricted year round: M-SA except holidays, 0745-0845 and 1645-1745 hrs, opens at 0815 and 1715 hrs.

830.7 Halifax River Yacht Club (0.3)
VHF 16; 386/255-7459
Exit ICW SSE of bridge. Proceed W to charted (northern) basin. Yacht club is ahead. [STR 1.0]
Accepts guests of members and offers reciprocal rights to members of accredited yacht clubs.
Facility to S is Daytona Beach Municipal Yacht Basin, the live-aboard and long-term transient area managed by Halifax Harbor Marina.

830.7 Memorial Bridge Anchorage (0.3)
Anchor 10-12 feet N29.12.443
STR 1.0 feet W081.00.370
Exit ICW SSE of bridge. Using charted Municipal Yacht Basin channel as a back range, proceed E then SSE to charted 11-foot pocket. Anchor behind G39.

831.1 Halifax Harbor Marina (0.3)
VHF 16; 386/671-3600
Exit ICW at G39 "A". Proceed WSW to large charted (middle) basin. Fuel dock and marina office are to starboard. [STR 1.0]

831.2 Daytona Marina & Boat Works (0.2)
VHF 16/72 N29.12.080
386/252-6421 W081.00.725
Exit ICW between R40 and G39 "A". Proceed WSW to marked channel and (southern) basin. Fuel dock and harbormaster are to starboard. [STR 1.0]

831.3 Daytona Anchorages
to Southbound/Northbound Navigation
833.4 ICW R40 to R50
Caution: For many years any of these "wide spots" were satisfactory anchorages. However, frequent shoaling and dredge spoil removal has made the bottom irregular and not as charted. These anchorages are not recommended.

835.1 Seven Seas Marina & Boatyard (0.1)
VHF 16/72; 386/761-3221
Exit ICW at R56. Proceed ENE in marked channel to marina. [STR 2.0]

835.5 Port Orange Bridge
Fixed; vertical 65 feet.

SAFETY INFO

NOAA Weather
WX-1 Jacksonville, FL
WX-2 Daytona Beach, FL
WX-1 Melbourne, FL

USCG
Station New Smyrna, FL
VHF 16 or 09/22A
386/428-9085

Sea Tow
Daytona/Ponce, FL
VHF 16/11 or 68 or 09
386/767-1508

TowBoatU.S.
Daytona Beach, FL
VHF 16/18
386/322-5582

HEADS UP!

775.0	St. Augustine Inlet Area (SB)
778.1	Bridge of Lions
779.0	St. Augustine Inlet Area (NB)
788.8	Crescent Beach Bridge
816.0	L.B. Knox Bridge
829.7	Daytona Beach Main St. Bridge
830.6	Daytona Beach Memorial Bridge
838.0	**Ponce de Leon Inlet Area (SB)**
845.0	**George Munson Bridge**
847.0	Ponce de Leon Inlet Area (NB)
869.1	Allenhurst Bridge
875.0	Bridge Caution (SB)
876.6	NASA RR Bridge
878.7	Max Brewer Bridge
885.0	NASA Causeway Bridge
890.0	Bridge Caution (NB)
964.8	Ft. Pierce North Bridge
984.9	Ernest Lyons Bridge

836.8 Adventure Yacht Harbor (0.4)
VHF 16/18 N29.07.879
386/756-2180 W080.57.713
Exit ICW between G59 and R60. Proceed E in privately maintained channel to marina. [STR 3.0]

838.0 Heads Up | Ponce de Leon Inlet Area
to Southbound Navigation Only
847.0 This area is consistently a problem for transiting cruisers due to frequent dredging and new marker placement. Be extremely vigilant.
SEE MONSTER'S LAST RESORT.

839.6 Junction | Ponce de Leon Inlet
Southbound Navigation Only
Exit ICW at G3. Favoring Live Oak Point, proceed SE for marinas and Ponce de Leon Inlet. [STR 3.4 (TS)]
SEE PONCE DE LEON LIGHT.
Caution: ICW aid numbers "re-start" at this junction. Carefully identify ICW G1, R2, and G3 (triangles and squares) versus Ponce Inlet Channel G1.

- **Sea Love Marina & Boat Works** (1.4)
  VHF 16/07 N29.04.885
  386/761-5434 W080.56.129
  Facility is to port.
- **Lighthouse Boat Yard** (2.0)
  VHF 16; 386/767-0683
  Exit channel into privately maintained channel. Facility is ahead.
- **Ponce de Leon Inlet** (4.1)
  This inlet, although frequently used by commercial and sport fishing boats, is not recommended without local knowledge.

842.3 Rockhouse Creek Anchorage (0.2)
Anchor 6-10 feet N29.03.661
STR 3.4 feet W080.55.873
Exit ICW between R10 and R12. Proceed NE to Rockhouse Creek.

843.5 Junction | Ponce de Leon Inlet (3.1)
Northbound Navigation Only
Exit ICW at G19. Proceed northerly to Ponce de Leon Inlet.
This inlet, although frequently used by commercial and sport fishing boats, is not recommended without local knowledge.

845.0 George Munson Bridge
(Coronado Beach Bridge)(New Smyrna Bridge)
VHF 09; 386/424-2024
Single bascule; vertical 24 feet.
Restricted year round: 0700-1900 hrs, opens on the hour, twenty minutes past, and forty minutes past the hour.

845.1 Riverview Hotel & Marina (0.1)
VHF 16; Tel.386/428-5858
Exit ICW S of bridge. Marina is to E. [STR 3.0]

845.5 Junction | Sheephead Cut Alternate Route
to Southbound Navigation Only
846.3 0.8-mile alternate route.
Exit ICW at GR Bn (eastern end of Chicken Island). Proceed southwesterly along well-aided channel.

Style, but was built with pink coquina mined from local beaches. The wraparound porch is built of local cedar and palm trunks.

The Princess also added a new architectural feature to her country home, the first in the state of Florida. Today Florida is dotted with millions of these amenities, visible from the air as tiny dots of turquoise blue...she built the state's first in-ground swimming pool.

Princess Place Reserve
www.flaglerparks.com
386/446-7658

MULLET SNACKS

During the early 1900s, broad and shallow Pellicer Creek at STM 797 was the popular spot to cast for mullet. Mullet, like herring, won't take a hook and must be caught with nets. Look for fishermen standing in the water, skillfully using a cast net, a 5,000-year-old technique to catch fish. When thrown properly, the circular net, seeded with weights around the perimeter, opens like an umbrella and falls over the school of fish.

Back in the 1930s, mullet were a popular food, eaten fresh, salted, or smoked. The roe was considered a delicacy. But as with turtle eggs, culinary trends come and go. Today mullet is an important baitfish.

HERNANDEZ'S PLANTATION

General Joseph Hernandez once owned the land along the Waterway, near STM 799, as part of his large Bella Vista Plantation.

Hernandez came from a long line of sub-tropical farmers, descended from Minorcans brought to the New World to establish tropical farming in Florida. In 1768, eight ships arrived in St. Augustine, carrying about 1400 men, women, and children from Greece, Italy, Turkey, and Minorca, the tiny island off the eastern coast of Spain.

Hernandez may have been a farmer, but he was also famous as a military leader during the Seminole Wars. Between uprisings, he quietly cultivated sea cotton and oranges here along the Waterway.

Unfortunately, his military success ultimately cost him his homestead. In retaliation for his leadership in the Seminole Wars, Seminole Indians burned his entire plantation to the ground.

Today much of Hernandez's land is preserved as parks, as the Washington Oaks State Gardens east of the ICW between R100 and R106, and Bings Landings a bit further south. Washington Oaks is now a formal garden owned by the state, formerly owned by the Chairman of the Board of General Electric. Bings Landing, located near the north end of the cut, is the small park with the picnic area and boat ramp. Archaeologists have discovered the foundations of Hernandez's early plantation buildings at this site and are currently excavating the foundations of his home.

Washington Oaks
www.floridastateparks.org
386/446-6780

Courtesy of Flagler County Chamber of Commerce

Flagler County ICW

STRAIGHTEN THIS CURVE

Notice anything unusual on the chart at STM 804? The Waterway, then called the East Coast Canal, originally took a sharp 90-degree turn at G1. You can still see the old route on the chart, marked "abandoned."

Apparently President Herbert Hoover was transiting the canal aboard the presidential yacht *Sequoia*. But when the *Sequoia* made the abrupt turn at G1, Hoover was thrown from his chair. As the story goes, Hoover angrily shouted, "Someone ought to straighten out this damn curve."

So they did. Now the Waterway proceeds nearly straight at STM 804. In

SAFETY INFO

NOAA Weather
WX-1 Jacksonville, FL
WX-2 Daytona Beach, FL
WX-1 Melbourne, FL

USCG
Station New Smyrna, FL
VHF 16 or 09/22A
386/428-9085

Sea Tow
Daytona/Ponce, FL
VHF 16/11 or 68 or 09
386/767-1508

TowBoatU.S.
Daytona Beach, FL
VHF 16/18
386/322-5582

HEADS UP!

778.1	Bridge of Lions
779.0	St. Augustine Inlet Area (NB)
788.8	Crescent Beach Bridge
816.0	L.B. Knox Bridge
829.7	Daytona Beach Main St. Bridge
830.6	Daytona Beach Memorial Bridge
838.0	Ponce de Leon Inlet Area (SB)
845.0	George Munson Bridge
847.0	**Ponce de Leon Inlet Area (NB)**
869.1	Allenhurst Bridge
875.0	Bridge Caution (SB)
876.6	NASA RR Bridge
878.7	Max Brewer Bridge
885.0	NASA Causeway Bridge
890.0	Bridge Caution (NB)
964.8	Ft. Pierce North Bridge
984.9	Ernest Lyons Bridge
995.9	Hobe Sound Bridge

the process, a new island was created, once overgrown and aptly named Snake Island, now the development of Island Estates. The name *Fox Cut* was given in thanks to Mr. Fox, the manager of a dredging company who cleared through a bad slide that blocked the steam-powered paddleboat traffic for several days.

BULOW PLANTATION RUINS

There comes a time when every mariner decides it's time to swallow the anchor: to trade the physical demands of a boat for a piece of land.

That's what happened to James Russel, who swapped his schooner for 5,000 acres of fertile high ground along the western banks of Halifax Creek at STM 815.5. He later sold the property to Charles Bulow, who during the 1800s developed the land into the largest sugar cane plantation in the country, now known as the Bulow Plantation Ruins Historic State Park.

Today only the scattered ruins of the mill, the manor house, and the workers' village remain as part of a large state park. In its better times, the plantation hosted John James Audubon, who wandered these marshes and woods to collect specimens for his famous paintings in *Birds of America*.

Bulow Plantation Ruins
www.floridastateparks.org
386/517-2084

A FREE WATERWAY

If it were 1925, you'd have to pay the equivalent of $31 to enter narrow Halifax Creek at STM 818. Back then, a $3 fee dropped the cross-canal chain so your boat could pass through.

Today the Intracoastal Waterway is entirely free and publicly owned. But the days of tolls and chains are a reminder of the value of a free, navigable inland passage.

ANCIENT TRASH HEAPS

The small peninsula at STM 820, jutting into the Tomoka Basin and formed by the intersection of Tomoka and Halifax Rivers, was once a Timucuan Native American village. The Spaniards documented a village called Nocoroco at this site in 1605, but Native Americans probably lived here since 5,000 BC.

Like modern societies, Native American communities produced refuse. But unlike our modern Mount Trashmores, their heaps of refuse are non-toxic: hundreds of years of discarded oyster and snail shells, fish bones, and tiny pieces of pottery shards.

Courtesy of NOAA

Photo by William B. Folsom

Brown Pelican

Native American landfills, called shell middens, remain along the ICW near Ormond Beach. Now overgrown, they are still visible as unusual mounds of high ground, often growing with different vegetation. For example, middens in a mangrove key might be covered with red-barked gumbo limbo trees. On the Tomoka peninsula, now part of the Tomoka State Park, the middens are visible as mounded high ground growing with wild coffee and tropical sage.

If you're walking in the town of Ormond, you'll find another midden located northeast of Ormond Beach Bridge (STM 824.9) at the corner of Mound Avenue and South Beach Street. It's one of the few remaining middens not lost to development, preserved by the community in 1982. But don't write it off as simply a mound of garbage. This ancient trash heap contained 125 skeletal remains and the refuse of a community that lived here in 800 AD.

ROCKEFELLER'S RETIREMENT HOME

Two unusual retirement hangouts overlook the Waterway near Ormond Beach Bridge.

John D. Rockefeller's retirement home—called The Casements after its many casement windows—is located at the southeast corner of the bridge, overlooking Halifax River. Rockefeller, Henry Flagler's partner in the Standard Oil Company, lived here until he died at age 97.

Rejoin ICW at GR Bn (N of Harris Saxon Bridge).
Caution: Not recommended as an anchorage because of swift currents and narrow channel.

846.1 North Causeway Marine (0.1)
No VHF Watch N29.01.697
386/427-5267 W080.55.187
Exit ICW NW of G37. Proceed westerly behind small island. [STR 3.0]

846.1 New Smyrna Beach City Marina (0.1)
VHF 16; Telephone TBA
Exit ICW at G39. Proceed WNW toward bridge. [STR 3.0]
Marina is undergoing extensive renovation. Completion expected in 2005.

846.2 Fishin' Cove Marina (0.1)
VHF 16; 386/428-7827
Exit ICW opposite Sheephead Cut. Proceed W. [STR 3.0]
Dry store with no transient dockage.

846.3 Junction | Sheephead Cut Alternate Route
to 845.5
Northbound Navigation Only
0.8-mile alternate route.
Exit ICW at GR Bn. Proceed northeasterly along well-aided channel. Rejoin ICW at GR Bn (eastern end of Chicken Island).
Caution: Not recommended as an anchorage because of swift currents and narrow channel.

846.5 Harris Saxon Bridge
(South Causeway Bridge)
Fixed; vertical 65 feet.

847.0 Smyrna Yacht Club (0.1)
VHF 16; 386/427-4040
Exit ICW between G43 and R46. Proceed ENE to yacht club. [STR 2.0]
Accepts guests of members and offers reciprocal rights to members of accredited yacht clubs.

847.0 Heads Up | Ponce de Leon Inlet Area
to 838.0
Northbound Navigation Only
This area is consistently a problem for transiting cruisers due to frequent dredging and new marker placement. Be extremely vigilant.

862.8 Mosquito Lagoon Anchorage (North)(0.2)
Anchor 8-10 feet N28.48.624
STR 0.0 feet W080.47.477
Exit ICW at R24. Proceed to charted 10-foot pocket behind charted submerged pile.
SEE MANGROVE MAZE.
Note: Government tide tables state, "From Oak Hill southward in Mosquito Lagoon the periodic tide is negligible."

864.1 Mosquito Lagoon Anchorage (South)(0.1)
Anchor 6-7 feet N28.47.776
STR 0.0 feet W080.46.974
Exit ICW between G27 and G29. Proceed ENE.
SEE MOSQUITO LAGOON.

868.5 Haulover Canal
to 869.7
Southbound Navigation Only
1.2-mile land cut.

SAFETY INFO

NOAA Weather
WX-2 Daytona Beach, FL
WX-1 Melbourne, FL
WX-3 West Palm Beach, FL

USCG
Station Port Canaveral, FL
VHF 16 or 09/22A
321/868-4200

Sea Tow
Port Canaveral, FL
VHF 16/11 or 69
321/868-4900

TowBoatU.S.
Titusville, FL
VHF 16/18
386/322-5582

HEADS UP!

816.0	L.B. Knox Bridge
829.7	Daytona Beach Main St. Bridge
830.6	Daytona Beach Memorial Bridge
838.0	Ponce de Leon Inlet Area (SB)
845.0	George Munson Bridge
847.0	Ponce de Leon Inlet Area (NB)
869.1	Allenhurst Bridge
875.0	**Bridge Caution (SB)**
876.6	**NASA RR Bridge**
878.7	**Max Brewer Bridge**
885.0	NASA Causeway Bridge
890.0	Bridge Caution (NB)
964.8	Ft. Pierce North Bridge
984.9	Ernest Lyons Bridge
995.9	Hobe Sound Bridge
1004.1	Jupiter Bridge
1004.8	Jupiter Federal Bridge
1005.9	Indiantown Road Bridge

No marinas, one anchorage, no fuel.
See Haulover Canal.

869.1 Allenhurst Bridge S N
(Haulover Bridge)(Kennedy Parkway Bridge)
VHF 09; 321/867-4859
Double bascule; vertical 27 feet; on request.

869.4 Haulover Canal Anchorage (0.1) S N
Anchor 6-8 feet N28.44.011
STR 0.0 feet W080.45.413
Exit ICW SW of bridge. Proceed SE into basin.
This is a tight anchorage. Arrive early if intending to stay overnight. Two anchors recommended. Area is thick with manatees.
See Manatee Divots.

869.7 Haulover Canal S N
to Northbound Navigation Only
868.5 1.2-mile land cut.
No marinas, one anchorage, no fuel.
See Haulover Canal.

875.0 Heads Up | Indian River Bridges S N
to Southbound Navigation Only
890.0 Over the next fifteen miles, there are two restricted bridges with extended morning and evening rush hour blackouts.
Southbound, there are multiple marina and anchorage options.

876.6 NASA RR Bridge S N
Automatic single bascule; vertical 7 feet; usually open.
Caution: Bridge unattended; span lowers automatically 8 minutes after red lights start flashing.

878.2 Titusville Basin S N
Exit ICW between G27 and bridge. Proceed WSW to Titusville Basin channel. [STR 0.0]
See Titusville.

- **Titusville Municipal Marina** (0.6)
  VHF 16/68 N28.37.259
  321/383-5600 W080.48.529
  Marina is ahead. Fuel dock is to port.
- **Westland Marine** (0.8)
  VHF 16; 321/267-1667
  Facility is in SSE corner of basin.
  Repair yard with weekly and monthly slips.

878.4 Titusville Anchorage (North)(0.2) S N
Anchor 8-10 feet N28.37.369
STR 0.0 feet W080.48.172
Exit ICW NNW of bridge. Proceed WSW.
Dinghy to municipal marina for free dinghy dockage.
See Dolphin Teamwork.

878.7 Max Brewer Bridge S N
(Titusville Bridge)(Route 402)
VHF 09; 321/264-5068
Single-pivot swing; vertical 9 feet.
Restricted year round: M-F except holidays, 0600-0715 and 1515-1630 hrs.

A much less famous retirement hangout overlooks the river at the northeast corner of the bridge. Look for an old two-story building jutting out into the river. In 1910, a group of 40 Ormond residents wanted a yacht club to moor their boats. So they cut a deal with the city to build the modest facility, which then included a long dock into the Waterway. But the deal was the building would never appear on the tax rolls. So this clandestine club, where its old-time members gather to play cards and shoot pool, still doesn't exist.

Courtesy of Florida Inland Navigation District

Daytona and Halifax Marina

BIRTHPLACE OF SPEED

Daytona is synonymous with car racing. Daytona may be the site of the International Speedway, but the city of Ormond also shares credit as the "birthplace of speed."

It was on the long stretch of hard-packed beach sand spanning Daytona and Ormond Beaches where race car driving began. Inventors—including Olds, Winton, Ford, Chevrolet, Stanley, and Packard—tested their engineering prowess on the only reliable flat track at the turn of the century: 23 miles of hard-packed sand naturally created by the receding tide.

They achieved astounding speeds on these sand flats. In 1903 a car was driven at 68 mph. In 1932, the famous British race driver, Sir Malcolm Campbell, came to test his skills. Rockefeller, a big fan of the auto races, was there handing out his signature "lucky dimes." He gave a lucky dime to Sir Campbell, who carried it with him when he drove 253 mph down the beach.

Eventually beach racing moved inland and off the sand. The National Association of Stock Car Racing (NASCAR) was founded in 1947 and the International Speedway opened in 1959. This $18 million facility remains a major draw for both races and tours. From the early days of races down the beach, stock car racing has emerged as the number one spectator sport in the United States.

If you transit Ormond Beach on the Friday after Thanksgiving, you can watch the city's Historic Antique Auto Beach Races. After the races, over 300 antique cars line up in chronological order at Rockefeller's former home for the Gaslight Parade.

Unfortunately, the legacy of driving on the beach has not entirely vanished. Private vehicles are allowed seaward of markers protecting the sea turtle nesting sites. If you prefer a pedestrian-only beach, vehicles are prohibited north of Granada Boulevard (Ormond Beach Bridge at STM 824.9).

Daytona International Speedway
www.daytonainternationalspeedway.com
386/254-2700

Ormond Beach Chamber of Commerce
www.ormondchamber.com
386/677-3454

MONSTER'S LAST RESORT

Thanks to an Academy Award winning performance by Charlize Theron, Daytona Beach is in the pop culture limelight as the setting for the film *Monster* (2003). It is a moving and troubling account of the true story of Aileen Wuornos, a homeless prostitute whose tragic life of abuse finally catches up with her, tipping her sanity until she starts killing her Johns. She is America's first female serial killer and Florida's first woman executed under the death penalty.

About five miles south of Halifax Marina in Daytona Beach on U.S. 1, at

Columbia/Tristar Promotional Image

Charlize Theron as The Monster

SAFETY INFO

NOAA Weather
WX-2 Daytona Beach, FL
WX-1 Melbourne, FL
WX-3 West Palm Beach, FL

USCG
Station Port Canaveral, FL
VHF 16 or 09/22A
321/868-4200

Sea Tow
Port Canaveral, FL
VHF 16/11 or 69
321/868-4900

TowBoatU.S.
Titusville, FL
VHF 16/18
386/322-5582

HEADS UP!

830.6	Daytona Beach Memorial Bridge
838.0	Ponce de Leon Inlet Area (SB)
845.0	George Munson Bridge
847.0	Ponce de Leon Inlet Area (NB)
869.1	Allenhurst Bridge
875.0	Bridge Caution (SB)
876.6	NASA RR Bridge
878.7	Max Brewer Bridge
885.0	**NASA Causeway Bridge**
890.0	**Bridge Caution (NB)**
964.8	Ft. Pierce North Bridge
984.9	Ernest Lyons Bridge
995.9	Hobe Sound Bridge
1004.1	Jupiter Bridge
1004.8	Jupiter Federal Bridge
1005.9	Indiantown Road Bridge
1009.4	Donald Ross Bridge
1012.3	PGA Blvd. Bridge

about STM 838 north of Rose Bay, is a gritty biker bar called The Last Resort. Wuornos hung out, and was arrested, at this bar. As the setting for much of the movie, the Last Resort Bar has now become a tourist attraction for film buffs.

PONCE DE LEON INLET LIGHT

Depending on your height of eye and boat traffic, you may be able to spot the Ponce de Leon Inlet lighthouse from the Waterway. Look for the tower as you come to the inlet junction at STM 840. At 159 feet, it's the tallest lighthouse in Florida and the second tallest in the nation.

If you can't spot it from the ICW and you'd like to see it from your boat, exit southbound at G1 Live Oak Point or northbound at G19 and take an alternative route parallel to the Waterway. This detour will take you right by the inlet and the lighthouse.

Ironically, coastal development conspired to save this historic lighthouse. In 1970, the lighthouse was taken out of service, made redundant by the beacon at the New Smyrna Coast Guard Station. But when a condominium development went up at New Smyrna Beach in 1983, it obscured the Coast Guard beacon. The Ponce de Leon Light was called back into service.

The lighthouse, part of Lighthouse Point Park, is now fully restored, including the keeper's house and all its outbuildings. Its original Fresnel lens, once a danger in Florida's strong sun, is on display. Every day the keeper needed to drape the lens or it could accidentally concentrate the sunlight and start a fire in the lantern room.

Ponce Inlet Lighthouse
www.ponceinlet.org
386/761-1821

THE MANGROVE MAZE

The Waterway runs a straight line along the western shore of Indian River. But outside, it's a maze of mangrove islands and winding natural channels.

Look on your chart between STM 850 and STM 858 and you can see evidence of previous routes through this mangrove maze. One route veered off the present Waterway near STM 850, in what was then called Hillsborough River. Another old cut is still visible near Cedar Creek.

In the 1930s the Waterway meandered much further east, passing by Turtle Mound, marked on the charts about two miles east of the ICW at R70. Although the new route is much shorter, it's a shame the Waterway no longer passes this historic site. In the days before lighthouses, Turtle Mound was a Native American lookout. It was built over 500 years ago out of oyster shells piled 50 feet high. The Spaniards spotted it from their galleons in 1605. Since it was also the site where the Surruque Indians launched their canoes to go to sea, the Spaniards called it the Mound of Surruque. In the 1820s the English called it Mount Tucker. But ultimately the descriptive name stuck, and today this dome-shaped hill is called Turtle Mound.

WALKING TREES

The Seminole people called Red Mangroves "walking trees." With their high arching roots, they seem to spread over tidal flats as if they were walking.

Courtesy of National Park Service

Mangrove Maze

Actually, mangroves don't cover the land; they create it. Their elevated stilt-like roots catch and hold silt, slowly building higher ground. Over time, Red Mangroves create new island clusters. Our English word *mangrove* probably comes from the Portuguese word for tree (*mangue*) and the English word for a stand of trees (*grove*).

Red Mangroves are everywhere along this part of the Waterway. The salty anaerobic conditions exclude other trees and the shifting tides exclude other species of mangrove. Only Red Mangrove can take the brunt of the salt and tides. It survives by being a living desalinization unit, separating freshwater from saltwater at the root and blocking the toxic tidal by-product of

878.8 Titusville Anchorage (South)(0.2)
Anchor 8-10 feet N28.37.003
STR 0.0 feet W080.47.897
Exit ICW SSE of bridge. Proceed WSW.

882.2 Indian River Anchorage (2.0)
Anchor 7-8 feet N28.34.742
STR 0.0 feet W080.44.964
Exit ICW at R38. Proceed easterly between charted spoil areas.
No protection. Fair weather overnight anchorage only. Excellent anchorage to view Cape Canaveral launches.
SEE ROCKETS AND ROOKERIES.

882.7 Kennedy Point Marina (1.3)
VHF 16; 321/383-0280
Exit ICW at G39. Proceed westerly in privately maintained channel to marina. [STR 0.0]

884.8 Addison Point Anchorage (North)(0.6)
Anchor 8-10 feet N28.31.759
STR 0.0 feet W080.45.330
Exit ICW N of bridge. Proceed E between charted 3-foot shoals to 8-foot pocket.
This is an excellent place to anchor in heavy south winds if you miss the timing of the NASA Causeway Bridge. You will still get all of the wind, but none of the surge.
Additionally, this is a better overnight anchorage when viewing Canaveral launch activities.

885.0 NASA Causeway Bridge
(JFK Causeway Bridge)(Route 405)
VHF 09; 321/867-7200
Double bascule; vertical 27 feet.
Restricted year round: M-F except holidays, 0630-0800 and 1530-1700 hrs.
SEE KENNEDY SPACE CENTER.

885.3 Addison Point Anchorage (South)(0.5)
Anchor 8-10 feet N28.31.472
STR 0.0 feet W080.45.345
Exit ICW S of bridge. Proceed E to charted 7-foot pocket.
See comments at STM 884.8.

890.0 Heads Up | Indian River Bridges
to 875.0 Northbound Navigation Only
Over the next fifteen miles, there are two restricted bridges with extended morning and evening rush hour blackouts.
Northbound, there are fewer options for marinas and anchorages so careful timing of the NASA Causeway Bridge is strongly advised.

893.7 Junction | Canaveral Barge Canal
Exit ICW N of bridge. Proceed E to charted canal entrance.

- **Harbor Square Marina** (1.5)
  VHF 16; 321/453-2464
  Marina is to S. [STR 0.0]
- **Christa McAuliffe Bridge** (1.8)
  VHF 09; 321/452-5220
  Bascule, vertical 21 feet.
  Restricted year round: 0600-2200 hrs, opens on

SAFETY INFO

NOAA Weather
WX-2 Daytona Beach, FL
WX-1 Melbourne, FL
WX-3 West Palm Beach, FL

USCG
Station Port Canaveral, FL
VHF 16 or 09/22A
321/868-4200

Sea Tow
Port Canaveral, FL
VHF 16/11 or 69
321/868-4900

TowBoatU.S.
Titusville, FL
VHF 16/18
386/322-5582

HEADS UP!

838.0	Ponce de Leon Inlet Area (SB)
845.0	George Munson Bridge
847.0	Ponce de Leon Inlet Area (NB)
869.1	Allenhurst Bridge
875.0	Bridge Caution (SB)
876.6	NASA RR Bridge
878.7	Max Brewer Bridge
885.0	NASA Causeway Bridge
890.0	Bridge Caution (NB)
964.8	Ft. Pierce North Bridge
984.9	Ernest Lyons Bridge
995.9	Hobe Sound Bridge
1004.1	Jupiter Bridge
1004.8	Jupiter Federal Bridge
1005.9	Indiantown Road Bridge
1009.4	Donald Ross Bridge
1012.3	PGA Blvd. Bridge
1013.5	Parker Bridge

the hour and half-hour; but no openings M-F except holidays, 0615-0815 and 1510-1759 hrs; three hour notice required, 2201-0559 hrs.

- **Tingley's Fish Resort** (1.9)
  VHF 16; 321/452-0504
  Marina is closed with no current plans to re-open. [STR 0.0]
- **Harbortown Canaveral Marina** (3.7)
  VHF 16/10 N28.24.567
  321/453-0160 W080.40.560
  Marina is to S. [STR 0.0]
- **Canaveral Lock** (5.8)
  VHF 16/13; 321/783-5421
  Open daily 0600-2130 hrs. Closes periodically for maintenance.
- **SR 401 Bridge** (6.2)
  VHF 09; 321/783-3759
  Bascule; vertical 25 feet.
  Restricted year round: M-F except holidays, 0630-0800 and 1530-1715 hrs; three hours notice required, 2200-0600 hrs.
- **Scorpions New Port Marina** (6.3)
  VHF 16; 321/784-5788
  Marina is to S. [STR 4.0]
- **Cocoa Beach Yacht Club** (6.6)
  VHF 16; 321/784-2292
  Yacht Club is to S. [STR 4.0]
  Accepts guests of members and offers reciprocal rights to members of accredited yacht clubs.
- **Cape Marina** (6.7)
  VHF 16; 321/783-8410
  Marina is to S. [STR 4.0]
- **Sunrise Marina** (7.9)
  VHF 16; 321/783-9535
  Marina is to S. [STR 4.0]
- **Port Canaveral** (11.0)
  Well Aided N28.23.820
  Well Lit W080.33.457
  Canal continues E, then SE to ocean. Waypoint is between G5 and R6.
  Because of Southeast Shoal, extending almost 10 miles seaward, this inlet is best used for southbound departures or northbound arrivals.

894.0 City Point Bridge S N
Fixed; vertical 65 feet.

897.5 Whitley Bay Marina (0.4) S N
VHF 16/68 N28.21.468
321/632-5445 W080.43.503
Exit ICW N of bridge. Proceed W in privately maintained channel to marina. [STR 0.0]

897.5 Indian Cove Marina (0.5) S N
VHF 16; 321/452-8540
Exit ICW N of bridge. Proceed E in privately maintained channel to marina. [STR 0.0]
Marina is closed. Transient wet slips are closed due to condo and dockominium development.

897.6 Cocoa Bridge S N
Fixed; vertical 65 feet.

hydrogen sulfide (the rotten egg smell of the tidal flats).

Although red mangroves may be all you see for long stretches along the Waterway, they are not invasive aliens. Mangroves create one of the most productive ecosystems in the world, dropping 7000 pounds of leaves, twigs, branches, and flowers into each acre of wetland. When a mangrove leaf first drops, it is about three percent protein. Give it another month, after being colonized by bacteria, fungi, and algae, and it contains about 20 percent protein—more than twice the protein of dog food. This high protein detritus then becomes food for crabs and small fish, which are in turn eaten by larger fish and crabs, turtles, snakes, wading birds, osprey, and eagles.

Courtesy of Smithsonian Marine Station

Photo by Barbara Zarrella

Red Mangrove Roots

But mangroves certainly create an impenetrable barrier. In Australia, foot races through the mangroves are a farcical pastime (presumably involving warm Foster's). The world record for the 100-meter "Mangrove Dash" is 22 minutes and 30 seconds. Not bad considering those roots.

No matter what you call 'em, no-see-ums, sand flies, or gnats can still get through the screens! If these tiny biting insects are winning, repel the boarders by spraying your screens with Shoo-fly Screen and Surface Insect Spray, available at True Value hardware stores.

MOSQUITO LAGOON

Not a very reassuring name for an anchorage, is it? But don't worry, Notre Dame biology professor George Craig estimates it would take roughly 1,120,000 mosquito bites to drain the blood from an adult human. You should be fine for the evening.

Contrary to popular belief, mosquitoes do breed in salt water. At least two species of mosquitoes breed like crazy in these salt marshes, laying eggs on damp ground in the higher swamp areas dominated by Black and White Mangroves. Florida has scores of mosquito species, each laying their eggs in a different niche. Some breed in the salt floodwaters, some in the little pools of water in the cypress knees, and some in the water pooled in the center of bromeliad air plants.

Before mosquito control districts and nighttime spraying of larvicides, locals relied on screens and mosquito beaters. A mosquito beater was like a feather duster, made of palmetto fronds bound together at the base and loose at the top. Locals hung one by each doorway and brushed the mosquitoes off their clothes before entering their houses.

MANATEE DIVOTS

For many boaters heading south, the eastern entrance to Haulover Canal is their first sighting of the endangered Florida Manatee (a sub-species of the West Indian Manatee).

Supposedly Christopher Columbus was the first European to report seeing a manatee. The crew thought they had sighted the mythical half-female, half-fish mermaids. So these cleft-faced, coarsely whiskered, thousand pound "beauties" became linked with the scientific order *Sirenia*, after the mythical women in Homer's *Odyssey*. Talk about delusional after months at sea without women!

Manatees use the deep waters of Haulover Canal for shelter. The key to spotting a manatee is to look for the "footprint" in the water. Since manatees must breath air, they generally float near the water surface. They are very graceful swimmers, pumping their large paddle-like tails and even doing barrel rolls. But as they pump their tails for a dive, they create a large disturbance or boil on the water's surface: a large ring like a raindrop echo several feet in diameter.

As you wait for the bridge opening, look north for these telltale divots near the scenic overlook.

SAFETY INFO

NOAA Weather
WX-2 Daytona Beach, FL
WX-1 Melbourne, FL
WX-3 West Palm Beach, FL

USCG
Station Port Canaveral, FL
VHF 16 or 09/22A
321/868-4200

Sea Tow
Port Canaveral, FL
VHF 16/11 or 69
321/868-4900

TowBoatU.S.
Titusville, FL
VHF 16/18
386/322-5582

HEADS UP!

838.0	Ponce de Leon Inlet Area (SB)
845.0	George Munson Bridge
847.0	Ponce de Leon Inlet Area (NB)
869.1	Allenhurst Bridge
875.0	Bridge Caution (SB)
876.6	NASA RR Bridge
878.7	Max Brewer Bridge
885.0	NASA Causeway Bridge
890.0	Bridge Caution (NB)
964.8	Ft. Pierce North Bridge
984.9	Ernest Lyons Bridge
995.9	Hobe Sound Bridge
1004.1	Jupiter Bridge
1004.8	Jupiter Federal Bridge
1005.9	Indiantown Road Bridge
1009.4	Donald Ross Bridge
1012.3	PGA Blvd. Bridge
1013.5	Parker Bridge

HAULOVER CANAL

For centuries, the isthmus at STM 869 was the obvious place to cross from Mosquito Lagoon to the Indian River. Native Americans and early settlers came here to portage or "haul over" their canoes and boats between the two large river basins. At one point, logs were cut and laid across the land, allowing mule teams to haul the boats, laden with goods, overland.

The first canal was hand dug by the slaves of a local citrus grower and was only three feet deep. But this 0.4-mile canal was a crucial link for commerce and by 1884 a deeper and wider canal was dug. By the 1920s the canal was widened again to accommodate logging and citrus traffic. Finally, in the 1950s the Army Corps came in with dynamite, blasting the coquina rock layer to its present depth.

ROCKETS AND ROOKERIES

Merritt Island National Wildlife Refuge includes most of the Haulover Isthmus, the barrier islands across from Mosquito Lagoon, and the land at Black Point to the south and east of the Waterway. It's a huge refuge, with 140,000 acres, but most of the land is inaccessible. If you'd like to visit the refuge, the main entrance and visitor center (all free of charge) are located about four miles east of Titusville Bridge at STM 878.7.

Courtesy of EROS Data Center, NASA

Kennedy Space Center

The refuge is unique because it shares land with the only place in the U.S. where men are launched into space. But the space program and the refuge have developed a symbiotic relationship. The refuge serves as a security buffer for the Space Center; in return, NASA protects the refuge from encroaching development. Since the refuge spans the transition line between temperate and sub-tropical zones, over 500 species commingle here, including 21 species on federal or state endangered or threatened lists.

Courtesy of Everglades Day Safari

Great Egret

The high-tech operations of the space program don't seem to bother the wildlife. According to NASA, the only wildlife fatalities caused by the launches are the minnows in the shallow water adjacent to the launch pad. For the rest of the residents, life returns to normal after a shuttle blast-off.

Merritt Island NWR
http://merrittisland.fws.gov
321/861-0667

TITUSVILLE

For years, Titusville had an enviable position at the junction of a railroad and steamship line. Indian River citrus, pineapples, and seafood arrived by steamboat at the old wharf, then were loaded onto a rail line called the "Tropical Trunk Line." The town was busy with packing plants: five citrus packing houses, a barrel factory to ship fish and vegetables, and a crabmeat picking and packing plant.

Indian River citrus is still grown in the area and shipped north, but Titusville no longer holds the railway monopoly. Eventually Henry Flagler's Jacksonville, St. Augustine & Indian River Railway (later the Florida East Coast Railway) ended Titusville's railroad reign.

Today Titusville is a town of 40,000 residents located at the gateway of the Space Center and Merritt Island. A city-owned dock has replaced the old commercial wharf (at the end of Broad Street) and the large municipal marina is the center of a new era of waterside commerce. But Titusville still holds a monopoly on great location: its an-

897.7 Cocoa Anchorage (0.3)
Anchor 7-10 feet — N28.21.258
STR 0.0 feet — W080.43.287
Exit ICW S of bridge. Proceed W.
SEE COCOA.

898.8 Rockledge Anchorage (North)(0.3)
Anchor 8-10 feet — N28.20.443
STR 0.0 feet — W080.42.996
Exit ICW at G77. Proceed WSW toward Rockledge.
SEE COQUINA ROCK.

901.2 Rockledge Anchorage (South)(0.3)
Anchor 8-10 feet — N28.18.587
STR 0.0 feet — W080.42.139
Exit ICW S of G83. Proceed WSW.

901.6 Jay's Harbor Lights Marina (0.6)
VHF 16; 321/453-6354
Exit ICW between G83 and G85. Proceed ENE in privately maintained channel to marina. [STR 0.0]
Annual contracts only. No transient dockage.

908.7 Palm Shores Bridge Anchorage (0.4)
Anchor 6-9 feet — N28.12.659
STR 0.0 feet — W080.38.736
Exit ICW NNW of bridge. Proceed E between two charted spoil areas.

909.0 Palm Shores Bridge
(Route 404)
Fixed; vertical 65 feet.

910.7 Diamond 99 Marina (0.6)
VHF 16/68 — N28.10.723
321/254-1490 — W080.38.888
Exit ICW NNW of G99. Proceed WSW in privately maintained channel to marina. [STR 0.0]

914.2 Junction | Indian Harbor Beach (Dragon Point)
Exit ICW NNW of bridge. Proceed easterly to Dragon Point G1. [STR 0.0]
SEE THE DRAGON.

- **Anchorage Yacht Basin** (1.2)
  VHF 16; 321/773-3620
  Marina is to SSE.
- **Dragon Point Anchorage** (1.1)
  Anchor 8-12 feet — N28.08.460
  STR 0.0 feet — W080.36.118
  Anchorage is SE of Dragon Point.
- **Telemar Bay Marina** (1.5)
  VHF 16; 321/773-2468
  Proceed northerly. Marina is before bridge to starboard.
- **Mathers Bridge** (1.6)
  VHF 09; 321/779-4019
  Swing; vertical 7 feet.
  Restricted year round: M-F except holidays, 2200-0600 hrs, two hour notice required.
- **Grand Canal Anchorage** (2.0)
  Anchor 6-7 feet — N28.09.722
  STR 0.0 feet — W080.36.434
  Continue NNW of bridge. Enter charted Grand Canal.

SAFETY INFO

NOAA Weather	Sea Tow
WX-2 Daytona Beach, FL	Port Canaveral, FL
WX-1 Melbourne, FL	VHF 16/11 or 69
WX-3 West Palm Beach, FL	321/868-4900
USCG	**TowBoatU.S.**
Station Port Canaveral, FL	Melbourne, FL
VHF 16 or 09/22A	VHF 16/10
321/868-4200	321/951-7955

HEADS UP!

838.0	Ponce de Leon Inlet Area (SB)	964.8	Ft. Pierce North Bridge
845.0	George Munson Bridge	984.9	Ernest Lyons Bridge
847.0	Ponce de Leon Inlet Area (NB)	995.9	Hobe Sound Bridge
869.1	Allenhurst Bridge	1004.1	Jupiter Bridge
875.0	Bridge Caution (SB)	1004.8	Jupiter Federal Bridge
876.6	NASA RR Bridge	1005.9	Indiantown Road Bridge
878.7	Max Brewer Bridge	1009.4	Donald Ross Bridge
885.0	NASA Causeway Bridge	1012.3	PGA Blvd. Bridge
890.0	Bridge Caution (NB)	1013.5	Parker Bridge

• **Banana River Anchorage** (2.4)
Anchor 11-13 feet N28.09.610
STR 0.0 feet W080.36.693
Proceed NNW of bridge, beyond Grand Canal entrance. Anchor under charted Merritt Island bump before R2.

914.3 Abaco Jack's Anchorage (0.3)
Anchor 8-10 feet N28.08.056
STR 0.0 feet W080.37.434
Exit ICW NNW of bridge. Proceed W toward restaurant. Anchor to NE of fishing pier.
Formerly Conchy Joe's; provides a dinghy dock.

914.4 Eau Gallie Bridge
Fixed; vertical 65 feet.

914.5 Eau Gallie Bridge Anchorage (0.3)
Anchor 10-12 feet N28.07.764
STR 0.0 feet W080.37.171
Exit ICW SSE of bridge. Proceed W.
See Eau Gallie and Melbourne.

915.0 Eau Gallie Harbor
Exit ICW NNW of R2. Proceed westerly to Eau Gallie channel. [STR 0.0]

• **Eau Gallie Boat Works** (0.7)
VHF 16 N28.07.528
321/254-1766 W080.37.530
Facility is to starboard.

• **Eau Gallie Yacht Basin** (0.8)
No VHF Watch N28.07.511
321/242-6577 W080.37.641
Marina is to starboard.

• **Waterline Marina** (1.0)
VHF 16/68 N28.07.423
321/254-0452 W080.37.746
Marina is to starboard, beyond G15.

916.7 Intracoastal Marina (0.6)
VHF 16; 321/725-0090
Exit ICW between G3 and G5. Proceed W in privately maintained channel to marina. [STR 0.0]

918.1 Melbourne Bridge Anchorage (North)(0.5)
Anchor 8-10 feet N28.05.283
STR 0.0 feet W080.35.141
Exit ICW NNW of bridge. Proceed E.

918.2 Melbourne Causeway Bridge
Fixed; vertical 65 feet.

918.3 Melbourne Bridge Anchorage (South)(0.4)
Anchor 8-10 feet N28.05.070
STR 0.0 feet W080.35.004
Exit ICW S of bridge. Proceed E along causeway.

918.7 Melbourne Harbor
Exit ICW at R6. Proceed W to Melbourne Harbor channel. [STR 0.0]
See The Melbourne Man.

• **Melbourne Harbor Marina** (0.8)
VHF 16; 321/725-9054
Marina is to starboard.

• **Melbourne Yacht Club** (0.9)
VHF 16; 321/768-9921

chorages, municipal marina, and waterfront parks are prime locations for viewing space shuttle launches.

LITTLE DOCKLINE ACROBAT

At night, walking down the dock to your boat, you may spot a silent dockline acrobat. These are Green Herons, tiny dark-colored waders in rufous and gray-green, crouching on the low-slung docklines at night.

Green Herons seem to defy gravity with their tightrope act. They hunker down on the catenary of a wobbly dockline, motionlessly watching the water. Then they dart forward and grab a small fish from the water. It makes no sense. How can they lean so far forward without swinging like a trapeze artist or splashing into the water?

The trick works because their necks are so long. Their necks can reach down to the water and back in a split second, keeping the bird's center of gravity aligned above the dockline.

In Japan, these little herons are even trickier: they've learned to scatter insects over the water to lure the fish up to the surface.

semi-local publications LLC

Photo by Author **Manatee at Titusville Marina**

MANATEE: THE OTHER WHITE MEAT

So reads the bumper sticker in Florida, a hint, if you haven't already noticed, of the less-than-friendly debate over the conservation status of the manatee. It's true: these large sea mammals were an important food source for Native Americans, who could easily capture the slow and docile creatures. The indigenous people ate the meat, used the bones for tools, the hide for leather, and the fat for lamp oil.

But Native Americans didn't decimate the manatee population, propellers did. Since manatees float just below the surface of the water, speeding boats kill them by impact or slice their backs with propeller blades.

Courtesy of Smithsonian Marine Station

Photo by Mary Bowman **Slow Speed for Manatees**

In 1974, when Florida passed the Manatee Sanctuary Act, there were only about 600 manatees. The state enacted manatee speed zones and launched public awareness campaigns. By 2003, using an aircraft count, the population was estimated at over 3,000 animals. In 2003, "only" 73 manatees died from collisions with watercraft —a record low despite an increasing number of boats.

As the manatee rebounds, the debate heats up. The environmental group Save the Manatee and the boaters' rights group Standing Watch continue a fierce battle over whether the manatee is ready to be downlisted to a threatened species.

Manatees are abundant in the Titusville basin during temperate fall and winter months. One of the manatees' favorite foods, not surprisingly called manatee grass, accumulates in the marina basin. The grass propagates by breaking off pieces that float to new locations. Depending on the wind direction, thick mats of floating manatee grass accumulate at the leeward end of the basin. Look for manatees feeding in the early morning or late evening. A manatee will feed five to eight hours a day to make its 30-pound recommended daily allowance of greens.

Manatees are very docile and are not bothered by people quietly sitting on the dock while they feed. You can see the scars scientists use like fingerprints to identify individuals. As they feed (and belch), you often can experience firsthand manatee grass halitosis (it's bad!).

Manatees love fresh water and may come alongside when you run a hose. They can get fresh water through their skin by a process that excludes the salt. But despite what others may do, do not attract them with fresh water, or feed or touch them. They are so close to the docks, it's tempting. But germs can cross from humans to manatees, so your touch could infect one of these rare creatures.

OSPREY

Waking up in Titusville, it's hard to believe the Osprey is endangered in many parts of the U.S. Every morning they circle the Titusville basin, waking boaters with their piercing high-pitched whistles. Their overhead silhouettes are distinctive: look for their long narrow wings with a crook at the wrist.

You have certainly passed their huge bulky nests of sticks and moss, often built on navigation dayboards. Ospreys generally mate for life and return to the same nest year after year, repairing and adding for each year's use. Not surprisingly, after all these annual remodels, an osprey nest can weigh more than half a ton.

The Coast Guard is willing to share navigation aids with these federally protected species, as long as the aid remains operational. You may notice experimental platforms that allow ospreys to use a dayboard for nesting, without compromising boater safety.

DOLPHIN TEAMWORK

Sometimes the water churns with hundreds of small fish. No wonder these 6- to 12-inch black or striped mullets are often simply called "jumping mullet."

The cause of the commotion is usually a dolphin pod, working together to trap a school of mullet. Dolphins herd fish cooperatively, like cowboys herding cattle, talking to each other with squeals and clicks.

One of their favorite local roundup sites is on the northeast side of Titusville Bridge, where the deep water of the Waterway meets a small cove and park. Look for churning water and arching dolphin dorsal fins as they cooperatively herd schools of mullet into the shallow beach crescent.

Group hunting and feeding fascinates animal biologists. Unlike humans, animals just seem to naturally "get it." At a minimum, if dolphins were humans, the team would need a manager to discourage slackers from *free-riding*, where team members don't help herd, but reap the benefits of easy feeding.

CANOPY FEEDING

You may observe another ingenious feeder along the Indian River: the Reddish Egret. Look for a wader that is smaller than a Great Blue Heron or Great Egret, usually seen with a slate gray body and reddish head and neck.

Unlike the staid Great Egret, Reddish Egrets are animated fishermen. They move about in shallow water, jumping, spinning, and chasing fish.

Courtesy of NASA

KSC Assembly Building

Reddish Egrets use an ingenious fishing trick. They stand in the water with their wings outstretched like a cormorant, making a patch of shade under their bodies. Minnows are attracted to the cool, dark shelter of the shade but, unfortunately for them, fail to notice the large gray feet and legs.

KENNEDY SPACE CENTER

The Vehicle Assembly Building at Kennedy Space Center is clearly visible from the Waterway. When this building was completed in 1965, it was the largest building in the world. Each stripe on its American flag logo used 6,000 gallons of paint.

The assembly building is no longer the largest building in the world, but it still claims the largest *doors*. The huge inverted T-shaped doors receive space shuttle components, which arrive by

Yacht club is to port.
Private sailing club. Limited space; "T-head sometimes open for sailboats passing through."

921.4 Palm Bay Harbor
Exit ICW between G13 and R14. Proceed WSW to Palm Bay Harbor. Marinas are beyond fixed bridge with 15-foot vertical clearance. [STR 0.0]
SEE LAGOON HOUSE.
Note: Government tide tables state, "In Indian River north of Palm Bay, in Banana River, and in Banana Creek, the periodic tides are negligible."

- **Pelican Harbor Marina** (1.1)
  VHF 16; 321/956-0960
  Marina is to starboard. 60-slip local facility with no transient dockage.
- **Palm Bay Marina** (1.1)
  VHF 16; 321/723-0851
  Facility is to port.
  Dry store and repair facility with no transient dockage.

925.2 Rocky Point Anchorage (North)(0.3)
Anchor 6-8 feet N27.59.431
STR 0.1 feet W080.32.712
Exit ICW at R20. Proceed W to anchor NW of spoil island.

926.4 Rocky Point Anchorage (South)(0.2)
Anchor 6-8 feet N27.58.499
STR 0.1 feet W080.32.323
Exit ICW at R24. Proceed W to anchor SE of spoil island.
SEE BEFORE AIR CONDITIONING.

934.0 Sebastian River Marina & Boatyard (0.5)
VHF 16; 772/664-3029
Exit ICW S of G55. Proceed W in privately maintained channel to marina. [STR 0.4]
SEE DREDGE ISLANDS.

937.3 Sebastian
Exit ICW at G65. Proceed southwesterly in privately maintained channel. [STR 0.4]
SEE SHOOTOUT AT SEBASTIAN.

- **Capt'n Butcher's Marina** (0.5)
  VHF 16; 772/589-2552
  Marina is to starboard.
- **Fins Marina** (0.5)
  VHF 16/11 N27.49.613
  772/589-4843 W080.28.330
  Marina & Restaurant is ahead.

937.7 Captain Hiram's Marina (0.4)
VHF 16; 772/589-4345
Exit ICW N of R66. Proceed W in privately maintained channel to marina. [STR 0.4]

940.7 Pauls Island Anchorage (0.1)
Anchor 5-6 feet N27.47.292
STR 0.4 feet W080.26.445
Exit ICW between R72 and G73. Proceed ENE toward Pauls Island.
SEE PELICAN ISLAND.

SAFETY INFO

NOAA Weather
WX-2 Daytona Beach, FL
WX-1 Melbourne, FL
WX-3 West Palm Beach, FL

USCG
Station Ft. Pierce, FL
VHF 16 or 09/22A
772/464-6100

Sea Tow
Treasure Coast, FL
VHF 16/11 or 69
772/288-2900

TowBoatU.S.
Vero Beach, FL
VHF 16/18
772/465-0709

HEADS UP!

845.0	George Munson Bridge
847.0	Ponce de Leon Inlet Area (NB)
869.1	Allenhurst Bridge
875.0	Bridge Caution (SB)
876.6	NASA RR Bridge
878.7	Max Brewer Bridge
885.0	NASA Causeway Bridge
890.0	Bridge Caution (NB)
964.8	**Ft. Pierce North Bridge**
984.9	Ernest Lyons Bridge
995.9	Hobe Sound Bridge
1004.1	Jupiter Bridge
1004.8	Jupiter Federal Bridge
1005.9	Indiantown Road Bridge
1009.4	Donald Ross Bridge
1012.3	PGA Blvd. Bridge
1013.5	Parker Bridge
1021.8	Flagler Memorial Bridge

943.2 Wabasso Bridge S N
Fixed; vertical 65 feet.

943.3 Wabasso Bridge Anchorage (0.1) S N
Anchor 8-10 feet N27.45.581
STR 0.4 feet W080.24.955
Exit ICW SE of bridge. Proceed WSW toward Environmental Learning Center docks.
See Environmental Learning Center.

944.4 Sea Oaks Town Docks (0.1) S N
VHF 16; 772/231-9828
Exit ICW between R90 and G91. Proceed ESE to marina. [STR 0.4]
Private residential facility with no transient dockage.

948.6 Grand Harbor Marina (0.4) S N
VHF 16; 772/770-4470
Exit ICW between G121 and G123. Proceed W in privately maintained channel to marina. [STR 0.5]

951.6 Vero Beach Municipal Marina (0.4) S N
VHF 16/66 N27.39.412
772/231-2819 W080.22.239
Exit ICW between G139 and bridge. Proceed E along bridge, then NNE. Fuel dock and marina office are to starboard. [STR 1.0]
No anchoring in Vero Beach. Vero Beach Municipal Marina provides dockage and two mooring fields. Expect to raft at moorings.
See Vero Beach.

951.7 Vero Beach Bridge S N
(Merrill Barbor Bridge)(Route 60)
Fixed; vertical 66 feet.

951.8 Vero Marine Center (0.3) S N
VHF 16; 772/562-7922
Exit ICW SSE of bridge. Proceed WSW in channel to facility. [STR 1.0]
Limited draft; call ahead. Repair facility with no transient dockage.

953.2 17th Street Causeway Bridge S N
Fixed; vertical 65 feet.
See Harbor Branch.

964.1 Riverside Marina (0.4) S N
VHF 16; 772/464-5720
Exit ICW S of R180. Proceed WSW in privately maintained channel to marina. [STR 1.4]
Repair yard with no transient dockage.

964.8 Ft. Pierce North Bridge S N
VHF 09; 772/468-3993
Double bascule; vertical 26 feet; on request.

964.9 Ft. Pierce Anchorage (0.1) S N
Anchor 8-12 feet N27.28.142
STR 1.5 feet W080.19.498
Exit ICW SSE of bridge. Proceed WSW.

965.1 Taylor Creek S N
Exit ICW SSE of R184. Proceed W to Taylor Creek. [STR 1.5]

barge and mobile launcher platform for their final stacking and fueling.

The Kennedy Space Center is open to the public and is a memorable all-day visit. Security is tighter since 9/11, but many sites are still viewable through a narrated bus tour. The attractions include twin IMAX theatres and up close views of historic rockets.

Kennedy Space Center
www.kennedyspacecenter.com
321/449-4444

Recorded Launch Info
321/867-4636

Photo Courtesy of Patricia Holm

Merrill Barbor Bridge (STM 951.7)

BIOLUMINESCENCE: FOR A SPARKLING BOWL

If you have a saltwater-flush toilet, you may notice your bowl glitters when you flush it at night. Or the water may sparkle around your hull or dinghy at dark nights at anchor.

This light is called *bioluminescence* (not phosphorescence) and is most likely produced by dinoflagellates, tiny drifting organisms that are part plant and part animal. A chemical reaction, which produces light, is triggered when they are jostled, such as by your hoses or dinghy.

Scientists believe bioluminescence is a strategy against predators, who may be startled or repelled by sudden light. Many marine animals produce light, including fish, squid, jellyfish, and worms. Scientists only recently discovered that snapping shrimp, which you may have heard at night, produce light when they snap. Their ten-nanosecond bursts of light produce temperatures near 8,000° F. What do scientists call light produced by shrimp? No joke: shrimpoluminescence.

Your joker valve will love you! To remove salt and calcium deposits in heads with rubber *(not leather)* parts, once a month pour two cups of vinegar into the bowl. Pump just enough to get the vinegar into the mechanism and let stand, then pump 2-3 strokes every half-hour for the next couple of hours.

COCOA

The town of Cocoa began as a small fishing and agricultural village called Indian River City, located at Magnolia Point across from R72. But when Indian River City aspired to a post office, their request was denied. The postal authorities of the 1880s said the name Indian River City was too long to use on a postmark.

So the town was renamed Cocoa, with several stories about the source of the name. It may have come from the coco plums that grew abundantly in the area. Or maybe it was from the old woman who lived along the Indian River and gave out hot cocoa to the sailors. They would call out "cocoa, cocoa" as they passed through.

Whichever story is true, Cocoa is now a town—with its own post office—and 16,000 people. The city hosts many activities at its waterfronts parks and the revitalized historic downtown has over 50 shops and restaurants. Unlike most Florida towns, Cocoa's largest age group is 20- to 44-year-olds.

Cocoa Village
www.cocoavillage.com
321/631-9075

COQUINA ROCK

The town of Rockledge, across from G77 at STM 899, is named for the coquina rock formations along its banks.

Florida was lucky to have coquina. It was a prized building material until the mid-1800s. The Native Americans, Spaniards, British, and Americans all quarried large blocks of coquina from this area. Areas without coquina, such as Georgia, had to develop complicated techniques of mixing sand and shells, called tabby, to build foundations.

Coquina, created by layers of compressed shell and coral, was the perfect material for foundation blocks. It's a soft limestone rock, so is easy to cut, but it hardens when exposed to air. Add

SAFETY INFO

NOAA Weather
WX-1 Melbourne, FL
WX-3 West Palm, FL
WX-1 Miami, FL

USCG
Station Ft. Pierce, FL
VHF 16 or 09/22A
772/464-6100

Sea Tow
Treasure Coast, FL
VHF 16/11 or 69
772/288-2900

TowBoatU.S.
Ft. Pierce, FL
VHF 16/18
772/465-0709

HEADS UP!

845.0	George Munson Bridge
847.0	Ponce de Leon Inlet Area (NB)
869.1	Allenhurst Bridge
875.0	Bridge Caution (SB)
876.6	NASA RR Bridge
878.7	Max Brewer Bridge
885.0	NASA Causeway Bridge
890.0	Bridge Caution (NB)
964.8	Ft. Pierce North Bridge
984.9	Ernest Lyons Bridge
995.9	Hobe Sound Bridge
1004.1	Jupiter Bridge
1004.8	Jupiter Federal Bridge
1005.9	Indiantown Road Bridge
1009.4	Donald Ross Bridge
1012.3	PGA Blvd. Bridge
1013.5	Parker Bridge
1021.8	Flagler Memorial Bridge

a coat of plaster and a coat of paint and it becomes waterproof.

As you walk through Florida's historic areas, take a look at the foundations of old city buildings or stately homes. They are probably built with coquina block foundations.

Courtesy of St. Lucie County TDC

Grouper Groupies

EAU GALLIE AND MELBOURNE

The city of Melbourne spans two Waterway bridges: the Eau Gallie Bridge at STM 914.4 and Melbourne Causeway Bridge at STM 918.2. Eau Gallie and Melbourne once were separate towns with their own harbors, marinas, and services. But Eau Gallie is now officially part of Melbourne. Many boaters still refer to Eau Gallie—no longer labeled on the charts—as the area on both sides of Eau Gallie Bridge, including the Banana River at the southern end of Merritt Island.

Every November, Eau Gallie is the site of the Seven Seas Cruising Association's Annual Gam. Historically, a *gam* is a social gathering of the crews of ships at sea, from the Scandinavian word *gams* meaning loose conversation. The SSCA Gam is a three-day gathering of hundreds of cruisers, with seminars, speakers, panel discussions, vendor exhibits, and socializing. The small community of Eau Gallie, on the western banks of the Eau Gallie Bridge, is a great location for a gam, providing a large anchorage, abundant dinghy docks, a small convention center, a beautiful waterfront library, and many small shops and restaurants.

The official center of Melbourne is further south, at Melbourne Harbor. Melbourne is the larger town, with many stores, repair facilities, restaurants, and the area's local airport.

SSCA Gam
www.ssca.org
954/771-5660

City of Melbourne
www.melbourneflorida.org
321/953-6282

THE DRAGON

The southern tip of Merritt Island, just north of the Eau Gallie Bridge, is affectionately called Dragon Point. For over 30 years, a huge cement sculpture of a dragon stood on the coquina rock point overlooking the Waterway. Locals gathered on the bridge or on their boats every July 4th to watch smoke pour from its nose and flames shoot out its mouth.

But a storm in 2002 destroyed the 65-foot long, 35-foot high dragon. The point stood empty, with only the concrete and steel vestiges of the dragon remaining.

As the locals point out, it's not really Dragon Point without a dragon. So momentum is gathering to rebuild the dragon. If everything goes as planned, a new green fiberglass dragon should be overlooking the Waterway by summer of 2005.

DRACO (SPRING)

The Dragon constellation, Draco, traveling around the North Star, is always visible at this latitude.

But the best time to see the Dragon is during spring, when the Big Dipper is well above the horizon. Look for the long string of stars winding around the Little Dipper, between the Big Dipper and the North Star, ending in a quadrangle-shaped head.

The faint star in the Dragon's tail, halfway between the bend in the Big Dipper's handle (Mizar) and the face of the Little Dipper, is Thuban. During the time of the Pyramids, Thuban was the Pole Star. The scale of time in astronomy is staggering. By 14,000 AD, the bright star Vega will be another life form's pole star.

THE MELBOURNE MAN

Go back in time 20,000 years. That's when this area, called the Melbourne

- **Harbortown Marina** (0.2)
  VHF 16; 772/466-7300
  Marina is large bulkheaded facility to NW.
- **Cracker Boy Boat Works** (0.3)
  No VHF Watch; 772/465-7031
  Facility is to port.
  Repair yard with no transient dockage.
- **Anchors Aweigh at Taylor Creek** (0.4)
  VHF 16; 772/465-2663
  Marina is to port.
  Formerly Taylor Creek Marina.

965.7 Junction | Ft. Pierce Inlet
Exit ICW in Ft. Pierce turning basin. Proceed easterly to Ft. Pierce Inlet. [STR 2.2]

- **Ft. Pierce Inlet Marina** (0.9)
  VHF 16; 772/464-8451
  Exit Ft. Pierce Inlet channel at G13. Proceed SE to charted Faber Point basin. Marina is to S.
  Local boats on yearly contracts; no transient dockage.
- **Pelican Yacht Club** (1.0)
  VHF 16; 772/464-1734
  Exit Ft. Pierce Inlet channel at G13. Proceed SE to charted Faber Point basin. Yacht club is to SE.
- **Ft. Pierce Inlet** (3.2)
  Well Aided N27.28.492
  Well Lit W080.16.193
  Continue easterly to inlet. Waypoint is between G3 and R4.
  This is a fine entry and exit point both north- and southbound. It is a very popular inlet for sailboats returning from the Bahamas, headed to Vero Beach.

965.8 Ft. Pierce South Bridge
(Peter P. Cobb Bridge)
Fixed; vertical 65 feet. [STR 1.5 (TS)]

966.2 Causeway Island Anchorages
Exit ICW at R188. Proceed ENE to privately maintained Causeway Island channel. [STR 1.5]
Ft. Pierce enforces a 96-hour anchoring limit.
SEE CROSSROADS OF MARINE RESEARCH.

- **Causeway Island Anchorage** (West)(0.5)
  Anchor 16-20 feet N27.27.250
  STR 1.5 feet W080.18.506
  Anchor opposite G5 in charted 18-foot pocket.
- **Causeway Island Anchorage** (East)(0.8)
  Anchor 16-20 feet N27.27.371
  STR 1.5 feet W080.18.177
  Anchor opposite G9 in charted 20-foot pocket.
- **Faber Cove Anchorage** (1.7)
  Anchor 6-10 feet N27.27.940
  STR 1.5 feet W080.17.731
  Charted Faber Cove is at the end of Causeway Island channel.

966.5 Ft. Pierce City Marina (0.4)
VHF 16; 772/464-1245
Exit ICW S of R188. Proceed NW in privately maintained channel to marina. [STR 1.5]
Marina nearly destroyed in 2004 hurricanes.

SAFETY INFO		
	NOAA Weather WX-1 Melbourne, FL **WX-3 West Palm, FL** WX-1 Miami, FL	**Sea Tow** Treasure Coast, FL VHF 16/11 or 69 772/288-2900
	USCG Station Ft. Pierce, FL VHF 16 or 09/22A 772/464-6100	**TowBoatU.S.** Stuart, FL VHF 16/11 or 18 772/286-8123

HEADS UP!				
	847.0	Ponce de Leon Inlet Area (NB)	995.9	Hobe Sound Bridge
	869.1	Allenhurst Bridge	1004.1	Jupiter Bridge
	875.0	Bridge Caution (SB)	1004.8	Jupiter Federal Bridge
	876.6	NASA RR Bridge	1005.9	Indiantown Road Bridge
	878.7	Max Brewer Bridge	1009.4	Donald Ross Bridge
	885.0	NASA Causeway Bridge	1012.3	PGA Blvd. Bridge
	890.0	Bridge Caution (NB)	1013.5	Parker Bridge
	964.8	Ft. Pierce North Bridge	1021.8	Flagler Memorial Bridge
	984.9	**Ernest Lyons Bridge**	1022.7	Royal Park Bridge

Slowly rebuilding.
SEE MANATEE WINTER HAVEN & FT. PIERCE.

979.2 Nettles Island S N
Exit ICW between R214 and G215. Proceed E to privately maintained channel. [STR 1.2 (TS)]

- **Nettles Island Marina** (1.1)
  VHF 16; 772/229-2811
  Marina is to port.
- **Nettles Island Anchorage** (1.2)
  Anchor 6-8 feet N27.17.039
  STR (TS) 1.2 feet W080.12.996
  Anchor beyond marina behind R10.

981.3 Jensen Beach Bridge Anchorage (North)(0.2) S N
Anchor 7-8 feet N27.15.263
STR 1.3 feet W080.13.380
Exit ICW NNW of bridge. Proceed W.

981.4 Jensen Beach Causeway Bridge S N
(Frank Wacha Bridge)
Fixed; vertical 65 feet.
Demolition of the old Jensen Beach Causeway Bridge (bascule) continues in 2005.

982.1 Jensen Beach S N
Exit ICW between R220 and G221. Proceed NNW in charted deep water toward causeway. [STR 1.3]

- **Jensen Beach Bridge Anchorage** (South)(0.7)
  Anchor 7-8 feet N27.15.002
  STR 1.3 feet W080.13.292
  Anchor in lee of bridge in charted 7-foot pocket.
- **Jensen Beach Anchorage** (0.6)
  Anchor 6-8 feet N27.14.826
  STR 1.3 feet W080.13.383
  Charted 7-foot pocket off Jensen Beach.
- **Sun Dance Marina North** (0.7)
  VHF 16; 772/334-1416
  Marina is in charted 7-foot tongue, beyond anchorage, at Jensen Beach.
  Dry store with no transient dockage.

982.8 A A Marina (0.6) S N
VHF 16 N27.13.887
772/334-0936 W080.13.021
Exit ICW between R222 and G223. Proceed W in privately maintained channel to marina. [STR 1.3 (TS)]
Formerly Anchors Aweigh Marina.

983.4 Outrigger Harbour Marina (0.5) S N
VHF 16; 772/286-7200
Exit ICW between G223 and R224. Proceed W in privately maintained channel to marina. [STR 1.3]

984.9 Ernest Lyons Bridge S N
(Indian River Bridge)(Sewall Point Bridge)
VHF 09; 772/221-4058
Double bascule; vertical 28 feet.
Restricted December 1-May 1: M-F except holidays, 0700-1800 hrs, opens every hour and half-hour.
Scheduled for replacement by 2007 with fixed 65-foot bridge.

Bone Bed, accumulated layers of sand and shells that embedded fossils of giant ground sloths, giant armadillos, saber-toothed cats, mastodons, and wooly mammoths.

As the sea withdrew and wind and water eroded the land, layers of archaeological history were exposed. The most famous of these discoveries was at Crane Creek, just south of Melbourne down the channel departing from R6. In 1925 a human skull was discovered at Crane Creek. The skull, called the Melbourne Man, generated a 30-year controversy between geologists and archaeologists.

Today it is accepted that Mr. Melbourne is about 12,000 years old. This ends the controversy: Native Americans did indeed live here on the Indian River alongside the last of the great Pleistocene mammals.

Equip your dinghy with a long (15-20') painter or locking cable. As dinghy docks become more crowded, you'll need to tie up then push your dinghy away from the dock. With the long-painter system, many more dinghies can share the same dock frontage.

THE LAGOON HOUSE

The Lagoon House, across from R10 on the western shore, is a new free visitor center highlighting the archaeological, historical, natural, cultural, and recreational resources of Indian River Lagoon. This $1 million facility, designed in traditional Florida style, is scheduled to open soon and is intended as the starting point of the Indian River Lagoon Scenic Highway.

Unfortunately for cruisers, there are no docks to access this facility. You can visit the Lagoon House by land, on U.S. 1 about two miles south of Melbourne. Or, as the facility and grounds are completed, call to inquire about possibilities for landing a dinghy.

Marine Resources Council
Lagoon House Info
321/725-7775

THE SNAKE BIRD

In the wilder areas of Indian River, you may spot an anhinga, also called a snakebird. When an anhinga swims, only its head and long curved black neck show above the water, looking like a dark upright snake. They're also called water turkeys because when they fly they look like a wild turkey with their long fanned tail. The formal name, anhinga, is a South American Indian word for water turkey.

Many people confuse anhinga with cormorants, because they are both black seabirds with long necks; but they are very different. Anhinga are tropical birds, found only in tropical swamps. Cormorants are abundant

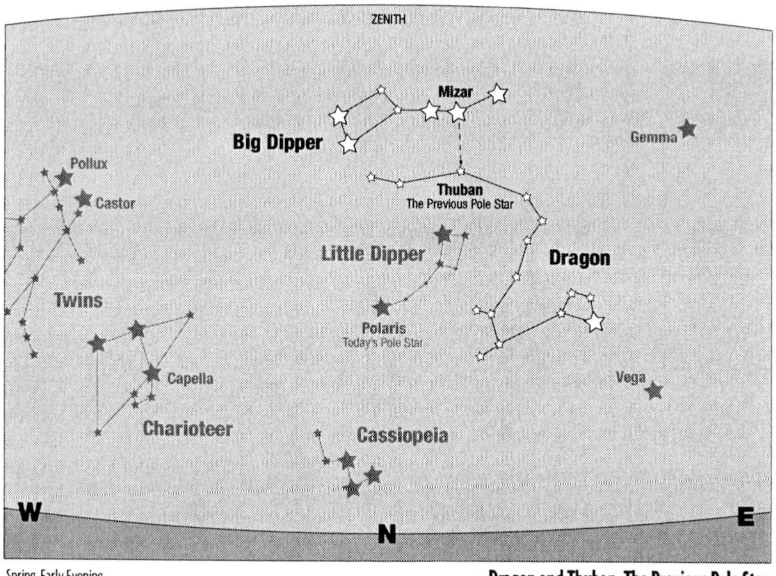

Spring, Early Evening

Dragon and Thuban, The Previous Pole Star

SAFETY INFO

NOAA Weather
WX-1 Melbourne, FL
WX-3 West Palm, FL
WX-1 Miami, FL

USCG
Station Ft. Pierce, FL
VHF 16 or 09/22A
772/464-6100

Sea Tow
Treasure Coast, FL
VHF 16/11 or 69
772/288-2900

TowBoatU.S.
Stuart, FL
VHF 16/11 or 18
772/286-8123

HEADS UP!

847.0	Ponce de Leon Inlet Area (NB)
869.1	Allenhurst Bridge
875.0	Bridge Caution (SB)
876.6	NASA RR Bridge
878.7	Max Brewer Bridge
885.0	NASA Causeway Bridge
890.0	Bridge Caution (NB)
964.8	Ft. Pierce North Bridge
984.9	Ernest Lyons Bridge
995.9	Hobe Sound Bridge
1004.1	Jupiter Bridge
1004.8	Jupiter Federal Bridge
1005.9	Indiantown Road Bridge
1009.4	Donald Ross Bridge
1012.3	PGA Blvd. Bridge
1013.5	Parker Bridge
1021.8	Flagler Memorial Bridge
1022.7	Royal Park Bridge

Courtesy of National Park Service

Anhinga Swallowing

along the Waterway as far north as the cold waters of Maine. Anhinga swim with only their head above water; cormorants swim with their bodies low in the water. Anhinga have much longer tails and are more snake-like than cormorants. But both species share a lack of waterproof feathers; cormorants and anhinga are often seen perched with their wings open to dry their feathers.

Like penguins, anhinga "fly" underwater to fish. They pull their long wings in to their bodies, swimming at high speed with shortened wings. In underwater pursuit, an anhinga darts its long neck forward, spearing a fish on its bill. Then it brings its speared catch to the surface, tosses the fish into the air, and swallows it headfirst in one (sometimes difficult) gulp.

WHAT'S A CRACKER?

Every day, about a thousand people move into Florida. In a state populated with transplants, it's hard to find someone whose family has lived here for more than two generations.

The early pioneers in Florida were called "Crackers," and the term is still used for Floridians whose families trace back to the original settlers. But as an out-of-towner, you need to be very careful calling someone a Cracker. In some parts of Florida, being a Cracker is a source of pride. In other parts, especially near the Georgia border, it's a racial slur meaning a bigoted redneck.

Historians are still not sure how the term originated as a name for rural multi-generational Floridians. One theory is from Florida's cattle industry, which began 500 years ago and still flourishes. Florida's pioneers were cattle ranchers who had a unique way of herding cattle. They used long whips made of braided leather that made a loud "crack" sound to drive the cattle back into line. So Florida cowboys were called Crackers. Still today there is a breed of horse, called a Florida Cracker horse, with ancestry to the Spanish stocks brought in the 1500s.

Whatever the source of the name, Florida Crackers had their own pioneer culture and language. Life was tough in the outposts of Florida at the turn of the century. Mosquitoes were euphemistically called "swamp angels." "Low-bush lightning" was the Cracker term for moonshine during Prohibition. And supper for these self-sufficient Cracker pioneers included "cooters" (soft-shelled turtles), "piney-woods rooter" (wild hog), and "scrub chicken" (gopher tortoises).

To remove black star mildew on non-porous surfaces, wipe with diluted chlorine bleach. To remove black mildew on canvas or sails, use an oxidizing laundry cleaner such as Oxy-Clean. To remove green mildew in the folds of canvas or sailcloth, use Mighty-Brite Mildew and Stain Remover.

Courtesy of U.S. Fish & Wildlife Service

Brown and White Pelicans

BEFORE AIR CONDITIONING

Florida is now experiencing a revitalization of its folk architecture, sometimes parodied as "Cracker Chic."

But the pioneers who built houses before air conditioning had some good ideas about design: local materials, smaller structures, steep roofs, sheltering porches for shade, crawl spaces underneath for ventilation, and room layouts with cross-breezes. But not all design features translate well into contemporary homes: some Cracker houses had floorboards intentionally spaced with large cracks for easy no-dustpan sweeping.

These simple houses were usually constructed by the owners or local self-

985.0 Hutchinson Island Resort (0.5) S N
VHF 16; 772/225-6989
Exit ICW SSE of bridge. Proceed ENE in privately maintained channel to marina. [STR 1.3]

987.8 Junction | "The Crossroads" S N
This area of the ICW is locally known as "The Crossroads," where the St. Lucie River crosses the ICW and leads easterly to St. Lucie Inlet or westerly to the Okeechobee Waterway.
Exit ICW SSE of R240.
SEE THE CROSSROADS.
Caution: ICW aid numbers "re-start" at this junction. Carefully identify ICW R240 and R2 (triangles and squares) versus St. Lucie River R2 and G3 (westward) as well as G17 (eastward).

St. Lucie Inlet (2.5)
Proceed easterly to St. Lucie Inlet.
This inlet, although frequently used by commercial and sport fishing boats, is not recommended without local knowledge.
SEE HOUSES OF REFUGE.

Manatee Pocket/Port Salerno (0.6)
Pick up St. Lucie River R2 and G3 pair and proceed westerly. Exit St. Lucie River at R6 "A" for charted Manatee Pocket. Proceed southwesterly into Manatee Pocket channel. [STR 1.1 (TS)]
Caution: Expect cross current at the Crossroads. Be sure to identify red nuns and green cans N of Rocky Point before proceeding. The initial stretch is shoal, but quickly deepens.

- **Sailfish Marina of Stuart** (0.9)
  VHF 16/73 N27.09.812
  772/283-1122 W080.11.568
  Marina is to starboard.
- **Finest Kind Marina** (1.0)
  VHF 16/73 N27.09.708
  772/223-4110 W080.11.729
  Marina is to starboard.
- **Mariner Cay Marina** (1.2)
  VHF 16; 772/287-2900
  Marina is to starboard.
  Limited space; may accept overnight transients on fuel dock.
- **Manatee Pocket Anchorage** (1.5)
  Anchor 5-7 feet N27.09.193
  STR (TS) 1.1 feet W080.11.765
  Continue southerly to center of bay. Water depths are greater than charted.
  72-hour anchoring limit.
- **Pirates Cove Resort & Marina** (1.8)
  VHF 68 N27.08.900
  772/223-9216 W080.11.750
  Marina is to starboard.
- **Stuart Corinthian Yacht Club** (1.9)
  VHF 16; 772/221-1900
  Yacht club is to port.
- **Manatee Marina** (2.0)
  VHF 16; 772/288-2888
  Marina is to starboard.
  Limited transient dockage; no shower facilities.

SAFETY INFO

NOAA Weather
WX-1 Melbourne, FL
WX-3 West Palm, FL
WX-1 Miami, FL

USCG
Station Lake Worth Inlet, FL
VHF 16 or 09/22A
561/844-4470

Sea Tow
Palm Beach, FL
VHF 16/06
561/844-8056

TowBoatU.S.
Jupiter, FL
VHF 16/11 or 18
561/842-1525

HEADS UP!

869.1	Allenhurst Bridge
875.0	Bridge Caution (SB)
876.6	NASA RR Bridge
878.7	Max Brewer Bridge
885.0	NASA Causeway Bridge
890.0	Bridge Caution (NB)
964.8	Ft. Pierce North Bridge
984.9	Ernest Lyons Bridge
995.9	**Hobe Sound Bridge**
1004.1	**Jupiter Bridge**
1004.8	Jupiter Federal Bridge
1005.9	Indiantown Road Bridge
1009.4	Donald Ross Bridge
1012.3	PGA Blvd. Bridge
1013.5	Parker Bridge
1021.8	Flagler Memorial Bridge
1022.7	Royal Park Bridge
1024.7	Southern Blvd. Bridge

City of Stuart Moorings | Okeechobee Waterway (7.5)
Southpoint Anchorage and the City of Stuart mooring field lies further up the St. Lucie River on the way to the Okeechobee Waterway.

992.1 Peck Lake Anchorage (0.2)
Anchor 8-10 feet N27.06.867
STR 1.5 feet W080.08.534
Exit ICW SSE of G19. Proceed ENE.
Avoid shoal S of sign. Deep water to shore.

992.3 Loblolly Marina (0.1)
VHF 16/10 N27.06.740
772/546-3136 W080.08.626
Exit ICW SSE of G19. Proceed WSW in privately maintained channel to marina. [STR 1.5 (TS)]

995.9 Hobe Sound Bridge
(Route 708/707)
VHF 09; 772/546-5234
Double bascule; vertical 21 feet; on request. [STR 1.8 (TS)]

998.4 Hobe Sound Anchorage (North)(0.1)
Anchor 6-8 feet N27.01.910
STR 2.1 feet W080.06.428
Exit ICW between R38 and R40. Proceed W to charted pocket.

998.9 Hobe Sound Anchorage (Mid)(0.1)
Anchor 7-9 feet N27.01.449
STR 2.1 feet W080.06.238
Exit ICW between R40 and G41. Proceed W.
See Hobe Sound.

1000.4 Hobe Sound Anchorage (South)(0.1)
Anchor 8-10 feet N27.00.289
STR 2.1 feet W080.05.706
Exit ICW between R44 and R46. Proceed W.

1001.6 Conch Bar Anchorage (0.1)
Anchor 7-9 feet N26.59.269
STR (TS) 2.0 feet W080.05.503
Exit ICW at G49. Proceed W.

1002.2 Jupiter Hills Lighthouse Marina (0.1)
VHF 16; 561/744-0727
Exit ICW at R52. Marina is to W. [STR 2.2]
Annual and monthly slip holders only. No transient dockage.

1002.3 Blowing Rocks Marina (0.1)
VHF 16; 561/746-3312
Exit ICW at R52. Marina is to W. [STR 2.2]
See Blowing Rocks.

1002.4 Seagate Marina (0.1)
VHF 16; 561/746-2600
Exit ICW at R54. Marina is to W. [STR 2.2]
Dry store with no transient dockage.

1004.1 Jupiter Bridge
(County Route 707)
VHF 09; Palm Beach County would not provide
Double bascule; vertical 25 feet; on request. [STR 2.4 (TS)]

taught builders. Most began as a single room, called a single pen house. Small additions were added over time as needed. Only a handful of simple floor plans were used, such as the double pen house called a Dog Trot: two rooms surrounded by an H-shaped porch creating a roofed-over breezeway.

You can see an original Cracker house, known as the Grant Historical House, across from Grant Farm Island on the mainland, just south of STM 930. It's a simple white house with a long pier, built from a mail order catalog by early settlers in 1913.

Grant Historical House
321/723-8543

SPOIL ISLANDS

Like beads on a necklace, scores of tiny spoil islands line the Waterway through mid-Florida's Brevard, Indian River, St. Lucie, and Martin Counties.

At first environmentalists were concerned about the impact of these spoil islands. But in Florida, plants rule: the islands were quickly covered by grass or mangrove or pines and created raccoon- and human-free nesting and feeding areas. Look for White Pelicans, usually in large flocks, sitting on the spoil islands.

Every one of these islands is named and has a designated use classification. For example, take the island just west of R50 near STM 932. This island is called "BC48" and is used for education. The next island south is BC49, designated for conservation and closed to the public. The next island in line, just across from R54, is BC50, designated for recreational use with a 5-foot depth boating access on the southwest side.

If you can figure out what "BC" stands for, you pass the Florida geography quiz. Need a hint? The next county's dredge islands are named IR1, IR2, and so on.

SHOOTOUT AT SEBASTIAN

Sebastian Inlet lies to the east of the Waterway, at about STM 936. In the early 1900s the reign of Florida's most notorious band of outlaws ended at the Sebastian Inlet Bridge. This foursome, the John Ashley Gang, robbed banks, hijacked trains, and bootlegged liquor for fourteen years, from 1910 to 1924.

Finally one night, local sheriffs staked out the bridge with red lanterns and a chain blockade. All four gangsters were killed in a spectacular half-hour shootout.

Don't forget bridges as anchorages. In crowded Central and South Florida, there are fewer anchorages. But most bridges offer four opportunities, albeit noisy, for moderate protection. Figure out that night's wind direction and choose the quadrant (NW, NE, SW, or SE) of the bridge that provides the most shelter.

Courtesy of U.S. Fish & Wildlife Service

Paul Kroegel

PELICAN ISLAND

East of G71, just south of STM 940, is a tiny island that made conservation history. Pelican Island was the first piece of land set aside by the national government to protect wildlife.

At the turn of the century, pelicans were shot for sport and for their plumes. Paul Kroegel, the Sebastian resident who spearheaded the creation of the refuge, would watch in frustration as pelicans were shot from what was then the only Brown Pelican rookery on Florida's Atlantic coast. He'd sail out from the mainland to try to discourage the shooting, but there was no legal protection for the birds. Even passing yachts thought it was great sport to pick off a few pelicans as they passed through Indian River Lagoon. And in those days the channel passed even closer to Pelican Island.

Then in 1903, America's conservation president, Theodore Roosevelt, set aside this tiny island as the nation's first "national wildlife refuge." Kroegel became the first national wildlife warden, earning $1 a month as the warden of the "Pelican Island Reservation."

SAFETY INFO

NOAA Weather
WX-1 Melbourne, FL
WX-3 West Palm, FL
WX-1 Miami, FL

USCG
Station Lake Worth Inlet, FL
VHF 16 or 09/22A
561/844-4470

Sea Tow
Palm Beach, FL
VHF 16/06
561/844-8056

TowBoatU.S.
Jupiter, FL
VHF 16/11 or 18
561/842-1525

HEADS UP!

878.7 Max Brewer Bridge
885.0 NASA Causeway Bridge
890.0 Bridge Caution (NB)
964.8 Ft. Pierce North Bridge
984.9 Ernest Lyons Bridge
995.9 Hobe Sound Bridge
1004.1 Jupiter Bridge
1004.8 Jupiter Federal Bridge
1005.9 Indiantown Road Bridge
1009.4 Donald Ross Bridge
1012.3 PGA Blvd. Bridge
1013.5 Parker Bridge
1021.8 Flagler Memorial Bridge
1022.7 Royal Park Bridge
1024.7 Southern Blvd. Bridge
1028.8 Lake Avenue Bridge
1031.0 Lantana Bridge
1034.4 South Florida Caution (SB)

From tiny Pelican Island, the National Wildlife Refuge system is now the world's largest network of managed wildlife lands, spanning over 500 refuges and protecting 94 million acres. Between Biscayne Bay and Hampton Roads, the Waterway transits through twelve National Wildlife Refuges, including Great Dismal Swamp, Mackay Island, Alligator River, Waccamaw, Cape Romain, Pinckney Island, Tybee Island, Blackbeard Island, Wolf Island, Merritt Island, Hobe Sound, and Pelican Island.

Today Pelican Island National Wildlife Refuge covers about 5,000 acres on the east side of Indian River Lagoon south to the Wabasso Bridge. Two-acre Pelican Island is closed to the public and is a breeding ground for sixteen bird species: Brown Pelicans, Great Egrets, Snowy Egrets, Cattle Egrets, Great Blue Herons, Little Blue Herons, Tricolored Herons, Green Herons, Black-crowned Night Herons, Reddish Egrets, Wood Storks, Double-crested Cormorants, Anhinga, White Ibis, American Oystercatchers, and Common Moorhens.

But you can visit the refuge and its visitor complex, south of Spratt Point across from Pelican Island. Today the Centennial Trail boardwalk and observation tower are busy with birders and spotting scopes, instead of sportsmen and rifles.

Pelican Island National Wildlife Refuge
www.pelicanisland.org
772/589-5969

WABASSO | OSSABAW

The coincidence is so unlikely. The small town of Wabasso (pronounced wuh-BASSO), on the eastern shore of the Wabasso Bridge at STM 943.2, is Ossabaw spelled backward.

Ossabaw Sound (pronounced AH-suh-baw) is in Georgia at about STM 602. As the story's told, settlers from Ossabaw Island migrated to Florida in 1898 and named their new home Wabasso. It's a stretch, but possible. Lucky they didn't move from Cincinnati.

ENVIRONMENTAL LEARNING CENTER

South of Wabasso Bridge, a long dock extends from Wabasso Island, the unlabeled island west of the bridge. This is the dock of the Environmental Learning Center, open for boaters visiting Wabasso Island.

The Environmental Learning Center, which includes most of Wabasso Island, was created to educate residents and visitors about Indian River Lagoon. In addition to labs and classrooms, the facility includes walking paths and boardwalks.

Wabasso Island prides itself on its Florida authenticity: all exotic invasive trees, such as Brazilian Peppers and Australian Pines, have been removed from the island, leaving only native plants such as Live Oaks, Cabbage Palms, Wax Myrtle, mangroves, and native salt marshes. A walk on Wabasso Island is a step back in horticultural time, a glimpse of Florida flora before the days of aggressive transplants from Asia, South America, and Australia.

Environmental Learning Center
www.elcweb.org
772/589-5050

Photo Courtesy of Patricia Holm

Vero Beach Mooring Field

VERO BEACH: A WARM THANKSGIVING

Vero Beach has always been popular with cruisers: it's convenient, offers great services, and serves up a mean Thanksgiving dinner. In fact, Vero Beach is so popular with cruisers many have trouble leaving, prompting cruising authors and musicians David Allester and Eileen Quinn to nickname it "Velcro Beach."

Every Thanksgiving, a group of cruisers organize the Annual Thanksgiving Feast at the municipal marina. A community hall is rented, caterers contracted, tickets sold, and chores assigned. Everyone buys a ticket, which pays for the turkey and trimmings, and brings a side dish to share. A community bus runs from the marina to the shopping district so you can provision for all

1004.2 JIB Yacht Club & Marina (0.1)
VHF 65 N26.57.059
561/746-4300 W080.04.708
Exit ICW S of bridge. Marina is to E. [STR 2.4]

1004.5 Junction | Jupiter Inlet (1.1)
Proceed E out inlet.
Used by local commercial and sport fishing boats.
SEE JUPITER INLET LIGHT.

1004.7 Jupiter Seasport Marina (0.1)
VHF 16; 561/575-0006
Exit ICW E of bridge. Marina is to S. [STR 2.4]
Limited transients accommodated on fuel dock.

1004.8 Jupiter Federal Bridge
(US 1)
VHF 09; 561/746-4907
Double bascule; vertical 26 feet; on request.

1005.9 Indiantown Road Bridge
(Route 706)
VHF 09; 561/746-7114
Single bascule; vertical 35 feet.
Restricted year round: opens on the hour and half-hour.

1006.0 Jupiter Anchorage (0.1)
Anchor 5-6 feet N26.55.988
STR (TS) 2.5 feet W080.04.984
Exit ICW S of bridge. Proceed E toward northern oxbow.

1007.0 Jonathan's Landing Marina (0.1)
VHF 16; 561/747-8980
Exit ICW between G17 and R18. Proceed W. [STR 2.5]

1007.6 Admiral's Cove Marina (0.2)
VHF 16; 561/745-2659
Exit ICW S of G19. Proceed W. [STR 2.5]
Ultra-private, gated residential community with no transient services.
SEE LIQUID GOLD.

1008.7 Bluffs Marina (0.1)
VHF 16; 561/627-6688
Exit ICW S of G25. Proceed E into charted basin. [STR 2.7]
Transients accommodated out of season (during summer months only).

1009.4 Donald Ross Bridge
(Juno Beach Bridge)
VHF 09; Palm Beach County would not provide
Double bascule; vertical 35 feet.
Restricted year round: opens on the hour and half-hour. [STR 2.8 (TS)]

1009.5 Loggerhead Club & Marina (0.2)
VHF 16/69 N26.52.811
561/627-7523 W080.04.395
Exit ICW S of bridge. Proceed W into charted basin. [STR 3.0]
Formerly Frenchman's Marina.

SAFETY INFO

NOAA Weather	**Sea Tow**
WX-1 Melbourne, FL	Palm Beach, FL
WX-3 West Palm, FL	VHF 16/06
WX-1 Miami, FL	561/844-8056
USCG	**TowBoatU.S.**
Station Lake Worth Inlet, FL	Palm Beach, FL
VHF 16 or 09/22A	VHF 16/11 or 18
561/844-4470	561/842-1525

HEADS UP!

890.0	Bridge Caution (NB)
964.8	Ft. Pierce North Bridge
984.9	Ernest Lyons Bridge
995.9	Hobe Sound Bridge
1004.1	Jupiter Bridge
1004.8	Jupiter Federal Bridge
1005.9	Indiantown Road Bridge
1009.4	Donald Ross Bridge
1012.3	**PGA Blvd. Bridge**
1013.5	**Parker Bridge**
1021.8	Flagler Memorial Bridge
1022.7	Royal Park Bridge
1024.7	Southern Blvd. Bridge
1028.8	Lake Avenue Bridge
1031.0	Lantana Bridge
1034.4	South Florida Caution (SB)
1035.0	Boynton Beach Bridge
1035.9	Briny Breezes Bridge

1011.9 E&H Boat Works (0.1)
No VHF Watch; 561/622-8550
Facility is to W. [STR 3.2]
Repair yard with no transient dockage.

1012.0 Seminole Boat Yard (0.1)
No VHF Watch; 561/622-7600
Facility is to W. [STR 3.2]
Dry store and Do-It-Yourself (DIY) yard with no transient dockage.

1012.1 Soverel Harbour Marina (0.2)
VHF 16/08 N26.50.764
561/691-9554 W080.04.232
Exit ICW N of bridge. Proceed W into charted basin. [STR 3.2]

1012.2 PGA Marina (0.1)
VHF 16; 561/626-0200
Marina is to W. [STR 3.2]
No transient dockage; annual contracts only.

1012.3 PGA Boulevard Bridge
(Route 74)
VHF 09; 561/624-3684
Double bascule; vertical 24 feet.
Restricted year round: opens on the hour and half-hour. [STR 3.2 (TS)]
SEE PGA BOULEVARD.

1012.5 Harbour Point Marina (0.1)
VHF 16; 561/622-6890
Marina is to W. [STR 3.2]
Marina has become a "brokerage" marina; wet slips occupied with boats for sale.

1013.1 North Palm Beach Waterway Anchorages
Exit ICW at bend between the two bridges. Proceed SW to charted North Palm Beach Waterway. [STR 3.3]

- **N. Palm Beach Waterway Anchorage** (North)(0.5)
  Anchor 5-7 feet N26.49.741
  STR 3.3 feet W080.04.182
  Exit W into first charted large basin.
- **N. Palm Beach Waterway Anchorage** (South)(1.1)
  Anchor 6-8 feet N26.49.319
  STR 3.3 feet W080.04.128
  Exit W into second charted large basin.

1013.5 Parker Bridge
(North Palm Beach Bridge)(US 1)
VHF 09; 561/626-5445
Double bascule; vertical 25 feet.
Restricted year round: opens on the quarter-hour and three-quarter hour.

1013.6 North Palm Beach Marina (0.2)
VHF 16/08 N26.49.702
561/626-4919 W080.03.528
Exit ICW SE of bridge. Proceed S into charted basin. [STR 3.4]

1014.1 North Lake Worth
Exit ICW at G27. Proceed northeasterly to North Lake Worth channel. [STR 3.4]

those cranberries, pumpkins, beans, yams, and mini-marshmallows on your list. But expect a crowd: in recent years the event has sold out and each mooring pennant anchors a flotilla.

If you don't make Thanksgiving, you can join the cruisers' breakfast, based on the popular Annapolis gathering, every Wednesday morning at 8:30 at 2002 Restaurant.

Indian River Chamber of Commerce
www.indianriverchamber.com
772/567-3491

Eileen Quinn's Music for Sailors
www.eileenquinn.com

CYCADS: THE JURASSIC PLANT

If you walk these subtropical streets or parks, you may notice a short palm-like plant that is a stereotype from a dinosaur mural. You can just imagine a prehistoric forest filled with these primitive, dark green fronded plants. This is a cycad (pronounced SY-kud), a relic of the Jurassic age back when Florida was inhabited by dinosaurs.

At about 200 million years old, cycads are one of the oldest living plants. They evolved after ferns but before modern flowering plants. In the U.S. they are native only to Florida.

Cycads were an important food source for the Seminoles. Cycad roots produce a starch that was used by Native Americans to make bread if corn was unavailable. You may have used a form of this starch in your own cooking: it's one version of arrowroot sold in health food stores.

Harbor Branch Oceanographic Institution

ICW and HBOI Canal

HARBOR BRANCH SUBMERSIBLES

The large Harbor Branch Ship Channel, running west from the Waterway at STM 960, is the site of the Harbor Branch Oceanographic Institution. Nicknamed HBOI, this marine research facility is home to two Johnson Sea-Link submersibles.

Harbor Branch Oceanographic Institution

Johnson Sea-Link Submersible

You may see one of HBOI's research vessels in the inlet area, heading out to conduct research on Florida's waters. The submersibles, equipped with acrylic viewing spheres, are launched from the Institution's two research vessels. The subs operate independently and are highly maneuverable, able to dive to depths up to 3,000 feet. Video cameras document the underwater scenes using special xenon arc lights that capture dark ocean bottom images in true color. Crewmembers collect ocean bottom samples with the sub's manipulator arms and suction devices.

Harbor Branch is open to the public, with a visitor center and tours of the Institution's aquaculture, research, and rehabilitation projects.

Harbor Branch Oceanographic Institution
www.hboi.edu
772/465-2400

MANATEE WINTER HAVEN

As Florida's temperatures drop for its short "cold" season, Florida Manatees must find warm water. Like a hypothermia victim who doesn't notice he's cold, manatees in water colder than 60° F become so sluggish they stop searching for food.

What better place for warm water than the outflow of a power plant? So every winter, manatees congregate near the Ft. Pierce power plant's outflow at Moores Creek. From the Waterway, the power plant is clearly visible with its tall stacks just southwest of the South Ft. Pierce Bridge, behind the Ft. Pierce City Marina.

To accommodate the congregation of manatees, the Florida Inland Navigation District funded the Manatee Observation and Education Center along the banks of the creek. For a $1 donation, you can view manatees in their natural habitat. Although the

SAFETY INFO

NOAA Weather
WX-1 Melbourne, FL
WX-3 West Palm, FL
WX-1 Miami, FL

USCG
Station Lake Worth Inlet, FL
VHF 16 or 09/22A
561/844-4470

Sea Tow
Palm Beach, FL
VHF 16/06
561/844-8056

TowBoatU.S.
Palm Beach, FL
VHF 16/11 or 18
561/842-1525

HEADS UP!

964.8	Ft. Pierce North Bridge
984.9	Ernest Lyons Bridge
995.9	Hobe Sound Bridge
1004.1	Jupiter Bridge
1004.8	Jupiter Federal Bridge
1005.9	Indiantown Road Bridge
1009.4	Donald Ross Bridge
1012.3	PGA Blvd. Bridge
1013.5	Parker Bridge
1021.8	Flagler Memorial Bridge
1022.7	Royal Park Bridge
1024.7	Southern Blvd. Bridge
1028.8	Lake Avenue Bridge
1031.0	Lantana Bridge
1034.4	South Florida Caution (SB)
1035.0	Boynton Beach Bridge
1035.9	Briny Breezes Bridge
1037.7	George Bush Blvd. Bridge

center is now open year-round (except Mondays), the manatees are usually in the area only between November and April.

Manatee Observation Center
www.manateecenter.com
772/466-1600

Courtesy of St. Lucie County TDC

Ft. Pierce City Marina

FT. PIERCE

Ft. Pierce's most famous resident was Zora Neale Hurston, the African American novelist and playwright. You can learn about her life by walking the Zora Neale Hurston Dust Tracks Heritage Trail. The first stop on the trail is St. Lucie County's Zora Neale Hurston Branch Library, the site of the 2003 dedication of the 37¢ postage stamp in her honor. The library also has a large collection of her works and other memorabilia of her writing career.

But Ft. Pierce was also home to many other African American artists. The Highwaymen were based in Ft. Pierce, artists who earned their name by traveling the South in the 1960s selling their landscape paintings from the trunks of their cars.

Today a Highwaymen landscape sells for thousands of dollars. The A.E. "Bean" Backus Gallery, named after their mentor Bean Backus, has several Highwaymen landscapes on display. It is located just north of the Ft. Pierce Yachting Center, on Indian River Drive near the waterfront.

In addition to tours, shops, and services, Downtown Ft. Pierce hosts several regular events, including a farmers' market, art walks, classic car cruise-ins, and jazz jams. The Farmers' Market is open Saturday mornings, October through April, at the downtown waterfront. Main Street Ft. Pierce hosts Friday Fest, the first Friday of every month from 5:30-8:30 pm, with food, arts and crafts, and live music.

City of Ft. Pierce
www.cityoffortpierce.com
772/465-5658

Main Street Ft. Pierce
www.mainstreetfortpierce.org
772/466-3880

Backus Gallery
www.backusgallery.com
772/465-0630

Always have an inexpensive air horn handy at the helm as the ICW becomes more crowded. It's fast and easy to grab the horn and blow if someone fails to notice your vessel.

CROSSROADS OF MARINE RESEARCH

The large ocean inlet and protected harbors of Ft. Pierce draw marine researchers from all over the world. Two research facilities are based on Causeway Island to the east of the Ft. Pierce South Bridge at STM 965.8.

The St. Lucie County Historical Museum, located on the northern shore of Causeway Island, focuses on offshore treasure searches. With displays of silver and gold from a fleet of eleven Spanish ships that sank during a 1715 hurricane, it's clear why this region is called Florida's "Treasure Coast."

The Smithsonian Marine Station, a research branch of the Smithsonian Institution, is located on the south side of Causeway Island. Its public branch, the Marine Center, displays six living Florida marine habitats. If you visit the Marine Center, you can experience a bit of the Bahamas without crossing the Gulf Stream: the highlight of the exhibit is the 3,000-gallon Caribbean coral reef.

Historical Museum
www.st-lucie.lib.fl.us/museum
772/462-1795

Smithsonian Marine Station
www.sms.si.edu/smee
772/462-3474

Courtesy of St. Lucie County TDC

Kingfish Tourney Early Morning Start

- **Old Port Cove Marina** (0.9)
  VHF 16/08 N26.49.950
  561/626-1760 W080.03.238
  Exit channel at G9. Proceed W to marina.
- **North Lake Worth Anchorage** (1.2)
  Anchor 8-14 feet N26.50.400
  STR 3.4 feet W080.03.207
  Anchorage is in extreme NE corner of basin.
  Many southbound cruisers believe Lake Worth is the official re-entry to "civilization." Be sure to lock your dinghy here.
  First day is free. Then a 5-day anchoring permit must be purchased.

1016.6 Lake Park Harbor Marina (0.3) S N
VHF 16; 561/840-0188
Exit ICW at G35. Proceed W in privately maintained channel to marina. [STR 3.3]
Private residential facility with limited transient dockage. If space is available, you may stay up to 10 days.

1017.2 Riviera Beach Bridge S N
(Blue Heron Boulevard Bridge)
Fixed; vertical 65 feet.

1017.3 Junction | Singer Island S N
Exit ICW S of bridge. Proceed easterly in Singer Island Channel. [STR 3.3]
See Peanut Island.

- **Singer Island Anchorage** (0.2)
  Anchor 8-10 feet N26.46.871
  STR 3.3 feet W080.02.432
  Proceed to NE elbow off Singer Island. Avoid charted cable area.
- **Cannonsport Marina & Resort** (0.3)
  VHF 16/07 N26.46.710
  561/848-7469 W080.02.410
  Marina is to E.
- **Buccaneer Marina** (0.4)
  VHF 16; 561/842-1620
  Marina is to E.
- **Sailfish Marina & Resort** (0.5)
  VHF 16/68 N26.46.627
  561/844-1724 W080.02.418
  Marina is to E.
- **Lake Worth Inlet** (3.0)
  Moderately Aided N26.46.423
  Well Lit W080.00.599
  Continue S, then E to Lake Worth Inlet.
  Waypoint is at RW "LW" sea buoy.
  See Junction | Lake Worth Inlet (STM 1018.4).

1017.5 New Port Cove Marine Center (0.3) S N
VHF 16; 561/844-2504
Exit ICW SW of G39. Proceed W in privately maintained channel to marina. [STR 3.3]

1017.8 Riviera Beach Yacht Center (0.2) S N
VHF 16; 561/863-4126
Exit ICW NE of G41. Marina is to W. [STR 3.3]
Repair facility with no transient dockage.

SAFETY INFO

NOAA Weather
WX-1 Melbourne, FL
WX-3 West Palm, FL
WX-1 Miami, FL

USCG
Station Lake Worth Inlet, FL
VHF 16 or 09/22A
561/844-4470

Sea Tow
Palm Beach, FL
VHF 16/06
561/844-8056

TowBoatU.S.
Palm Beach, FL
VHF 16/11 or 18
561/842-1525

HEADS UP!

984.9 Ernest Lyons Bridge
995.9 Hobe Sound Bridge
1004.1 Jupiter Bridge
1004.8 Jupiter Federal Bridge
1005.9 Indiantown Road Bridge
1009.4 Donald Ross Bridge
1012.3 PGA Blvd. Bridge
1013.5 Parker Bridge
1021.8 Flagler Memorial Bridge
1022.7 Royal Park Bridge
1024.7 Southern Blvd. Bridge
1028.8 Lake Avenue Bridge
1031.0 Lantana Bridge
1034.4 South Florida Caution (SB)
1035.0 Boynton Beach Bridge
1035.9 Briny Breezes Bridge
1037.7 George Bush Blvd. Bridge
1039.6 Atlantic Avenue Bridge

1017.9 Riviera Beach Municipal Marina (0.2)
VHF 16 N26.46.397
561/842-7806 W080.03.080
Exit ICW at R42. Marina is to W. [STR 3.3]

1018.1 Cracker Boy Boat Works (0.1)
No VHF Watch; 561/845-0357
Exit ICW at G43. Proceed W to facility. [STR 3.3]

1018.4 Junction | Lake Worth Inlet (3.0)
Moderately Aided N26.46.423
Well Lit W080.00.599
Exit ICW in Port of Palm Beach turning basin. Proceed easterly to Lake Worth Inlet. Waypoint is at RW "LW" sea buoy.
Many cruisers bounce in and out of the Waterway between Lake Worth and Biscayne Channel. It is a nice alternative to the bridges and congestion of the ICW and a welcome opportunity to get back out to the ocean.
See Lake Worth.
Caution: Southbound, if your vessel height is greater than 56 feet, you must exit the ICW at this inlet or at Port Everglades (Ft. Lauderdale) to proceed outside and re-join the ICW at Government Cut (Miami) or Biscayne Channel (Key Biscayne).

1018.4 Lake Worth Anchorage (North)(1.2)
Anchor 8-10 feet N26.45.431
STR 3.3 feet W080.02.559
Exit ICW in Port of Palm Beach turning basin. Proceed toward Lake Worth Inlet. At G11, turn S and follow charted Palm Beach channel along shore. Anchorage is beyond R6, between cable areas.

1019.7 Rybovich Spencer (0.1)
VHF 16/08 N26.44.905
561/844-1800 W080.02.983
Exit ICW between R4 "A" and R6. Facility is to W. [STR 3.3]

1021.6 Palm Beach Yacht Club Marina (0.1)
VHF 16; 561/655-1944
Exit ICW N of bridge. Marina is to W. [STR 3.1]

1021.7 Flagler Memorial Bridge Anchorage (0.1)
Anchor 6-8 feet N26.43.158
STR 3.1 feet W080.02.866
Exit ICW N of bridge. Proceed W.

1021.8 Flagler Memorial Bridge
(Quadrille Boulevard Bridge)
VHF 09; 561/833-7339
Double bascule; vertical 17 feet.
Restricted year round: opens on the quarter-hour and three-quarter hour.
See Flagler's Whitehall.

1022.0 Palm Harbor Marina (0.1)
VHF 16; 561/655-4757
Exit ICW S of bridge. Marina is to W. [STR 3.1]

1022.3 Lake Worth Anchorage (South)(0.1)
Anchor 8-10 feet N26.42.700
STR 3.1 feet W080.02.835
Exit ICW between R12 and R14. Proceed W.

INVASION OF THE ALIENS

Florida, with its welcoming climate, battles exotic species, called "invasive aliens," from all over the world. When the weather is this mild, it truly is a jungle out there. Florida faces a massive weed control problem, part of what the Audubon Society estimates is a $130 billion cost to the U.S. economy.

Courtesy of NASA

Merritt Island Wild Pigs

On Merritt Island, feral hogs have taken over, consuming huge quantities of sea turtle eggs and tearing up native vegetation. The refuge has brought in trappers to hunt the hogs for meat, but the population keeps replenishing itself: every year 3,000 hogs are removed from Merritt Island.

Along the spoil islands, another invasive alien has taken hold. Australian Pines, or casuarinas, were originally brought from Australia as wind breaks for the pineapple plantations. Unfortunately this wispy-branched member of the eucalyptus family went wild, covering the ground with smothering needles that prevent any other plants from surviving nearby.

In the water, look for the Water Hyacinth: round bright green leaves floating on a ping-pong-sized bladder of air with trailing water roots. These plants were brought over from Venezuela in 1884 as ornamentals for garden pools. They do have nice purple flowers, but the fast-breeding escapees now choke navigable waterways.

In some sections along the banks of the Waterway, Brazilian Peppers reign. These scrubby trees were brought from South America in the 1840s as an ornamental plant for their attractive red berries, clusters of white flowers, and evergreen leaves. Unfortunately, Brazilian Peppers spread like wildfire: they're so aggressive they've earned a place on Florida's official "Noxious Weeds List" and are now illegal to cultivate. But beekeepers use the trees, bringing their beehives into the monocultures during pollination to produce the popular Brazilian Pepper honey.

THE TREE THAT CAN'T BE KILLED

Susan Orleans, author of *The Orchid Thief*, describes Melaleuca as one of Florida's "deathless plants." Nothing seems to kill this prodigious tree, identified by its spongy, whitish, peeling bark and leaves like a eucalyptus.

In the early 1900s, Melaleuca was the panacea to the swamps of Florida. This fast-growing water-hungry plant was brought from Australia to drain the wetlands. In the 1930s, Florida developers scattered Melaleuca seeds by airplane to dry up their land.

But Melaleuca didn't work out as planned. The trees spread fifty acres a day, creating massive monocultures and covering a half-million of the Everglade's 7.6 million acres. When Ted Levin, author of *Liquid Land: Journey through the Florida Everglades*, asked a state forester how long it takes Melaleuca to reach flowering age, he replied, "About fifteen minutes."

Courtesy of U.S. Fish & Wildlife Service

Spraying Melaleuca

Melaleuca is nearly impossible to kill. The government tried girdling the trees and painting the exposed cambium with Arsenal, but any branches touching the water grow roots and become new trees. If you try to kill it by

SAFETY INFO

NOAA Weather
WX-1 Melbourne, FL
WX-3 West Palm, FL
WX-1 Miami, FL

USCG
Station Lake Worth Inlet, FL
VHF 16 or 09/22A
561/844-4470

Sea Tow
Palm Beach, FL
VHF 16/06
561/844-8056

TowBoatU.S.
Palm Beach, FL
VHF 16/11 or 18
561/842-1525

HEADS UP!

1004.1 Jupiter Bridge
1004.8 Jupiter Federal Bridge
1005.9 Indiantown Road Bridge
1009.4 Donald Ross Bridge
1012.3 PGA Blvd. Bridge
1013.5 Parker Bridge
1021.8 Flagler Memorial Bridge
1022.7 Royal Park Bridge
1024.7 Southern Blvd. Bridge
1028.8 Lake Avenue Bridge
1031.0 Lantana Bridge
1034.4 South Florida Caution (SB)
1035.0 Boynton Beach Bridge
1035.9 Briny Breezes Bridge
1037.7 George Bush Blvd. Bridge
1039.6 Atlantic Avenue Bridge
1041.1 Linton Blvd. Bridge
1044.9 Spanish River Bridge

freezing, chopping, poisoning, or burning, the tree immediately responds by releasing 20 million seeds right before it dies.

Courtesy of St. Lucie County TDC

Green Turtle

So you have to sneak up on it with its own mortality. The current technique is called "hack-and-squirt": slowly hacking off sections and squirting it with low doses of herbicide. But efforts at removing this invasive plant are so extensive that melaleuca control has its own line item in Florida's state budget.

Florida recently imported an Australian weevil called the Melaleuca Snout Beetle, which eats the leaves and buds of the melaleuca tree. Let's hope this latest experiment in an exotic species fares better than the last few imports.

Make your own custom dinghy security cable with coated stainless wire (lifelines) and two Nicopress sleeves. Take 30' of wire and create a loop on each end by crimping the Nicopress sleeves. Attach a stainless steel eyebolt, with washers and bedding compound, to your dinghy transom. Secure the cable with a small combination lock.

ENERGY ENCOUNTER

The large towers and high-voltage lines at STM 974 identify Florida Power and Light's St. Lucie Nuclear Plant.

Because of recent security upgrades, boaters are no longer allowed to anchor in its man-made basin. The security zone now provides land protected from further development for nesting sea turtles and other wildlife. But the plant is open to visitors through FP&L Energy Encounter, a free visitor center.

FP&L Energy Encounter
www.fpl.com
877/375-4386

HOUSES OF REFUGE

This may be the Treasure Coast of Florida, but lost treasures also mean treacherous seas. Shipwrecks were a constant concern along these uninhabited shores. If you didn't die by drowning, your prospects stranded on land weren't much better. You may have noticed the names along the Waterway near STM 957: Starvation Cove, Starvation Point...you get the idea.

In the late 1800s, the federal government stepped in and offered to construct ten lifesaving stations, called "houses of refuge," as havens for shipwrecked sailors. Florida's frontier coastline received five houses of refuge.

The only refuge left standing is on Gilbert's Bar, the narrow bar on Hutchinson Island to the east of the Waterway at about STM 986. Over the years, many sailors were rescued from this lookout and brought to the shelter of the house. Today the station, which closed in 1945, is on the National Register of Historic Places and is open to the public for a small fee.

Gilbert's Bar House of Refuge
772/225-1875

THE CROSSROADS

To locals, the four-way intersection at STM 987.8 is known simply as "The Crossroads." St. Lucie Inlet, a small inlet used by locals, departs to the east. St. Lucie River turns off to the west, connecting to the Okeechobee Waterway and Ft. Myers on the Gulf Coast.

The 152-mile Okeechobee Waterway opened in 1937, intended for commercial traffic. But mostly recreational vessels use it now. Like many Florida names with "ee," Okeechobee is a Seminole word. Any word in the Seminole language ending in a double-e denotes water. So Kissimmee means winding water, a wampee is a water plant, hatchee means river, and Okeechobee means big water.

1022.7 Royal Park Bridge
(Route 704)
VHF 09; 561/655-5617
Double bascule; vertical 14 feet.
Restricted year round: opens on the hour and half-hour.
Replacement bridge (vertical 21 feet) has estimated completion of Spring 2005. [STR 3.1 (TS)]

1022.8 Town of Palm Beach Marina (0.1)
VHF 16; 561/838-5463
Exit ICW S of bridge. Marina is to E. [STR 3.1]
Also known as Australian Avenue Docks.
SEE PALM BEACH AND WEST PALM.

1022.9 Royal Park Bridge Anchorage (0.1)
Anchor 10-12 feet N26.42.176
STR 3.1 feet W080.02.889
Exit ICW S of bridge. Anchor opposite town docks in charted 11-foot pocket.

1024.7 Southern Boulevard Bridge
(Route 700)
VHF 09; 561/833-8852
Double bascule; vertical 14 feet.
Restricted year round: opens on the hour and half-hour.

1024.9 Southern Boulevard Bridge Anchorage (0.1)
Anchor 8-10 feet N26.40.363
STR 3.0 feet W080.02.722
Exit ICW S of bridge. Proceed E toward island.

1026.7 West Palm Beach Anchorage (0.1)
Anchor 12-14 feet N26.38.859
STR 3.0 feet W080.02.599
Exit ICW N of R26. Proceed W.

1028.8 Lake Avenue Bridge
(Route 802)
VHF 09; 561/540-2516
Single bascule; vertical 35 feet; on request.

1030.4 Loggerhead Club & Marina (0.2)
VHF 16; 561/582-4422
Exit ICW at R38. Proceed W to marina. [STR 3.0]
Formerly GMC of Lantana.

1030.5 Murrelle Marine (0.2)
No VHF Watch; 561/582-3213
Exit ICW S of R38. Proceed W to facility. [STR 3.0]

1031.0 Lantana Bridge
(Ocean Avenue Bridge)
VHF 09; Palm Beach County would not provide
Double bascule; vertical 13 feet.
Restricted year round: opens on the hour and half-hour.

1031.2 Lantana Anchorage (0.2)
Anchor 6-8 feet N26.34.960
STR 3.0 feet W080.02.931
Exit ICW S of bridge. Proceed W.
Permit with $30 fee allows 96-hour anchoring within 30 days.

SAFETY INFO		
	NOAA Weather WX-3 West Palm Beach, FL **WX-1 Miami, FL** WX-2 Sugarloaf Key, FL	**Sea Tow** Palm Beach, FL VHF 16/06 561/844-8056
	USCG Station Lake Worth Inlet, FL VHF 16 or 09/22A 561/844-4470	**TowBoatU.S.** Boynton, FL VHF 16/08 561/704-1144

HEADS UP!

1013.5	Parker Bridge	**1037.7**	**George Bush Blvd. Bridge**
1021.8	Flagler Memorial Bridge	**1039.6**	**Atlantic Avenue Bridge**
1022.7	Royal Park Bridge	1041.1	Linton Blvd. Bridge
1024.7	Southern Blvd. Bridge	1044.9	Spanish River Bridge
1028.8	Lake Avenue Bridge	1047.4	Palmetto Park Bridge
1031.0	Lantana Bridge	1048.2	Camino Real Bridge
1034.4	**South Florida Caution (SB)**	1050.0	Hillsboro Blvd. Bridge
1035.0	**Boynton Beach Bridge**	1055.0	Northeast 14th Street Bridge
1035.9	**Briny Breezes Bridge**	1056.2	Atlantic Blvd. Bridge

1032.7 Palm Beach Yacht Center (0.2) S N
VHF 16; 561/588-9911
Exit ICW S of G43. Proceed W to marina. [STR 2.9]

1033.1 Gateway Marina (0.2) S N
VHF 16; 561/588-1211
Exit ICW at G45. Proceed W to marina. [STR 2.9]
Dry store with no transient dockage.

1034.4 Heads Up | South Florida S N
to Southbound Navigation Only
1091.8 From Boynton Canal to the Rickenbacker Bridge, this 57-mile stretch is the most congested collection of narrow canals, opening bridges (6 in next 10 STM alone!), personal watercraft, and "weekend warriors" of your ICW experience.

Dotted with multimillion-dollar estates and eccentric lawn and house trimmings we always enjoy the "tour," but with a steady hand on the wheel and an extra cautious eye.

1035.0 Boynton Beach Bridge S N
(Ocean Avenue Bridge)(Route 804)
VHF 09; 561/733-0214
Double bascule; vertical 21 feet.
Restricted year round: opens on the hour and half-hour. [STR 3.1 (TS)]

1035.9 Briny Breezes Bridge S N
(SE 15th Street Bridge)(Woolbright Road)
VHF 09; Palm Beach County would not provide
Double bascule; vertical 25 feet; on request.
SEE IN HER SHOES.

1037.7 George Bush Boulevard Bridge S N
(Northeast 8th Street Bridge)
VHF 09; Palm Beach County would not provide
Double bascule; vertical 9 feet; on request.
SEE BODY HEAT.

1037.8 Marina Delray (0.1) S N
VHF 16/69 N26.28.406
561/276-7666 W080.03.730
Exit ICW S of bridge. Marina is to W. [STR 3.0 (TS)]

1039.5 Free Dock (0.1) S N
Exit ICW N of bridge. Proceed W to tie-up on park wall. [STR 3.0]
2-hour tie-up allowed.

1039.6 Atlantic Avenue Bridge S N
(Route 806)
VHF 09; 561/276-5435
Double bascule; vertical 12 feet.
Restricted year round: opens on the quarter-hour and three-quarter hour.
SEE DELRAY BEACH.

1039.8 Delray Beach Yacht Club (0.1) S N
VHF 16; 561/272-2700
Exit ICW S of bridge. Yacht club is to W. [STR 3.0]

1040.7 Delray Harbor Club Marina (0.1) S N
VHF 16; 561/276-0376
Exit ICW opposite charted 9- and 7-foot pocket. Marina is to W. [STR 3.0 (TS)]
SEE KABOOM! BAD BOYS II

Courtesy of Florida Inland Navigation District

Hobe Sound

UV sunlight is tough on dinghies, especially PVC inflatables. Buy or make a dinghy cover out of Sunbrella fabric. And remember to treat your new inflatable to a sunscreen coating of 303 Aerospace Protectant, available at West Marine and other marine stores.

HOBE SOUND

Martin County keeps a low profile. As you enter from the north at STM 981.4 near Jensen Beach Bridge, or from the south at STM 1003 near Jupiter Inlet, watch the buildings change height. Martin County, unlike St. Lucie County to the north and Palm Beach County to the south, strictly enforces a four-story building height limit.

Martin County is also a quiet county. Hobe Sound, an unincorporated area of the county, is a residential community of golf courses and government parks. Most of the area through Peck Lake, South Jupiter Narrows, and Hobe Sound are part of Hobe Sound National Wildlife Refuge. The refuge's headquarters are located on the west bank of Hobe Sound, about two miles south of Hobe Sound Bridge. The refuge also includes nearly all the eastern shore, to the Atlantic Ocean, from about STM 992 to north of the bridge.

Hobe Sound National Wildlife Refuge
http://hobesound.fws.gov
772/546-6141

BLOWING ROCKS

On the Atlantic side of narrow Jupiter Island, there is an unusual outcropping of limestone called Blowing Rocks. If the tide is high and the winds are strong, the sea breaks against the rocks and sprays saltwater up to 50 feet in the air. Spectacular in itself, but many accounts also claim you can hear a musical humming sound if the wind blows across the rocks at a certain angle.

Today Blowing Rocks is part of a nature preserve, owned by the Nature Conservancy and open to the public. The preserve spans from the Atlantic to the Waterway between R58 and R60.

Blowing Rocks
http://nature.org
561/747-3113

JUPITER INLET LIGHT

Jupiter Inlet Lighthouse was a tough project back in 1850. Imagine trying to build this structure in the middle of a jungle, with no accessible materials, swarms of biting insects, and Indians raiding the site.

Simply transporting materials was a challenge. Over 500 tons of material were brought to the site, but back then the inlet was too shallow for navigation. So supplies were unloaded from larger sailing vessels at the Indian River and ferried using small shallow-draft boats. It took fifty long, hot, and tedious trips to move the building materials.

To add insult to injury, as the lighthouse was completed, someone stole the lens. Supposedly Confederate raiders hid the Fresnel lens as an attempt to confuse blockading Union ships.

Courtesy of Smithsonian Marine Station

Photo by Arlene Brooks **Jupiter Lighthouse**

At the end of the Civil War, the lighthouse keeper conveniently found the lens, buried in Jupiter Creek.

You pass this bright red lighthouse as you meet Jupiter Inlet coming from Jupiter Sound or Loxahatchee River. The lighthouse is open to the public. You can climb its 105 steps for $6, a signature on a liability waiver, and a shoe inspection (closed back shoes only). Only in South Florida would people even think of climbing narrow lighthouse steps in stilettos or flip-flops.

Jupiter Inlet Lighthouse
www.lrhs.org
561/747-6639

SAFETY INFO

NOAA Weather
WX-3 West Palm Beach, FL
WX-1 Miami, FL
WX-2 Sugarloaf Key, FL

USCG
Station Fort Lauderdale, FL
VHF 16 or 09/22A
954/927-1611

Sea Tow
Fort Lauderdale, FL
VHF 16/73
954/525-0037

TowBoatU.S.
Hillsboro, FL
VHF 16
954/783-7821

HEADS UP!

1031.0	Lantana Bridge
1034.4	South Florida Caution (SB)
1035.0	Boynton Beach Bridge
1035.9	Briny Breezes Bridge
1037.7	George Bush Blvd. Bridge
1039.6	Atlantic Avenue Bridge
1041.1	**Linton Blvd. Bridge**
1044.9	**Spanish River Bridge**
1047.4	**Palmetto Park Bridge**
1048.2	**Camino Real Bridge**
1050.0	**Hillsboro Blvd. Bridge**
1055.0	Northeast 14th Street Bridge
1056.2	Atlantic Blvd. Bridge
1059.1	Commercial Blvd. Bridge
1060.6	Oakland Park Bridge
1062.7	East Sunrise Blvd. Bridge
1064.1	East Las Olas Blvd. Bridge
1066.0	Brooks Memorial Bridge

THE CELESTIAL RAILROAD

Back in the 1880s, Titusville was the area's railroad hub. Goods arrived by rail in Titusville and were shipped south by the Indian River Steamboat Company to the south side of Jupiter Inlet. A seven-mile narrow-gauge railroad between Jupiter and Lake Worth moved goods and people along this next stretch of coastline.

Courtesy of NOAA

Photo by Marge Beaver

Jupiter Inlet

This line was originally called the Jupiter & Lake Worth Railroad. But since it stopped at Jupiter, Mars, Venus, and Juno, it was nicknamed "The Celestial Railroad." The town of Jupiter obviously still exists. You pass the town of Juno at STM 1010. Mars and Venus were never much more than loading platforms; supposedly Venus had a population of one man and two cats.

The fare was high and the train was late, but it was the only show in town for years. It cost 10¢ a mile to ride and the crew often delayed the train to visit with friends along the route. But the train stopped for anyone waving from the bushes.

Henry Flagler tried to purchase the line to carry freight for his Palm Beach project, but like many acquisitions, negotiations broke down over price. So Flagler extended his own line, the Florida East Coast Railway, bypassing the Celestial Line. Within two years the Celestial Line was out of business.

Lubricate your key(s) and ignition switch(es) with Corrosion Block or T-9 Boeshield every few months. Spray directly into the switch, insert the key, then turn the key to the on and off position several times.

LIQUID GOLD

"Liquid Gold" is how the community of Admiral's Cove describes itself. South of Indiantown Road Bridge, at STM 1005.9, the Waterway extends into a collection of natural-looking canals and oxbows. This gated community boasts private luxury waterfront homes, listing for about $4 million. Its residents include Tom Cruise and other celebrities seeking Florida luxury and privacy.

PGA BOULEVARD

With affluence, comes golf. With over 150 courses, Palm Beach County has more golf courses than any other area of Florida. The county is also home to the Professional Golfers Association, hence the "PGA Boulevard Bridge" at STM 1012.3.

You may have also noticed the Donald Ross Bridge, just north of the PGA Boulevard Bridge, named after the legendary golf course designer. Ross was a Scottish immigrant who transformed golf course design in the 1920s. He revolutionized southern golf courses by changing the putting surfaces from oiled sand to Bermuda grass.

Courtesy of St. Lucie County TDC

So Many Holes, So Little Time

The Seminole Golf Club, designed in 1929 and located to the east of the Waterway on the barrier island between these two golf-history bridges, is listed as one of Ross's finest designs. Most of Palm Beach County's golf courses are private, but there are 18 courses open to the public.

Palm Beach County CVB
www.palmbeachfl.com
561/233-3000

PEANUT ISLAND

In 1961, tiny Peanut Island, a dredge island in the middle of the Waterway at STM 1017, found itself at the center of

1041.1 Linton Boulevard Bridge
VHF 09; Palm Beach County would not provide
Single bascule; vertical 30 feet.
Restricted year round: opens on the hour and half-hour.

1042.2 Pelican Harbor Anchorage (0.2)
Anchor 6-8 feet N26.25.419
STR 3.0 feet W080.04.032
Exit ICW at charted stomach-shaped basin. Proceed W over 5-foot shoal into basin.

1044.9 Spanish River Bridge
(40th Street Bridge)
VHF 09; 561/395-5417
Double bascule; vertical 25 feet.
Restricted year round: opens on the hour and half-hour.

1047.4 Palmetto Park Bridge
(Route 798)
VHF 09; Palm Beach County would not provide
Double bascule; vertical 19 feet.
Restricted year round: opens on the hour and half-hour.

1047.7 Lake Boca Raton Anchorage (0.2)
Anchor 6-8 feet N26.20.775
STR (TS) 2.7 feet W080.04.342
Exit ICW at G65. Proceed E along shore to anchor in NE charted 8-foot pocket.
Return to ICW along same path. Lake Boca Raton is shoal near its center.

1048.0 Boca Raton Resort & Club (0.1)
VHF 16; 561/447-3474
Exit ICW NNE of R66. Proceed WNW to marina. [STR 2.7]
SEE BOCA RATON.

1048.1 Junction | Boca Raton Inlet (0.8)
Exit ICW at G67. Proceed easterly to inlet.
Approached through bascule bridge (vertical 23 feet). Used by local commercial and sport fishing boats.

1048.2 Camino Real Bridge
VHF 09; Palm Beach County would not provide
Double bascule; vertical 9 feet.
Restricted year round: opens on the hour, twenty minutes past, and forty minutes past the hour.

1050.0 Hillsboro Boulevard Bridge
(Deerfield Beach Bridge)(Route 810)
VHF 09; 954/428-1090
Double bascule; vertical 21 feet.
Restricted October 1- May 31: M-TH, 0700-1800 hrs, opens on the hour, twenty minutes past, and forty minutes past the hour; F-SU and holidays, 0700-1800 hrs, opens on the hour and half-hour.

1050.1 Cove Marina (0.1)
VHF 16; 954/427-9747
Exit ICW S of bridge. Marina is to W. [STR 2.8]
Facility is currently undergoing reconstruction.

SAFETY INFO

NOAA Weather
WX-3 West Palm Beach, FL
WX-1 Miami, FL
WX-2 Sugarloaf Key, FL

USCG
Station Fort Lauderdale, FL
VHF 16 or 09/22A
954/927-1611

Sea Tow
Fort Lauderdale, FL
VHF 16/73
954/525-0037

TowBoatU.S.
Hillsboro, FL
VHF 16
954/783-7821

HEADS UP!

1035.9 Briny Breezes Bridge
1037.7 George Bush Blvd. Bridge
1039.6 Atlantic Avenue Bridge
1041.1 Linton Blvd. Bridge
1044.9 Spanish River Bridge
1047.4 Palmetto Park Bridge
1048.2 Camino Real Bridge
1050.0 Hillsboro Blvd. Bridge
1055.0 Northeast 14th Street Bridge
1056.2 Atlantic Blvd. Bridge
1059.1 Commercial Blvd. Bridge
1060.6 Oakland Park Bridge
1062.7 East Sunrise Blvd. Bridge
1064.1 East Las Olas Blvd. Bridge
1066.0 Brooks Memorial Bridge
1069.4 Dania Beach Blvd. Bridge
1070.8 Sheridan Street Bridge
1072.3 Hollywood Blvd. Bridge

1052.2 Lighthouse Point Yacht & Racquet (0.2) S N
VHF 16; 954/942-6688
Exit ICW between R68 and R68 "A". Proceed W into canal. Marina is to port. [STR 2.9]

1053.6 Lighthouse Point Marina (0.1) S N
VHF 16; 954/941-0227
Exit ICW between G69 and R70. Proceed NW into canal. Marina is to port. [STR 3.0]

1053.9 Junction | Hillsboro Inlet (1.1) S N
Exit ICW between G71 and R72. Proceed southeasterly to inlet.
Approached through bascule bridge (vertical 13 feet). Used by local commercial and sport fishing boats.
See Hillsboro Inlet Light.

1054.8 Merritt's Boat & Engine Works (0.1) S N
No VHF Watch; 954/941-0118
Exit ICW N of bridge. Facility is to W. [STR 3.0]
Repair facility with no transient dockage.

1054.8 Hidden Harbour Marina (0.4) S N
VHF 16; 954/786-5210
Exit ICW N of bridge. Proceed W into canal to marina. [STR 3.0]
Dry store with no transient dockage.

1055.0 Northeast 14th Street Bridge S N
(Pompano Beach Bridge)
VHF 09; 954/942-6909
Double bascule; vertical 15 feet.
Restricted year round: 0700-1800 hrs, opens on the quarter-hour and three-quarter hour.
See Pompano.

1056.1 Sands Harbor Hotel & Marina (0.1) S N
VHF 16; 954/942-9100
Exit ICW N of bridge. Marina is to east. [STR 3.0]

1056.2 Atlantic Boulevard Bridge S N
(Route 814)
VHF 09; 954/941-7119
Double bascule; vertical 15 feet.
Restricted year round: 0700-1800 hrs, opens on the hour and half-hour.

1056.8 Lake Santa Barbara Anchorage (0.1) S N
Anchor 5-7 feet N26.13.375
STR 3.0 feet W080.05.848
Exit ICW between R74 and R76. Proceed W into charted Lake Santa Barbara.

1056.9 Lettuce Lake S N
Exit ICW between R74 and R76. Proceed E into charted Lettuce Lake. [STR 3.0]

- **Lettuce Lake Anchorage** (0.1)
  Anchor 8-10 feet N26.13.261
  STR 3.0 feet W080.05.715
  Anchor in SE corner.
- **Ramada Inn Pompano** (0.3)
  VHF 16; 954/941-7300
  Continue eastward into canal. Hotel and marina are to port.
  Annual contracts only. No transient dockage.

the Cuban Missile Crisis. Before the crisis, this island, created in 1919 with dredging spoils, housed a small Coast Guard Station.

But in December of 1961, U.S. Navy Seabees arrived to covertly build an underground emergency fallout shelter for President Kennedy and his family. The site was so secret many of Kennedy's closest advisors didn't even know of its existence. During the Cuban Missile Crisis, the president and his family could be quickly moved to Peanut Island from their nearby vacation home in the event of an imminent nuclear catastrophe.

The facility is a stark reminder of how close Kennedy and his advisors feared the nation was to nuclear war with the former Soviet Union.

Today the island is managed by Palm Beach County. The Coast Guard station closed in 1996 but you can still view both the station and the nuclear bunker. The island itself is a 79-acre county park with a 19-slip boat dock and fishing pier.

Palm Beach Maritime Museum
www.pbmm.org
561/832-7428

LAKE WORTH

As its name suggests, Lake Worth was once a freshwater lake. Now it is brackish, connected to the ocean by tiny Boynton Inlet and larger Lake Worth Inlet. Although it's technically "Lake Worth Lagoon," locals simply call it the Intracoastal Waterway.

According to a 1925 account, a runaway soldier began the transformation of Lake Worth to a saltwater lagoon. The story tells of a deserter from the Confederate army, fleeing as far south as present-day Palm Beach, where he dug a connection to the ocean with a conch shell from an Indian midden. The wave action deepened the canal over time and began the influx of salt water into Lake Worth.

But Henry Flagler's efforts to open Lake Worth to the Atlantic Ocean were much more concerted. Flagler realized sheltered ocean access would make Palm Beach even more attractive for his development plans. In 1877 a stable inlet was completed, then deepened and widened over the next few decades.

As Flagler intended, Lake Worth is now full of luxury yachts with easy ocean access. Today the lake—or lagoon—is dredged and flanked with bulkheads to shelter thousands of deep-draft boats at its 28 marinas.

Many cruisers hang a 12V light out at night either as a primary or secondary anchor light. Consider locating this in the cockpit rather than the foredeck. This adds additional light where you need it and deters thieves from boarding your boat by entering the cockpit.

FLAGLER'S WHITEHALL

Look for Whitehall, a large white house with a red tile roof, on the east bank of the Waterway, in the bight near STM 1022. Whitehall is Henry Flagler's 55-room estate, built in 1901 as a wedding present for his third wife. It's quite a home for a man who was born the son of a poor Presbyterian minister. But Flagler went on to make millions as a railroad magnate and a partner in Standard Oil with John D. Rockefeller. Today the house is a museum, showcasing Flagler's vast art and furnishings collection.

Courtesy of Greater Ft. Lauderdale CVB

Plenty of Beachside Pit Stops

Flagler also built a walking path for his hotel guests to stroll along the lagoon. It's now a paved bike path, called the Lake Trail, running from North Palm Beach to the Flagler Bridge, with spectacular views of the Intracoastal Waterway and the extravagant homes along Palm Beach. The trail can be accessed at the end of any cul-de-sac north of Flagler Memorial Bridge.

Flagler Museum
www.flaglermuseum.us
561/655-2833

PALM BEACH AND WEST PALM

Henry Flagler developed Palm Beach and West Palm as complemen-

SAFETY INFO

NOAA Weather
WX-3 West Palm Beach, FL
WX-1 Miami, FL
WX-2 Sugarloaf Key, FL

USCG
Station Fort Lauderdale, FL
VHF 16 or 09/22A
954/927-1611

Sea Tow
Fort Lauderdale, FL
VHF 16/73
954/525-0037

TowBoatU.S.
Ft. Lauderdale, FL
VHF 16
954/525-5577

HEADS UP!

1044.9	Spanish River Bridge
1047.4	Palmetto Park Bridge
1048.2	Camino Real Bridge
1050.0	Hillsboro Blvd. Bridge
1055.0	Northeast 14th Street Bridge
1056.2	Atlantic Blvd. Bridge
1059.1	**Commercial Blvd. Bridge**
1060.6	**Oakland Park Bridge**
1062.7	**East Sunrise Blvd. Bridge**
1064.1	**East Las Olas Blvd. Bridge**
1066.0	Brooks Memorial Bridge
1069.4	Dania Beach Blvd. Bridge
1070.8	Sheridan Street Bridge
1072.3	Hollywood Blvd. Bridge
1074.0	Hallandale Beach Blvd. Bridge
1078.0	Sunny Isles Bridge
1081.3	Broad Causeway Bridge
1084.6	JFK Causeway Bridge

tary towns. West Palm, on the west or mainland side of the Waterway was originally the commercial and less pretentious adjunct of Palm Beach, saving Palm Beach as the playground for the wealthy.

Flagler's flagship development was the Palm Beach Inn, still one of the most famous beachfront hotels along the East Coast. Located on the ocean across from Flagler Bridge, the hotel was eventually renamed "The Breakers" because the guests always asked for rooms "down by the breakers." If you need a rest from your boat, but still want to see the ocean, a room at The Breakers will set you back about $800 a night.

For cruisers, Palm Beach offers access to affluence and luxury. The ornate architecture, much of it by architect Addison Mizner, sets a tone of opulence. Worth Avenue, south of Royal Park Bridge, is Florida's Rodeo Drive, the place to people-watch and window-shop.

COCONUT PALMS

Nothing symbolizes the tropics like a coconut palm leaning over a sandy beach. Coconut palms grow in warmer southern Florida, both near the sandy beaches and in town. You may even notice the clusters of green or mature brown coconuts.

But coconut palms regularly drop their two-pound seeds—onto whatever lies below. Native Floridians joke you can identify tourists as the "coconuts" who unwittingly park their rental car under a coconut palm. Every year thousands of dollars of claims are filed from coconut dents on the hoods of rental cars.

But seriously, killer coconuts are out there. It's estimated about 150 people worldwide die every year from coconuts on the noggin. A mature coconut dropping 50 feet from a tree hits at about 40 mph and can fatally bonk a pedestrian. To prevent an unfortunate drop, some communities now neuter their coconut palms, pruning the heavy clusters of dangerous nuts.

If your outboard engine stores on the dinghy transom, prevent engine theft by locking the handles of the motor's mounting clamps. Tighten up the clamps until they face each other, then lock the handles into this position with a sturdy combination lock. It's simple, if a thief cannot unscrew the clamp, they can't make off with the engine!

Courtesy of National Park Service

Coconut Palms

IN HER SHOES

The Briny Breezes Bridge, at STM 1035.9, connects the quiet community of Briny Breezes to the mainland. Filmmakers have recently discovered this "authentic Florida community," where they can capture Florida on film without the hassles of a Miami shoot.

In the spring of 2004, the movie *In Her Shoes*, starring Cameron Diaz, Shirley MacLaine, and Toni Collette, was filmed at Briny Breezes. If you catch the movie in theatres in 2005, you may recognize the Briny Breezes beach and clubhouse, and Abbey Delray South, the retirement community that is the home of MacLaine's character.

BODY HEAT

It worked for Frank and Lola, when he took her to this movie called *Body Heat*. She said, "The Junior Mints were mushy and the sex was neat." The movie, a low-budget steamy thriller that turned into a modern classic, was immortalized in the Jimmy Buffett song, "Frank and Lola."

1059.1 Commercial Boulevard Bridge
VHF 09; 954/772-3987
Double bascule; vertical 15 feet.
Restricted year round: 0700-1800 hrs, opens on the hour, twenty minutes past, and forty minutes past the hour.

1060.6 Oakland Park Bridge
VHF 09; 954/566-3711
Double bascule; vertical 22 feet.
Restricted November 15-May 15: M-F, 0700-2200 hrs, opens on the hour, twenty minutes past, and forty minutes past the hour; SA-SU and holidays, 1000-2200 hrs, opens on the hour, quarter-hour, half-hour, and three-quarter hour.

1062.5 Coral Ridge Yacht Club (0.1)
VHF 16; 954/566-7886
Exit ICW N of bridge. Yacht club is to W. [STR 3.0]
Accepts guests of members and offers reciprocal rights to members of accredited yacht clubs.

1062.6 Sunrise Harbor Marina (0.1)
VHF 16; 954/667-6720
Exit NNE of bridge. Marina is to W. [STR 3.0]
Mega-yacht facility (200-plus feet). $4.00/ft.

1062.7 East Sunrise Boulevard Bridge
(Route 838)
VHF 09; 954/564-6986
Double bascule; vertical 25 feet.
Restricted November 15-May 15: 1000-1800 hrs, opens on the hour, quarter-hour, half-hour, and three-quarter hour.
Restricted first weekend in May: SA-SU, 1600-1800 hrs; and SA 2145-2245 hrs (due to vehicle traffic from Air and Sea Show).

1064.0 Las Olas Municipal Marina (0.1)
VHF 16/71 N26.07.207
954/828-7200 W080.06.514
Exit ICW N of bridge. Marina is to E. [STR 3.0]

1064.1 East Las Olas Boulevard Bridge
VHF 09; 954/463-0842
Double bascule; vertical 31 feet.
Restricted first weekend in May: SA-SU, 1600-1800 hrs; and SA 2145-2245 hrs (due to vehicle traffic from Air and Sea Show).

1064.2 Las Olas Municipal Moorings (0.1)
VHF 16/71 N26.07.140
954/828-7200 W080.06.596
Exit ICW S of bridge. Proceed W into charted basin. [STR 3.0]
The city provides 9 moorings at $20/night. 30-day limit. No reservations.

1064.2 Las Olas Bridge Anchorage (0.1)
Anchor 7-10 feet N26.07.092
STR 3.0 feet W080.06.561
Room for 2-3 boats to anchor off ICW channel at S edge of mooring basin.

1064.3 Hall of Fame Marina (0.1)
VHF 16/08 N26.06.976
954/764-3975 W080.06.497

SAFETY INFO

NOAA Weather
WX-3 West Palm Beach, FL
WX-1 Miami, FL
WX-2 Sugarloaf Key, FL

USCG
Station Fort Lauderdale, FL
VHF 16 or 09/22A
954/927-1611

Sea Tow
Fort Lauderdale, FL
VHF 16/73
954/525-0037

TowBoatU.S.
Ft. Lauderdale, FL
VHF 16
954/525-5577

HEADS UP!

1047.4 Palmetto Park Bridge
1048.2 Camino Real Bridge
1050.0 Hillsboro Blvd. Bridge
1055.0 Northeast 14th Street Bridge
1056.2 Atlantic Blvd. Bridge
1059.1 Commercial Blvd. Bridge
1060.6 Oakland Park Bridge
1062.7 East Sunrise Blvd. Bridge
1064.1 East Las Olas Blvd. Bridge
1066.0 Brooks Memorial Bridge
1069.4 Dania Beach Blvd. Bridge
1070.8 Sheridan Street Bridge
1072.3 Hollywood Blvd. Bridge
1074.0 Hallandale Beach Blvd. Bridge
1078.0 Sunny Isles Bridge
1081.3 Broad Causeway Bridge
1084.6 JFK Causeway Bridge
1087.2 Julia Tuttle Bridge

Exit ICW N of G11. Proceed into northernmost of three charted basins. Marina is to starboard. [STR 2.9]

1064.5 Bahia Mar Yachting Center (0.1)
VHF 16; 800/755-9558
Exit ICW at R12. Marina is to E. [STR 2.9 (TS)]
Bahia Mar has facilities in the middle and southern of the three charted basins. You will be directed to one of these depending on boat size. Smaller, transient boats are typically berthed in the southernmost basin.
SEE THE BUSTED FLUSH.

1064.7 Lake Sylvia Anchorage (0.6)
Anchor 7-9 feet N26.06.338
STR 2.9 feet W080.06.704
Exit ICW NE of G13. Proceed southerly following charted deep water, favoring Burnham Point and eastern shore. 24-hour limit.

1065.0 Junction | New River
Southbound Navigation Only
Exit ICW at RG "A". Proceed northwesterly to New River and South Fork New River facilities. [STR 2.6]
Note: Bridges have 0730-0830 hrs and 1630-1730 hrs blackouts. Otherwise on request.
Note: It takes approximately one hour to travel from Hyatt Regency Pier 66 Marina to Roscioli Yachting Center (last facility on New River).

- **Southeast Third Avenue Bridge** (1.7)
VHF 09; 954/765-4080
Bascule; vertical 16 feet.
- **New River Municipal Marina** (1.8)
VHF 16; 954/828-5423
City has dockage on both sides of river to Andrews Avenue Bridge, and on south side from FEC RR to William Marshall Bridges.
No facilities; may use Cooley's Landing facilities.
- **Andrews Avenue Bridge** (1.9)
(South Andrews Avenue Bridge)
VHF 09; 954/765-4033
Bascule; vertical 60 feet; will open only when railroad bridge is open. [STR 2.6 (TS)]
- **Las Olas Riverfront Complex** (2.0)
No VHF; No Telephone
Tie-up to starboard. First come-first served. No overnight dockage. No charge. No facilities.
- **FEC RR Bridge** (2.1)
(Florida East Coast Railroad Bridge)
No VHF; No Telephone
Bascule; vertical 4 feet; usually open.
- **Riverfront Marina** (2.2)
VHF 16 N26.07.108
954/527-1829 W080.08.754
Facility is to port.
Dry store with no transient dockage. Look for Shirttail Charlie's.
- **Sun Power Diesel** (2.3)
No VHF; No Telephone
Facility to port.
Facility is closed with operations moved to Dania Beach.

Over twenty years ago, a group of no-name actors, including Kathleen Turner, William Hurt, Ted Danson, and Mickey Rourke, arrived at Ft. Worth to film *Body Heat* (1981). George Bush Boulevard Bridge, at STM 1037.7, is the bridge in the movie where Oscar the cop is stuck waiting on his way to arrest Ned (William Hurt) at the home of seductive Mattie (Kathleen Turner).

DELRAY BEACH

Delray Beach, often just known as Delray, has always been an ethnically diverse town. It began when white and black northerners arrived to homestead new agricultural areas. Japanese immigrants arrived shortly afterward to raise pineapples. More recently, Delray has attracted Caribbean, Haitian, and Latin American communities.

Delray is a year-round town rather than a resort town. Houses line the Waterway, but remain more affordable than Palm Beach to the north or Boca Raton to the south. Houses in most parts of Delray cost about $150,000 to $200,000, with houses along the Waterway starting at $400,000.

Delray went through some tough times during its rapid development in the 1960s and 1970s. Like many Florida cities, Delray over-developed, covering 90% of its area, then went to seed. But having no where else to go, the residents decided to focus on revitalizing what it already had. The downtown area, on the west side of Atlantic Avenue Bridge at STM 1039.6, transformed from a vacant depressed area to a trendy location for restaurants, galleries, and shops.

Courtesy of U.S. Army Corps of Engineers

Photo by Tony Santana **Hillsboro Inlet**

The transformation has been so staggering the town has twice been named an All-American City. Recently the progressive magazine, *Utne Reader*, chose Delray Beach as one of the nation's "Top 10 Enlightened Suburbs" for its planning and livability.

Delray Beach
www.delraybeach.com
561/278-0424

KABOOM! BAD BOYS II

There once was a waterfront mansion at STM 1041 that became a drug lord estate. There was machine gun fire, and in the end, a climatic scene where the mansion exploded and a bikini-clad woman flees from a poolside chair!

Columbia/Tristar Promotional Image

Bad Boys Lawrence and Smith

No, not for real—in the movies. Will Smith and Martin Lawrence (a.k.a. "the Bad Boys") raided this "Cuban drug lord's mansion," located at the head of the canal across from the Delray Harbor Club Marina, in *Bad Boys II* (2003). According to Dockmaster Jena Willoughby, boaters and marina staff stood on the fuel docks and watched the residence explode in a black mushroom cloud. The explosion set off car alarms for miles.

You might wonder how anyone—even Hollywood—could afford to blow up a waterfront mansion in Palm Beach County. The house was originally built for the Coca-Cola heir, Michael Bird, but he aborted construction after kidnappers tied up and threatened his family nearby. The unfinished and abandoned mansion became the perfect dealmaker: Hollywood needed a mansion to blow up and Delray Beach needed a mansion torn down so the lot could be divided and re-sold for three new houses.

BOCA RATON

A luxury community like Boca Raton named after Boca de Ratones—Spanish for "rat's mouth"? The name

SAFETY INFO

NOAA Weather
WX-3 West Palm Beach, FL
WX-1 Miami, FL
WX-2 Sugarloaf Key, FL

USCG
Station Fort Lauderdale, FL
VHF 16 or 09/22A
954/927-1611

Sea Tow
Fort Lauderdale, FL
VHF 16/73
954/525-0037

TowBoatU.S.
Ft. Lauderdale, FL
VHF 16
954/525-5577

HEADS UP!

1047.4	Palmetto Park Bridge
1048.2	Camino Real Bridge
1050.0	Hillsboro Blvd. Bridge
1055.0	Northeast 14th Street Bridge
1056.2	Atlantic Blvd. Bridge
1059.1	Commercial Blvd. Bridge
1060.6	Oakland Park Bridge
1062.7	East Sunrise Blvd. Bridge
1064.1	East Las Olas Blvd. Bridge
1066.0	Brooks Memorial Bridge
1069.4	Dania Beach Blvd. Bridge
1070.8	Sheridan Street Bridge
1072.3	Hollywood Blvd. Bridge
1074.0	Hallandale Beach Blvd. Bridge
1078.0	Sunny Isles Bridge
1081.3	Broad Causeway Bridge
1084.6	JFK Causeway Bridge
1087.2	Julia Tuttle Bridge

only makes sense if you remember what Spanish explorers found when they arrived at this bay: jagged teeth-like rocks that guarded the bay and threatened their vessels.

Entrepreneurs saw something very different when they arrived at Boca: a snug protected harbor where wealthy yachtsmen could moor with a deep inlet for ocean access. The Boca Raton Resort and Club, designed by architect Addison Mizner in the 1920s, was part of this tourism and development boom. Although Mizner ultimately went bankrupt, the resort, located at STM 1048, is still thriving. Described as one of Florida's finest examples of Spanish-Gothic architecture, the resort's historic palatial buildings are visible behind the new 27-story resort tower.

If you are receiving multiple envelopes of forwarded mail at a marina or post office, be sure the sender numbers each item: 1 of n, 2 of n, 3 of n, etc. It's very easy to unknowingly leave a straggler behind!

Hold for Arrival Template

HILLSBORO INLET LIGHT

The Hillsboro Inlet Light is a Midwest transplant, built in Chicago and shipped down the Mississippi to the 1904 St. Louis World's Fair. This modern lighthouse impressed the crowds with its high-tech steel skeleton painted in black and white, anchored with six huge iron piles.

In 1907 the light was purchased by the government and placed in service here at Hillsboro Inlet, where the new design was ideally suited to ride out the wind and waves of this hurricane-prone coast. The light proved its design over the years, withstanding a tidal surge from Hurricane Donna in 1960 that washed over the dunes and the base of the lighthouse. The lighthouse is still in operation today, its 28-mile light visible nearly halfway to the Bahamas.

As you approach the inlet at STM 1053.9, you may catch a glimpse of the lighthouse by looking seaward through the bascule bridge. But this junction is often hectic with traffic and current, so it may be difficult to sightsee for a lighthouse. If you want a better view from the water, request a bridge opening into Hillsboro Inlet (13 foot clearance) and proceed the short distance past the bridge to the lighthouse.

POMPANO

The town of Pompano is a member of a tiny group of towns—including Wahoo, Nebraska and Chinook, Washington—named after fish.

Pompano (pronounced PAWM-puh-no), or butterfish, are locally prevalent and have been exported from this area since the 1800s. Supposedly engineers surveying the area were served a fried fish dinner of the local fish, noted for its unusual flavor and texture. An engineer was so impressed with the dinner he decided to name the new region in honor of the local fish.

Pompano's seafood heritage is still celebrated annually at the Pompano Beach Seafood Festival in late April. The gathering, to the west of Atlantic Boulevard Bridge at STM 1056.2, includes music and lots of seafood. Proceeds from the event benefit local charities and civic organizations.

Pompano Seafood Festival
www.pompanoseafoodfestival.com
954/570-7785

THE CAPRON TRAIL

It's nearly impossible to imagine Ft. Lauderdale as it was in the 1800s: dense jungle with an isolated military fort to keep Seminoles at bay. The Native American villages were to the northwest, where they lived in huts thatched with palmettos, spoke their own language, and self-governed under tribal laws.

The only road to Ft. Lauderdale was the Capron Military Trail, which ran through the jungle along the Waterway from Palm Beach to Miami. The trail was blazed during the Seminole Wars, allowing soldiers to move through the jungles and block the Seminoles' sup-

- **William H. Marshall Memorial Bridge** (2.4)
  (SW 7th Avenue)(SW 4th Avenue)
  VHF 09; 954/765-4081
  Bascule; vertical 20 feet.
- **Cooley's Landing Municipal Marina** (2.5)
  VHF 16; 954/828-4626
  Marina is to starboard.
- **Davie Boulevard Bridge** (3.7)
  (Route 736)(Southwest 12th Street)
  VHF 09; 954/523-6701
  Bascule; vertical 21 feet.
- **River Bend Marina** (4.2)
  No VHF Watch N26.05.847
  954/523-1832 W080.09.673
  At charted 90-degree bend, marina is to port.
- **Summerfield Boat Works** (4.3)
  No VHF; No Telephone
  Facility is to starboard.
  Facility is closed. Property sold for planned condo and dockominium development.
- **Lauderdale Marine Center** (4.5)
  VHF 16; 954/713-0333
  Facility is to port.
- **Mango Marine** (4.6)
  No VHF N26.05.846
  954/585-1041 W080.10.092
  Facility is to port.
- **Interstate 95 Bridges** (4.8)
  Fixed; vertical 55 feet.
- **SCL/CSX RR Bridge** (4.9)
  No VHF; No Telephone
  Bascule; vertical 2 feet; usually open.
- **Jackson Marine Center** (5.0)
  No VHF Watch N26.05.796
  954/792-4900 W080.10.188
  Facility is to starboard. Repair yard with no transient dockage.
- **Marina Bay Club & Resort** (5.1)
  VHF 16; 954/791-7600
  Marina is to port.
- **Yacht Haven Marina** (5.2)
  VHF 16; 954/583-2322
  Marina is to port.
- **Cable Marine West** (5.5)
  VHF 16; 954/587-4000
  Facility is to port.
  Repair facility with no transient dockage.
- **Rolly Marine** (5.6)
  VHF 16; 954/583-5300
  Facility is to port.
  Repair facility with no transient dockage.
- **Billfish Marina** (6.0)
  VHF 16; 954/587-6226
  Marina is to port. Repair yard with no transient dockage.
- **New River Marine** (6.1)
  VHF 16; 954/584-2500
  Marina is to port.
  Repair facility with no transient dockage.

SAFETY INFO

NOAA Weather
WX-3 West Palm Beach, FL
WX-1 Miami, FL
WX-2 Sugarloaf Key, FL

USCG
Station Fort Lauderdale, FL
VHF 16 or 09/22A
954/927-1611

Sea Tow
Fort Lauderdale, FL
VHF 16/73
954/525-0037

TowBoatU.S.
Ft. Lauderdale, FL
VHF 16
954/525-5577

HEADS UP!

1048.2	Camino Real Bridge
1050.0	Hillsboro Blvd. Bridge
1055.0	Northeast 14th Street Bridge
1056.2	Atlantic Blvd. Bridge
1059.1	Commercial Blvd. Bridge
1060.6	Oakland Park Bridge
1062.7	East Sunrise Blvd. Bridge
1064.1	East Las Olas Blvd. Bridge
1066.0	**Brooks Memorial Bridge**
1069.4	Dania Beach Blvd. Bridge
1070.8	Sheridan Street Bridge
1072.3	Hollywood Blvd. Bridge
1074.0	Hallandale Beach Blvd. Bridge
1078.0	Sunny Isles Bridge
1081.3	Broad Causeway Bridge
1084.6	JFK Causeway Bridge
1087.2	Julia Tuttle Bridge
1088.6	West Venetian Causeway Bridge

- **Bradford Marine** (6.1)
  No VHF Watch; 954/791-3800
  Stay in New River, bearing right, N of bridge. Proceed W. Facility is to port.
  Repair facility with no transient dockage.
- **Roscioli Yachting Center** (6.2)
  No VHF Watch N26.05.226
  954/581-9200 W080.11.241
  Stay in New River, bearing right, N of bridge. Proceed W. Facility is to port.
- **State Route 84 Bridge** (6.3)
  VHF 09; 954/583-4760
  Bascule; vertical 21 feet; on request with 24-hour notice.

1065.3 Junction | New River S N
Northbound Navigation Only
Exit ICW at R20. Proceed northwesterly, leaving R20 to starboard, to enter charted New River.
For New River and South Fork New River facilities information, see STM 1065.0.

1065.6 Lauderdale Yacht Club (0.2) S N
VHF 16; 954/524-5500
Exit ICW between R24 "A" and R26. Proceed NW in privately maintained channel to charted Lauderdale Yacht Club. [STR 3.0]
Accepts guests of members and offers reciprocal rights to members of accredited yacht clubs.

1065.8 Lauderdale Marina (0.1) S N
VHF 16; 954/523-8507
Exit ICW at G27. Marina is to W. [STR 3.1]

1065.9 Cable Marine East (0.4) S N
VHF 16/09 N26.06.156
954/462-2840 W080.07.613
Exit ICW S of G27. Proceed W into charted canal. Marina is to port. [STR 3.1]

1065.9 Hyatt Regency Pier 66 Marina (0.1) S N
VHF 16/71 N26.06.135
954/728-3578 W080.07.064
Exit ICW S of G27. Proceed E into charted canal. Marina is to starboard. [STR 3.1]

1065.9 Marriott Portside Marina (0.1) S N
VHF 16; 954/527-6781
Exit ICW N of bridge. Marina is to W. [STR 3.1]

1066.0 Brooks Memorial Bridge S N
(E. Clay Shaw Bridge)(SE 17th St. Causeway)
VHF 09; 954/524-7783
Double bascule; vertical 55 feet.
Restricted year round: 0700-1900 hrs, opens on the hour and half-hour.
This new bridge is restricted but now has a 55-foot vertical clearance.
SEE THREE ONE-OF-A-KINDS.

1066.1 Best Western Marina (0.1) S N
VHF 16; 954/525-3484
Exit ICW S of bridge. Marina Is to E. [STR 3.1]

plies from Cuba.

But the trail was abandoned at the end of the Seminole Wars and quickly became impassable, quickly returning to jungle. Without the Capron Trail, the safe route to Ft. Lauderdale was a long slow slog down the beach sand.

Or one could link up with the postman, who moonlighted as a trail guide. For $5, he'd let you follow him along his jungle shortcut—which included a stash of small boats for river crossings—as he traveled his mail route between the two settlements.

Courtesy of gssites.com/miami

Draining the Swamps (circa 1910)

SWAMPS TO CANALS

Charles Rodes and his wife moved to Ft. Lauderdale from West Virginia, intending to farm a small ten-acre plot and run a feed store. But one day Rodes sat looking over the land around his farm and envisioned a "Venice of America."

The idea was nutty but ingenious: transform miles of swampy jungle into miles of waterfront property. So he began platting subdivisions, digging canals, and building narrow peninsulas of land.

By the 1920s, Rodes was one of South Florida's most famous and richest land developers. Today Ft. Lauderdale has 270 miles of canals, compared to only 45 miles of canals in Venice, Italy. And the value of all this waterfront real estate? You do the math!

Nasty-looking dinghies and outboards are much less appealing to thieves. Spray paint with ugly colors and scratch the cowlings. Or if you just can't bear to do this, at least remove the decals to hide brand or horsepower. As a bonus, to easily identify our dink at crowded dinghy docks, we use a fluorescent green!

WATERWAY CLEANUP

For nearly thirty years, on the first Saturday in March, Broward County residents clean up their 300 miles of canals and shorelines. Last year over 3,500 volunteers gathered along the Waterway, hauling out 55 tons of trash.

If you're transiting the area in early March, you can pitch in. With 30 cleanup sites, there's a gathering near your mooring. Previous locations included Deerfield Island Park at STM 1050; Pompano Beach Bridge at STM 1055; the west side of East Sunrise Boulevard Bridge at STM 1062.7; near the Hall of Fame Marina at STM 1064.3; and the Anne Kolb Nature Center at STM 1070. The cleanup runs from 9:00-1:00 and each year's locations are listed on their website.

Waterway Cleanup
www.waterwaycleanup.org
954/524-2733

THE BUSTED FLUSH

"It was to have been a quiet evening at home. Home is the *Busted Flush*, 52-foot barge-type houseboat, Slip F-18, Bahia Mar, Lauderdale."

Recognize those words? You will if you're a Travis McGee fan, the main character in John D. MacDonald's phenomenally successful and long-running mystery novels. These are the first lines from MacDonald's first book, *The Deep Blue Good-by*. McGee's houseboat, the Busted Flush, named after a card game that won him the vessel, was fictionally docked at the Bahia Mar Yachting Center at STM 1064.5.

Courtesy of Florida Inland Navigation District

Ft. Lauderdale Boat Show

The Marina has honored this literary legacy with a brass plaque at slip F-18. The landmark was rededicated in 2004 with a ceremony including

SAFETY INFO

NOAA Weather	Sea Tow
WX-3 West Palm Beach, FL	Fort Lauderdale, FL
WX-1 Miami, FL	VHF 16/73
WX-2 Sugarloaf Key, FL	954/525-0037
USCG	**TowBoatU.S.**
Station Fort Lauderdale, FL	Ft. Lauderdale, FL
VHF 16 or 09/22A	VHF 16
954/927-1611	954/525-5577

HEADS UP!

1050.0	Hillsboro Blvd. Bridge	**1070.8**	**Sheridan Street Bridge**
1055.0	Northeast 14th Street Bridge	**1072.3**	**Hollywood Blvd. Bridge**
1056.2	Atlantic Blvd. Bridge	1074.0	Hallandale Beach Blvd. Bridge
1059.1	Commercial Blvd. Bridge	1078.0	Sunny Isles Bridge
1060.6	Oakland Park Bridge	1081.3	Broad Causeway Bridge
1062.7	East Sunrise Blvd. Bridge	1084.6	JFK Causeway Bridge
1064.1	East Las Olas Blvd. Bridge	1087.2	Julia Tuttle Bridge
1066.0	Brooks Memorial Bridge	1088.6	West Venetian Causeway Bridge
1069.4	**Dania Beach Blvd. Bridge**	1089.3	Dodge Island Bridges

authors such as Randy Wayne White, whose Doc Ford character is considered by many to be the successor to Travis McGee.

Bahia Mar was once the location of a Coast Guard Station, but at the end of World War II, the Coast Guard decided to sell the property. The asking price was $1 million, but the City of Ft. Lauderdale only agreed to $600,000. On a Friday the 13th, during a raging hurricane, a proposal was accepted to build the first modern world-class marina on the site. Bahia Mar opened in 1949 as the largest marina in the world: three miles of concrete piers with dockage for 450 40-foot boats.

Many cruisers leave their boat in Florida to return home for the summer. If so, arrange for someone to rotate your boat monthly at the dock. Florida's summer sun is ruthless: yellowing, chalking, and bleaching whatever surface it repetitively touches. And don't forget to cover sun-vulnerable interior woods and fabrics with old bed sheets.

FT. LAUDERDALE

Arrive in Ft. Lauderdale with a list: spares to find, supplies to purchase, repairs to complete, and systems to upgrade. You won't be disappointed. If you think Ft. Lauderdale is expensive and crowded, you're missing the point. This is the place to hunker down and prepare (or repair) your boat for the miles. If you're planning to chase supply lists in the Bahamas or Georgia, you're not managing the Waterway.

Courtesy of USCG, 7th District

Andrews Avenue Bridge, New River

There is nothing marine you can't buy or hire in Ft. Lauderdale. If you can't find a marine part in this town, you simply haven't looked in the right place. The big marine stores are in town of course, and scores of smaller independent chandleries with new and used equipment. Hundreds of marine industrial suppliers are located in Ft. Lauderdale, providing parts or refitting of plumbing, refrigeration, heating and cooling, hydraulic steering, engines, electrical, electronics, rigging, sail or canvas, and stainless work. Contact the Marine Industries Association of South Florida (MIASF) for referral information by category.

Courtesy of Greater Ft. Lauderdale CVB

Ft. Lauderdale Water Bus

For leisurely transportation, you can get around by dinghy or by the Water Bus. Soundings Magazine lists Ft. Lauderdale's Water Bus as the best public transportation for cruisers. The fleet of hybrid diesel/electric canal boats run hourly along the Intracoastal Waterway and New River, stopping at marinas, downtown, and the beach. But to really take advantage of Ft. Lauderdale's marine services, a rental car is the best bet. If you're going to rent a car someplace and justify it as part of the expense of cruising boat maintenance, Ft. Lauderdale is the place.

MIASF
www.miasf.org
954/524-2733

Water Bus
www.watertaxi.com/ftlaud
954/467-6677

THREE ONE-OF-A-KINDS

Boaters have strange ideas for a fun afternoon. They ogle the gear at Cabela's, go bargain hunting for stainless hardware at a wholesaler, or browse cruising guides for regions not on their itinerary.

If you've done any of these things, with apologies to Jeff Foxworthy, "You might be a cruiser." In which case, there are three unique Featured Attractions waiting for you in Ft. Lauderdale: Sailorman, Home Base, and Bluewater Books & Charts.

1066.5 Junction | Port Everglades (1.7) S N
Well Aided N26.05.616
Well Lit W080.05.413
Exit ICW in Port Everglades turning basin. Proceed easterly to inlet. Waypoint is between R2 and G3. [STR 3.1 (TS)]
Caution: Southbound, if your vessel height is greater than 56 feet, you must exit the ICW at this inlet to proceed outside and re-join the ICW at Government Cut (Miami) or Biscayne Channel (Key Biscayne).

1066.8 USCG Station Ft. Lauderdale S N
Charted USCG station is to E.

1068.6 Dania Cut-off Canal S N
Exit ICW at G35. Proceed WSW into Dania Cut-off Canal. [STR 2.8 (TS)]
Caution: Be sure you have correctly identified Dania Cut-off Canal versus the charted Dania Town Canal to S.

- **Harbour Towne Marina** (1.1)
  VHF 16; 954/926-0300
  Marina is to port.
- **Dereckter-Gunnell of Florida** (1.2)
  No VHF Watch; 954/920-5756
  Facility is to starboard.
  Repair facility with no transient dockage.
- **Royale Palm Yacht Basin** (1.3)
  VHF 16; 954/923-5900
  Marina is to port.

1069.4 Dania Beach Boulevard Bridge S N
VHF 09; 954/922-7833
Double bascule; vertical 22 feet; on request.

1070.8 Sheridan Street Bridge S N
VHF 09; 954/923-2597
Double bascule; vertical 22 feet; on request.

1071.0 Sheridan Street Bridge Anchorage (0.2) S N
Anchor 8-10 feet N26.01.951
STR (TS) 2.4 feet W080.06.953
Exit ICW S of bridge. Proceed E, then N into narrow basin.

1072.0 Hollywood Municipal Marina (0.1) S N
VHF 16/08 N26.00.892
954/921-3035 W080.07.180
Exit ICW N of bridge. Marina is to W. [STR 2.4]

1072.3 Hollywood Boulevard Bridge S N
(Route 820)
VHF 09; 954/922-3366
Double bascule; vertical 25 feet.
Restricted November 15-May 15: 1000-1800 hrs, opens on the hour and half-hour.
Restricted May 16-November 14: SA-SU and holidays, 0900-1900 hrs, opens on the hour and half-hour.

1072.8 Harbor Islands Marina (0.1) S N
VHF 16/68 N26.00.217
954/457-8557 W080.07.208
Exit ICW S of R42. Marina is to W. [STR 2.4]

SAFETY INFO

NOAA Weather	Sea Tow
WX-3 West Palm Beach, FL	Miami, FL
WX-1 Miami, FL	VHF 16/18
WX-2 Sugarloaf Key, FL	305/673-2869
USCG	**TowBoatU.S.**
Station Miami Beach, FL	Haulover Inlet, FL
VHF 16 or 09/22A	VHF 16/11
305/535-4368	305/864-1736

HEADS UP!

1060.6	Oakland Park Bridge
1062.7	East Sunrise Blvd. Bridge
1064.1	East Las Olas Blvd. Bridge
1066.0	Brooks Memorial Bridge
1069.4	Dania Beach Blvd. Bridge
1070.8	Sheridan Street Bridge
1072.3	Hollywood Blvd. Bridge
1074.0	**Hallandale Beach Blvd. Bridge**
1078.0	**Sunny Isles Bridge**
1081.3	Broad Causeway Bridge
1084.6	JFK Causeway Bridge
1087.2	Julia Tuttle Bridge
1088.6	West Venetian Causeway Bridge
1089.3	Dodge Island Bridges
1091.8	South Florida Caution (NB)
SB	No Southbound Heads Up!
SB	No Southbound Heads Up!
SB	No Southbound Heads Up!

1074.0 Hallandale Beach Boulevard Bridge
(Route 824)
VHF 09; 954/456-6630
Double bascule; vertical 31 feet.
Restricted year round: 0715-1815 hrs, opens on the quarter-hour and three-quarter hour.

1075.2 Waterways Marina (0.3)
VHF 16/12 N25.58.205
305/935-4295 W080.07.693
Exit ICW into charted basin. [STR 2.5]

1075.9 Fairmont Turnberry Isle Resort (0.4)
VHF 16/68 N25.57.507
800/327-7028 W080.07.658
Exit ICW NNE of bridge. Proceed WNW into basin. Marina is to port. [STR 2.5]

1076.3 Golden Beach Bridge
(NE 192nd Street Bridge)
Fixed; vertical 65 feet.

1076.9 Golden Beach Anchorage (0.1)
Anchor 6-8 feet N25.56.662
STR 2.5 feet W080.07.557
Exit ICW at G49. Proceed E to charted pocket.
See Trump Towers South.

1077.4 Maule Lake
Exit ICW at R54. Proceed W through canal to charted Maule Lake. [STR 2.3]
Caution: Channel may have as little as 4 feet at low tide.

- **Williams Island Marina** (0.5)
  VHF 16; 305/937-7813
  Marina is to starboard.
- **Maule Lake Anchorage** (0.9)
  Anchor 7-12 feet N25.56.037
  STR 2.3 feet W080.08.759
  Anchor along lake edges according to wind conditions.
- **Loggerhead Club & Marina** (1.1)
  VHF 16; 305/945-0808
  Marina is to W.
  Formerly Maule Lake Marina.

1078.0 Sunny Isles Bridge
(Northeast 163rd Street Bridge)(Route 826)
VHF 09; DOT District 6 would not provide
Double bascule; vertical 30 feet.
Restricted year round: M-F, 0700-1800 hrs; and SA-SU and holidays, 1000-1800 hrs; opens on the quarter-hour and three-quarter hour.

1079.5 Haulover Beach
Exit ICW at G5. Proceed S toward inlet. [STR 2.2]

- **Haulover Beach Park Marina** (0.2)
  VHF 16; 305/945-3934
  Marina is to E.
  Dry store with no transient dockage.
- **A1A Bridge** (0.7)
  Fixed; vertical 32 feet.
- **Bakers Haulover Inlet** (1.5)
  Proceed E out inlet.

Sailorman is a sight like no other. It's a completely different kind of marine store, described as the world's largest marine emporium of new, used, and consignment marine gear. Cruisers swoon over barrels of anchor chain, browse aisles of marine supplies, locate or advertise for crew, and bring their used gear in for cash. It's located about 1.5 miles from the Lauderdale Marine Center on the New River.

"Home Base" is how members of the Seven Seas Cruising Association refer to the association's main office, located on 2501 East Commercial Boulevard. You can justify this visit as an "errand," since the office provides members access to a phone, fax, copier, and computer. While you're there, the office has one of the most complete marine libraries in the country and boxes of charts from all over the world as part of a free chart exchange.

Finally, need a courtesy flag for the Turks and Caicos? A cruising guide to Belize? Or the latest book by solo-sailor Ellen MacArthur? Bluewater Books & Charts, with over 35,000 items in stock, is where cruisers stock up on anything marine on paper or computer chip. If you're going to winter charter in the Adriatic, there will be a member of the staff who once cruised extensively there. If you haven't yet made your plans for the Bahamas, ask an expert for the latest advice on chart kits, cruising guides, and customs issues.

The store recently moved to their new location at 1811 Cordova Road, southwest of Brooks Memorial Bridge (S.E. 17th Street) at STM 1066. There is a dinghy dock at Southport Raw Bar at the west end of the canal between 15th and 16th Streets (just northwest of the causeway bridge). If you have a drink or appetizer, you can leave your dinghy and walk the few blocks south on Cordova to grocery shop at a large Publix or visit Bluewater.

Sailorman
www.sailorman.com
800/523-0772

Seven Seas Cruising Assoc.
www.ssca.org
954/771-5660

Bluewater Books & Charts
www.bluewaterweb.com
800/942-2583

FERAL PARROTS

If you hear hoarse and penetrating "squaaaaks" overhead, look up and you'll likely see a noisy flock of parrots flying over your boat. And if you own a sailboat, they may even land on your rigging, raucously squawking as they perform acrobatics hanging onto your stays. At times, we've had more parrot-heads than a Jimmy Buffet concert dress our rigging.

semi-local publications LLC

Photo by Paul Pregent **Jimmy Buffett, Eat Your Heart Out**

These parrots or parakeets are not native to the Southeast. The only native parakeet, the Carolina Parakeet, was extirpated in the 1920s. Most Florida parrots are descendants of airport jailbreaks. Over 65 species of pet store parrots from Asia, Central or South America have re-flocked and naturalized in Florida's mild climate.

One of the most common feral species is the monk parakeet: bright green with dark blue wings and a pale face. Look—or listen—for them in the trees near the marinas.

Recycle old fire hose or water hose for dockline chafe guard. Cut 6- to 8-inch lengths, split lengthwise, and wrap around your docklines at chafe points for storms or long absences.

BIG GAME FISHING

Dania is the Cooperstown of fishing. The International Game Fish Association Fishing Hall of Fame and Museum is located in Dania. It opened about six years ago in a new $32 million facility. They're located about

SAFETY INFO

NOAA Weather	Sea Tow
WX-3 West Palm Beach, FL	Miami, FL
WX-1 Miami, FL	VHF 16/18
WX-2 Sugarloaf Key, FL	305/673-2869
USCG	**TowBoatU.S.**
Station Miami Beach, FL	Haulover Inlet, FL
VHF 16 or 09/22A	VHF 16/11
305/535-4368	305/864-1736

HEADS UP!

1062.7	East Sunrise Blvd. Bridge	**1084.6**	**JFK Causeway Bridge**
1064.1	East Las Olas Blvd. Bridge	1087.2	Julia Tuttle Bridge
1066.0	Brooks Memorial Bridge	1088.6	West Venetian Causeway Bridge
1069.4	Dania Beach Blvd. Bridge	1089.3	Dodge Island Bridges
1070.8	Sheridan Street Bridge	1091.8	South Florida Caution (NB)
1072.3	Hollywood Blvd. Bridge	SB	No Southbound Heads Up!
1074.0	Hallandale Beach Blvd. Bridge	SB	No Southbound Heads Up!
1078.0	Sunny Isles Bridge	SB	No Southbound Heads Up!
1081.3	**Broad Causeway Bridge**	SB	No Southbound Heads Up!

three miles inland near the terminus of the Dania Cut-off Canal at STM 1068.6.

The facility is spectacular, with a great hall filled with life-size replicas of world-record game fish. The highlight of the facility is the Catch Gallery of Virtual Fishing. You can strap into a fighting chair and feel what it's like to battle a 300-lb Blue Marlin or a 15-lb Largemouth Bass, all without getting blood and guts on your gelcoat.

Fishing Hall of Fame
www.igfa.org
954/922-4212

Courtesy of Dania Jai-Alai

180 mph Fastball!

JAI ALAI

In Dania, you need to know about jai alai. But unless you hail from near Milford, Connecticut or Newport, Rhode Island, you will probably call it "jay-ah-lay." It's pronounced HI-lie.

Jai alai is a fast-paced betting sport. According to *Guinness Book of World Records* it's the fastest ballgame in the world, with its rock-hard *pelota* traveling up to 180 mph. Each game is short and fast, lasting only about ten minutes. Two players face off in a court, trying to hurl a small hard ball against the front wall of the court with so much speed and spin the opponent cannot catch or return it before the second bounce. Each player retrieves and throws the ball with a scoop-shaped *cesta*. The winner stays on the court to meet the next player in rotation.

The game originated in the Basque region of Spain, where it's been played against church walls since the 15th century. It was a popular game during religious holidays, so the name jai alai means "merry festival" in Basque.

By the 1800s, jai alai had immigrated with the Basques to Mexico, Cuba, and South America. Its debut in the United States was at the 1904 St. Louis World's Fair. Today there are still only seven *frontons*, or arenas, in the U.S.: five in Florida; one in Milford, Connecticut; and one in Newport, Rhode Island.

Dania Jai-Alai was the second jai alai fronton built in the U.S., opening in 1953. It's located about a mile west of the Waterway between the Dania Cut-off Canal at STM 1068.6 and the Dania Town Canal. For a wild cultural experience, general admission is only $1.50.

Dania Jai-Alai
www.dania-jai-alai.com
954/920-1511

TRUMP TOWERS SOUTH

Unlike Florida cities to the north, Miami is a city of waterfront high-rises. For example, Donald Trump's latest luxury development is visible east of STM 1077. The two 55-story towers, topped with tubular white structures, overlook the Atlantic Ocean and Intracoastal Waterway. In true Trump style, a one-bedroom condo starts at a cool half-million dollars; penthouses are available for $25 million.

Quiet down! Silence rattling lockers and cabinets by placing self-adhesive felt or cork pads on inside corners. Foam insulation strips will do the trick for deck hatches or cockpit lockers. Fit doors with an eye on the bulkhead *and* an eye on the door to keep the hook from noisily swinging when not in use.

MIAMI

Miami, Florida would have been "Flagler, Florida," if not for the modesty of Henry Flagler, the man who envisioned South Florida as more than a jungle swamp and put his own money behind those ideas.

But Flagler, despite becoming incredibly rich, was the son of a minister and a modest man. So when Miami incorporated in 1896, Flagler politely declined having the new city named after him. Instead the name was adapted from *Mayami*, the Spaniards' name for Lake Okeechobee, derived from a

Approached through fixed bridge (vertical 32 feet). Used by local commercial and sport fishing boats. [STR 2.2 (TS)]

1079.9 FIU Anchorage (0.5)
Anchor 8-16 feet N25.54.550
STR 2.2 feet W080.08.148
Exit ICW NNE of R6 "A". Proceed NW to Florida International University basin. Anchor in basin according to wind conditions.

1080.4 Indian Creek Anchorage (0.5)
Anchor 8-10 feet N25.53.553
STR 2.6 feet W080.07.761
Exit ICW between G9 and G11. Proceed SE to charted Indian Creek. Anchor S of Bal Harbour basin, before bridge.

1080.9 Keystone Point Marina (2.0)
VHF 16; 305/940-6236
Exit ICW at R12. Proceed WNW in privately maintained channel to charted New Arch Creek. Marina is ahead. [STR 2.6]
Dry store with no transient dockage.

1081.3 Broad Causeway Bridge
VHF 09; 305/891-2221
Double bascule, vertical 16 feet.
Restricted year round: 0800-1800 hrs, opens on the quarter-hour and three-quarter hour.

1082.0 Jockey Club Marina (0.9)
No VHF Watch; No Telephone
Marina is closed indefinitely.

1083.8 Gator Racquet Club & Marina (0.5)
No VHF Watch; No Telephone
Marina is closed indefinitely.

1084.5 Pelican Harbor Marina (0.1)
No VHF Watch N25.50.950
305/754-9330 W080.10.087
Exit ICW N of bridge. Proceed E. [STR 2.6]

1084.6 John F. Kennedy Causeway Bridge
(West 79th Street Causeway Bridge)
VHF 09; DOT District 6 would not provide
Double bascule; vertical 25 feet; on request.

1084.7 79th Street Causeway Anchorage (0.5)
Anchor 5-7 feet N25.50.733
STR 2.6 feet W080.09.866
Exit ICW S of bridge. Proceed E toward charted 7-foot pocket W of North Bay Island.

1085.3 Palm Bay Club & Marina (0.4)
VHF 16; 305/751-3700
Exit ICW at G29. Proceed W in privately maintained channel to marina. [STR 2.6]

1087.0 Miami Beach Marinas
Exit ICW N of bridge. Proceed E along causeway to Miami Beach. Follow charted red aids northerly (leave to port) to Normandy Isle. At R10, turn easterly for charted Indian Creek. Pass N of Allison Isle, through bascule bridge (vertical 11 feet), into Indian Creek. [STR 2.6]

SAFETY INFO

NOAA Weather	**Sea Tow**
WX-3 West Palm Beach, FL	Miami, FL
WX-1 Miami, FL	VHF 16/18
WX-2 Sugarloaf Key, FL	305/673-2869
USCG	**TowBoatU.S.**
Station Miami Beach, FL	Biscayne Bay, FL
VHF 16 or 09/22A	VHF 16/11
305/535-4368	305/358-1486

HEADS UP!

1069.4	Dania Beach Blvd. Bridge	1089.3	Dodge Island Bridges
1070.8	Sheridan Street Bridge	1091.8	South Florida Caution (NB)
1072.3	Hollywood Blvd. Bridge	SB	No Southbound Heads Up!
1074.0	Hallandale Beach Blvd. Bridge	SB	No Southbound Heads Up!
1078.0	Sunny Isles Bridge	SB	No Southbound Heads Up!
1081.3	Broad Causeway Bridge	SB	No Southbound Heads Up!
1084.6	JFK Causeway Bridge	SB	No Southbound Heads Up!
1087.2	**Julia Tuttle Bridge**	SB	No Southbound Heads Up!
1088.6	**West Venetian Causeway Bridge**	SB	No Southbound Heads Up!

- **Indian Creek Bridge** (4.8)
  VHF 09; No Telephone
  Bascule; vertical 11 feet; on request.
- **Wyndham Miami Beach Resort** (6.0)
  VHF 16; 305/532-3600
  Marina is to port near Surprise Lake Creek.
  Dockage for hotel guests only.
- **Fontainebleau Hilton Resort** (6.4)
  VHF 16; 305/538-2000
  Hotel and marina are to port.

1087.2 Julia L. Tuttle Bridge S N
Fixed; vertical 56 feet.
Caution: At vertical 56 feet, the Tuttle Bridge is the lowest fixed bridge along the ICW.
SEE JULIA TUTTLE.

1088.5 Sealine Marina & Yachting Center (0.2) S N
VHF 16/10 or 11 N25.47.443
305/377-3625 W080.10.996
Exit ICW at G49. Proceed W to privately maintained channel. Marina is charted semi-circular breakwater ahead. [STR 2.6]

1088.5 Sealine Anchorage (0.4) S N
Anchor 7-10 feet N25.47.569
STR 2.6 feet W080.11.064
Exit ICW at G49. Proceed W to privately maintained channel. Anchorage is N of Sealine Marina in charted pocket.

1088.5 Municipal Island Anchorages (North) S N
Exit ICW at G49. Proceed E.

- **Biscayne Island Anchorage** (0.3)
  Anchor 6-8 feet N25.47.515
  STR 2.6 feet W080.10.548
  Proceed E to middle of Biscayne Island.
- **Municipal Island Anchorages**
  Depending on wind direction, you may also anchor in lee of the other Venetian Causeway islands. Anchor in 8-12 feet.
  Caution: Move off marked channel carefully, avoiding charted submerged obstructions.

1088.5 Sunset Harbour Yacht Club (2.3) S N
VHF 16; 305/398-6800
Exit ICW at G49. Proceed E along privately maintained channel to Belle Isle. Marina is on Miami Beach, to port. [STR 2.6]
Dockominiums with no transient dockage.

1088.6 West Venetian Causeway Bridge S N
VHF 09; DOT District 6 would not provide
Double bascule; vertical 12 feet.
Restricted November 1-April 30: M-F except holidays, 0700-0900 and 1630-1830 hrs, opens on the hour and half-hour.

1088.7 Miami Yacht Club (0.6) S N
VHF 16; 305/377-9877
Exit ICW S of bridge. Proceed E, favoring Biscayne Island, through charted 6-foot pass. Yacht club is on NE corner of charted Watson Park. [STR 2.6]
SEE PARROT JUNGLE ISLAND.

Tequesta Indian word some say means "sweet water" and others document as meaning "vast."

Flagler may have initially developed Miami, but air conditioning was what put Miami on the world map. Historians point out Miami didn't take off as a major metropolitan area until the mass availability of air conditioning. Climate-controlled buildings and homes allowed people and businesses to move into the area and sustain a world-class modern city. Today Miami-Dade is a banking and finance center, home to many Fortune 500 companies, and the 8th largest county by population in the U.S. And its population continues to grow: Miami's Chamber of Commerce projects another 30% increase over the next 15 years.

Courtesy of gssites.com/miami

Venetian Causeway (circa 1930)

Courtesy of gssites.com/miami

Venetian Causeway (circa 1990)

For boaters, Miami is a contradiction. On one hand, it's a major metropolitan area with all the services and activities one could imagine. But as we pointed out in Virginia, it isn't the gold at the end of the rainbow. Most boaters find they don't spend much time in downtown Miami.

But Miami is a landmark for boaters: the terminus or beginning of what most boaters think of as the Atlantic Intracoastal Waterway. And as beginning or end, most boaters are psyched to move on: either to get started on the long journey north or looking forward to the Keys or Bahamas. Goals are fleeting fancies, quickly replaced when achieved.

JULIA TUTTLE

To tall-rigged sailboaters, the name Julia Tuttle is associated with a fixed bridge that is too short. The 56-foot span of the Julia L. Tuttle Bridge at STM 1087.2 is the single glaring exception to the Waterway's 65-foot bridge standard. Vessels with masts over 56 feet are forced outside to transit between Miami and Ft. Lauderdale.

But Julia Tuttle should be remembered as a pioneer in urban planning. She arrived in this frontier area in 1891 from Cleveland and bought several hundred acres along the banks of the Miami River. It was Tuttle who convinced New York financier Henry Flagler to extend his Florida East Coast Railway south to Miami.

Flagler obliged in 1896, the year the city was incorporated, and embraced Tuttle's vision: dredging the harbor, building the Royal Palm Hotel, and promoting the area to northerners as a tourist destination. Miami became the thriving metropolis it is today and goes down in history as the only U.S. city planned by a woman.

PARROT JUNGLE ISLAND

The island to the southeast of the MacArthur Causeway, at STM 1088.8, is the recently re-named Parrot Jungle Island (formerly Watson Park). This island, in the middle of Biscayne Bay, is the new home of Parrot Jungle, the famous facility formerly located on the mainland near Monkey Jungle.

The concept of a Parrot Jungle started in 1936, when Austrian-born Franz Scherr imagined a property where people could see tropical birds flying free. The first 25 macaws arrived from Texas and visitors paid 25¢ to walk along a nature trail and listen to Scherr describe the tropical birds and plants.

Today the $47 million park at Parrot Jungle Island boasts over 1,100 tropical birds, 2,000 varieties of plants and flowers, trained bird shows, an Everglades exhibit, and exotic birds flying in natural habitats. One of the

SAFETY INFO

NOAA Weather	**Sea Tow**
WX-3 West Palm Beach, FL	Miami, FL
WX-1 Miami, FL	VHF 16/18
WX-2 Sugarloaf Key, FL	305/673-2869
USCG	**TowBoatU.S.**
Station Miami Beach, FL	Biscayne Bay, FL
VHF 16 or 09/22A	VHF 16/11
305/535-4368	305/358-1486

HEADS UP!

1070.8	Sheridan Street Bridge	1091.8	South Florida Caution (NB)
1072.3	Hollywood Blvd. Bridge	SB	No Southbound Heads Up!
1074.0	Hallandale Beach Blvd. Bridge	SB	No Southbound Heads Up!
1078.0	Sunny Isles Bridge	SB	No Southbound Heads Up!
1081.3	Broad Causeway Bridge	SB	No Southbound Heads Up!
1084.6	JFK Causeway Bridge	SB	No Southbound Heads Up!
1087.2	Julia Tuttle Bridge	SB	No Southbound Heads Up!
1088.6	West Venetian Causeway Bridge	SB	No Southbound Heads Up!
1089.3	**Dodge Island Bridges**	SB	No Southbound Heads Up!

exhibits, the Manu Encounter with more than 200 parrots and macaws, is the world's only aviary replicating the clay cliffs of Manu, Peru.

You can enjoy the views without the admission fee at the Lakeside Café, which overlooks a lake filled with (real, not lawn) pink flamingos and tropical fish. To see the full exhibits, admission to the park is $23.95.

Parrot Jungle
www.parrotjungle.com
305/258-6453

STAR ISLAND

As you transit Miami's dense series of bridges (Venetian Causeway, MacArthur Causeway, and Dodge Island Highway Bridges), you may notice the islands of these bridges are perfect oval shapes. These man-made islands are refuges for the rich and famous, even back in the 1920s when Al Capone had his estate on Palm Island.

Courtesy of gssites.com/miami

Star Island

Star Island, visible from the Flagler Memorial anchorage at STM 1088.7 or Miami Beach Marina at STM 1089.8, is one of the most exclusive island communities in Miami. A 10,000-square-foot residence on Star Island, complete with a pool, four-car garage, and seven bathrooms, lists for about $12 million. Cuban-born singer Gloria Estafan, who is adored by her adopted hometown for her community efforts, lives on Star Island.

MIAMI BOAT SHOW

As you pass under Dodge Island Highway Bridge at STM 1089.3, Miamarina is visible to the southwest. This marina is one of the three locations of the Miami International Boat Show. The "largest in-water boat show in the world" takes place every February. Miamarina hosts the Strictly Sail portion of the boat show. Powerboats

Courtesy of Greater Miami CVB

Port of Miami

are displayed in-water at the Sealine Marina & Yachting Center, northwest of the Venetian Causeway Bridge at STM 1088.6. The Miami Beach Convention Center is the third location, chockerblock-full with every nautical goodie one could imagine.

Miami International Boat Show
www.discoverboating.com/boatshows

BISCAYNE BAY

Southern Biscayne Bay was a refuge for early sailors: a source of drinking water during their travels along the coast from Key West or the Caribbean. During the 1800s, freshwater springs occurred in the middle of this brackish bay. Native people and explorers filled pots of sweet water by dipping them overboard. A photograph from 1888 shows a boatman dipping freshwater from the middle of the bay.

But taking a look around, it's obvious the ecology of Biscayne Bay has been drastically altered over the last hundred years. A shallow freshwater aquifer still allows some freshwater to reach Biscayne Bay, but the springs are gone. As South Florida's land use changed, the hydrology of Biscayne Bay also changed. After the Everglades were drained, sheets of fresh water no longer flowed into Biscayne Bay. The freshwater springs disappeared as the natural water table lowered.

Today the bay is very salty and turbid. And although spiny lobsters and coral still manage here, agricultural run-off and industrial pollution continue to negatively impact the bay's ecology. Land development has removed the cleansing buffers of mangroves and careless recreational boaters damage the sea grass that keeps the bay productive and clean.

1088.7 Municipal Island Anchorages (South)
Exit ICW S of bridge. Proceed E, favoring Biscayne Island, through charted 6-foot pass.

- **Flagler Memorial Anchorage** (1.7)
  Anchor 8-10 feet N25.47.071
  STR 2.6 feet W080.09.241
  Anchor to SW of small island with charted Flagler Memorial Monument.
  SEE STAR ISLAND.
- **Belle Isle Anchorage** (2.3)
  Anchor 8-12 feet N25.47.348
  STR 2.6 feet W080.08.735
  Anchor SE of Belle Isle near mouth of charted Collins Canal.
- **Municipal Island Anchorages**
  Depending on wind direction, you may also anchor in lee of the other Venetian Causeway islands. Anchor in 8-12 feet.

1088.8 MacArthur Causeway Bridge
Fixed; vertical 65 feet.

1089.0 Junction | Port of Miami (4.6)
Exit ICW in turning basin. Proceed easterly, through Government Cut, to inlet.
Caution: Security Zone. Since 9/11, this channel has been increasingly restricted to cruise ship and commercial vessel use only. Typically, you will be directed to use the Dodge Island and Lummus Island Cuts (STM 1089.8).

1089.3 Dodge Island Highway Bridge
Fixed; vertical 65 feet.

1089.3 Dodge Island RR Bridge
No VHF; No Telephone
Bascule; vertical 22 feet; usually open.

1089.4 Miamarina at Bayside (0.1)
VHF 16/18 N25.46.724
305/579-6955 W080.11.088
Exit ICW SSW of bridges. Proceed WNW to charted basin. [STR 2.6 (TS)]
SEE MIAMI BOAT SHOW.

1089.8 Junction | Port of Miami
Exit ICW at G57. Proceed ENE to charted Dodge Island Cut, then E in Lummus Island Cut. [STR 2.8]
Caution: Northbound, if your vessel height is greater than 56 feet, you must exit the ICW at this inlet and re-join the ICW at Port Everglades (Ft. Lauderdale) or Lake Worth (Palm Beach).

- **Fisher Island Anchorage** (2.8)
  Anchor 8-12 feet N25.45.427
  STR 2.8 feet W080.08.637
  Exit Lummus Island Cut E of G5. Proceed southeasterly along Fisher Island western shore. Anchor beyond charted basin.
- **USCG Station Miami Beach** (1.6)
  As Lummus Island Cut joins Government Cut, charted USCG station is to NNW.
- **Miami Beach Marina** (1.8)
  VHF 16; 305/673-6000
  As Lummus Island Cut joins Government Cut, marina is large bulkheaded facility to NNE.

SAFETY INFO

NOAA Weather	Sea Tow
WX-3 West Palm Beach, FL	Biscayne Bay, FL
WX-1 Miami, FL	VHF 16/18
WX-2 Sugarloaf Key, FL	305/361-9500
USCG	**TowBoatU.S.**
Station Miami Beach, FL	Biscayne Bay, FL
VHF 16 or 09/22A	VHF 16/11
305/535-4368	305/358-1486

HEADS UP!

1072.3	Hollywood Blvd. Bridge	SB	No Southbound Heads Up!
1074.0	Hallandale Beach Blvd. Bridge	SB	No Southbound Heads Up!
1078.0	Sunny Isles Bridge	SB	No Southbound Heads Up!
1081.3	Broad Causeway Bridge	SB	No Southbound Heads Up!
1084.6	JFK Causeway Bridge	SB	No Southbound Heads Up!
1087.2	Julia Tuttle Bridge	SB	No Southbound Heads Up!
1088.6	West Venetian Causeway Bridge	SB	No Southbound Heads Up!
1089.3	Dodge Island Bridges	SB	No Southbound Heads Up!
1091.8	**South Florida Caution (NB)**	SB	No Southbound Heads Up!

- **Port of Miami** (Government Cut)(4.5)
  Well Aided N25.45.403
  Well Lit W080.06.884
  Follow Government Cut easterly out inlet. Waypoint is at turning mark between R6 "A", R6, and G7.

1091.6 Marine Stadium
Exit ICW N of bridge. Proceed E along causeway. [STR 2.5]

- **Rickenbacker Marina** (0.5)
  VHF 16; 305/361-1900
  Marina is in charted fork.
  Dry store with no transient dockage.
- **Marine Stadium Marina** (0.8)
  VHF 16; 305/361-3316
  Continue beyond charted fork and round SE into large charted Marine Stadium basin. Marina is to starboard.
  Dry store with no transient dockage.
- **Marine Stadium Anchorage** (1.0)
  Anchor 6-9 feet N25.44.659
  STR 2.5 feet W080.10.152
  Anchor E of Marine Stadium Marina, in front of charted grandstand.

1091.7 Rickenbacker Bridge
Fixed; vertical 76 feet.

1091.8 Heads Up | South Florida
to Northbound Navigation Only
1034.4 From the Rickenbacker Bridge to Boynton Canal, this 57-mile stretch is the most congested collection of narrow canals, opening bridges, personal watercraft, and "weekend warriors" of your ICW experience.

Dotted with multimillion-dollar estates and eccentric lawn and house trimmings we always enjoy the "tour," but with a steady hand on the wheel and an extra cautious eye.

1092.2 Virginia Key Anchorage (0.9)
Anchor 10-12 feet N25.44.177
STR 2.4 feet W080.10.196
Exit ICW S of G69. Proceed E toward charted dome.

1093.7 Crandon Park Marina (2.3)
VHF 16; 305/361-1281
Exit ICW WNW of West Point (Key Biscayne). Proceed E to Bear Cut channel. Marina is in charted basin, before bridge, at Northwest Point. [STR 2.4 (TS)]

1094.3 Coconut Grove
Exit ICW W of West Point (Key Biscayne). Proceed WNW to charted Dinner Key Channel. [STR 2.3]
There are three channels to Coconut Grove. This is the main, and preferred, channel.
See Dinner Key Terminal.

- **Coconut Grove Anchorage** (South)(2.7)
  Anchor 6-8 feet N25.43.438
  STR 2.3 feet W080.13.908
  Exit channel before R14. Proceed westerly, outside of spoil islands, to anchor among permanent fleet.

Lubricate your marine toilet every few weeks by pouring two tablespoons of vegetable oil into the bowl and slowly pumping it through. For heads with leather parts, use an approved marine toilet lubricant such as Sea-Lube.

DINNER KEY TERMINAL

Dinner Key Channel leads west from STM 1094.3 to the community of Coconut Grove.

In our grandparents and parents day, if you could afford the $35, you could come out to Dinner Key and fly one of the new Pan Am Clippers to exotic ports like Havana and Nassau. Or for free you could do what many families did: come out to Dinner Key for a picnic dinner to simply watch the Flying Boats take off and land.

Until 1945, Dinner Key was Pan American Airways' Latin American Hub for its flying boat, or clipper ship, fleet. Passengers arrived and passed through customs at a barge moored alongside the Key.

Courtesy of gssites.com/miami

Dinner Key Terminal (circa 1945)

Courtesy of gssites.com/miami

Pan Am Clipper Over Miami (circa 1930)

Little remains of this legendary American company. Two hangars are still on Dinner Key, one a sailing and kayaking center and another converted in the 1950s to city hall. The tracks where the Clippers were towed out of the water are still visible in the boat basin. And Pan American Drive runs along the waterfront.

COCONUT GROVE

Coconut Grove is technically part of the city of Miami. What was once a radical bohemian art colony is now a thriving upscale art community. It's the chic location for trendy restaurants, galleries, and shops where Miamians come to see and be seen.

Courtesy of gssites.com/miami

Vizcaya Estate

Every February, Coconut Grove hosts one of the area's largest outdoor art festivals, organized for over 40 years. For the rest of the year, the community is busy with art and music events and an active nightlife. During the day, the Shopping District and Cocowalk bustle with shops, street performers, and café activity. For mariners who no longer have a nightlife and don't need to "be seen," mundane services such as laundry, drugstores, and banks are also available in town.

Just north of town, behind the tiny island appropriately called Tidal Flat, is the U.S. Sailing Center, one of the training sites for the U.S. Olympic sailing team. A bit further north up the coast, just past the hospital at Hospital Pier, is the Villa Vizcaya, also on Biscayne Bay. Millionaire James Deering (as in Deering Channel west of STM 1092.8) built this Italian Renaissance-style villa in 1916. The house, with 42 rooms, 28 acres of formal Mediterranean-style gardens, and a waterfront teahouse is open to the public.

Coconut Grove Art Festival
www.coconutgroveartsfest.com
305/447-0401

Vizcaya Museum
www.vizcayamuseum.com
305/250-9133

THE BARNACLE

Before there were roads to Miami, yacht designer Ralph Middleton Munroe ventured into shallow Biscayne Bay with one of his shoal-draft yachts

SAFETY INFO

NOAA Weather
WX-3 West Palm Beach, FL
WX-1 Miami, FL
WX-2 Sugarloaf Key, FL

USCG
Station Miami Beach, FL
VHF 16 or 09/22A
305/535-4368

Sea Tow
Biscayne Bay, FL
VHF 16/18
305/361-9500

TowBoatU.S.
Biscayne Bay, FL
VHF 16/11
305/358-1486

HEADS UP!

1072.3	Hollywood Blvd. Bridge	SB	No Southbound Heads Up!
1074.0	Hallandale Beach Blvd. Bridge	SB	No Southbound Heads Up!
1078.0	Sunny Isles Bridge	SB	No Southbound Heads Up!
1081.3	Broad Causeway Bridge	SB	No Southbound Heads Up!
1084.6	JFK Causeway Bridge	SB	No Southbound Heads Up!
1087.2	Julia Tuttle Bridge	SB	No Southbound Heads Up!
1088.6	West Venetian Causeway Bridge	SB	No Southbound Heads Up!
1089.3	Dodge Island Bridges	SB	No Southbound Heads Up!
1091.8	South Florida Caution (NB)	SB	No Southbound Heads Up!

and settled on the western shores of the bay. He designed and built his own home in 1891, called The Barnacle, then constructed a large boathouse where he built and designed his boats.

Today the house is the oldest home in Miami-Dade still in its original location. The grounds are a state park and the house is open to visitors. As you enter or exit Dinner Key Channel, you may spot the Barnacle Historic State Park just south of Coconut Grove. The homestead's historic yellow boathouse, dock, and marine railway are visible along the shore.

Barnacle Historic State Park
www.floridastateparks.org/thebarnacle
305/442-6866

Courtesy of gssites.com/miami

Barnacle Boathouse (circa 1895)

KEY BISCAYNE

Key Biscayne is divided into two areas: exclusive homes for the rich and famous and preserved lands open to public access.

The middle of the island, visible if you anchor to the north of Southwest Point, is developed with homes for the wealthy, who coveted the exclusiveness of a Miami island accessible by a single bridge. Former President Richard Nixon had his "Winter White House" overlooking this anchorage. The house went down in history as the place where the Watergate break-in at the Democratic headquarters was planned.

You can no longer see the Nixon home, although many boaters still talk about it. In 2004 the *Miami Herald* reported the ranch-style house was torn down to make way for a new home. You may see new construction at the site, located across from the piling symbol shown on the chart.

The southern end of Key Biscayne is one of the state's most coveted parks: the Bill Baggs Cape Florida State Recreation Area, famous for its beaches, sunsets, and views of Miami. The easiest way to access the park is to dinghy into the protected keyhole at No Name Harbor. The park has been completely refurbished since Hurricane Andrew with native plantings, boardwalks over the dunes, and two rustic waterfront cafés.

Key Biscayne
www.key-biscayne.com

Bill Baggs State Recreation Area
www.floridastateparks.org/capeflorida
305/361-5811

CAPE FLORIDA LIGHT

Cape Florida Light has had a tough history. First it was fraudulently built with hollow walls, secretly saving the contractor half the cost of the bricks. Then the lighthouse was damaged in the Seminole Wars and couldn't be repaired because of Indian raids. Finally Confederates destroyed its illuminating apparatus. Ultimately the project was given up and replaced by the light at Fowey Rocks two miles southeast.

But with the renaissance of lighthouse appreciation, the Coast Guard refurbished the structure in the 1970s. It was transformed from a crumbling structure of spalling brick to a well-maintained white tower described as one of the most attractive lighthouses in America.

Courtesy of gssites.com/miami

Coconut Grove

The best way to see Cape Florida Light is to anchor nearby—either north of Southwest Point, in Hurricane Harbor, or in No Name Harbor—and dinghy ashore at No Name Harbor. From there you can walk to the lighthouse through the Bill Baggs Cape Florida State Recreational Area. If you don't stop at Key Biscayne, you can also see the lighthouse from the Waterway near the southern end of Biscayne Bay.

- **Dinner Key Marina** (2.9)
  VHF 16/68 N25.43.543
  305/579-6980 W080.14.084
  Marina is to port. [STR 2.3 (TS)]
- **Grove Key Marina** (2.9)
  No VHF Watch N25.43.668
  305/858-6527 W080.13.956
  Marina is to starboard. Dry store with no transient dockage.
- **Coconut Grove Anchorage** (North)(3.0)
  Anchor 6-10 feet N25.43.710
  STR 2.3 feet W080.13.918
  Proceed northerly beyond Grove Key Marina.
- **Bayshore Landing Marina** (3.2)
  VHF 16; 305/854-7997
  Proceed beyond anchorage. Marina is to N.
  Formerly Monty's Marina Coconut Grove.
- **Coral Reef Yacht Club** (3.3)
  VHF 16; 305/858-1733
  Proceed beyond anchorage to yacht club.
  Accepts guests of members and offers reciprocal rights to members of accredited yacht clubs.

1095.2 Key Biscayne Anchorages S N
Exit ICW NW of Southwest Point (Key Biscayne). Proceed easterly to a point N of R2 (Hurricane Harbor).
SEE KEY BISCAYNE.

- **Key Biscayne Anchorage** (1.2)
  Anchor 8-14 feet N25.41.695
  STR 2.4 feet W080.10.581
  Anchor between R2 and G3.
- **Hurricane Harbor Anchorage** (1.6)
  Anchor 10-14 feet N25.41.208
  STR 2.4 feet W080.10.399
  Proceed SE into charted Hurricane Harbor.

1095.9 Junction | Cape Florida Channel S N
Exit ICW W of Southwest Point (Key Biscayne). Proceed easterly to charted Cape Florida Channel R2. [STR 2.4]
SEE CAPE FLORIDA LIGHT.

- **No Name Harbor Anchorage** (2.3)
  Anchor 8-12 feet N25.40.601
  STR 2.4 feet W080.09.778
  Favoring Key Biscayne shore, proceed SE to charted No Name Harbor.
  This anchorage is within the Bill Baggs State Recreation Area so there is a $1/person fee for going ashore.
- **Cape Florida Channel** (5.5)
  If you intend to run outside to the Bahamas or Florida Keys, you can continue out Cape Florida Channel to Biscayne Channel Light. However, Biscayne Channel (STM 1097.9) is much preferred.
  Caution: This route should only be taken in excellent light and sea conditions; it is extremely easy to stray southerly onto charted Biscayne Flats.

1097.8 Matheson Hammock Marina (3.8) S N
No VHF Watch N25.40.727
305/665-5475 W080.15.561

SAFETY INFO

NOAA Weather
WX-3 West Palm Beach, FL
WX-1 Miami, FL
WX-2 Sugarloaf Key, FL

USCG
Station Miami Beach, FL
VHF 16 or 09/22A
305/535-4368

Sea Tow
Biscayne Bay, FL
VHF 16/18
305/361-9500

TowBoatU.S.
Biscayne Bay, FL
VHF 16/11
305/358-1486

HEADS UP!

1072.3	Hollywood Blvd. Bridge	SB	No Southbound Heads Up!
1074.0	Hallandale Beach Blvd. Bridge	SB	No Southbound Heads Up!
1078.0	Sunny Isles Bridge	SB	No Southbound Heads Up!
1081.3	Broad Causeway Bridge	SB	No Southbound Heads Up!
1084.6	JFK Causeway Bridge	SB	No Southbound Heads Up!
1087.2	Julia Tuttle Bridge	SB	No Southbound Heads Up!
1088.6	West Venetian Causeway Bridge	SB	No Southbound Heads Up!
1089.3	Dodge Island Bridges	SB	No Southbound Heads Up!
1091.8	South Florida Caution (NB)	SB	No Southbound Heads Up!

Exit ICW WNW of charted Biscayne Channel. Proceed WNW in privately maintained channel to marina. No transient dockage. [STR 2.4]

1097.9 Junction | Biscayne Channel (5.0) S N
Well Aided N25.38.302
Poorly Lit W080.07.846

Exit ICW W of charted Biscayne Channel. Proceed easterly across Biscayne Flats to Biscayne Channel Light. Waypoint is Biscayne Channel Light.

Many cruisers bounce in and out of the Waterway between Biscayne Channel and Lake Worth. It is a nice alternative to the bridges and congestion of the ICW and a welcome opportunity to get back out to the ocean.

See Stiltsville.

Note: Biscayne Channel is not an inlet. It is a passage across Biscayne Flats avoiding numerous coral heads and shoals. It is reasonably straight and well-marked, but poorly lit. It is popular for twilight Bahamas departures.

Caution: Northbound, if your vessel height is greater than 56 feet, you must exit the ICW at this inlet or at Government Cut (Miami) to proceed outside and re-join the ICW at Port Everglades (Ft. Lauderdale) or Lake Worth Inlet (Palm Beach).

If you have roller furling, remove the polyester core from the length of braided line that wraps around your roller-furling drum. The line will be lighter, dry more quickly, and lie flatter around the drum, preventing roller furler wraps and tangles.

STILTSVILLE

South of Key Biscayne, a historical community literally clings to Biscayne Flats for its life. This is Stiltsville, a cluster of structures built on the finger flats of Biscayne Bay. The homes in Stiltsville survived decades of hurricanes, but may not weather the changing legal landscape.

Stiltsville began as a cluster of fishing shacks, evolving over the decades to clubs, getaways, and eventually homes. In the early days before government regulation, fishermen picked a site, built a structure, and convinced their buddies to build a fishing shack nearby. Boaters would hang out on the flats, fishing and resting in the shade of the structures.

Courtesy of www.key-biscayne.com
Photo by Eddie Dziura
Save Our Stiltsville

But now Stiltsville finds itself in the middle of a land-ownership regulatory nightmare. After Hurricane Betsy hit in 1965, the county ended all new construction. It condemned structures with more than 50% damage and required the remaining buildings to comply with building codes. In 1974 the State of Florida issued 25-year bay bottom leases to the remaining homeowners. Meanwhile, Biscayne National Park extended its boundary north to encompass Stiltsville. When the lease ended in 1999, the National Park Service wanted the structures removed.

Today seven houses remain, survivors of countless hurricanes, including a direct hit by Hurricane Andrew in 1992. Efforts continue to save the structures, but attempts to renew leases or place the homes on the National Register of Historic Places have not been successful. Organizations, such as Save Old Stiltsville (S.O.S.), continue the battle. Hopefully when you pass by Key Biscayne, the silhouette of this unique community will still be visible on the horizon.

Courtesy of NOAA
Photo by Ralph F. Kresge
Biscayne Bay

Save Old Stiltsville
www.stiltsville.org

A PARTING OR JOINING

For many boaters, Biscayne Bay is the end or the beginning of the Intracoastal Waterway. Of course, it's not a terminus: the Waterway continues another 1,965 miles to Brownsville or 1,879 miles to Boston.

But for most, the Waterway bifurcates at Biscayne Bay. Some boaters transit Biscayne Bay to or from the Keys, choosing either Hawk Channel or the Florida Bay route. Other boaters use Biscayne Bay as the jumping-off port for the Bahamas.

If you are heading north, welcome aboard for the next 1098 miles. If you are heading south or east, *buen viaje*, wind to your back, and stay in the deep water! ▲

Florida Waterway Business Cards

Palm Cove Marina
STM 746.9
www.palmcovemarina.com

14603 Beach Boulevard
Jacksonville, FL 32250

904/223-4757 (phone)
904/223-6601 (fax)

VHF 16/69

Depth	6	**Laundry**	On-Site
Diesel/Gas	D/G	**Pool**	Yes
Pumpout	Yes	**Internet/WiFi**	I
Mail/Fax	M/F	**Car/Bike**	No
Service	On-Site	**Groceries**	Walk
Parts	On-Site	**Restaurant**	On-Site
Haulout	35T	**Post Office**	Taxi
Propane	Walk	**Library**	Walk

Beach Marine
STM 747.3
www.jaxbeachmarine.com

2315 Beach Boulevard
Jacksonville Beach, FL 32250

904/249-8200 (phone)
904/249-2050 (fax)

VHF 16/68

Depth	6	**Laundry**	On-Site
Diesel/Gas	D/G	**Pool**	No
Pumpout	Yes	**Internet/WiFi**	I
Mail/Fax	M/F	**Car/Bike**	No
Service	On-Call	**Groceries**	Walk
Parts	On-Call	**Restaurant**	Walk
Haulout	No	**Post Office**	Walk
Propane	Walk	**Library**	Walk

Camachee Cove Yacht Harbor
STM 775.6
www.camacheeisland.com

3070 Harbor Drive
St. Augustine, FL 32084

904/829-5676 (phone)
904/829-0396 (fax)

VHF 16/68

Depth	7	**Laundry**	On-Site
Diesel/Gas	D/G	**Pool**	Yes
Pumpout	Yes	**Internet/WiFi**	I
Mail/Fax	M/F	**Car/Bike**	C
Service	On-Call	**Groceries**	Taxi
Parts	On-Call	**Restaurant**	On-Site
Haulout	No	**Post Office**	Taxi
Propane	Taxi	**Library**	Taxi

Conch House Marina Resort
STM 776.8
www.conch-house.com

57 Comares Avenue
St. Augustine, FL 32080

800/940-6256 (phone)
904/829-6998 (fax)

VHF 16/69

Depth	8	**Laundry**	On-Site
Diesel/Gas	D/G	**Pool**	Yes
Pumpout	Yes	**Internet/WiFi**	I/W
Mail/Fax	M/F	**Car/Bike**	No
Service	On-Call	**Groceries**	Walk
Parts	On-Call	**Restaurant**	On-Site
Haulout	No	**Post Office**	Taxi
Propane	Walk	**Library**	Taxi

St. Augustine Municipal Marina
STM 778.2
www.staugustinemarina.com

111 Avenida Menendez
St. Augustine, FL 32084

904/825-1026 (phone)
904/825-1025 (fax)

VHF 16/71

Depth	8	**Laundry**	On-Site
Diesel/Gas	D/G	**Pool**	No
Pumpout	Yes	**Internet/WiFi**	I
Mail/Fax	M/F	**Car/Bike**	No
Service	On-Call	**Groceries**	Walk
Parts	On-Call	**Restaurant**	Walk
Haulout	No	**Post Office**	Walk
Propane	Walk	**Library**	Walk

St. Augustine Marine
STM 780.0
www.staugustinemarine.com

404 South Riberia Street
St. Augustine, FL 32084

904/824-4394 (phone)
904/824-9755 (fax)

VHF 16

Depth	11	**Laundry**	Taxi
Diesel/Gas	No	**Pool**	No
Pumpout	Yes	**Internet/WiFi**	No
Mail/Fax	M/F	**Car/Bike**	No
Service	On-Site	**Groceries**	Taxi
Parts	On-Site	**Restaurant**	Walk
Haulout	100T	**Post Office**	Walk
Propane	Walk	**Library**	Taxi

Palm Coast Marina
STM 802.8
www.oceanhammock.com

200 Clubhouse Drive
Palm Coast, FL 32137

386/446-6370 (phone)
386/445-9563 (fax)

VHF 16/69

Depth	8	**Laundry**	On-Site
Diesel/Gas	D/G	**Pool**	Yes
Pumpout	Yes	**Internet/WiFi**	I/W
Mail/Fax	M/F	**Car/Bike**	B
Service	On-Call	**Groceries**	Taxi
Parts	On-Call	**Restaurant**	On-Site
Haulout	No	**Post Office**	Walk
Propane	Taxi	**Library**	Taxi

Daytona Marina & Boat Works
STM 831.2
www.daytonamarine.com

645 South Beach Street
Daytona Beach, FL 32114

386/252-6421 (phone)
386/253-8174 (fax)

VHF 16/72

Depth	8	**Laundry**	On-Site
Diesel/Gas	D/G	**Pool**	No
Pumpout	Yes	**Internet/WiFi**	I/W
Mail/Fax	M/F	**Car/Bike**	C/B
Service	On-Site	**Groceries**	Taxi
Parts	On-Site	**Restaurant**	On-Site
Haulout	55T	**Post Office**	Walk
Propane	Walk	**Library**	Walk

Photocopy the "business card" of any Waterway facility. Then cut out the copy and take it ashore for easy reference!

Adventure Yacht Harbor
STM 836.8

www.adventureyachtharbor.com

3948 South Peninsula Drive
Daytona Beach, FL 32127

386/756-2180 (phone)
386/756-0693 (fax)

VHF 16/18

Depth	7	**Laundry**	On-Site
Diesel/Gas	D/G	**Pool**	No
Pumpout	Yes	**Internet/WiFi**	I/W
Mail/Fax	M/F	**Car/Bike**	No
Service	On-Call	**Groceries**	Taxi
Parts	On-Call	**Restaurant**	On-Site
Haulout	No	**Post Office**	Taxi
Propane	Taxi	**Library**	Taxi

Sea Love Marina & Boat Works
STM 839.6

4877 Front Street
Ponce Inlet, FL 32127

386/761-5434 (phone)
386/760-4210 (fax)

VHF 16/07

Depth	6	**Laundry**	Taxi
Diesel/Gas	D	**Pool**	No
Pumpout	No	**Internet/WiFi**	I
Mail/Fax	M/F	**Car/Bike**	No
Service	On-Site	**Groceries**	Taxi
Parts	On-Site	**Restaurant**	Walk
Haulout	70T	**Post Office**	Taxi
Propane	Taxi	**Library**	Taxi

North Causeway Marine
STM 846.1

www.northcausewaymarine.com

Four North Causeway
New Smyrna Beach, FL 32169

386/427-5267 (phone)
386/427-5620 (fax)

No VHF Watch

Depth	6	**Laundry**	Walk
Diesel/Gas	D/G	**Pool**	No
Pumpout	Yes	**Internet/WiFi**	No
Mail/Fax	No	**Car/Bike**	No
Service	On-Call	**Groceries**	Taxi
Parts	On-Call	**Restaurant**	Walk
Haulout	No	**Post Office**	Walk
Propane	Taxi	**Library**	Taxi

Titusville Municipal Marina
STM 878.2

451 Marina Road
Titusville, FL 32796

321/383-5600 (phone)
321/383-5602 (fax)

VHF 16/68

Depth	7	**Laundry**	On-Site
Diesel/Gas	D/G	**Pool**	No
Pumpout	Yes	**Internet/WiFi**	I
Mail/Fax	M/F	**Car/Bike**	No
Service	On-Call	**Groceries**	Walk
Parts	On-Call	**Restaurant**	Walk
Haulout	No	**Post Office**	Walk
Propane	Walk	**Library**	Walk

Harbortown Canaveral Marina
STM 893.7

www.harbortownmarina.com

2700 Harbortown Drive
Merritt Island, FL 32952

321/453-0160 (phone)
321/453-1512 (fax)

VHF 16/10

Depth	6	**Laundry**	On-Site
Diesel/Gas	D/G	**Pool**	Yes
Pumpout	Yes	**Internet/WiFi**	I/W
Mail/Fax	M/F	**Car/Bike**	No
Service	On-Site	**Groceries**	Taxi
Parts	On-Site	**Restaurant**	On-Site
Haulout	70T	**Post Office**	Taxi
Propane	Taxi	**Library**	Taxi

Whitley Bay Marina
STM 897.5

90 Delannoy Avenue
Cocoa, FL 32922

321/632-5445 (phone)
321/635-8434 (fax)

VHF 16/68

Depth	8	**Laundry**	On-Site
Diesel/Gas	No	**Pool**	No
Pumpout	Yes	**Internet/WiFi**	I
Mail/Fax	M/F	**Car/Bike**	No
Service	On-Call	**Groceries**	Walk
Parts	On-Call	**Restaurant**	Walk
Haulout	No	**Post Office**	Walk
Propane	Walk	**Library**	Walk

Diamond 99 Marina
STM 910.7

www.diamond99marina.com

4399 North US Hwy. 1
Melbourne, FL 32935

321/254-1490 (phone)
321/242-7404 (fax)

VHF 16/68

Depth	6	**Laundry**	On-Site
Diesel/Gas	D/G	**Pool**	No
Pumpout	No	**Internet/WiFi**	I/W
Mail/Fax	M/F	**Car/Bike**	No
Service	On-Site	**Groceries**	Walk
Parts	On-Site	**Restaurant**	On-Site
Haulout	No	**Post Office**	Taxi
Propane	Taxi	**Library**	Taxi

Eau Gallie Boat Works
STM 915.0

www.eaugallieboatworks.com

589 Young Street
Melbourne, FL 32935

321/254-1766 (phone)
321/242-8212 (fax)

VHF 16

Depth	5	**Laundry**	Walk
Diesel/Gas	No	**Pool**	No
Pumpout	No	**Internet/WiFi**	No
Mail/Fax	No	**Car/Bike**	No
Service	On-Site	**Groceries**	Walk
Parts	On-Site	**Restaurant**	Walk
Haulout	70T	**Post Office**	Walk
Propane	Walk	**Library**	Walk

Eau Gallie Yacht Basin
STM 915.0

587 Young Street
Melbourne, FL 32935

321/242-6577
321/724-6173

No VHF Watch

Depth	8	**Laundry**	On-Site
Diesel/Gas	No	**Pool**	No
Pumpout	Yes	**Internet/WiFi**	I
Mail/Fax	M	**Car/Bike**	No
Service	On-Call	**Groceries**	Walk
Parts	On-Call	**Restaurant**	Walk
Haulout	No	**Post Office**	Walk
Propane	Walk	**Library**	Walk

Waterline Marina
STM 915.0

www.waterlinemarina.com

905 N. Harbor City Blvd.
Melbourne, FL 32935

321/254-0452
321/254-0516

VHF 16/68

Depth	9	**Laundry**	On-Site
Diesel/Gas	No	**Pool**	No
Pumpout	Yes	**Internet/WiFi**	W
Mail/Fax	M/F	**Car/Bike**	No
Service	On-Call	**Groceries**	Walk
Parts	On-Call	**Restaurant**	Walk
Haulout	No	**Post Office**	Walk
Propane	Walk	**Library**	Walk

Fins Marina
STM 937.3

www.finsmarina.com

1600 Indian River Drive
Sebastian, FL 32958

772/589-4843
772/589-4843

VHF 16/11

Depth	6	**Laundry**	Walk
Diesel/Gas	D/G	**Pool**	No
Pumpout	Yes	**Internet/WiFi**	W
Mail/Fax	M/F	**Car/Bike**	No
Service	On-Call	**Groceries**	Walk
Parts	On-Call	**Restaurant**	On-Site
Haulout	No	**Post Office**	Taxi
Propane	Walk	**Library**	Taxi

Vero Beach Municipal Marina
STM 951.6

www.covb.com

3611 Rio Vista Boulevard
Vero Beach, FL 32963

772/231-2819
772/231-6893

VHF 16/66

Depth	8	**Laundry**	On-Site
Diesel/Gas	D/G	**Pool**	No
Pumpout	Yes	**Internet/WiFi**	I/W
Mail/Fax	M/F	**Car/Bike**	No
Service	On-Call	**Groceries**	Taxi
Parts	On-Call	**Restaurant**	Walk
Haulout	No	**Post Office**	Walk
Propane	Taxi	**Library**	Taxi

A A Marina
STM 982.8

2225 NE Indian River Drive
Jensen Beach, FL 34957

772/334-0936
772/334-0953

No VHF Watch

Depth	8	**Laundry**	Taxi
Diesel/Gas	No	**Pool**	No
Pumpout	No	**Internet/WiFi**	No
Mail/Fax	M/F	**Car/Bike**	No
Service	On-Site	**Groceries**	Taxi
Parts	On-Site	**Restaurant**	Walk
Haulout	No	**Post Office**	Taxi
Propane	Walk	**Library**	Taxi

Sailfish Marina of Stuart
STM 987.8

3565 SE St. Lucie Boulevard
Stuart, FL 34997

772/283-1122
772/220-6811

VHF 16/73

Depth	7	**Laundry**	On-Site
Diesel/Gas	D/G	**Pool**	No
Pumpout	Yes	**Internet/WiFi**	No
Mail/Fax	M/F	**Car/Bike**	No
Service	On-Site	**Groceries**	Taxi
Parts	On-Site	**Restaurant**	Taxi
Haulout	50T	**Post Office**	Taxi
Propane	Taxi	**Library**	Taxi

Finest Kind Marine
STM 987.8

www.finestkind.com

3585 SE St. Lucie Boulevard
Stuart, FL 34997

772/223-4110
772/220-9605

VHF 16/73

Depth	7	**Laundry**	Taxi
Diesel/Gas	D/G	**Pool**	No
Pumpout	No	**Internet/WiFi**	I
Mail/Fax	F	**Car/Bike**	No
Service	On-Call	**Groceries**	Taxi
Parts	On-Call	**Restaurant**	Walk
Haulout	No	**Post Office**	Walk
Propane	Taxi	**Library**	Walk

Pirates Cove Resort & Marina
STM 987.8

www.piratescoveresortandmarina.com

4307 SE Bayview Street
Stuart, FL 34997

772/223-9216
772/223-0863

VHF 16/68

Depth	7	**Laundry**	On-Site
Diesel/Gas	D/G	**Pool**	Yes
Pumpout	Yes	**Internet/WiFi**	No
Mail/Fax	M/F	**Car/Bike**	C
Service	On-Call	**Groceries**	Taxi
Parts	On-Call	**Restaurant**	On-Site
Haulout	No	**Post Office**	Walk
Propane	Taxi	**Library**	Taxi

Loblolly Marina

STM 992.1

www.loblollyinfo.com

8000 SE Little Harbor Drive
Hobe Sound, FL 33455

772/546-3136 (phone)
772/546-3997 (fax)

VHF 16/10

Depth	8	**Laundry**	Taxi
Diesel/Gas	No	**Pool**	No
Pumpout	No	**Internet/WiFi**	No
Mail/Fax	M/F	**Car/Bike**	No
Service	On-Call	**Groceries**	Taxi
Parts	On-Call	**Restaurant**	Taxi
Haulout	No	**Post Office**	Taxi
Propane	Taxi	**Library**	Taxi

JIB Yacht Club & Marina

STM 1004.2

www.jibmarina.com

46 Beach Road
Tequesta, FL 33469

561/746-4300 (phone)
561/743-8680 (fax)

VHF 16/65

Depth	8	**Laundry**	On-Site
Diesel/Gas	D/G	**Pool**	Yes
Pumpout	Yes	**Internet/WiFi**	I
Mail/Fax	M/F	**Car/Bike**	No
Service	On-Call	**Groceries**	Walk
Parts	On-Call	**Restaurant**	Walk
Haulout	No	**Post Office**	Walk
Propane	Walk	**Library**	Walk

Loggerhead Club & Marina

STM 1009.5

2700 Donald Ross Road
Palm Bch. Gardens, FL 33410

561/627-6358 (phone)
561/627-7523 (fax)

VHF 16/69

Depth	8	**Laundry**	On-Site
Diesel/Gas	D/G	**Pool**	No
Pumpout	Yes	**Internet/WiFi**	I
Mail/Fax	M/F	**Car/Bike**	B
Service	On-Call	**Groceries**	Walk
Parts	On-Call	**Restaurant**	Walk
Haulout	No	**Post Office**	Taxi
Propane	Taxi	**Library**	Taxi

Soverel Harbour Marina

STM 1012.1

www.soverelharbour.com

2401 PGA Bouldevard
Palm Bch. Gardens, FL 33410

561/691-9554 (phone)
561/691-9557 (fax)

VHF 16/08

Depth	7	**Laundry**	Taxi
Diesel/Gas	D/G	**Pool**	No
Pumpout	No	**Internet/WiFi**	I
Mail/Fax	M/F	**Car/Bike**	No
Service	On-Call	**Groceries**	Walk
Parts	On-Call	**Restaurant**	On-Site
Haulout	No	**Post Office**	Walk
Propane	Taxi	**Library**	Walk

North Palm Beach Marina

STM 1013.6

www.opch.com

1037 Marina Drive
N. Palm Beach, FL 33408

561/626-4919 (phone)
561/626-8857 (fax)

VHF 16/08

Depth	10	**Laundry**	On-Site
Diesel/Gas	D/G	**Pool**	Yes
Pumpout	Yes	**Internet/WiFi**	I
Mail/Fax	M/F	**Car/Bike**	No
Service	On-Call	**Groceries**	Taxi
Parts	On-Call	**Restaurant**	Walk
Haulout	No	**Post Office**	Walk
Propane	Taxi	**Library**	Walk

Old Port Cove Marina

STM 1014.1

www.opch.com

112 Lakeshore Drive
N. Palm Beach, FL 33408

561/626-1760 (phone)
561/626-1249 (fax)

VHF 16/08

Depth	12	**Laundry**	On-Site
Diesel/Gas	D	**Pool**	No
Pumpout	Yes	**Internet/WiFi**	I/W
Mail/Fax	M/F	**Car/Bike**	No
Service	On-Call	**Groceries**	Walk
Parts	On-Call	**Restaurant**	Walk
Haulout	No	**Post Office**	Taxi
Propane	Taxi	**Library**	Taxi

Cannonsport Marina & Resort

STM 1017.3

www.cannonsport.com

178 Lake Drive
Palm Beach Shores, FL 33404

561/848-7469 (phone)
561/844-9007 (fax)

VHF 16/07

Depth	12	**Laundry**	On-Site
Diesel/Gas	D/G	**Pool**	Yes
Pumpout	No	**Internet/WiFi**	I/W
Mail/Fax	No	**Car/Bike**	No
Service	On-Call	**Groceries**	Walk
Parts	On-Call	**Restaurant**	Walk
Haulout	No	**Post Office**	Walk
Propane	Walk	**Library**	Taxi

Sailfish Marina & Resort

STM 1017.3

www.sailfishmarina.com

98 Lake Drive
Palm Beach Shores, FL 33404

561/844-1724 (phone)
561/848-9684 (fax)

VHF 16/68

Depth	5	**Laundry**	On-Site
Diesel/Gas	D/G	**Pool**	Yes
Pumpout	No	**Internet/WiFi**	I/W
Mail/Fax	M/F	**Car/Bike**	No
Service	On-Call	**Groceries**	Walk
Parts	On-Call	**Restaurant**	On-Site
Haulout	No	**Post Office**	Walk
Propane	Walk	**Library**	Taxi

Riviera Beach Municipal Marina

STM 1017.9

200 East 13th Street
Riviera Beach, FL 33404

561/842-7806
561/845-8197

VHF 16/11

Depth	8	**Laundry**	On-Site
Diesel/Gas	D/G	**Pool**	No
Pumpout	Yes	**Internet/WiFi**	I
Mail/Fax	M/F	**Car/Bike**	No
Service	On-Call	**Groceries**	Walk
Parts	On-Call	**Restaurant**	Walk
Haulout	No	**Post Office**	Taxi
Propane	Taxi	**Library**	Walk

Rybovich Spencer

STM 1019.7

www.rybovich.com

4200 North Flagler Drive
West Palm Beach, FL 33407

561/844-1800
561/844-8393

VHF 16/08

Depth	12	**Laundry**	Walk
Diesel/Gas	D/G	**Pool**	No
Pumpout	Yes	**Internet/WiFi**	I
Mail/Fax	M/F	**Car/Bike**	No
Service	On-Site	**Groceries**	Taxi
Parts	On-Site	**Restaurant**	Taxi
Haulout	300T	**Post Office**	Walk
Propane	Walk	**Library**	Taxi

Marina Delray

STM 1037.8

www.marinadelray.com

777 Palm Trail
Delray Beach, FL 33483

561/276-7666
561/265-0666

VHF 16/69

Depth	5	**Laundry**	Walk
Diesel/Gas	D/G	**Pool**	Yes
Pumpout	No	**Internet/WiFi**	No
Mail/Fax	No	**Car/Bike**	No
Service	On-Call	**Groceries**	Walk
Parts	On-Call	**Restaurant**	Walk
Haulout	No	**Post Office**	Taxi
Propane	Taxi	**Library**	Taxi

Las Olas Municipal Marina

STM 1064.0

www.ftlauderdale.gov

240 Las Olas Circle
Ft. Lauderdale, FL 33316

954/828-7200
954/762-4912

VHF 16/71

Depth	7	**Laundry**	On-Site
Diesel/Gas	No	**Pool**	No
Pumpout	Yes	**Internet/WiFi**	I
Mail/Fax	M/F	**Car/Bike**	No
Service	On-Call	**Groceries**	Taxi
Parts	On-Call	**Restaurant**	Walk
Haulout	No	**Post Office**	Walk
Propane	Taxi	**Library**	Taxi

Las Olas Municipal Marina

STM 1064.2

www.ftlauderdale.gov

240 Las Olas Circle
Ft. Lauderdale, FL 33316

954/828-7200
954/762-4912

VHF 16/71

Depth	10	**Laundry**	On-Site
Diesel/Gas	No	**Pool**	No
Pumpout	Yes	**Internet/WiFi**	I
Mail/Fax	M/F	**Car/Bike**	No
Service	On-Call	**Groceries**	Taxi
Parts	On-Call	**Restaurant**	Walk
Haulout	No	**Post Office**	Walk
Propane	Taxi	**Library**	Taxi

Hall of Fame Marina

STM 1064.3

www.halloffamemarina.com

435 Seabreeze Boulevard
Ft. Lauderdale, FL 33316

954/764-3975
954/779-3658

VHF 16/08

Depth	8	**Laundry**	On-Site
Diesel/Gas	No	**Pool**	Yes
Pumpout	Yes	**Internet/WiFi**	I/W
Mail/Fax	M/F	**Car/Bike**	No
Service	On-Call	**Groceries**	Taxi
Parts	On-Call	**Restaurant**	Walk
Haulout	No	**Post Office**	Taxi
Propane	Taxi	**Library**	Taxi

Riverfront Marina

STM 1065.0

www.riverfrontmarina.com

420 SW Third Avenue
Ft. Lauderdale, FL 33315

954/527-1829
954/527-1842

VHF 16/71

Depth	6	**Laundry**	Walk
Diesel/Gas	D/G	**Pool**	Yes
Pumpout	No	**Internet/WiFi**	No
Mail/Fax	F	**Car/Bike**	No
Service	On-Site	**Groceries**	Walk
Parts	On-Site	**Restaurant**	On-Site
Haulout	No	**Post Office**	Walk
Propane	Taxi	**Library**	Walk

River Bend Marina

STM 1065.0

1515 SW 20th Street
Ft. Lauderdale, FL 33315

954/523-1832
954/523-1876

No VHF Watch

Depth	8	**Laundry**	Walk
Diesel/Gas	No	**Pool**	No
Pumpout	No	**Internet/WiFi**	No
Mail/Fax	M/F	**Car/Bike**	No
Service	On-Site	**Groceries**	Walk
Parts	On-Site	**Restaurant**	Walk
Haulout	70T	**Post Office**	Walk
Propane	Walk	**Library**	Taxi

Mango Marina

STM 1065.0

www.mangomarine.com

2005 SW 20th Street
Ft. Lauderdale, FL 33315

954/585-1041
954/585-1043

VHF 16

Depth	10	**Laundry**	On-Site
Diesel/Gas	No	**Pool**	No
Pumpout	Yes	**Internet/WiFi**	I
Mail/Fax	F	**Car/Bike**	No
Service	On-Site	**Groceries**	Walk
Parts	On-Site	**Restaurant**	Walk
Haulout	200T	**Post Office**	Taxi
Propane	Taxi	**Library**	Taxi

Jackson Marine Center

STM 1065.0

www.jacksonmarine.com

1915 SW 21st Avenue
Ft. Lauderdale, FL 33312

954/792-4900
954/587-8164

No VHF Watch

Depth	6	**Laundry**	Taxi
Diesel/Gas	G	**Pool**	No
Pumpout	No	**Internet/WiFi**	No
Mail/Fax	F	**Car/Bike**	No
Service	On-Site	**Groceries**	Walk
Parts	On-Site	**Restaurant**	Walk
Haulout	70T	**Post Office**	Taxi
Propane	Taxi	**Library**	Walk

Roscioli Yachting Center

STM 1065.0

3201 W. State Road 84
Ft. Lauderdale, FL 33312

954/581-9200
954/791-0958

No VHF Watch

Depth	10	**Laundry**	Walk
Diesel/Gas	No	**Pool**	No
Pumpout	No	**Internet/WiFi**	No
Mail/Fax	M/F	**Car/Bike**	No
Service	On-Site	**Groceries**	Walk
Parts	On-Site	**Restaurant**	Walk
Haulout	225T	**Post Office**	Taxi
Propane	Walk	**Library**	Taxi

Cable Marine East

STM 1065.9

www.cablemarine.com

1517 SE 16th Street
Ft. Lauderdale, FL 33312

954/462-2840
954/523-5339

VHF 16/09

Depth	18	**Laundry**	Walk
Diesel/Gas	D	**Pool**	No
Pumpout	Yes	**Internet/WiFi**	I
Mail/Fax	M/F	**Car/Bike**	C
Service	On-Site	**Groceries**	Walk
Parts	On-Site	**Restaurant**	On-Site
Haulout	40T	**Post Office**	Walk
Propane	Taxi	**Library**	Taxi

Hyatt Regency Pier 66 Marina

STM 1065.9

www.pier66.hyatt.com

2301 SE 17th Street
Ft. Lauderdale, FL 33316

954/728-3578
954/728-3588

VHF 16/71

Depth	15	**Laundry**	On-Site
Diesel/Gas	D/G	**Pool**	Yes
Pumpout	Yes	**Internet/WiFi**	W
Mail/Fax	M/F	**Car/Bike**	No
Service	On-Call	**Groceries**	Taxi
Parts	On-Call	**Restaurant**	On-Site
Haulout	No	**Post Office**	Walk
Propane	Taxi	**Library**	Taxi

Hollywood Municipal Marina

STM 1072.0

www.hollywoodfl.org

700 Polk Street
Hollywood, FL 33019

954/921-3035
954/921-3032

VHF 16/08

Depth	8	**Laundry**	On-Site
Diesel/Gas	D/G	**Pool**	No
Pumpout	Yes	**Internet/WiFi**	I
Mail/Fax	M/F	**Car/Bike**	No
Service	On-Call	**Groceries**	Walk
Parts	On-Call	**Restaurant**	Walk
Haulout	No	**Post Office**	Walk
Propane	Taxi	**Library**	Walk

Harbor Islands Marina

STM 1072.8

www.harborislandsmarina.com

1400 Marina Drive
Ft. Lauderdale, FL 33019

954/457-8557
954/458-5927

VHF 16/68

Depth	8	**Laundry**	On-Site
Diesel/Gas	No	**Pool**	Yes
Pumpout	Yes	**Internet/WiFi**	I
Mail/Fax	M/F	**Car/Bike**	B
Service	On-Call	**Groceries**	Taxi
Parts	On-Call	**Restaurant**	Taxi
Haulout	No	**Post Office**	Taxi
Propane	Taxi	**Library**	Taxi

Waterways Marina

STM 1075.2

www.waterwaysmarina.com

3601 NE 207th Street
Ft. Lauderdale, FL 33180

305/935-4295
305/933-1753

VHF 16/12

Depth	10	**Laundry**	On-Site
Diesel/Gas	No	**Pool**	No
Pumpout	Yes	**Internet/WiFi**	I
Mail/Fax	M/F	**Car/Bike**	B
Service	On-Call	**Groceries**	Walk
Parts	On-Call	**Restaurant**	On-Site
Haulout	No	**Post Office**	Walk
Propane	Taxi	**Library**	Walk

Fairmont Turnberry Isle Resort
STM 1075.9

www.fairmont.com

19735 Turnberry Way
Aventura, FL 33180

305/933-6934 (phone)
305/933-6908 (fax)

VHF 16/68

Depth	9	**Laundry**	On-Site
Diesel/Gas	No	**Pool**	Yes
Pumpout	Yes	**Internet/WiFi**	I/W
Mail/Fax	M/F	**Car/Bike**	No
Service	On-Call	**Groceries**	Taxi
Parts	On-Call	**Restaurant**	On-Site
Haulout	No	**Post Office**	Taxi
Propane	Taxi	**Library**	Taxi

Pelican Harbor Marina
STM 1084.5

www.miamidade.gov

1275 NE 79th Street
Miami, FL 33138

305/754-9330 (phone)
305/756-4105 (fax)

No VHF Watch

Depth	6	**Laundry**	Walk
Diesel/Gas	D/G	**Pool**	No
Pumpout	Yes	**Internet/WiFi**	No
Mail/Fax	M/F	**Car/Bike**	No
Service	On-Call	**Groceries**	Walk
Parts	On-Call	**Restaurant**	Walk
Haulout	No	**Post Office**	Walk
Propane	Taxi	**Library**	Walk

Sealine Marina & Yachting Center
STM 1088.5

www.sealinemarina.com

1635 N. Bayshore Drive
Miami, FL 33132

305/377-3625 (phone)
305/377-1016 (fax)

VHF 16/10 or 11

Depth	8	**Laundry**	On-Site
Diesel/Gas	D/G	**Pool**	Yes
Pumpout	Yes	**Internet/WiFi**	I/W
Mail/Fax	M/F	**Car/Bike**	No
Service	On-Call	**Groceries**	Taxi
Parts	On-Call	**Restaurant**	Walk
Haulout	No	**Post Office**	Taxi
Propane	N/A	**Library**	Taxi

Miamarina at Bayside
STM 1089.4

www.miami-marinas.com

401 Biscayne Boulevard
Miami, FL 33132

305/579-6955 (phone)
305/579-6957 (fax)

VHF 16/18

Depth	11	**Laundry**	On-Site
Diesel/Gas	No	**Pool**	No
Pumpout	Yes	**Internet/WiFi**	I
Mail/Fax	M/F	**Car/Bike**	No
Service	On-Call	**Groceries**	Taxi
Parts	On-Call	**Restaurant**	On-Site
Haulout	No	**Post Office**	Walk
Propane	N/A	**Library**	Walk

Dinner Key Marina
STM 1094.3

www.miami-marinas.com

3400 Pan American Drive
Miami, FL 33133

305/579-6980 (phone)
305/579-6952 (fax)

VHF 16/68

Depth	5	**Laundry**	On-Site
Diesel/Gas	No	**Pool**	No
Pumpout	Yes	**Internet/WiFi**	I
Mail/Fax	M/F	**Car/Bike**	No
Service	On-Call	**Groceries**	Walk
Parts	On-Call	**Restaurant**	Walk
Haulout	No	**Post Office**	Walk
Propane	Taxi	**Library**	Walk

Grove Key Marina
STM 1094.3

3385 Pan American Drive
Miami, FL 33133

305/858-6527 (phone)
305/858-0250 (fax)

No VHF Watch

Depth	7	**Laundry**	Walk
Diesel/Gas	D/G	**Pool**	No
Pumpout	No	**Internet/WiFi**	No
Mail/Fax	M	**Car/Bike**	No
Service	On-Call	**Groceries**	Walk
Parts	On-Call	**Restaurant**	Walk
Haulout	No	**Post Office**	Walk
Propane	Taxi	**Library**	Walk

Matheson Hammock Marina
STM 1097.8

www.miamidade.gov

9610 Old Cutler Road
Coral Gables, FL 33156

305/665-5475 (phone)
305/669-4008 (fax)

No VHF Watch

Depth	5	**Laundry**	Taxi
Diesel/Gas	D/G	**Pool**	No
Pumpout	Yes	**Internet/WiFi**	No
Mail/Fax	No	**Car/Bike**	No
Service	On-Call	**Groceries**	Taxi
Parts	On-Call	**Restaurant**	On-Site
Haulout	No	**Post Office**	Taxi
Propane	Taxi	**Library**	Taxi

Florida Waterway Marine Facilities

This table summarizes all known Waterway Marine Facilities, their location along the ICW, and their telephone number. Each is listed as either offering transient (T) dockage or not—and whether they have a fuel dock with diesel (D), gas (G), or neither.

715.4	Tiger Point Marina & Boat Works	904/277-2720	T	No
716.5	Florida Petroleum Corporation	904/261-3200	No	D
716.8	Fernandina Harbor Marina	904/491-2090	T	D/G
720.6	Amelia Island Yacht Basin	904/277-4615	T	D/G
740.0	Jacksonville Marina	904/246-8929	T	D/G
744.8	Pablo Creek Marina	Closed	No	No
746.9	**Palm Cove Marina**	904/223-4757	T	D/G
747.3	**Beach Marine**	904/249-8200	T	D/G
775.6	**Camachee Cove Yacht Harbor**	904/829-5676	T	D/G
776.8	**Conch House Marina Resort**	904/824-4347	T	D/G
778.2	**St. Augustine Municipal Marina**	904/825-1026	T	D/G
779.8	Fish Island Marina	904/471-1955	T	D/G
780.0	**St. Augustine Marine**	904/824-4394	T	No
780.0	Oasis Boat Yard & Marina	904/824-2520	No	No
780.0	Oyster Creek Marina	904/827-0520	T	No
796.5	Marineland Marina	Future	No	No
802.8	**Palm Coast Marina**	386/446-6370	T	D/G
829.4	Caribbean Jack's Marina	386/523-3000	T	D/G
830.7	Halifax River Yacht Club	386/255-7459	T	No
831.1	Halifax Harbor Marina	386/671-3600	T	D/G
831.2	**Daytona Marina & Boat Works**	386/252-6421	T	D/G
835.1	Seven Seas Marina & Boatyard	386/761-3221	T	D/G
836.8	**Adventure Yacht Harbor**	386/756-2180	T	D/G
839.6	**Sea Love Marina & Boat Works**	386/761-5434	T	D
839.6	Lighthouse Boat Yard	386/767-0683	T	D/G
845.1	Riverview Hotel & Marina	386/428-5858	T	No
846.1	**North Causeway Marine**	386/427-5267	T	D/G
846.1	New Smyrna Beach City Marina	Future	No	No
846.2	Fishin' Cove Marina	386/428-7827	No	No
847.0	Smyrna Yacht Club	386/427-4040	No	No
878.2	**Titusville Municipal Marina**	321/383-5600	T	D/G
878.2	Westland Marine	321/267-1667	No	No
882.7	Kennedy Point Marina	321/383-0280	T	No
893.7	Harbor Square Marina	321/453-2464	T	No
893.7	Tingley's Fish Resort	Closed	No	No
893.7	**Harbortown Canaveral Marina**	321/453-0160	T	D/G
893.7	Scorpions New Port Marina	321/784-5788	T	D/G
893.7	Cocoa Beach Yacht Club	321/784-2292	No	No
893.7	Cape Marina	321/783-8410	T	D/G
893.7	Sunrise Marina	321/783-9535	T	D/G
897.5	**Whitley Bay Marina**	321/632-5445	T	No
897.5	Indian Cove Marina	Closed	No	No
901.6	Jay's Harbor Lights Marina	321/453-6354	No	No
910.7	**Diamond 99 Marina**	321/254-1490	T	D/G
914.2	Anchorage Yacht Basin	321/773-3620	T	D/G
914.2	Telemar Bay Marina	321/773-2468	T	D/G
915.0	**Eau Gallie Boat Works**	321/254-1766	No	No
915.0	**Eau Gallie Yacht Basin**	321/242-6577	T	D/G
915.0	**Waterline Marina**	321/254-0452	T	No
916.7	Intracoastal Marina	321/725-0090	T	D/G
918.7	Melbourne Harbor Marina	321/725-9054	T	D/G
918.7	Melbourne Yacht Club	321/768-9921	No	No
921.4	Pelican Harbor Marina	321/956-0960	No	No
921.4	Palm Bay Marina	321/723-0851	No	G
934.0	Sebastian River Marina & Boatyard	772/664-3029	T	D/G
937.3	Capt'n Butcher's Marina	772/589-2552	T	D/G
937.3	**Fins Marina**	772/589-4843	T	D/G
937.7	Captain Hiram's Marina	772/589-4345	T	D/G
944.4	Sea Oaks Town Docks	Private	No	No
948.6	Grand Harbor Marina	772/770-4470	T	D/G
951.6	**Vero Beach Municipal Marina**	772/231-2819	T	D/G
951.8	Vero Marine Center	772/562-7922	No	No
964.1	Riverside Marina	772/464-5720	No	No
965.1	Harbortown Marina	772/466-7300	T	D/G
965.1	Cracker Boy Boat Works	772/465-7031	No	No
965.1	Anchors Aweigh at Taylor Creek	772/465-2663	T	D/G
965.7	Ft. Pierce Inlet Marina	772/464-8451	No	No
965.7	Pelican Yacht Club	772/464-1734	T	D/G
966.5	Ft. Pierce City Marina	772/464-1245	T	D/G
979.2	Nettles Island Marina	772/229-2811	T	D/G
982.1	Sun Dance Marina North	772/334-1416	No	G
982.8	**A A Marina**	772/334-0936	T	No
983.4	Outrigger Harbour Marina	772/286-7200	T	D/G
985.0	Hutchinson Island Resort	772/225-3700	T	D/G
987.8	**Sailfish Marina of Stuart**	772/283-1122	T	D/G
987.8	**Finest Kind Marina**	772/223-4110	T	D/G
987.8	Mariner Cay Marina	772/287-2900	No	D/G
987.8	**Pirates Cove Resort & Marina**	772/223-9216	T	D/G
987.8	Stuart Corinthian Yacht Club	772/221-1900	No	No
987.8	Manatee Marina	772/288-2888	T	D/G
992.3	**Loblolly Marina**	772/546-3136	T	No
1002.2	Jupiter Hills Lighthouse Marina	561/744-0727	No	No
1002.3	Blowing Rocks Marina	561/746-3312	T	D/G
1002.4	Seagate Marina	561/746-2600	No	No
1004.2	**JIB Yacht Club & Marina**	561/746-4300	T	D/G
1004.7	Jupiter Seasport Marina	561/575-0006	No	D/G
1007.0	Jonathan's Landing Marina	561/747-8980	T	D/G
1007.6	Admiral's Cove Marina	Private	No	No
1008.7	Bluffs Marina	561/627-6688	No	No
1009.5	**Loggerhead Club & Marina**	561/627-6358	T	D/G
1011.9	E&H Boat Works	561/622-8550	No	No
1012.0	Seminole Boat Yard	561/622-7600	No	No
1012.1	**Soverel Harbour Marina**	561/691-9554	T	D/G
1012.2	PGA Marina	561/626-0200	No	D/G
1012.5	Harbour Point Marina	561/622-6890	No	No
1013.6	**North Palm Beach Marina**	561/626-4919	T	D/G
1014.1	**Old Port Cove Marina**	561/626-1760	T	D
1016.6	Lake Park Harbor Marina	561/840-0188	T	D/G
1017.3	**Cannonsport Marina & Resort**	561/848-7469	T	D/G
1017.3	Buccaneer Marina	561/842-1620	T	D/G
1017.3	**Sailfish Marina & Resort**	561/844-1724	T	D/G
1017.5	New Port Cove Marine Center	561/844-2504	T	D/G

1017.8	Riviera Beach Yacht Center	561/863-4126	No	No
1017.9	**Riviera Beach Municipal Marina**	561/842-7806	T	D/G
1018.1	Cracker Boy Boat Works	561/845-0357	No	No
1019.7	**Rybovich Spencer**	561/844-1800	T	D/G
1021.6	Palm Beach Yacht Club Marina	561/655-8711	No	No
1022.0	Palm Harbor Marina	561/655-4757	T	D/G
1022.8	Town of Palm Beach Marina	561/838-5463	T	No
1030.4	Loggerhead Club & Marina	561/582-4422	T	G
1030.5	Murrelle Marine	561/582-3213	No	No
1032.7	Palm Beach Yacht Center	561/588-9911	T	D/G
1033.1	Gateway Marina	561/588-1211	No	G
1037.8	**Marina Delray**	561/265-0666	T	D/G
1039.8	Delray Beach Yacht Club	561/272-2700	T	No
1040.7	Delray Harbor Club Marina	561/276-0376	T	D/G
1048.0	Boca Raton Resort & Club	561/447-3000	T	No
1050.1	Cove Marina	954-427-9747	No	No
1052.2	Lighthouse Point Yacht & Racquet	954/942-7244	T	No
1053.6	Lighthouse Point Marina	954/941-0227	T	D/G
1054.8	Merritt's Boat & Engine Works	954/941-0118	No	No
1054.8	Hidden Harbour Marina	954/786-5210	No	No
1056.1	Sands Harbor Hotel & Marina	954/942-9100	T	D/G
1056.9	Ramada Inn Pompano	954/941-7300	No	No
1062.5	Coral Ridge Yacht Club	954/566-7886	No	No
1062.6	Sunrise Harbor Marina	954/667-6720	T	No
1064.0	**Las Olas Municipal Marina**	954/759-5200	T	No
1064.2	**Las Olas Municipal Moorings**	954/759-5200	T	No
1064.3	**Hall of Fame Marina**	954/764-3975	T	No
1064.5	Bahia Mar Yachting Center	954/764-2233	T	D/G
1065.0	New River Municipal Marina	954/828-5423	T	No
1065.0	Las Olas Riverfront Complex	Docks	No	No
1065.0	**Riverfront Marina**	954/527-1829	No	D/G
1065.0	Sun Power Diesel	Closed	No	No
1065.0	Cooley's Landing Municipal Marina	954/468-1626	T	No
1065.0	**River Bend Marina**	954/523-1832	T	No
1065.0	Summerfield Boat Works	Closed	No	No
1065.0	Lauderdale Marine Center	954/713-0333	T	No
1065.0	**Mango Marine**	954/585-1041	T	No
1065.0	**Jackson Marine Center**	954/792-4900	No	G
1065.0	Marina Bay Club & Resort	954/791-7600	T	No
1065.0	Yacht Haven Marina	954/583-2322	T	No
1065.0	Cable Marine West	954/587-4000	No	No
1065.0	Rolly Marine	954/583-5300	No	No
1065.0	Billfish Marina	954/587-6226	No	No
1065.0	New River Marine	954/584-2500	No	No
1065.0	Bradford Marine	954/791-3800	No	No
1065.0	**Roscioli Yachting Center**	954/321-1250	No	No
1065.6	Lauderdale Yacht Club	954/524-5500	No	No
1065.8	Lauderdale Marina	954/523-8507	T	D/G
1065.9	**Cable Marine East**	954/462-2822	T	D
1065.9	**Hyatt Regency Pier 66 Marina**	954/728-3578	T	D/G
1065.9	Marriott Portside Marina	954/527-6781	T	No
1066.1	Best Western Marina	954/525-3484	T	No
1068.6	Harbour Towne Marina	954/926-0300	T	D/G
1068.6	Derecktor-Gunnell of Florida	954-920-5756	No	No
1068.6	Royale Palm Yacht Basin	954/923-5900	T	No

1072.0	**Hollywood Municipal Marina**	954/921-3035	T	D/G
1072.8	**Harbor Islands Marina**	954/457-8557	T	D/G
1075.2	**Waterways Marina**	305/935-4295	T	No
1075.9	**Fairmont Turnberry Isle Resort**	305/932-6200	T	No
1077.4	Williams Island Marina	305/937-7813	T	No
1077.4	Loggerhead Club & Marina	305/945-0808	T	D/G
1079.5	Haulover Beach Park Marina	305/945-3934	No	G
1080.9	Keystone Point Marina	305/940-6236	No	D/G
1082.0	Jockey Club Marina	Closed	No	No
1083.8	Gator Racquet Club & Marina	Closed	No	No
1084.5	**Pelican Harbor Marina**	305/754-9330	T	D/G
1085.3	Palm Bay Club & Marina	305/751-3700	T	D/G
1087.0	Wyndham Miami Beach Resort	305/532-3600	No	No
1087.0	Fontainebleau Hilton Resort	305/538-2000	T	No
1088.5	**Sealine Marina & Yachting Center**	305/377-3625	T	D/G
1088.5	Sunset Harbour Yacht Club	305/398-6800	No	No
1088.7	Miami Yacht Club	305/377-9877	T	No
1089.4	**Miamarina at Bayside**	305/579-6955	T	No
1089.8	Miami Beach Marina	305/673-6000	T	D/G
1091.6	Rickenbacker Marina	305/361-1900	No	G
1091.6	Marine Stadium Marina	305/361-3316	No	G
1093.7	Crandon Park Marina	305/361-1281	T	D/G
1094.3	**Dinner Key Marina**	305/579-6980	T	No
1094.3	**Grove Key Marina**	305/858-6527	T	D/G
1094.3	Bayshore Landing Marina	305/854-7997	T	No
1094.3	Coral Reef Yacht Club	305/858-1733	No	No
1097.8	**Matheson Hammock Marina**	305/665-5475	No	D/G

Boldface type indicates the facility completed a survey and is highlighted in a Waterway Business Card. Each facility received multiple fax, email, and telephone requests. A final telephone call was made to verify the accuracy of transient, fuel, and contact information.

Florida Waterway Chandleries

This table lists marine equipment suppliers within easy reach of the ICW, their telephone number and address, and their location relative to ICW marinas and anchorages.

The Boat House	904/261-0167	30 S. 2nd Street, Fernandina Beach, FL 32034	0.1 miles from Fernandina Harbor Marina
Orvis Tidewater Outfitters	904/261-2202	6800 First Coast Highway, Amelia Island, FL 32034	3.2 miles from Amelia City anchorage
West Marine Jacksonville Beach	904/821-5033	14180 Beach Blvd., Jacksonville, FL 32250	0.8 miles from Palm Cove Marina
Home Depot Jacksonville Beach	904/220-0822	12721 Atlantic Blvd., Jacksonville, FL 32225	5.3 miles from Palm Cove Marina
BoatU.S. Jacksonville	904/642-6505	8595 Beach Blvd., Jacksonville, FL 32216	8.4 miles from Palm Cove Marina
Proctor Ace Hardware	904/249-5622	525 3rd Street N., Jacksonville Beach, FL 32250	3.2 miles from Beach Marine
West Marine Jacksonville	904/737-4360	5951 University Blvd. W., Jacksonville, FL 32216	12.5 miles from Beach Marine
First Mate Yacht Services	904/829-0184	235 Yacht Club Drive, St. Augustine, FL 32084	On-site Camachee Cove Yacht Harbor
First Mate Ships Store	904/824-9300	111 Avenida Menendez Drive, St. Augustine, FL 32084	On-site St. Augustine Municipal Marina
Hamblen True Value Hardware	904/824-1529	111 King Street, St. Augustine, FL 32084	0.4 miles from St. Augustine Municipal Marina
Marine Supply & Oil Company	904/829-2271	150 Riberia Street, St. Augustine, FL 32084	0.7 miles from St. Augustine Municipal Marina
Sailor's Exchange	904/808-0667	222 W. King Street, St. Augustine, FL 32084	1.0 miles from St. Augustine Municipal Marina
West Marine St. Augustine	904/810-5353	1030 S. Ponce de Leon Blvd., St. Augustine, FL 32084	1.7 miles from St. Augustine Municipal Marina
Home Depot St. Augustine	904/824-3657	1750 US Highway 1 S., St. Augustine, FL 32084	1.2 miles from Oyster Creek Marina
Home Depot Palm Coast	386/445-2497	10 Garden Street N., Palm Coast, FL 32137	2.9 miles from Palm Coast Marina
West Marine Daytona Beach	386/226-9966	125 Basin Street, Daytona Beach, FL 32114	0.5 miles from Halifax Harbor Marina
Home Depot Daytona	386/257-5114	2455 W. Int'l. Speedway Blvd., Daytona, FL 32114	4.9 miles from Halifax Harbor Marina
Boater's World Daytona	386/257-5006	2200 W. Int'l. Speedway Blvd., Daytona, FL 32114	5.3 miles from Halifax Harbor Marina
West Marine South Daytona	386/760-0660	2400 S. Ridgewood, South Daytona, FL 32119	2.8 miles from Daytona Marina & Boat Works
Madden's Ace Hardware	386/322-3377	2580 S. Atlantic Ave., Daytona Beach, FL 32118	2.3 miles from Seven Seas Marina & Boatyard
Marine Hardware	386/304-9945	3131 Opportunity Court, South Daytona, FL 32119	2.5 miles from Seven Seas Marina & Boatyard
Fishin' Shack	386/788-2120	3514 S. Atlantic Ave., Daytona Beach Shores, FL 32118	1.4 miles from Adventure Yacht Harbor
Beach Variety & Hardware	386/428-8069	311 Flagler Ave., New Smyrna Beach, FL 32169	0.2 miles from Riverview Hotel & Marina
Ace Handiman Hardware	321/267-1030	2300 S. Washington Ave., Titusville, FL 32780	2.4 miles from Titusville Municipal Marina
Lowe's Titusville	321/267-9221	4660 South Street, Titusville, FL 32780	3.8 miles from Kennedy Point Marina
Captain Jack's Bait & Tackle	321/783-3694	780 Mullet Road, Cape Canaveral, FL 32920	0.9 miles from Sunrise Marina
Marine Pro Central Florida	321/636-8950	2150 W. King Street, Cocoa, FL 32926	3.0 miles from Whitley Bay Marina
Boater's Exchange	321/638-0090	2101 US Highway 1, Rockledge, FL 32955	4.1 miles from Whitley Bay Marina
Lowe's Rockledge	321/631-0696	3790 Fiske Blvd., Rockledge, FL 32955	5.2 miles from Whitley Bay Marina
West Marine Merritt Island	321/452-4661	320 W. Merritt Island Causeway, Merritt Island, FL 32953	0.3 miles from Indian Cove Marina
Home Depot Merritt Island	321/453-5855	200 N. Courtenay Parkway, Merritt Island, FL 32953	0.6 miles from Indian Cove Marina
Ace Hardware Merritt Island	321/452-3484	1005 N. Courtenay Parkway, Merritt Island, FL 32953	1.7 miles from Indian Cove Marina
Ace Hardware Pineda	321/254-2346	5970 N. Wickham Road, Melbourne, FL 32940	3.7 miles from Diamond 99 Marina
West Marine Express	321/777-7622	274 E. Eau Gallie Blvd., Indian Harbour, FL 32937	0.2 miles from Anchorage Yacht Basin
Eau Gallie Ace Hardware	321/254-3261	590 W. Eau Gallie Blvd., Melbourne, FL 32935	0.3 miles from Eau Gallie Yacht Basin
Boathouse Discount Marine	321/254-2535	557 North Harbor City Blvd., Melbourne, FL 32935	0.4 miles from Waterline Marina
West Marine Eau Gallie	321/242-9600	1509 North Harbor City Blvd., Melbourne, FL 32935	0.7 miles from Waterline Marina
West Marine Melbourne	321/723-1878	1024 South Harbor City Blvd., Melbourne, FL 32901	1.3 miles from Melbourne Harbor Marina
Boater's World	321/722-3990	2585 W. New Haven Ave., West Melbourne, FL 32904	4.0 miles from Melbourne Harbor Marina
Home Depot Melbourne	321/728-1900	2829 W. New Haven Ave., West Melbourne, FL 32904	4.2 miles from Melbourne Harbor Marina
Home Depot Palm Bay	321/956-6805	1140 Malabar Road NE, Palm Bay, FL 32907	6.0 miles to Pelican Harbor Marina
West Marine Express	772/562-2166	474 21st Street, Vero Beach, FL 32960	2.3 miles from Vero Beach Municipal Marina
Boathouse Discount Marine	772/562-6797	2746 US Highway 1, Vero Beach, FL 32960	4.0 miles from Vero Beach Municipal Marina
Home Depot Vero Beach	772/794-0566	1885 58th Ave., Vero Beach, FL 32966	5.4 miles from Vero Marine Center
West Marine Ft. Pierce	772/460-9044	1875 North US Highway 1, Ft. Pierce, FL 34946	0.9 miles from Riverside Marina
Marine Connection Liquidators	772/465-6460	2970 North US Highway 1, Ft. Pierce, FL 34946	1.0 miles from Riverside Marina
Ace Hardware	772/334-4626	1140 NE Jensen Beach Blvd., Jensen Beach, FL 34957	0.8 miles from Sun Dance Marina North
Home Depot Jensen Beach	772/692-9000	3451 NW Federal Highway, Jensen Beach, FL 34957	3.3 miles from Sun Dance Marina North
Lowe's Jensen Beach	772/692-7745	4100 NW Federal Highway, Jensen Beach, FL 34957	3.6 miles from Sun Dance Marina North
West Marine Jensen Beach	772/692-3092	3523 NW Federal Highway, Jensen Beach, FL 34957	3.8 miles from Sun Dance Marina North
Boater's World	772/692-1150	3193 NW Federal Highway, Jensen Beach, FL 34957	4.1 miles from A A Marina
SPS True Value Hardware	772/334-2700	657 NE Dixie Highway, Jensen Beach, FL 34957	2.1 miles from Outrigger Harbour Marina
West Marine Stuart	772/223-1515	4545 SE Dixie Highway, Stuart, FL 34997	0.8 miles from Sailfish Marina of Stuart
Lewis Marine Supply	772/286-2118	3385 SE Dixie Highway, Stuart, FL 34997	2.1 miles from Sailfish Marina of Stuart

BoatU.S. Stuart	772/283-2335	2595 SE Federal Highway, Stuart, FL 34994	3.5 miles from Finest Kind Marina
Chapman Marine Supply	800/245-3622	2201 SE Indian Street, Stuart, FL 34997	2.5 miles from Pirates Cove Resort & Marina
Lowe's Stuart	772/283-4229	3620 SE Federal Highway, Stuart, FL 34997	2.5 miles from Pirates Cove Resort & Marina
Home Depot Stuart	772/223-7216	3030 SE Federal Highway, Stuart, FL 34994	2.8 miles from Pirates Cove Resort & Marina
Hobe Sound Ace Hardware	772/546-0597	8863 SE Bridge Road, Hobe Sound, FL 33455	4.3 miles from Loblolly Marina
Jupiter Outdoor Center	561/747-9666	18095 North A1A, Jupiter, FL 33477	0.2 miles from Jupiter Seasport Marina
West Marine Jupiter	561/745-3013	161 North US Highway 1, Jupiter, FL 33469	0.7 miles from Jupiter Seasport Marina
Home Depot Jupiter	561/747-6561	1694 W. Indiantown Road, Jupiter, FL 33458	3.4 miles from Jupiter Seasport Marina
Seagull True Value Hardware	561/624-0220	885 Donald Ross Road, Juno Beach, FL 33408	0.8 miles Loggerhead Club & Marina
Marine Supply Store	561/775-6207	2208 Idlewilde Road, Palm Beach Gardens, FL 33410	On-site Seminole Boat Yard
Intracoastal Ship Store	561/627-2707	2385 PGA Blvd., Palm Beach Gardens, FL 33410	Adjacent to Soverel Harbour Marina
West Marine North Palm Beach	561/775-1434	12189 US Highway 1, North Palm Beach, FL 33408	2.5 miles from North Palm Beach Marina
Park Center True Value	561/848-1515	556 Northlake Blvd., Lake Park, FL 33408	1.5 miles from Old Port Cove Marina
Kahn's Marine Service	561/863-5132	115 Federal Highway, Lake Park, FL 33403	0.1 miles from Lake Park Harbor Marina
Home Depot Lake Park	561/627-9555	3860 Northlake Blvd., Lake Park, FL 33403	4.8 miles from Lake Park Harbor Marina
West Marine Lake Park	561/863-1440	1401 Old Dixie Highway, Lake Park, FL 33403	3.8 miles from Cannonsport Marina & Resort
Village Marine	561/844-3320	155 E. Blue Heron Blvd., West Palm Beach, FL 33404	1.2 miles from Sailfish Marina & Resort
Fisherman's Center	561/844-5150	56 E. Blue Heron Blvd., Riviera Beach, FL 33404	0.5 miles from New Port Cove Marine Center
Boat Owners Warehouse	561/845-7777	2230 Broadway, Riviera Beach, FL 33404	0.6 miles from Riviera Beach Municipal Marina
Hopkins Marine	561/832-4206	207 6th Street, West Palm Beach, FL 33401	0.2 miles from Palm Harbor Marina
Home Depot West Palm Beach	561/683-7221	1550 Palm Bch. Lakes Blvd., West Palm Beach, FL 33401	2.4 miles from Palm Harbor Marina
Lowe's Lake Park	561/207-9037	401 N. Congress Ave., Lake Park, FL 33403	3.3 miles from Palm Harbor Marina
West Marine West Palm Beach	561/684-4900	1900 Okeechobee Blvd., West Palm Beach, FL 33409	2.4 miles from Palm Beach Town Docks
Outdoor Sports World	561/833-7539	3415 S. Dixie Highway, West Palm Beach, FL 33405	2.5 miles from Palm Beach Town Docks
Boater's World	561/967-1937	3678 S. Congress Ave., Lake Worth, FL 33461	2.7 miles from Loggerhead Club & Marina
Home Depot Lake Worth	561/642-2626	4241 Lake Worth Road, Lake Worth, FL 33461	3.9 miles from Murrelle Marine
Ace Hardware	561/585-0247	1212 Lantana Road, Lantana, FL 33462	2.9 miles to Palm Beach Yacht Center
Ace Hardware & Marine	561/732-2161	510 E. Boynton Beach Blvd., Boynton Beach, FL 33435	1.8 miles from Gateway Marina
Lowe's Boynton Beach	561/733-1397	1500 Corporate Drive, Boynton Beach, FL 33426	3.8 miles from Gateway Marina
Home Depot Boynton Beach	561/364-9600	1500 SW 8th Street, Boynton Beach, FL 33426	4.0 miles from Gateway Marina
Ace Hardware	561/278-1144	50 SE 6th Ave., Delray Beach, FL 33483	1.2 miles from Marina Delray
West Marine Delray Beach	561/266-8489	2275 S. Federal Highway, Delray Beach, FL 33483	0.9 miles from Delray Harbor Club Marina
Home Depot Delray Beach	561/272-5127	1400 Waterford Place, Delray Beach, FL 33444	1.7 miles from Delray Harbor Club Marina
Lost Bwana Outfitters	561/955-9348	870 NW 6th Drive, Boca Raton, FL 33486	2.8 miles from Boca Raton Resort & Club
West Marine Deerfield Beach	954/427-6165	110 N. Federal Highway, Deerfield Beach, FL 33441	0.9 miles from Cove Marina
Home Depot Deerfield Beach	954/427-0028	60 SW 12th Ave., Deerfield Beach, FL 33442	0.9 miles from Cove Marina
KMC Marine Center	954/941-9193	3896 N. Federal Highway, Lighthouse Point, FL 33064	0.9 miles from Lighthouse Point Yacht & Racquet
Simons Hardware	954/941-6213	1827 NE 25th Street, Lighthouse Point, FL 33064	1.1 miles from Lighthouse Point Marina
Point Marine	954/946-7840	3330 N. Federal Highway, Lighthouse Point, FL 33064	1.7 miles from Lighthouse Point Marina
Sample Road Hardware	954/942-3961	1601 E. Sample Road, Pompano Beach, FL 33064	2.1 miles from Lighthouse Point Marina
Boat Owners Warehouse	954/946-6930	750 E. Sample Road, Pompano Beach, FL 33064	2.8 miles from Lighthouse Point Marina
Lowe's Pompano Beach	954/545-7381	1851 N. Federal Highway, Pompano Beach, FL 33062	0.3 miles from Hidden Harbour Marina
Boater's World	954/781-0007	960 N. Federal Way, Pompano Beach, FL 33062	0.9 miles from Hidden Harbour Marina
Bait Busters Tackle	954/942-3474	2303 NE 5th Ave., Pompano Beach, FL 33064	1.6 miles from Hidden Harbour Marina
Home Depot Pompano Beach	954/978-6100	1151 W. Copans Road, Pompano Beach, FL 33064	3.2 miles from Hidden Harbour Marina
West Marine Pompano Beach	954/960-0560	1951 W. Copans Road, Pompano Beach, FL 33064	3.7 miles from Hidden Harbour Marina
West Marine Bargain Center	954/960-0562	1951 W. Copans Road, Pompano Beach, FL 33064	3.7 miles from Hidden Harbour Marina
BoatU.S. Pompano Beach	954/782-6181	451 S. Federal Highway, Pompano Beach, FL 33062	1.2 miles from Sands Harbor Hotel & Marina
Beach Ace Hardware	954/776-5811	232 Commercial Blvd., Lauderdale-By-The-Sea, FL 33308	2.3 miles from Ramada Inn Pompano
West Marine N. Ft. Lauderdale	954/564-6767	1201 N. Federal Highway, Ft. Lauderdale, FL 33304	1.2 miles from Sunrise Harbor Marina
Home Depot Ft. Lauderdale	954/763-1932	1000 NE 4th Ave., Ft. Lauderdale, FL 33304	1.9 miles from Sunrise Harbor Marina
BoatU.S. Ft. Lauderdale	954/523-7993	505 W. Broward Blvd., Ft. Lauderdale, FL 33312	0.5 miles from Cooley's Landing Municipal Marina
Boat Owners Warehouse	954/522-7998	311 SW 24th Street, Ft. Lauderdale, FL 33315	1.5 miles from Marina Bay Club & Resort
Southport Hardware	954/522-5541	1025 SE 16th Street, Ft. Lauderdale, FL 33316	0.7 miles from Lauderdale Marina
Bluewater Books & Charts	954/763-6533	1811 Cordova Road, Ft. Lauderdale, FL 33316	0.8 miles from Lauderdale Marina
Boats & Motors (West Marine)	954/761-3830	2214 S. Federal Highway, Ft. Lauderdale, FL 33316	1.5 miles from Lauderdale Marina
West Marine Ft. Lauderdale	954/527-5540	2300 S. Federal Highway, Ft. Lauderdale, FL 33316	1.6 miles from Lauderdale Marina
Nautical Niche	954/524-6722	2301 S. Federal Highway, Ft. Lauderdale, FL 33316	1.6 miles from Lauderdale Marina
Sailorman New & Used Marine	954/522-6716	350 SE 24th Street, Ft. Lauderdale, FL 33316	1.8 miles from Lauderdale Marina
McDonald's Hardware	954/463-2000	245 SW 24th Street, Ft. Lauderdale, FL 33315	2.2 miles from Lauderdale Marina
Claire's Marine Outfitters	954/523-4301	2921 SW 2nd Ave., Ft. Lauderdale, FL 33315	2.4 miles from Lauderdale Marina
Hawthorne Marine	954/763-2653	180 SE 29th Street, Ft. Lauderdale, FL 33316	1.8 miles from Cable Marine East
US 1 True Value Hardware	954/922-0054	110 S. Federal Highway, Dania Beach, FL 33004	1.3 miles from Harbour Towne Marina

Intermarine	954/922-5500	4550 Anglers Ave., Ft. Lauderdale, FL 33312	3.2 miles from Harbour Towne Marina
Home Depot Hollywood	954/922-7886	3401 Oakwood Blvd., Hollywood, FL 33020	4.5 miles from Hollywood Municipal Marina
West Marine Hollywood	954/921-1800	3350 N. 28th Terrace, Hollywood, FL 33020	4.7 miles from Hollywood Municipal Marina
Boat Owners Warehouse	954/457-5081	1720 E. Hallandale Bch. Blvd., Hallandale Bch., FL 33009	2.8 miles from Harbor Islands Marina
West Marine North Miami	305/947-6333	16215 Biscayne Blvd., Aventura, FL 33160	0.7 miles from Loggerhead Club & Marina
BoatU.S. North Miami	305/895-1870	12195 Biscayne Blvd., North Miami, FL 33181	1.0 miles from Keystone Point Marina
Silver Paint & Hardware	305/866-5929	1138 Normandy Drive, Miami Beach, FL 33141	1.3 miles from North Bay Landing Marina
Sykes Ace Hardware	305/754-2556	284 NE 79th Street, Miami, FL 33138	2.5 miles from Pelican Harbor Marina
Central Ace Hardware	305/531-0836	545 41st Street, Miami Beach, FL 33140	0.7 miles from Fontainebleau Hilton Resort
Budget Hardware	305/379-5444	1644 NE 2nd Ave., Miami, FL 33132	0.4 miles from Sealine Marina & Yachting Center
Hopkins-Carter Hardware	305/534-0300	300 Alton Road, Miami Beach, FL 33139	On-site Miami Beach Marina
South Beach Hardgoods Co.	305/672-7070	1668 Alton Road, Miami Beach, FL 33139	1.3 miles from Miami Beach Marina
Home Depot Miami	305/643-3777	3030 SW 8th Street, Miami, FL 33135	3.0 miles from Dinner Key Marina
Complete Angler Fishing Supply	305/665-2771	6827 SW 40th Street, Miami, FL 33155	5.2 miles from Dinner Key Marina
West Marine Miami	305/444-5520	3635 S. Dixie Highway, Miami, FL 33133	1.9 miles from Grove Key Marina